Oxford Re

Greek Religion

Oxford Readings in
Greek Religion

Edited by

RICHARD BUXTON

OXFORD
UNIVERSITY PRESS

OXFORD
UNIVERSITY PRESS

Great Clarendon Street, Oxford OX2 6DP

Oxford University Press is a department of the University of Oxford.
It furthers the University's objective of excellence in research, scholarship,
and education by publishing worldwide in

Oxford New York

Athens Auckland Bangkok Bogotá Buenos Aires Cape Town
Chennai Dar es Salaam Delhi Florence Hong Kong Istanbul Karachi
Kolkata Kuala Lumpur Madrid Melbourne Mexico City Mumbai Nairobi
Paris São Paulo Shanghai Singapore Taipei Tokyo Toronto Warsaw

with associated companies in Berlin Ibadan

Oxford is a registered trade mark of Oxford University Press
in the UK and in certain other countries

Published in the United States
by Oxford University Press Inc., New York

British Library Cataloguing in Publication Data
Data available

Library of Congress Cataloging in Publication Data
Data applied for
ISBN 0–19–872190–0

3 5 7 9 10 8 6 4 2

Typeset in Photina
by RefineCatch Limited, Bungay, Suffolk
Printed in Great Britain by
T.J. International Ltd., Padstow, Cornwall

CONTENTS

ABBREVIATIONS

Certain books or articles referred to very frequently are cited from the outset in the abbreviated forms given below. In other cases, publications are cited in full on their first occurrence within each chapter; in subsequent citations within a chapter, they are referred to by short title only. Authors and titles of ancient works, collections of inscriptions, and titles of modern periodicals, are normally abbreviated according to the system used in *The Oxford Classical Dictionary*, 3rd edn., ed. Simon Hornblower and Antony Spawforth (Oxford, 1996).

ANRW	*Aufstieg und Niedergang der römischen Welt*
Burkert, *GR*	W. Burkert, *Greek Religion: Archaic and Classical* (Oxford, 1985); Germ. orig. Stuttgart, 1977
—— *HN*	id., *Homo Necans: The Anthropology of Ancient Greek Sacrificial Ritual and Myth* (Berkeley, 1983); Germ. orig. Berlin, 1972/1997
—— *SH*	id., *Structure and History in Greek Mythology and Ritual* (Berkeley, 1979)
CID	G. Rougemont, *Corpus des inscriptions de Delphes*, i. *Lois sacrées et règlements religieux* (Paris, 1977)
Crux	P. A. Cartledge and F. D. Harvey (eds.), *Crux: Essays Presented to G. E. M. de Ste. Croix on his 75th Birthday* (Exeter, 1985)
de Polignac, *Naissance*	F. de Polignac, *La Naissance de la cité grecque: cultes, espace et société VIIIᵉ–VIIᵉ siècles avant J.-C.* (Paris, 1984)

Detienne and Vernant, *Cuisine*	M. Detienne and J.-P. Vernant (eds.), *The Cuisine of Sacrifice among the Greeks* (Chicago, 1989); Fr. orig. Paris, 1979
Deubner, *AF*	L. Deubner, *Attische Feste*, 2nd edn. (Darmstadt, 1966)
FGrHist	F. Jacoby, *Die Fragmente der griechischen Historiker* (Berlin, 1923–)
Frazer, *GB*	Sir James Frazer, *The Golden Bough*, 3rd edn. (London, 1911–15)
GDI	*Sammlung der griechischen Dialekt-Inschriften*, ed. H. Collitz *et al.* (Göttingen, 1884–1915)
Gifts	T. Linders and G. Nordquist (eds.), *Gifts to the Gods: Proceedings of the Uppsala Symposium 1985* (Uppsala, 1987)
Graf, *NK*	F. Graf, *Nordionische Kulte* (Rome, 1985)
IG	*Inscriptiones Graecae*
LSAM	F. Sokolowski, *Lois sacrées de l'Asie mineure* (Paris, 1955)
LSCG	F. Sokolowski, *Lois sacrées des cités grecques* (Paris, 1969)
LSS	F. Sokolowski, *Lois sacrées des cités grecques. Supplément* (Paris, 1962)
Malkin, *RC*	I. Malkin, *Religion and Colonization in Ancient Greece* (Leiden, 1987)
Magika	C. A. Faraone and D. Obbink (eds.), *Magika Hiera: Ancient Greek Magic and Religion* (New York and Oxford, 1991)
ML	R. Meiggs and D. Lewis (eds.), *A Selection of Greek Historical Inscriptions to the End of the Fifth Century BC*, rev. edn. (Oxford, 1988)
Nilsson, *Cults*	M. P. Nilsson, *Cults, Myths, Oracles, and Politics in Ancient Greece* (Lund, 1951)
——*GF*	id., *Griechische Feste von religiöser Bedeutung mit Ausschluss der attischen* (Leipzig, 1906)

——*GGR*	id., *Geschichte der griechischen Religion*, i, 3rd edn. (Munich, 1967)
Parke, *FA*	H. W. Parke, *Festivals of the Athenians* (London, 1977)
P/W	H. W. Parke and D. E. W. Wormell, *The Delphic Oracle* (Oxford, 1956). P/W no. 10 = no. 10 in vol. ii, 'The Oracular Responses'
RE	A. Pauly/G. Wissowa, *Real-Encyclopädie der klassischen Altertumswissenschaft* (Stuttgart, 1894–)
SEG	*Supplementum epigraphicum Graecum*
*SIG*³	W. Dittenberger, *Sylloge Inscriptionum Graecarum*, 3rd edn. (Leipzig, 1915–24)
Sinn, *Perachora*	U. Sinn, 'Das Heraion von Perachora. Eine sakrale Schutzzone in der korinthischen Peraia', *AM* 105 (1990), 53–116
Travlos, *PD*	J. Travlos, *Pictorial Dictionary of Ancient Athens* (London, 1971)
van Straten, 'Gifts for the Gods'	F. T. van Straten, 'Gifts for the Gods', in H. S. Versnel (ed.), *Faith, Hope and Worship: Aspects of Religious Mentality in the Ancient World* (Leiden, 1981), 65–151
Vernant, *MT*	J.-P. Vernant, *Myth and Thought among the Greeks* (London, 1983); Fr. orig. Paris, 1965/1985
Welcker, *Prometheus*	F. G. Welcker, *Die aeschyleische Trilogie Prometheus und die Kabirenweihe zu Lemnos* (Darmstadt, 1824)

ILLUSTRATIONS

Introduction

RICHARD BUXTON

However tasty and nutritious when originally prepared, most dishes, when reheated, tend to become unappetizing, indigestible, and ultimately toxic. Scholarship does not decay in the same way as food, but it is surprising how, even in the area of the humanities, a book or article can come to seem dated after just one decade, let alone two or three. Nevertheless, for the present collection I have indeed looked, in two instances, as far back as the 1970s, the remaining contributions being divided about equally between the 1980s and 1990s. How can such an act of re-presentation be justified?

One not insignificant consideration is that, in almost all cases (see *Details of Original Publication*) the authors have updated their contributions, either by inserting corrections and modifications along the way, or by writing a section of 'Addenda', or both. Then, one chapter (that by van Straten) has the benefit of illustrations, which were absent from the original version; two other chapters (those by Sourvinou-Inwood), though designed to be read as a pair, appeared first in separate works published in different countries; and the paper by Graf has been translated into English specifically for this collection. However, it is true that in the case of every chapter the substance of the argument and most of the phrasing remain unaltered compared with the original publication. Yet in spite of this I have absolutely no sense of behaving like an unhygienic chef. At the moment of writing, no single interpretative paradigm dominates the study of Greek religion; hence, to highlight a variety of approaches which have been influential in the recent past may be taken to illustrate at the same time the menu of choices available to the interpreter *now*.

Having set out to display the range of perspectives currently on offer, I must immediately bow to the inevitable. So numerous and diverse have been interpretations of Greek religion in the last thirty years that anyone attempting to construct a one-volume collection of readings is bound to omit, not just many fine individual studies, but whole areas and methodological angles which would have fully merited inclusion if space had permitted.[1] I propose, then, to follow a strategy which the user of this book may find idiosyncratic or even annoying: namely, to take him/her on a detour before the journey proper has begun. Introductions are meant to announce what a book will contain; here are some things which will *not* be in this book.

We may begin with the placing of the religious experience and practices of the Greeks in relation to those of their predecessors and neighbours. Debates about these matters have continued apace. Walter Burkert and Martin West have marshalled formidable scholarly expertise to demonstrate the extent of the Greeks' debt to the Near East, an emphasis which has not been without its detractors.[2] Far more controversial, in view of its overtly political agenda, has been Martin Bernal's attempt to attack Hellenocentrism on its southern flank, by arguing for the profound indebtedness of Greece to its neighbours in Africa.[3] Work has continued too (albeit with fewer fanfares) on the religious aspect of another society antecedent to that of Classical Greece: Minoan Crete. Here, stress has been laid on the extent to which, in spite of the limitations of the evidence, we can reconstruct Minoan religion as a functioning system of ritual action, rather than simply as a set of foreshadowings of the Classical future.[4]

---

[1] For a good survey of recent work, with rich bibliography, see J. N. Bremmer, *Greek Religion*, Greece and Rome New Surveys in the Classics, 24 (Oxford, 1994; revised edn. 1999, with Addenda).

[2] e.g. W. Burkert, *The Orientalizing Revolution: Near Eastern Influence on Greek Culture in the Early Archaic Age* (Cambridge, Mass., 1992); M. L. West, *The East Face of Helicon: West Asiatic Elements in Greek Poetry and Myth* (Oxford, 1997). Detractors: there was a rumpus in the Greek press over the decision to give one of the 1998 Runciman Awards to West's *East Face*; the then sponsor went so far as to withdraw funding from the Awards, though a new backer stepped into the breach.

[3] M. Bernal, *Black Athena: The Afroasiatic Roots of Classical Civilization*. i: *The Fabrication of Ancient Greece 1785–1985* (London, 1987); ii: *The Archaeological and Documentary Evidence* (London, 1991). For a massive assault on Bernal's views, see M. R. Lefkowitz and G. M. Rogers (eds.), *Black Athena Revisited* (Chapel Hill, NC, 1996), on which assault see in turn the review article by M. Myerowitz Levine, 'The Marginalization of Martin Bernal', *CPh* 93 (1998), 345–63. It is not without interest that, in an interview with a Greek newspaper, Bernal has prudently demonstrated that he is really on the side of the angels by arguing for the return of the Elgin Marbles to Greece (see pp. 8–11 of the literary supplement of *ΕΛΕΥΘΕΡΟΤΥΠΙΑ* for 27 Aug. 1999).

[4] See N. Marinatos, *Minoan Religion: Ritual, Image, and Symbol* (Columbia, SC, 1993); cf. also P. M. Warren, *Minoan Religion as Ritual Action* (Gothenburg, 1988).

In parallel with such investigations, scholars have continued to probe the religious experience of Mycenaean Greeks.[5] One of the thorniest issues remains that of deciding how far it is indeed justifiable to distinguish between 'Minoan' and 'Mycenaean'.[6] Finally, the 'Indo-European' background to Greek society, and in particular to Greek religion, still has its devotees. The theory of Georges Dumézil concerning the three 'functions' (sovereignty and law; warfare; agricultural production) allegedly characteristic of 'Indo-European peoples' has proved increasingly resistant to export beyond the boundaries of France. But scholars from various intellectual traditions have exploited similarities between societies falling within the 'Indo-European' language group to throw light on institutions within the ancient Greek world; several such studies have dealt directly with ritual and myth.[7]

Homing in, now, on the religious mentality of Archaic/Classical/ Hellenistic Greece, we must first register the excitement generated by the discovery of the Derveni papyrus[8] and the Orphic gold

[5] Cf. B. Rutkowski, *The Cult Places of the Aegean* (New Haven, 1986); R. Hägg, 'Mycenaean Religion: The Helladic and the Minoan Components', in A. Morpurgo Davies and Y. Duhoux (eds.), *Linear B: A 1984 Survey* (Louvain, 1985), 203–25; id., 'Ritual in Mycenaean Greece', in F. Graf (ed.), *Ansichten griechischer Rituale. Geburtstags-Symposium für Walter Burkert* (Stuttgart, 1998), 99–113; R. Hägg and G. C. Nordquist (eds.), *Celebrations of Death and Divinity in the Bronze Age Argolid* (Stockholm, 1990).

[6] P. Scarpi's account of 'Le religioni preelleniche di Creta e Micene' (in G. Filoramo (ed.), *Storia delle religioni*. i: *Le religioni antiche* (Rome and Bari, 1994), 265–81) begins with a section entitled precisely 'La difficoltà di distinguere'; cf. R. Hägg and N. Marinatos (eds.), *Sanctuaries and Cults in the Aegean Bronze Age* (Stockholm, 1981), 213–14.

[7] Within France, B. Sergent is a staunch supporter of an Indo-European perspective; cf. his *Les Indo-Européens: histoire, langues, mythes* (Paris, 1995). On the problems with Dumézil's ideas, see now M. Beard, J. North, and S. Price, *Religions of Rome*, i (Cambridge, 1998), 14–16. A notable I.-E. comparatist outside France is J. Puhvel; see his *Comparative Mythology* (Baltimore, 1987). A number of papers written by J. N. Bremmer in the 1970s and 1980s have an I.-E. dimension, for example, 'Avunculate and Fosterage', *J. Indo-European Stud.* 4 (1976), 65–78; 'An Enigmatic Indo-European Rite: Paederasty', *Arethusa*, 13.2 (1980), 279–98; and the Bremmer-authored sections of J. N. Bremmer and N. M. Horsfall, *Roman Myth and Mythography*, Univ. of London Institute of Classical Studies Bulletin Supplement 52 (1987). See also B. Lincoln, 'The Indo-European Myth of Creation', *HR* 15 (1975), 121–45 (for a more recent, Near-Eastern perspective on the same subject, see W. Burkert, 'The Logic of Cosmogony', in R. Buxton (ed.), *From Myth to Reason? Studies in the Development of Greek Thought* (Oxford, 1999), 87–106); id., 'The Indo-European Cattle-raiding Myth', *HR* 16 (1976), 42–65, developed by P. Walcot in 'Cattle Raiding, Heroic Tradition, and Ritual: The Greek Evidence', *HR* 18 (1978–9), 326–51.

[8] Cf. A. Laks and Glenn W. Most (eds.), *Studies on the Derveni Papyrus* (Oxford, 1997).

4 Richard Buxton

leaves.[9] The papyrus, dating from the fourth century BC, preserves a remarkable commentary on a poetic theogony embodying the ideas of the marginal religious movement known as 'Orphism'; the gold leaves, for their part, constitute 'passports to the underworld',[10] and as such illuminate assumptions about the afterlife made by members of the same sect. Next, iconography: study of the representation of individual divinities and heroes has been transformed by the collaborative enterprise which culminated in the multi-volume lexicon known as LIMC;[11] in addition, several more specific contributions have been made to the interpretation of Greek religious imagery.[12] So far as study of interrelationships between divinities is concerned, the movement which came to be known as 'structuralism' devoted much productive energy to the drawing of symbolic maps and the exploration of meaningful contrasts.[13] As a complement and partial corrective to such a global enterprise, scholars have also extensively researched the idiosyncrasies of local religious phenomena, often on the basis of epigraphical evidence relating to calendars and festivals.[14] Finally, several individual aspects of religious experience have been explored in monographs or shorter publications; for example, pollution, prayer, oath-taking, and the opposition between 'Olympian' and 'chthonian' deities.[15]

[9] R. Parker, 'Early Orphism', in A. Powell (ed.), The Greek World (London, 1995), 483–510; C. Riedweg, 'Initiation—Tod—Unterwelt. Beobachtungen zur Kommunikationssituation und narrativen Technik der orphisch-bakchischen Goldblättchen', in Graf, Ansichten griechischer Rituale, 359–98.

[10] Bremmer, Greek Religion, 87.

[11] Lexicon Iconographicum Mythologiae Classicae (Zürich, 1981–97).

[12] I would single out J.-M. Moret, Oedipe, la Sphinx et les Thébains. Essai de mythologie iconographique, Institut Suisse de Rome, Bibliotheca Helvetica Romana, 23 (Geneva, 1984), and F. Lissarrague, The Aesthetics of the Greek Banquet: Images of Wine and Ritual (Princeton, 1990), as well as C. Bérard et al., A City of Images: Iconography and Society in Ancient Greece (Princeton, 1989). Also worthy of mention, thanks to the breadth of its repertoire, is the splendidly illustrated five-volume work edited by I. Kakridis, Ελληνική Μυθολογία (Athens, 1986–7).

[13] Cf. P. Ellinger, 'Vingt ans de recherches sur les mythes dans le domaine de l'antiquité grecque', REA 86 (1984), 7–29.

[14] Some examples: Graf, NK; M. Jost, Sanctuaires et cultes d'Arcadie (Paris, 1985); J. D. Mikalson, 'Religion in the Attic demes', AJP 98 (1977), 424–35; A. Schachter, Cults of Boeotia (London, 1981–); R. Parker, 'Spartan Religion', in A. Powell (ed.), Classical Sparta: Techniques behind her Success (London, 1989), 142–72; C. Sourvinou-Inwood, 'Reading' Greek Culture: Texts and Images, Rituals and Myths (Oxford, 1991), 147–88 (on a cult of Persephone at Locri Epizephyrii); R. Parker, Athenian Religion: A History (Oxford, 1996).

[15] Pollution: R. Parker, Miasma: Pollution and Purification in Early Greek Religion (Oxford, 1983); a fine analysis of a particular case is to be found in M. H. Jameson,

All these trends and developments will, as I have hinted, figure at best indirectly in the pages which follow. The overwhelming reason for this is lack of space, but three other considerations have influenced my decisions about what to leave out, none of which considerations has anything to do with the intellectual importance of the studies involved. First, certain approaches to Greek religion are best exemplified in an entire book or books, rather than in articles or excerpts: I think here of West's *East Face*, where the force of the argument depends on the sheer accumulation of evidence, and where an excerpt would miss the point.[16] Second, the ready availability of English translations of some works, especially those of the French structuralists, makes the need to republish here less pressing[17] (incidentally, the article by Vernant which I have chosen happens not to be particularly 'structuralist'). Third, I took note of the fact that some fundamental articles are expected soon to be republished in collections of papers by their authors; the pragmatic solution in these cases seemed to me to be to omit the papers here, so as to leave room for studies which, while no less important, are at present less widely available.[18]

D. R. Jordan, and R. D. Kotansky (eds.), *A Lex Sacra from Selinous*, Greek, Roman, and Byzantine Monographs 11 (Durham, NC, 1993). Prayer: H. S. Versnel, 'Religious Mentality in Ancient Prayer', in Versnel (ed.), *Faith, Hope and Worship: Aspects of Religious Mentality in the Ancient World* (Leiden, 1981), 1–64; D. Aubriot-Sévin, *Prière et conceptions religieuses en Grèce ancienne jusqu'à la fin du Ve siècle av. J.-C.* (Lyon, 1992); S. Pulleyn, *Prayer in Greek Religion* (Oxford, 1997). Oath-taking: Ch. 5 of J. D. Mikalson, *Athenian Popular Religion* (Chapel Hill, NC, 1983); C. A. Faraone, 'Molten Wax, Spilt Wine and Mutilated Animals: Sympathetic Magic in Near Eastern and Early Greek Oath Ceremonies', *JHS* 93 (1993), 60–80. Olympian/chthonian: R. Schlesier, 'Olympian versus Chthonian Religion', *Scripta Class. Israel.* 11 (1991–2), 38–51 (reprinted in her *Kulte, Mythen und Gelehrte: Anthropologie der Antike seit 1800* (Frankfurt am Main, 1994), 21–32), seeing the distinction as a modern construct; S. Scullion, 'Olympian and Chthonian', *Class. Ant.* 13 (1994), 75–119, directly opposing Schlesier's view.

[16] See n. 2 above.

[17] See e.g. R. L. Gordon (ed.), *Myth, Religion and Society: Structuralist Essays by M. Detienne, L. Gernet, J.-P. Vernant and P. Vidal-Naquet, with an Introduction by R. G. A. Buxton* (Cambridge, 1981); M. Detienne and J.-P. Vernant (eds.), *The Cuisine of Sacrifice among the Greeks* (Chicago, 1989); M. Detienne, *The Gardens of Adonis: Spices in Greek Mythology* (Hassocks, 1977); P. Vidal-Naquet, *The Black Hunter: Forms of Thought and Forms of Society in the Greek World* (Baltimore, 1986); J.-P. Vernant, *Myth and Society in Ancient Greece* (Hassocks, 1980), and *MT*.

[18] The *primus inter pares* is J. Gould, a sizeable handful of whose articles would otherwise have demanded inclusion in the present collection. In particular, his 'On Making Sense of Greek Religion' (in P. E. Easterling and J. V. Muir (eds.), *Greek Religion and Society* (Cambridge, 1985), 1–33) is a fundamental and innovative introduction to

Given these various absences, it might be thought that nothing of much consequence can remain. Yet the material which is left forms a corpus of formidable scholarship whose contours illustrate some of the most distinctive emphases from the last thirty years of research. From this corpus I have tried to select papers which seem to me to be both thought-provoking and representative, though into my judgement of what belongs to these two overlapping categories there inevitably enters a measure of personal preference—it could not be otherwise. I have divided the material into four parts: (I) Religion in Society; (II) Archaeology of the Sacred; (III) Myths and Rituals; (IV) Boundary Disputes.

Parts (I), (II), and (III) represent different ways of exploring one basic yet complex question: how was the religious experience of the ancient Greeks integrated into, shaped by, embedded in its socio-political, topographical-material, and ceremonial contexts? (By 'religious experience' I intend to mean actions and beliefs involving reference to some thing ('the sacred') or some being or beings perceived as 'superhuman' or 'divine'.[19]) The extent of this multiple embeddedness has been emphasized often enough,[20] but the papers reprinted here reinforce the point in depth and in detail. Many central interpretative problems are aired: the relationships between *polis* religion and individual religion (Sourvinou-Inwood), between religion and politics (Connor, Parker, Vernant), between myth and ritual (Burkert, Graf, Bremmer), between men and

---

the whole topic, while his '*Hiketeia*' (*JHS* 93 (1973), 74–103) is an exemplary analysis of the ritual of supplication, a theme taken up from a different angle by Sinn in the present collection. Gould's collected papers will appear with Oxford University Press under the title *Myth, Ritual, Memory, and Exchange: Essays in Greek Literature and Culture*. An article by M. H. Jameson which is particularly valuable for the understanding of Greek sacrifice is 'Sacrifice and Animal Husbandry in Classical Greece', in C. R. Whittaker (ed.), *Pastoral Economies in Classical Antiquity=Proc. Camb. Phil. Soc. Suppl.* 14 (Cambridge, 1988), 87–119; this will be republished in Jameson's *Cults and Rites of Ancient Greece: Selected Essays on Religion and Society* (Cambridge University Press, forthcoming). Last but not least, A. Henrichs has renewed the understanding of Dionysus thanks to a series of articles, from which may be singled out 'Changing Dionysiac Identities', in B. F. Meyer and E. P. Sanders (eds.), *Jewish and Christian Self-definition*, iii (London, 1982), 137–60 and 213–36. A collection of these Dionysiac papers is projected.

[19] Cf. Filoramo, *Le religioni antiche*, 3.
[20] See L. Bruit Zaidman and P. Schmitt Pantel, *Religion in the Ancient Greek City* (Cambridge, 1992); R. Buxton, 'Religion and Myth', in P. Cartledge (ed.), *The Cambridge Illustrated History of Ancient Greece* (Cambridge, 1998), 320–44.

women in their religious behaviours (Osborne). Along the way, a spectrum of modes of religious action is analysed: procession (Connor), divination (Parker), supplication (Sinn), sacrifice (Osborne), the cult of heroes (Snodgrass), the making of dedications (van Straten).

Three broad kinds of evidence are deployed: first, ancient texts; second, the fruits of archaeological excavations and surveys, including not only material finds such as votive offerings, written oracular responses, and inscriptions recording cultic regulations, but also reconstructions of the ancient landscape (cf. Cole); third, comparative, 'ethnographic' data, together with the perspectives developed by historians (cf. Connor) and anthropologists for the study of 'their' societies. None of these three kinds of evidence deserves to be privileged over the others; 'best practice' in this field consists of the simultaneous weighing of all these sources of information. Above all, it is imperative that cultural historians should feed off the insights of archaeologists, and *vice versa*. In the study of Greek religion, this has not always happened, and one of my principal aims in making my selection has been to discourage such tunnel vision. If proof of the value of such cross-fertilization is needed, it can be found in Macedonia, more precisely at Vergina: there, the tomb decorated with the wall-paintings depicting Hades' abduction of Persephone transfigures into breath-taking, heart-stopping reality the academic doctrine that myth and ritual 'go together'.[21] More such excitement is sure to follow. The editor, for one, finds it hard to contain his sense of anticipation in advance of the publication of well over a thousand new oracular responses from Dodona, in the light of which our view of the religious assumptions of ordinary Greeks is unlikely to remain unchanged.[22]

Attempts to *situate* Greek religion are, it goes without saying, far from new,[23] but there can perhaps have been no other period at which that enterprise has been carried out so intensively. Archaeology has been an important influence here,[24] but so has

---

[21] See M. Andronicos, *Vergina: The Royal Tombs and the Ancient City* (Athens, 1994), 86–95 ('The Tomb of Persephone').

[22] This is thanks to the labours of A.-Ph. Christidis, S. Dakaris, and I. Vokotopoulou.

[23] Two earlier works by M. Nilsson are especially noteworthy: *Greek Popular Religion* (New York, 1940), and *Cults, Myths, Oracles, and Politics in Ancient Greece* (Lund, 1951).

[24] See e.g. S. E. Alcock and R. Osborne (eds.), *Placing the Gods: Sanctuaries and Sacred Space in Ancient Greece* (Oxford, 1994).

anthropology. From Sir Edward Evans-Pritchard and Julian Pitt-
Rivers[25] to Claude Lévi-Strauss[26] and Clifford Geertz,[27] anthropologists have been regarded by classicists as valued advisers in the
formulation of method. Particular mention must be made of Arnold
van Gennep and Victor Turner, the grandfather and father, respectively, of the emphasis on initiatory patterns which has exercised such
a dominant hold over the last generation of researchers. Fertility has
been 'out', rites of passage 'in'. But not everyone has been convinced
(echoes of the debate can be found in the contrasting chapters by
Graf and Fowler).[28] Finally, before leaving the issue of 'outside influences', we can hardly pass over the combination of ethology and
palaeoanthropology which has lent such a distinctive intellectual
infrastructure to the work of one of the most remarkable modern
historians of Greek religion. For Walter Burkert, the religious
behaviour of the Greeks can only be understood when situated
within the context of the rituals practised by palaeolithic humans
and, beyond that, by primates and other mammals.[29]

   Behind all such 'situational' enquiries there lies, however, a set of
prior questions. What *is* Greek religion? What is religion *tout court?* Is
there such a thing as '(Greek) religion'? This is where the inverted
commas go into overdrive, framing and thus problematizing such
concepts as 'ritual', 'myth', 'magic', as well as 'religion' itself. The
posing of such prior questions has until recently occupied a relatively
small proportion of the energies of scholars of Greek religion, but
that proportion has noticeably increased within the last decade.[30]

[25] Both scholars are influential in Gould, '*Hiketeia*'.

[26] Lévi-Strauss's presence is very strong in Detienne, *The Gardens of Adonis*.

[27] See Gould, 'On Making Sense', and E. Kearns, 'Order, Interaction, Authority:
Ways of Looking at Greek Religion', in A. Powell (ed.), *The Greek World* (London,
1995), 511–29.

[28] For some wise words on rites of passage, marginality, and much else, see H. S.
Versnel, 'What's Sauce for the Goose is Sauce for the Gander: Myth and Ritual, Old and
New', in L. Edmunds (ed.), *Approaches to Greek Myth* (Baltimore, 1990), 25–90. A very
large initiatory dossier can be found in A. Moreau (ed.), *L'Initiation* (Montpellier,
1992); in my contribution to that work (R. Buxton, 'Le Centaure anglais: l'espace
"initiatique" dans *Henri IV* de Shakespeare', ii. 153–61), I offered some brief sugges-
tions about how far the notion of initiation can be useful.

[29] The seminal work here is *HN*.

[30] See e.g. C. Calame, ' "Mythe" et "rite" en Grèce: des catégories indigènes?', *Kernos*,
4 (1991), 179–204, and Ch. 1 ('Illusions de la mythologie') in C. Calame, *Mythe et
histoire dans l'Antiquité grecque* (Lausanne, 1996); A. B. Lloyd (ed.), *What is a God?
Studies in the Nature of Greek Divinity* (London, 1997); J. N. Bremmer, ' "Religion",
"Ritual" and the Opposition "Sacred vs. Profane". Notes towards a Terminological
"Genealogy" ', in Graf, *Ansichten griechischer Rituale*, 9–32.

The distinction between 'religion' and 'magic', or rather the issues raised by the drawing of such a distinction, have generated an especially large bibliography.[31] Also coming to prominence at the moment of writing is another boundary dispute, which concerns how far investigations into *Roman* religion have been affected by a particular model, implicit or explicit, about *Greek* religion, the model, namely, which sees Greek religion as 'organic' to the society within which it developed.[32] It is these developments that Part IV (Fowler, Phillips) is designed to register. The fact that this part is briefer than any of the other three reflects, as I have suggested, a general emphasis within the relevant literature. It is not that definitional problems have been totally ignored, either in the discipline as a whole or in the fragment of it which is reproduced below—Snodgrass's chapter, for example, is centrally concerned with the definition of 'the hero'. Nor have *methodological* issues been entirely set aside: Sourvinou-Inwood, for example, has consistently laid stress upon them (see her chapters, and those of several other contributors, below). But what is the case is that certain definitional questions have tended to remain implicit, while attention has been productively directed elsewhere. Not everything is possible at every time. If the present exercise of selection were to be repeated twenty years from now, the balance in this respect might, I suspect, be quite different.

Two final points. First, there is nothing 'Oxford' about the readings in this volume of *Oxford Readings*, beyond the bald fact that that city is the home of the publisher who commissioned this book. Of those whose views are reproduced below, only a small minority work in Oxford, the others being based elsewhere in Britain, or in continental Europe, or in the United States; some, for all I know, have never set foot in Oxford. The contributors (and, for that matter, the editor) do not constitute a 'school'—certainly not an 'Oxford School' to rival the misleadingly named 'Cambridge School' of the early twentieth

---

[31] This can be seen from the references in Fowler Ch. 14, below; cf. also H. S. Versnel, 'Some Reflections on the Relationship Magic-Religion', *Numen*, 38 (1991), 177–97; S. Ribichini, 'La magia nel Vicino Oriente antico. Introduzione tematica e bibliografica', in *Magic in the Ancient Near East* (=*Studi epigrafici e linguistici sul Vicino Oriente antico*, 15 (Verona, 1998)), 5–16. J. N. Bremmer has recently given an unequivocal thumbs-down to the utility of the magic–religion dichotomy for the study of antiquity, in 'The Birth of the Term "Magic" ', *ZPE* 126 (1999), 1–12, at 9–12.

[32] The case is powerfully made by D. Feeney, *Literature and Religion at Rome: Cultures, Contexts, and Beliefs* (Cambridge, 1998); cf. also M. Beard, 'Looking (Harder) for Roman Myth: Dumézil, Declamation and the Problems of Definition', in F. Graf (ed.), *Mythos in mythenloser Gesellschaft: Das Paradigma Roms* (Stuttgart, 1993), 44–64.

century. If this collection stimulates the interest of a public as diverse and international as the group of scholars upon whose work it is based, then it will have more than served its purpose.

Second, as I was preparing to send off the typescript of this volume to the publisher, I read a thoughtful review of two earlier titles in the *Oxford Readings* series. The reviewer describes the producing of such an anthology as a 'closural act which confers a "pastness" upon the included essays'.[33] I am by no means out of sympathy with this point of view: embalming is doubtless an honourable profession, but it is not a calling towards which I find myself strongly drawn. That is precisely why I thought it would be appropriate to end this set of *Readings* with a chapter which expresses unease at the current state of the study of Greek religion. The present volume claims for itself not finality, but mere provisional utility. Every conclusion is a fresh stimulus, and a new beginning.[34]

[33] R. Hunter, *Joint Association of Classical Teachers Review*, 2nd ser. 26 (Autumn 1999), 21–2.

[34] A number of colleagues helped me during the gestation of this volume, notably Jan Bremmer, Robert Fowler, Pantelis Michelakis, Robert Parker, Peter Warren, and Martin West; the Press's anonymous readers also gave valuable advice. I hope all these people will accept my thanks via the modesty of a footnote, rather than the grandeur of a Preface. None of them should be held responsible for the choice of papers made here, or for editorial shortcomings of any kind.

PART I
Religion in Society

I

What is *Polis* Religion?

CHRISTIANE SOURVINOU-INWOOD

The attempt to reconstruct, and make sense of, a religious system to which we have extremely limited access, and which is very different from those which have conditioned our own understanding of the category 'religion', demands a methodology which, as far as possible, prevents our own—culturally determined—assumptions from intruding into, and thus corrupting, the investigation. We also need to discard the layers of earlier interpretations which form distorting filters structuring the data on the basis of the assumptions and expectations of scholars of earlier generations, when it was not fully realized that all reading and interpretation, and all 'common sense', are culturally determined. Here I present highly compressed versions of selected parts of my arguments, to define the parameters within which, on my analysis, *polis* religion operated in the Classical period.

The *polis* provided the fundamental framework in which Greek religion operated. Each *polis* was a religious system which formed part of the more complex world-of-the-*polis* system, interacting with the religious systems of the other *poleis* and with the Panhellenic religious dimension; thus direct and full participation in religion was reserved for citizens, that is, those who made up the community which articulated the religion. One belonged to the religious community of one's own *polis*, (or *ethnos*, tribal state);[1] in the *sacra* of others, even in Panhellenic sanctuaries, one could only participate as a *xenos* (foreigner). On at least some occasions a *xenos* could take part in cult only with the help of a citizen,

I am very grateful to Professor W. G. Forrest, Professor D. M. Lewis, and Dr R. Parker for discussing various aspects of this paper with me.
[1] I cannot consider *ethnos* religion here. The differences between *ethnos* and *polis* religion do not impinge on our investigation.

normally the *proxenos* (consul) of his city, who acted as 'intermediary'.[2]

It would seem that the transgression of these rules did not involve disrespect to the gods, that the prohibition was perceived to pertain to the human articulation of the divine world, which was not considered inviolable. For Kleomenes, disregarding the priest's ban on him as a *xenos*, had the priest removed and performed a sacrifice on the altar at the Argive Heraion.[3] Later, Kleomenes was believed by the Spartans—who took religious prohibitions and other prescriptions especially seriously even when at war[4]—when he claimed that he had obtained omens there; this suggests that his action was not seen as liable to offend the goddess and preclude her from sending him an omen. Furthermore, although Apollodoros in [Dem.] 59 states that it was impious for Phano who was allegedly not an Athenian citizen to have become *basilinna* (queen), his tone and arguments (94–107 and 110–11), and the fact that he also brings up (85–7, 110) the accusation of adultery (a woman taken in adultery was not allowed to attend the public rites), suggest that it was not quite as self-evident as one might have expected that the illegitimate officiating of a *xenos* in the most central and secret rites of the *polis* (59; 73) was a clear-cut, unambivalent, case of serious impiety—as opposed to being merely an offence against the *polis*.

The idea that the transgression of the rules excluding *xenoi* did not offend the gods is connected with another point (to which I shall return), that the ownership of sanctuaries was perceived as belonging to the human, not the divine, sphere, which is why sanctuaries could change hands without it being felt that any disrespect to the gods had been committed. This contrasts with the transgression of different types of exclusion which did offend the gods.[5] One such offence, the sacrilegious nature of which was confirmed by the Pythia, and which brought divine punishment, was Miltiades'

---

[2] On *proxenoi*: C. Marek, *Die Proxenie* (Frankfurt, etc., 1984); M.-F. Baslez, *L'Étranger dans la Grèce antique* (Paris, 1984), 39–40, 111–25; Ph. Gauthier, *Symbola: Les étrangers et la justice dans les cités grecques* (Nancy, 1972), 17–61; cf. also M. B. Walbank, *Athenian Proxenies of the Fifth Century BC* (Toronto and Sarasota, 1978), *passim*, esp. p. 2.

[3] Hdt. 6. 81–2. It is unclear whether *xenoi* were totally forbidden to sacrifice, or had to sacrifice elsewhere in the precinct, or through a *proxenos*.

[4] A. J. Holladay and M. D. Goodman, *CQ* 36 (1986), 151–60. The validity of the representations encoded in the story does not depend on its historicity.

[5] Of course, what counted as sacrilegious behaviour liable to attract divine punishment was variously perceived (cf. e.g. Andoc. 2. 15).

attempt to enter the *megaron* (chamber) of the Thesmophorion of Paros, from which men were excluded (Hdt. 6. 134–5). Another sacrilegious transgression was entering a sanctuary in one's *polis* while forbidden to do so after being deprived of citizen rights (e.g. Andoc. 1. 71; cf. 32–3; 72). The transgression of this exclusion, which was punishable with death (Andoc. 1. 33), constituted impiety and threatened the effectiveness of all the religious practices of the *polis*.

The *polis* anchored, legitimated, and mediated all religious activity. This is true even in the Panhellenic sanctuaries where the *polis* mediated the participation of its citizens in a variety of ways. At Delphi the *polis* schema articulated the operation of the oracle. The oracle's religious personnel consisted of Delphians, and the participation of non-Delphians was mediated by Delphians who acted as *proxenoi* and offered the preliminary sacrifice before consultation by non-Delphians. On regular consultation days this sacrifice was offered by the Delphic *polis* for all the enquirers; on other days it was offered on behalf of the enquirer by the *proxenos* of his city.[6] The non-Delphians, then, were treated on the model of *xenoi* worshipping at the sanctuary of another *polis*. The same dominance of the *polis* articulation occurred, it appears, in other Panhellenic sanctuaries. In the sanctuary of Zeus at Olympia *proxenoi* again played a role,[7] the judges of the Olympic Games were Eleans (Hdt. 2. 160; Paus. 5. 9. 5), and the Eleans made decisions as to who was allowed to participate in the Games and worship at the sanctuary (cf. e.g. Thuc. 5. 50).[8]

Another manifestation of the fact that the *polis* mediated the individual's participation in Panhellenic cult can be seen in the order of consultation of the Delphic oracle.[9] Greeks came before barbarians; among the Greeks, the Delphians before all other Greeks; after the Delphians and before the other Greeks came the other ethnic groups

[6] Cf. Eur. *Androm.* 1102–3. Cf. Marek, *Die Proxenie*, 168–70; G. Roux, *Delphes: Son oracle et ses dieux* (Paris, 1976), 75; G. Daux, in *Le Monde grec: Pensée, littérature, histoire, documents: Hommages à Claire Préaux* (Brussels, 1975), 480–95; Baslez, *L'Etranger*, 40; L. Gernet and A. Boulanger, *Le Génie grec dans la religion* (Paris, 1970; first edn., 1932), 264; cf. also *CID* 5 (p. 17) and perhaps also nos. 4 (pp. 15–16) and 6 (pp. 18–19); cf. also p. 76.

[7] Gauthier, *Symbola*, 41–6; Marek, *Die Proxenie*, 169; cf. also Baslez, *L'Étranger*, 40.

[8] On Dodona see Hyp. 4. 24–6; cf. 19. 26; these passages suggest that it was arguable that expensive dedications to sanctuaries should not be made by outsiders without the permission of the *polis/ethnos* which owned the sanctuary, which (irrespective of the underlying 'political' reasons) confirms that even in Panhellenic cultic contexts the *polis* articulation was felt to be basic.

[9] Roux, *Delphes*, 76–9.

and *poleis* who were members of the Delphic Amphictiony. Consultation by the remaining Greeks was, apparently, arranged according
to some geographical order. Within this basic articulation operated
the *promanteia*, a privilege which the Delphic *polis* granted to individuals, *poleis*, or other collectivities. Here again, that is, the oracle is
treated as a sanctuary of the Delphic *polis* in which the latter could
grant special privileges to its benefactors. The *promanteia* did not
transcend categories, it only involved priority over people belonging
to the same category: given to a barbarian it meant he could consult
the oracle before other barbarians, not before Greeks; an Athenian
could consult before other Athenians, an Amphictionic *polis* before
all other Amphictionic peoples, but after the Delphians.

    Another example of the mediation of the *polis* in Panhellenic
religious activities is the *theōriai* (sacred embassies) sent by individual
poleis to the Panhellenic sanctuaries and also to other *poleis*.[10] The
theōroi (ambassadors) of each *polis* conducted ritual acts in the Panhellenic sanctuaries in the name of that *polis* (e.g. [Andoc.] 4. 29).
The treasuries erected by individual *poleis* in the great Panhellenic
sanctuaries are the physical expression of this mediation, the symbolic representation of the *polis* religious systems in those sanctuaries. They housed the offerings dedicated by their citizens and the
ritual furnishings for the various cult activities, and were also a visual reminder of the cities which had built them, whose achievement
and wealth they advertised and glorified.

    A major context of inter-*polis* religious interaction, besides the
Panhellenic, is that of the Amphictionies or Leagues, associations of
poleis or *ethnē*, or a combination of the two, which celebrated one
or more festivals together and were focused on one or, as in the case
of the Delphic Amphictiony, two sanctuaries. They developed their
own institutions, such as the amphictionic council of the Delphic
Amphictiony, the duties of which included the conduct of the Panhellenic Pythian Games and the care of the finances of the sanctuary
and upkeep of the temple. Even in the case of the Panhellenic Games
the Delphic *polis* was the symbolic centre: it was the Delphic *polis*
that sent *theōroi* to announce the Pythian Games;[11] and the laurel
for the victors' crowns was brought from Tempe in the course of a
ritual (of an initiatory type) involving male adolescents from the

---

[10] Nilsson, *GGR*, 549–52, 826–7; Baslez, *L'Étranger*, 59.
[11] e.g. *CID* 10. 45–6 (cf. pp. 118–19).

Delphic *polis*.[12] Thus the same articulation pertains in the Pan-hellenic Games as in the order of the oracular consultation: the Delphic *polis* at the centre, the Amphictiony forming the inner circle, the other Greeks the outer one. Here the barbarians were excluded from competing—for this was one of the rites defining membership of the group 'Greeks'. That it is the *polis* which mediates the participation of individuals in the cult activities of the Leagues is also illustrated by a story according to which the transgression of one individual during the games of Triopian Apollo was punished through the expulsion of his city, Halikarnassos, from the religious League of Dorian cities (Hdt. 1. 144). This reveals a mentality[13] in which the individual is perceived as participating in the ritual (including the agonistic) activities in the name of his *polis*, which mediates and guarantees that participation. This made the whole *polis* guilty of impiety.

Even in international contexts cult remained *polis*-based: at Nauk-ratis, which down to the fourth century had the double character of *emporion* (trading station) and *polis*, some Greek cities singly set up sanctuaries that belonged to them and were 'their' *polis* shrines in a foreign land; others acting in combination set up a sanctuary called the Hellenion (Hdt. 2. 178). But (as is shown by Herodotus' insist-ence that only the *poleis* he names were involved in its foundation and had a share in it) this was not a supra-*polis* 'Greek' shrine, but the common sanctuary of an *ad hoc* combination of cities, in which the *polis* was the basic unit.

Greek religion, then, consists of a network of religious systems interacting with each other and with the Panhellenic religious dimension. The latter is articulated in, and through, Panhellenic poetry and the Panhellenic sanctuaries; it was created, in a dispersed and varied way, out of selected elements from certain local systems, at the interface between the (interacting) *polis* religious systems—which it then also helped to shape.[14] The Greeks saw themselves as part of one religious group; the fact that they had common sanctuar-ies and sacrifices—as well as the same language and the same blood, a perceived common ancestry, and the same way of life—was one of

---

[12] A. Brelich, *Paides e parthenoi* (Rome, 1969), 387–405; C. Sourvinou-Inwood, *CQ* 29 (1979), 233–4.
[13] The historicity of the story is irrelevant; truth or invention, it is an expression of the relevant Greek perceptions.
[14] Cf. e.g. on divine personalities C. Sourvinou-Inwood, *JHS* 98 (1978), 101–21.

the defining characteristics of Greekness (Hdt. 8. 144. 2). This identity was cultically expressed in, and reinforced through, ritual activities in which the participating group was 'all the Greeks' and from which foreigners were excluded, of which the most important was competing in the Olympic Games (Hdt. 2. 160; 5. 22). But each person was a member of this Panhellenic group in virtue of being a member of a *polis*. It is not simply that being a citizen of a particular *polis* guarantees one's Greekness; as we saw, the *polis* mediated participation in Panhellenic cult.

The gods who were worshipped in the different *poleis* were, of course, perceived to be the same gods (cf. also Hdt. 5. 92–3). What differed was the precise articulation of the cult, its history, its particular modalities, which aspect of each deity each city chose to emphasize, which deities were perceived to be more closely connected with, and so more important to, the city, and so on. Such differences were to a very large extent perceived as relating to the past, to a deity's relationships to particular places and to the heroic ancestors of the individual cities and the cults that these had founded—which were hallowed, both by tradition and because many of these founders belonged to the heroic past in which men had a closer connection with the divine, and thus mediated between man's limitations and the unknowability of the divine. The perception that different needs gave rise to different cults was most unambiguous in the case of cults articulating social groups. Common cult was the established mode for expressing communality in the Greek world, for giving social groups cohesion and identity; it would therefore have been perceived as inevitable that the particular social realities of the particular *poleis* would be reflected in the articulation of their cults. This was not a matter of a 'state' 'manipulating' religion; the unit which was both the religious body carrying the religious authority and the social body, acting through its political institutions, deployed cult in order to articulate itself in what was perceived to be the natural way.

All Greeks were bound to respect other cities' sanctuaries and cults if they did not wish to offend the gods. The 'law' of the Greeks as reported in Thucydides 4. 98. 2 (cf. 4. 97. 2–3) was that whichever *polis* had control over a land also owned its sanctuaries, and they should worship as far as possible according to the rites that were customary there before the change of ownership.[15] The underlying

[15] Malkin, *RC*, 149–50.

perceptions here are that since the gods were the same, and since *polis* religion (including its sanctuaries) was part of the wider *polis* system, possession of the land naturally entailed ownership of the sanctuary; and that, since the way the gods were worshipped in any particular *polis* and sanctuary was partly a result of its past history, traditional practices, hallowed by their connections with a heroic founder and/or by custom, should be respected as far as possible; but not absolutely, since those sanctuaries and cults could not but be affected by the different religious system which they entered, by the articulation of religion in the rest of the *polis*; thus the rites practised after the conquest would be the result of the interaction between those already established and—to a lesser, but varying degree—the religious system of the *polis* that now controlled it. In my view, underlying it all is the notion that the articulation of religion through the systems of particular *poleis* is a human construct, created by particular historical circumstances and open to change under changed circumstances (Thuc. 4. 98. 3–4).

Greek religion is, above all, a way of articulating the world, of structuring chaos and making it intelligible; it is a model articulating a cosmic order guaranteed by a divine order which also (in complex ways) grounds human order, perceived to be incarnated above all in the properly ordered and pious *polis*, and providing certain rules and prescriptions of behaviour, especially towards the divine through cult, but also towards the human world—prescribing, for example, that one must not break one's oaths (e.g. Hom. *Il.* 3. 276–80; 19. 259–60), or that one must respect strangers and suppliants who have the special protection of the gods, especially Zeus, precisely because they are most vulnerable.[16] The *polis* was the institutional authority that structured the universe and the divine world in a religious system, articulated a pantheon with certain particular configurations of divine personalities, and established a system of cults, particular rituals and sanctuaries, and a sacred calendar. In a religion without a canonical body of belief, without revelation, without scriptural texts (outside certain marginal sects which did have sacred books but are irrelevant to our present discussion), without a professional divinely anointed clergy claiming special knowledge or authority, without a church, it was the ordered community, the *polis*, which assumed the role played in Christianity by the Church

---

[16] Pl. *Leg.* 729e–730a. Cf. Nilsson, *GGR*, 419–21; J. Gould, *JHS* 93 (1973), 90–4.

—to use one misleading comparison (for all metaphors derived from Christianity are inevitably misleading) to counteract and destroy alternative, implicit models. It assumed the responsibility and authority to set a religious system into place, to mediate human relationships with the divine world.[17] Connected with this is the fact that, as we shall see, *polis* religion embraces, contains, and mediates all religious discourse—with the ambiguous and uncertain exception of some sectarian discourse. Even festivals common to different *poleis*, such as the Thesmophoria, the most widespread Greek festival, were articulated by each *polis*, at *polis* level. Hence, the same festival could take different forms in different, even neighbouring, *poleis*. For example, the Agrionia at Orchomenos was celebrated differently from the festival of the same name at Chaironeia;[18] and at Eretria the Thesmophoria had certain unique features: Kalligeneia was not invoked, and the meats were grilled in the sun, not on the fire (Plut. *Mor.* 298b–c).

Connected with the absence of revelation, of scriptures, and of a professional divinely anointed priesthood is the fact that a central category of Greek religion is unknowability, the belief that human knowledge about the divine and about the right way of behaving towards it is limited and circumscribed. The perception that the articulation of religion through the particular *polis* systems is a human construct, created by particular historical circumstances and open to change under changed circumstances, is in my view connected with this awareness of the severe limitations of human access to the divine, of the ultimate unknowability of the divine world, and the uncertain nature of human relationships to it. The Greeks did not delude themselves that their religion incarnated the divine will.

The only anchoring for the *polis'* endeavour to ensure the optimum behaviour towards the gods was prophecy, which offered the only direct means of access to the divine world in Greek religion. But this access also was flawed, because, according to Greek ideas about divination, human fallibility interferes, and the word of the gods is often misinterpreted. Nevertheless, through the Delphic oracle (above all), the *polis* could ensure some, if ambiguous, assurance of the

---

[17] We can observe the *polis* putting into place its religious system, and through this creating itself, its own 'centre', in the foundation of colonies (on which cf. Malkin, *RC*, *passim*, esp. pp. 1–2).

[18] Orchomenos: A. Schachter, *Cults of Boiotia*, i (London, 1981), 179–81. Chaironeia: ibid. 173–4; ii (1986), 146.

correctness of its religious discourse.[19] Thus cities consulted the oracle to ensure that the appropriate worship was offered to the appropriate deities either on a particular occasion such as that of a portent (e.g. [Dem.] 43. 66) or more generally for health and good fortune;[20] a vast number of cults and rites were established at the Delphic oracle's instigation and/or on its advice or with its simple approval (e.g. *LSCG* 5. 4–5, 25–6; *LSCG* 178. 2–3; Hdt. 4. 15).[21] The introduction of new cults[22] was connected with the awareness of the fallibility of human knowledge of the divine and the appropriate forms of worship, which entailed that potentially there was always room for improvement. Especially in times of crisis or difficulties, the question 'is there some god we have neglected?', or more generally 'how can we improve our relationship with the divine?' would have arisen, generating pressures towards innovation, especially the introduction of new cults (e.g. Hdt. 7. 178–9). The oracle provided the authority for such changes; but because prophecy is flawed, the danger of getting things wrong could not be eliminated.

It is in this context that we must place the tension between conservatism and innovation in *polis* religion, which is revealed and exploited in Lysias 30, on Nikomachos' codification of the Athenian sacred calendar.[23] The most important argument for religious conservatism in this speech[24] is that the ancestral rites have served the Athenians' ancestors and themselves well, and thus should not be changed. On the desirability of the new sacrifices the

---

[19] One safeguard against the flawed nature of the prophetic vehicle was to consult more than one oracle (cf. e.g. Hyp. 4. 14–15). But even this could not guarantee unflawed access to the gods. On the role of oracular divination cf. R. Parker, Ch. 4, below.

[20] Cf. Dem. 21. 52; P/W, pp. 114–15, no. 282. Cf. Parker, Ch. 4, p. 83.

[21] The poets' mythological/theological articulations were not authoritative; for the Muses who inspired them often lied. Cf. Hes. *Theog.* 27–8; M. L. West (ed.), *Hesiod: Theogony* (Oxford, 1966), p. 163 on 28; K. J. Dover, *Greek Popular Morality in the Time of Plato and Aristotle* (Oxford, 1974), 130. On Greek poetry and religion, P. E. Easterling, in P. E. Easterling and J. V. Muir (eds.), *Greek Religion and Society* (Cambridge, 1985), 34–49.

[22] See e.g. J. K. Davies, *Democracy and Classical Greece* (Glasgow, 1978), 180–1, and below, 28.

[23] See esp. S. Dow, *Proc. Massachusetts Historical Soc.* 71 (1953–7), 3–36; id., *BCH* 92 (1968), 177–81; id., *Historia*, 9 (1960), 270–93; K. Clinton, *Studies in Attic Epigraphy, History and Topography Presented to Eugene Vanderpool, Hesperia*, Suppl. 19 (Princeton, 1982), 27–37.

[24] I am concerned with the rhetorical strategy, which operates within the parameters of collective assumptions; the speaker's 'real' beliefs and motivations are irrelevant.

speech is ambivalent—an attitude which certainly fits the rhetorical context. In classical Athens, the tension between conservatism and innovation tended to be 'resolved' with the former drifting towards the non-abandonment of old cults and the latter towards the introduction of new ones.

The Greek *polis* articulated religion and was itself articulated by it; religion became the *polis'* central ideology, structuring, and giving meaning to, all the elements that made up the identity of the *polis*, its past, its physical landscape, the relationship between its constituent parts. Ritual reinforces group solidarity, and this process is of fundamental importance in establishing and perpetuating civic and cultural, as well as religious, identities.[25] Its heroic cults in particular gave the religious system of each *polis* much of its individuality, its sense of identity and difference, which were connected with the mythical past and sanctified the connection of the citizens with that past to which they related through those cults. This is an important reason for the density of heroic cults (often for figures who appear to us insignificant) in Athenian deme religion: they helped define the deme's identity, both through the performance of distinctive rites and also through the fact that they related the deme to its territory and its mythical past. In the colonies the heroic cult offered to the founder played a similar role.[26] Religion continued to provide the one stable cohesive force in the Classical *polis*, even in Athens after the development of a new Athenian self-definition—whose focus was anyway very largely religious, namely the Acropolis, the Panathenaia, Theseus as Athenian hero par excellence and good democratic king, and the burial of the war dead.[27] This was especially true in a time of crisis, when there was the danger—and sometimes the reality—of sections of the *polis* preferring ideology over country and rupturing the *polis*. This is a prime reason why the profanation of the Mysteries and the mutilation of the Herms was taken by many to be part of an oligarchic or tyrannical conspiracy, an attempt to overthrow democracy (Thuc. 6. 28. 1, 6. 60–1; cf. also Diod. Sic. 13. 2. 3). Religion is the facet of *polis* ideology that all citizens should respect most; thus a

---

[25] I cannot discuss this complex notion; in the simplified form in which it is put here it goes back to Durkheim's work, but it does not depend on acceptance of the latter *in toto*. Cf. also the not-unrelated perception in Pl. *Leg.* 738d–e; 771b–772a.

[26] Malkin, *RC*, 189–266.

[27] See esp. N. Loraux, *The Invention of Athens* (Cambridge, Mass., and London, 1986).

sign of disrespect towards religion is a sign of disloyalty towards the *polis* and the *politeia* (constitution).

The central place of religion in civic life[28] is an expression of the close relationship between the two. The perception that religion was the centre of the *polis* also explains, and is revealed in, a variety of stories[29] and practices.[30] It is also related to the perception that it is the relationship of the *polis* with its gods that ultimately guarantees its existence, that in the origins of the *polis* there is often (explicitly or implicitly) located a form of 'guarantee' by the gods, of a finite and relative protection, which the cultic relationships of the *polis* with the gods—above all with its principal deity—strives to maintain. Such a guarantee is surely perceived to be at the root of the oracular sanction for the foundation of colonies. Cities whose origin was perceived to lie in the mythical past expressed their divine guarantee through myth. In Athens the myths embodying, among other things, this 'guarantee' of protection are that of the earth-born king Erichthonios and, above all, that of the contest between Athena and Poseidon for Attica;[31] the gift of an olive tree by Athena brought about and was the sign sealing the relationship between Athena and Athens, and the olive-tree was thus the symbolic core of Athenian *polis* religion and the guarantee of Athens' existence.[32] This perception is expressed in the story (in Hdt. 8. 55) that this olive-tree which had been burnt by the Persians together with the rest of the Acropolis had by the next day miraculously germinated[33] a cubit-long shoot. (It is significant that Herodotus begins this story with the 'history' of the sacred olive-tree and the salt-water spring which were the tokens of the contest between Athena and Poseidon.) The fact that the olive-tree sprouted again immediately and miraculously signified that the

---

[28] Some instances in Athens: homicide trials were conducted in a sanctuary, *Ath. Pol.* 57. 4; sacred structures were situated in 'political' buildings, e.g. the altar in the Bouleuterion, Xen. *Hell.* 2. 3. 52, 53, 55; Antiph. 6. 45; political and social life functioned with the help of rites, prayers, oaths, and curses; the election for office by lot entailed selection by the gods.

[29] e.g. Hdt. 7. 153 (cf. de Polignac, *Naissance*, 119–21).

[30] e.g. the important place of religion in the Athenian ephebic oath (on which cf. e.g. P. Siewert, *JHS* 97 (1977), 102–11; also the mirror-image of lines 8–9 of the oath, Lycurgus, *Leocr.* 2; the oath is cited in *Leocr.* 76–8).

[31] On Erichthonios, R. Parker, in J. Bremmer (ed.), *Interpretations of Greek Mythology* (London and Sydney, 1987), 193–7; on the contest, ibid. 198–200.

[32] See also M. Detienne, in M. I. Finley (ed.), *Problèmes de la terre en Grèce ancienne* (Paris and La Haye, 1973), 295.

[33] Detienne ibid.

burning of the Acropolis did not entail the end of the Athenian *polis*, for it was the sign that Athena's guarantee was still valid, and at the same time the act which renewed that guarantee and thus signalled Athens' continued existence.[34] The story of the Trojan Palladion which Odysseus and Diomedes stole from Troy because otherwise Troy could not be taken[35] is an expression of the same perception: it had been given to Dardanos, the ancestor of the Trojans, by his father Zeus and was thus a sign of the 'divine guarantee', of the benign relationship between Troy and the gods. Its loss was a sign that the guarantee had come to an end.

As will become clear, in the Classical period the *polis* had ultimate authority in, and control of, all cults, and *polis* religion encompassed all religious discourse within it.[36] *Polis* cults may be classified in broad categories on the basis of their worshipping group.[37]

One category is that in which the worshipping group encompasses the whole *polis*, the cults administered on behalf, and for the welfare, of the whole *polis*, which I shall call 'central *polis* cults'. They are varied in type. A first group of central *polis* cults is located at, and pertains symbolically to, the geographical, social, political, and symbolic centre of the *polis*. To this group belong the cults of the civic divinities who, above all, are explicitly concerned with the identity and the protection of the *polis* as one whole, and thus focus and express the *polis*-holding aspects of *polis* religion. In Athens the two main civic deities were Athena Polias and Zeus Polieus. Next to, and symbolically connected with, this pair was the pair Athena Polias and Poseidon Erechtheus. A poliad Athena was associated with Zeus Polieus elsewhere too (e.g. Kos: *LSCG* 151 A 55 ff. for Athena; 156A

---

[34] Whether or not Herodotus believed this event had happened is irrelevant. What matters is the perception embodied in the story. The inferred departure of the sacred snake from the Acropolis at the time of the evacuation of Athens, which was taken to mean that Athena had abandoned the Acropolis (Hdt. 8. 41), did not entail that she was abandoning the *polis*; it could be seen as a sign of her approval of the evacuation.

[35] Nilsson, *GGR*, 435; Sir James Frazer (ed.), *Apollodorus: The Library* (London, 1921) ii. 226–9 n.2, with a list of the sources.

[36] Cf. below, *passim*, and also the discussion in 'Further Aspects of *Polis* Religion' (Ch. 2, below, 38–55). In my view, the *polis* had had this authority from its beginning, and the changes pertained only to who administered its authority and how. I hope to argue elsewhere against the prevailing model according to which 'the state' took over cults which had originally belonged to—as opposed to being administered on behalf of the *polis* by—the *genē* (clans) and other kinship groups.

[37] I concentrate on Athens, where the available evidence allows us to consider the system of *polis* religion as a whole; this is necessary in order to try to make sense of Greek religion.

19–20). Athena was Polias/Poliouchos in many cities.[38] In Troezen we find a pair reminiscent of the Athenian Athena Polias and Poseidon Erechtheus, Athena Polias and Sthenias and Poseidon Basileus, whose quarrel for the sovereignty of the land ended with an agreement to share it.[39] One set of cults in this group was generally centred on the Agora, the civic and social centre which also had a religious aspect.[40] In many *poleis*, the common hearth of the *polis*, the *koinē hestia*, which was also an altar-hearth for Hestia, was located in the *prytaneion*.[41] At Kos the hearth-altar of Hestia was in the Agora, clearly not in a building, and it was the focus of an important ritual during the festival of Zeus Polieus.[42] The common hearth in the Prytaneion, and Hestia's cult, was the symbolic centre of the *polis*. The common hearth of a colony was lit with fire from the *prytaneion* of the mother-city, and this was a significant act in the establishment of the new *polis*.[43] Among the cults situated in the centre were the cults of deities connected with, and presiding over, the central *polis* institutions: in Athens, Zeus Boulaios and Athena Boulaia (Antiph. 6. 45; Xen. *Hell.* 2. 3. 53, 55), Zeus Agoraios,[44] Artemis Boulaia.[45] Zeus Agoraios also occurs in other *poleis*,[46] as does Zeus Boulaios, sometimes paired with Hestia Boulaia.[47]

One of the gods often associated with the civic life of the *polis* is

---

[38] Graf, *NK*, 44 and n. 4; R. F. Willetts, *Cretan Cults and Festivals* (London, 1962), 280–1 (cf. also 207–8, 233); L. R. Farnell, *The Cults of the Greek States*, i (Oxford, 1896), 299.

[39] Paus. 2. 30. 6; cf. C. M. Kraay, *Archaic and Classical Greek Coins* (London, 1976), 100.

[40] R. Martin, *Recherches sur l'Agora grecque* (Paris, 1951), 164–201, 229–48; R. E. Wycherley, *How the Greeks Built Cities*, 2nd edn. (London, 1962), 51–2; F. Kolb, *Agora und Theater, Volks- und Festversammlung* (Berlin, 1981), 5–15 and *passim*; cf. also G. Vallet, F. Villard, and P. Auberson, *Megara Hyblaea*, i: *Le quartier de l'Agora archaïque* (Rome, 1976), 412–13.

[41] S. G. Miller, *The Prytaneion: Its Function and Architectural Form* (Berkeley, 1978), 13–14; Vernant, *MT*, 147, 157; P. J. Rhodes, *A Commentary on the Aristotelian Athenaion Politeia* (Oxford, 1981), p. 105 on 3. 5; Burkert, *GR*, 170.

[42] *LSCG* 151 A; S. M. Sherwin-White, *Ancient Cos* (Göttingen, 1978), 322–3. Cf. also Nilsson, *GGR*, 153–4; Burkert, *HN*, 138 n. 10; Vernant, *MT*, 150. For Hestia, Zeus, and Athena at the centre of the *polis* cf. also Pl. *Leg.* 745b, 848d.

[43] Malkin, *RC*, 114–34.

[44] R. E. Wycherley, *GRBS* 5 (1964), 162, 176; Travlos, *PD*, 466; Kolb, *Agora und Theater*, 57.

[45] Travlos, *PD*, 553.

[46] Graf, *NK*, 197–8; Willetts, *Cretan Cults*, 233–4.

[47] Graf, *NK*, 176–7 and cf. 363.

Apollo Delphinios.[48] In some cities, as at Miletos and Olbia, his cult was at the centre of civic life; in others, as in Athens, it was less central, but also associated with important institutions. At Miletos the cult of Apollo Delphinios and the Delphinion, his sanctuary,[49] were intimately connected with the civic life of the *polis*. The Delphinion was the main sanctuary with which were associated the Molpoi, a college with religious functions which was also closely connected with the civic life of the *polis*: their leader was the annual chief magistrate of the city, and the college had responsibilities pertaining to civic law; in the Delphinion were set up the sacred laws of the Molpoi and also state treaties, proxeny decrees, and the like. At Miletos Apollo Delphinios was associated with Hekate (*LSAM* 50. 25 ff.) who apparently had a civic aspect in that city. In Athens Apollo Delphinios and his sanctuary were again associated with civic law;[50] he also had a shrine in at least some demes, certainly at Erchia (*LSCG* 18 A 23–30) and almost certainly also at Thorikos.[51]

Heroic cults, involving both the alleged graves of mythical heroes and those of the heroized historical founders of new cities, are an important category of cult located in the Agora.[52] Since the Athenians claimed to be autochthonous, Athens did not have a founder, but it did have founder-like figures: Theseus the synoecist, Erichthonios/ Erechtheus, and Kekrops. In, or associated with, the Athenian Agora—conceivably in the Old Agora[53]—lay the shrine of Theseus, which housed Theseus' alleged bones brought back by Kimon and

---

[48] F. Graf, 'Apollon Delphinios', *Mus. Helv.* 36 (1979), 2–22.

[49] G. Kleiner, *Die Ruinen von Milet* (Berlin, 1968), 33–5; W. Koenigs, in W. Müller-Wiener (ed.), *Milet 1899–1980: Ergebnisse, Probleme und Perspektiven einer Ausgrabung: Kolloquium Frankfurt-am-Main 1980* (Tübingen, 1986), 115–16; Graf, 'Apollon Delphinios', 7–8. In the Archaic period the Delphinion appears to have been outside the walls (F. Graf, *Mus. Helv.* 31 (1974), 215 n. 26). After the Persian Wars the centre of the city shifted to this area (G. Kleiner, in R. Stillwell (ed.), *The Princeton Encyclopedia of Classical Sites* (Princeton, 1976), 578).

[50] Graf, 'Apollon Delphinios', 9–10; Travlos, *PD*, 83–90.

[51] G. Daux, *Ant. Class.* 52 (1983), 150–74 (cf. R. Parker in *Gifts*, 144–7 and passim), text of the deme Thorikos (hereafter *Thorikos*), 6, 63–5, cf. 11.

[52] Martin, *Recherches*, 194–201; Kolb, *Agora und Theater*, 5–8, 19, 24–5, and esp. 47–52; W. Leschhorn, '*Gründer der Stadt*' (Stuttgart, 1984), 67–72, 98–105, 176–80; Malkin, *RC*, 187–260; de Polignac, *Naissance*, 132–52; C. Bérard, in G. Gnoli and J.-P. Vernant (eds.), *La Mort, les morts dans les sociétés anciennes* (Cambridge and Paris, 1982), 89–105.

[53] The location is controversial. Cf. Travlos, *PD*, 1–2, and now esp. G. S. Dontas, *Hesperia*, 52 (1983), 62–3.

which played a small role in the civic life of the *polis*.[54] The shrines-and-graves of Erechtheus and Kekrops are situated on the Acropolis, at the Erechtheion, and are intimately connected with the cult of Athena Polias and Poseidon.

Central *polis* festivals connected with the poliad divinities and/or the constitution of the *polis* are, for example, the Panathenaia, the Synoikia, the Dipoleia in Athens, the festival of Zeus Polieus in Kos. There are very many other central *polis* cults of different kinds in the different *poleis*, some located in the *polis* centre and others not. Many were centred on shrines located within the city but not in its central core (for example, in Athens the Lykeion), others on peri-urban or extra-urban shrines. Processions connected the *polis* centre with some of these shrines. The most important sanctuaries outside the Athenian city, ritually connected with its centre, were those of Demeter and Kore at Eleusis and of Artemis at Brauron. Eleusinian cult was intimately intertwined with the other central *polis* cults; its symbolic place in the centre of Athenian religion was given material expression in the Eleusinion in the centre of Athens, whence began the procession to Eleusis and in which took place rites and acts pertaining to the relationship between the Eleusinian nexus and the Athenian *polis* (e.g. Andoc. 1. 111). In Argos a very important central *polis* rite was the procession to the extra-urban Heraion. In Sparta the major procession was at the Hyakinthia, linking Sparta with the sanctuary of Apollo at Amyklai.[55]

Each significant grouping within the *polis* was articulated and given identity through cult. In Greece all relationships and bonds, including social and political ones, were expressed, and so defined, through cult (cf. also Pl. *Leg.* 738d). This is why the creation of new *polis* subdivisions entailed cultic changes. Thus Kleisthenes' reforms did not involve the subordination of cult to politics, but the ordinary creation of group identity. The *polis* had set in place a particular organization of *polis* religion; now it was changing it because the

[54] J. P. Barron, *JHS* 92 (1972), 20–2; cf. Dontas, *Hesperia*, 52 (1983), 60–3 *passim*; Travlos, *PD*, 578–9; cf. Plut. *Thes.* 36. 2; Paus. 1. 17. 2. 6. On other *hērōa* in the Athenian Agora, H. A. Thompson, in *Athens Comes of Age: From Solon to Salamis* (Princeton, 1978), 96–108.

[55] [I have now discussed the place of the Eleusinian cult in Athenian religion in 'Reconstructing Change: Ideology and Ritual at Eleusis', in M. Golden and P. Toohey (eds.), *Inventing Ancient Culture: Historicism, Periodization and the Ancient World* (London, 1997), 132–64.] Argos: Burkert, *HN*, 162–8; de Polignac, *Naissance*, 41–92 *passim*, esp. 88. Sparta: Brelich, *Paides*, 141–7.

polis organization as a whole was changing. This change was sanctioned by the Delphic oracle: the Pythia selected the eponymous heroes for the ten tribes out of a hundred names submitted to her, and since the tribes were the new major subdivisions of the *polis*, this selection was a symbolic *pars pro toto* for all the cultic changes connected with the reorganization of the *polis*. In Classical Athens the deme was the most important religious subdivision after the *polis*. The cults and rites that went into the making of the cult of these demes were undoubtedly not new; most would have been local rituals, now brought under the administration of the demes. Some may have been significantly reshaped, others not.[56] Cultic innovation, we saw, was accepted without problems; Kleisthenes' reforms were clearly not perceived to have involved the abandonment of long-established practices for which there was a much greater reluctance;[57] they seem similar to the course recommended by Plato (*Leg.* 738b–c). Moreover, articulations of this type were not, we saw, perceived as sacred and unchangeable—not surprisingly, given the role of religion in the definition of sociopolitical units which themselves changed considerably over the years.

In so far as we can judge, the *polis* subdivisions had, first, cults in which only their members could participate, which helped define those groups through the exclusion of non-members; second, some at least also had cults to which outsiders could be admitted; finally, they had cults which pertained to their interaction with the other *polis* groupings: for example, the demes participated in festivals which were primarily central *polis* festivals, either by celebrating

---

[56] At least some may have been phratry cults before (cf. Humphreys, cited by R. Parker in *Gifts*, 138 n. 13; D. Whitehead, *The Demes of Attica* (Princeton, 1986), 177). If, as I believe, phratries began as local units, perhaps by the late 6th cent. phratry membership had become radically dissociated from locality, and there had been in any case a need for a new locality-bound articulation.

Some classical demes formed cultic units which appear to reflect older groupings articulated through cult, whether or not they had been exclusively cultic, variable associations of three or four demes, focused (in different ways) on religious practice: the Marathonian Tetrapolis (D. M. Lewis, *Historia*, 12 (1963), 31–2; *LSCG* 20; Dow, *BCH* 92 (1968), 174–5, 181–2; Whitehead, 190–4; Parke, *FA*, 181–2; J. D. Mikalson, *A. J. Phil.* 98 (1977), 425, 427); the Tetrakomoi (Lewis, 33); the League of Athena Pallenis (Lewis, 33–4; R. Schlaifer, *HSCP* 54 (1943), 35–67; S. Solders, *Die ausserstädtischen Kulte und die Einigung Attikas* (Lund, 1931), 13–14); and the Trikomoi (Lewis, 34). On these associations cf. also P. Siewert, *Die Trittyen Attikas und die Heeresreform des Kleisthenes* (Munich, 1982), 118–20.

[57] *Ath. Pol.* 21. 6; cf. Rhodes, *Commentary on Ath. Pol.*, ad loc. (pp. 258–9); cf. E. Kearns in *Crux*, 190.

them also in the deme, or by taking part in the central *polis* rites as a deme. The cults of the *genos* (clan) are a category of *polis* cult which separately defined the members of each group, of each *genos*, who had exclusive right to one or more priesthoods specific to the *genos*. There were also in the various cities 'private' cultic associations, based on personal choice (e.g. Isaeus 9. 30). The cult of private associations often became part of *polis* religion. Thus, for example, the cult of a god, almost certainly Apollo Delios, who had hitherto had an informal cult to which shipowners contributed a voluntary levy, became a *polis* cult shortly before 429/8.[58]

We shall now consider the cults of the subdivisions of the *polis*. In Athens the new Kleisthenic tribes had their own tribal cults;[59] in addition, the Athenians were tribally articulated in many activities, including cultic ones such as chorus competitions and the *ephēbeia* (military training with initiatory overtones). The connection of the old tribe G[e]leontes and the *phylobasileis* (tribal kings) with the Synoikia, the festival celebrating the birth of the Athenian *polis*, in Nikomachos' calendar,[60] shows the continuing involvement of the old Ionian tribes in cult and suggests an early, certainly pre-Kleisthenic, intertwining of *polis* subdivisions and *polis* formation. Tribes had a cultic role also in the other cities.[61] In the college of the Molpoi at Miletos one representative from each tribe was acting as a college official (*LSAM* 50. 1–3). In the rites for Zeus Polieus and Hestia in Kos it was the tribes which provided the primary articulation of the worshipping group *polis*.[62] The tribes' participation in the cults of the civic deities is comparable to their connection with the formation of the Athenian *polis* through the Synoikia: they and other *polis* subdivisions participated in the cults symbolizing the unity of the *polis* because this reinforced that unity and defined the subdivisions as parts of a symbolically potent whole. The Kleisthenic *trittyes*

---

[58] D. M. Lewis, *BSA* 55 (1960), 190–4.
[59] U. Kron, *Die zehn Phylenheroen* (Berlin, 1976), *passim*; R. Schlaifer, *HSCP* 51 (1940), 253–7; Gernet and Boulanger, *Le Génie grec*, 255; Kearns in *Crux*, 192–9.
[60] *LSS* 10. 35 ff.; cf. Dow, *Proc. Mass. Hist. Soc.* 71 (1953–7), 15–21, 25–7; also Rhodes, *Commentary on Ath. Pol.*, 151; Dow, *BCH* 92 (1968), 174; J. D. Mikalson, *The Sacred and Civil Calendar of the Athenian Year* (Princeton, 1975), 29–30. Cf. also Deubner, *AF*, 36–8; Parke, *FA*, 31–2; E. Simon, *Festivals of Attica* (Madison, Wisc., 1983), 50.
[61] Gernet and Boulanger, *Le Génie grec*, 255; D. Roussel, *Tribu et cité* (Paris, 1976), 207 n. 38, 216.
[62] *LSCG* 151 A 5–15, on which see Sherwin-White, *Ancient Cos*, 322–3. Cf. also Roussel, *Tribu et cité*, 207 n. 38, 261.

(subdivisions of the tribes) also had a cultic role,[63] and so did the old pre-Kleisthenic ones, even after Nikomachos' reforms.[64] In terms of cult the deme was the most important *polis* subdivision in Classical Athens. A few deme calendars have survived.[65] The first category of deme rites consists of rites performed in the deme. It includes: (*a*) local celebrations of central *polis* festivals and cults which were also—and sometimes predominantly—*polis* cults such as that of the poliad deities; (*b*) cults and rites which were specific to the specific demes, above all of local heroes and heroines, including that of the eponymous hero; and (*c*) major festivals celebrated only in the demes, of which the most important was the Rural Dionysia. The second main category of deme ritual activity involved the participation of the demes as demes in the central *polis* cults. This second category and the type (*a*) of the first category represent the two main ways in which deme and central *polis* cults were interwoven.

The Erchia calendar offers an example of type (*a*), that is, of a deme cult involving rites and offerings in the deme to deities which functionally above all pertained to the central *polis* nucleus, on days which were ritually significant in the central *polis* calendar. Zeus Polieus, Athena Polias, Kourotrophos, Aglauros, and Poseidon (and perhaps also Pandrosos) received sacrifices on the Erchia Acropolis on the third Skirophorion, which was almost certainly the day of the Arrhephoria in Athens.[66] Athena Polias and Zeus Polieus were concerned with the *polis* as a whole; their local worship in the demes expressed ritually the interdependence between demes and *polis*; another symbolic strand in this complex interweaving of the whole

---

[63] Lewis, *Historia*, 12 (1956), 35; cf. esp. *IG* I³ 255. In *IG* I³ 258 the deme of the Plotheians makes contributions to the festivals of the Epakreis, probably the *trittys* to which they belonged—though we cannot exclude that it may have been a religious association of neighbouring demes. (Cf. Lewis, 27–8; Siewert, *Die Trittyen*, 15 n. 67, 102 n. 91, 112–13 n. 140; Parker in *Gifts*, 140; cf. also R. J. Hopper, *BSA* 56 (1961), 217–19.) Epakria may also have been the name of a pre-Kleisthenic *trittys* (cf. Siewert, 15 n. 67, 112–13 n. 140).

[64] The Leukotainioi, one of the *trittyes* of the Geleontes (*LSS* 10 A 35ff.; cf. Dow, *Proc. Mass. Hist. Soc.* 71 (1953–7), 26; Siewert, *Die Trittyen*, 15 n. 67; Rhodes, *Commentary on Ath. Pol.*, 68; W. S. Ferguson, in *Classical Studies Presented to Edward Capps on his Seventieth Birthday* (Princeton, 1936), 151–8, esp. 154–7), are involved in a sacrifice associated with the Synoikia (cf. Mikalson, *Sacred and Civil Calendar*, 29).

[65] On deme religion, Whitehead, *Demes*, 176–222; Parker in *Gifts*, 137–47; R. Osborne, *Demos: The Discovery of Classical Attika* (Cambridge, 1985), 178–81; Kolb, *Agora und Theater*, 62 ff.

[66] *LSCG* 18 *A* 57–65; *B* 55–9; *Γ* 59–64; *Δ* 55–60. Cf. M. Jameson, *BCH* 89 (1965), 156–8; Whitehead, *Demes*, 179.

polis (symbolized through its centre) and the subdivisions that constitute it and their cults was the Erchia deme's sacrifices to Zeus Polieus (*LSCG* 18 *Γ* 15–18) and to Athena Polias (*LSCG* 18 *Δ* 13–17) in the acropolis in the *asty* (city). Poseidon was associated with Athena Polias at the cultic centre of the city and the two represent an alternative poliad pair. Aglauros and Pandrosos were part of the same central *polis* cultic nexus and were also associated with the Arrhephoria[67]—in which Athena was the main deity. The cults of Aglauros and Pandrosos were associated with that of Kourotrophos: all three were served by the same priestess.[68] Kourotrophos, who was concerned with the *polis* in so far as she was concerned with the growth of the children that will make up the *polis*, also received many other offerings at Erchia. Her cult was important in other demes too[69] and was thus an important common element between the demes and the centre. The celebration of the central *polis* nexus in the demes helped articulate the cohesion of the *polis*.

Another form of interconnection of type (*a*) involved local celebration of central *polis* festivals. The Hieros Gamos/Theogamia was celebrated in Athens on 27 Gamelion, and on this date the Erchia calendar lists sacrifices to Hera, Zeus Teleios, Kourotrophos, and Poseidon in the sanctuary of Hera at Erchia, which indicate a local celebration of the same rite.[70] At Thorikos there were sacrifices for Athena and Aglauros at the Plynteria (*Thorikos* 52–4), celebrated on a different date from that of the central *polis* festival.[71] This may have allowed the demesmen to participate in both local and central *polis* celebration if they so wished, and suggests that the local rite and the central one were seen as complementary, the purifications and washing of the local statue of Athena being a counterpart to (and perhaps also symbolically dependent on) that of the ancient image of Athena Polias. The cult of Zeus Herkeios was practised in the demes[72]

---

[67] Burkert, *GR*, 228–9; Simon, *Festivals of Attica*, 45–6. On the cult of Aglauros cf. also Dontas, *Hesperia*, 52 (1983), 48–63.

[68] On Kourotrophos, *Salaminioi*, ll. 12, 45–6 and p. 21; *Suda* s.v. *kourotrophos, paidotrophos*, cf. e.g. *LSS* 10 A 24. Cf. Th. Hadzisteliou-Price, *Kourotrophos* (Leiden, 1978); Nilsson, *GGR*, 457.

[69] *Thorikos*, 20–3, 42–3; Tetrapolis calendar: *LSCG* 20 B 6; B 14; B 31; B 37; B 42; B 46; A 56. Cf. also Parker in *Gifts*, 146.

[70] 18 *B* 32–9; *Γ* 38–41; *Δ* 28–32. Cf. F. Salviat, *BCH* 88 (1964), 647–54; Mikalson, *A.J. Phil.* 98 (1977), 429; Parker in *Gifts*, 142–3.

[71] Deubner, *AF*, 17–22; Parker in *Gifts*, 152–5; R. Parker, *Miasma* (Oxford, 1983), 26–8.

[72] *Thorikos*, 22 and left and right side (cf. Daux, 157–60).

and in the central *polis* cult nexus, as well as in the *oikos* with which
it is symbolically associated.[73] The participation of the demes as demes in the central *polis* cults
(e.g. *IG* I³ 258. 25–7; cf. 30–1), in the *asty* and elsewhere, is the
second main way in which the relationship between the central *polis*
cults which pertain to the whole *polis* and those of the *polis* subdivisions is expressed. Among the central *polis* festivals in which the
demes participated as demes was the Panathenaia, in which the meat
of the sacrificial victims was distributed deme by deme, among the
participants sent by each deme.[74] The deme of Skambonidai at least
is known to have participated in the Synoikia (*LSCG* 10 C 16–19),
which, as we saw, celebrated the formation of the *polis* and with
which the old tribes and the old *trittyes* were also associated. The
absence of religious activities in Erchia during some major *polis* festivals may be indicative of a general tendency, suggesting that the
demesmen attended the rites at Athens (or Eleusis).[75] This 'comple-
mentarity' is another sort of interconnection between the Athenian
central *polis* cult and those of the demes. Another category of festival
was celebrated both in Athens and in some at least of the demes. The
Thesmophoria and a group of closely related women's rites, particularly the Skira, probably belong to this class.[76] The Plotheia decree
suggests that there may have been also a third category of cult,
participation in the cult of the *trittys*.[77]

   In so far as we can judge, in other *poleis* too there was similar
participation of the subdivisions in central *polis* cults. We glanced
at tribal participation above, and we shall consider some aspects

---

[73] I discuss the significance of this fact in 'Further Aspects of *Polis* Religion' (Ch. 2,
below, 52–3).

[74] *LSCG* 33 B 25–7; cf. 10 A 19–21; Mikalson, *A.J. Phil.* 98 (1977), 428; Parke, *FA*,
48; Osborne, *Demos*, 180; Parker in *Gifts*, 140–1.

[75] Mikalson, *A.J. Phil.* 98 (1977), 428.

[76] Cf. Parker in *Gifts*, 142. The deme Eleusinia are, in my view, comparable to the
deme Thesmophoria. The central *polis* nexus pertaining to the Eleusinian cult was
focused above all on Eleusis and the *asty* Eleusinion. I hope to discuss this cult
elsewhere.

[77] Unless the Epakreis were a religious association comparable to the Tetrapolis
(above n. 56). Guarducci (*Historia*, 9 (1935), 211) suggested that the *pentetērides*
(festivals celebrated every fifth year), the third category of sacrifices to which the
Plotheians contribute in ll. 25–8, besides deme and central *polis* cults, may have been
celebrated by the Epakreis, for they correspond to the Epakreis category in the tripartite articulation of ll. 30–1; Mikalson, *A. J. Phil.* 98 (1977), 427, believes they are
analogous to the Marathonians' biennial sacrifices. Parker in *Gifts*, 140 n. 32, noted
that the central *polis pentetērides* are another possibility.

pertaining to phratries below. Here I shall say something very briefly about the Spartan religious system. The same type of cultic interconnections between the *polis* and its subdivisions is also seen in Sparta. In the celebration of the extremely important festival of the Karneia an articulation by phratries came into play (Demetrius of Skepsis *ap.* Ath. 141e–f), while another articulation was involved in the selection of the Karneatai for the liturgy of Apollo Karneios.[78] There is also unambiguous, if fragmentary, evidence showing that girls' choruses were organized according to the *polis* subdivisions, by tribe and/or by *ōbē* (village).[79] Cults associated with the subdivisions of the Spartan *polis* are not attested in the Classical period, but given the paucity of evidence that is perhaps due to chance.[80]

Phratries[81] everywhere appear to have had cults common to all the phratries of the *polis*, of the gods who were the protectors of the phratries in that city and were also worshipped at the central *polis* level, and also to have all celebrated, each phratry separately, certain *polis* festivals. One of these was the main festival of the phratries at which new members were admitted; this was known as the Apatouria in most Ionian cities and was, in Athens at least, celebrated by each phratry in its own local centre (cf. *IG* II² 1237. 52 ff.)—and as the Apellai in the Dorian–North-West Greek world.[82] These were central *polis* festivals.[83] Another group of phratry cults were cults which were distinctive and exclusive to each phratry, which thus helped define it as a group.[84]

[78] Hesychius s.v. *Karneatai* tells us that five unmarried youths were selected from each [= tribe? obe?] for this *leitourgia* (cf. Brelich, *Paides*, 149–50).

[79] C. Calame, *Choruses of Young Women in Ancient Greece* (Lanham, Md., 1997), 154–6, 219–21.

[80] R. Parker, 'Spartan Religion', in A. Powell (ed.), *Classical Sparta: Techniques behind her Success* (London, 1989), 142–72.

[81] On phratries see esp. A. Andrewes, *JHS* 81 (1961), 1–15; S. C. Humphreys, *Anthropology and the Greeks* (London, 1978), 194–8, cf. 206–8; Roussel, *Tribu et cité*, 93–157; most recently, M. A. Flower, *CQ* 35 (1985), 232–5. On phratry cults and ceremonies, J. Labarbe, *Bull. de l' Académie royale de Belgique*, Classe des Lettres, 5th ser., 39 (1953), 358–94; C. Rolley, *BCH* 89 (1965), 441–83; Roussel, 133–5; Nilsson, *Cults*, 162–70; cf. Graf, *NK*, 32–7; cf. *CID*, pp. 28–88 *passim*; also Latte in *RE* s.v. *Phratrioi theoi*.

[82] Rougemont in *CID*, pp. 46–7, suggests that only the *apellaia*, the sacrifice at a male's achievement of majority, had to be offered on the day of the Apellai, and that the sacrifices for infants and weddings did not have a fixed date. In Athens, in special circumstances, one could be presented to the phratry at another festival, such as the Thargelia (cf. Isaeus 7. 15).

[83] According to schol. Ar. *Ach.* 146 the Apatouria is a '*dēmotelēs*' festival.

[84] Nilsson, *Cults*, 162–4.

In Athens the main deities of all the phratries were Zeus Phratrios and Athena Phratria, who had a temple in the Agora and also another shrine with an altar but no temple.[85] Apollo Patroos may conceivably also have been worshipped by all the phratries; he also had a temple in the Agora.[86] Andrewes suggested that his cult was in the custody of the *genē* but all members of the phratry were perceived as sharing in it. This may well be right. The fact that, as *Ath. Pol.* 55. 3 shows, having a cult of Apollo Patroos was a prerequisite of archonship[87] does indeed suggest that by that time at least there was a direct connection with (citizenship through) the phratries. In my view, it was perceived as a cult of the phratries which was administered by the *genē* at the centre of each phratry—and also a cult of the *polis* as a whole. This was perhaps not seen as radically different from the priesthood of Zeus Phratrios being held by the *genos* at the centre of the phratry.[88]

The fact that all the phratries in Athens had the same main deities suggests that their most important cults resulted from a central articulation of cult, an articulation of the *polis* given symbolic expression and cohesion through cult. The cults of Zeus Phratrios and Athena Phratria, a central *polis*, cultic nexus almost certainly created at the formation of the *polis*, expressed the phratries' communality and their identity as constituent elements of the city. The latter was signalled especially strongly because the two Phratrioi deities were also the two poliad deities. Thus the protection of the *polis* includes the protection of the phratries that make it up; and the protection of the phratries contributes to the protection of the *polis*. The hypothesis

[85] X. de Schutter, *L'Antiquité classique*, 56 (1987), 116; Nilsson, *Cults*, 165–7; Kearns in *Crux*, 204–5; Travlos, *PD*, 96, 572–5.

[86] de Schutter (n. 85), 104, cf. 108; Roussel, *Tribu et cité*, 73; Kearns in *Crux*, 205; Travlos, *PD*, 96.

[87] Rhodes, *Commentary on Ath. Pol.*, ad loc. (pp. 617–18); Andrewes, *JHS* 81 (1961), 7–8.

[88] As e.g. it is surely implied in Andoc. 1. 126 that Kallias did. A comparable custodianship may have been the background to the move of the common *hiera* from private houses to a common house of the Chiot phratry Klytidai (cf. *LSCG* 118; Graf, *NK*, 428–9 (*I. Ch.* 3), and cf. also 32–7; Forrest, *BSA* 55 (1960), 179–81)—if they are indeed a phratry and if the private individuals in whose houses the *hiera* had been kept before were *gennētai* holding the priesthoods. The fact that annually elected priests in central *polis* cults sometimes also kept the statue of the god in their house (cf. Paus. 4. 33. 2; 7. 24. 4) suggests that 'keeping the statue/other *hiera* in one's house' is symbolically correlative with 'being in charge of the administration of' and does not necessitate possession through a hereditary connection. The privileged position of the *genos* within the classical phratry cannot be doubted (cf. Andrewes, *JHS* 81 (1961), 3–9).

that there was a connection between this cultic nexus, the phratries, and the act of constitution of the *polis* is supported by the fact that a sacrifice was made to Zeus Phratrios and Athena Phratria at the Synoikia.[89] Again, the fact that this sacrifice was made on the authority of the law of the *phylobasileis* and was associated with the old Ionian tribe Geleontes suggests that this cultic connection with the formation of the *polis* was old, certainly pre-Kleisthenic. In Kos also Athena and Zeus were both Phratrioi and Polieis.[90]

But of course the situation was not as tidy everywhere—as is to be expected when the pantheon of each city was a different system which could vary considerably in each case. At Erythrai it was Poseidon who was worshipped as Phratrios while Athena was Polias; the epithet of Zeus more directly connected to the *polis* as a central unit was Agoraios.[91] Zeus Patroos seems to be the—or at least one of the—phratry god[s] also at Chios (*LSCG* 118) where Athena is *poliouchos* (city-protecting) and where we lack evidence for Zeus in the type of '*polis*-holding' persona considered in this connection.[92] Despite the variety between the *phratrioi* gods of the different *poleis*, the forms of the relationship between phratry and central *polis* cults seem constant.

Another manifestation of this close relationship between the two, and of the fact that the phratries' cult is dependent on, and derives its authority from, the central *polis* religion, is seen in Thasos, where the altars of the *patrai* (here equivalent to the phratries) were set up in what is almost certainly the Thesmophorion.[93] This arrangement also expresses the links between the different phratries, especially since some of them may have shared an altar—with each group who sacrificed there having a boundary stone of their own. Each of the *patrai* had a different divinity whom they called Patroos/Patroa. Several have Zeus, some Athena, some the Nymphs, some other divinities without the epithet Patroos, and one Demeter Patroa Eleusinia. In this case—though not usually—'Patroos' seems equivalent to 'Phratrios' in other *poleis*.[94] The fact that these altars

[89] *LSS* 10; cf. Nilsson, *Cults*, 166; Mikalson, *Sacred and Civil Calendar*, 29–30.
[90] Sherwin-White, *Ancient Cos*, 158, 293, 295, 298–9.
[91] Graf, *NK*, 207, 209ff., 197–9.
[92] Cf. Graf, *NK*, 141.
[93] Rolley, *BCH* 89 (1965), 441–83; id., 'Le Sanctuaire d'Évraiokastro: Mise à jour du dossier', in Μνήμη Δ. Λαζαρίδη. Πόλις καὶ χώρα στὴν αρχαία Μακεδονία καὶ Θράκη (Salonica, 1990), 405–8.
[94] Cf. Rolley, *BCH* 89 (1965), 458 f; id., Μνήμη.

were situated in the sanctuary of Demeter may perhaps suggest
that Demeter was a major protector of the *patrai*, as well as being a
goddess who, in the same sanctuary, was closely connected with the
centre, and with the foundation, of the *polis*.[95]
     The oath of the commanders (*tagoi*) of the Delphic phratry of the
Labyadai invokes Zeus Patroos (*CID* 9 A 21–2), while the oath taken
by the assembly of all the Labyadai before voting—that they will vote
fairly, according to the laws of the Delphians—invokes Apollo,[96]
Poseidon Phratrios, and Zeus Patroos (B 10–17). Side D of the Labyadai inscription deals with festivals and other cultic matters. First the
regulations specify that in a series of central *polis* festivals (D 3–11)
all the Labyadai had to participate in the common banquet of the
phratry.[97] Then the inscription lists certain contributions made to the
Labyadai by others who consulted the Delphic oracle—that is, by
those participating in the Panhellenic cult, here treated on the model
of *xenoi* participating in a *polis* cult.[98] The 'sacrifices of the Labyadai'
listed in ll. 43–9[99] are clearly phratry rites. Dionysos receives a sacrifice in the month Apellaios, Zeus Patroos receives a sacrifice at the
Boukatia, and on the same occasion Apollo receives the first fruits.
The phratry of the Labyadai was a subdivision of the Delphic *polis*. It
regulated admissions to the phratry, participation in the central *polis*
festivals, and all interactions with the *polis*, including the Panhellenic
sanctuary. It also issued funerary regulations (*CID* 9 C 19 ff.). It functioned like a mini-*polis*—though interacting with, and under the
authority of (e.g. B 15–17), the Delphic *polis*. It can be argued that it
combines functions similar to those of both the Athenian phratry
and the Athenian deme. No village-like subdivisions comparable to
the Athenian demes are known in the *polis* of Delphi, which was of
course very much smaller than Athens. (The coexistence of phratries
and village-like subdivisions was not limited to Athens; there were,
for example, phratries and obes in Sparta, and phratries and demes at
Locri Epizephyrii.)
     I hope to have shown in this chapter that, and how, the *polis*

---

[95] Rolley, *BCH* 89 (1965), 483; id., Μνήμη.
[96] The most important Delphic god, and also especially concerned (W. Burkert,
Rhein. Mus. 118 (1975), 1–21) with the Apellai and the youths' initiation and
achievement of maturity, and thus of full phratry membership.
[97] *CID*, ad loc., esp. p. 64.
[98] *CID*, ad loc., esp. p. 80; Ch. Kritzas, *BCH* 110 (1986), 611–17.
[99] Cf. *CID*, pp. 59, 62, 82–5.

provided the fundamental, basic framework in which Greek religion operated. I also set out the complex ways in which the Greek *polis* articulated, and was articulated by, religion, and I proposed certain reconstructions of ancient religious perceptions pertaining especially to the articulation of *polis* religion. The role of the *polis* in the articulation of Greek religion was matched by the role of religion in the articulation of the *polis*: religion provided the framework and the symbolic focus of the *polis*. Religion was the very centre of the Greek *polis*.

2

Further Aspects of *Polis* Religion

CHRISTIANE SOURVINOU-INWOOD

In the Classical period priests and priestesses[1] functioned under the authority and control of the *polis*. Each served one (or sometimes more than one) deity and could not officiate in cults beyond their prescribed domain. Even within the same cultic nexus, each priest had definite prescribed ritual duties and was not entitled to perform any other ritual acts (cf. e.g. [Dem.] 59. 116–17). Some priesthoods were limited to the members of a particular *genos*.[2] Non-gentilicial priesthoods were open to all the citizens (cf. Isoc. 2. 6) who were of the appropriate sex (and, where appropriate, age group and status (e.g. virgin)—provided that they were physically unblemished[3] and had not performed an action which made them ineligible (for example, a man who prostituted himself was debarred from holding certain offices, including priesthoods (cf. Aeschin. 1. 19–21)). Such priests were appointed by the community or elected by lot—which allowed the gods to choose; from the later fourth cent. onwards in particular geographical areas priesthoods were increasingly frequently sold. Priestly perquisites varied. Some priests and priestesses served for life, others for a set period, usually a year. They were not

The following abbreviations are used in this chapter: *Salam.* = inscription of 363/2 BC of the *genos* Salaminioi, publ. by W. Ferguson, *Hesperia* (1938), 1–74; *Thorik.* = text of calendar of deme Thorikos; see G. Daux, 'Le Calendrier de Thorikos au Musée J. Paul Getty', *Ant.Class.* 52 (1983), 150–74, with Parker in *Gifts*, 144–7 and *passim*.

[1] On whom cf. Burkert, *GR*, 95–8; E. Sinclair Holderman, 'Le sacerdotesse: requisiti, funzioni, poteri', in G. Arrigoni (ed.), *Le donne in Grecia* (Rome and Bari, 1985), 299–330. In Athens: R. Garland, 'Religious Authority in Archaic and Classical Athens', *BSA* 79 (1984), 75–8; J. Martha, *Les Sacerdoces athéniens* (Paris, 1882); D. D. Feaver, 'Historical Development of the Priesthoods of Athens', *YCS* 15 (1957), 123–58; on Eleusinian sacred officials: K. Clinton, *The Sacred Officials of the Eleusinian Mysteries* (Philadelphia, 1974). On the categories of religious roles in Athens cf. S.C. Humphreys, *Anthropology and the Greeks* (London, 1978), 254; cf. also Garland, 75–123.

[2] On *genē* cf. esp. Humphreys, *Anthropology*, 196–7.

[3] Cf. Burkert, *GR*, 98, 387 n. 48.

obliged to dedicate themselves exclusively to priestly duties (cf. e.g. *LSCG* 69. 1–6 for one example of the minimum amount of time a priest had to spend in the sanctuary in one cult). There were certain requirements of ritual purity during the period of office.[4] They had liturgical and administrative duties (cf. e.g. for the latter *LSCG* 115. 7–8; *LSCG* 69. 5ff.; *LSCG* 37). Sometimes some of these administrative duties were hived off to others. Aristotle, *Pol.* 1322[b]11–12 notes that in some places, for example in small cities, the superintendence of cults is concentrated in the priesthood, while elsewhere it is divided among several offices, such as *hieropoioi*, *naophylakes*, and *tamiai* of the sacred monies. The 'warden' of the sanctuary was the *neokoros* and in some cases at least (cf. e.g. *LSCG* 69. 6–8) the priest had the responsibility to compel him to take care of the sanctuary and its visitors. There were varying numbers of other administrators in the different sanctuaries in the different periods, often with different names in the different *poleis*.[5] There were also colleges of religious officials concerned with the administration of certain rites, such as the *hieropoioi* in Athens;[6] the finances of the sanctuaries were overseen by committees, such as the *tamiai* in Athens, or *hierotamiai* in some other places, the Treasurers of the various gods.[7]

Not all sacrifices required a priest. Private sacrifice, even in a sanctuary, could usually be performed by the private individual himself. The sanctuary regulations governing the conduct of sacrifice by an individual rather than the priest suggest that the two were not perceived to be significantly different (cf. e.g. *LSCG* 69. 25–8; *LSS* 129. 7–11); though of course, such assessments are inevitably culturally determined.[8] However, in certain cults and sanctuaries the presence of the priest/priestess was decreed to be necessary (cf. e.g. *LSCG* 36. 3–7). It appears that sacrifices for, and on behalf of, the *polis* are always performed by a priest. Some of those on behalf of a deme

---

[4] Cf. R. Parker, *Miasma* (Oxford, 1983), 87–94; 52–3; 175.

[5] Cf. e.g. B. Jordan, *Servants of the God* (Göttingen, 1979), 22, cf. 23–8.

[6] *Ath. Pol.* 54. 6–7, cf. P. J. Rhodes, *A Commentary on the Aristotelian Athenaion Politeia* (Oxford, 1981), ad loc. (pp. 605 ff.). On administrative religious offices in Athens cf. also Garland, 'Religious Authority', 116–18.

[7] Cf. Jordan, *Servants*, 66; Burkert, *GR*, 95–6.

[8] For a private person sacrificing in the absence of a priest cf. also Lyc. fr. 4. 1. In at least one *genos* cult (*LSCG* 119; Graf, *NK*, 430, *I.Ch.* 5; cf. p. 101) in the absence of the priest the sacrifice is apparently conducted by a person belonging to a particular category, the nature of which is unclear.

were performed by the demarch (mayor).[9] In Arist. *Pol.* 1322[b] 11–12 the first category of religious officials consists of priests and others concerned with the state of preservation of the sacred buildings and related matters; the second of the officials on whom devolves the responsibility for those common rites which the law does not ascribe to the priests, and who derive their authority from the common hearth, whom some call *archontes* (magistrates), others *basileis* (kings), and others *prytaneis* (presidents)—demarchs may be added as another example.[10] In my view, Aristotle distinguished this category because these particular offices expressed the communality of a particular group, of the whole *polis* (in the case of the *basileus*, for example), or the deme, its character as a community, and performed a cultic role in their character as embodiments, 'symbolic representations', of that communality. (The question of the magistrate called *basileus* in the Classical *polis* is too complex to be properly discussed here).

In his liturgical duties the priest was acting as a symbolic mediator between men and gods; it was the *polis* who placed him in that symbolic position; in the same way the *polis* (in its role of articulator of the relationships between men and gods) decreed that magistrates could assume that role on certain occasions—while the priest was above all the embodiment of that role. It is because priests held that role of mediator that the community—in the form of whoever was the sovereign authority in the individual cities at a particular time—determined their duties and exercised control over them. It is because it was the community who determined the forms of the relationship between man and god, including the particular modalities of cult, and ensured their proper observance, that the Athenian *dēmos* punished Archias the hierophant, holder of a gentilicial priesthood of the highest prestige, from the *genos* of the Eumolpids (which can be said to have been deemed to have a special religious status more than any other, since it furnished the Eumolpid *exēgētai* (expounders, interpreters)) for impiously performing a sacrifice not in accordance with the ancestral custom: he had, among other things, sacrificed for a *hetaira* (courtesan) on the Haloa on the *eschara* in the courtyard at Eleusis,

---

[9] R. Osborne, *Demos: The Discovery of Classical Attika* (Cambridge, 1985), 234 n. 27 suggests that priests are indispensable for public sacrifices, citing Ar. *Birds* 848, cf. 862 which, in my view, pertains to sacrifices for, and on behalf of, the whole *polis*, and so does not necessarily invalidate the notion that the demarch performed the sacrifices in which he is said to be sacrificing (cf. e.g. *LSCG* B 23; cf. D. Whitehead, *The Demes of Attica* (Princeton, 1986), 128; 180).

[10] Cf. Whitehead, *Demes*, 180–1.

while it was not customary (*nomimon*) to sacrifice on that day, nor was he entitled to perform the sacrifice, for it belonged to the priestess ([Dem.] 59. 116–17). Once again, it is not a matter of 'the state' encroaching over a religious authority: it is the community articulated in the ordered *polis* which is represented in the ritual activities, and the authority that speaks for it—in the case of Classical Athens the *dēmos*—acts on its behalf.

The fact that the priests acted on behalf of the community is expressed in the priests' obligation in Classical Athens to give account for, to be publicly examined on, their performance in office (cf. Aeschin. 3. 18). Aeschines thought that this was paradoxical, since being a priest did not involve receiving or administering large sums, only the receiving of perquisites and the duty to pray to the gods on behalf of the *polis* (Aeschin. 3. 18); for he did not see (or did not, in that particular forensic context, choose to acknowledge) that this obligation was, above all, not financial in nature, and that it expressed symbolically the relationship between *polis* and priest. (This relationship was not different from that between priest and community in Homer: *Il.* 6. 300 tells us of Theano 'her the Trojans had made priestess of Athena'; what has changed by the fourth century is where the power to act in the name of the *polis* lay). Priests and priestesses accounted for their conduct in office both individually and all together; also, both each on their own account, and each priestly *genos* together, as a unit (Aeschin. 3. 18). I take the collective accounting to be an expression of the relationship between the Athenian community and all its representatives in their relationships with the gods, all the mediators with the divine taken together, as though they symbolically made up one mediator. The accounting of each *genos* as a unit I take to be an expression of a notion that the *polis* had 'appointed' each *genos* to be responsible for a priesthood or set of priesthoods, which the *genos* then assigned to one of its members, thus expressing the relationship between the *polis* and gentilicial priesthoods in a modality that can be accommodated in, and appears comparable to, the established modalities of *polis* religion in the democratic *polis*.[11] The same mentality, that the priests acted on

[11] Which inherited this institution, which had originated in a *polis* in which, in my view, the religious mentality and modalities were not essentially different, but operated in a different sociopolitical framework in which power-holding and administering was limited to one segment of the population, the Eupatrids, membership in which depended on membership of a *genos*. The *genē* shared out permanently between them one particular set of 'magistracies', the priesthoods.

behalf of the community, underlies, and is expressed in, the institution of the priests' reports to the Boule (Council) concerning the sacrifices at which they officiated and the Boule's acceptance of 'the good things that had occurred in the sacrifice'.[12]

Apart from priests and cult administrators there were also certain religious personnel with specialized duties, such as *exēgētai*, who expounded on sacred matters, and prophets. Some prophets, like the Pythia, were institutionally appointed in an established cult and sanctuary; others, such as the professional interpreters of omens accompanying military expeditions, performed a particular function; finally others were charismatic individuals who offered solicited and unsolicited advice. There were also many other religious offices with varying ritual responsibilities and duration in the different *poleis* (in Athens, for example, the *arrhēphoroi* and the *arktoi* (bears), girls serving Athena and Artemis respectively, or the office of *archousa* (president) at the Thesmophoria (cf. *LSS* 124. 3 ff.; cf. Isaeus 8. 19–20), to name but a very few).

I shall now consider extremely briefly the financing of Classical cults (but not its changes, nor the gods' loans to the *polis*). The gods' wealth came from a variety of sources. First, votive offerings[13] given by individuals, civic bodies or the whole *polis*. It has now been shown that in all but the most exceptional circumstances the offerings stayed in the god's possession and were withdrawn from circulation.[14] A source of revenue which provided income for the upkeep of the sanctuary and conduct of the cult was property owned by the sanctuary and the rents derived from it; another was fees paid to the cult[15] and also property expropriated and given to the deity (cf. e.g. Andoc. 1. 96) and fines.[16] The final source of revenue was endowments and also regular contributions by, and on the responsibility and authority of, its worshipping group. In the case of the central *polis* cults this was the whole *polis*; the rites financed by and on the authority of the *polis* as a whole were called *dēmotelē hiera*.

[12] Cf. e.g. *IG* II² 410; 661; 689; 775; 780; 783. Cf. also P.J. Rhodes, *The Athenian Boule* (Oxford, 1972), 43 n. 6; R. Parker in *Gifts*, 138.
[13] Cf. esp. van Straten, 'Gifts for the Gods'; Linders in *Gifts*, 115–22.
[14] Cf. Linders in *Gifts*, 115–22, esp. 116.
[15] Cf. e.g. *LSCG* 69. 20–24; and cf. A. Petropoulou, 'The *Eparche* Documents and the Early Oracle at Oropus', *GRBS* 22 (1981), 39–63, at 53–4.
[16] Cf. e.g. *LSCG* 69. 9–13; G. Pfohl, *Griechische Inschriften als Zeugnisse der privaten und öffentlichen Lebens*, 2nd edn. (Munich, 1980), no. 94. On fines paid to the gods cf. K. Latte, *Heiliges Recht* (Tübingen, 1920), 48–61 and *passim*.

The central *polis* funds used for the financing of central *polis* cults came mostly from the general *polis* revenues but also from special taxes the income from which was reserved for specific cults—the modalities of collection varied as between cults and *poleis*.[17] When the worshipping group was the deme, cult was financed on the responsibility of the deme (through modalities which are, up to a point, comparable to those through which the *polis* financed cults), and the rites called *dēmotika*.[18] The participation of the demes as demes in the central *polis* rites[19] and their contributions to them do not affect this distinction. For the complex modalities through which the *polis* provided the necessary revenues and animals included contributions made directly by the *polis*, individual liturgies, and contributions of at least some of the constituent groups, such as the demes. In an important Koan rite (*LSCG* 151 A) the tribes, or, if the animals sent in the name of the tribes failed to be selected, the *chiliastyes* (another *polis* subdivision), provided the sacrificial animal.

Genē also participated as a group in at least some central *polis* cults, making sacrifices and providing the victims (cf. e.g. *Salam.* 1. 88). Another category making a contribution in some central *polis* cults in some cities, whose participation is comparable to, and modelled on, that of the *polis*' constituent groups, is, we shall see, colonists and 'allies'. Each worshipping group provides the organizing framework and authority for the contributions pertaining to its cults, and also for its participation as a group in the 'superior' order group cults—deme for *polis*, *genos* for phratry and *polis*. In the case of the *genos* Salaminioi, the Salaminioi themselves finance the sacrifices which they make as a *genos*—be it in cults confined to the *genos*, or in central *polis* cults in which the *genos* contributes as a *genos* (cf. e.g. *Salam.* 88) or in phratry cults (*Salam.* 97). This contrasts with the sacrifices in which the Salaminioi played a role on behalf of the whole *polis*, namely the central *polis* cults in which they held the priesthoods, for which victims were provided by the *polis*, and by the *deipnophoroi* (the carriers of meat offerings) and *oschophoroi* (the carriers of vine branches with grapes) who may have been members of the *genos*, and who may have offered this contribution as a

---

[17] Cf. e.g. *LSS* 85; for Athens: cf. R. Schlaifer, 'Notes on Athenian Public Cults', *HSCP* 51 (1940), 233–60.
[18] Cf. Whitehead, *Demes*, 178–80; cf. 163–75.
[19] I discuss this participation in 'What is *Polis* Religion?' (Ch. 1).

liturgy.[20] The provision of victims to the Salaminioi in the context of
these cults is surely comparable, *mutatis mutandis*, to the provision
of victims to the Molpoi by the *polis* of Miletos in the course of
certain *polis* festivals (*LSAM* 50. 19–23).

The fact that the central focus, and the central mode of articulation, of Greek religion was ritual, and not the personal inner spiritual
experience, and that much ritual activity took place in groups, must
not be taken to entail that Greek religion is a 'group religion' in the
sense that group worship was the norm and individual cultic acts
somehow exceptional. In my view, the individual was without doubt
the primary, the basic, cultic unit in *polis* religion—and not, for
example, a small group such as the *oikos* (household). The following
arguments make this clear. First, the modalities of individual acts of
worship are the same as those of group worship, be that group the
polis as a whole or any of the *polis* subdivisions. This suggests a
religious mentality in which the individual's act of worship is not
different in nature from that of the group's, and thus a religious
system in which the basic cult units are individuals, who are also
grouped in a variety of ways and participate in group cults. Personal
prayers have a counterpart in *polis* prayers, offered for, and on behalf
of, the *polis*, indeed prayers are a constituent part of all cultic acts
(cf. e.g. Aeschin. 3. 18; cf. *LSCG* 69. 25–30). Personal curses have a
counterpart in *polis* curses. More importantly, the category 'individual cultic act' comprises a very important aspect of Greek cult
activity, the many votive gifts dedicated to deities by individuals,
which begin at an early period[21] and cannot convincingly be considered marginal in religious significance. They have a counterpart in
dedications made by the whole *polis* or other groups within it. The
irregularity and *ad hoc* nature of individual dedications does not
mean that they were perceived to be different in nature or importance from the cult acts performed on a regular basis. Cities, as well as
individuals, made votive offerings to the gods on special occasions.
Individuals offered votive gifts on a variety of occasions[22] and not
only in times of crisis.[23] Dedications by individuals, like *polis* and

---

[20] Cf. *Salam.* 20ff. Cf. W. Ferguson, 'The Salaminioi of Heptaphylai and Sounion',
Hesperia, 7 (1938), 28, 34.

[21] Cf. n. 22. On the underlying mentality cf. also Burkert in *Gifts,* 43–50.

[22] Cf. van Straten, 'Gifts for the Gods', 88–102.

[23] As is suggested by J. D. Mikalson, *Athenian Popular Religion* (Chapel Hill, NC, and
London, 1983), 89. Cf. a sample of dedications not pertaining to an occasion of need or
crisis: van Straten, 'Gifts for the Gods', 92–6.

group dedications, were often commemorated through inscriptions,[24] which perpetuated the memory of the donor's action and his/her claim to a special relationship with the divine;[25] this shows that the dedication was perceived as a permanent act of worship, and that individual dedications were not simply crisis acts, but were an important modality in the relationship between men and gods. The same mentality, of course, underlies humbler and less permanent and uninscribed gifts.

Another important individual cultic act is the individual sacrifice. In many sacred laws the category 'sacrifice of a private individual at a sanctuary' is treated as normal, for regulations are set out on the one hand for *polis* sacrifices and on the other for a private individual's sacrifice (cf. e.g. *Horos* 3 (1985), 105–7, ll. 2–10, 16–21). Nor are the regulations or the modalities pertaining to the latter significantly different from those for the former, so as to suggest that they were thought of as different in nature, a different category—except that the *polis* commands, naturally enough, a hierarchical superiority. Obviously, the people who sacrificed did not consume the sacrificial meat on their own, but what concerns us is not who participated on an *ad hoc* basis, but the fact that this was considered to be an individual cultic act, an individual sacrifice, and that this was a significant category. The individual sacrifice is a recognized cult act also in gentilicial sanctuaries, where the regulations for 'when a private individual sacrifices' contrast with those for 'when the *genos* sacrifices' (cf. *LSCG* 119. 2–9). 'Individual sacrifice' and 'individual votive gift' are combined in the dedication of votive offerings inscribed with an inscription commemorating a sacrifice offered by an individual (cf. e.g. Pfohl (n. 16) no. 49). The foundation of altars and shrines by individuals as a result of individual experiences was apparently not uncommon, at least in the fourth century (cf. Pl. *Leg.* 909e–910e),[26] and though Plato disapproved, the custom was clearly perfectly acceptable to the actual *polis*. Consequently, it is clear that individual cult acts were not abnormal in *polis* religion, or different in nature

---

[24] Cf. samples in van Straten, 'Gifts for the Gods', *passim*; Pfohl, *Griechische Inschriften*, nos. 45–7, 49, 51.

[25] Cf. Burkert in *Gifts*, 49. Cf. also Lyc. *Leocr.* 136.

[26] Cf. also M. Guarducci, 'L'offerta di Xenokrateia nel santuario di Cefiso al Falero', in D. W. Bradeen and M. F. McGregor (eds.), *Phoros: Tribute to Benjamin Dean Meritt* (Locust Valley, NY, 1974), 59, on the dedication of altars. For the 5th cent. cf. Themistokles' dedication of a temple to Artemis Aristoboule (Plut. *Them.* 22; *Mor.* 869c–d; Travlos, *PD*, 121).

from cult activities performed in groups; individual worship was one of the main modalities of Greek cult.

Another argument in favour of the view that the individual was the basic cultic unit in *polis* religion is the fact that in cult individuals were grouped in various types of groupings, according to age, sex, and, perhaps most significantly, profession (at the Chalkeia for example[27]), as well as affiliation to *polis* subdivisions. That is, the cultic articulation of the citizen body was manifold, and the individual was deployed in a variety of ways which signalled a variety of identity elements, not all of which were dependent on the others. It was not the case that one participated in the higher cult unit simply in virtue of being a member of the lower unit until the all-encompassing *polis* level was reached. This articulation, then, seems to be governed by a religious mentality in which the individual was the basic cult unit. Individuals participated as individuals in some central *polis* rites (cf. e.g. LSCG 92. 38 for a procession in a central *polis* cult). They were, of course, always excluded as individuals when they had committed certain types of offence (cf. e.g. [Dem.] 59. 85–6). The perception that the individual was the primary cultic unit surely also underlies the existence of individual liturgies linked to the performance of ritual duties (cf. e.g. LSS 124; cf. Isaeus 8. 19–20 for a deme liturgy of this type involving women). This view makes best sense also because it entails a less radical 'rupture' between the 'normal' *polis* cults and those involving an individual initiation and/or choice, such as the Eleusinian Mysteries, or cults practised in the private cult associations, and can thus best explain the absence of a radical discontinuity between the two types and also the observable intimate relationship between the Eleusinian Mysteries and the rest of Athenian central *polis* religion. Yet another argument in its favour is provided by the religious restrictions accompanying the grant of citizenship, which do not extend to the next generation if the latter are the legitimate children of an Athenian woman (cf. e.g. [Dem.] 59. 106)—clearly a practice governed by a mentality in which the individual is the basic cult unit. Finally, also more naturally explained if

---

[27] Cf. E. Simon, *Festivals of Attica* (Madison, Wis., 1983), 38–9. On professional groups in cult cf. also L. Gernet and A. Boulanger, *Le Génie grec dans la religion* (Paris, 1970 (orig. publ. 1932)), 249. The levy of tax destined to finance a particular cult on groups such as shipowners can also be perceived as part of this type of articulation— and this is not affected by the fact that non-citizens were also involved (cf. Schlaifer, 'Notes on Athenian Public Cults', 233–4).

the individual was the basic cultic unit is the fact that—besides private associations—*ad hoc* collections of individuals also formed themselves into cultic groups with their own community of cult; thus we learn from Dinarchos 2. 9 that prisoners formed a cult group sufficiently conscious of its identity as a group to exclude those felt not to be worthy of their communion. This may appear 'natural', but only because, in our society—as on my model also in the Greek *polis*—the basic cult unit is the individual. It is clear, then, that the basic cult unit in *polis* religion is the individual, and the basic religious framework, the significant higher-order cult group, is the *polis*. As we saw, this is also the main articulation of participation in Panhellenic cult, in which the two main types of worshipping unit are the *polis* and the individual, whose participation is mediated by the *polis*.

In so far as religion defines, and plays a considerable role in giving identity to, the group—the *polis* and each of its subdivisions—there are closures in *polis* cults. But other factors, among them the perception of common Greekness and the Panhellenic dimension of religion, create pressures towards openings. Similar pressures were also created by religious activities which involved worship at sanctuaries other than those of one's *polis*, such as the consultation of oracles, pilgrimages, and the dedication of votives at particular sanctuaries, already attested in the eighth century. The *poleis* emerged, and their religious systems were set in place, at a moment in which most parts of the Greek world were opening up much more drastically than before towards each other and towards the outside world— most strikingly through colonization, and, in religion, through the emergence of Panhellenic sanctuaries and the radiation of Homer and Hesiod, who articulated a Panhellenic religion. Thus the openings as well as the closures were built into these religious systems from the beginning. Delphi's increasingly important role helped strengthen the Panhellenic dimension. Eventually, the four Panhellenic Games gave a focus, and greater regularity and intensity, to inter-*polis* ritually focused contacts in which the Panhellenism of the international Archaic aristocracy played a crucial role. The openings and the closures of the *polis* towards outsiders varied from city to city and from period to period. At the closed end of the spectrum should be situated Sparta and Lyttos,[28] at the open Athens (cf. Strabo

---

[28] Cf. H. and M. van Effenterre, 'Nouvelles lois archaïques de Lyttos', *BCH* 109 (1985), 179–88.

10. 3. 18). A particular type of opening, of link, exists between colony and mother city; the latter retained some share in the cults of the
former,[29] who, in addition, participated with offerings to some
religious festivals of the mother-cities.[30] Thus, while the religious
system of the colony was autonomous—though open and
interacting—when viewed from the inside, when viewed from the
mother-city it could also be seen as a dependent part of the latter's
religious system—in which it had originated. (At the foundation of a
colony *sacra* and the sacred fire were carried from the mother city,[31]
but with the establishment of the new cults and sanctuaries a new
system was created, in which the oecist's cult represented the colony's first own, new, cult which helped give it identity.[32]) This symbolic
dependence, and the colony–mother-city cultic relationship, which
became a schema for expressing a (real, perceived or manufactured)
genetic (or metaphorically genetic) relationship between cities, did
not only have negative connotations for the colony. It could be perceived as a privilege when the relationship was with a prestigious
polis, especially one with prestigious cults.[33]

   In every *polis* non-citizens could only worship as *xenoi*. But not all
xenoi had the same status: some were admitted into the system more
than others. An important distinction is that between foreigners
passing through and metics settled in the *polis*.[34] Metics in Athens[35]
were allowed a certain measure of participation. Of the various levels
of participation in the cult of a Greek *polis*, the highest, being eligible

---

[29] Cf. e.g. Thuc. 1. 25. 4; cf. A.J. Graham, *Colony and Mother City in Ancient Greece*
(Manchester, 1964), 10; 14–15; 49–51; 100–3; 153; 154–65; W. Leschhorn, *Gründer der
Stadt* (Stuttgart, 1984), 96–7; Malkin, *RC*, 266.
[30] Graham, *Colony*, 154–65 esp. 161; cf. R. Meiggs, *The Athenian Empire* (Oxford,
1972), 293. On this relationship was modelled the participation in Athenian cult of
Athens' allies, who, after the Treasury of the League was transferred to Athens,
brought the tribute, and attended theatrical performances, during the Dionysia, and
were eventually obliged to bring a cow and a panoply to the Great Panathenaia (cf.
Meiggs, 290–5).
[31] Cf. Malkin, *RC*, 70–2; 114–34.
[32] Cf. Malkin, *RC*, 189–240.
[33] Cf. e.g. *IG* IV². 1. 47; Graham, *Colony*, 163–4.
[34] Cf. Aesch. *Suppl.* 611; Ar. *Ach.* 502–8; M. F. Baslez, *L'Étranger dans la Grèce antique*
(Paris, 1984), 48; D. Whitehead, *The Ideology of the Athenian Metic* (Cambridge, 1977),
39–40 and 41 ff. Cf. also *LSAM* 59. 3–6.
[35] On whom there is most evidence (cf. Whitehead, *Ideology, passim*; Ph. Gauthier,
Symbola. Les Étrangers et la justice dans les cités grecques (Nancy, 1972), 108–49; Baslez,
L'Étranger, 127–49; on cult participation cf. also A. Pickard-Cambridge, *The Dramatic
Festivals of Athens*, 2nd edn. revised by J. Gould and D. M. Lewis (Oxford, 1968), 61 and
n. 6; Deubner, *AF*, 28 nn. 3–6.

for priesthoods, was limited to Athenian citizens.[36] The lowest, being present at a rite and prayer, was extended to *xenoi* and slaves for the *dēmotelē* rites,[37] though slaves were excluded from certain cults and certain temples (cf. Isaeus 6. 50). A more significant type of ritual participation involves sharing in the sacrificial meat; metics did so in certain particular contexts, both in central *polis* cults (cf. *LSCG* 13. 25–6, a sacred law pertaining to the Hephaisteia) and in the context of the demes in which they were resident.[38] At the Panathenaia metics took part in the procession, holding an honorific office, *skaphēphoria* (carrying of trays) for men, *hydriaphoria* (carrying of water jars) and *skiadēphoria* (carrying of sun-shades) for women,[39] while freedmen and other barbarians carried an oak branch through the Agora (Bekker, *Anecd.* 1. 242, 3–6). The Panathenaia could thus be said to have articulated the Athenian *polis* as an open system, with the citizens at the centre. An important Athenian cult in which all Greeks, including slaves, could participate was the Eleusinian Mysteries—from which barbarians and those who had impure hands were excluded.[40] Metics were excluded from the cults of phratries and tribes.[41] Metics also practised their own cults, mostly in private religious associations, which, at least eventually, and by the fourth century almost all of them, included both citizens and noncitizens.[42] Metics had probably had their own associations from an early date, which can be said to have been 'encompassed', in the diluted sense of being sanctioned, by the *polis* perhaps from an early date, if the Solonian law quoted (probably with accretions) in a corrupt passage in *Dig.* 47. 22. 4, which permitted the regulations of various associations to be binding so far as they did not conflict with the laws of the *polis*, had indeed contained a reference to private

[36] Cf. Dem. 57. 47–8; [Dem.] 59. 92, 104, 106; cf. also Whitehead, *Ideology*, 86.
[37] Cf. [Dem.] 59. 85. Cf. also Callim. *Aet.* 178. 1–2; Deubner, *AF*, 94–5; 96; 118; 152; Whitehead, *Demes*, 214.
[38] Cf. the deme law of the Skambonidai (*IG* I³ 244 C 4–9; *LSCG* 10 C 4–9. Cf. on it Whitehead, *Ideology*, 86–7, cf. also pp. 28, 75, 145; Baslez, *L'Étranger*, 77): in the festival of the tribal hero Leos the metics living in Skambonidai share in the sacrifice.
[39] On these offices cf. Whitehead, *Ideology*, 87–8.
[40] Isocr. 4. 157; Hdt. 8. 65; cf. G. E. Mylonas, *Eleusis and the Eleusinian Mysteries* (Princeton and London, 1961), 247–8; A. R. W. Harrison, *The Law of Athens: The Family and Property* (Oxford, 1968), 166.
[41] Whitehead, *Ideology*, 86. Also from *genē* cults, but so were most Athenians, who were not members of a *genos*.
[42] Cf. A. Andrewes, 'Philochoros on Phratries', *JHS* 81(1961), 1–15, at 11; Whitehead, *Ideology*, 88–9.

religious associations.[43] A stricter and more significant form of 'encompassing' and sanctioning religious associations of foreigners is that involving the grant of land to them by the *ekklēsia* (Assembly) so that they could own a sanctuary.[44] A much more radical opening of the *polis* religious system took place in Athens in the third quarter of the fifth century, before 429/8, when that system took up a foreign deity, the Thracian goddess Bendis, who was incorporated in Athenian *polis* religion.[45] Divine sanction had been sought and obtained for this action (cf. *LSS* 6. 15–17; *LSCG* 46. 6–7).

As in Athens, slaves were excluded from certain cults and shrines also in other cities (cf. e.g. Plut. *Mor.* 267d). *Xenoi* were also excluded from certain rites and shrines, especially those which defined the citizen group. Thus, for example, at Delos a marble lintel which almost certainly came from a door in the shrine of Archegetes Anios, the *hērōs archēgetēs* (founder) of the Delians, bears the inscription 'It is not lawful for a *xenos* to enter'.[46] It is significant that it is the cult of *archēgetēs* Anios, from which foreigners are excluded; for the cult of the Archegetes stands also for, and helps define, the identity of the *polis*.[47] A particular category of exclusion concerns particular groups of foreigners.[48] We know that barbarians were explicitly excluded from some cults, and we can surmise that they were excluded from many others also. Non-Greeks were not prevented from consulting the major Panhellenic oracle at Delphi, but they were not allowed to seek consultation in all oracles.[49] With regard to openings and exclusions in the *polis* subdivisions, we saw that in Athens, demes, unlike phratries, allowed some participation to outsiders, not only other citizens, but also metics. But deme rites also had their closures, rites

[43] Cf. Andrewes, 'Philochoros on Phratries', 2 n. 7 and 12 n. 40; Whitehead, *Ideology*, 88; M. L. Freyburger-Galland, G. Freyburger, and J.-Ch. Tautil, *Sectes religieuses en Grèce et à Rome dans l'antiquité païenne* (Paris, 1986), 61–3.

[44] Thus cf. *IG* II² 337 (on which cf. J. Pečírka, *The Formula for the Grant of Enktesis in Attic Inscriptions* (Prague, 1966), 59–61; Whitehead, *Ideology*, 88).

[45] Cf. Pl. *Rep.* 327a–328b; *IG* I³ 136; *LSS* 6; cf. also *LSCG* 45, 46; Nilsson, *GGR*, 833–6; Deubner, *AF*, 219–20; Parke, *FA*, 149–52; Pečírka, *Formula*, 122–30.

[46] *LSS* 49; cf. Ph. Bruneau, *Recherches sur les cultes de Délos à l'époque hellénistique et à l'époque impériale* (Paris, 1970), 423, 427.

[47] Cf. also Malkin, *RC*, 189–266 *passim*, esp. 241–50.

[48] Cf. Hdt. 8. 134: Thebans at the Amphiaraion. Hdt. 5. 72. 3: Dorians not allowed in the temple of Athena Polias on the Acropolis, the most important central *polis* cult. *LSCG* 110: Dorians excluded from certain rites or a festival, of Kore (almost certainly city-protector in function) at Paros.

[49] For example, they were excluded from those of Trophonios and Amphiaraos: cf. Hdt. 8. 134; Petropoulou, 'The *Eparche* Documents', 51–2.

in which only demesmen could participate,[50] which helped define the membership of the group 'deme'.

A different and ritually very significant type of exclusion was that of one or the other sex from certain rites or cults. (The exclusion of men from the Thesmophoria has been immortalized by Aristophanes; for examples of the exclusion of women, cf. *LSS* 63; *LSCG* 89. 5–6.)

In the Classical period *polis* religion encompassed all religious activity within the *polis*. All such activity was perceived as symbolically legitimated through the religious system of the *polis*, which shaped the perception of the gods and articulated the relationships between men and the divine—with the help of the anchoring provided by the oracle; and the *polis* was the authority which sanctioned all cult activity within its boundaries and mediated it beyond them. Of course, the process of recovering perceptions of this type is vulnerable to the danger that our assessments may be shaped by our own culturally determined assumptions and expectations and thus distort the ancient realities. A strategy which helps block as far as possible such corruption is to begin by locating the cults under consideration within the relevant network of articulated relationships. (This I have done in the preceding chapter.) As a result, we can see that the *polis* encompasses and regulates the religious discourse of its subdivisions. A point that needs to be stressed is that all cult acts, including those which some modern commentators are inclined to think of as 'private', are (religiously) dependent on the *polis*. *Oikos* cults also derive their religious authority from, and are regulated by, the *polis*. This is made clear in Xen. *Mem.* 1. 3. 1 and 4. 3. 16 where we are told that to those who enquire how they should make themselves agreeable to the gods, or how they should act either with regard to sacrifices or with regard to cult offered to their ancestors, the Pythia replies that they would be acting piously by acting according to the law of the *polis*.

A series of other arguments supports this interpretation. First, the *polis* regulated *oikos* cults by law in a variety of ways.[51] (1) It regulated 'private' funerals through funerary legislation. (2) It

---

[50] Cf. Whitehead, *Demes*, 205.

[51] The *polis* had a say in the affairs, even the membership, of the *oikos* in general: it legislated to ensure its continuation through adoption (cf. e.g. Isaeus 2. 10, 25, 45; 7. 30), and to determine who should marry girls with no brothers, through whom inheritance was transmitted (cf. e.g. [Dem.] 43. 52–5).

sometimes took over the responsibility for the disposal of the body of certain categories of people; thus the *polis* in classical Athens gave an honorary funeral to its war-dead and disposed dishonourably of the bodies of traitors. (3) The *polis* defined and policed obligations between members of the *oikos*, especially of sons towards parents and grandparents (cf. e.g. Isaeus 8. 32), which included burial and the offer of the customary rites thereafter (cf. Xen. *Mem.* 2. 2. 13; Dem. 24. 107; Din. 2. 8; cf. also [Dem.] 43. 57–8). Even more significantly, both practice and such explicit articulations as we have suggest that the burial and offering of the customary rites was perceived as affecting not simply the individual dead person, but above all the law and the gods, and so also the *polis'* relationships to the gods (cf. Aeschin. 1. 14). (4) The *polis* prescribed that the most solemn commemorations of the dead took place as a central *polis* ritual, when everyone commemorated their immediate ancestors at the same time at the festival of the Genesia.[52]

Second, the cults which appear to be the *oikos* cults *par excellence*, above all that of Zeus Herkeios which seems to symbolize the *oikos* as a group,[53] are also part of the cultic nexus of the central *polis* and of the *polis* subdivisions, part of the network of interwoven relationships between the cults of the central *polis* and those of its subdivisions. Since, we shall now see, the modality of the relationship between *oikos* cults and other *polis* cults is the same as, for example, that between the phratries' and the central *polis'* cults of the Phratrioi gods, we may conclude that the relationship between *oikos* cult and other *polis* cults is similar to that between phratry cults and other *polis* cults. Zeus Herkeios had a deme cult[54] and a central *polis* cult in Athens,[55] including an altar on the Acropolis, in the Pandroseion, under the sacred olive-tree (Philochoros *FGrHist* 328 F 67), and thus in connection with the most central cults of the Athenian *polis* which are associated with the constitution of that *polis*. 'Having' a

[52] Cf. esp. the discussion in S. C. Humphreys, *The Family, Women and Death* (London, 1983), 87–8.
[53] Cf. Soph. *Ant.* 486–7; Hdt. 6. 68, cf. 67. The hearth and the cult of Hestia is above all the ritual centre of the *oikos*.
[54] Cf. *Thorik.* line 22 and left and right side (cf. Daux 157–60).
[55] Cf. Travlos, *PD*, 302, 478, fig. 602. Cult of Zeus Herkeios at Olympia: Paus. 5. 14. 7. On this god cf. also Harpocration s.v. Herkeios Zeus; R. E. Wycherley, 'The Olympieion at Athens', *GRBS* 5 (1964), 161–79, at 177; Nilsson, *GGR*, 402–3; Burkert, *GR*, 130, 248, 255–6; Andrewes, 'Philochoros on Phratries', 7–8.

cult of Zeus Herkeios (and a cult of Apollo Patroos) was a necessary qualification for archonship in Athens (*Ath. Pol.* 55. 3). The exact significance of this requirement is problematic. But it is possible that, as Andrewes suggested,[56] the cult of Zeus Herkeios was in the symbolic custody of the *genos* which presided over each phratry, in which case the altar of Zeus Herkeios in the individual house courtyards would have been symbolically dependent on that of the *genos*. In my view, this may well have begun this way, but—even leaving open the question of the institution of the central *polis* cult of Zeus Herkeios with its higher-order legitimation—in post-Kleisthenic times the house altars and household cult of Zeus Herkeios would probably have come *de facto* to be seen as symbolically dependent on, and sanctioned by, other higher-order cults of Zeus Herkeios, especially of the deme—and the central *polis*. In any case, if the notion of symbolic custody by the *genē* is correct, it fits well with the articulation presented here, according to which the cult of Zeus Herkeios in the *oikos* was not a self-contained 'private' cult, but was intertwined with, and derived its authority from, the higher-order cult, and ultimately the central *polis* cult. Since it is the *polis* which defines religion, including the cult of Zeus Herkeios, the individual manifestations of this cult, in the individual houses, derive their authority, their religious validity, from that central *polis* representation. Zeus Ktesios also had both a domestic and a central *polis* cult.[57]

Third, Lyc. *Leocr.* 25–6 (cf. 56) makes clear that the *oikos* cult was perceived to be part of the *polis* religious system from which it derived its forms. For one of the many blameworthy and treasonable things that Leocrates is said to have done when he fled Athens was that he transferred his ancestral *sacra* (*hiera ta patrōa*) to Megara. Various statements in this passage make clear that the head of the *oikos* was perceived as an 'administrator' of the *oikos* cult, without the authority to do what he liked with his ancestral *sacra* which were perceived to be a part of *polis* religion as a whole. (1) It is stressed that these *sacra* had been handed down to Leocrates by his ancestors who had established them according to the *polis*' laws and ancestral customs, and thus that it is thanks to, and in the framework of, the *polis* that he came in possession of

---

[56] Andrewes, 'Philochoros on Phratries', 7–8.
[57] On the latter cf. Dem. 21. 53; cf. Wycherley, 'The Olympieion', 177.

them. (2) The implication is that he committed impiety when he
forced these *sacra* to abandon the temples and the land in which
they had been established and to settle in an alien land in which
they were strangers—to the land and also to the traditional rites
of the Megarian *polis*. This shows that all cults, including *oikos*
cults, were closely connected to the geographical, sociopolitical,
and religious entity '*polis*' which helped shape them. (3) It is
claimed that this export of the *sacra* created the danger that the
divine help for the *polis* would have been diminished, exported
with them. This reveals a mentality in which the protection of the
gods depended on *polis* religion in all its individual articulations,
cults, rites, images, in all their manifestations, central *polis* cults,
deme cults, *oikos* cults, and so on; and in which the abstraction of
one element diminishes, and renders less effective, the whole system. (The forensic context and orator's aims do not affect this; for
this argument could only have been effective if it was credible, able
to strike a chord with the audience.) This, therefore, is another
argument in favour of the view that *oikos* cults were perceived to
be part of the *polis* cults and were interdependent with the whole
system of *polis* religion.

A further point that needs to be stressed is that cult activities
which in culturally determined terms would appear to pertain to
'personal' religion are in fact also part of *polis* religion. We saw that
individual cult activities were but one particular manifestation of
polis cult. The other side of this phenomenon can be illustrated by the
example of a personal dedication to an oecist (hero founder),[58] a type
of cult which in modern culturally determined assumptions would be
considered a *par excellence* 'state' artificial cult unlikely to attract
what some call 'personal piety'. *Polis* religion also encompassed the
Eleusinian Mysteries and Dionysiac rites—which involve personal
initiation and personal salvation. The intimate connection between
the Eleusinian Mysteries and the Athenian *polis* which regulated
them and had authority over them is too well documented to need
discussion. With regard to Dionysiac rites, which differed widely in
different places and periods,[59] in Classical Athens, where the evidence
is sufficient for us to form a picture, Dionysiac rites are wholly

---

[58] To Antiphemos (Malkin, *RC*, 194–5).
[59] Cf. A. Henrichs, 'Changing Dionysiac Identities,' in B. F. Meyer and E. P. Sanders
(eds.), *Jewish and Christian Self-definition, iii, Self-definition in the Graeco-Roman World*
(London, 1982), at 151–3.

integrated into the socio-religious structures of the *polis*.[60] Limitations of space prevent me from discussing the relationship between *polis* religion and non-institutionalized sectarian discourse of the Orphic type; it seems possible that at least some manifestations of the latter may have been perceived as lying outside the authority of the *polis* discourse—some important aspects of which they did in fact challenge, unlike, for example, the tragedians, whose alleged challenge to the religious discourse of the *polis* is a modern mirage, resulting from the culturally determined reading both of the tragedies and of a religious discourse which was not a dogmatic schema demanding faith, but an open system proposing certain articulations of the world and transversed by the fundamental Greek category of unknowability.

---

[60] C. Bérard and C. Bron, 'Bacchos au coeur de la cité. Le thiase dionysiaque dans l'espace politique', in *L'Association dionysiaque dans les sociétés anciennes*, Actes de la table ronde organisée par l'École française de Rome, Rome 24–25 mai 1984 (Rome, 1986), 27, cf. 13–30. Cf. also the later Miletos decree *LSAM* 48. On the group aspect of Dionysiac cult activity: cf. Henrichs, 'Changing Dionysiac Identities', 150–1.

3

Tribes, Festivals, and Processions: Civic Ceremonial and Political Manipulation in Archaic Greece

W. R. CONNOR

I

In recent years classicists and ancient historians have devoted renewed attention to the Archaic Age in Greece, the period from approximately the eighth century to the fifth century BC. Important articles, excavation reports and monographs, as well as books by Moses Finley, L. H. Jeffery, Oswyn Murray, Chester Starr and others, not to mention a recent volume of the *Cambridge Ancient History*, bear witness to the vigour of recent scholarship in this area.[1] Among many of these treatments of the period, moreover, is evident an increasing recognition of the close connection between social and economic developments and the political life of the Greek cities of the period. At the same time that this renewed interest in the Archaic Age has become so prominent in classical studies, a group of scholars working in more modern periods has developed a fresh approach to the role of ritual and ceremonial in civic life, especially

Thomas Figueira and several colleagues at Princeton helped improve earlier drafts of this chapter. The final version was completed while enjoying the hospitality of the Institute for Advanced Study. This chapter is dedicated to the memory of Gerald Else.

[1] J. Boardman and N. G. L. Hammond (eds.), *CAH*[2] iii. 3 (Cambridge, 1982); M. I. Finley, *Early Greece: The Bronze and Archaic Ages* (New York, 1970); R. J. Hopper, *The Early Greeks* (New York, 1976); L. H. Jeffery, *Archaic Greece* (New York, 1976); Oswyn Murray, *Early Greece* (Brighton, 1980); A. M. Snodgrass, *Archaic Greece: The Age of Experiment* (London, 1980); Chester Starr, *The Economic and Social Growth of Early Greece, 800–500 BC* (Oxford, 1977). Among the older studies A. Heuss, in *Antike und Abendland*, 2 (1946), 26–62 is especially important. See now his 'Von Anfang und Ende', *Gnomosyne, Festschrift W. Marg* (Munich, 1981), 1–31. Recent periodical literature is too extensive to mention but note W. G. Runciman, *Comparative Studies in Society and History*, 24 (1982), 351–77.

during the European Middle Ages and Renaissance. Deeply influenced by cultural anthropology, they have found in the often surprisingly rich documentation about festivals, processions, charivaris etc. important insights into the societies in which these activities took place.[2] Classicists looking upon this movement may be inclined to undervalue its originality and perhaps its controversiality, pointing out that a serious interest in ancient festivals has long been prominent in classical scholarship and is well represented in recent books such as those by Mikalson, Parke, and Simon, and such older works as Martin Nilsson's frequently cited *Cults, Myths, Oracles and Politics in Ancient Greece* (Lund, 1951).[3] Yet there is a great difference both in method and in results between the traditional approaches to ceremonial represented in the study of ancient Greece and those being developed in more recent fields.[4] That difference is reflected in Simon Price's comment on 'methodological individualists', that is on scholars who couch their explanations of events in terms of the beliefs and goals of individuals:

methodological individualists can study only the organization of ritual by the elite and the exploitation of . . . ritual for propaganda purposes. That is, they draw a sharp distinction between symbolism and the 'real' world of individuals and they cannot treat ritual as an articulation of collective representations.[5]

Thus traditional approaches to ancient Greek ritual have emphasized the link between specific political movements or leaders and the

---

[2] See e.g. Robert Darnton, 'A Bourgeois Puts his World in Order: The City as a Text', *The Great Cat Massacre* (New York, 1985), 107–43; Natalie Z. Davis, *Past and Present*, 59 (1971), 41–75; E. Le Roy Ladurie, *Carnival in Romans*, trans. M. Feeney (New York, 1979); Edward Muir, *Civic Ritual in Renaissance Venice* (Princeton, 1981); R. C. Trexler, *Public Life in Renaissance Florence* (New York, 1980) and 'Ritual Behaviour in Renaissance Florence', *Medievalia & Humanistica*, NS 4 (1973), 125–44. Two essays in *The Pursuit of Holiness in Late Medieval and Renaissance Religion*, ed. C. Trinkaus and H. A. Oberman (Leiden, 1974) are also helpful: Natalie Z. Davis, 'Some Tasks and Themes in the Study of Popular Religion', 307–36, and R. C. Trexler, 'Ritual in Florence: Adolescence and Salvation in the Renaissance', 200–64. Among the works dealing with earlier periods Sabine MacCormack, *Art and Ceremony in Late Antiquity* (Berkeley, 1981) and Simon Price, *Rituals and Power* (Cambridge, 1984) are especially important. Many of these works rely on studies in symbolic anthropology, e.g. Clifford Geertz, *The Interpretation of Cultures* (New York, 1973).

[3] Parke, *FA*; E. Simon, *Festivals of Attica* (Madison, Wis., 1983); J. D. Mikalson, *The Sacred and Civil Calendar of the Athenian State* (Princeton, 1975).

[4] See also Nilsson's 'Die Prozessionentypen im gr. Kult', *Jahrbuch des k. Archäolog. Instituts*, 31 (1916), 309ff. (reprinted in his *Opera Selecta*, i. 166–214).

[5] Price, *Rituals and Power*, 11.

development of cult and festival. They emphasize the distance between the leader and his followers, and the consequent 'manipulation' of myth and religion for propaganda purposes. Although M. I. Finley and others have pointed out the limitations of this approach, works outside the field of ancient Greek history continue to provide the clearest articulation of the advantages of a new approach to ritual and ceremony.[6] These works often see ceremony as part of the symbolic expression of civic concerns and as a difficult to read but ultimately eloquent text about the nature of civic life, as in Edward Muir's observations about Renaissance Venice:

Civic rituals were commentaries on the city, its internal dynamics, and its relationship with the outside world. In commenting upon civic realities, the rituals illustrated an ideal arrangement of human relationships, created a homily that stimulated or altered some formal political and social ideas, and provided a medium for discourse among the constituent classes and the literate elite and the masses. Although civic rituals often served the rulers' interests they were not just propaganda and did not pass messages in only one direction.[7]

This emphasis on civic rituals as a means of communication, and especially on communication in two directions, derives from one of the central concerns of the newer scholarship on ceremonial, and is a major point of difference between this approach and that more familiar in the study of early Greece. This essay investigates the possibility of applying the newer approach to Archaic Greece and thereby exploring the nature of political life and leadership, the role of propaganda, manipulation etc., and the significance of ritual festivals and ceremonial in civic life. Even a cursory study of the history of Archaic Greece points to the need for a closer examination of these issues. There is, for example, an apparent convergence between festivals and political disturbances. Cylon attempted his unfortunate coup at the time 'of the greatest festival of Zeus' (Thuc. 1. 126. 4), although he perhaps misinterpreted the oracle which urged this

---

[6] See M. I. Finley, *Politics in the Ancient World* (Cambridge, 1983), 95 f.

[7] Edward Muir, *Civic Ritual*, 5. A similar approach has suggested that even the delivery of panegyrics on imperial occasions in late antiquity, often regarded as one of the most extreme examples of flattery and propaganda, is to be seen 'not merely as a method of making propaganda; it was also a token of legitimate rule and a form of popular consent, demonstrated by the presence of an audience' (MacCormack, *Art and Ceremony*, 9). The study of French festivals has shown their tendency to turn into protests, *trouble-fêtes*, and thereby communicate popular anger or demands. See C. Rearick, *Journal of Contemporary History*, 12 (1977), 437.

timing upon him. Harmodius and Aristogiton carried out their plot against the Pisistratids at the time of the Great Panathenaea of 514. Recently Thomas Figueira has suggested that the principal periods of instability in the early sixth century in Athens coincide with the years of the Great Panathenaea.[8] Clisthenes' career provides a further instance of the significance of civic ritual in political life, particularly when we bear in mind that the tribes which he created were not purely administrative conveniences. Each had as its namesake a traditional hero, and these in turn had their own myths and legends, most fully attested in the elaborate rendition in the sixtieth oration in the Demosthenic corpus. Cult places, shrines, treasuries, officials, meetings, communal meals on festival occasions are attested for many of the new Clisthenic tribes and may safely be presumed to have existed in all ten cases.[9] A monument with statues of the ten tribal heroes stood in a prominent place in the Athenian agora and served as a mustering place for the citizens and as a civic bulletin board. The tribes also competed with each other for the prestige conferred by the Athenian system of individual services to the state, especially in the choral competitions at the Dionysia. The tribes also passed honorary decrees, awarded honorific crowns, and sponsored dinners for all members at the time of the Dionysiac and Panathenaic festivals.[10]

Perhaps the most productive topics for examination, however, come from earlier parts of the sixth century—Pisistratus' return to power in the 550s and Solon's establishment of a 'census' system in the preceding generation. These episodes provide an opportunity to test some of the approaches discussed above and to clarify the connection between ceremonial and civic life.

---

[8] Thomas Figueira, *Hesperia*, 53 (1984), 447–73. Note, however, that the events of 579/8 come in a year of preparation for the Panathenaea, rather than in the year of its celebration.

[9] See G. Busolt and H. Swoboda, *Griechische Staatskunde*, xi (Munich, 1926), 973–8, and Nilsson, *Cults*, 30–7.

[10] On the role of cults and ceremonial in Clisthenes' reforms see E. Kearns, 'Change and Continuity in Religious Structures after Cleisthenes', in *Crux*, 189–207.

II

Pisistratus' return from his first exile in the 550s BC escorted in a chariot by a tall woman dressed as Athena has often produced perplexity and interpretive distress. Herodotus, again our earliest source, confesses his amazement at the apparent gullibility of the Athenians:

at last Megacles, wearied with the struggle, sent a herald to Pisistratus, with an offer to re-establish him . . . if he would marry his daughter. Pisistratus consented, and on these terms an agreement was concluded between the two, after which they proceeded to devise the mode of his restoration. And here the device on which they hit was the silliest to be found in all history, more especially considering that the Greeks have been from very ancient times distinguished from the barbarians by superior sagacity and freedom from foolish simpleness, and remembering that they contrived this for Athenians, who have the reputation of surpassing all other Greeks in cleverness. There was in the Paeanian district a woman named Phye, whose height was almost six feet, and who was altogether comely to look upon. This woman they clothed in complete armour, and, showing her the fashion in which she would appear most becoming, they placed her in a chariot and drove into the city. Heralds had been sent forward to precede her, and to make proclamation to this effect, 'Citizens of Athens, receive again Pisistratus with friendly minds. Athena, who of all men honours him the most, herself conducts him back to her own citadel.' This they proclaimed in all directions, and immediately the rumour spread through the country districts that Athena was bringing back Pisistratus. They of the city also, fully persuaded that the woman was the veritable goddess, worshipped her and received Pisistratus back. (Hdt. 1. 60. 2–5, trans. Rawlinson, with modifications)

Herodotus is greatly amused and somewhat perplexed by the episode, but he has no doubts that it took place. Modern scholarship commonly reverses the pattern. Many scholars deny its historicity; only a few deal with the interpretive problem posed by the procession. Most studies dismiss the reports of the procession as a 'legend' or as a story that 'even for Herodotus . . . [was] more than he could believe.'[11] Those who accept the story regularly treat it as manipulation of the

---

[11] Among the other sources reporting the procession are: Arist. *Ath. Pol.* 14. 4, Clidemus *FGrHist* 323 F 15, Polyaenus *Strat.* 1. 21. 1, Athen. 13. 609; cf. J. B. Bury, *History of Greece*, 4th edn., rev. R. Meiggs (New York, 1975), 128, which treats it as a legend that Herodotus did not himself believe.

masses by Pisistratus (or sometimes by Megacles) labelling it a 'charade' or 'propaganda blatant to the point of absurdity' etc.[12] Only a small minority of scholars has accepted the episode as historic and attempted to read the messages implicit in it. But agreement has not been easy. Louis Gernet viewed the chariot as a symbol both of triumph and of marriage.[13] Pisistratus

est le roi qui agrée la déesse du pays, et sa royauté est proclamée à l'occasion et par la vertu de son mariage. Pour la pensée mythique, les deux choses sont liées; et c'est la femme qu'on épouse qui confère la royauté.[14]

Was this, as Helmut Berve has explicitly suggested, part of a *hieros gamos*, a ritual re-enactment of divine fertility?[15] Surely there are marriage elements in the tale—later elaborated into the story that one of Pisistratus' sons married Phye.[16] But the notion of a ritual marriage between Pisistratus and the analogue of Athena, a perpetual virgin, gives other scholars pause. Athena is, after all, not elsewhere associated with such rites.

John Boardman has also attempted to interpret rather than simply dismiss the procession. Like Gernet he focuses on the procession by chariot but his analogies are drawn from art rather than fertility rituals. He notes that while before the period of Pisistratus' rule Athena was only occasionally depicted in chariots, 'later she is increasingly associated with them', especially in the company of Heracles.[17] He concludes that Pisistratus was, on this occasion as on others, associating himself with Heracles and hinting that his procession to the Acropolis was an analogue to Heracles' elevation to Olympus.[18] The procession then reflects a major theme in Pisistratid propaganda—the association of Pisistratus with Heracles.

---

[12] See e.g. J. Boardman, *Revue archéologique*, (1972), 62; Snodgrass, *Archaic Greece*, 114; W. G. Moon, 'The Paris Painter', in W. G. Moon (ed.), *Ancient Greek Art and Iconography* (Madison, Wis., 1983), 101f.

[13] L. Gernet, 'Mariages des tyrans', *Éventail de l'histoire vivante, Hommage à L. Febvre*, ii (Paris, 1953), 52. The essay is reprinted in Gernet, *Anthropologie de la Grèce antique* (Paris, 1968), 344–59, and is also included in the collection of Gernet's works trans. J. Hamilton and B. Nagy (Baltimore, 1981).

[14] Ibid.

[15] H. Berve, *Die Tyrannis bei den Griechen* (Munich, 1967), 545, paraphrasing and expanding on Gernet.

[16] Clidemus *FGrHist* 323 F 15. On the problems in chronology see J. K. Davies, *Athenian Propertied Families* (Oxford, 1971), 450–5.

[17] Boardman, *Revue archéologique*, (1972), 60f.

[18] For an important challenge to Boardman's views see Moon, 'The Paris Painter', 97–118; R.M. Cook, 'Pots and Pisistratan Propaganda', *JHS* 107 (1987), 167–9.

Boardman's discussion of the scenes showing Athena and Heracles is a useful reminder that the episode is far richer than his characterization of it as a 'charade' suggests. But it is precisely the identification of Pisistratus with Heracles that is missing in the story. Have our sources suppressed the most interesting detail of all—that Pisistratus donned a lion skin and club? Or did Pisistratus for some reason avoid making explicit the parallel between himself and Heracles? If so, why, and just what message was conveyed by the form of this procession?

Other scholars have turned to literary parallels. Gerald Else noted that the story echoed in some respects Athena's support for Odysseus. 'Surely it depends integrally upon the *Odyssey* and upon the *Odyssey* being well known to the whole population of Athens at the time.'[19] The closest Homeric analogue, however, is *Iliad* 5, as Stein long ago pointed out in his commentary on Herodotus (1.60). In this passage Athena elbowed Sthenelos aside, entered the chariot next to Diomedes 'and drove the horses hard and straight at Ares' (trans. R. Fitzgerald). Athetized lines follow saying that the 'dread goddess led on the man who was the bravest'. But Else's essential point is well taken. The ceremony calls to mind many stories of Athena's willingness to become involved with human favourites—Odysseus, Diomedes, Heracles, and now Pisistratus.

All these explications of the ceremony have something to commend them, even if none seems precisely right. They pose, moreover, rather sharply the more general interpretive problem of how one explicates, or 'reads', a ceremony of this sort. Surely we are not forced to choose a single model for the procession. Elements from marriage processions, epic interventions, arrival ceremonies, parades celebrating athletic or military victories, myths, rituals, and legends may all be present simultaneously.[20] No single 'explanation', no minimalist aetiology, can catch the richness and multivalence of the event. But in determining which elements are most revealing about the ceremony it is important to look not only at the similarities but also to try to understand the contrasts between the ceremony and other patterns within the culture. As in literary criticism, a powerful interpretation will be recognized not by precise parallelism in all

[19] G. F. Else, *Hermes*, 85 (1957), 36f.

[20] On the possibility that the arrival ceremonies of late antiquity have an origin in much earlier phases of Greek civilization see MacCormack, *Art and Ceremony*, 19ff. and 281 n. 14.

elements but by its ability to make sense of both similarities and differences.

It is important then to look widely at the elements present in such a ceremony. The list may be a long one. The procession, for example, acts out a verbal pattern of praise in which a young woman is likened to a goddess. The pattern of praise goes back to the earliest Greek literature, for example, Odysseus' smooth words to Nausicaa when, branch in hand, he first meets her:

> Mistress: please: are you divine, or mortal?
> If one of those who dwell in the wide heaven,
> you are most near to Artemis, I should say —
> great Zeus' daughter—in your grace and presence.
> If you are one of earth's inhabitants,
> how blest your father, and your gentle mother,
> blest all your kin.
>
> (*Od.* 6. 149–55, trans. R. Fitzgerald)

But this is not merely a pattern of verbal praise. In processions the formula can actually be acted out, as can be seen in the much later novelistic account by Xenophon of Ephesus of a procession in honour of Artemis. The heroine of his *Ephesian Tale*, Anthia, is introduced dressed as Artemis in a procession where all can behold her beauty:

The girls in the procession were all decked out as if to meet lovers. Of the band of maidens the leader was Anthia . . . a prodigy of loveliness [who] far surpassed the other maidens. Her age was fourteen, and she had bloomed into mature shapeliness . . . Her eyes were lively, shining sometimes like a girl's and sometimes severe as of a chaste goddess. Her dress was a frock of purple . . . Her wrap was a fawn skin, and a quiver hung down from her shoulder. She carried bow and javelins and dogs followed at her heels. Time and again when the Ephesians saw her in the sacred procession they bowed down as to Artemis. And now too when Anthia came into view the entire multitude cried out in astonishment; some of the spectators asserted that she was the very goddess, others declared she was a replica fashioned by the goddess. But all did obeisance to her and bowed down and called her parents blessed.[21]

These parallels to the chariot ride with Phye help elucidate the likely relationship between those in the procession and the surrounding

---

[21] Xenophon of Ephesus, *An Ephesian Tale*, 1. 2. 2f. trans. Moses Hadas. The description is paralleled in other novels, e.g. Heliodorus 3. 4.

crowds. The on-lookers are not deluded by the similarity between Anthia's dress and the conventions for representing Artemis. They know perfectly well this girl is a human but they delight in her beauty and express that delight by their responses. The populace joins in a shared drama, not foolishly, duped by some manipulator, but playfully, participating in a cultural pattern they all share. We may assume that a similar situation existed when Pisistratus and Phye processed. The crowds might have chosen to express coolness, disinterest, or downright hostility. Instead it appears that they delighted in the shared drama and let their enthusiasm be known. The ceremony thus served as an expression of popular consent—two-way communication, not, as so often assumed, mere manipulation.[22]

But there is more to be gleaned from this analogy. The pattern of ceremonial appearance in the guise of a god is not restricted to females. Xenophon says that Anthia's lover-to-be, Habrocomes, also brought thoughts of divinity to mind when he marched among the *ephebes* in the procession:

The people gazed at him, were smitten by the sight, and cried out, 'Habrocomes is beautiful!' 'None is so fair!' 'He is the image of a beautiful god!'[23]

There is no reason to think that Habrocomes adopted a special dress to make himself resemble a god. But we know that some Greeks who enjoyed special success or claimed special powers dressed from time to time as divinities, perhaps thereby drawing on exceptional sources of psychic energy, expressing their gratitude for divine support, or making clear to all the role and status they claimed for

---

[22] The other side of manipulation is flattery, and this is the common interpretation of the Athenians' response to another famous ceremonial arrival, that of Demetrius Poliorcetes at Athens. One would like to know much more about this occasion, e.g. how Demetrius dressed etc., but the close association between himself and Athena is evident in the stories in Plut. (*Demetr.* 10–12) about his conduct in Athens. See also A. D. Nock, 'SUNNAOS THEOS', *HSCP* 41 (1930), reprinted in *Essays on Religion and the Ancient World*, i, ed. Z. Stewart (Cambridge, Mass., 1972), 202–51, esp. 204, and Ch. Habicht, *Gottmenschentum*, 2nd edn. (Munich, 1970), 232f.

[23] Xen. Eph. *Ephesian Tale* 1. 2. 8, trans. M. Hadas. The passage raises the important question whether the formula *male name in nominative* + *kalos* ('X is beautiful'), so common on Greek vase painting, may sometimes reflect acclamation and community consensus rather than purely individual erotic attachments. Note, for example, the scene on the *psyktēr* in the Metropolitan Museum 10. 210. 18 (*c.*520–510 BC) on which the boy Epainetos is being presented with garlands and *tainiai*. Next to him is the inscription *kalos*. (On Epainetos cf. the *haltēr* found at Eleusis, *IG* i² 802). This inscription seems likely to reflect an acclamation at or on returning from the games, analogous to *kallinikos*. Cf. Pi. *Ol.* 9. 1 ff.

themselves.[24] The use of divine dress both by men and women on cult occasions is well attested.[25] Chresmologoi and other claimants to exceptional wisdom—Pythagoras, Empedocles, Hippias, and Gorgias —are said to have appeared in exotic, perhaps god-like, garb, as did Menecrates, the healer at Syracuse.[26] Nikostratos of Argos, Milo of Croton, Dionysius I of Syracuse are all said to have dressed as a divinity at some point in their careers.[27] The historian Ephippus claimed that Alexander the Great put on the horns of Ammon and at other times appeared as Artemis, Hermes, and Heracles—he was certainly represented as Heracles from time to time.[28] There are, of course, Hellenistic and Roman analogues, perhaps the best known of which concern Marc Antony and Cleopatra.[29]

But although there was a cultural pattern among the Greeks of dressing as a divinity on certain ceremonial occasions, Pisistratus did not use it. Similarly, although there *are* similarities between this procession and the representations in the visual arts of Athena and Heracles in a chariot, Pisistratus avoided representing himself as Heracles.[30] His message is much more restrained: he comes back accompanied by Athena, honoured and approved by her, but as a human being not a superman or god-to-be. He is her associate and her assistant, but a fully human one.

This restraint is all the more striking if we may accept a detail reported in both the *Athēnaiōn Politeia* (14. 4) and Clidemus' *Atthis* I (*FGrHist* 323 F 15): Pisistratus drove the chariot and Phye was the *parabatēs*. This is often interpreted to mean simply that Phye was 'standing at his side'. But the Greek is stronger and perhaps more technical. The *parabatēs* or *apobatēs* was a person who in certain festivals leaped from the chariot in full armour and nimbly back

---

[24] See O. Weinreich, *Menekrates Zeus und Salmoneus* (Stuttgart, 1933) and E. Wunderlich, *Die Bedeutung der roten Farbe . . . , RGVV*, xx 1.

[25] Paus. 4. 27, 7. 18. 7; F. Back, *de Graecorum ceremoniis* (Berlin, 1883) and Burkert, *GR*, 97, 100, 186, 279.

[26] Hdt. 1. 62. 4; Ael. *VH* 12. 32; Empedocles *VS* 31 B 112. On Menecrates see Athen. 7. 289 a–c and the parallel passages cited in Weinreich, *Menekrates*, 92.

[27] Nikostratos: Diod. Sic. 16. 44. 2f; Milo of Croton: Diod. Sic. 12. 9. 6; Dionysius I: Dio Chrys. *Or*. 37. 21 (as emended by Casaubon). The prominence of Western Greek settings for these stories may be significant. The appearances may in part be modelled on the ritual of the Great Oath described in Plut. *Dion* 56.

[28] Ephippus (*FGrHist* 126 F 5) *apud* Athen. 537d ff. On the passage see A. B. Bosworth, *JHS* 100 (1980), 8.

[29] Plut. *Ant*. 24 and 26. On Roman examples see esp. F. Drexel, *PhW* 46 (1926), 157–60, and A. Alföldi, *Mitt. d.A.I. Rom* 49 (1934), 1–118.

[30] See M. B. Moore, *AJA* 40 (1986), 35–9.

again.[31] Athena is represented this way in art from time to time, perhaps in reflection of her original arrival in Athens at the time of the contest with Poseidon.[32] The Panathenaic and Eleusinian festivals included contests of this sort.[33] Walter Burkert has detected a ritual of kingship underlying this performance, whereby a new king seizes the kingship and sets himself within a complex context of deeply rooted Athenian myths and rituals.[34]

Surely there can be something very special in the ritual descent from a chariot, as the arrival of Demetrius Poliorcetes in Athens reminds us. When he arrived in the city the Athenians dedicated an altar to Demetrius *katabatēs* on the spot where he first stepped down.[35] But Pisistratus' procession reverses the expected pattern. Not Pisistratus but Phye acts as the *parabatēs*. The reversal is eloquent, perhaps even programmatic.[36] Pisistratus is not seizing the

[31] See Dion. Hal. *AR* 7. 73, esp. sec. 3 where he discusses the relationship between the terms *apobatēs* and *parabatēs*. The practice seems concentrated in Attica and Boeotia and a few other areas: see Harpocration s.v. *'apobatēs'*, and F. Brommer, *Der Parthenonfries* (Mainz, 1977), 221 f. In Thebes the practice gave a name to the military elite, the Heniochoi and Parabatai: Diod. Sic. 12. 70 and M. Detienne, 'La phalange', in J.-P. Vernant (ed.), *Problèmes de la guerre* (Paris, 1968), 134 f. Perhaps Herodotus' observation that Megacles and Pisistratus showed Phye 'the fashion in which she would appear most becoming' masks instruction given her in the art of leaping in and out of the chariot.

[32] On the representation of Athena in the west pediment of the Parthenon see J. Binder, 'The West Pediment of the Parthenon: Poseidon', *Studies . . . S. Dow* (Durham, NC, 1984), 15–22.

[33] Cf. *Il.* 5. 837. Artistic representations of the activity include the Parthenon Frieze, see Brommer, *Der Parthenonfries*, 221f. On the *parabatēs*' role in the Eleusinia see A. Mommsen, *Feste der Stadt Athen* (Leipzig, 1898), 188 n.4; in the Panathenaea, Mommsen, *Feste*, 89–92, Plut. *Phoc.* 20. See also H. A. Thompson, *Archäologischer Anzeiger*, 76 (1961), 228 (and fig. 4) and Simon, *Festivals of Attica*, 62.

[34] W. Burkert, *Hermes*, 94 (1966), 24 f.; cf. his *GR*, 232 f.

[35] Plut. *Demetr.* 10. There was also an altar of Zeus Kataibates in the Academy: Scholia Soph. *OC* 705 = Apollodorus *FGrHist* 244 F 120. See Burkert, *GR*, 126. The moment of descent from the chariot is often the crucial one. Hence one must be very cautious in interpreting vase scenes showing Athena (or other figures) with one foot in a chariot and another out. These are often construed as representations of the start of a journey, but in some cases, e.g. the Elvehjen Museum hydria described by Moon, 'The Paris Painter', 98, the scene may actually be another way of representing the arrival of Heracles and Athena at Olympus. Note the presence of Hebe, and the motion of Hermes to check the forward movement of the horses—both suggestive of the completion of the journey.

[36] In a less elaborate fashion the ceremony serves one of the functions that Muir, *Civic Ritual*, 187, detects in some Renaissance ceremonies: 'In Renaissance Europe ceremonies were in broadest terms an expression of the world order and more narrowly a formulation of political rules that usually appeared in written theory much later. Civic ceremonies thus provided a continuous discourse in the constitutional order.'

kingship but serving as the subordinate and helper of Athena. He is not claiming to be Heracles, or a monarch, but Athena's attendant, a brave but subordinate charioteer, and thereby the agent of the true protector and ruler of the land, Athena.[37]

The reversal of an ancient kingship ritual which may be suspected in this procession, corresponds to another reversal closer to the surface of recent events. In the recently expanded Panathenaic festival the citizens of Athens processed, some by chariot, many with spear and shield (Thuc. 6. 58), to honour Athena at her shrine on the Acropolis.[38] In the procession under investigation Phye, representing Athena, is armed and moves through the citizenry to her citadel and sanctuary.[39] Like the exiled Pisistratus, she too has been away from Athens. The reversal of the festival pattern may then hint that under the previous regime the goddess had been offended and withdrawn from the Acropolis, but was now returning to her proper place and traditional role as Athens' protector.

As one looks more closely at the procession of Pisistratus and Phye it appears constantly richer and more evocative of underlying cultural patterns and more eloquent as an expression of the closeness between Pisistratus and the residents of Attica at this point in his career. The leader seems not to stand at a great distance from the attitudes and the behaviour of his fellow countrymen. Rather both appear to be linked by shared patterns of thought and united in a communal drama. The citizens are not naive bumpkins taken in by the leader's manipulation, but participants in a theatricality whose rules and roles they understand and enjoy. These are alert, even sophisticated, actors in a ritual drama affirming the establishment of a new civic order, and a renewed rapport among people, leader, and protecting divinity.

The episode, attested by relatively early and reliable authorities, cannot then be dismissed as a fabrication of ancient storytellers or as

---

[37] I see no hint of impiety as has sometimes been suspected, e.g. by Moon, 'The Paris Painter', 101.

[38] There may be a further echo of the Panathenaea in the presence of those crowned with the *thallos* in Polyaenus' account of the Phye episode (1. 21. 1) and the *thallophoroi* of the Panathenaea (Mommsen, *Feste*, 102 n. 4).

[39] On the appearance of a priestess of Athena dressed as the goddess in full armour see Polyaenus 8. 59.

mere manipulation by a cynical politician.[40] Its rich symbolism evokes patterns deeply rooted within the culture. Why then has it produced such scepticism and interpretive difficulty? Part of the answer may be our reluctance to enter into the playful and mimetic mentality of what Gerald Else has called 'the histrionic period' of Greek history.[41] We are not, however, alone in our difficulties. Even Herodotus, our earliest source, reports it with a mixture of amusement and puzzlement. He perhaps underestimates the popularity of Pisistratus, and the spontaneity and enthusiasm for his return. He may also be carried away by his amusement that the Athenians, who in his day made pretensions to the greatest urbanity and sophistication, acted so differently in an earlier period. His story builds to a climax as he shows that it was not only the country-dwellers who were involved but the residents of the town themselves. But the story simultaneously attests Herodotus' perplexity at the great change in the style of Athenian politics from Pisistratus' time to his own.[42] Yet his reporting of episodes such as this attests his familiarity with older traditions and his ability in transmitting them. It challenges us to attempt to attune ourselves to the Archaic Greeks, even as it underlines the difficulties that confront any such effort.

III

Our third case study concerns a problem central to the agrarian reform achieved by Solon in the early sixth century BC. Solon established, as is well known, a new basis for political privileges and prerogatives within his city, by substituting wealth for birth as the principal criterion. Citizens were classified into four groups, determined by the number of units of agricultural production each year. Those with 500 such units, the *pentēkosiomedimnoi*, constituted the

---

[40] Cf. the remarks of Nicole Loraux on the myth of Attic autochthony in *Annales: ESC* 34. 1 (1979), 19f.: 'soucieux de décrire les multiples manipulations dont le mythe est l'objet dans le monde des cités, les historiens de la Grèce ont trop souvent réduit ce qu'ils appellent sa "fonction politique" à celle, purement instrumentale, de support inerte et malléable, au service de toutes les propagandes . . .'.

[41] Else, *Hermes*, 85 (1957), 36. On the dramatic element in processions during Venetian festivals see Muir, *Civic Ritual*, 141f.

[42] In Pericles' day it is hard to imagine a similar event (*pace* Frontinus, *Strategemata* 1. 11. 10) but the leader might allow a more subtle artistic analogue: the representation of his likeness on the shield of the Athena Parthenos (Plut. *Per.* 31).

highest class and enjoyed the widest range of political privileges. Those with 300 or more were classified as 'knights', with somewhat reduced privileges, and so on, down to the fourth class, the *thētes*, with very restricted prerogatives. This much is clear. Far less evident is the way wealth was assessed and the classification determined. The one serious attempt to deal with these questions, by K. M. T. Chrimes in *Classical Review* for 1931, posited an elaborate census—a sensible way of handling the problem, but one without good parallels from Greece of this period. It seems most unlikely that the Attic state in Archaic times possessed a mechanism of assessment and enforcement of such complexity.

There is a further difficulty with the conventional view of the Solonian system of classification, clearly set forth by A. Andrewes in the new *Cambridge Ancient History*:

the base was the dry measure, *medimnos*. Wheat and barley, however, differed in value and *Athēnaiōn Politeia* 7. 4 says that dry and wet measures . . . were to be taken together, a more serious disparity in that the standard wet measure (*metrētēs*) of oil was worth a good deal more than a *medimnos* of any produce, and a measure of wine had another value. A tariff of equivalents for the *medimnos* of wheat is not in principle impossible, but there is no trace of any such arrangement . . . [43]

The classification of those whose wealth was based in significant part on the production of salt, honey, or from the wool, meat and milk products from flocks of sheep or goats, or from fishing, or services such as hauling, quarrying, carpentry, or blacksmithing must have been even more troublesome. I omit entirely the question of income derived from manufacturing or trade, a controversial subject at this point in the study of the Attic economy, and one made more difficult by the belief that the Solonian classification system is itself evidence that there was little trade or manufacturing in Solon's time.

The Aristotelian *Athēnaiōn Politeia* (7. 3) indicates that the classification system was not an invention of Solon's but had in some form already existed: 'he divided the people into four property classes according to wealth, *as had been done before*.'[44] Where in the Athenian

---

[43] A. Andrewes, *CAH*[2] iii. 3. 385. The equivalencies in Plut. *Sol.* 23. 3 imply an economy making extensive use of coinage, hence considerably later than Solon's time.

[44] Cf. Plut. *Sol.* 18. This statement may be an allusion to the 'Constitution of Draco' in ch. 4 of the *Ath. Pol.*, as C. Hignett, *History of the Athenian Constitution* (Oxford, 1952), 99 f. suggested. See also R. Sealey, *Hist.* 9 (1960), 161, and P. J. Rhodes's commentary on the *Ath. Pol.* 7. 3.

system would such a classification have existed, and why would it have made sense to Solon to adopt it for his new political schema? The efforts to find an occasion where a legal or constitutional schema of this sort would have arisen have not been successful.[45] But the use of *medimnoi* may provide a clue: the other place where *medimnoi* of grain figure prominently in Athenian civic life are the first-fruit offerings presented in agricultural festivals.[46] The number of *medimnoi* of agricultural produce determines the amount of offering to the divinity, and one's relative position among those making the offering. Thus a person who had enjoyed divine favour resulting in at least 500 *medimnoi* of production would be expected to present the divinity with an offering of the various types of produce reflecting his gratitude for the blessings enjoyed. Presumably he would then rank among the first citizens in his contribution, and take a prominent place in the procession presenting the offerings. Citizens of such prominence are likely to have driven chariots and hence may be identified with *hēniochoi* attested in some late sources as rich Athenian citizens who maintained chariots.[47] Their close association with Athena is reflected in her representation as a chariot driver.[48] If this suggestion is correct the Pentekosiomedimnoi in the early Archaic period would drive their chariots in the festival procession; the Hippeis would ride horses; the Zeugitae would march.

The advantages of using such a system for the new political arrangements introduced by Solon were considerable. It was familiar, adaptable, and self-enforcing. The major innovation of the Solonian system would be legitimized by the use of a pattern sanctioned by long custom and religious usage. The public display of the first-fruit offerings would provide a control on those who might otherwise exaggerate their wealth and claim a disproportionate role in society. In a relatively small community in which status was carefully watched and jealously guarded social pressure would provide

---

[45] Cf. Hignett, *History*, 99f.

[46] See e.g. the Eleusinian first-fruits decree of the 5th cent. BC, *IG* I³ 78. This decree specified a minimum contribution of a *hekteus* from every *medimnos* for the offering to Demeter and Kore.

[47] Photius, *Lexicon* s.v. 'hēniochoi'; Aelius Dionysius fr. 196 (Schwabe) *apud* Eustathius 576. 44 on *Il.* E 505 (ii p. 136, ll. 22ff., van der Valk). On the Heniochos of Pallas as a civic official see *IG* II/III² 2245, 299 and W. Burkert, *Zeitschrift für Rel. u. G.geschichte* 22 (1970), 358 n. 8. On Heniochides as a personal name see *PA* 6427ff. See also n. 31 above.

[48] Ar. *Nu.* 602; cf. Eur. *Hec.* 467.

effective enforcement.[49] Even much later in Attica inappropriate participation in a festival might become a cause célèbre calling for immediate action.[50] In an earlier period less formal action is perhaps more likely—expressions of scorn, derision or even outright threats. At the same time this arrangement could respond to public attitudes about various types of wealth. Grain producers were of course the standard-setters. But lavish contributions of purchased grain by the producers of grapes, olive oil, or perhaps even by traders and manufacturers might win the donors a place among the *pentēkosiomedimnoi*, if public sentiment were favourable. The state would not be forced to develop an elaborate tariff of equivalencies, any more than it would need to conduct a formal census. Although the system might eventually be formalized and codified, there was no need at the outset to give the various classes 'a precise meaning defined by law'.[51] Social pressure would suffice.

The Solonian system of political classification is likely then to depend not upon a Roman-style census or a Byzantine-like bureaucracy, but upon a characteristic pattern of Archaic Greek civic life, the festival with its parade and offerings.[52] Solon need have done little more than utilize a festival pattern that antedated his reform and extend it to the political privileges as allocated in his new system.

Along with privileges, of course, went responsibilities, especially military ones. The hypothesis that the Solonian system utilized a festival procession can thus help with a further problem in the interpretation of the Solonian reforms. It has often been questioned whether the system was essentially a political classification or

---

[49] Note the treatment of social outcasts reported in Plut. *Mor.* 538a, and Aelian fr. 245.

[50] Isaeus 6. 50.

[51] A. Andrewes in *CAH*[2] iii. 3. 385.

[52] Which festival? Since grain production seems so central, one expects a major festival with an offering procession, occurring not far from the time of the grain harvest—roughly the end of June. (For the date of the wheat harvest see P. Deane, *Thucydides' Dates* (Don Mills, Ont., 1972), Appendix, p. 135.) The Thargelia is perhaps not impossible: see Hesychius s.v., but an early form of the Panathenaea is perhaps more attractive. This may have included first-fruit offerings (see Mommsen, *Feste*, 57 f.) especially before the Eleusinian festivals were fully developed and integrated into the state festival cycle. Note Hdt. 5. 82 f. and Mommsen's discussions of the passage, *Feste*, 147 and 156 n. 1. On Athena as a goddess associated with the fertility of grain see L. R. Farnell, *Cults of the Greek States*, i (Oxford, 1896), 289–93. On the date of the incorporation of the Eleusinian festivals see J. Boardman, *RA* (1972), 52 f., and *JHS* 95 (1975), 1 f.

whether military considerations were paramount.[53] But many such festivals combine several kinds of display: individual status, civic order and affluence, and military strength. The procession in such festivals showed an individual's affluence and status in the community, and also reflected his military obligation to that community. The procession in honour of Artemis Amarynthia at Eretria, for example, was described on an inscription reported by Strabo: 'they are said to have made their festival procession with three thousand heavy-armed soldiers, six hundred horsemen, and sixty chariots.'[54] Likewise Dionysius of Halicarnassus (*AR* 7. 71–2) described a Roman festival based on Greek models in which young Romans whose fathers had the assessments of knights rode on horseback, and those who were to fight on foot marched on foot in the parade, etc. The festival procession then becomes a reflection of divine favour, social status, military obligation and, in Solon's case, political privilege as well.

Felix Jacoby long ago showed how much attention Solon paid to festivals and civic ritual and how important they were to his political reforms.[55] Part of their rationale may have been to provide a civic alternative to the lavish aristocratic displays at funerals and on other occasions. Festivals such as the Genesia may thus reflect a similar tendency to that of sixth century sumptuary legislation—a curtailing of the political advantage enjoyed by those who could make a lavish display of their wealth and status. In any event, Solon, like many politicians of the Archaic period, worked in large part with and through ceremonies, rituals, and festivals. Indeed even the name of his famous *Seisachtheia*, the shaking-off-of-burdens, may echo those of festivals ending in -eia.[56] And Plutarch *Solon* 16 suggests the actual event may have taken the form of a festival, perhaps a

---

[53] This position has been argued most recently by D. Whitehead, *CQ* 31 (1981), 282–6.

[54] Strabo 10. 1. 10, 448 C. with F. W. Walbank's commentary on Polyb. 2. 416. Is there also a hint of a military structure behind the Samian Tonaia festival in the corrupt last line of the fragment of Asius *apud* Athen. 12. 525e ff.? On the importance of processions in ancient festivals see Nilsson, 'Die Prozessionentypen' and *Cults*; Burkert, *GR*, 99–102; J. Mikalson, *GRBS* 23 (1982), 213–21. On the Amarynthia festival see I. C. Ringwood, *AJA* 33 (1929), 384–92; D. Knoepfler, *BCH* 96 (1972), 283–301; L. Breglia, *Contribution à l'étude . . . Eubéennes* (Naples, 1975), 37–47. Cf. also Pl. *Leg.* 947c on a procession arranged in part by military roles.

[55] F. Jacoby, *CQ* 38 (1944), 65–75, reprinted in Jacoby's *Abhandlungen zur griechischen Geschichtsschreibung* (Leiden, 1956), 243–59.

[56] e.g. the Chalkeia, Dipoleia, and Nemeseia.

procession through some of the countryside or a ritualized destruction of the boundary markers.[57] When we think of this reform, then, we should envision not only legislative and legal measures (although certainly not a complex series of administrative arrangements) but also a ceremony expressing a new community consensus, the celebration of the end of past abuses by the pulling up of the old *horoi*, with all the symbolism implicit in such an act, a proclamation that those who had been sent abroad as virtual slaves under the old system might return with impunity, and, surely, thanksgiving sacrifices to the gods.[58]

IV

The examples we have examined indicate the importance of festival and ritual in the political life of Archaic Athens. Such acts of ceremonial were a central part of civic life and some of the principal means and objects of political activity. At the same time the episodes we have examined raise some more general questions about the relation between leader and follower and even the nature of politics in the Archaic Greek state.

The leader, in the examples we have studied, often uses tribal structures, processions, or festivals to articulate community values and emerging consensuses about state policy. But while he utilizes various forms of ceremony and civic religion, the distance between the leader and his followers seems rather smaller than has commonly been thought. The successful politician is closely linked to his community and shares many of its values, recognizes emerging consensuses and knows how to utilize familiar patterns to express and confirm new patterns of civic life. His success derives not so much from his intellectual or emotional distance from the community or

[57] It may be significant that none of these *horoi* has ever been found. This may suggest exceptionally thorough destruction or a removal of the stones over the boundaries of Attica, as was sometimes done with the bones of polluted individuals or with other objects.

[58] Compare the burning of written mortgages in Hellenistic Sparta at the time of Agis' reform: Plut. *Agis* 13. Solon's claim (fr. 36 West) that he freed those who had been sold into slavery need not reflect an elaborate plan to negotiate or buy back their freedom but simply the assurance that if they could escape to Attica no effort would be made to deport them.

his cleverness at seeking his own advantage at the expense of the community, as in his attunement to civic needs and aspirations, and his ability to give them form and expression. Thus leader and follower are linked by a shared, even if often rapidly evolving, set of expectations. They play different roles in a shared drama.

Hence it may be neither accidental nor trivial that in each of the cases we have studied, *mimēsis* (best thought of not as 'imitation' but as 'creative adaptation') has an important role to play.[59] The actual term is used in Herodotus' account of Clisthenes' reforms, which he alleges were a *mimēsis* of those made by his maternal grandfather. It is implicit in Phye's dressing as Athena and in Pisistratus' restrained adaptation of procession patterns deeply rooted in the culture. In Solon's case the *mimēsis* is both more direct and more subtle. A traditional festival form, if we are correct, is reshaped to fulfil a further function—arranging and displaying a new ordering of the civic body. The leader, like a tragic poet or actor, adapts familiar material to a new setting and structure.

Approached in this way Archaic politics shares elements with drama and other creative arts. It can be a histrionic activity, not simply in the tension and drama often implicit in political events, but in the importance of mutually understood roles and expectations. Its creativity derives from the fact that the effective politician has the skill and knowledge, the *technē* and *sophia*, to use traditional forms and inherited material to develop new patterns of civic order and to give expression to evolving civic feeling, and beliefs.

This is not to deny that individual politicians, including some very effective ones, sought their own personal advantage. Surely many of them did. But it would appear that this goal was most likely to be achieved not solely by their careful calculation of personal or family self interest, but by merging their sense of individual advancement into the community's evolving sense of its needs and aspirations. 'Manipulation', then, is an inadequate formulation of

---

[59] In the visual arts *mimēsis* 'usually implied something beyond the simple process of copying a natural model' as J. Pollitt points out in a useful discussion in his *Ancient View of Greek Art* (New Haven, 1974), 37–52. The term can betoken not a literal replication but 'imitation by psychological association'. This is not to suggest that political leaders of the Archaic period would themselves have used the term *mimēsis*, but that the concept, later of such prominence in Greek culture, may usefully be retrojected into this period. On the development of the term *mimēsis* see the suggestive observations of H. Koller, *Die Mimesis in d. Antike* (Berne, 1954) and the cautious assessment by G. F. Else, *CPh* 53 (1958), 73–90.

the relationship between leader and follower. The merging of individual and community interest, the sense of shared goals and well-being, the ability of the effective leader to recognize and give expression to new civic attitudes are all central to political leadership in this period. Success in politics in the last analysis depended on the ability to understand the needs, hopes, and anxieties of the community, to give them expression through rite and ritual, and to find the patterns of speech and act that console or that celebrate an underlying order. The politics of that age cannot be fully understood as the manipulation of those patterns, but must also be seen as the invention, articulation, and adaptation of ceremonial to the changing needs and consciousness of the community.

4

Greek States and Greek Oracles[1]

ROBERT PARKER

I

The influence of oracles on the life of Greek states has long been a controversial theme. Apollo of Delphi is, of course, at the centre of the debate, and the subtle god has not ceased even in modern times to puzzle the enquirer. Often the question has been posed in terms of the political allegiances and aspirations of the oracular shrines. But it may be more interesting to consider the matter from the side of the states that approached the oracles. To what extent were Greek states prepared to cede to the god an important share in decisions that affected their own interests?

Consultation of an oracle is the most powerful of several forms of divination through, in Roman terms, 'besought' indications. The important distinction between 'besought' and 'self-offering' signs is that the authority of the former was increased by the decision to seek them. Where matters of collective importance were concerned, that decision was a public one and was taken by whatever individual or body normally determined policy.[2] The corollary is that the group that had resolved to seek a sign came close to a commitment to accepting the god's advice or verdict. No clear case of disobedience to a specifically solicited oracular response is recorded.[3] Such a response, therefore, had quite different authority from the 'oracles of Bacis' and the like that oracle-collectors chanted, influential though

---

[1] For reasons of space I have had to compress some discussions, curtail documentation (particularly of anthropological writings) and say nothing of such relevant and controversial issues as the actual oracular mechanisms and the general trustworthiness of transmitted responses. I am most grateful to Simon Hornblower, Simon Price, and the editors of *Crux* for valuable comments on a draft of this chapter.

[2] See the still most valuable study of Ph.E. Legrand, *Quo animo Graeci divinationem adhibuerint* (Paris, 1898), 72 f.

[3] Hdt. 7. 148–9 is probably apologetic fiction.

these could be as precipitants of public opinion. An 'oracle of Bacis' adduced by a speaker was one argument in a debate, not an agreed means of resolving it. But by the decision to consult an oracle the reins of state were put in the hands of a divine charioteer. If important issues were indeed 'referred to the god' (Hdt. 1. 157. 3, 6. 66. 2; Polyb. 36. 17. 2; SIG^3 633. 17) in a way that gave him freedom to choose, Greek political processes can scarcely be studied in purely secular terms.[4] We need, therefore, to consider the kind of problems on which oracles were publicly consulted, the terms in which the questions were phrased, and the degree of volatility and independence that the oracles actually displayed in their responses. The last factor matters because it was obviously hazardous to consult the Pythia even about crop-failure if she was liable to respond with a demand, for instance, to 'recall all exiles'.

As a preliminary it may be useful to look outside Greece, and to mention some of the conclusions of the many anthropologists who have studied divinatory practices in contemporary societies.[5] From them we learn, first, that divination is normally used as a guide to action, and not as a means of stripping the veil from the future to satisfy simple curiosity. This is, of course, also true of Greece: Xenophon says that we learn by this means 'what we ought to do and what not', and the god can be spoken of as an 'adviser'.[6] Divination often relates to the past ('what offence caused this disease?') rather than the future ('will I benefit from marrying this girl?'): in either case the problem is one of deciding what is to be done now. The oracle is seldom expected to suggest lines of conduct on its own initiative, but passes judgment on possibilities put forward by the consultant ('shall I build my house at x or y?').[7]

Even within the range of practical questions further restrictions are normally observed. Questions that have an obvious answer in human terms are not put. 'Is it better for me to employ a skilled or

---

[4] As M.I. Finley recommends, *Politics in the Ancient World* (Cambridge, 1983), 93–5.

[5] Cf. the pioneering article of C. R. Whittaker, 'The Delphic Oracle: Belief and Behaviour in Ancient Greece—and Africa', *Harvard Theological Review*, 58 (1965), 21–47. The classic anthropological study is E. E. Evans-Pritchard, *Witchcraft, Oracles and Magic among the Azande* (Oxford, 1937; abridged edn. with introd. by E. Gillies, 1976).

[6] Xen. *Mem.* 1. 4. 15, and often (Legrand, *Quo animo*, 7 n. 1). Adviser: e.g. Hdt.1. 157. 3; Xen. *Cyrop.* 1. 6. 46, *Hipparch.* 9. 9; and see B. Haussoullier, *Rev. Phil.* 44 (1920), 272f.

[7] For such question-forms in Greece see P. Amandry, *La Mantique apollinienne à Delphes* (Paris, 1950), 150–9.

unskilled charioteer?' is Xenophon's example (*Mem.* 1. 1. 9). It seems that consultants do not ask about moral problems, or seek permission to violate clear moral norms. This principle is explicitly formulated in classical sources, sometimes with cautionary tales to emphasize it.[8] Questions about issues that are very specific, particularly in time, are also excluded. 'Will I catch a buffalo if I hunt tomorrow?' is not asked, although 'should I marry x?' is common. The precise enquiry about the present by which king Croesus 'tested' the oracles would seem as irregular to an African as it did to Greeks.[9] Normal questions relate to a limited and conventional range of problems.

Divination helps the consultant to move from doubt to action by providing counsel that is apparently objective and uniquely authoritative. The individual enquirer receives reassurance that among all available courses of action the one he chooses is the most advantageous. For a group, consultation also acts as a kind of referral to binding arbitration.[10] This may be a significant motive even for enquiries that are at first sight purely personal. Behind a seemingly innocent question about where to site a house, for instance, delicate issues of group affiliation may lie concealed. Was it to satisfy his own mind, or to silence his relatives, that a Coan asked Delphi, in a recently published document, whether he should 'divide his ancestral [*oikos*]' (*SEG* 18. 329)? We can feel sure that it was primarily to prevent opposition from his troops that king Agesipolis checked with two oracles that it 'was safe to reject a truce unjustly offered', when the Argives were about to obstruct his invasion by fraudulent declaration of a sacred truce (Xen. *Hell.* 4. 7. 2).

Divination fails of its function if its objectivity is not convincingly demonstrated. Though clients seldom go away with an answer that is unsatisfactory, the possibility must always be present. Divination is a drama that leads through many a perilous reversal to a satisfactory dénouement. The oracular mechanism must be such as to provide what has been called 'resistance' (see n. 10). The general cannot control the state of the sacrificial victim's liver (though he can of course sacrifice another if the first proves uncomplaisant). Where divination is by trance-mediumship the prophet is often a stranger, a

[8] Hdt. 1. 157. 3–159, 6. 86; Diod. Sic. 15. 10. 2; Epict. *Ench.* 32. 3; cf. Cic. *Div.* 2. 11.
[9] Hdt. 1. 46–9, cf. H. Klees, *Die Eigenart des griechischen Glaubens an Orakel und Seher* (Tübinger Beiträge zur Altertumswissenschaft, 43, Stuttgart, n.d.), 95–8.
[10] Cf. S. K. Park, 'Divination and its Social Contexts', *Journal of the Royal Anthropological Institute*, 93 (1963), 195–209.

person deemed free from partisan interests. In Greece too the influential 'healer-seers' and seers of the Archaic and early Classical periods were often strangers (witness the famous Teisamenos, who won for himself and his brother the unique honour of admission to Spartan citizenship).[11] The most influential shrine lay outside the territory of the great Classical city-states not because these had no use for it, but because the most convincing prophecy comes from afar. In the fourth century the yet more remote Ammon became popular. Ambassadors were dispatched abroad to put a question of perhaps high moment not to a competent authority but to an entranced, uneducated woman. The brusque contemptuous tone that the Pythia sometimes adopted towards persons of rank (P/W, ii. xxv), so different from anything possible for her as a humble peasant woman of Delphi, was a sure sign that through her spoke the god. Her riddling speech too provided a kind of resistance to the understanding. And we can take as a model of resistance Herodotus' story of the Athenian envoys' consultation in 481 or 480 about the Persian threat (7. 140–3). Eventually they depart with an answer that is at least tolerable, but only after they have forced the god by threats of suicide to think again, only after Athene has laboured on their behalf to 'win round Olympian Zeus, beseeching him with many a plea and close cunning'. The recent claim[12] that Apollo always said simply 'yes' when asked 'is it advantageous for me to do x?' is therefore psychologically implausible. One looks for more art from the most famous of oracular gods.

Not that prophets are normally at a deeper level unobliging. Observers of spirit-mediums have noted again and again the skill with which they induce those who consult them virtually to provide the answer to their own questions. Those forms of divination termed 'technical' by the ancients (lot-oracles and the like) appear more truly objective, but it seems that even these, when applied to a delicate issue such as the identification of a witch, can be controlled (unconsciously, of course) by the choice of questions so that a socially unacceptable verdict cannot emerge. In Ifa divination, the diviner recites a set of obscure verses, selected by a procedure comparable to throwing dice, and the client himself decides which verse

---

[11] Hdt. 9. 33–5; on such wandering seers cf. I.Löffler, *Die Melampodie* (Meisenheim, 1963), 11–29; J. D. Mikalson, *Athenian Popular Religion* (Chapel Hill, NC, and London, 1983), 41.

[12] J. Fontenrose, *The Delphic Oracle* (Berkeley, 1978), 222.

relates to his problem, and what its significance is. He thus of course
provides his own answer. After describing an oracular diagnosis in a
case of sickness the ethnographer of the Tiv concludes: 'the oracle
itself is primarily a distracting device that allows the principals to
construct an explanation that can be handled'.[13]

This is the perspective from which Apollo's riddling oracles should
be viewed. Often Apollo gave simple answers to simple questions. But
if he did sometimes respond to delicate enquiries with riddles,[14] he
was, like the Ifa diviner with his verses, forcing the client to construct
by interpretation his own response. The perplexed Athenians turned
to Apollo for advice on how to resist the approaching Persian hordes.
By the 'wooden walls' oracle, Apollo referred the problem back to
them; discussion resumed, though in appearance at a different level:
no longer a problem of tactics or politics, but of philology. Arguments about the interpretation of particular oracles are so common
as to suggest that they are not a by-product but an essential part of
the institution's working.[15]

The attitudes to divination of those who consult oracles are an
intriguing theme. The clients of diviners are by no means
unreservedly credulous. They are often suspicious or openly contemptuous of particular forms of divination or individual diviners,
happy indeed to assert that 'most' diviners are charlatans. Such scepticism supports rather than subverts belief in the possibility of divination, since failures can be explained through the incompetence or
fraud of particular diviners. The society that abuses diviners is the
society that consults them. Manipulation of oracles to further one's
own interests is also commonplace.[16] By a careful choice of question
even a quite objective oracle can be prevented from obstructing

[13] W. Bascom, *Ifa Divination* (Indiana, 1969), 68 f.; P. Bohannan, 'Tiv Divination', in
J. H. M. Beattie and R. G. Lienhardt (eds.), *Essays in Social Anthropology in Memory of E.
E. Evans-Pritchard* (Oxford, 1975), 149–66, at 166.
[14] Cf. J. Hart, *Herodotus and Greek History* (London, 1982), 183–6. Note too Aesch.
Ag. 1255; Soph. fr. 771 Radt; Eur. *Supp.* 138; Pl. *Apol.* 21b (αἰνίττομαι), cf. Pacuvius fr.
308 Ribbeck². *Contra*, mistakenly, Fontenrose, *Delphic Oracle*, 236.
[15] Hdt. 7. 140–3, cf. 5. 79–80; Ar. *Eq.* 1025, 1045, 1070, 1084, *Plut.* 51; Xen. *Hell.* 3.
3. 3, and already Hom. *Od.* 2. 180.
[16] Cf. Evans-Pritchard, *Witchcraft*, 350 (with the example that I mention); E. L.
Mendonsa, *The Politics of Divination* (Berkeley, 1982). P. *Oxy.* 1148 (= *Select Papyri* i:
Non-literary Papyri, ed. A. S. Hunt and C. C. Edgar (London and Cambridge, Mass.,
1932), no. 193), is a delightful Greco-Egyptian instance: the enquirer asks Sarapis
'whether it is beneficial that my son Phanias and his wife should disagree with his
father and oppose him'. Young Phanias will certainly have been informed of the god's
response.

a cherished project. Such artifice is perhaps not always quite un-conscious. A wife, eager to visit her relatives, may find a veto imposed by an oracle that her considerate but dependent husband has con-sulted. Readers of *David Copperfield* may be reminded of the so obstructive invisible partner of the obliging Mr Spenlow.

It follows that much of the mockery of oracle-mongers and abuse of mercenary seers that occurs in Greek texts should not be taken as evidence of deep disenchantment.[17] The blatant venality and incompetence of the street-corner seer often serves to emphasize by contrast the unique insight and honesty of the distant Apollo.[18] As for manipulation, a prime offender is the pious Xenophon, who asked Apollo at Delphi what gods he should sacrifice to in order to partici-pate with success in the expedition of Cyrus. Only later was he reminded by Socrates that he should have asked whether it was advantageous to go at all.[19] Xenophon's original form of question was in fact very common.[20] Similarly, on the occasion already mentioned, Agesipolis foreclosed the gods' options in two ways. He asked Zeus at Olympia whether it was safe to 'reject a truce unjustly offered', and then, since Zeus could scarcely say no to a question so put, turned to Apollo to enquire whether he 'agreed with his father'. As Aristotle notes, filial piety demanded assent (*Rhet.* 1398^{b}33–5). The incident is often taken as evidence of fourth-century cynicism, but it is scarcely clear that such a stratagem would have been unthinkable two hundred years before.

There are, of course, features that set Delphi apart from most of the oracles described by the ethnographers. Above all, Apollo's prac-tice was decisively influenced by the unique position that he acquired as 'ancestral exegete to all the Greeks, seated at the centre of the earth' (Pl. *Rep.* 427c). A shrine patronized by clients from various states with conflicting interests faced difficulties from which, say, the seers of the Athenian army were exempt. Late in the fifth century the Eleans announced, to spite the Spartans, that 'ancestral custom

---

[17] Cf. G. E. R. Lloyd, *Magic, Reason and Experience* (Cambridge, 1979), 17. On Greek attitudes to divination see A. D. Nock's classic essay 'Religious Attitudes of the Ancient Greeks', *Proc. Amer. Philos. Soc.* 85 (1942), ii. 472–82 = *Essays on Religion and the Ancient World* (Oxford, 1972), 534–50.

[18] Cf. Soph. *OT* 497–503; Eur. *El.* 399f., *Phoen.* 954–9. Such was even Thucydides' attitude, according to N. Marinatos, *JHS* 101 (1981), 138–40.

[19] Xen. *Anab.* 3. 1. 5–7. Xenophon learnt his lesson: cf. Xen. *Poroi* 6. 2–3.

[20] See e.g. n. 36 below, and on question formulae Legrand, *Quo animo*, 7–32; Amandry, *Mantique*, 149–68.

forbad consulting oracles about wars against other Greek states' (Xen.
Hell. 3. 2. 22); but this was an ancestral custom of the most recent
origin, and Apollo had in fact often been asked for guidance and help
by one set of clients in compassing the defeat of another. Even if the
will was present, it would not be easy to remain impartial without
sinking into the most transparent evasiveness. Nor was it easy to
rebuff clients who had enriched the shrine, who had been granted
particular privileges as 'benefactors' of Delphi, and who probably
had ties of friendship with individual Delphians. And in one area at
least, that of the control of the shrine, the Delphians had political
interests of their own.

Delphi's international position had a further consequence. We
have seen that individuals habitually use oracles as moral levers
against one another: so too the attempt could be made to exploit
Delphi as a lever against other states. This becomes quite clear in
the third century, when cities seeking *asylia* (freedom from attack)
for their shrines approach Delphi before soliciting their neighbours.
'Apollo has consented, how can you refuse?' we almost hear them
say.[21] Scholars are perhaps too ready to read back this strongly
propagandist intention into earlier centuries, forgetting that 'is it to
our advantage to fight the Athenians?' was a matter Spartans could
be genuinely worried about, whereas it did not take a god to answer
the later question 'is it to our advantage to proclaim *asylia* for
our shrine?'. But even an oracle elicited in good faith might also be
suitable for brandishing before the world, and when, already in the
fifth century, the Athenians asked (probably) whether 'it was better
that all Greek states send first-fruits to Athens',[22] they were scarcely
moved by a simple desire for information.

II

A central function of oracles, ancient and durable, was to prescribe
a 'release from evils' (λύσις κακῶν). Plague, crop-failure, an
abnormal mortality-rate among human and animal young, drought,

---

[21] P/W nos. 341–51; Fontenrose, *Delphic Oracle*, 422 nos. 19 f. (Didyma); *SIG*³ 635b
(Lebadea).
[22] *IG* I³ 78. 24–6 (ML 73). Brandishing: e.g. Thuc. I. 25. 2, 123. 1; Hdt. I. 69. 2;
Hyperides *Euxen.* 26.

even unnaturally violent storms, unseasonable hail and frost: these were all god-sent banes on which in primitive Greece the healer-seers and subsequently their successors the oracular shrines could advise.[23] Many states, particularly large ones, may have become less quick to turn to oracles about these problems in and after the fifth century, but Polybius implies that such consultations still occurred in his own day, and allows that they were perhaps 'reasonable', since the causes of such afflictions are 'hard to find' (but it would have been absurd, he adds, to consult an oracle about the 'childlessness' and 'population shortage' of the Greece of his day, when their causes were all too clear). In later antiquity questions about crop-failure were typical of the humdrum concerns of Plutarch's Delphi, and it was largely on such business that the oracle of Claros thrived.[24]

Sometimes vaguer requests for guidance on relations with the gods were made: 'the Corcyraeans and Oricians ask Zeus Naios and Dione by sacrificing to what god or hero they can live in their cities best and most safely, and have good and abundant produce, and enjoyment of all the good produce' (*SEG* 23. 474; cf. *GDI* 1562, 1567; Dem. 21. 51–3 = P/W no. 282). Such questions were a kind of prophylaxis against afflictions of the kind just mentioned. Communities might ask 'what to do or sacrifice' to make portents (such as 'the sign in the sky') turn out for the best (e.g. Dem. 43. 66 = P/W no. 283). A state might, it seems, even ask 'how long will our good fortune last?', expecting not a prediction in years but a warning ('until x occurs') entailing precautionary measures.[25]

Plato's Socrates indicates the commonest area of consultation in the Classical period, when he reserves for Apollo all legislative activity concerning 'the establishment of shrines, sacrifices, and other forms of cult for gods and daimons and heroes; and also the graves of the dead and the service we must do them to have their favour'. He goes on to explain that 'this god is the ancestral exegete for all mankind on such matters and expounds them to them, seated on the *omphalos* at the centre of the earth' (*Rep.* 427b–c). Despite Socrates' claim,

[23] Cf. R. Parker, *Miasma* (Oxford, 1983), Ch. 9.

[24] Polyb. 36. 17; Plut. *De Pyth. or.* 408c; Claros: cf. L. Robert, *CR Acad. Inscr.* 1968, pp. 591 f., and below n. 60; cf. too the question to the Gryneian Apollo, *JHS* 74 (1954), 85 no. 21 (*Bull.epigr.* 1959 no. 401).

[25] Hdt. 3. 57. 3, cf. Hdt. 1. 55, P/W no. 73, and the 'but when . . . ' oracular opening formula (Fontenrose, *Delphic Oracle*, 168–70).

questions about innovations in cult were put to oracular gods throughout the Greek world. The Athenian deme of Acharnae, for instance, sought Apollo's permission before building a temple of Ares and Athene Areia; the men of Tanagra asked, probably, Apollo Ptoïos about a change in the site of a temple of Demeter; the Chaones put a similar question at Dodona.[26] These questions too were a prophylaxis, a way of guaranteeing well-being by ensuring that one's cultic arrangements were punctiliously correct. They were also, of course, the mechanism through which religious innovations could be declared legitimate in a society that otherwise lacked authoritative religious experts and institutions.

Occasionally even questions about cult had implications outside the ritual sphere. A favourable answer to certain enquiries could have value as propaganda, as the first-fruits oracle given to the Athenians shows (above, p. 82). It was as part of a broader anti-Argive policy that Cleisthenes of Sicyon asked permission to expel the tomb of the Argive Adrastus—and was rebuffed (Hdt. 5. 67). Perhaps prudent men pondered this snub, and learnt caution. The Athenians seem not to have asked permission from any oracle to finance the Peloponnesian war out of temple-treasures, or to put temple-land out to lease. It was on a religious question with military implications that Agesipolis framed his tendentious questions to Zeus and Apollo (above, pp. 78 and 81). Only twice do we hear of gods being invited to sanction the cult paid to Hellenistic rulers.[27] (A question was, however, put about the heroization of the controversial Aratus of Sicyon (Plut. Arat. 53 = P/W no. 358). The Pythia answered obscurely, and Aratus' supporters went ahead.) In 352/1 the Athenians did, it is true, seek permission before cultivating some part of the Eleusinian sacred orgas, so often violated by the Megarians with such weighty consequences. To do so, however, they devised an unparalleled procedure that forced the Pythia willy-nilly to give a fair answer (a refusal, as it turned out).[28] A mark of suspicion, perhaps, in a case

---

[26] P/W no. 281; LSCG 72 line 4 (cf. A. Schachter, Cults of Boiotia (London, 1981), i. 67 n. 1); SEG 15. 397. On the term pythochrēstos, used of rites and persons, see most recently L. Robert, Fouilles d'Amyzon en Carie (Paris, 1983), 110–13.

[27] Diod. Sic. 20. 100. 3 (Rhodians consult Ammon about worship of Ptolemy in 304); M. Segré, Bull. Soc. Alex. 31 (1937), 286–98 (Coans consult unknown shrine about posthumous cult of Arsinoe II, but possibly only about the site of the temple: cf. S. M. Sherwin-White, Ancient Cos (Göttingen, 1978), 100).

[28] IG II² 204. 23–54 (LSCG 32): cf. G. E. M. de Ste. Croix, The Origins of the Peloponnesian War (London, 1972), 254–6; and n. 95 below.

with political implications (but we know too little of normal procedures to be quite sure).

We turn now to issues that are more directly political in modern terms. Delphi is famous above all for its patronage of colonization. Unfortunately, though the fact of the shrine's involvement is certain, its precise character in the early centuries is beyond our knowledge. It is doubtful whether any of the recorded colonial prophecies are genuine,[29] and even if a few are, they do not resolve the crucial question of where the initiative to colonize came from. Herodotus offers an ideal picture in which a state with thoughts of colonization consults Delphi 'about what land it should settle in' (cf. 5. 42. 2), or the god even suggests projects to those who had approached him on other matters (e.g. 4. 155). It is not at all ridiculous to suppose that Delphi caught the mood of a colonizing age, and sometimes suggested the possibility of colonization to states that had not yet considered this particular 'release from evils' (particularly the evil of famine). But Herodotus also illustrates a more limited role for the oracle, whereby it merely confirms that a project already formed by a state will turn out well. This seems to be the pattern in the two instances he mentions (from the late sixth century) that fall closest in time to his own day. Dorieus of Sparta, having resolved to settle Heracleia in Sicily, asked Apollo 'whether he would take the land he was setting out for' (5. 43). Despite certain picturesque elaborations in Herodotus' account (6. 34–6; contrast Nepos, *Miltiades*, 1. 1–3), Miltiades the elder perhaps did no more before leading Athenian settlers to Thrace.[30] Certainly, the presence of an Athenian colony in Thrace at this period causes no surprise; nor does the role of Miltiades as leader.[31] Nothing demands the postulate of a significant intervention by Delphi.

In the fifth century Athens dispatched some twelve overseas settlements of various kinds. It is clear, from Aristophanes for instance (*Nub.* 332, *Av.* 959–91), that such projects still went forward amid a flurry of divination, but not certain that the Athenians often put them to the hazard of an oracular consultation. Delphi was

---

[29] Cf. H. Berve, *Gnomon*, 30 (1958), 422. On Delphi and colonization see most recently A. J. Graham in *CAH*[2] iii.3 (1982), 144–6.

[30] Note especially the form of his question in Hdt. 6. 35. 3. In general, on the question formula 'should I do *as I intend?*', see *Bull. épigr.* 1959 no. 299.

[31] For Athens and Thrace see How and Wells on Hdt. 6. 35. 2, for Miltiades ML pp. 10–12; J. K. Davies, *Athenian Propertied Families 600–300 BC* (Oxford, 1971), 299–300.

possibly consulted about the most ambitious of these, that sent to Amphipolis in 437.[32] If so, the form of question was probably 'by appeasing what god or hero can we settle Ennea Hodoi?'. The foundation-decree for Brea of (probably) c.445 contains a reference to 'getting good omens by sacrifice on behalf of the colony' (IG I³ 46. 9 = ML 49). This sounds like a domestic means of ensuring divine support, probably intended to supplant rather than supplement a verdict from Delphi. A decree of 446/5, the settlement-decree after the revolt of Chalcis, ordains that 'three men along with Hierocles make the sacrifices for Euboea prescribed by the oracles'. We do not know either the origin or the content of these oracles that receive such respectful mention in a public decree, nor whether they are to be connected with Athenian colonial projects in Euboea.[33] Nothing is said of any involvement of Delphi in other Athenian settlements. We should probably conclude that the Athenians normally now looked elsewhere than to Apollo for divine support in their colonial schemes.

About the panhellenic settlement at Thurii, however, Apollo probably was consulted. If he was not, it is hard to see on what grounds he later claimed to be himself oecist of the colony (see P/W nos. 131, 132, with P/W's commentary on no. 131). The Spartans certainly sought Apollo's approval for their settlement of 426 at Heraclea in Trachis. Thucydides explains most clearly the secular reasons for which 'they were eager to found the colony'. He continues, 'and so first of all they consulted the god at Delphi. And when he told them (to proceed), they sent out settlers . . . ' (3. 92. 5). Though leaving no doubt as to where the initiative lay, Thucydides does not seem to regard the consultation as an absolute formality.

In 385 the Parians planted a colony on the Adriatic island of Pharos, with the aid of Dionysius I of Syracuse, 'in accordance with an oracle' (probably a Delphic oracle, to judge from the Pharians' subsequent devotion to the shrine).[34] But the story ends here. With one doubtful exception,[35] there is no evidence that the Hellenistic

---

[32] See P/W no. 133. The form of this anonymous oracle is that of a Delphic response. If genuine, it must have been issued in 437 (note 'again').

[33] Euboea: IG I³ 40. 64–7 (ML 52). If the oracles had been Delphic, this would probably have been stated. Settlements in Euboea: cf. R. Meiggs, The Athenian Empire (Oxford, 1972), 120–3, 565–8. Much later, there is no hint of Delphi in Tod no. 200 (235/4 BC)—though note the oecist's name, Miltiades.

[34] Diod. Sic. 15. 13. 4, cf. SEG 23. 489 (subsequent contacts), and on Dionysius' interest A. G. Woodhead, Klio, 52 (1970), 503–12.

[35] Steph. Byz. s.v. Laodicea, quoting an oracle of uncertain origin.

kings ever consulted oracles before dispatching their military colonies. Throughout the ancient world, warfare was the sphere of operation *par excellence* for divination. As Xenophon points out (*Hipparch.* 9. 8–9), this is largely because war was very unpredictable and very dangerous. At every stage in a campaign the disposition of the gods was tested by divinatory sacrifice (see for example Xen. *Lac. Pol.* 13). Consultation of an oracle before a campaign was an alternative form of conspicuous objectivity, because it transferred the onus of investigation away from two members of the army (the general and his seer) to a foreign arbiter. Many such enquiries from the fifth and fourth centuries are recorded, both in open ('will I capture x?/will I benefit from attacking x?') and closed ('how can I defeat x?') form.[36] The open form seems to belong particularly to a state planning to instigate a war, the closed form to one that faces a battle or that has been suffering unexpected setbacks. Herodotus' Croesus adds a further, practical question: 'should I seek allies?' (1. 53. 3). The victims of aggression might counter by asking 'about salvation', that is, of course, not 'should we?' but 'how can we?' defend ourselves (Hdt. 6. 19. 1; Paus. 10. 1. 4 = P/W no. 68; Cic. *Div.* 1. 76). It was presumably an Athenian question 'about salvation' to which the Pythia replied with the famous 'wooden walls' oracle (above, p. 80).

This is the last certainly attested Athenian military enquiry. They may perhaps have asked a little later 'how can we capture Scyros?'.[37] A poignant document of the mid-century, the epigram on the fallen at (as is commonly believed) the battle of Coroneia (P. A. Hansen, *Carmina Epigraphica Graeca* (Berlin, 1983), no. 5), shows the ideal regard and practical disregard in which oracles were often held. It concludes with the claim that the Athenian defeat has 'made the fulfilment of oracles certain for all men to heed in future'. As so often in myth and tragedy, so here in the real experience of the 440s a seer's words have been disastrously disbelieved. But we have no

---

[36] Cf. W. K. Pritchett, *The Greek State at War*, iii (Berkeley, 1979), 296–321; R. Lonis, *Guerre et religion en Grèce à l'époque classique*, Annales Littéraires Univ. Besançon 238 (Paris, 1979), 69–94. Open: e.g. probably Hdt. 1. 53. 3, 66. 1, 6. 76. 1, 7. 169. 1; Thuc. 1. 118. 3. Closed: e.g. Hdt. 1. 67. 2, 5. 79. 1; Paus. 10. 18. 2 (P/W no. 181).

[37] So by implication Paus. 3. 3. 7, cf. A. J. Podlecki, *JHS* 91 (1971), 141–3. The other main source for the bringing home of Theseus' bones, Plutarch (*Thes.* 36. 1–3, *Cim.* 8. 5–7), is quite vague about the occasion of the enquiry.

strong reason to think that these 'oracles' were actually the response of an oracular shrine to a specific question. It is possible that the Athenians put a military question to Delphi late in the Ten Years' War. Thucydides tells how in 421 they 'restored the Delians, because they were worried about their misfortunes in the war and because the god at Delphi had told them to'.[38] This is a striking instance of significant action undertaken, if we believe Thucydides, for purely religious motives, but it is not certain that the original question was precisely 'about their misfortunes in the war'. As for the Sicilian expedition, Thucydides tells of the influence exercised by oracle-mongers, but only late sources know of actual embassies sent to Delphi, Dodona, and Zeus Ammon (one by Alcibiades personally, to ask 'I lust for Sicily. How can I have her?'). They brought back piquantly appropriate or delusive answers, piquant enough to condemn the stories.[39] But we have Thucydides' evidence that in 432 the Spartans decided that 'the treaty had been broken and the Athenians were doing wrong' and so 'asked the god if they would benefit from going to war' (1. 118. 3). It is interesting, though, that the whole long war shows no other certain instance of a military consultation. Some seem still to have occurred in the first half of the fourth century, before Leuctra, for instance, but they peter out later.[40] Perhaps the shrines began indeed to apply the putative 'ancestral custom' (above, pp. 81–2) that forbad consultation by one Greek state in a war against another. If so, they were responding to the ideal of peace between Greeks that was widely canvassed in the fourth century. The new restriction left Philip free to ask Delphi, so the story goes, 'if he would conquer the king of Persia'. Much later, too, the Romans could for a brief period court Delphi with enquiries about their war with the barbarian Hannibal (P/W nos. 266–7, cf. 270 (Alexander); P/W nos. 354–6).

Perhaps the oracles could be transformed from warmongers into peacemakers. Xenophon notes in describing the peace-conference of 368, held at Delphi, that 'they did not consult the god as to how peace

[38] Thuc. 5. 32. 1: but Ephorus had a rationalizing account of these events (Diod. Sic. 12. 73. 1) which Meiggs, *Athenian Empire*, 302, accepts.

[39] Thuc. 8. 1. 1; P/W nos. 166–7; Plut. *Nic.* 13. 2 (cf. 14. 7); Paus. 8. 11. 12. Cf. P/W i. 199; H. W. Parke, *The Oracles of Zeus* (Oxford, 1967), 136 (who considers an enquiry at Dodona possible); C.A. Powell, *Historia*, 28 (1979), 17f.

[40] Cic. *Div.* 1. 76; Paus. 4. 32. 5 (P/W no. 253); cf. too Xen. *Hell.* 3. 2. 22 (Agis' consultation, late fifth century); Paus. 10. 18. 2 (P/W no. 181); Diod. Sic. 16. 25. 3 (P/W no. 261).

could be brought about, but considered it by themselves' (and got nowhere). But the criticism displays bias, as there is no evidence that before that date an oracle had ever even approved a treaty, still less given effective advice as to its terms. The first treaty to be sent to a god for approval, to our knowledge, is that of 356 between Philip and the Chalcidians, and it is surely correct to ascribe the innovation to Philip's genius for propaganda. The only other recorded consultation about a treaty is by the Milesians early in the second century, at a period when they were referring an unusually wide range of issues to their own oracle at Didyma.[41]

On two or perhaps three occasions we find Delphi actually or potentially involved in an arbitration between states. The god was suggested in 435 as an arbiter in the dispute between Corinth and Corcyra over Epidamnus. According to an ingenious interpretation of a fragmentary document, he was called in to reconcile Thasos and Neapolis in the last decade of the fifth century, but passed the responsibility on to Paros. He certainly adjudicated the dispute between Clazomenae and Cyme in the 380s over the island of Leuke: it was to belong to whichever state, starting from home on a given day, first made sacrifice in it. The Clazomenians won by a ruse. After this whimsical verdict no further appeals to Delphic arbitration are recorded. We cannot postulate a process by which the power of arbitrament gradually passed from god to man, since in all the earliest attested instances the judge is in fact human. Apollo is the temporary intruder, and then only for cases that touched on his special concerns: the first two disputes were about relations between colony and mother-city, while the object of the third was an island on which stood a majestic ancient temple of the god.[42]

Questions about other aspects of interstate relations were occasionally put. The Epidamnians in 435 asked Delphi whether they should transfer their allegiance from their unobliging mother-city Corcyra to Corcyra's own mother-city Corinth (Thuc. 1. 25. 1). The

---

[41] Xen. *Hell.* 7. 1. 27; Tod ii no. 158 (P/W no. 260); *SIG*[3] 633. 17: cf. Nock, *Essays*, 534 n.2.

[42] Thuc. 1. 28. 2; J. Pouilloux, *Recherches sur l'histoire et les cultes de Thasos* 1 (= Études Thasiennes III, Paris, 1954), 178–92 (but the postulate of actual arbitration goes beyond what is needed to explain Delphi's role, cf. L. Robert, *BCH* 59 (1935), 501); Diod. Sic. 15. 18 (= P/W no. 178), mentioning the temple. On early arbitrations see L. Piccirilli, *Gli arbitrati interstatali greci* (Pisa, 1973).

question was an appropriate one for Delphi, since it concerned ritual
ties arising from colonization; but there were serious political issues
at stake too, as the angry reaction of the Corcyraeans (Thuc. 1. 26.
3) made clear.[43] A note of real anxiety can perhaps be heard in the
question put to Zeus of Dodona by an Epirote community 'is it safe
for us to share a sympolity with the Molossians?' (GDI 1590).
Innumerable sympolity agreements were made in the period (probably the early third century) without, we presume, benefit of oracles.
In the same way, when the Milesians asked their Apollo of Didyma
on several occasions in the 220s about the admission of bands of
Cretans to citizenship, they were referring to the god an issue that
seems normally to have been handled on the secular level: such
'citizen-recruitment' was common in the Hellenistic world.[44] We can
scarcely divine their precise motives—though one can well imagine
that not every good burgher of Miletus would welcome a mercenary
from piratical Crete as a neighbour.

There is one very significant reserved area about which oracles
were almost never consulted in the historical period: the internal
politics, legislation (except occasionally religious legislation) and jurisdiction of the state. We can take as an emblem of this reservation
the extraordinary scene in Aeschylus' Eumenides (470–88) where
Athene, a goddess, declares that she cannot try the case of Orestes
without mortal aid. A most important exception from the proto-
historical period is the constitution of Sparta, which is already presented by Tyrtaeus (fr. 4 West) as originating in a response of Apollo.
We cannot know the historical reality behind Apollo's sanction,
though the practical consequence ('so don't think you can argue
about it') is clear enough in Tyrtaeus. But there is no hint that the
other great lawgivers sought even a formal ratification for their
codes. Cleisthenes of Athens asked Delphi what heroes should be
patrons of his new tribes (Arist. Ath.Pol. 21. 6: cf. Emily Kearns's
article in Crux, 189–207), but not to our knowledge whether the
new tribal structure itself was advantageous. Xenophon's proposal
at the end of Poroi (6. 2–3) that his suggested financial reforms
should be submitted to Dodona and Delphi for approval has a quaint

---

[43] Cf. J. B. Salmon, Wealthy Corinth (Oxford, 1984), 282–4.
[44] Milet 1. 3, ed. T. Wiegand (Berlin, 1914), nos. 33f, g; 36a; ?37b. 32–5. Ibid. nos.
40–93 are further citizenship grants, without oracular consultation (perhaps because
made to individuals). On citizen recruitment cf. LSJ s.v. λαογραφία. On the dangers in
it see Arist. Pol. 1303^{a}25–^{b}3.

anachronistic air. And even Xenophon seeks only an *imprimatur*; he does not contemplate enlisting the god as an active legislator.[45] Nor do we find oracles involved in jurisdiction, except very occasionally in relation to specifically religious cases ('deorum iniuriae dis curae').[46] Private clients put questions about thefts to the god of Dodona, but not as far as we know as part of formal legal procedure.[47] At Sparta, one quasi-judicial case of the highest importance was referred to the god, but the circumstances were so unusual and problematic that it can scarcely be taken as a norm. For what is a society without blood-tests to do when the purity of the queen mother comes into doubt?—and with it the legitimacy of a reigning king? In the case of Demaratus, the god was asked to pronounce on a question of fact that could be settled in no other way.[48] For the same reason individuals consulted oracles about problems of paternity (Eur. *Ion* 540f., 1547f.; *GDI* 1565 = *SIG*³ 1163), but only at Sparta could such a question have public implications. Even then it was only, according to Herodotus, on the proposal of Cleomenes, who had corrupted the Pythia, that an approach was made to Delphi. In a similar dispute almost a century later the Spartans preferred to make up their own minds about the legitimacy of Leotychidas (Xen. *Hell.* 3. 3. 2–4, cf. Paus. 3. 8. 10).

Once, perhaps, the oracles had had more influence even in internal affairs. In some early Greek societies they may have been occasionally involved in the making of kings. (Their informal role in the unmaking of kings will be mentioned later.) Such divine election of rulers is a common phenomenon, and though it is sometimes a mere ceremonial form, where no fixed rules of succession apply a seer may have real power.[49] One legend shows the Pythia drawing lots among

---

[45] We do not know why or in what sense the Locrian land law (ML 13) was 'sacred to Apollo Pythios' (A 14). *IG* XII 2. 213 (P/W no. 351; Eretria, late 3rd cent. BC) is the start of a law sanctioned by the oracle, but the lost content may have been religious.

[46] Hdt. 6. 135. 2–3; Schwyzer 661; Pl. *Leg.* 914a; Hyperides, *Euxen.* 14–17; Ath. 606b. In each case except the special one of the Hyperides passage the god is merely invited to pass sentence on an already identified sacral offender (Legrand, *Quo animo*, 29).

[47] Parke, *Oracles of Zeus*, 271–3; cf. in relation to adultery Eur. *Hipp.* 1055–9.

[48] Hdt. 6. 66. 1. Problems of legitimacy at Athens were sometimes tackled (one could scarcely say solved) by another 'pre-legal' procedure, challenge to a binding oath before an arbitrator (Dem. 59. 60, 40. 10f., cf. Isaeus 12. 9).

[49] See e.g. J. Goody (ed.), *Succession to High Office* (Cambridge, 1966), 21f.; Bascom, *Ifa Divination*, 69f.; G. Kingsley Garbett, 'Religious Aspects of Political Succession', in *The Zambesian Past*, ed. E. Stokes and R. Brown (Manchester, 1966), 137–70; for ancient Egypt, *Ancient Near Eastern Texts*, ed. J. B. Pritchard, 3rd edn. (Princeton, 1969), 446–8.

the qualified candidates to choose a Thessalian king; in another she is invited to advise on the choice of a successor when the king of Argos dies heirless; in a third she mediates in a dispute about the Lydian throne.[50] Even at a later period advice may occasionally have been sought about political disorder (for to the religious mind class struggle is a 'disease'). Two legends show (characteristically) the Spartans approaching Delphi for counsel about 'division of mind' among the citizens (P/W nos. 223–4). It is more important that according to Herodotus the Cyrenaeans asked Delphi in the mid-sixth century, after a prolonged period of civil strife, 'how they should organize themselves to fare best'. Apollo prudently suggested the solution that they might otherwise have tried themselves, to summon an arbiter from Mantinea. There is no specific reason to doubt the story, except that it forms part of a Cyrenaean excursus which contains demonstrably spurious oracles.[51] That an oracle might be consulted on such an issue is shown by a document rich in pathos (for it is tentatively ascribed to the late fifth century): 'the Corcyraeans ask Zeus Naios and Dione by sacrificing and praying to what god or hero they may be of one mind for the common good' (GDI 1563). The Corcyraeans use a closed formula (not 'how?' but 'by sacrifice to whom?') but it is not incredible that the open formula was employed a century earlier.

An adjudication by Apollo stayed what Diodorus describes as a slide towards civil strife in Thurii in the 430s.[52] The point at issue was whether Athenians, Peloponnesians or some other group should be considered true founders of the mixed colony. Behind the formal problem doubtless lay a bitter dispute about a matter of real importance, ceremonial precedence, the visible expression of the status of the various groups within the colony. Apollo, true statesman, declared when consulted that he himself should be honoured as the founder.

Herodotus records one case of a consultation about a particular political problem, hard of solution. In the mid-sixth century the

---

[50] P/W nos. 316, 483, 51, cf. 62. For oracular choice of priests (later in antiquity) see SEG 30. 1286 with references.

[51] Hdt. 4. 161. 1 (P/W no. 69: for the formula cf. GDI 1562). On the role of such arbitrators, particularly those from Mantinea, in the 6th cent. see F. Chamoux, Cyrène sous la monarchie des Battiades (Paris, 1953), 139 n. 1; Piccirilli, Arbitrati.

[52] Diod. Sic. 12. 35. 1–3; on the importance of such issues cf. ibid. 11. 1–2, and Burkert, HN, 37.

refugee Pactyes supplicated the Cymaeans, who found themselves threatened with war unless they handed him over to the Persians. What follows is intriguingly ambiguous. They asked Apollo at Didyma 'what they should do to please the gods' (note the evasive formulation) and were told to 'surrender the suppliant'—but only, it turned out later, 'so that they might commit impiety and so perish all the sooner, and not come to the oracle again to ask about handing over suppliants'. The Cymaeans were breaking the oracular rules by seeking exemption from a basic religious obligation; but one can well see how attractive it would have been to hope that the god might somehow see this as a special case.[53]

The main subjects of consultation have now been mentioned. There remains a penumbra of isolated or doubtful enquiries. According to late sources the Pythia was asked a momentous question, doubtless the most momentous ever put to her, by the victorious allies at the end of the Peloponnesian war. The issue was no less than whether Athens should be destroyed, and she rose to the occasion with the fine injunction to 'spare the common hearth of Greece'. No analogy, however, is available for such an enquiry, which is unknown to the contemporary sources. On the other hand, 'should we resettle our city or build another?' (Pellene or Aegina, early in the sixth century) seems a possible question to put to the god who founded cities. Some enquiries show the states taking the god's role as 'adviser' very literally: 'where shall we buy gold from?' (perhaps not impossible, from the Spartans); 'how can we get in this miraculous shoal of tunny?'; 'what are we to do about a plague of hares?'. But vainglory, no practical concern, lay behind a question which provoked a famous snub: the men of Aigion or Megara, bringing a tithe to Apollo and asking eagerly 'who are the best Hellenes?', learnt with mortification that their fellow-citizens were 'not third, nor fourth, nor twelfth, no not even in the reckoning' (P/W nos. 171; 25; 57, cf. 521; 126; 333; 1).

It is hard to know how often a given state might approach an oracle on political issues. There are important events even in Herodotus' narrative (the Marathon campaign, and the Ionian revolt) in connection with which consultations by the prime actors are not recorded. Herodotus implies that Croesus' barrage of enquiries was

---

[53] Hdt. 1. 157. 3–160. 1. Agesipolis' question, Xen. *Hell.* 4. 7. 2–3, concerned a comparable religious rule; note too Hom. *Od.* 16. 400–5, Plut. *Quaest. Graec.* 300d.

excessive (1.55). A community that had an oracle near at hand, though, could turn to it on quite trivial matters: the Dodonaeans asked their Zeus whether 'it was because of some mortal's impurity that he was causing the storm' (*SEG* 19. 427). A rough and fallible indicator of the proportions of different forms of business at one shrine is given by the lead question-tablets from Dodona. Of some eighty enquiries so far published, nine are public.[54] Of these, three are general questions about the ritual measures necessary to ensure prosperity, one about ritual measures to ensure concord, two about cultic reforms, one about a disturbance in nature, one about sympolity, while one is obscure. What is most interesting is the preponderance of enquiries of the type we termed prophylactic over those relating to a specific impending decision. None of the surviving tablets, though, seems to antedate the middle of the fifth century.

We turn to the responses. In cultic matters the normal tenor seems to be conservative and emollient. Clients are told to sacrifice 'according to the custom of the city'; a sanction for ritual change is granted either simply, or accompanied by a modest independent suggestion (e.g. Xen. *Mem.* 1. 3. 1; P/W no. 335; Diod. Sic. 15. 49. 1). There was scope for disruptive answers to questions about portents and disturbances in nature: for portents may portend political change, and by the doctrine of pollution natural disasters can be a product of human crime. Here too, however, the normal policy of the oracles seems to have been conciliatory. A 'sign in the sky' indicates to the Athenians no more than that they should make certain sacrifices, while a miraculously large spider's web observed in a temple evokes the deep diagnosis: 'the web being woven is an evil for some, better for others' (Dem. 43. 66 = P/W no. 283; Diod. Sic. 17. 10. 3). Plagues and the like were perhaps occasionally interpreted as consequences of pollution, but it is likely that in such cases the diagnosis was due to the consulting state.[55] The oracle provided confirmation, and suggested a remedy that seems normally happily to have avoided the need actually to punish the guilty parties: 'honour the dead with

---

[54] Cf. Parke, *Oracles of Zeus*, 259–62. [1999 addendum: In C. Brixhe (ed.), *Poikila Epigraphika*, Études d'archéologie classique 9 (Nancy, 1997), 105–10, A. -Ph. Christidis, S. Dakaris, and I. Vokotopoulou announce that a further 1400 tablets are 'nearly ready for publication'.]

[55] As explicitly in *SEG* 19. 427; Hdt. 1. 167. Conceivably P/W no. 169 is a counter-case where the Pythia threw an offence against a friend of the shrine (Sparta) in the enquirers' teeth unexpectedly; but P/W's historical location of the response is insecure (Fontenrose, *Delphic Oracle*, 332). P/W no. 130 is unclear.

heroic honours', 'set up two images of Pausanias'.[56] Only in stories that stand condemned on other grounds do we find such troublesome requirements as 'all the guilty must be expelled' or 'recall all exiles'.[57] Possibly something as non-committal as 'holding the unhonoured in honour you will plough the land' (P/W no. 388) might be hazarded. Otherwise, natural disasters could be explained through a ritual omission (suggested, inevitably, by the consultants); or a ritual cure, by foundation of cult or shrine, could be prescribed without a cause being found.[58] Seldom will the ritual cure have been as demanding as the Locrian maiden-tribute, which was probably revived in the third century BC on Delphi's suggestion to stay a plague.[59] According to an unverifiable though not implausible tradition (above, p. 85), in early times afflicted states were occasionally urged to dispatch a colony. Nothing so dramatic is recorded in the Classical period, and the oracles of late antiquity seem to have relied exclusively on ritual prescriptions in times of plague.[60]

But one could never be absolutely sure that the Pythia would respond meekly. She was perhaps being a little tendentious when she told the Lydian Alyattes that he would not recover his health until he rebuilt the Greek temple that his troops had burnt down.[61] She pressed the Athenians to restore the Delians, her fellow-servants of Apollo (Thuc. 5. 32. 1). (From the fourth century a more obvious interest appears, with reminders to 'send gifts to Apollo' or the like: Dem. 21. 52–3, 43. 66; P/W no. 284.) And we have already noted signs of suspicion and unease in those who posed cultic questions that touched on politics. According to Herodotus, Cleisthenes of Sicyon's request to expel the tomb of Adrastus was actually refused.

---

[56] Hdt. 1. 167; Thuc. 1. 134. 4 (P/W nos. 64, 114, but in the latter case the occasion of the enquiry is unknown). Sometimes (but not in reliably historical material) 'compensation' has to be paid, perhaps whatever the victim or his relatives/fellow-countrymen demand: Hdt. 2. 134. 4, 6. 139. 1, 9. 93–4 (P/W nos. 58, 83, 107). There are stern reproaches for communal crimes also in P/W nos. 130 and 74 (both probably spurious).

[57] Plut. de mul. virt. 244e (Fontenrose, Delphic Oracle, 276: aition for a colony); P/W no. 389 (Theagenes legend).

[58] Cf. Parker, Miasma, 271–6.

[59] P/W no. 331: cf. Graf, Ch. 11, below, with lit. But note the doubts of Fontenrose, Delphic Oracle, 136 f.

[60] Colony: e.g. Hdt. 4. 151. 1. Late antiquity: see e.g. Kaibel nos. 1034–5 (on the latter cf. Bull. épigr. 1956 no. 274a); IG Rom iv. 1498; M. L. West, 'Oracles of Apollo Kareios', ZPE 1 (1967), 183–7, at 184.

[61] Hdt. 1. 19. 2: cf. L. H. Jeffery, Archaic Greece (London, 1976), 213.

We do not know the Pythia's motive, but it is too easy to suppose that she was merely standing out for tradition; for though here she followed Homer, who knew Adrastus as king of Sicyon, in the matter of Orestes' homeland she went against him.[62] As an expounder of that most political of subjects, mythology, she must often have had to pick her way with care. But even a quite innocent question could occasionally provoke a startling response, as a famous incident of 339 shows. While bathing in preparation for the Mysteries some unfortunate Athenians had been killed by a shark. One Ameiniades proposed that the Pythia be consulted about the portent, but Demosthenes resisted, saying that 'the Pythia is Philippizing' (Aeschin. 3. 130 with schol.). He must have feared that she would exploit the opportunity offered by the humdrum enquiry to let loose a demoralizing political prophecy. Something of the kind actually occurred, if we believe Herodotus (1. 174), in 545. The Cnidians, eagerly digging their ditch to resist Harpagus' advance, were troubled by an exceptional number of eye injuries caused by flying stone-chips. They asked Apollo 'what the obstacle was'. The predictable response would surely have been an instruction to placate an appropriate god. They were told instead that Zeus would have made Cnidos an island had he wanted it to be one, and so abandoned themselves to Harpagus. If true, the story is striking evidence of Delphic defeatism, since the Cnidians themselves are portrayed as eager to resist. Many scholars judge it a fabrication, designed to disguise a failure of will in Cnidos itself.[63] The unfinished ditch has been found, and the Cnidians' devotion to Delphi is well attested; but the shrine was a long way off to consult about such a matter at such a moment.

About responses to many of the categories of political question, there is nothing of note to record. We never hear of specific proposals (to found a colony, for instance) being rejected. In connection with one colony, the Pythia is said to have done a little advertising, announcing that anyone who 'came too late to lovely Libya' would 'regret it later' (Hdt. 4. 159). There is more interesting evidence on warfare, though even of this much is very fragile. To questions of the open from ('is it better for me to go to war?', 'will I capture x?') we

[62] Hdt. 5. 67. 2; cf. Hom. *Il.* 2. 572. Orestes: Hdt. 1. 67. 2. Other political bringings-home of bones sanctioned or suggested by Delphi are P/W no. 113 (Theseus, by Cimon, whose interest it served: cf. note 37 above); P/W no. 163.

[63] See Fontenrose, *Delphic Oracle*, 306, with references. Could this response in fact (note the iambic metre) be from nearby Didyma?

find one clear answer of 'yes', that to the Spartans at the start of the Peloponnesian war (though even here an escape clause was included: they would win 'if they fought with full force'). Several questionable stories present a 'yes' that proved equivocal in the event: 'you will capture Argos' (the grove, not the town), 'you will capture all the Syracusans' (their names on a list, not their bodies). Such stories imply the possibility of simple assent.[64] Deliberate equivocation ('you will destroy a great empire') is a familiar legendary theme, but scholars have wondered with some reason whether historical consultants would have been credulous enough to tolerate it (P/W nos. 53, 441, cf. 266).[65] One possibly historical answer offers an alternative: if the Athenians wait thirty years they will defeat the Aeginetans with ease, but if they attack now, only after many setbacks (Hdt. 5. 89. 2). Once in Herodotus the Pythia says 'no' to 'will I capture?' (the Spartan request for Arcadia, in the sixth century) and twice to 'should I fight?' (the Argives and Cretans in 481/0) (1. 66. 1, 7. 148. 3, 169. 2). In the latter two cases, the refusal doubtless came to the consultants as a welcome excuse, but the Spartans in Herodotus' account genuinely change plans. Questions of the 'how are we to?' form were often answered with a ritual prescription: 'bring home the bones of Orestes', 'pray to the winds' (P/W nos. 32, 96; cf. e.g. nos. 102, 326). The question itself might indicate that such an answer was required: 'by placating what god or hero can we prevail over Tegea?' (Hdt. 1. 67. 2). An alternative was the riddle: 'trust the wooden walls', 'refer it to the many-voiced and ask the nearest', and the inextricable obscurities presented to the Argives before the battle of Sepeia in the 490s (P/W nos. 95, 81, 84; cf. e.g. no. 68, Hdt. 7. 189. 1). The familiar legendary theme of a city saved by a sacrificial death occasionally appears, but never very reliably: 'find one hundred Oresthasians to die for you' (a curious blend of the pragmatic and the religious), 'one Spartan king must die' (P/W nos. 30, 100).[66] In a few stories of uncertain authenticity advice is offered, perhaps lightly disguised: 'cut off their water supply', 'persuade a Greek state to found a colony near you'.[67] (It is clear from a response of 205 (P/W

---

[64] Thuc. 1. 118. 3; Hdt. 6. 76. 1, cf. 80; Plut. *Nic.* 13. 2, cf. 14. 7; also e.g. Paus. 8. 11. 12.

[65] See e.g. P/W i. 135; M. Delcourt, *L'Oracle de Delphes* (Paris, 1955), 105.

[66] But note L. E. Rossi's argument for the authenticity of P/W no. 100, in the collective work *I poemi epici rapsodici non omerici* (Padua, 1981), 208f.

[67] P/W nos. 181, 60: cf. e.g. no. 30, Plut. *Phoc.* 28. 4.

no. 356) that the Pythia might occasionally descend to practicalities: a Roman embassy was told that it would 'get what it desired through king Attalus'.) On the other hand Croesus, specifically seeking advice about allies, was told only to 'attach to himself the strongest Greeks' (Hdt. 1. 53).

Historians regularly seek signs of bias and predilection in these military responses. It is important to be clear, however, about the limits of the Pythia's power to aid a state, even given the will. She could perhaps help wars to occur but, unless the value of an encouraging prophecy as propaganda was extraordinarily high, she could scarcely influence their outcome. One cannot therefore argue that a lukewarm or non-committal answer, such as that given to Thebes against Athens in 506 (Hdt. 5. 79. 1), expresses disfavour: more probably it reflects the realities of the situation. Sometimes a modern interpretation in political terms is less convincing than the ancient criticism that the god, having a business to run, was prone to equivocate. Some see in the alternatives offered to the Athenians (either attack Aegina now and prevail after much suffering, or wait thirty years and win with ease) an attempt to protect Aegina from attack, others a helpful warning to the Athenians not to tangle with the mighty Aeginetan fleet too soon.[68] It seems, rather, a neat way of referring the issue back to Athens undecided. Again, it is a common modern belief that Delphi 'medized' in 481/0. Indeed, scholars often assert, in bold defiance of the evidence, that it was this humiliating misjudgment that brought the oracle's political influence to an end. But Delphi's prestige was perhaps never higher than in the aftermath of the Persian wars.[69] There are serious uncertainties about the authenticity of almost all the responses ascribed to 481/0 (P/W nos. 92–101), but if one merely accepts them as reported in Herodotus the pattern seems to be one of confirming the consultants in their own inclinations. (And the more of them one rejects, the more does the evidence for Delphi's medism diminish.)[70] The Cretans and Argives are told to keep well clear, natural policy for, respectively, a distant state and one crippled by recent disasters. For the heroic Spartans

[68] Respectively P/W i. 150 and W. G. Forrest, CAH[2] iii. 3, 319, on Hdt. 5. 89. 2 (on which see too Forrest, CR NS 8 (1958), 123; A. Andrewes, BSA 37 (1936–7), 1–7).
[69] Cf. P/W i. 180; H. Lloyd-Jones, 'The Delphic Oracle', Greece and Rome, 23 (1976), 60–73, at 69.
[70] Cf. M. Delcourt, L'Oracle, 127–31; R. Crahay, La Littérature oraculaire chez Hérodote (Paris, 1956), Ch. 7.

there is talk of the saving sacrifice of a king's life, and then of 'demanding justice from Mardonius for the killing of Leonidas'. The two responses to the Athenians mention the three policies that were being discussed in Athens at the time (flight abroad, cf. Hdt. 8. 62. 2; standing a siege; evacuation) but not the possibility of medism, which was not. Earlier the oracle had apparently condemned the Ionian revolt as a wild venture in which it was best not to be involved.[71] In doing so it was echoing the view of many mainland Greek states, including perhaps the one to which this answer was made.

There remains a final category of response to consider, rare and spectacular, the 'spontaneous' response by which the Pythia issued an order unrelated to the question posed. (She did not normally, however, dispatch oracles to a city from which no enquiry had come. It was only by consultation that one exposed oneself to divine commands.)[72] The cases are these. According to Herodotus, the Alcmaeonids induced the Pythia to urge all Spartan enquirers to 'liberate Athens' by expelling the Peisistratids. King Pleistoanax was recalled in 427 or 426 because, at his prompting, all Spartan sacred embassies were ordered to 'bring home the seed of the demigod son of Zeus. Otherwise they would plough with a silver ploughshare'. In 332 the Pythia told all Athenian consultants that she would not answer them until Athens paid the sacred Olympic fine imposed by Elis. And finally, if Lysander had succeeded in his plot to bribe the authorities of a major oracular shrine, it would probably have been through a spontaneous utterance that the order was given for the Spartan kingship to be elective henceforth.[73]

In the third case Delphi was merely showing solidarity in the cause of piety with another panhellenic shrine. In the others we find something much more interesting, oracular authority exploited as a lever to shift the Spartans in areas where they could not be moved by ordinary political processes. It is rather striking how often oracles obtrude in one form or another in debates about the kingship at Sparta. Delphi was involved in the deposition of Demaratus and the

---

[71] Hdt. 6. 19. 2 (but perhaps *post eventum*, or all but).

[72] Legrand, *Quo animo*, 41. Hdt. 6. 19. 2 is an apparent exception—but what were the circumstances? On spontaneous commands cf. H. W. Parke, *JHS* 82 (1962), 145–6.

[73] Hdt. 5. 63. 1 (on which see Jacoby on Philochorus, *FGrHist* 328 fr. 115); Thuc. 5. 16. 2 (on which see F. D. Harvey, *Crux*, 79); Paus. 5. 21. 5 (P/W no. 274); Ephorus, *FGrHist* 70 frr. 206 f. with Jacoby.

recall of Pleistoanax (above, pp. 91 and 99); the controversy about
the accession of Agesilaus was conducted around the old prophecy
warning the Spartans against a 'lame kingship' (Xen. *Hell.* 3. 3. 2–4),
and Lysander hoped to open the throne to merit through a bought
oracle. It is as though problems about the kingship could not readily
be resolved by political means because the kingship was itself the
foundation of the political structure.

Legend suggests that in early times, when kingship was general in
Greece, oracles could quite often have influence in unseating
unpopular kings (though whether through spontaneous commands,
or in answer to a request for 'release from evil', is hard to say). We
hear of kings stoned, or 'led out as a purification', or executed, or at
least 'hated' in consequence of an oracular response.[74] Since 'it is a
dire thing to kill one of royal blood' (Hom. *Od.* 16. 401), and there
was no formal mechanism for dethroning a king, a 'voice of god'
(Hom. *Od.* 3. 215) could have a special function in raising popular
discontent to the pitch of action. (But since a voice of god proceeds
from human lips, there must always have been someone of the
stamp of Cleomenes and Lysander to whisper in the prophetess's ear.)
Extraordinarily enough, a formalized divinatory mechanism for
unseating a king existed in Sparta even in the third century. Every
nine years the ephors had the right to observe the heavens on a clear
night. If a shooting star appeared, it indicated that a king had committed a religious offence: he could then be tried and dethroned 'until
an oracle came from Delphi and Olympia in his defence' (perhaps it
never would).[75] The doctrine that the behaviour of, precisely, the king
can affect the natural order is a check set upon him, and it would be a
little naive to suppose that the ephors often observed the heavens
with a quite impartial eye.

Even in warnings given to the Athenians in the fifth and fourth
centuries there peeps through the ancient oracular function of
focusing opposition to a leader. Advice (scarcely necessary) from Zeus
of Dodona to 'be suspicious of your leaders' made an impression: it

[74] Plut. *Quaest. Graec.* 26, 297c; Hdt. 7. 197. 3; Apollod. 3. 5. 1; Hom. *Od.* 3. 215; cf.
ibid. 16. 400–5.
[75] Plut. *Cleom.* 11. 3–6. H.W. Parke, *CQ* 39 (1945), 107–12, argues ingeniously on
chronological grounds that this procedure was used in the deposition of Demaratus; F.
Zeilhofer, *Sparta, Delphoi und die Amphiktyonen* (diss. Erlangen, 1959), 17 n. 33, is
sceptical. P. Rahe, *Lysander and the Spartan Settlement, 407–403 BC.* (diss. Yale, 1977),
278–9 n. 145, extends the argument to Pausanias' trial in 403/2, Paus. 3. 5. 1–6 (I owe
this reference to Paul Cartledge).

was twice quoted in political speeches, at a distance of nineteen years.[76] A response that was applied, according to Plutarch, to Phocion, 'the rest of the citizens are in harmony. One man alone is opposed to the state', was, if genuine, a similar invitation to turn against a chosen leader. And the theme of 'the villainy of the shepherds' of the people appears in oracles of the Sibyl and Musaeus that came to be taken as prophecies of the defeat at Aegospotami.[77]

III

The 'cessation of oracles' is a theme that has interested scholars since ancient times. As Plutarch, who wrote a treatise on it early in the second century AD, was priest of a Delphi that was still busy with private and ritual enquiries, it is clear that the real subject was the oracle's loss of authority in political affairs. Several aspects of the 'cessation' have been mentioned already. The influence of oracles on internal politics, implied by legend and even in the *Odyssey* (e.g. 16. 400–5), is scarcely demonstrable in the historical period. It is hard to prove that the Athenians consulted an oracle on any important issue of public policy after the Persian wars. From Greek states at large, questions about colonization come to an end early in the fourth century, about wars perhaps around the middle. No appeals to an oracle for arbitration are attested after the 380s. Even enquiries about cultic reform by whole states seem to become rarer after 300.

The pattern is, certainly, by no means uniform. Thus it was perhaps early in the third century that an Epirote *koinon* put its question at Dodona about sympolity. Throughout the third century the Boeotian *koinon* sent delegations to the oracle of Apollo Ptoïos, though we do not know what they asked (for advice about precautionary sacrifices, perhaps).[78] In the period of roughly 230–180 we seem to see something of a revival. Into this period fall the many requests for confirmation of the right of particular sanctuaries to *asylia*. The Romans made military enquiries at Delphi during the second Punic war, while both in the 220s and 180s we find the Milesians putting

---

[76] Dem. 19. 297; Dinarch. 1. 78, 98. On another occasion (or conceivably the same?) Dodona no less safely declared Athens' luck to be good (Dem. 18. 253).

[77] Plut. *Phoc.* 8. 4; Paus. 10. 9. 11; for oracular abuse of a king cf. Diod. Sic. 8. 30. 1.

[78] N.G.L. Hammond, *Epirus* (Oxford, 1967), 563 n. 2; Schachter, *Cults*, i. 67 n. 3.

political proposals, about the recruitment of new citizens and about alliance, to their oracle at Didyma for confirmation. (It was precisely in the low-water period of the early third century that Didyma had re-emerged as an oracular centre, and that a great new temple had been laid out at Claros.)[79] At some time in the first half of the second century the Parians sent an embassy to Delphi to ask what sacrifices their colonists the Pharians in the Adriatic should make to ensure their city's safety in a time of difficulty: the god urged them, in verse, to 'send Praxiepes the Parian(?) to the west', presumably to take charge of sacrifices in Pharos.[80] The occasion for this enquiry was secular, though the form of question invited the god to respond only in religious terms. Comparable evidence for later in the century, however, has yet to be found. Public enquiries are still occasionally attested, even at some new shrines, but they are confined to the themes of health, growth of crops, and ritual change.[81] Alexander had consulted Ammon at Siwa, to spectacular effect, but the Hellenistic kings took no great interest in oracles (except for the early Seleucids in the case of Didyma),[82] and did not even pretend to shape their policies by oracular guidance. As for the Romans, Strabo could blame the decline of oracular shrines on their reliance on indigenous forms of divination. For Cicero it was an agreed fact that the well of Delphic inspiration was dry. The blooming of Claros as a public oracle which could advise states not just about plagues but even about attacks of brigands still lay in the future.[83]

The evidence reveals no sudden failure of the oracles but a gradual and uneven decline. The abruptest break seems to come with the emergence of the Hellenistic kingships. Delphi was no longer the navel of the Greek world, acknowledged point of reference for the competing states. The traditional pattern of Greek warfare, of which oracular consultation formed a part, had been transformed. For the states there was now a higher authority outside themselves other than that of the gods, in the person of the king. The psephism

[79] See W. Günther, Das Orakel von Didyma in hellenistischer Zeit (Tübingen, 1971), 23–95; L. Robert, Les Fouilles de Claros: Conférence (Limoges, 1954), 13–16.
[80] See L. Robert, Hellenica, 11–12 (Paris, 1960), 505–41; Bull. épigr. 1963 no. 129 (SEG 23. 489).
[81] Above n. 24; for Delphic and Didyman evidence see Fontenrose's catalogues in Delphic Oracle; note too SIG³ 735 (Apollo Pythios at Argos).
[82] See esp. OGI 227. 3–5; and further Günther, Das Orakel, 23–95.
[83] Strabo 17. 1. 43 (813); Cic. Div. 2. 117. Brigands: L. Robert, Documents de l'Asie Mineure méridionale (Paris, 1966), 91–100.

of Dromocleides, frivolous though it was and suggested by special circumstances, none the less has an emblematic significance: Athenian ambassadors to Demetrius Poliorcetes were to be 'sacred envoys' and his pronouncements 'oracles'.[84] And the mortal oracles did not sustain by patronage the prestige of their traditional divine counterparts.

The earlier change, the gradual decline in influence, especially over the fifth and fourth centuries, is harder to explain. Particular misjudgments by oracles are often invoked, the supposed medism of Delphi in 481/0 or its too evident favour for Sparta in the Peloponnesian war or the periodic scandals over bribery. In fact, as we have seen, the Persian invasion brought to Delphi nothing but glory, and it is hard to prove that the oracle's stance at the start of the Peloponnesian war was ever criticized. As for bribery, most of our evidence comes from the oracle's most enthusiastic devotee, Herodotus. All such explanations are unsatisfactory because they underestimate the true believer's power to forgive and forget, to explain away particular failures and even misdeeds. At most one would expect disillusioned clients to transfer their custom to a less discredited shrine.

Perhaps public divination gave way because its function had been absorbed by other institutions.[85] Oracles traditionally set the seal of absolute rightness on a crucial collective decision. There seem to be two requirements if a decision is to be generally accepted: it must be reached by procedures that are admitted to be fair, and it must be believed to be based on the best available information. On the second point, the role of 'experts' and statistics in creating conviction in modern debates is obvious. As for the first, two procedures designed to display fairness (not quite everyone agrees, of course) are legislation by delegated democracy, and trial by jury. On some issues in some countries delegated democracy ceases to seem sufficiently representative, and the question is 'put to the people' by referendum. Often these are issues of constitutional structure or national sovereignty that are felt to lie outside the scope of normal political

---

[84] Plut. *Demetr.* 13: on the circumstances see C. Habicht, *Untersuchungen zur politischen Geschichte Athens im 3.Jahrhundert v. Chr.* (Munich, 1979), 34–44: the date is 292/1, when Delphi itself was inaccessible to Athens through the presence of the hostile Aetolians. Compare earlier Arr. *Anab.* 7. 23. 2; Plut. *Dem.* 29. 3.

[85] For this approach (which I owe to a comment of Richard Gordon) see in general J.-P. Vernant, *The Origins of Greek Thought* (Ithaca, NY, 1982), esp. Ch. 4; Lloyd, *Magic*, Ch. 4.

procedure. Thus several modern European monarchs have been
deposed by referendum, the voice of the people proving as fatal to
them as that of Apollo could be for Spartan kings. Joining the Common Market, too, may require a special mandate, much like entering
into sympolity with the Molossians. Referendums also occur on
moral issues such as abortion and divorce; we may compare the
Cymaeans' supposed question about surrendering a suppliant.
Under a radical democracy, of course, every vote is a referendum.
The guarantee for the propriety of a decision is that it has been
passed in the sovereign assembly. We noted earlier (p. 90) that
Aeschylus in *Eumenides* shows Athene referring a judicial decision to
human jurors, and similarly in *Supplices* his king Pelasgus puts a
choice between surrendering suppliants and incurring war to the
'controlling hand of the people'. Herodotus' Cymaeans, by contrast,
had referred the same issue to Apollo; by 'Cymaeans' here we must
doubtless understand the ruling oligarchs.[86] As a procedural guarantor of decisions, therefore, an oracle is redundant in a democracy.
Of course the argument cannot be applied too simply, since the
Spartans consulted Apollo about the decision to invade Attica (Thuc.
I. 118. 3), which had been taken in the citizen assembly; but
the individual decision is less important than the habitual pattern
of decision-making, which was at Sparta by no means truly
democratic.[87] The ordinary Athenian, by contrast, learnt by daily
experience of issues great and small to believe that the sovereignty
of the assembly was a reality, and a beneficent one. To consult an
oracle with a view to doing what the god 'ordered' ($\kappa\epsilon\lambda\epsilon\acute{u}\omega$, Thuc.
3. 92. 5) could perhaps be seen as a surrender of the right of
self-determination. A Spartan, of course, was never happier than
when doing what he was told.

Nor could Apollo's standing as a uniquely expert adviser go
unchallenged in the fifth century. Thucydides' Athenians draw a
contrast in the Melian debate (5. 103. 2) between 'having recourse to
divination' and 'saving oneself by human means' ($\dot{a}\nu\theta\rho\omega\pi\epsilon\acute{\iota}\omega s$).
Even a firm believer would agree that the proper sphere of divination
only begins where that of human capacity and understanding
ends (Xen. *Mem.* I. I. 6–9). Even a pragmatist might be willing to

---

[86] Aesch. *Supp.* 365–401, 480–5, 600–24; note Pelasgus' fear of popular criticism
(401, 485). On the Cymaean oligarchy see Halliday on Plut. *Quaest. Graec.* 2. 291e–f.
[87] De Ste. Croix, *Origins*, 124–51.

admit the aid of divination on issues genuinely uncontrollable or indeterminate in human terms (Polyb. 36. 17). But there was scope for conflict as to where the boundary between the two spheres should be put; and new skills were developed in the fifth century that claimed to make inroads on the realm of the indeterminate. Rhetoric was a secular mode of divination, probing past and future by the light of 'probability', through 'signs' no longer magical. There is thus a special aptness in the much-quoted Euripidean tag 'the best prophet is the man who's good at guessing' (literally, 'at calculating what's probable').[88] Politics and generalship were becoming professions and skills, no longer merely one of the varied activities of the gently born.[89] In many traditional contexts for divination the new professionals would have been devaluing their expertise if they had accepted that there was no clearly preferable choice in human terms. By ceding Apollo's unique authority in matters of cult—'for we ourselves know nothing of such matters' (Pl. Rep. 427b)—one might be quietly disputing it in matters of more pressing concern.

The decline of oracles, however, was a loss of the semblance of power as much as the reality. The Greek evidence that we have reviewed supports the general proposition of anthropologists that on important issues men seldom allow divination to stand in their way. A few instances can be offered where the oracles genuinely deflected the course of events, but it is rather striking that the most obvious (the restoration of Pleistoanax, or the expulsion of the Peisistratids) are precisely cases where the ancients believed corruption to have been at work (see n. 91 below). For an oracle actually to influence affairs was somehow a perversion of its proper nature. We have already noted the two scenes that best convey this obdurate capacity not to expose oneself to unpalatable advice, or at least to evade it when it comes: Xenophon asking Apollo what sacrificial preparations he should make for the Anabasis, not whether he should join the expedition at all, and the Athenians in 481/0 refusing to leave the shrine at Delphi until the god 'gave them some more favourable prophecy about their native land'.

---

[88] Eur. fr. 973 N.²; cf. Thuc. 1. 138. 3 on Themistocles, and the valuable brief study of J.-P. Vernant, 'Parole et signes muets' in Vernant et al., Divination et rationalité (Paris, 1974), 9–25, at 14. On the 'divination' of doctors and rhetoricians see Lloyd, Magic, 45; D. Lanza, Lingua e discorso nell' Atene delle professioni (Naples, 1979), 96–113.

[89] On professionalism see S. Hornblower, The Greek World 479–323 BC (London, 1983, corr. impr. 1985), 123f., 156–9.

APPENDIX: 'WITHOUT FEAR OR FAVOUR'?

We noted above (p. 82) the general factors that might have pushed the Pythia occasionally into partiality. None the less, the case for Delphic bias, spasmodic or perpetual, needs to be built up rather than assumed *a priori*. To start with the strongest evidence, Demosthenes in 339 accused the Pythia of 'Philippizing'. At that time Philip was posing as champion of the Amphictyonic league and Apollo in a holy war; perhaps the priestess was honestly beguiled by his professions, but whatever her feelings it would have been hard for her to 'Atticize' at a time when honorary inscriptions show Delphi to have been aswarm with influential Macedonians.[90] Most Greeks believed that earlier the Pythia had occasionally yielded to improper 'persuasion', whether by words or by gold.[91] By isolating this abnormal category of corrupted response they defended the purity of others, but the neat distinction, essential of course for the believer, perhaps locates the source of 'persuasion' too narrowly in gold passing from hand to hand, or other forms of explicit approach to the Pythia. Of the supposed corrupters two were Spartan kings, persons always esteemed at Delphi, while the Alcmaeonids were based at the shrine and had contracted to rebuild part of the temple. Such factors may always have had their influence. Lysander, by contrast, who had no such claims to consideration, failed in his attempts to buy up a priestess (Ephorus, *FGrHist* 70 frr. 206 f. with Jacoby).

This seems to be the sum of the wholly reliable, because explicit, evidence for Delphic partisanship. Various items can also be cited as evidence by implication: the repeated attempts of the Athenians in the fifth century to put Delphi under Phocian control, and the corresponding Spartan interventions to restore Delphic autonomy (only relevant if we think that the Athenians were chiefly moved by the hope of securing favourable prophecies, such as the famous one from roughly this period comparing Athens to 'an eagle in the clouds');[92] perhaps consequent on this, the oracle's promise of Apollo's aid to the Spartans in the Peloponnesian war, and the use of Delphi itself as a place of muster for Peloponnesian armies (Thuc. 1. 118. 3, 3. 101. 1, and cf. 1. 121. 3); apparent boycotts of Delphi by particular states at particular periods (most obviously by Athens under

[90] 'Philippizing': Aeschin. 3. 130. Holy War: cf. P/W i. 235–8. Influential Macedonians: *SIG*[3] 267–9.

[91] Hdt. 5. 63. 1 (cf. n. 73 above), 6. 66. 2–3; Thuc. 5. 16. 2. For another form of alleged influence, bribery of Delphians to report discouraging portents from the shrine, see Plut. *Nic.* 13. 5–6 (?cf. Cic. *Div.* 1. 75).

[92] Cf. P/W i. 184–6. Eagle: P/W no. 121. On the Athenian alliance, of uncertain date, with the Delphic Amphictyony (the council of 'neighbouring' states that administered the shrine) see Meiggs, *Athenian Empire*, 418–20.

Peisistratus, perhaps too by Sparta when Delphi was under Phocian control);[93] a harsh rebuff supposedly issued in 479 to Themistocles, arch-rival of two families who had good friends at Apollo's court;[94] the suspicion that the technique of enquiry used by the Athenians in 352/1 (above pp. 84–5) perhaps implies;[95] possibly even Euripides' hostility to the oracle in certain plays of the war years. Further evidence from the seventh and sixth centuries has been adduced, but it is too uncertain to base an argument upon.[96]

On the other side we have many statements of faith in the truthfulness of Apollo (see e.g. n. 18 above); consultations by both parties to a war;[97] the shock created by Demosthenes' claim about a Philippizing Pythia; dedications or consultations by states whose enemies Apollo might be thought recently to have favoured.[98] Despite Delphi's stance in 432, for instance, the Athenians were certainly consulting it in the late 420s, and if they turned to Dodona in 429 that was probably merely because the more prestigious shrine was inaccessible.[99] Free access to Delphi was a generally desired good that was specifically guaranteed in the peace of Nicias of 421 (Thuc. 5. 18. 2, cf. 4. 118. 1–3). Such evidence of course illustrates merely belief in Apollo's fairness, not the fact of it, but it weakens the common modern assumption that Delphi was often very blatantly partisan. The reality is complex: the interests of the Pythia and of her advisers as persons and citizens in some degree conflicted with the impartiality of shrewd professional prophets, and with whatever measure of honest faith (probably in most cases a large one) they brought to their

[93] Peisistratids: see e.g. J. Bousquet, *BCH* 80 (1956), 570; J. Boardman, *Rev. Arch.* 1978, 234; and note the extraordinary rumour in Schol. Pind. *Pyth.* 7. 9b that the Peisistratids started the fire that destroyed the temple. Sparta: the dedication after Tanagra seems to have been at Olympia only (ML 36), while for Athenian and Argive dedications at Delphi in this period see Paus. 10. 10. 3–4, with G. Daux, *Pausanias à Delphes* (Paris, 1937), 88–92.

[94] Paus. 10. 14. 5, cf. Forrest, *CR* NS 8 (1958), 69.

[95] But it is hard to see the ground for suspicion at just this time, when Delphi was in the hands of the Phocians and the pro-Phocian, pro-Athenian faction (cf. *SIG³* 175, with Pomtow's notes) of Delphians. Was the point rather to show Megara that the verdict was fair?

[96] W. G. Forrest, 'Delphi, 750–500 B.C.', in *CAH²*, iii.3, 305–20.

[97] Hdt. 6. 76. 1 with 77. 2 (not, certainly, indisputable evidence).

[98] For dedications by Athens or her allies during the Peloponnesian war see Paus. 10. 11. 6 (Phormion's campaign of 429; perhaps not installed till 423); *SIG³* 81; Thuc. 4. 134. 1 (both sides send spoils); Paus. 10. 9. 12, with Daux, *Pausanias*, 87. In 506 the Thebans consulted the oracle about revenge (Hdt. 5. 79) for a defeat in commemoration of which the Athenians apparently dedicated their Delphic portico (Daux, *Pausanias*, 131–3).

[99] Athenians: Thuc. 5. 32. 1. Dodona in 429: Parke, *Oracles of Zeus*, 136, 149 on *IG* II² 1283. 6 with *IG* I³ 383, 143 and *SIG³* 73. Inaccessible: so Zeilhofer, *Sparta, Delphoi und die Amphiktyonen*, 67 n. 32.

high calling. Sometimes what will have seemed to the Pythia like simple piety (defence at all costs of the shrine's interests) may have looked like partisanship to an outsider. A general formula will scarcely exhaust the possibilities.

5
From Oedipus to Periander: Lameness, Tyranny, Incest in Legend and History

J.-P. VERNANT

In *Structural Anthropology*, as an example of his method, Lévi-Strauss proposes an analysis of the myth of Oedipus which has become classic.[1] His interpretation has two characteristics. First, in the eyes of the Hellenist, it appears erroneous from beginning to end. Second, it has so radically modified the field of mythological studies that after it, in Lévi-Strauss's work and in the work of other scholars, reflection on the legend of Oedipus has taken new and, I think, fruitful paths.

I will recall just one aspect of this revival. Lévi-Strauss is, to my knowledge, the first to have brought out the importance of a trait common to three generations of the Labdacids' line: a disequilibrium in walking, a lack of symmetry of the two sides of the body, a defect in one of the two feet. Labdacus, that is, the lame, he whose legs are not alike, not of the same size or strength; Laius, the asymmetrical, all left feet, the left-handed; Oedipus, he who has a swollen foot. Lévi-Strauss, evoking a defect in walking or a malformation of the foot, thought at first he could read these names of Greek personages in light of Native American myths. According to these myths, men born from the earth, the autochthonous, remain attached to the soil from which they have just barely emerged, by an anomaly in their mode of locomotion, in the manner in which they move on the earth while walking. This is an interpretation difficult to sustain, since the application of the American models to the Greek ones reveals it to be gratuitous and arbitrary.[2]

---

[1] C. Lévi-Strauss, *Structural Anthropology* (London, 1963), 206–31.
[2] In Greek myths of autochthony, men 'born of the earth' as such present no anomalies of foot or walking. In the very case of Thebes, the Spartoi—that is, the 'Sown Men' who came directly from the earth and whose descendants interfere with

But Lévi-Strauss himself, as if obsessed by this myth to which he continually returns, either directly or indirectly, gave up this first hypothesis while enlarging and modifying his reading on essential points. I will mention two. First, in his *Inaugural Lecture* at the Collège de France,[3] he linked the theme of the riddle, curiously 'forgotten' in his first analysis, where he breathed not a word of it, to the theme of walking: the riddle should be understood as a question separated from its response, that is, formulated in such a way that the response cannot catch up with it. Thus the riddle translates a defect or an impossibility of communication in the verbal exchange between two interlocutors: the first poses a question to which only the silence of the second can reply. Afterwards, in a recent study,[4] placing himself at the level of highest abstraction and trying to draw out the purely formal frame of the mythical armature, he advanced the following hypothesis: lameness, when a man does not walk straight— stuttering, when a man, limping with his tongue instead of his foot, drags the foot of his discourse and does not pursue his course directly toward the listener—finally, forgetting, when a man cannot tie up inside himself the thread of his memories—all these are so many converging markers which the myth uses, bound up with the themes of indiscretion and misunderstanding, in order to express the failures, distortions or blockages of communication between different levels of social life: sexual communication, the transfer of life (normal childbirth being opposed to sterility or monstrosity), communication between successive generations (fathers transmitting their status and their functions to their sons), verbal exchanges, communication of the self with the self (presence of mind, the transparency to one's self contrasting with forgetting, division, the doubling of the self, as in Oedipus.)[5]

I would like to test this new orientation—closer to the reading which Terence Turner proposed of the myth and which I myself

---

the line of the Labdacids in the royal legend of the city—carry on their body the mark of their origin, but it has nothing to do with the foot. The sign of autochthony is the figure of a lance on the shoulder of the sons of the earth, authenticating their line and recalling their vocation as warriors.

[3] C. Lévi-Strauss, *Structural Anthropology*, ii (Harmondsworth, 1976), 22–4.

[4] C. Lévi-Strauss, 'Mythe et oubli', in *Langue, discours, société. Pour Émile Benveniste* (Paris, 1975), 294–300.

[5] See, in the *Annuaire de l'École Pratique des Hautes Études*, Ve section, Sciences religieuses, the summary of the seminar which J.-P. Vernant devoted to these questions (161–2), and Vernant, *Religions, histoires, raisons* (Paris, 1979), 30–1.

suggested in an analysis of Sophocles' tragedy—as an experimental exercise, in what it says about lameness. For now I leave aside stuttering, that is, for us Hellenists, the tales concerning the origins of Cyrene, whose foundation, delayed and deflected by a memory lapse of the Argonauts, was realized in spite of the communication blocks with the Delphic god, at the end of many wanderings and detours, by Battos, the stutterer, the eponymous founder of the royal dynasty of the Battiads, which ended with a last Battos, the latter 'lame and unsound of foot', χωλός τε ἐὼν καὶ οὐκ ἀρτίπους, as Herodotus notes.[6]

I will examine to what extent such an interpretative frame allows us to draw out the traits common to two narratives of very different sorts, on the one hand a myth, the legend of the Labdacids, on the other, the 'historical' narrative, in Herodotus, of the dynasty of the tyrants of Corinth, the Cypselids, descended from Labda the lame.

This attempt presupposes a preliminary condition. It is necessary that for the Greeks themselves the category of 'lame', 'limping', not be strictly limited to a defect of the foot, the leg, or of walking, but that it be susceptible to a symbolic extension to domains other than simple displacement in space, that it can express metaphorically all forms of behaviour which seem unbalanced, deviated, slowed down or blocked. On the values of lameness Marcel Detienne and I have explained ourselves at sufficient length in *Cunning Intelligence in Greek Culture and Society* that it is not necessary to return to them.[7] Let me just recall the equivocal character of lameness, its ambivalence.[8] Compared to a normal walk, it ordinarily constitutes a defect; the lame person lacks something; one of his legs has less than is needed (in size, in strength, in straightness). But this exception to the rule can also confer on the lame the privilege of an uncommon status, of an exceptional qualification; no longer a defect, but a sign or a promise of a singular destiny, the asymmetry of the two legs then presents itself in another way, positive rather than negative. It adds a new dimension to ordinary walking by liberating the walker from the

---

[6] Hdt. 4. 161. 2; the whole passage in Book 4, from 147 to 162, must be read, and Pindar *Pyth.* 4. 57–123 and 452–66.

[7] Especially in the chapter entitled 'The Feet of Hephaestus', in M. Detienne and J.-P. Vernant, *Cunning Intelligence in Greek Culture and Society* (Hassocks, 1978), 259–75, at 270–3.

[8] See E. Cassin, 'Le droit et le tordu', *Ancient Near Eastern Studies in Memory of J.J. Finkelstein* (Connecticut Academy of Arts & Sciences, 19, 1977), 29–37, and A. Brelich, 'Les monosandales', *La Nouvelle Clio*, 7–9 (1955), 469–89, at 483.

common necessity of advancing in a straight line, within the limits of a single direction.
Let me explain this point in more detail. Since the lame man's two feet are not on the same plane, the limping produces a walk which is zigzagging, oscillating, unbalanced; its trail is winding. Compared to normal displacement, where each foot is placed after the other in order to progress in a constant balance on the same path, it certainly is defective. But pushed to the ultimate extreme, its furthest point, the sort of waddling gait which the progress of the lame produces, this see-saw motion, reaches at its limit another form of locomotion, that entirely waddling gait, completely circular, which characterizes in the eyes of the Greeks various categories of exceptional beings: instead of pushing straight in front of them, thrusting their legs, each foot following the other, these beings all go around in circles, turning cartwheels, all spatial directions mixed up in a whirling in which the opposition between forward and backward is done away with—an opposition which, while giving a direction to the walk of the normal man, at the same time imposes rigorous limits on him. Thus the gait of Hephaestus appears circular, Hephaestus the divine lame one, when he 'rolls' in his workshop around his bellows.[9] Also circular is the gait of those primordial men, those 'complete' beings, compared to human beings of today who are cut in two (following the axis which determines the forward-backward cleavage), like those presented by the speech of Aristophanes in the *Symposium*.[10] Thanks to the staggering of each one of their four legs in relation to the three others (not to mention the four arms which are paired with their lower limbs), these extremely lame creatures, these lame in all directions—advance and retreat equally, turning cartwheels,[11] resembling in their circular mode of locomotion the tripods mounted on wheels which the magic of Hephaestus fabricates (in the image of the god) so that these animated automata move about as easily backward as forward[12]—resembling also those animals of the island of the Sun whose rotary walk, attested to by Iambulus, bears witness,

[9] *Il.* 18. 372: ἐλισσόμενον περὶ φύσας.
[10] Pl. *Symp.* 184e4 ff. Zeus cut these primordial men in two so that thus 'they walk straight on two legs' (190d3-4).
[11] 'Since, in that time, they had eight limbs to serve as support, turning cartwheels they advanced with great speed' (190a7-9: κυβιστῶσι κύκλῳ ... ταχὺ ἐφέροντο κύκλῳ).
[12] *Il.* 18. 375-8.

among other wonders, to the superiority of the islanders compared to the majority of mortals.[13] But that there is not just lameness of the feet, that for the Greeks there are the lame of the mind, opposed to those who are agile, quick, steady on their two feet, βέβαιοι, opposed to those who walk straight (ἰθύς, ὀρθῶς)—we see in particular in the seventh book of the Republic,[14] where Plato distinguishes between well-born souls, made for philosophy, and those which are 'crippled and lame'. In so doing, as if it were self-evident, he assimilates intellectual lameness to the illegitimacy of the soul, the χωλός, being a νόθος, a bastard, not a γνήσιος, of straight and legitimate descent,[15] as in the case where the son 'resembles his father', who has engendered him regularly, without swerving, without deformity, because the descent is maintained in a straight line, not limping. Two texts are of decisive value concerning the relations between lameness and filiation: Xenophon, Hellenica 3. 1–3, and Plutarch, Agesilaus 3. 1–9. The king of Sparta, Agis, having died, it is necessary to designate his successor. Agis has one son, Leotychidas, and a brother Agesilaus. Normally the succession falls to the son, not to the brother of the deceased. In addition, Agesilaus is lame, physically lame. However, Leotychidas is suspected of being in reality the son of Alcibiades, who had been commonly known to be the lover of Timaea, Agis' wife, during his stay in Sparta. Meanwhile the seer Diopeithes, to support the cause of Leotychidas, pulls out of a drawer an 'ancient oracle' warning Sparta in something like these terms: 'Beware, Sparta, steady on your two feet (ἀρτίπους), lest someday your royalty become lame, χωλὴ βασιλεία. You will then be overcome by evils.'[16] Thus the contest for the royal successor to Agis opposes his lame brother to his presumably bastard son. Between the χωλός and the νόθος, which is the more lame of the two? The response of Lysander and of the Spartans left no room for doubt. According to Xenophon, 'the god did not command you to beware of a man who would limp because of a fall, but of a man who would reign without being of the true race, μὴ οὐκ ὢν τοῦ γένους. It is then that the royal house would be lame.' And Plutarch: 'A man

---

[13] Diod. Sic. 2. 18.
[14] Rep. 535 ff.
[15] Ibid. 536a6: χωλοῖς τε καὶ νόθοις.
[16] A kingship 'steady on its own two feet' or 'lame': the formula applies so much better in the case of Sparta since the city relies on two royal lines which must each be equally intact.

having become lame would reign, but if a king was neither legitimate nor descended from the Heraclids, μὴ γνήσιος ὢν μηδ' Ἡρακλείδης, that would make the royal house lame.'[17]

Let us examine from this point of view the series Labdacus, Laius, Oedipus, and his two sons Eteocles and Polyneices.

Labdacus, the lame, dies when his son is still a year-old baby. The legitimate line is interrupted, as is the normal link between father and son. The throne is occupied by an outsider, Lycus. The young Laius is not only removed from the throne, but also distanced from it, turned away from Thebes to take refuge with Pelops.

Laius, the left-handed [gauche], shows himself when he grows up to be unbalanced and unilateral in his sexual relations and in his relations with his host. He fumbles [gauchit] his erotic behaviour with an excessive homosexuality, with the violence he inflicts on young Chrysippus, son of Pelops, thus breaking the rules of symmetry and of reciprocity which are required between lovers as between guest and host. Chrysippus kills himself. Pelops hurls a curse against Laius which condemns his kind to extinction: the γένος of Labdacids is no longer to perpetuate itself.

Having returned to Thebes, re-established on the throne, married to Jocasta (or Epicasta), Laius is warned by the oracle. He must not have children. His line is condemned to sterility, his descent pledged to disappearance. If he disobeys and procreates, this 'legitimate' child, instead of keeping him alive rightly, in his resemblance to his father, will destroy him and will sleep with his mother. The γνήσιος, the well-born, will be revealed as worse than a νόθος, beyond illegitimacy, a monster.

Laius has 'left-handed' relations with his wife, homosexual ones, in order not to conceive a child. But one drunken evening, he does not take precautions: he plants a child in the furrow of his wife. This son, both legitimate and cursed, is expelled from Thebes at birth, thrown out onto Cithaeron where he must die of exposure. In reality, he goes both nearer and further away. He escapes death; he remains here below, but he is distanced, turned away from his proper place, deflected to a path which leaves on one of his feet the trace of both his origin and his rejection; he finds himself at Corinth, in the house of strangers whose son he thinks he is, bearer of a name which recalls and hides the lineage to which he belongs and from which he was at birth excluded.

The story of Oedipus is that of his return to his place of origin, his reintegration into the lineage of which he is the legitimate son and the forbidden child. Like a boomerang, the return occurs not in the proper time, under the required conditions, in the rightness of a succession respecting the regular order of generations, but in the violence of an excessive identification: Oedipus does not come to occupy in his turn the place which his father gave up, to leave it free for him; he takes his father's place through parricide and maternal incest; he goes back too far; he finds himself a husband in the womb which gave birth to him as son, and which he was not entitled to leave.

Two sequences of the story make very clear these aspects of the myth. At the same moment when, having crossed the threshold of adolescence, Oedipus the man leaves Corinth to flee from those he believes his parents and when he turns by way of Delphi toward the Thebes of his origin, Laius leaves Thebes for Delphi, travelling in the opposite direction, to consult the oracle about the calamity which has struck the city: the Sphinx. The two men meet at the intersection of three roads, but they encounter each other in a place too narrow to pass abreast. Father and son, instead of following along the same road which would lead them to occupy successively the same places—without jostling each other or getting lost—reunite, after having been brutally separated, in a place of passage where they can only meet face to face. The two generations of the lame collide rather than succeed each other. Oedipus kills his father, who topples from the height of his chariot to the same level as he.

Second sequence: the riddle of the Sphinx. We must read one of the versions which Pausanias brought back from Thebes and which is precious from our point of view since the Sphinx is the illegitimate daughter of Laius and since her role is to test all the sons of the sovereign in order to distinguish the νόθοι from the γνήσιοι.[18]

'The Sphinx, according to what some say, was an illegitimate daughter of Laius, νόθη θυγάτηρ; he, because of the particular goodwill he felt for her, revealed to her the oracle which Delphi had given to Cadmus. No one except the kings knew this oracle. Then

---

[18] Paus. 9. 26. 3–5.

when one of her brothers came to debate with her his right to the throne—Laius had sons by concubines, but the Delphic oracle concerned only Epicasta and those sons Laius had with her—she used trickery against her brothers, saying that if they were Laius' sons they should know the oracle given to Cadmus. When they could not answer, she punished them with death, since they had no valid right to the lineage, nor to the throne. But Oedipus, having learned it in a dream, presented himself as knowledgeable about the contents of the oracle.'

Let us examine finally, and especially, the riddle itself. There is decidedly a relationship between the riddle and walking, but in the case of Oedipus it goes much further than Lévi-Strauss thought. The riddle of the Sphinx defines man by his mode of locomotion, his walk. And it defines him in opposition to all other living creatures, to all animals which progress, which move on the earth, in the air, in the water, that is, which walk, which fly, which swim (which have four feet, two feet, no feet).[19] In fact all creatures are born, grow, live and die, always using the same mode of locomotion. Man is the only one to change the nature of his mobility, taking on three different types of walking: four feet, two feet, three feet. Man is a being who at once is always the same (he has one voice, φωνή, one essence) and who becomes other: in opposition to all the animal species he knows three different states of existence, three 'ages': child, adult, old man. He must go through them one after another, each in its time, because each one implies a particular social status, a transformation of his position and of his role in the group. The human condition involves a temporal order because the succession of ages, in the life of each

---

[19] Recall the text of the riddle as it appears in the argument to Euripides' *Phoenissae*: 'There is on earth a being with two, four, three feet, with a single voice. He alone changes his nature, among all those who move on the surface of the earth, in the air, in the sea. But when he walks by leaning on more of his feet, it is then that his members have least strength.' The text was also transmitted to us by Athenaeus 10. 456b; *Anthologia Palatina* 14. 64; Scholia to Lycophron, *Alexandra* 7. 1. 22 Scheer 2. 11. A few variants to note: in the first line, instead of 'with a single voice (φωνή)' we have 'with a single form (μορφή)'; in the second line: 'he changes his nature', we have sometimes φυήν, sometimes φύσιν, and once βοήν, his cry (which supposes, due to the incorrect writing of οὖ towards the end of the last line, that we read: 'his voice is not single' instead of 'with a single voice'). Diodorus Siculus sums up the statement as follows: 'what is it that, remaining always the same, is two-, three-, four-footed?' (4. 64). Note that in all versions the riddle scrambles the normal chronological order, beginning with the adult (two feet), then passing sometimes to the old man (three feet), sometimes to the child (four feet). In Athen. 13. 558d we find an erotic transposition of the riddle, the prostitute then taking the Sphinx's place.

individual, must be articulated on the sequence of generations, must respect that sequence to harmonize with it, at the risk of a return to chaos.

Oedipus, Οἰδίπους, guesses the answer to the riddle: he is himself the δίπους, the man with two feet. But the result of his flaw, or rather of the curse which weighs on the lame line of descendants, is that in guessing the answer, in reuniting the response and the question, he also 'rejoins' his own place of origin, on his father's throne, in his mother's bed. Instead of making him equal to the man who progresses in life by walking in a straight line, his success identifies him with the monster the Sphinx's words evoke: the being who is at one and the same time two-, three-, four-footed, the man who as he advances in age jumbles up and confuses the social and cosmic order of the generations instead of respecting it. Oedipus, the two-footed adult, is in fact identical to his father, the old man who walks with a staff, this 'three-footed one' whose place he has taken at the head of Thebes, even in the bed of Jocasta—identical also to his children, walking on all fours, who are at the same time his sons and his brothers.[20]

The two sons he produced, Eteocles and Polyneices, will communicate normally neither with him nor with one another. Oedipus will curse them as Pelops cursed Laius. They will meet face to face, like Oedipus and Laius, to find themselves united only in the death each inflicts on the other. Thus, at the end of this long detour, the theme of which is lameness, the line of the Labdacids instead of continuing in a straight line comes back to its point of origin, destroying itself. The 'left-handed one', Laius, son of the lame one, can have no direct descent.

Before passing to Herodotus in order to confront 'history' and legend, let me formulate, as so many others have, the questions which the myth tests through the tale of the calamities of the limping walk, the problems which as it were underlie the terrain which the narrative explores:

How can man participate in the same, be rooted solidly in the same, in becoming throughout the course of his existence thrice

---

[20] On the equality or identity which Oedipus has at the same time with his father and his children, see J.-P. Vernant, 'Ambiguity and Reversal: On the Enigmatic Structure of *Oedipus Rex*', in J.-P. Vernant and P. Vidal-Naquet, *Myth and Tragedy in Ancient Greece* (New York, 1990), 113–40. As Leonidas of Alexandria (*Anth. Pal.* 6. 323) says, Oedipus is he who 'was the brother of his children, the husband of his mother.'

different? How can the permanence of an order be maintained with creatures who must at every stage of life submit to a complete change in their status? How can the rights and functions of king, father, husband, grandfather, son, remain intact, immovable, while others successively assume them and while the same person must be son, father, husband, grandfather, young prince and old king in turn?

Or again: under what conditions should a son travel straight in the wake of his father, coming to occupy his place, sufficiently like his father that this place remains indefinitely the same, sufficiently distinct from him that this replacement of one by the other does not result in chaotic confusion?

Let us see now if this schema throws any light on the articulation of Herodotus' account in 5. 92 and 3. 50–4, and on the image the Greeks had of the tyrant in the fifth century.

If we are to believe Herodotus, it was to warn the Lacedemonians and their allies against tyranny, 'the most unjust and bloodiest thing on earth', that Socles of Corinth chose to recount an adventure he was well placed to know about, that of the Cypselids, tyrants of his own city. In Herodotus' hands this 'history' is at the same time related to an old wives' tale, to a fantastic story, and to tragedy. In the course of extraordinary episodes, of unexpected rebounds, an inexorable necessity comes to light. 'It was fated,' writes Herodotus, 'that Eëtion's descent be the seed of misfortune for Corinth'[21]—as if calamity, which the gods had decided he would install as master in the heart of the city, must be incarnated in a marginal family, at once cursed and elect, a lineage of persons whose deviance from their lineage predestined them from birth to play the figure of the tyrant.

Up to that time there had been an oligarchy at Corinth's head. The Bacchiads—such was the name of the little group of men who monopolized power—to keep for their own profit the privileges of a kingship they held in common, married exclusively among themselves, reserving their daughters to be exchanged inside the group, giving them as wives to one another. The Bacchiads thus not only exercise the monarchy in the plural; they constitute, at the height of the city, a sort of collective Father for the royal line.

---

[21] 5. 92. δ1–2.

Now one of them had a lame daughter named Labda. No Bacchiad wanted to marry her. Labda's infirmity places her on the margin of the descent to which she belongs. Being lame, she is thrust aside from direct descent, turned away from the straight line which she normally would have perpetuated. Or perhaps, as Louis Gernet would suggest, we should invert the terms of the relationship between marriage and limping. 'Having been married out of order, the girl was named the lame.'[22] In any case, whether she could not marry according to the rules because of her limp, or whether she was called the Lame because married against the rules, Labda was disqualified from giving birth to an authentic Bacchiad, a legitimate son, resembling the father who produced him and of whom he ought to be a true copy. With respect to the group of King-Fathers, Labda's child will inherit from his mother a lame birth.

Rejected by her normal suitors, Labda finds a Corinthian husband, Lapith in origin, a descendant of Caeneus. This Caeneus was considered to be an androgyne, both man and woman, like Teiresias. By its deviance, its strangeness, its ambivalent character (the androgyne can be effeminate just as well as a superman), hermaphroditism evokes a form of lameness in the sexual status of individuals (the androgyne is not entirely male on both sides; he has one male half, the other female). We are in fact so much the more tempted to admit this analogy since a fragment of Hesiod establishes, concerning another person, a complete equivalence between bisexuality and lameness; according to this text, Pleisthenes, whom Hesiod makes the father of Agamemnon and Menelaus, 'was hermaphrodite or lame.'[23]

Like Laius, sexually lame in his own way, Labda's husband goes off to Delphi to consult the oracle on the subject of his descendance, περὶ γόνου—he had no children, by Labda or any other woman. Again like Laius he desires to learn from the god's mouth if he can ever have any. Apollo had replied to Laius with a prohibition and a threat: you must not have a son; if you have one, he will kill you, he will sleep with his mother. To Labda's husband, Eëtion, the god announces straight off: 'Labda is pregnant; she will give birth to a

[22] L. Gernet, *The Anthropology of Ancient Greece* (Baltimore, 1981), 293.
[23] See in M. Papathomopoulos, *Nouveaux fragments d'auteurs anciens* (Ioannina, 1980), the text of the fragment as it appears in *Schol. ad Exeg. in Iliadem* A 122 and the very pertinent commentary (11–26).

rolling stone who will swoop down on the rulers and will punish Corinth.'[24]

Cast out of the right line, the lame girl gives birth to an offspring who, by rolling, whirling like a stone rushing down from a mountain, will return to the place from which he has been distanced through his mother.[25] And like a bowling ball, this exile's return will create disaster for Corinth, knocking down the ἄνδρες μούναρχοι, grown men, adults with two feet (the collective Fathers) who are at the same time the legitimate masters of power (the Royal Ones).

The analogies with the schema we believe we have deciphered in the Oedipus story are more especially striking as the differences of situation between the protagonists come to reinforce them. In one case we have a legitimate son, rejected *after* his birth by his real parents, excluded from the royal (and lame) line of the Labdacids to which he belongs. When he returns to Thebes, it is in the hope that by fleeing Corinth he will save his false parents, who have welcomed him like a son, whose legitimate son he thinks he is, while in reality he is illegitimate. Those whom he destroys by returning and putting himself in his father's place are his real parents, whom he treats as strangers, not recognizing them. In the second case everything happens *before* the child's birth; the child is thrown out of the line in the mother's person. He is reduced to a lame, inferior, illegitimate descendance compared to what ought to have been. And it is in perfect agreement with his true, lame parents, whose legitimate son

[24]Hdt. 5. 92. β7–13, to be compared, on Laius, with Eur. *Phoen.* 13–20. We accept the translation of the text of the oracle given by the edition of P. Legrand. *Contra*, see Edouard Will, *Korinthiaka* (Paris, 1955), 450 f. Will understands 'who will fall upon the monarchs and deliver justice to Corinth.' Herodotus seems to be using here a tradition of popular narratives favourable to the Cypselids, and the oracle, in the version taken up by Herodotus, would have been itself published under Cypselus. Thus it would establish a clear distinction between the Bacchiads, monopolizing power, justly punished, and the city of Corinth, innocent. However, one of the oracles recounted by Herodotus is addressed directly to the Corinthians to warn them of the imminent arrival, in the person of Cypselus, of a 'powerful, fierce (ὠμηστής: eater of raw flesh) lion, who will break many men's knees.' The prospect is not very reassuring to the Corinthians, and it is indeed for Corinth itself, for the city, that 'it was necessary that Eëtion's descendance be the seed of troubles, κακὰ ἀναβλαστεῖν.' If we want to find a point of comparison for the oracle's formula, we must look—with Nicole Loraux, to whom we owe this comparison—in Theognis, expressing (39 f.) his fear lest a tyrant come to reestablish order at Megara. To 'Labda is pregnant, she will give birth to a rolling stone' corresponds Theognis' 'Our city is already pregnant and I fear lest she give birth to someone who will redress our deplorable excesses.'

[25] On what the 'rolling stone', ὀλοίτροχος, evokes, see *Il.* 13. 136 ff.; Hdt. 7. 52. 10; Xen. *Anab.* 4. 2. 3.

he is, that he will swoop down like a stone on the Fathers, who represent in Corinth the straight descendance and who, dedicating him in advance to a limping, lame birth, made him not their authentic son but a stranger to the very line of the Bacchiads which he will destroy by his return.

These original divergences in the familial status of the actors lead to differing modifications of the theme of exposure which, in the historical account as in the myth, occupies a central position. Oedipus is exposed by his legitimate mother and father, who give him to their shepherd so he will die. Unable to kill the new-born, the shepherd passes him to another shepherd, who himself puts the child in the hands of his masters, the sovereigns of Corinth. From this death by exposure, from which he escaped against all expectations, Oedipus takes his name, a name which is the sign of his fate, since it recalls an infirmity of which one can say it is as much the trace left on his body by his rejection as it is the mark of his perfect membership in the lame family of the Labdacids.[26]

The new-born child given birth by Labda undergoes himself, from the moment of birth, an ordeal which recalls the exposure of the tiny Oedipus, but which recalls it like a counterfeiting, by reversing its values. The lame mother makes her child disappear for the necessary period by placing him in hiding within the enclosure of a terra cotta container which serves as a bee-hive;[27] this seeming rejection, this

---

[26] Euripides retains a remarkably vivid sense of the multiple and ambiguous relations among Oedipus' name, his wounded feet, his personal fate and the lame line of the Labdacids, represented by his father, whose legitimate son and murderer he is, both at the same time. In the *Phoenissae* he is not content merely to recall the iron pins which pierced the middle of the heels of the new-born, given up for exposure. The whole episode of the fatal encounter at the crossroads between Laius and Oedipus stresses the theme of the feet. 1) The meeting of father and son, who are reunited in the same place by the action of walking, is expressed by the formula ξυνάπτετον πόδα ἐς ταὐτὸν ... σχιστῆς ὁδοῦ, they were joined together both with the same foot on a road which forked (37). ξυνάπτειν πόδα, to meet, is to join feet, like ξυνάπτειν χεῖρα, join hands, link hands (as a sign of friendship) and ξυνάπτειν στόμα, join mouths, kiss. The effect of the meaning is reinforced by the position of πόδα at the end of the line. 2) When the driver orders Oedipus to move away, to let his master's chariot pass, he exclaims: 'Move aside, do not stand at the king's feet, τυράννοις ἐκποδών' (40). 3) Finally, as Oedipus continues on his way without faltering, he springs forward, 'bloody the tendons of his feet, τένοντας ποδῶν, with their hooves (χηλαῖς)' (42).

[27] Herodotus does not tell us where the κυψέλη was placed—this rustic object, this bit of rural, even wild space—inserted in the domestic enclosure. Georges Roux supposes with good reason that it must have been in the court of Eëtion's house, where the ten Bacchiads first presented themselves to Labda.

fictive absence of the baby, suddenly not to be found in the domestic space, unlike exposure aims not at sending him far away to let him die at the mercy of fierce beasts in the emptiness of a mountain wilderness, but rather on the contrary intends his salvation, intends saving his life by hiding him in the very enclosure of the house, to make him invisible. Those who do not want the child to live are the ἄνδρες μούναρχοι, the Bacchiads, masters of legitimate power and legitimate descendance. When they understand the meaning of the oracle given to Eëtion, without breathing a word of it they decide to kill the new-born baby. As soon as Labda delivers, the collective Father entrusts to a delegation of ten of its members the mission of suppressing the child. On the way to the house of the lame woman, who suspects nothing, the group decides that the first to receive the new-born from the arms of his confident mother will have the burden of smashing him to the ground. But 'it was fated' that the lame descent bring to Corinth its ransom of tears. By providential chance, 'divine luck', as Herodotus says,[28] the minute the baby is in the arms of one of the Bacchiads, he smiles, and the man, pitying him, in a great hurry passes him on to his neighbour, who does the same with the next man. The child thus passes from hand to hand, through the whole series of the ten appointed to the murder, to find himself at the end where he began, in the arms of his lame mother. The Bacchiads leave; on the threshold they quarrel, deluging each other with reproaches. They then decide to go back into Labda's house and to accomplish the murder all together. But the woman hears them from

---

Before George Roux's study appeared, the term κυψέλη was interpreted according to information given by Pausanias at 5. 17. 5. At Olympia he had seen, in the temple of Hera, a wooden chest (λάρναξ) which he had been told was the very one in which Cypselus had been hidden. But a λάρναξ is not a κυψέλη; Pausanias knew this very well and was obliged to claim that only at the time of Cypselus, and only among the Corinthians, a wooden chest whose Greek name is λάρναξ was called a κυψέλη. A terra cotta container used as a beehive, the κυψέλη could also serve as a vase in which to store wheat. (See Aristophanes, Peace 631.) Note that the wooden chest (λάρναξ) and the earthen jar (χύτρα) are the two types of container in which, according to heroic legend, parents conceal their children for exposure. In a certain sense, in putting him in the terra cotta beehive to hide him, Labda 'exposes' her baby in her own house: most certainly it is the semblance of exposure, an inverted exposure, to which Plutarch's text clearly testifies when he takes up Herodotus' narrative to summarize it. The Bacchiads, Plutarch writes (164a), searched for but did not find the new-born deposited (ἀποτεθέντα) in a beehive (κυψέλη) by his mother. The verb ἀποτίθημι, the noun ἀπόθεσις are, along with ἐκτίθημι and ἔκθεσις, the technical terms designating exposure (see Vernant, MT, 173 n. 153).

28   5. 92. γ14–15.

the other side of the door. She has the time to hide the child where no one would think to find him, in a κυψέλη, a beehive deserted by its bees. The Bacchiads will search the house in vain. The child is not to be found, as if he had in fact disappeared from the family home. Thus the child of the lame woman, like Oedipus, escapes the death to which he seemed promised. Like Oedipus, his name comes to him from this episode, evoking both the extreme peril of his birth, and his unexpected salvation: he was called Cypselus, the child of the κυψέλη.[29] The episode reveals a whole series of convergences between Oedipus and Cypselus: the new-born escapes death by passing from hand to hand, from one shepherd to another, then to the Corinthian king, or from one Bacchiad to his neighbours. In both cases the executors of the murder take care not to tell what has happened; the ten Bacchiads, like Laius' shepherd, decide to say nothing, and claiming that their mission was accomplished, let it be believed that the maleficent child has been suppressed.

As soon as he has crossed the threshold of adolescence and become an adult, standing on his own two feet, Oedipus goes to Delphi, interrogates the oracle about his birth and, terrified by the response, instead of returning to Corinth makes his way toward Thebes where he will become tyrant.

At the same stage of his life, as soon as he attains manhood, Labda's son also goes off to consult the Delphic oracle. Greeting him as 'King of Corinth', the god urges him without ambiguity to go and seize the city. Thus Cypselus, established tyrant of Corinth, put to death a good number of the ἄνδρες μούναρχοι.

But it is his son Periander who gives the person of the tyrant his true dimensions. We might say that Periander, in succeeding Cypselus, completes him; he realizes in all its fullness the tyrannical vocation of his father. 'All that Cypselus left undone, in killing, in banishing,' writes Herodotus, 'Periander finished.'[30] Men first of all. All those whose heads were a little higher than the others' Periander mows and throws down, as Oedipus striking Laius with his staff made him fall from the height of his chariot to the ground at Oedipus' feet. Next the women. Greek tradition makes Periander, the model tyrant, a new Oedipus: he supposedly had sexual intercourse in secret with his mother, Crateia.[31] The royal Fathers slain,

[29] 5. 92. ε2–3.   [30] 5. 92. η5–6.   [31] Diog. Laert. I. 96.

what was left for a descendant of the lame one but to sleep in the bed of a mother whose name proclaims so clearly what she represents: Sovereignty over a city which the tyrant makes entirely his own?

In Herodotus' account, where the episode of maternal incest does not occur, a curious sequence perhaps occupies an analogous position with respect to the murder of the father. Immediately after having recalled the fate of the males of the whole group of the Fathers, noting that 'all that Cypselus left undone, in killing, in banishing, Periander finished,' Herodotus adds, concerning the women: 'In one day Periander had all the women of Corinthia stripped of their clothing in honour of his own wife Melissa.'[32] When he orders the whole female population of the city to assemble at the temple of Hera, free women and servants together, in order to strip them of their clothing and the festive attire they had put on, it is all of feminine Corinth which the tyrant undresses *en masse*, which he strips with one blow for the benefit of his own dead wife, as if the whole feminine race of Corinth were obliged to take the place at his side which the death of his companion had left vacant.

But the tyranny, that limping kingship, could not continue successful for very long. The oracle which gave the green light to Cypselus, opening the route to power to him, began by fixing the limit beyond which the lineage of Labda could no more perpetuate itself than that of Laius. 'Cypselus, Eëtion's son, king of illustrious Corinth,' the god had proclaimed; but only to add immediately: 'He and his sons, but not the sons of his sons.'[33] In the third generation the shock effect produced by the 'rolling stone' which came from the womb of Labda no longer made itself felt. For the line of the lame, installed on the throne of Corinth, the moment came when fate staggered, tumbled, sank into misfortune and into death.

This reversal is the subject of Herodotus' detailed account in the long excursus he consecrates in Book 3 to the theme of the hostility between Corinth and her colony Corcyra.[34] Above I briefly evoked the disappearance of the lineage of the Labdacids, prophesied at the start to Laius, and which was realized after the ephemeral elevation of Oedipus because of the tragic death of his two sons who, both opposed to their father as they were to one another, found themselves reunited only in reciprocal murder. Let us look a little more closely,

[32] Hdt. 5. 92. η5–7.   [33] 5. 92. ε8–9.   [34] 3. 50–3.

with Herodotus, at the end of the Cypselids, Labda's descendants. Periander also had two sons of about the same age by his wife Melissa. These two young men had nothing in common.[35] Periander's misfortune can be summed up as follows: his older son, who is close and devoted to him, but who is his opposite in his slowness of mind, his inattention, his lack of reflection, does not communicate with himself, within his own mind; he remembers nothing. His younger son, an exact copy of Periander in the sense that he has a quick intelligence, obstinate character, precise and accurate memory, refuses to communicate with his father; he speaks not a word to him; he does not answer him. On the one side forgetting, on the other, silence; in both cases, in Labda's descendance, the communication network is blocked.

The drama begins with the death of Melissa, whom Periander beats to death in a furious rage. The maternal grandfather of the two boys, Procles, tyrant of Epidaurus, sends for them and treats them with the greatest affection. Before returning them to Corinth, he says to them, 'My children, do you know who killed your mother?' The older boy makes nothing of the remark; not having understood it, he does not store it in his mind; he doesn't remember it.[36] The younger, Lycophron, is so overcome by this revelation that when he returns, seeing his father as the murderer of his mother, he says not one word to him, 'not responding if his father talked, answering nothing if he questioned him.'[37] The furious Periander expels him from the palace.

When the father, having forced questions on the son who could not 'understand' and remember, finally succeeds in 'understanding' what his younger son had in mind,[38] he forbids anyone to receive his son in his house. The order is given to all to turn him away. His refusal to communicate with his father makes Lycophron an exile within the city, expelled from everywhere, a being without house or home, like a child rejected by his own family. But the status of Lycophron is ambiguous. If Periander's orders put him in the position of

[35] On the contrast between the two sons, see Diog. Laert. 1. 94: 'He had two sons, Cypselus and Lycophron, the younger intelligent (συνετός), the older simple-minded (ἄφρων).'
[36] 3. 50. 10–11.
[37] 3. 50. 13–15.
[38] The opposition is marked by the repetition, three lines later, of the same formula; the older son does not understand (οὐ νόῳ λαβών), and Periander does understand (νόῳ λαβών); 3. 51. 4–5, 3. 51. 8.

an ἄπολις, cut off in his solitude from all social bonds, his legitimate birth nonetheless designates him to succeed his father as tyrant; it projects him in advance to the height of the city, as high above the common as his condition of exile threw him down below. 'Seeing in him Periander's son, in spite of their fears people received him anyway.'[39]

To force Lycophron to a last-ditch stand, Periander has his herald declare that whoever received or even conversed with him would have to pay a very heavy fine. No one from then on wants to speak to the young man. In his obstinacy Lycophron accepts this state of complete isolation, of non-communication. For want of the desire to follow his father in the straight path of a succession which would lead him to his place in the palace, he goes astray, he wanders from one side to the other, 'rolling under porches'.[40] The grandson of Cypselus, the rolling stone whose impetus threw the royal Fathers to the ground, is now himself like a rolling stone, but this time he is like the one of which the proverb says, when it evokes the misfortune of someone who cannot stay in one place: 'a rolling stone gathers no moss.'

Lycophron has nothing to eat. He is wasting away. Periander meets him, dirty and wasted. His anger abates; he asks him which he prefers: the tyranny or a life of wandering (ἀλήτης βίος)? 'You are my son,' he says, 'the king of wealthy Corinth . . . come back to the palace.'[41] Without another answer, Lycophron declares that his father should pay the fine for having spoken to him.

Periander banishes his son, like a φαρμακός, to Corcyra, far from his eyes (ἐξ ὀφθαλμῶν μιν ἀποπέμπεται).[42] The tyrant does not stab out his eyes in order to see no more, like Oedipus; he rejects his son so as to see him no more.

But time progresses too; it walks like men. With the advance of time (ἐπεὶ δὲ τοῦ χρόνου προβαίνοντος)[43] Periander grows old. The

[39] 3. 51. 14–15.
[40] 3. 52. 6: ἐν τῆσι στοιῆσι ἐκαλινδέετο. The verb καλινδέομαι, roll, very probably results (Chantraine, *Dictionnaire étymologique de la langue grecque* 2. 485) from a cross between ἀλινδέομαι and κυλινδέομαι, roll. On the use of κυλίνδω in the active sense, with the meaning: knock down by whirling a rolling stone, see Xen. *Anab.* 4. 2. 3: ἐκυλίνδουν ὀλοιτρόχους; and Theoc. 22. 49–50: πέτροι ὀλοίτροχοι οὔστε κυλίνδων . . . ποταμὸς . . . περιέξεσε.
[41] 3. 52. 9–20.
[42] 3. 52. 24–5.
[43] 3. 53. 1.

man with two feet now has three; he no longer feels himself capable
of assuming the responsibilities of power. The hour has come for him
to give up his place to his son. But the oldest one will not do; his
mind, which drags its feet, does not move quickly enough: he is too
slow (νωθέστερος)[44] to walk in his father's footsteps. Periander
therefore sends his younger son first a messenger, then his sister, to
convince him to return to Corinth and to occupy the place which falls
to him by right: 'Tyranny,' his sister explains to Lycophron, 'is an
unstable, wavering thing (χρῆμα σφαλερόν); it has many lovers.
Your father is old now, he is past his prime; don't give away to others
the goods that belong to you.'[45] But Lycophron, inflexible, confirms
his decision: he will not return to Corinth as long as he knows his
father is still alive. A decision similar to that Oedipus makes at Delphi
when he promises himself not to set foot in Corinth as long as his
father is still alive there. Similar, but with the exception however that
the father whose presence Oedipus flees—because of love, not hate—
is in reality a stranger, and that to avoid this false parent, Oedipus
crosses paths with a stranger against whom he throws himself with
violence and who is in fact his real father.

To overcome his son's resistance Periander perfects a solution
which ought to have allowed him to settle this difficult problem of
succession between two beings who at the same time are closest in
kinship, and furthest apart in feelings, as in their place of residence,
all the while avoiding the misfortunes of the line of the Labdacids.
The tyrant proposes to his son, by a third messenger, to change positions with him, without the risk of meeting, of finding themselves
together in the same place, Lycophron coming back to Corinth to
preserve the tyranny there, while he would go to Corcyra, which he
would not leave. Lycophron accepts; all seems settled by this
exchange of places that reestablishes the desired moment, the legitimate son in his place, on his father's throne, without the young man
and the old, to this point radically dissociated, having to face each
other, to reunite, to run into each other like Oedipus who, in order to
return to the land of his birth, had to clash *en route* with Laius
travelling in the opposite direction.[46] All seems settled—settled

---

[44] 3. 53. 6.

[45] 3. 53. 17–19.

[46] Oedipus' sons, Polyneices and Eteocles, planned a solution analogous to Periander's to settle the fundamental misunderstanding which opposed them to one another.
After Oedipus was locked up by his children so his fate would be forgotten, he cursed

'logically'. But an oracle is an oracle: 'King of Corinth, you, your son, but not the sons of your sons,' the Pythia had decreed. At the last moment the Corcyrans, warned of the plan, kill the son in order not to inherit the father. Labda's lineage, like Labdacus', falls into nothingness instead of continuing in the right order of successive generations.

What conclusion to draw from this strange parallelism in the destiny of the Labdacids of legendary Thebes and of the Cypselids of historical Corinth? In 'Marriages of Tyrants' Louis Gernet observed that the tyrant, innovator though he was, proceeded 'naturally' from the past: 'his excesses,' he writes, 'had their models in legends.'[47] These are the models which orient Herodotus' narration from beginning to end. When the father of history recounts as fact the events which installed a line of tyrants at the head of Corinth, quite 'naturally' he mythologizes, and his account lends itself to a type of analysis analogous to that we can apply to the legend of Oedipus. 'From the point of view of legend,' Gernet also said, à propos precisely of Corinth, 'tyranny could only be the result of a disruptive marriage.'[48] If, in order to tie them so clearly together, Herodotus' text retains the themes we were perhaps able to locate in the saga of the Labdacids: lameness, tyranny, power gained and lost, the continuous or blocked sequence of generations, straight or indirect succession, straightness or deviation in sexual relations, agreement or misunderstanding in the communication between fathers and sons, or among sons, presence of mind or forgetfulness—it is because in the Greek 'imagination' the figure of the tyrant, as it is sketched out in the fifth and fourth centuries, adopts the features of the legendary hero, at once elect and cursed. In rejecting all the rules which, for the Greeks, are the foundation of communal life, the tyrant puts himself socially out of play. He is external to the network of relations which unites citizen with

---

them, willing them to divide the palace with a sword blade. The two boys, 'afraid the gods would grant his wish if they lived together, agreed that the younger, Polyneices, would begin by voluntarily exiling himself from the land, while Eteocles would stay to hold the sceptre, during one year, in his turn' (Eur. *Phoen.* 69–74). But there too the foreseen exchange did not occur. Once in place Eteocles refuses to abandon the throne and sends Polyneices into exile. The two brothers will not reunite until they meet face to face, arms in hand, to kill one another.

[47] Gernet, *Anthropology*, 289.
[48] Ibid. 294.

citizen, man with woman, father with son according to precise norms. For better or worse, he turns away from all the channels through which individuals enter into communication with each other and constitute themselves in a civilized community. The path, solitary and indirect, onto which the tyrant ventures, with contempt for the well-beaten path, well-marked itineraries, is exile far from the city of men, with its settled exchanges, its reciprocal contact, in an isolation comparable as much to a god's—too far above human laws to accept submission to them—as to a wild beast's, too dominated by his appetites to respect any prohibition.[49] Despising the rules which preside over the ordering of the social fabric and which, through the regular inter-crossing of sons, determine the positions of each in relation to the others—or, as Plato puts it more crudely, ready to kill his father, sleep with his mother, eat the flesh of his own children,[50] the tyrant, at once equal to god[51] and equal to a ferocious beast, incarnates in his ambivalence the mythic figure of the lame man, with his two opposing aspects: a gait beyond the human because in rolling, faster and more agile in all directions at once, he transgresses the limitations to which walking straight must submit; but also this side of the normal mode of locomotion because mutilated, unbalanced, vacillating, he advances, limping in his singular fashion all the better to fall in the end.

(Translated by Page duBois)

[49] See Vernant, 'Ambiguity and Reversal'. P. Schmitt Pantel writes: 'An effeminate being or a super-male both at the same time, or occasionally each in turn, the tyrant fails to keep the proper distance with his sexuality which would make him a possible citizen.' ('Histoire de tyran ou comment la cité grecque construit ses marges', in *Les Marginaux et les exclus dans l'histoire*, Cahiers Jussieu 15 (Paris, n.d.), 299.) 'Effeminate and super-male': such indeed is the status of the sexually lame, of the hermaphrodite Caeneus whose descendant, by his marriage with Labda the lame, founds the dynasty of the Cypselid tyrants.

[50] Pl. *Rep.* 571–4 and 619b6–c2.

[51] On tyranny ἰσόθεος, equal to god, see Eur. *Tro.* 1168; Pl. *Rep.* 360c3 and 568b3.

PART II
Archaeology of the Sacred

6

Demeter in the Ancient Greek City and its Countryside

SUSAN GUETTEL COLE

Greek conceptions of space and time were shaped by ideas that identified the world of nature with the world of the gods. The gods were thought to control the forces of nature and were believed to have their own place in the natural world. The countryside was thought to have been the home of the gods long before the birth of the first humans, and local political charter myths always placed human struggle for survival or human competition for political dominance in the context of the divine world. With the development of the walled city (*asty*) marked off as separate from its countryside (*chōra*), the divine pantheon was standardized, and the functions of the gods were adapted to the new communal organization of the city-state. The gods of the countryside, however, never lost their vitality, and the history of the religious life of the Greek city is very much a history of rituals that helped the *polis* to maintain a balance between its nucleated centre and its rural periphery. These rituals defined the community and kept the *polis* embedded in the land that was believed to sustain it.

The issues of the relation between a *polis* and its land are stated with elegant simplicity in a late fourth-century decree from Kolophon, a small *polis* in western Ionia. Freed from Persian domination after the death of Alexander, the city took the opportunity to enlarge its core by extending the city wall:

to enclose the old city within the same wall as the existing city, the old city which the gods handed over to our ancestors and which our ancestors settled by building temples and altars, thereby becoming famous among all Greeks.

Addendum 1999: The text of this chapter remains substantially the same as published in 1994, with only minor corrections. The notes have been to some extent brought up to date, especially where new publications augment the argument.

And so, that this might be accomplished quickly, on the fourth day of the coming month, the priest of Apollo and the other priests and priestesses and the *prytanis* (eponymous magistrate) together with the *boulē* and those appointed in this decree, are to go down to the old agora, and at the altars of the gods that our ancestors left behind for us, they are to pray to Zeus Soter, Poseidon who brings security, Apollo of Klaros, Mother Antaia, Athena Polias, and to all the other gods and heroes who dwell in our city (*polis*) and land (*chōra*); and when benefits are bestowed, they are to hold a procession and sacrifice just as the *dēmos* decides.[1]

The ancient city is described as given to the people of Kolophon in former times by the gods themselves. Founding a new city is described in terms of building temples and altars, as recognition to the gods for the gift of the city. The decree requires that the priests and priestesses of Kolophon visit the altars in the old agora to acknowledge the ties between the old site and the current site of the city. The decision to build the wall is ratified by sacrifices to the major gods of the city and to all other gods and heroes who inhabit the walled city (here, *polis*) and its territory (*chōra*). The inscription justifies the city's claim to its territory by describing that territory as a gift from the gods who dwell in the land itself. According to such beliefs, sanctuaries existed in precisely those places thought of as the natural home of the individual deity, whether in the city itself or scattered in the landscape of the city's territory.

Each *polis* had its own constellation of divinities. Citizens of fourth-century Kolophon knew from experience which of their gods 'dwelt' in the town and which in the countryside, and it was natural for them to consider all of these gods as belonging to the *polis*, just as they considered the countryside as well as the walled town to be their own. They found reassurance and derived a sense of stability from the assumption that their gods had founded their city for them. The real history of city foundation, urban planning, and community development, to be sure, was much more complex, but competition between cities required foundation myths that recognized the power of the gods in order to justify claims to territory.

Common cultural consciousness, a common economic experience, and constants of social organization shaped the *polis* physically as

[1] L. Robert, 'Décrets de Kolophon', *RPh* 10 (1936), 158–68 (*Opera Minora Selecta*, ii (Amsterdam, 1969), 1237–47). Robert dates the decree after 315, and before 306. See also Malkin, *RC*, 151–2 (Greek text and trans.); N. H. Demand, *Urban Relocation in Archaic and Classical Greece* (Norman, Okla., 1990), 161–2.

well as spiritually. As a result, where and how a city placed its sanctuaries is significant. The motivation for spatial order has been explained by others in terms of the power of the landscape,[2] political competition with other cities for space and territory,[3] rational planning,[4] or peculiarities of local history coupled with the function of the particular deity.[5] All of these factors may have played a role, but other issues were also important in the development of the community. I would like to propose another combination of considerations, which seems to have influenced choices of cult sites, by examining the ways in which the function of the divinity, the demands of ritual, and the social organization of the community influenced the placement of sanctuaries in relation to the city and its land. By concentrating on a single divinity and focusing on the location, arrangement, history, and uses of the relevant sanctuaries, it may be possible to isolate those features that transcended local conditions. I have chosen Demeter because she was a divinity worshipped throughout the Greek Mediterranean, she had clearly defined functions, and her main festival, the Thesmophoria, was one of the most widely observed of any Greek festival. Moreover, the general uniformity of her votives implies a certain consistency in ritual, she was often worshipped by groups clearly defined by gender, and although her sanctuaries are found both inside and outside Greek cities, there are certain striking features associated with their position, natural resources, and architectural features. A survey of her cult sites will show that the perceived character of the goddess and the demands of ritual always exerted a considerable influence.

Demeter was rarely the principal god of an ancient Greek city, but she was worshipped by the Greeks wherever agriculture was practised. Although her functions extended beyond the protection of

---

[2] I. E. M. Edlund, *The Gods and the Place* (Stockholm, 1987), 29, distinguishing between urban, extra-urban, and rural sanctuaries, recognizes that function may have determined the location of sanctuaries just outside the city's walls, but describes rural sanctuaries in terms of 'the mysterious forces of nature'. She follows Eliade, who argues that sacred places are natural places of communion with the divine, discovered and marked by human use, but defined by an absolute holiness not dependent upon human acts.

[3] de Polignac, *Naissance*.

[4] Malkin, *RC*, 135–86, describing the process by which colonial *poleis* organized their sanctuaries, emphasizes the rational planning that determined not only the regular streets within the city's walls, but the location of sanctuaries outside the walls in the city's territory.

[5] M. Jost, *Sanctuaires et cultes d'Arcadie* (Paris, 1985), 545–59.

grain, agriculture was her special province. Grain was the primary staple throughout the Mediterranean,[6] and unlike oil or wine, was not practical to store for protection against lean years.[7] This is perhaps the explanation for the importance of festivals linked with Demeter as a goddess of agriculture. It may explain as well the relative prominence of her sanctuaries in the landscape of the *polis* when compared to Athena as goddess of the olive or even Dionysos as god of wine. For the Greeks the growing, storage, and distribution of grain was a matter of life and death.[8] Many of the epithets of Demeter reflect these concerns: Chloe ('Green Shoot'), Sito ('Grain'), Himalis ('Abundance'), Ompnia ('Nourisher with Grain'), Achaia ('Reaper'), Ioulo ('Goddess of Grain Sheaves'), Haloïs ('Goddess of the Ploughed Field'), Megalartos and Megalomazos ('Goddess of Wheat (or Barley) Bread'), Hamalophoros ('Bearing Sheaves of Grain'), Polusoros ('Rich in Piles of Grain'), Soritis ('Giver of Heaps of Grain'), Karpophoros ('She who brings forth fruit'), and Anesidora ('She who sends up gifts').[9] Her epithet Kalligeneia ('She who brings forth beautiful offspring'), referring to the fruits of the earth, could also be used of the earth itself. As the name of the third day of the Thesmophoria, Kalligeneia could also be associated with the women who celebrated her festival and suggested a homology between the earth, the goddess, and the bodies of the women invoking her aid.

Demeter could bring food, but, as cause of deprivation, she could also take it away. In Phokis she was called Steiritis ('Barren', Paus. 10. 35. 10), and Hesychius associates her epithet Azesia with a Greek verb that means 'parch' (ἀζαίνω; Hsch. s.v. Ἀζησία). Some of Demeter's epithets are not so transparent. Even where she was clearly associated with the agricultural cycle, it is often difficult to determine what a particular epithet means. For instance, the Thesmophoria was associated with the sowing of grain, but her epithet 'Thesmophoros', 'the one who carries what has been set down', is difficult to

---

[6] L. Foxhall and H. A. Forbes, 'Sitometreia: The Role of Grain as a Staple Food in Classical Antiquity', *Chiron*, 12 (1982), 43–90.

[7] P. Garnsey and I. Morris, 'Risk and the *Polis*: The Evolution of Institutionalised Responses to Food Supply Problems in the Ancient Greek State', in P. Halstead and J. O'Shea (eds.), *Bad Year Economics: Cultural Responses to Risk and Uncertainty* (Cambridge, 1989), 102–5, for control of grain trade.

[8] Issues and strategies are discussed by T. W. Gallant, *Risk and Survival in Ancient Greece* (Stanford, Calif., 1991), 34–59, 111–16.

[9] Nilsson, *GF*, 311–12; for a more complete list, see L. Farnell, *Cults of the Greek States*, iii (London, 1906), 311–25.

explain. 'Thesmophoros' may refer both to the actions of the ritual (bringing up of ritual objects that had been 'set down' into pits in the earth) or to the establishment of the laws and institutions (*thesmoi*) of civilized life by her contribution of grain.[10] Where Demeter was not clearly associated with agriculture, the explanation is even more problematic. For instance, her Arkadian titles Melaina ('Black') and Erinys ('Avenging Fury'), not associated elsewhere with Demeter, can possibly be understood as relics of very old forms of her cult.[11]

Agricultural concerns are reflected in the many sacrifices and festivals for Demeter associated with the agricultural year.[12] In Attica the Proerosia took place during the Attic month Pyanopsion in the autumn, before the ploughing for the winter crop. Ploughing is followed by sowing, and the Stenia and Thesmophoria followed in the same month, to safeguard the planting of the grain crop. In mid-winter Greeks sacrificed to Demeter Chloe, who protected the growing green shoots of grain, and they also celebrated the Haloa, in honour of the *halōs* (threshing-floor), barren in winter, but commemorated in anticipation of the later harvest. At the time of harvest itself, in early summer, many Greek cities celebrated the Kalamaia to protect the grain stalks. The Stenia and the Thesmophoria were festivals for women from which men were excluded; the Haloa also included rituals restricted to women. In Attica many of the festivals of Demeter were celebrated at deme level, and a single modest deme sanctuary of Demeter could have served at different times throughout the year for all the various individual festivals. The Thesmophorion in the Piraeus was used only for women's festivals, for the Plerosia, the Kalamaia, the Skira, and, as the inscription says: 'also if the women come together on any other day according to ancestral tradition'.[13] At Eleusis Demeter's sanctuary was used for

[10] On the much debated etymology of the epithet, see Burkert, *GR*, 243, for *thesmos* as what is set in the ground when the women imitate the sowing; cf. 246, for Thesmophoros as 'one who brings order'.

[11] Jost, *Sanctuaires*, 309.

[12] A. C. Brumfield, *The Attic Festivals of Demeter and their Relation to the Agricultural Year* (New York, 1984); see also L. Foxhall, 'Women's Ritual and Men's Work in Ancient Athens', in R. Hawley and B. Levick (eds.), *Women in Antiquity, New Assessments* (London, 1995), 97–110.

[13] *IG* II² 1177; *LSCG* 36, 4th cent. BC. Others were also limited to a female clientele; J. Delemarre, 'Décrets religieux d'Arkésiné', *REG* 16 (1903), 166 (Amorgos, 4th cent. BC), *LSAM* 16 (Gambreion, 3rd cent. BC). From votive dedications it is obvious that some precincts of Demeter, even some specifically labelled 'Thesmophorion', could sometimes be open to men; P. Bruneau, *Recherches sur les cultes de Délos à l'époque hellénistique et à l'époque impériale* (Paris, 1970), 284, for the inventories of the Thesmophorion at Delos.

the local deme celebrations of the Thesmophoria as well as for the mysteries.[14] Demeter's rituals restricted to women could also be connected with other cults. At Thasos the same sanctuary, located just outside the wall, served for both the ancestral divinities of the local phratries (οἱ πατρῷοι) and the Thesmophoria,[15] perhaps a recognition of the need for different institutions for assimilating male and female to communal life. Strict consistency was never achieved. Demeter's calendar of festivals varied somewhat from city to city, and even the Thesmophoria, celebrated wherever grain was grown, were not fixed to the same month in every city.[16] Nevertheless Demeter's agricultural functions remained the basis of most forms of her worship.

Agricultural concerns are often reflected symbolically or indirectly in the votives dedicated to Demeter. These are so regular in type that many minor sanctuaries of Demeter may be identified by the votives alone. The most striking characteristics of Demeter's votives are their number, simplicity, and modesty. Several types of dedications to Demeter, remarkably similar from site to site, seem to reflect activities of the rites themselves. Miniature vessels for carrying water (especially small *hydriai*)[17] or vessels for grain (*kernoi*) predominate among the small ceramic objects. Figurines representing female worshippers carrying *hydriai*, plants, or animals (especially pigs) are also very common in sanctuaries of Demeter. These objects were dedicated by women as tokens of their participation in the rites. Small female figurines dedicated to Demeter number in the thousands, tiny *hydriai* in the hundreds of thousands. Small ceramic sows and piglets reflect not only the Thesmophoria, where

[14] K. Clinton, 'Sacrifice at the Eleusinian Mysteries', in R. Hägg, N. Marinatos, and G. C. Nordquist (eds.), *Early Greek Cult Practice* (Stockholm, 1988), 72. For the Thesmophoria as a deme festival in Attika, see K. Clinton, 'The Thesmophorion in Central Athens and the Celebration of the Thesmophoria in Attica', in R. Hägg (ed.), *The Role of Religion in the Early Greek Polis* (Stockholm, 1996), 111–25.

[15] C. Rolley, 'Le Sanctuaire des Dieux Patrooi et le Thesmophorion de Thasos', *BCH* 89 (1965), 441–83.

[16] At Athens the Thesmophoria were celebrated in the month of Pyanopsion, just before winter; at Delos the festival was celebrated in Metageitnion (late summer). The Delian schedule seems to correspond to that of Thasos, where the Thesmophoria were celebrated in the month after Hekatombaion; see F. Salviat, 'Une nouvelle loi thasienne', *BCH* 82 (1950), 218, 248; cf. Nilsson, *GF*, 316–18.

[17] E. Diehl, *Die Hydria* (Mainz, 1964), 187–92, where inventories of excavated examples make it clear that more *hydriai* are associated with Demeter than with any other divinity.

the rotted remains of sacrificed piglets were brought up from underground chambers, but also bear witness to the numbers of pregnant sows offered as a special sacrifice to Demeter at many sites and festivals throughout the year.[18] Ceramic pigs correspond to bones of pigs and piglets found in ash pits in sanctuaries of Demeter. Ceramic sows found at Thasos, slit open to show the foetuses inside, must reflect sacrifices similar to those performed at Mytilene, where bones of pig foetuses were found in ash pits, mixed with bones of infant and adult pigs. The fecundity of the sacrificial animal reflects a concern for female fecundity, apparent in the many kourotrophic dedications found in Demeter's sanctuaries.[19] As with any divinity, more personalized dedications show variation from these norms,[20] and Demeter's votives may not be identical at every sanctuary.[21] Nevertheless, the masses of modest dedications from individual women indicate a general consistency in the kind of ritual performed, and show that the rites of Demeter must have been open to the majority of local women, and not reserved for representative ritual specialists or small groups selected from prominent families to represent the whole. No single votive type can identify a sanctuary of Demeter if there are no inscriptions or literary accounts, but the compounding of several distinctive types

[18] Attica: *LSCG* 20 A. 43, B. 48, 49; *LSS* 18 B. 29–30. Mykonos: *LSCG* 96. 11, 16. Lindos: *LSS* 87 A. 3, B. 2. Delos: *IG* IX 287. 68–70, 372. 103–6, 440. 36–41, 442. 198–202, 460. 66–7.

[19] T. H. Price, *Kourotrophos: Cults and Representations of the Greek Nursing Deities* (Leiden, 1978), for kourotrophic figurines in sanctuaries of Demeter.

[20] P. Gregory Warden, 'Gift, Offering, and Reciprocity', *Expedition*, 34 (1992), 51–8, for heirlooms and luxury items (Egyptianizing scarabs, gems, a bronze falcon, silver satyr-mask, etc.) as dedications at Cyrene. C. Dengate, 'The Sanctuaries of Apollo in the Peloponnesos' (Ph.D. diss., University of Chicago, 1988), 116–17, on 'votive drift' and the difficulty of always correlating type of votive with nature of cult or function of deity.

[21] Ceramic cakes are common for Demeter in the Peloponnese, but not so common elsewhere. For ceramic cakes at Corinth, see A. Brumfield, 'Cakes in the Liknon: Votives from the Sanctuary of Demeter and Kore on Acrocorinth', *Hesperia*, 66 (1997), 147–72. Agricultural tools, surprisingly, are relatively rare; C. G. Simon, 'The Archaic Offerings and Cults of Ionia' (Ph.D. diss., University of California, Berkeley, 1986), 224, 228. They do, however, occur in connection with Demeter. See U. Kron, 'Frauenfest in Demeterheiligtümern: Das Thesmophorion von Bitalemi', *AA* 44 (1992), 635–9. In some places the votives seem exclusively from female donors, but elsewhere men and women made dedications in the same sanctuary. For instance, Demeter Malophoros at Selinus, whose epithet associates her with agriculture, received weaving equipment, apparently from women, and also spears, arrowheads, and full-sized shields used in war, apparently from male worshippers; ibid. 237, 240, 249, 265.

together is a strong indication for Demeter at a site known only from archaeological finds.

Agricultural concerns are often reflected in the choice of sites for sanctuaries of Demeter. Rites associated with Demeter, designed to encourage agricultural success, required natural features often available only in the countryside. The ubiquitous votives associated with water indicate a concern for water, and the same concern seems to have determined the choice for sites appropriate for worship. Demeter's sanctuaries were often located near a spring or stream.[22] Water was necessary for agriculture,[23] and pure water was required for her rites.[24] Other features have been noticed. Béquignon has argued that the typical sanctuary of Demeter was located on the side of a hill,[25] and de Polignac has observed that, during the formative stages of the *polis*, the typical sanctuary of Demeter was located just outside or near a city's walls, providing a transition between the inhabited city and its agricultural territory. Not every sanctuary, however, fits these descriptions. Many sanctuaries of Demeter were located on hillsides, a fact reflected in the *Homeric Hymn to Demeter* when Keleus instructs the Eleusinians to build a temple and altar for Demeter 'upon a projecting hill' (ἐπὶ προὔχοντι κολωνῷ, 298),[26] but sanctuaries of Demeter could also be located in the plain or at the base of a hill. And while it is true that many sanctuaries of Demeter were located between the walls of the city and the city's agricultural territory, others were placed within the walls (even on the acropolis), or far outside the walls, deep in the city's rural area. Pausanias mentions sanctuaries of Demeter in 51 cities on the Greek mainland; 21 of these cities had sanctuaries of Demeter inside the city (*asty*), either on the acropolis or in the agora, 18 had a sanctuary of Demeter in a village outside the city, and 24 had sanctuaries of Demeter deep in the countryside. Pausanias rarely concerns himself with the location

---

[22] S. G. Cole, 'The Uses of Water in Greek Sanctuaries', in Hägg, Marinatos, and Nordquist, *Early Greek Cult Practice*, 164–5.

[23] *POxy* 2. 221, col. 9. 18–20: '. . . and many sacrifice to Acheloos before Demeter because Acheloos is a name of all rivers and water is the source of fruit . . .'

[24] Water flowing into sanctuaries of Demeter was protected from pollution. See *IG* XII (5) 569 and XII Suppl. p. 114 (Keos); *LSCG* 65. 103–6 (Andania).

[25] Y. Béquignon, 'Déméter, déesse acropolitaine', *RA* (1958), 149–77.

[26] This line is curiously ignored by Béquignon, p. 177, in his attempt to associate Demeter with Rhea, called μήτηρ ὀρείη in the Homeric hymn. For reservations about the association, see N. Richardson, *The Homeric Hymn to Demeter* (Oxford, 1974), 295–6.

of a Demeter sanctuary in relation to the walls of a city.[27] When he does record distance, it is the great distance of rural sanctuaries of Demeter from towns and inhabited settlements that interests him. Recorded distances vary from the 0.7 kilometre between Akakesion (Arkadia) and the *peribolos* of Demeter and Despoina (Paus. 8. 37. 2) to the 11 kilometres that separated the grove and spring of Demeter Mysia from Pellene (Paus. 7. 27. 9).[28]

De Polignac's observations about peri-urban sanctuaries of Demeter are more consonant with colonial *poleis* than with cities of the Greek mainland. Colonial foundations, at least in their original stages, were more likely to have been built according to a deliberate plan. Cities on the Greek mainland, however, grew more slowly, and the positioning of sanctuaries is often obscured by later adjustments resulting from political change. There are important differences between Greek cities on the mainland, Aegean cities whether on the islands or the Asian coast, and cities in other colonial areas, like Magna Graecia, Sicily, and North Africa. Historical factors like synoecism (e.g. at Kos[29]), dioecism (e.g. at Mantineia[30]), refoundation (Siris[31]), and movement of cities from one site to another (e.g. Teos[32]), as well as the ravages of decline (Tanagra[33]) could affect the placement of local sanctuaries relative to other important urban features.

Many of the mainland cities described by Pausanias had more

---

[27] He makes the relation clear only in his description of Troizen, where he describes the sanctuary of Demeter Thesmophoros as located outside the wall, on the road to Hermione, above the temple of Poseidon Phytalmios ('nourisher' or 'parent'; 2. 32. 8). The sanctuary has been located above the village of Damala by G. Welter, *Troizen und Kalaureia* (Berlin, 1941), 20–2 and pls. 2, 9.

[28] The cave of Demeter Melaina on Mt. Elaios, with grove and spring, was 5.5 km. from Phigaleia (Arkadia, Paus. 8. 42. 1–2), and an unfinished temple of Demeter and Kore was 7.36 km. from Plataiai (Paus. 9. 4. 4). Jost, *Sanctuaires*, 300, stresses regional characteristics, pointing out that Demeter in Arkadia is a rural divinity, only rarely (at Tegea and Mantineia) worshipped together with Kore.

[29] After synoecism at Kos in the 4th cent. there were at least nine sanctuaries of Demeter in the territory of a single *polis*; the earliest was an Archaic sanctuary at a spring just north of the town of Kos. See S. Sherwin-White, *Ancient Cos* (Göttingen, 1978), 305–12.

[30] S. and H. Hodkinson, 'Mantineia and the Mantinike: Settlement and Society in a Greek Polis', *BSA* 76 (1981), 261–5, on the dioecism of 385 BC, when the sanctuary of Demeter at Nestane might have reverted to the village. Jost, *Sanctuaires*, 345–8, discusses the problems of the Koragion and Megaron at Mantineia itself.

[31] See below, p. 152.

[32] See below, p. 148.

[33] See below, p. 154.

than one sanctuary of Demeter. Leaving aside Attica (where the evidence for Demeter is far richer than Pausanias indicates) Megara, with four Demeter sanctuaries, and Hermione, with seven or more, indicate the possible diversity. At Megara there was a *megaron* on the main acropolis, a sanctuary of Demeter Thesmophoros on the second acropolis, another of Demeter Malophoros at the harbour, and a fourth sanctuary (with a well) in the border territory between Megara and Eleusis. Hermione, located in the southern Argolid, had at least seven sanctuaries of Demeter. Within the territory of Hermione in the southern Argolid there were four sanctuaries at some distance from the city: a sanctuary of Demeter at the village of Eileoi near the border with Troizen, a sanctuary of Demeter Thermasia on the coast north of the city, one on the mountainous headland on the sea south of the city, and a fourth at the village of Didymoi, about 3.6 kilometres from Hermione's port city of Mases. A fifth sanctuary was located in the city itself, and a sixth on Mt. Pron, not far from the city's walls.[34] Synoecism with Halieis in the Hellenistic period would have brought yet a seventh Demeter sanctuary within the province of Hermione. Clearly some Demeter sanctuaries were originally associated with local villages rather than with the central *polis*. Pausanias gives some indication of the vitality of the cult of Demeter in the Imperial period, but his survey does not indicate the historical complexity of sanctuary planning.

Recent excavations of Demeter sanctuaries show that in the Archaic period the older cities of Greece often kept their primary sanctuary of Demeter within the city's walls. Corinth and Eretria are both examples. At Corinth from the seventh to the fourth century BC the sanctuary of Demeter developed on a series of three terraces on the lower, gradual slope of the acropolis, some distance from the agora and densely inhabited areas of the city. The earliest buildings, a sacred *oikos* (perhaps the Thesmophorion) and a group of dining-rooms, date from the second half of the sixth century BC.[35] Activity

---

[34] According to Michael Jameson, 'on the slope of a long hill', but not 'visible from much of the land'; 'Cultic Map of the Greek City-State', Paper presented at the American Philological Association, December 1987; see also M. Jameson, C. Runnels, T. H. van Andel, *A Greek Countryside: the Southern Argolid from Prehistory to the Present Day* (Stanford, Calif., 1994), 72, 262–3.

[35] N. Bookidis and J. E. Fisher, 'The Sanctuary of Demeter and Kore on Acrocorinth, Preliminary Report IV: 1969–1970', *Hesperia*, 41 (1972), 284; eid. 'Sanctuary of Demeter and Kore on Acrocorinth, Preliminary Report V: 1971–73', *Hesperia*, 43 (1974), 272.

continued in the Hellenistic period, stopped after 146, and revived in the Roman period, when three small temples were built on the upper terrace in the last half of the first century. In spite of the lack of a natural source of water in the sanctuary itself, water seems to have been important, both for purification (several of the dining-rooms were equipped with small shower stalls near the entry) and as a constituent of the ritual. Hundreds of thousands of miniature vases were among the dedications, with *kalathiskoi, hydriai* or *hydriskai*, and *phialai* predominating,[36] and the highest concentrations in the period from the sixth to the fourth century BC. Many of the votives were found in rectangular stone-lined pits or in pits cut into bedrock.[37] Miniature terracotta figurines include girls and women carrying piglets and torches.[38] From the sanctuary the buildings of the agora are clearly visible in the distance, but the sanctuary itself is remote from the city centre and would have looked out over agricultural territory as well as the city.

Like the sanctuary of Demeter and Kore at Corinth, the sanctuary of Demeter at Eretria, bounded by a double *temenos* wall on the lower side, was located on the slope leading to the acropolis, at some distance from the harbour, the agora, and the areas of domestic habitation.[39] Eretria was founded in the eighth century, but the earliest cult activity in the area of the Thesmophorion dates only from the sixth century BC. In the eighth and seventh centuries Demeter seems to have been worshipped near the major temple of Apollo Daphnephoros. A votive deposit near the temple contained more than 600 miniature *hydriai*, some showing women in procession.[40] The major votive deposits at the Thesmophorion on the side of the acropolis hill parallel for the most part those at Corinth, with the highest concentrations in the sixth to fourth centuries. The temple and altar date from the late sixth or early fifth century; it is not known whether they survived the Persian destruction of 480.[41] A falling off of

---

[36] E. G. Pemberton, *Corinth* xviii. 1: *The Sanctuary of Demeter and Kore: The Greek Pottery* (Princeton, 1989), 65.

[37] N. Bookidis and R. Stroud, *Corinth* xviii. 111: *The Sanctuary of Demeter and Kore, Topography and Architecture* (Princeton, 1997), for the complete report.

[38] *Hesperia*, 41 (1972), pl. 62d; Bookidis and Stroud (n. 37), 15 fig. 13.

[39] I. R. Metzger, *Eretria* vii: *Das Thesmophorion von Eretria* (Bern, 1985), 14 and pl. 1. The building is definitely a Thesmophorion. Roof tiles on the site are inscribed ΘΕΣΜ- (personal observation by author on site).

[40] *AR* (1982–3), 18.

[41] Metzger, *Das Thesmophorion*, 52.

votives in the third century indicates either decline or that the
worship of Demeter moved away from the Thesmophorion on the
acropolis at that time.

In some older Greek cities Demeter's sanctuary was located
between the urban centre and the agricultural territory, the pattern
attributed by de Polignac to cities in the formative stage. This was the
case at Knossos. Some of the earliest votives to Demeter have been
found at Knossos, where from the eighth century to the second century Demeter was worshipped in what was originally an open-air
sanctuary near a spring, on the lower slope of a hill about a kilometre from the acropolis and separated from the acropolis (and the
Minoan palace) by a stream. If Knossos had had a wall, this could
have been an extramural sanctuary. As it is, the site is well removed
from the main habitation area to the west of the palace and lies at
least 200 metres away from the nearest traces of houses.[42] Early
votives indicate nocturnal ceremonial meals in the sanctuary. Bones
of sacrificial victims show that sheep predominated, with pigs com-
prising only 17 per cent. Most of the early (late eighth- and early
seventh-century BC) terracotta figurines are female, including at least
one kourotrophic figure.[43] By the late fifth century, when a small
temple was built, the bones of sacrificial victims had become primarily those of pigs (as many as 90 per cent).[44] Votives associated with
water were common: *hydriskai* and *hydrophoroi*.[45] Until the second
century, when votives seem to cease, lamps and miniature vases,
especially *krateriskoi* and *hydrophoroi*, were popular dedications.
Votive figurines (loomweights, jewellery, and *hydrophoroi*)[46] indicate
a primarily female clientele, but male figurines have also been found,
as well as agricultural tools, weapons, and an inscribed ring dedicated 'to the Mother', by a man named Nothokrates, winner in the
games.[47] Like the sanctuary of Demeter at Corinth, the sanctuary at
Knossos experienced a decline in the Hellenistic period,[48] but revived
again in the second half of the first century BC (when Octavian

---

[42] S. Hood, *Archaeological Survey of the Knossos Area* (London, 1958), 20 no. 119.

[43] J. N. Coldstream, *Knossos: The Sanctuary of Demeter* (Oxford, 1973), 55 no. 60.

[44] For a marble pig's head as a dedication, see Coldstream, *Knossos*, 96 no. 12 and pl.
77a.

[45] Ibid. 68–70, 184.

[46] Including a ring inscribed *ΔAMATP-*, Coldstream, *Knossos*, 134 no. 25.

[47] Ibid. no. 14.

[48] Ibid. 186, compares the falling off of votives to Demeter at Axos and Gortyn in
the Hellenistic period.

settled Campanians at Knossos) and continued into the second century AD.

Other sanctuaries of Demeter in Greece were located at some distance from town centres. A sanctuary of Demeter at Kalyvia tes Sokhas, situated in a grove near a stream on a mountain side in the foothills of Mt. Taygetos, would have been about an hour and a half's walk for the women of Sparta.[49] Roof tiles inscribed $\Delta AMATPO[\Sigma]$ identify the sanctuary as Demeter's.[50] The earliest traces of cult activity go back to the sixth century.[51] Recognized ritual specialists in charge of women's banquets were exclusively female, and filled an office known from similar sanctuaries throughout Lakonia and Messenia.[52]

Literary references from the Classical period, usually describing a political or military crisis, give some hints about the location of Demeter sanctuaries elsewhere in Greece. Two of these occur in the context of violation of the boundaries of sanctuaries normally restricted to female worshippers and illustrate the punishments for men who violated these boundaries. The first pertains to the sanctuary of Demeter Thesmophoros on Aigina during an early fifth-century conflict between Aigina and Athens. Herodotos tells us about a man condemned to death who attempted to take refuge in the temple and held on to the door handles so tightly that when his pursuers cut his hands off to apprehend him, the hands remained gripped to the door (Hdt. 6. 91). Herodotos does not give the exact location of the sanctuary, but it could not have been far from the town centre because the execution was scheduled in or near the agora. The second crisis occurred after the battle of Marathon, when Miltiades violated the sanctuary of Demeter Thesmophoros during the siege of Paros. Miltiades was trying to find a way into the city and injured his leg jumping over the wall (herkos) of the temenos of Demeter, described by Herodotos as located on a hill in front of the city (πρὸ τῆς πόλιος, 6. 134). Miltiades was not able to open the door to the megaron and

---

[49] R. M. Dawkins, 'Laconia. Sparta', BSA 16 (1909–10), 12–14.

[50] This is probably the sanctuary associated by Pausanias with the Eleusinian goddesses (3. 20. 5, 7).

[51] A Corinthian terracotta figurine and early Lakonian pottery; Dawkins, 'Laconia. Sparta', 14, and J. M. Cook, 'Lakonia', BSA 45 (1950), 274.

[52] Cook, 'Lakonia', 276–81; M. N. Tod, 'Notes and Inscriptions from S. W. Messenia', JHS 25 (1905), 49–53, for the office of thoinarmostria (female official in charge of banquets), a Peloponnesian title associated with the cult of Demeter and Kore. For Sparta, see LSS 64, 2nd cent. BC.

later died of gangrene as a result of his injuries. Herodotos says the priestess who told Miltiades how to get in had revealed secrets not to be divulged to males, and implies that the injury was understood as punishment from the goddess. Two other mainland sanctuaries of Demeter can be located because they figure in battle narratives. The first was just outside Plataiai, protected from pollution by Demeter herself during the battle of 479 BC. Herodotos describes a temple with *temenos* and grove located on a hill not far from the city (Hdt. 9. 57, 65). Although the battle of Plataiai raged all around the *temenos*, no Persian corpses fell in the sanctuary because, as Herodotos reports, Demeter was angry over the burning of Eleusis (9. 67).[53] Another mainland sanctuary played a pivotal role in a Spartan attack on Thebes. The Spartans were able to sneak on to the Theban Kadmeia and capture it because the Theban men, displaced by the women holding the Thesmophoria in Demeter's sanctuary on the Kadmeia, had to stay down in the agora (Xen. *Hell.* 5. 2. 29).

The archaeological as well as the literary evidence shows that in the Archaic and Classical periods sanctuaries of Demeter in Greece and the Cyclades could be located on top of the acropolis, on the side of the acropolis, or outside the walls of the city. Many acropolis sanctuaries of Demeter, like those at Eretria and Corinth, were at some distance from the agora. Demeter at Thebes, however, was right in the centre. At Thebes Demeter combined agricultural and political functions, and her location, squarely in the centre of town, reflects her central political role. She was called Demeter Thesmophoros (Paus. 9. 16. 5), had a temple on the Kadmeia (Ael. *VH* 12. 57), and was represented both as an agricultural divinity rising from the earth[54] and as a political divinity, seated on a throne, wearing a crown, and holding a sceptre.[55] Euripides recognized both functions of Theban Demeter when he identified her with Ge and called her possessor of Thebes, protector of the land (*Phoen.* 683–8).[56] Theban Demeter received the sacrifice of a bull, leaders took omens at her

---

[53] See Paus. 9. 4. 3; Plut. *Arist.* 11. 3–7. Pritchett locates the *temenos* at the site of building foundations he found at Hysai on the Pantanassa ridge; see A. Schachter, *Cults of Boiotia*, i (London, 1981), 152–3.

[54] Shown rising from the earth: Paus. 9. 16. 1.

[55] Kadmos and the dragon with audience of divinities marked with non-Attic names, *ARV*[2] 1187, 33; Schachter, *Cults of Boeotia*, i. 167 n. 4.

[56] For the double function and the central location, see Schachter, *Cults of Boeotia*, i. 165–8.

altar both when magistrates took office[57] and before battle,[58] and soldiers dedicated booty in her sanctuary if a battle was won.[59] Demeter nevertheless, as goddess of agriculture, continued to be the major divinity of Theban women, and the Thesmophoria, celebrated in midsummer, remained a major festival.[60]

Demeter was also an acropolis divinity at Lepreon, Mytilene, and Iasos, but it is not likely that she played a central political role in any of these cities. The fourth-century sanctuary of Demeter at Lepreon, the only excavated building in this tiny Peloponnesian *polis*, was located at the very top of the acropolis and enclosed within the city's fortification wall, overlooking the town and surrounding fields, visible in the plain below.[61] At Mytilene Demeter was located on a rocky height overlooking the sea. Her sanctuary dates from the Archaic period, but remained rather modest until the late Classical and Hellenistic periods, when expansion is indicated by additional building and heavy votive activity. The sanctuary at Mytilene seems to have been used for a variety of ceremonies. Over fifteen hundred terracotta figurines have been found, representing men, women, children, birds, and animals. The building identified as the Thesmophorion dates from the late Hellenistic period, but the Thesmophoria had a long history at Mytilene as the many *hydrophoroi* and over five hundred lamps in the sanctuary attest.[62] Iasos had a structure for Demeter with the earliest foundations dating from the period just before the Persian wars. It was located within the wall, on the lower slope of the acropolis, not far from a series of cisterns for collection of water. Although within the wall, Demeter was not the major acropolis divinity at Iasos, and her sanctuary was situated on the lower slope of the hill, about as far away as possible from the theatre, public buildings, and main gate of the city.

Thebes, Mytilene, and Lepreon were exceptional. In most other cities sanctuaries of Demeter were either within the wall but removed

---

[57] Plut. *De gen. Soc.* 586f, 587c.

[58] Paus. 9. 6. 5–6; Ael. *VH* 12. 57.

[59] Pind. *Isthm.* 7. 1–5; Diod. Sic. 7. 10. 2–4.

[60] An unusual time for a festival elsewhere timed to coincide with the autumn planting. As Schachter points out, *Cults of Boeotia*, i. 168 n. 2, other Boiotian cities must have been more conventional. The Boiotian month Damastros coincided with Attic Pyanopsion, the month of the Athenian Thesmophoria.

[61] H. Knell, 'Lepreon: Der Tempel der Demeter', *AM* 98 (1983), 113–47.

[62] C. Williams and H. Williams, 'Excavations at Mytilene, 1990', *EMC* 35, NS 10 (1991), 175–91.

from the central area or outside the wall altogether. Paros is a good example of the second pattern. Here the sanctuary was just outside the wall, or, as Herodotos says, πρὸ τῆς πόλιος, standing 'in front of the city' (6. 134). The pattern of Demeter πρὸ πόλεως was common in cities founded from Greece during the two great periods of diaspora and colonial expansion. At the time of the Ionian revolt the Ephesian Thesmophoria were celebrated near the borders of the city's territory (Hdt. 6. 16). At Smyrna an inscription describes the sanctuary of Demeter Thesmophoros as πρὸ πόλεως.[63] The sanctuary of Demeter at Miletos was located 'a short way from the city' (Parth. 8. 1). The same arrangement was carried to colonial cities and refoundations from Asia Minor. For instance, at Olbia, a colony of Miletos, the temple of Demeter was located outside the walls, across a river on Cape Hippolaos (Hdt 4. 53).[64] Teos, a city with a poor excavation record, had a temple of the Eleusinian goddesses,[65] as yet not located, but Abdera, refounded and rebuilt by Tean immigrants in 545 BC, and possibly preserving a pattern already established at Teos, had an open-air *temenos* of Demeter on a terrace outside the walls where terracottas and vases, including 6,000 miniature *hydriai*, dating from the sixth to the third century BC were found.[66]

Demeter πρὸ πόλεως was also the most common pattern in colonial cities founded during the second phase of the Greek diaspora. Thasos, founded from Paros, had a Thesmophorion on a small hill above the sea, on a narrow strip of land just outside the city wall.[67] A variation on this arrangement was prevalent in the western coastal colonies, but in these and other coastal cities Demeter's extramural sanctuaries usually faced not the sea, but the interior. This was the arrangement at Cyrene, where the sanctuary of Demeter was established in about 600 BC, about a generation after the city was founded. Here Demeter was located outside the wall, separated from the city by a waterway. Originally an open-air *temenos* near a spring, the sanctuary eventually occupied three terraces leading up from the

---

[63] *ISmyrna* 655.

[64] The sanctuary is located by a graffito recording a dedication to Demeter, Persephone, and Iakchos; A.-S. Roussiaéva, 'Les Cultes agraires à Olbia pontique', *DHA* 9 (1983), 187–8. For Demeter at other colonies of Miletos along the coast of the Black Sea, see Graf, *NK*, 274.

[65] *SEG* 4. 598. 54. late 1st cent. BC.

[66] *AR* (1988–9), 84–95. For the Thesmophoria at Abdera, see Diog. Laert. 9. 43; Athen. 2. 26.

[67] Rolley, 'Le Sanctuaire des Dieux Patrooi', 441–83.

city to the agricultural plains above the coast, linking the town centre to its agricultural territory. The sixth century BC was a time of vigorous activity at Cyrene, with what White calls a 'flood of repetitious pottery', when the sanctuary was enlarged to include two precincts with the first small buildings.[68] This development corresponded to the period of expansion into the agricultural territory of the interior. Heavy votive dedication continued until the fourth century BC, when votives began to fall off. Cyrene nevertheless continued to be an important supplier of grain to the rest of Greece, as we know from an important inscription detailing the sale of grain to forty-three cities of Greece at a time of shortage and famine in 330–326.[69] The significance of Demeter and Kore as goddesses of grain continued to be emphasized at Cyrene by a Hellenistic *defixio* that calls Demeter 'Aglaokarpos' ('She who bears splendid fruit') and an Imperial dedication to Kore 'who looks after the wheat'.[70]

Demeter was also associated with agricultural expansion in the colonial foundations in Sicily and Magna Graecia. There seem to have been several stages in the development and permanent placement of sanctuaries in the process of colonial foundation. In the first stage, when Greeks as traders and not yet permanent settlers were still only temporary residents, their sanctuaries remained on the periphery of local settlements. At Etruscan Gravisca, Greek merchants and early settlers concentrated the sanctuaries of their divinities in a small area at the edge of the town's territory, where Demeter was worshipped in close proximity to Aphrodite, Hera, and Apollo.[71] In the second stage, when Greek colonists founded their own permanent settlements in new territory, the movement was from the centre to the periphery, with Demeter often one of the first divinities to appear outside a new city's walls. The best example, with clearest stratification, is Gela, where a Thesmophorion on a hill at Bitalemi was separated from the city not only by the wall, but by a river. Demeter at Gela is like Demeter at Cyrene both in the orientation of the sanctuary and in the timing of the establishment of her

---

[68] D. White, *The Extramural Sanctuary of Demeter and Persephone at Cyrene*, i. *Background Introduction to the Excavations* (Philadelphia, 1984); id., 'Cyrene's Sanctuary of Demeter and Persephone', *AJA* 85 (1981), 13–30.

[69] M. N. Tod, *A Selection of Greek Historical Inscriptions*, ii (Oxford, 1948), no. 196.

[70] White, 'Cyrene's Sanctuary', 23. The history of the architectural development of the sanctuary is covered in D. White, *The Extramural Sanctuary of Demeter and Persephone at Cyrene, Libya*, v. *The Site's Architecture* (Philadelphia, 1997).

[71] Edlund, *The Gods and the Place*, 76–7.

extramural cult. Demeter's first votives at Gela date from 650 BC, about forty years after the founding of the city.[72] Buildings followed by the middle of the sixth century, and by the fifth the piglets and kourotrophic figurines characteristic of the worship of Demeter began to appear.[73] As the new polis established and expanded its agricultural territory in the generation after foundation, Demeter became one of the first extramural divinities, placed outside the city (at Bitalemi) to protect and nourish the new agricultural territory. As a token of this function farming tools were common dedications. At both Gela and Akragas there were eventually at least four extramural sanctuaries of Demeter.[74] The same pattern of extramural sanctuaries for Demeter was also followed at Selinus.[75]

The sanctuaries of Demeter at Corinth, Eretria, and Iasos illustrate a general characteristic of many sanctuaries of Demeter found within a city's walls. Although located in the 'inner' space of the city, their orientation and design exploits topographical or geographical features of the site in order to preserve the sense of isolation associated with sanctuaries outside the walls. Inside the wall, within the 'inner' space, they are nevertheless somewhat remote, either removed by distance or because they occupy an isolated level or terrace of a rising hill. Demeter could be close to the city centre, but even in these cases she often seems to turn away from inhabited areas, the agora, and other sanctuaries. The sanctuary of Demeter at Priene, for example, illustrates the remoteness of Demeter in 'inner' space. At Priene, a city that enjoyed expansion and rebuilding in the fourth century BC,[76] the sanctuary of Demeter and Kore (identified by

[72] de Polignac, *Naissance*, 114; Malkin, *RC*, 180.

[73] Price, *Kourotrophos*, 183, on the historical development of the sanctuary. For the dedications, see M. Sguaitamatti, *L'Offrande de porcelet dans la coroplathie géléenne: Étude topologique* (Mainz, 1984). The sanctuary remained in heavy use, with new buildings constructed after a fire in 450, and lasted until the Carthaginian attack in about 405 BC. For Demeter's rites, sanctuary, and votives at Bitalemi, see Kron, 'Frauenfest'.

[74] R. R. Holloway, *The Archaeology of Ancient Sicily* (London and New York, 1991), 56–60.

[75] Holloway (n. 74), 61–3. At Morgantina there may have been at one time as many as seven; M. Bell, *The Terracottas. Morgantina Studies*, i (Princeton, 1981), 81. For a similar pattern of multiple sanctuaries and rural development, see J. C. Carter, 'Sanctuaries in the *chora* of Metaponto', in S. Alcock and R. Osborne (eds.), *Placing the Gods* (Oxford, 1994), 161–98. For other colonial evidence, see G. Gasparro Sfameni, *Misteri e culti mistici di Demetra* (Rome, 1986).

[76] N. Demand, 'The Relocation of Priene Reconsidered', *Phoenix*, 40 (1986), 35–44, argues that 4th-cent. Priene was an expansion of a smaller settlement on the same site, not a refoundation of a city originally located in the plain.

inscribed statue bases at the entrance)[77] was located in a bounded precinct on the west end of a terrace, a steep climb above the main temple area and theatre, on the way up the cliff to the acropolis heights above. The location was perhaps chosen to take advantage of the spring that fed the lion's head fountain at the entrance to the *temenos*.[78] Terracotta votives from the third to the early first century BC were found deposited in the *megaron* beside the temple.[79] From the sanctuary worshippers could look down over the temple of Athena to the agora and further, to the fields of the city in the plain below.

The situation at Pergamon to some extent parallels that at Priene. When Eumenes II created the great acropolis sanctuaries there in the early second century, his architects seem to have been conscious of the problem of maintaining elements of Demeter's rural character within the 'inner space' of the city's sacred area. Demeter Thesmophoros had occupied her own terraced sanctuary on the side of the acropolis before the third century BC,[80] and through at least three major periods of expansion and construction, the successive architects of Philetairos, Attalos I, and Eumenes II respected the isolation of Demeter and kept her terrace separate from the upper level of the major acropolis cults above and the three gymnasium levels below. The separation was marked by a *propylon*, built by benefactions from Apollonis, wife of Attalos I, and not visible to people approaching the sanctuary until they turned the last corner and stood in the forecourt. The forecourt, bordered by a fountain enclosed in a natural rock niche, emphasized the segregation of the *temenos* by providing a transitional space between the communal gymnasia below and the restricted area of Demeter's sanctuary just above. Water at the entrance to sanctuaries of Demeter seems to have been more integral to the operation of the cult than water for purification contained in *perirrhantēria* at the entrance to other sacred precincts.[81] The

---

[77] T. Wiegand, *Priene* (Berlin, 1904), 148, 151; M. Schede, *Die Ruinen von Priene* (Berlin, 1964), 90 fig. 104, and 92 fig. 106, for a *hydrophoros*.

[78] Wiegand (n. 77), 148 fig. 119, with fountain at location C.

[79] E. Toppferwein-Hoffman, *Ist Mitt* 21 (1971), 125–60. For the Thesmophoria at Priene, see *IPriene* 196.

[80] C. H. Bohtz and W.-D. Albert, 'Die Untersuchungen am Demeter-Heiligtum in Pergamon', *AA* (1970), 391–412; C. H. Bohtz, *Altertümer von Pergamon*, xiii: *Das Demeter-Heiligtum* (Berlin, 1981).

[81] Cole, 'The Uses of Water', 162. For miniature *hydriai* from the sanctuary at Pergamon, see Bohtz and Albert, (n. 80), 402 fig. 26. For the Thesmophoria at Pergamon, see *IPergamon* 315.

fountain at Pergamon, like the fountain at the entrance to Demeter's *temenos* at Priene, was a permanent architectural structure, integrated into the architecture of the sanctuary, not simply a temporary or removable water vessel.

Characteristics of a countryside sanctuary could also be imitated by a later sanctuary that brought Demeter into the *asty*. At Gela, where Demeter's original sanctuary was outside the wall, separated from the city by a river, a second sanctuary was built later in the Archaic period inside the wall, on the acropolis. The votive terracottas of the later sanctuary were similar to the dedications at the earlier site, and both continued to be used through the Classical period.[82] The same doubling of Demeter's sites occurred at Akragas and Heloros. At Akragas, founded from Gela, the older sanctuary, dating from the period of foundation in the early sixth century, developed outside the city around a site with two caves and springs. About a century later a more substantial temple was built on a slope along the circuit wall, closer to the other major sanctuaries of the city.[83] Providing a central sanctuary that mimicked a peripheral sanctuary might have been a response to the needs of a growing urban society and may have reflected a growing complexity in the functions of the goddess, but it also provided the opportunity for a more complex ritual with processions linking the two sanctuaries and connecting the city with its external territory.

There were other ways by which a country sanctuary could become a city sanctuary. If a city increased its walled territory, sanctuaries once outside the walls could become sanctuaries inside the walls. When Siris in Magna Graecia was founded by colonists from Kolophon in about 700 BC, the sanctuary of Demeter was located at a spring on a slope outside the city. Later, after refoundation from Taras in 433/2, the rural area was incorporated into the walled city and the sanctuary endured 'like an island' within the city.[84] Country-like sanctuaries could also be artificially preserved. The acropolis sanctuary of Demeter at Syracuse must have also been like a garden in the city. At Syracuse, Demeter had a very early sanctuary on Ortygia, with votives dating from the

---

[82] de Polignac, *Naissance*, 115.

[83] Polyaen. *Strat.* 5. 1, for Thesmophoria at Akragas.

[84] Edlund, *The Gods and the Place*, 112, for the idea of a formerly rural sacred territory preserved as an island within the city.

eighth century.[85] Later she assumed a special political importance when Gelon chose her in 491 as the divinity by which he united two populations brought together by his forced synoecism of Syracuse with Gela. Gelon's family had controlled the hereditary priesthood of Demeter at Gela, and when he brought a major part of the population from Gela to Syracuse, he built temples to Demeter and Kore on the acropolis[86] where he required suspected traitors to swear allegiance to the newly reorganized *polis* with a great oath sworn for Demeter and Kore.[87] This sanctuary was also the site for the Thesmophoria, a ten-day festival described later as celebrated 'in a garden' on the acropolis (Pl. *Epist.* 7. 349d).

We have observed three patterns of sanctuary location for cults of Demeter: within the city, just outside, and at the borders of the city's territory. All three patterns seem to occur in all parts of the Greek world, and common to all is the identification of Demeter with the land, whether inside or outside the city. Two points should be stressed. First, establishment of extramural sanctuaries of Demeter was not confined to the period of colonization. The practice existed before colonization, for instance at Paros, the metropolis of Thasos, and continued elsewhere on the Greek mainland after the period of colonization. Hellenistic sanctuaries of Demeter at Dion and Pella were extramural.[88] Second, Demeter's votives do not seem to vary with location of her sanctuary, whether inside or outside the city wall, and the major types of votives usually fall into similar chronological ranges, whether found in sanctuaries in Old Greece or in colonial foundations. Demeter's ritual required water in a natural setting. The need for secrecy, whether for the mysteries or the Thesmophoria, dictated isolation. Such requirements could be most easily met outside the city, but nature and isolation could also be artificially created within the city.

Finally, we should remember that although place, space, and ritual could be closely related, space could be re-created in a new place. An

---

[85] *AR* (1976–7), 65; Malkin, *RC*, 177 n. 282. There seems to have been an early Thesmophorion at Piazza Vittoria; see G. Voza, *Kokalos*, 22–3 (1976–7), 551–3, and 26–7 (1980–1), 680–5.

[86] Diod. Sic. 11. 26. 7; Cic. *Verr.* 4. 53. 119.

[87] Diod. Sic. 19. 5. 4; Plut. *Dion* 57. For the political meaning of Demeter at Syracuse, see D. White, 'Demeter's Sicilian Cult as a Political Instrument', *GRBS* 5 (1964), 261–79.

[88] Dion: *AR* (1985–6), 56; Pella: *AR* (1980–1), 29, (1982–3), 38–9.

inscription from Tanagra demonstrates how this process worked.[89]
Sometime during the early second century BC the *dēmos* of Tanagra
consulted Apollo about their temple (*hieron*) of Demeter and Kore,
which apparently needed to be rebuilt. They asked the god whether
they should leave it where it was, move it to a site called Topos tes
Euemerias ('Place of Good Weather'), or bring it into the city (*polis*).
Apollo chose the city site, and commanded, 'Receive within the
crown of the walls the goddesses who are just outside the city
(προϝαστίδας) . . .' (7). Demeter and Kore, who had been formerly
located 'in front of the city (*asty*)' like Demeter at Paros or Smyrna,
now would have their sanctuary moved inside the walls of the city.
The procedure required a committee of three men over 30 to consult
with the architect and the leaders of the city, in order to construct
the temple of Demeter 'as beautifully as possible in the *polis*, in the
place where it seems best' (9–10). Ninety-eight women, probably all
the married women of the community, contributed almost 500
drachmas, most paying five drachmas each; all of their names are
listed in the text. Moving the temple was not costly, but the *dēmos*
allowed three years for planning and reconstruction. During his visit
to Tanagra Pausanias failed to notice either the sanctuary of Demeter or the 'Place of Good Weather', but he did remark that the
people of Tanagra were exceptional among the Greeks for their consideration of the gods, because they built their sanctuaries 'far away
from their houses, in an unpolluted place, kept separate from human
affairs' (9. 22. 2). Demeter's new sanctuary may have been modest,
but I think we can be sure that it was carefully placed.

[89] T. Reinach, 'Un temple élevé par les femmes de Tanagra', *REG* 12 (1899), 53–115;
Schachter, *Cults of Boiotia*, i. 163. For the date, see D. Knoepfler, 'Zur Datierung
der großen Inschrift aus Tanagra im Louvre', *Chiron*, 7 (1977), 67–87. The text is
most recently discussed by L. Migeotte, *Les Souscriptions publiques dans les cités grecques*
(Geneva, 1992), 75–81.

7

Greek Sanctuaries as Places of Refuge

ULRICH SINN

If a person in Greece found himself in a threatening situation he had the option of taking refuge in a sanctuary.[1] At first glance the ancient sources do not create the impression that sheltering people seeking asylum was one of the everyday responsibilities of the sanctuaries. We learn about personalities in political life who turned to sanctuaries seeking help when they had been stripped of office or had fallen into disfavour among the people.[2] The sources name victims of war and civil war in particular as making use of the protection provided in sanctuaries.[3]

We consistently hear about the sanctuaries as places of refuge in exceptional situations. This naturally led scholars to compare the protection afforded by Greek sanctuaries with modern institutions officially recognized as places of refuge, such as Christian churches, diplomatic missions or universities; in practice only occasional use is made of the privilege of guaranteeing protection enjoyed by these present-day institutions.

Thus it is readily understandable that this topic, which apparently played a rather minor role in the everyday life of the Greeks, attracted little interest among scholars. The right of sanctuaries to grant asylum is, indeed, counted as an exemplary feature of the Greek social order, but how this idea worked in reality has hardly been explored.

[1] The topic of Greek sanctuaries as places of refuge has been treated *in extenso* by the author; see Sinn, *Perachora*.
[2] e.g. the Athenian statesmen Kylon (*c*. 630 BC, Hdt. 5. 71; Thuc. 1. 126. 10–11) and Demosthenes (after 322 BC, Arrian (*FGrHist* 156 F 9. 13); Strabo 8. 6. 14; Paus. 1. 8. 2f., 2. 33. 2f.). Members of various Greek royal families availed themselves of the protection afforded by sanctuaries: Queen Deïdameia of Epirus (Polyain. *Strat.* 8. 52), King Perseus of Macedonia (Livy 44. 45. 5–45. 6. 10) and Cleopatra IV (Justin 39. 3. 10–11). For Spartan kings seeking asylum, see nn. 49–53 below.
[3] e.g. the inhabitants of Plataia sought refuge in a sanctuary when the Spartans captured their town (427 BC, Thuc. 3. 58. 3) and so did the Thebans when Alexander the Great took their town (335 BC, Arr. *Anab.* 1. 8. 8 and 1. 9. 6–10; Diod. Sic. 17. 8–15).

It does in fact seem as if it were hardly possible to find concrete
evidence of how the protection afforded by sanctuaries worked in
practice. In the ancient sources, and especially in pictorial representations, the action of seeking sanctuary takes place among objects
which in any case are the obligatory components of a sanctuary: at
the altar (Fig. 1) or at the image of the god (Fig. 2). It seems that there
are no specific arrangements for looking after suppliants which the
archaeologist could find by means of excavation and could analyse.

Under these circumstances would one then be justified in considering that protection offered in sanctuaries—in theory such an
august institution—is in fact nothing more than an occasional
obligation, which the sanctuaries rather casually fulfilled?

Fig. 1 Suppliants on the altar. The daughters of Danaos in the Argive
sanctuary.

Fig. 2 Suppliants at the image of the god. The daughters of Proitos in the
sanctuary of Artemis Hemera at Lusoi(?).

Our views on the right of sanctuaries to grant asylum have been
thrown off balance by the reports written by ancient historians, mentioned above. In accordance with the genre, they focus on the lives of
outstanding figures and tell us almost exclusively about spectacular
individual cases. On the other hand many different aspects of the
daily life of the normal citizen are mirrored in ancient drama, in the
texts of the orators or in philosophical treatises. These types of literary evidence mention the protective function of sanctuaries much
more often than do the works of the historians—but mostly by
allusion and indirect implication, rather than by outright statements.

Taking into consideration sources which have not been properly
evaluated up until now, we gain a much broader spectrum of the
ways in which sanctuaries were invoked for protection—especially
in the realm of private life: for example, girls turned to sanctuaries for
help in order to escape a forced marriage.[4] We also hear about a
woman who became a suppliant because she had left her husband
and wanted to reach her lover.[5] Orphans were placed under the protection of a guardian by means of action taken by a sanctuary.[6]
Members of a family who had been cast out tried to bring about a
reconciliation with their relatives in the same way.[7] The same sort of
thing also occurs in public life: diplomatic missions, the personal
safety of whose members was already guaranteed (see below), placed
themselves under the protection of a sanctuary at their destinations
in order to make it difficult for the negotiators on the other side to
reject their requests.[8]

---

[4] Flight to a sanctuary in order to get married or for escaping the unwanted atten-
tions of a lover is a common topic in ancient drama, even in tragedy (Aesch. *Supp.*), as
well as in burlesque (Plaut. *Rud.*); see also Paus. 8. 5. 11 f.

[5] The legend about the local Naxian heroine Polykrite originates in the tale of the
Milesian Neaira, who falls in love with the Naxian Promedon, follows him to Naxos
and, pursued by her husband, takes refuge there in the sanctuary of Hestia (Parth.
Amat. narr. 18 (from Theophrastus); Plut. *Mor.* 254b–c *de mul. vir.*).

[6] This convention is mentioned in ancient commentaries in connection with a myth
about Medea (Kreophylos in Didymos in: Schol. Eur. *Med.* 264).

[7] In *Oedipus at Colonus* Sophocles describes such a case (1158 ff.): Polyneikes is a
suppliant at the altar of Poseidon in Athens in order to force his father, who has cursed
him, to speak to him.

[8] Thucydides (1. 24. 3–7) describes this use of sacred protection in Corcyra. The
events that took place in the sanctuary of Zeus in Olympia in 428 BC are particularly
informative. After Mytilene had left the Athenian League the Mytileneans wanted to be
taken into the Peloponnesian League; this was deliberated in a session of the League,
which convened at the Olympic Games (sic!). Realizing that their position as former
partners of Athens was weak, the Mytileneans, at the end of the speech in which they

These examples serve to show that the concept 'asylum' is not a suitable term for characterizing the sort of protection the Greek sanctuaries were in a position to offer. It is true that the ancient world had the institution of asylum (*asylia*), but this should not be confused with the specific form of guaranteeing protection afforded by the sanctuaries. This important distinction must be briefly elucidated.[9]

Ancient Greece was broken up into many independent towns and districts. There was no law code valid for all of the Greeks. Here the institution of *asylia* provided some sort of compensation. It limited the consequences bound to result from the lack of a common set of laws by means of a network of contracts and agreements between the various states. *Asylia* (literally translated: 'prohibition against stealing') guaranteed safe conduct for all those who, acting in the interests of their home towns, crossed the city-state boundaries and therefore were outside the jurisdiction of local justice. Those who profited from *asylia* were envoys—as mentioned above—and especially negotiators, but also artists and athletes whose professions involved travelling around. This kind of protection was effective only when it had been previously agreed on or when it had been formally granted to individuals as an honour.

Sanctuaries are involved in this kind of *asylia* only insofar as the agreements and documents were usually publicly displayed in sacred places which acquired greater effectiveness through the authority possessed by the sanctuary.

But the sanctuaries themselves were protected by *asylia*. One of the basic tenets of Greek religion was that everything inside sacred territory was owned by the god—and the possessions of divinities were of course taboo for human beings. Hence every sanctuary had the status of an inviolable precinct (*asylon hieron*). The inviolability of the sanctuaries guaranteed pilgrims and festival participants security. In the same way it served to protect the often valuable votive offerings. The sanctuaries were predestined to fulfil other functions by virtue of the security afforded by *asylia*. For example they could perform the function of banks. The sanctuary of Artemis in Ephesus

---

request membership, interpose the observation that, in view of the fact that they are convening in Olympia, they are basically suppliants of Zeus, so that reverence for the god should hinder rejection of their application for membership (Thuc. 3. 14. 1; F. E. Adcock, *Thucydides and his History* (London, 1963), 8).

[9] This differentiation is extensively set forth and the earlier, basic literature cited in Sinn, *Perachora*, 71–83.

is the most noteworthy example of this. Thanks to its status of inviolability the Sacred Island of Delos became one of the most important trading centres of the Mediterranean.

It is important to make a distinction between this general guarantee of protection and the granting of a specific type of protection, the avowed aim of which was to help people in their daily need. The inviolable precincts were the most suitable places for this purpose too. They did not have to be limited to sanctuaries; according to old beliefs the gods were also present in the fires on the hearths of private houses, so that they also counted as *asyla hiera*. And of course this also held true of images of the gods and altars in civic institutions, as in the bouleuterion or the agora. But one most often sought refuge in sanctuaries.

If a person in trouble entered a sanctuary, he was protected by *asylia* as explained above. But his trouble would not be solved simply by staying in a sanctuary. If someone were being pursued on account of a misdeed, he could of course attempt to hide in a sanctuary, but in the long run that was of no help. We know from regulations governing conduct in sanctuaries that anonymous stay on sacred land was not tolerated. For example, whoever wanted to enter the Amphiaraion at Oropos had to hang a wooden tablet with his name clearly visible at the entrance of the sanctuary.[10]

If someone really wished to avail himself of the protection of a sanctuary he had to appear openly and set forth the reasons for his coming. After such a presentation the sanctuary was in turn obliged to work towards a solution of the problem, as a rule by undertaking the role of go-between. This assistance was set in motion through a fixed ritual. This is the rite of *hiketeia* according to which the person in need of help sat down on the altar or at the image of the god holding a certain symbol identifying him as a suppliant, either a freshly broken-off twig or a strand of wool (Figs. 1 and 3). From this moment on he was no longer an ordinary visitor to the sanctuary. He had acquired the status of suppliant (male: *hiketēs*; female: *hiketis*) and thus had a claim to special treatment, mentioned above. This was the decisive moment for the person in trouble. That is why one used the short-hand phrase 'he sat down in the sanctuary' for a person who sought refuge in a sanctuary. This is also the reason, of course, why artistic representations reduced the subject matter of

---

[10] IG VII no. 235 lines 39 ff.

Fig. 3 Warriors threatening two suppliants at the altar.

sacred protection to the motif of settling down at the cult monument (Figs. 1–3).

If the person in trouble had become a suppliant, he now had a legal adviser in the person of the priest. This was not always an easy assignment. Since criminals, even convicted murderers, had the right to perform the rite of *hiketeia*,[11] it was all too often a matter of calming emotions running high, hindering acts of revenge, and instead setting in motion orderly criminal proceedings—since the suppliant could not avoid paying for his crime. The priest's obligation was particularly ticklish when the claim for protection was politically motivated and that was doubtless very often the case. Rejecting a person begging for protection counted as sacrilege. The demand for entry into the sanctuary on the part of the person seeking protection could bring about retaliatory measures from the political opponents, and expose the sanctuary and/or the town to which it belonged to great danger. This burden on the priests was in fact the weak point in the system of sacred immunity. Complaints over breakdowns run like a red thread through the ancient literature on the protective function of sanctuaries. The suppliants, as we shall see later on, drew their own conclusions and acted accordingly.

Historians record only examples where the law of sacred immunity was disregarded. It is blood-curdling to read how suppliants are forcibly driven out of sanctuaries, starved to death in sanctuaries,

---

[11] In *Ion* (1312 f.) Euripides has one of the actors utter a complaint (such as we are accustomed to hearing nowadays) about the allegedly over-liberal regulations of right to asylum.

massacred or burnt to death. Scenes such as these have also been
represented on vases (Fig. 3). Over and over again the priests were
not able to endure the pressure and strain and found ways of hypocritically circumventing the sacred law. Many a suppliant was the
victim of malicious deception. When a sanctuary wanted to rid itself
of an undesirable suppliant, there was, for example, a much favoured
method of pretending to ask an oracle how to deal with the suppliant. The oracular answer was, as a rule, ambiguously formulated
and could be interpreted at will as being unfavourable to the suppliant. Faced with reproach for having left the suppliant in the lurch,
one could talk one's way out by claiming to have misunderstood the
oracular response. This happened, for example, in Kyme after the
oracle at Didyma had been hypocritically consulted.[12]

Athens, which prided itself on being the 'bulwark for all suppliants', is no exception. Just at the time when Euripides has one of his
actors say in the *Heraclidae*: 'Here suppliants are not driven away as
they are elsewhere', (i.e. in the second half of the fifth century BC) the
Athenians put up a police station at the entrance to the Acropolis
with the clear aim of keeping undesirable suppliants away from the
sanctuaries in the fortress.[13] In Athens, too, it could happen that a
priest would not scruple to guarantee a suppliant safe conduct to the
borders of the state and that once across the border he would be
caught at once by his pursuers, who had been tipped off by the priest
as to the route by which the suppliant was to be sent 'to freedom'.[14]

Many similar accounts have played a decisive role in influencing
scholars to adopt the present consensus, namely that the protection
afforded by sanctuaries was effective only in the early period, if at all,
and that this institution had lost its effectiveness by the fifth century
BC at the latest.[15]

The emotional laments over failures to provide sacred protection
could, nonetheless, be explained in quite another way: that every
violation against this indispensable institution was recorded with
misgivings and at the same time branded with sharp disapproval,
whereas all mentions of the cases with positive outcomes were

---

[12] Hdt. I. 159.
[13] *IG* I Suppl. 26A; K. Wernicke, 'Die Polizeiwache auf der Burg von Athen', *Hermes*,
26 (1891), 51–7.
[14] Eur. *Heraclid.* 257.
[15] J. Gould claims a virtually complete failure ('Hiketeia', *JHS* 93 (1973), 101); so
does H. Schaefer, *Staatsform und Politik* (Leipzig, 1932), 46 ff.

omitted because they were normal. This way of interpreting the sources is supported by the fact that reports of bad treatment of suppliants always have moralistic undertones. The great number of legends that grew up around instances where sacred protection was either disregarded or abused are evidence of the unremitting struggle to preserve the effectiveness of sacred protection. The legends give awe-inspiring accounts of the gods mercilessly punishing sacrilege: when Kleomenes, the king of Sparta, went mad in his old age it was considered to be punishment for having ordered thousands of suppliants in Argos to be put to death.[16] A crime against suppliants was thought to be the cause of Sulla's stomach troubles.[17] When an earthquake and a tidal wave buried the town of Helike on the north coast of the Peloponnese together with all of its inhabitants in 373 BC it was thought to be the response of the gods to a crime committed shortly before against suppliants in the Poseidon sanctuary of the town.[18] And elsewhere in Greece natural catastrophes and military defeats were directly linked to preceding mistreatment of suppliants, for example in Sparta, Sybaris, Metapontum, Croton, and Aegina.[19]

These dramatic legends are evidence that the institution of *hiketeia* was deeply rooted in popular belief. The harshness of the divine retribution is a measure of how highly the institution of sacred protection was valued by the people—a measuring stick also for the tenacity with which people continually claimed the right to sacred protection.

Considering how strongly people were aware of the protective function of sanctuaries, it is not surprising that politicians exploited the popularity of *hiketeia* for their own purposes. The topic was well suited for stirring up emotions both in a positive and in a negative sense: thus the Spartans claimed superiority for the law code of Lykurgus because, among other things, they glorified the lawgiver as a man who valued the observance of sacred protection more than his own life.[20] The historian Xenophon praised the same attitude in the Spartan general Agesilaus whom he esteemed so highly.[21] Even the Romans attempted to set themselves up as champions of the right of

[16] Hdt. 6. 75. 3.
[17] Paus. 1. 20. 7.
[18] Paus. 7. 25. 1.
[19] For a collection of such legends, see Sinn, *Perachora*, 115f. (Appendix III).
[20] Plut. *Mor.* 227.
[21] Xen. *Ages.* 11. 1.

protection in order to worm their way into the good graces of the Greeks. This occurred in 192 BC in a speech held at Corinth by the Roman general Flamininus.[22] In the same way hate could be whipped up against political opponents. On the eve of the Peloponnesian War the chief rivals, Athens and Sparta, went through the pretence of conducting negotiations long after they had decided on war because they still had to deal with the problem of convincing their own citizens and allies who were unwilling to fight to back them up. One of their methods in this situation was to summon up remembrance of times when the opponent had disregarded *hiketeia*—coupled with the rhetorical question, whether it is conceivable that one would enter into a peaceful agreement with such evil-doers.[23]

Even this selective glance at the sources serves to show that the institution of *hiketeia* was an ever-present factor in the thinking and dealings of the Greeks. And one could expand the list of examples by pointing out the great number of legends and anecdotes clustered around this topic. *Hiketeia* appears as the main theme for plots not only in drama but also in comedy and even in erotic farce. There was even a code of behaviour advising suppliants how to behave towards hesitant priests: the suppliant should lay claim to compassion and give an impression of humility, but at the same time show unequivocally that he is determined to take his life on the spot, should his call for help be rejected[24]—a powerful means of exerting pressure, for suicide under these conditions would have meant terrible disgrace for the priest himself and the sanctuary in his care.

The everyday routine in activating sacred protection shows up just as it actually was with no retouching in the information referred to above. Mention has already been made of the evil tricks used in the sanctuaries to get rid of undesirable suppliants, while ostensibly keeping to the letter of the law. These reports, reflecting raw reality, are very important documents for determining that the function of granting protection, brought about by means of the rite of *hiketeia*, was not merely an idea up in the air, but was really put into practice

[22] Diod. Sic. 29. 1.
[23] Thuc. I. 126–8. For a collection of passages in which mistreatment of those seeking asylum is exploited for propaganda, see Sinn, *Perachora*, 113f. (Appendix III.)
[24] Aesch. *Supp.* 194ff.; cf. Aesch. *Eum.* 415ff., 443ff.; Soph. *OC* 237ff.; Plut. *Agis* 16–18, is clearly referring to the code of behaviour in Classical drama when he describes the request for protection made by the Spartan kings Kleombrotos II and Chilonis in the sanctuary of Poseidon at Tainaron.

—though subject to breakdowns through human weakness—and
it can be shown that it was practised far into the period of Roman
rule in Greece.

Just as each person had to reckon with having to rely at some point
on the protection given by sanctuaries, so the sanctuaries must have
held themselves in readiness to respond to the appeals of suppliants.
How did the sanctuaries prepare for these continual claims on their
hospitality?

In order to answer this question it is sufficient to recall that protection in a sanctuary was put into effect by means of a rite; that the
granting of protection and help from the priest as an intermediary
was a matter of practising a cult, comparable with proclaiming an
oracle, holding musical or athletic contests or taking care of sick
people. And so, just as it was taken for granted that lodging inside the
sanctuary would be temporarily provided for pilgrims to the oracular
shrines, for athletes and artists competing in contests and for patients
in sacred places of healing,[25] in the same way it was also taken for
granted that suppliants would live in sanctuaries, until a solution to
their problems was brought about.

There are several different indications that suppliants and other
cult participants lived side by side in the sanctuaries. In this case
too, sources outside official histories have proved to be particularly
revealing.

For example, the poet Alcaeus bewails his lot in one of his poems[26]
as being politically persecuted and having to seek refuge in a sanctuary, but he at once adds that his status as suppliant has the advantage that he can enjoy watching the ritual ring dances performed by
the girls of his homeland every day. It is clear that he lived among the
other pilgrims. Herodotus tells the story of how three hundred suppliant boys were rescued in a Samian sanctuary of Artemis: when
their pursuers threatened to starve them to death in their place of
refuge, the Samians simply included the refugees in the cult ceremonial involving meals—once again we see the suppliants mixed
together with the other participants in the cult.[27]

Such testimonia indicate how natural it was for pilgrims and suppliants to be together, and there were also several regulations for

---

[25] Inscriptions show that patients in healing sanctuaries were actually termed
suppliants; see e.g. R. Herzog, *Die Wunderheilungen von Epidauros* (Leipzig, 1931), 9 ff.
[26] P. *Oxy.* 18. 2165 fr. 1 col. II 9–32.
[27] Hdt. 3. 48.

Greek sanctuaries giving us more definite information about this question. There is an inscription from the Demeter and Apollo sanctuary in Andania, Messenia, dating to 92 BC, in which the organization of the cult ceremonies is regulated to the last detail. One of the sections pertains specifically to suppliants living in the sanctuary—which is, by the way, an uncommonly strong indication that suppliants continually stayed in sanctuaries. The rule is laid down that participants in the cult and suppliants are to be separated for the duration of the cult festival (celebration of mysteries!). We may infer that for the rest of the time pilgrims and suppliants were sharing the living quarters of the sanctuary.[28] One may infer from an inscription from the Heraion on Samos that the suppliants—except those who were slaves—are allowed to frequent the eating places and lodgings in the sanctuary and even to accept temporary employment.[29]

This information leads us to the further question, where exactly inside the sanctuary were all of these long-term guests living? We do not need to consider the suppliants alone. We can now say that it is a matter of the infrastructure for taking care of all the pilgrims living for longer periods in the sanctuaries.

An extensively excavated sanctuary such as Olympia lends itself particularly well to an investigation of the arrangements for lodging and feeding cult participants. Guest houses, bath installations and even shops have been cleared right around the Altis at some distance from the temple and altar (Fig. 5). In most of the literature about Olympia it is stated that these structures lay outside the sacred precinct. But this formulation is not correct. We are able to state this with such certainty because we have an authentic testimonium about the sacred territory in Olympia. The poet Pindar, in one of his victory odes, recounts the legend of how Herakles founded the sanctuary.[30] Herakles first marked the bounds of the smaller sacred precinct. Pindar speaks of the 'Altis'. He is referring to the precinct, bounded by a low wall with a few entrances, where later the temples of Hera and Zeus were built, and where the treasuries and the masses of statues were erected. But a further passage in Pindar's text shows

[28] H. Sauppe, 'Die Mysterieninschrift aus Andania', Abhandlungen der königlichen Gesellschaft der Wissenschaften zu Göttingen, 7 (1859), 253, 265f.; LSCG 120ff. no. 65.
[29] Chr. Habicht, AM 87 (1972), 210ff.; G. Thür and H. Taeuber, Anzeiger der Österreichischen Akademie der Wissenschaften, 115 (1978), 205ff.
[30] Pind. Ol. 10. 42ff.

that the sacred area extended far beyond the area enclosed with a wall; marking off a large area destined for visitors to live in was part of the foundation ceremony. In Pindar's words 'and he set apart the plain right round as a resting-place for the banquet'.

Excavations in Olympia show that the land around the Altis was, in fact, used in this way. By the early seventh century at the latest, hundreds of wells had been dug, from which the visitors to the sanctuary could draw water (Fig. 4).[31] Household wares and bones were found in many of these wells, remains of the meals mentioned by Pindar. After a short period of use these wells were filled in and the dumped fillings contained a great number of votive offerings that had been discarded. This provides proof that the land around the Altis (first occupied by wells, later on by practical structures) was sacred, because according to Greek sacred law votive offerings were inalienable possessions of the divinity and even after they had been discarded could be deposited only inside the sanctuary.

The division into a smaller and larger precinct, as exemplified by Olympia, is an absolutely typical feature of Greek sanctuaries in general as may be demonstrated by a basic review of cult sites everywhere. As a rule the inner precinct with the altar, a temple (if there is one) and votive offerings is separated off from the outer precinct. This can be achieved by means of a low wall, as in the case of Olympia, or by a large artificial terrace, as in the case of the sanctuary of Aphaia on Aigina (Fig. 6).[32] As a rule one took advantage of the natural terrain to separate the two areas, siting the sacred centre at the top or on the slope of a hill with the larger area spreading out below. The Zeus sanctuary on Mt Lykaion is an outstanding example. The place of sacrifice is on the second highest peak of Lykaion, 1400 m. high, while the subsidiary sacred structures, including the facilities for the athletic contests, are located on a highland plateau 200 m. below. Strabo's description of the Apollo sanctuary at Actium also fits into this scheme: the temple stands on a hill; down below in the plain is a grove with all facilities for conducting the sacred contests held in Actium.[33] A variant of this

---

[31] A. Mallwitz, 'Cult and Competition at Olympia', in *The Archaeology of the Olympics*, Wisconsin Studies in Classics (Los Angeles, 1988), 79 ff.

[32] U. Sinn, 'Der Kult der Aphaia auf Aegina', in R. Hägg, N. Marinatos, and G. C. Nordquist (eds.), *Early Greek Cult Practice. Proceedings of the Fifth International Symposium at the Swedish Institute at Athens (26–29 June, 1986)* (Stockholm, 1988), 154 ff.

[33] Strabo 7. 7. 6, p. 325.

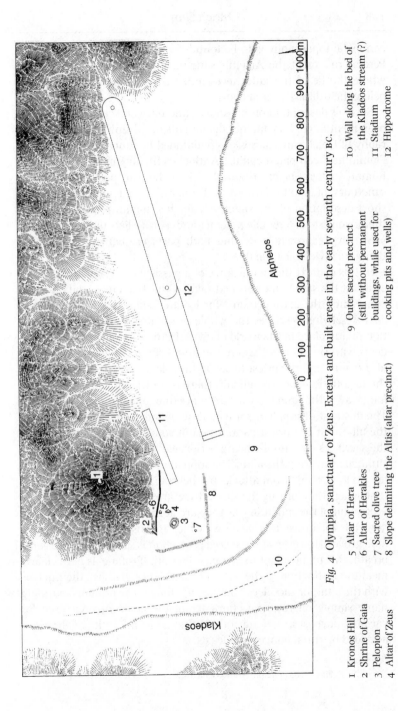

Fig. 4 Olympia, sanctuary of Zeus. Extent and built areas in the early seventh century BC.

1 Kronos Hill
2 Shrine of Gaia
3 Pelopion
4 Altar of Zeus

5 Altar of Hera
6 Altar of Herakles
7 Sacred olive tree
8 Slope delimiting the Altis (altar precinct)

9 Outer sacred precinct
  (still without permanent
  buildings, while used for
  cooking pits and wells)

10 Wall along the bed of
   the Kladeos stream (?)
11 Stadium
12 Hippodrome

canonical topography is to be found, for example, at the Heraion at Perachora[34] or at the Artemis sanctuary in Arcadian Orchomenos where the lie of the land necessitated placing the temple precinct below the utilitarian area above.

Strabo's description of the Apollo sanctuary at Actium has already been mentioned. Livy further documents our definition of the topography of Greek sanctuaries as conditioned by function: in reporting Flamininus' campaign against Antiochos III, Livy mentions how the Roman soldiers, before the outbreak of the war, paid a visit to the sanctuary of Apollo (Delion) at Tanagra.[35] In passing, Livy gives a short description of the sanctuary for his Roman readers and says that it consists of a temple precinct and a grove like all Greek sanctuaries. Livy expressly adds that both parts are equally sacred and therefore inviolable (asyla).

In this context the significance of a passage in Aeschylus becomes clear. At the same time this text takes us back to our initial question concerning the arrangements for lodging suppliants. In the Suppliants Aeschylus describes the whole procedure of requesting protection taking place in the world of myth. In the course of events he also deals with the moment where the initial rite of hiketeia is performed at the altar and the priest takes up his role as intermediary. Because the negotiations are so difficult, there is no way of getting around a long stay in the sanctuary for the more than one hundred suppliants. The mistrustful suppliants are loath to abandon their secure place at the altar, but the priest cannot permit something so detrimental to the sacrifices continually being performed. He sends them to a grove situated away from the altar. The suppliants are afraid that there they are no longer safe from attacks by their pursuers; the priest explains that when they are in the grove they are just as much under the protection of the sanctuary as they are at the altar. Aeschylus in line 509 calls the grove 'bebēlon alsos', which means something like 'profane grove'. However, since sacred protection is spoken of in the same breath, this name is not to be taken literally. 'Profane' is here clearly meant in distinction to the 'Holy of Holies' (hieron alsos), the nucleus with the altar for sacrifices and the cult image. The profane-sounding name simply mirrors the character of the adjacent area used for various purposes, among other things joyful cult celebrations attended by ritual dances and feasts.

[34] Sinn, Perachora, pl. 11 and Beilage 4.   [35] Livy 35. 51. 1–4.

These subsidiary areas had an infrastructure with a water supply and either permanent structures or simply shady places for temporary shelters, that is, huts made of branches or tents. Thus all Greek sanctuaries, with their subsidiary areas indispensable for cult requirements, were in a position to put up large numbers of cult participants—and therefore suppliants too—for a long period of time on sacred ground (Figs. 4, 5, 7, 9, 10). The protective function of Greek sanctuaries was not associated with any one particular divinity. As guarantor of the concept, Zeus was accorded the epithet 'hikesios', just as he guarded the rights of guest-friendship as Zeus Xenios and the validity of an oath as Zeus Horkios. In Greece there were no sanctuaries which were specifically sanctuaries for asylum, in contradistinction to the practices of the Jews and Egyptians.[36] The rite of hiketeia could be performed in any sanctuary, no matter what kind of sanctuary it was or to whom it was dedicated. The right and the duty of extending protection was valid for all sanctuaries without distinction. As the result of bitter lessons, however, suppliants always attempted, if they had the time, to reach sanctuaries they trusted. The effort to choose a sanctuary which would favour the best possible mediation by priests is a recurring theme in drama. One preference shows up clearly: if at all feasible the suppliants turned to the main sanctuaries of the towns or districts.

It is easy to make out the reasons for this preference. The psychological factors should not be underrated: the aversion encountered by the suppliants in the sanctuaries has already been described. The risk of being rejected was much lower in the larger sanctuaries. For one thing there was a certain awareness of what went on in these well-frequented cult centres making it less easy for a priest to avoid fulfilling his responsibilities. An observation in Euripides' Heraclidae (44) indicates that the presence of other visitors to the sanctuary was reassuring. In Oedipus Coloneus (47 f.) Sophocles suggests that in a

---

[36] For the regulated right of asylum among the Jews, see L. Fuld, 'Das Asylrecht in Alterthum und Mittelalter', Zeitschrift für vergleichende Rechtswissenschaft, 7 (1887), 102 ff.; M. Siebold, Das Asylrecht der römischen Kirche mit besonderer Berücksichtigung seiner Entwicklung auf germanischem Boden, Universitas-Archiv, Historische Abteilung, Band 4 (1930), 9 ff.
For the right of asylum in Egypt in which the government played a role, see F. v. Woess, Das Asylrecht Ägyptens in der Ptolemäerzeit und die spätere Entwicklung, Münchner Beiträge zur Papyrusforschung und antiken Rechtsgeschichte, 5 (Munich, 1923); L. Wenger, 'Asylrecht', in Reallexikon für Antike und Christentum, i (1950), 838 ff.

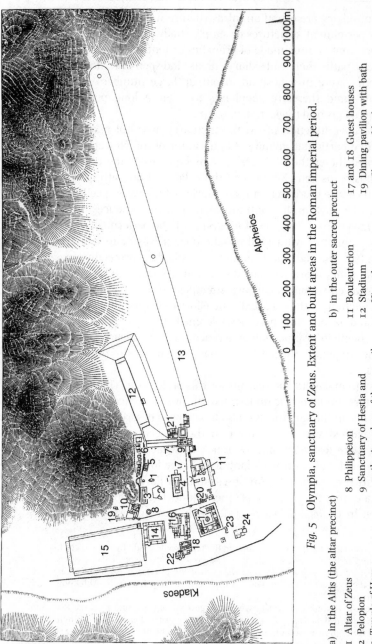

Fig. 5   Olympia, sanctuary of Zeus. Extent and built areas in the Roman imperial period.

a) in the Altis (the altar precinct)

1 Altar of Zeus
2 Pelopion
3 Temple of Hera
4 Temple of Zeus
5 Temple of Meter
6 Terrace of the treasuries
7 Statue bases
8 Philippeion
9 Sanctuary of Hestia and
 gathering place of the council
 ('Prytaneion')
10 Sanctuary of Hestia and
 Prytaneion in Roman
 times

b) in the outer sacred precinct

11 Bouleuterion
12 Stadium
13 Hippodrome
14 Palaestra
15 Gymnasium
16 Building for the
 administration
 of the sanctuary

17 and 18 Guest houses
19 Dining pavilion with bath
20 Shops and bath
21 Multi-purpose complex with meeting-
 hall, dining rooms and baths
22 and 23 Baths
24 Club building of athletes (?)

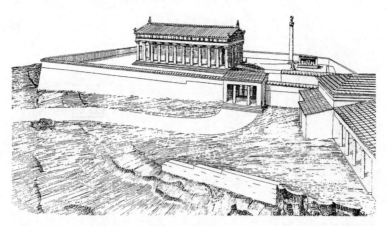

Fig. 6 Aigina, sanctuary of Aphaia. View of the separate temple precinct on the podium.

small sanctuary not frequented by the public it could easily happen that a suppliant could be driven out of the precinct.

The religious centre of a town or region offered the further advantage, especially for a political fugitive, that the priest was backed up by the authority of a whole town or even a whole district. The demand of a political opponent, coupled with threats, to surrender a suppliant would have less effect. We encounter this argument too in Classical drama.[37]

The chief sanctuaries of the towns and districts, where a large general public regularly came together for common cult ceremonies, offered much more favourable conditions for a stay lasting some length of time. The areas set aside for the convenience of visitors in these religious centres were more extensive, the infrastructure was doubtless of a higher standard in respect to hygiene and maintenance. But this consideration is still not sufficient to explain why the suppliants were so powerfully drawn to the main sanctuaries.

One turns to consider the known phenomenon that the main sanctuaries of a town or region were often situated far outside the inhabited areas. One may profitably enquire if there may not be some causal connection between the site of a sanctuary and its function as

---

[37] e.g. in the *Suppliants* of Aeschylus and in the *Heraclidae* of Euripides.

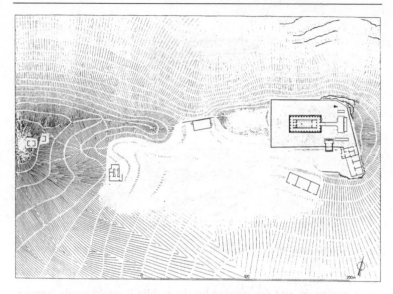

Fig. 7 Aigina, sanctuary of Aphaia. Ground plan of the sanctuary.
Dotted: the temple precinct; white: the outer precinct.

Fig. 8 Perachora. View of the Perachora peninsula from the east, with the
sacred precinct on the rocky spur at the tip.

a place of asylum. Of course one has to take into consideration the fact that within the settlements there would have scarcely been enough land available for the necessarily extensive subsidiary areas of the religious centres. But if a question of space were the only reason for siting the sanctuaries outside of the settlements, the distance between town and sanctuary need not have been so great as it actually is in most cases. It is not only a question of measurable distance. The geographical placement of many of these sanctuaries is striking: they are sited on particularly exposed spots remarkably often.

The sanctuary of the Messenian League is sited on the edge of the Messenian plain on the steep ridge of Ithome 700 m. high. The Arcadians had their joint sanctuary at an even more remote place on the peak of Mt Lykaion 1400 m. high. The inhabitants of the Epidaurian region gathered together for the common cult ceremonies in the sanctuary of Apollo Maleatas far inland on the edge of a highland plain enclosed by mountains far inland. The temple of Apollo at Bassae in its oft-mentioned mysterious lonely mountain setting belongs in this category. The main sanctuary in Phigalia, just as in the case of so many other regional cult centres, is sited on the highest mountain of the region—and occupies the whole peak.[38]

The exposed position of these sanctuaries was an advantage with regard to their function as potential places of asylum, as the example of the sanctuary of Apollo at Thermon (Fig. 9) clearly indicates. The historian Polybius has some very suggestive observations to make concerning the sanctuary of the Aetolian League.[39] He emphasizes the fact that the site of this sacred precinct is on a highland plain enclosed by mountains and difficult of access and describes this as the ideal place for a sanctuary under whose protection the inhabitants of a large region come together for their religious festivals, their political gatherings, and their annual trade fair. Polybius explicitly states that in times of war the Aetolians were accustomed to deposit their personal belongings and a supply of food in houses maintained in their so well protected league sanctuary. Because the site served a protective function, the sanctuary of the Aetolian League was also called 'the Acropolis of all Aetolia'.

For the same reasons sanctuaries were sited at the tip of capes or

[38] The author is preparing a full treatment of the geographical position and the topography of these and other sanctuaries under the title: 'Die griechischen Heiligtümer, Funktion—Organisation—Topographie.'

[39] Polyb. 5. 7–8.

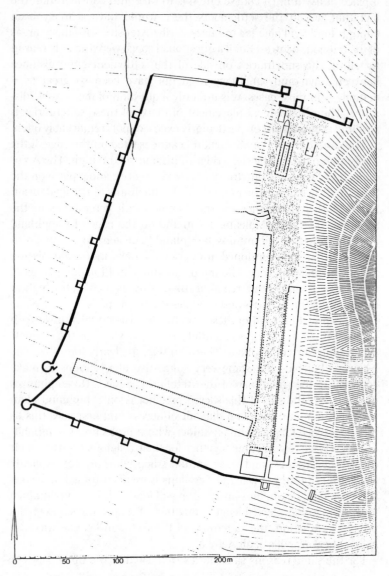

Fig. 9 Plan of the fortified sanctuary of Apollo at Thermon.
Dotted: the temple precinct; white: the outer precinct.

peninsulas or on an island close to the mainland. For example, the sanctuary of Poseidon at Cape Taenaron (the religious centre of the Laconian helots) or the sanctuary of Athena and Poseidon at Cape Sounion (Fig. 10), which had had the descriptive name of 'holy land's end of Attica' since the time of Homer.[40] The island of Kalaureia with its sanctuary of Poseidon, highly esteemed by all the Greeks as a place of asylum, lies directly off the coast of Troizen.[41]

Just as information about Thermon demonstrates that sanctuaries in out-of-the-way hill districts are specially well suited as places of asylum, so testimonia on the sanctuary of Hera at Perachora (Fig. 8) provide striking information about sanctuaries at the ends of capes being specially suitable for guaranteeing protection. Xenophon reports that in times of danger the inhabitants of the entire peninsula of Perachora were accustomed to hasten to the sanctuary on the cape.[42] On these occasions they even drove all of their flocks into the sanctuary. This was nothing unusual in an agrarian region. In times of danger, the inhabitants of the Chelmos region in Arcadia used to drive their flocks, their most valuable possessions, into the sanctuary of Artemis at Lusoi. During their stay there the animals, like the suppliants, belonged to the god.[43] Xenophon's report on how the Heraion at Perachora was used is so important for our investigation because excavations have made it possible to show what additional practical arrangements were made in a sanctuary so that it could serve as a place of refuge. Extensive subterranean cisterns and wells were installed in order to provide men and animals with water. In addition some houses were constructed here, as in Thermon, either as storerooms for food supplies or as lodgings for people who could not be expected to live out in the open or in temporary dwellings.

The living arrangements that are comparatively well attested at Thermon and Perachora may reasonably be assumed to have existed at those sites where the historical sources inform us that protection

[40] Hom. *Od.* 3. 278 ff. On the names of the cult precincts and for the topography of sacred territory on Cape Sounion, see U. Sinn, 'Sunion. Das befestigte Heiligtum der Athena und des Poseidon an der "Heiligen Landspitze Attikas"', *Antike Welt*, 23 (1992), 175 ff.

[41] Strabo 8. 6. 14.

[42] Xen. *Hell.* 4. 5.

[43] Polyb. 4. 18. 10–12, 4. 19. 4. On this topic, see U. Sinn, 'The "Sacred Herd" of Artemis at Lusoi', in R. Hägg (ed.), *The Iconography of Greek Cult in the Archaic and Classical Periods*, Proceedings of the First International Seminar on Ancient Greek Cult, organized by the Swedish Institute at Athens and the European Cultural Centre of Delphi (Delphi 16–18 Nov. 1990). Kernos, Suppl. 1 (Liège, 1992), 177 ff.

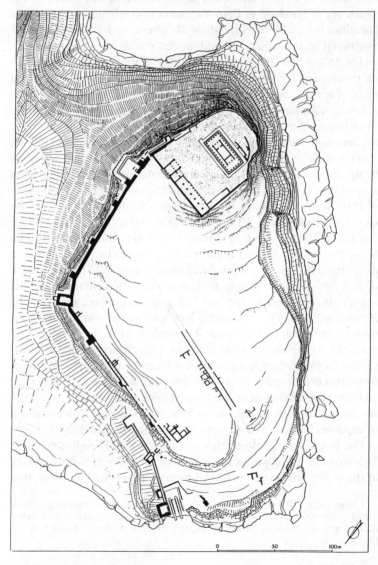

Fig. 10 Plan of the fortified Athena–Poseidon sanctuary at Cape Sounion.
Dotted: the temple precinct; white: the outer precinct.

was extended on a large scale. Without such living arrangements it would not have been possible for thousands of Messenians to hold out as suppliants in the sanctuary of Zeus on Ithome in the 460s BC until they finally obtained safe conduct to their new home at Naupactus.[44] A few years earlier the sacred precinct on Mt Lykaion had served as a collecting point for the inhabitants who had been driven out of the town of Ira and who were distributed among various localities in Arcadia from there.[45] In the early fifth century BC, when the people of Phigalia decided to abandon their town in the face of Laconian superior power, they doubtless took this decision knowing that they could temporarily settle in their cult centre on Mt Kotilion.[46]

It surely would not be right to consider the exposed position of these sanctuaries as a measure adopted for strategic reasons. The unassailable sanctuary of Zeus on Ithome is certainly an exception. If religious awe no longer acted as a deterrent, then geographical isolation would not hinder a determined opponent from attacking sacred land. Not even if the sanctuaries were enclosed within fortification walls, as for example on the Acropolis of Athens, the sanctuary of Apollo at Thermon (Fig. 9), the Athena-Poseidon sanctuary at Sounion (Fig. 10), or at the Demeter sanctuary at Lepreon. But as long as one had it in one's power to choose the site where people would come together to practise the rites of a cult, then why not consider the conditions under which the site could function as effectively as possible as a place of refuge?

In reading the literary sources, one becomes aware of a further reason for the often very sharp separation of inhabited areas from sacred places of refuge: there is a passage in Thucydides' history where no attempt is made to conceal the strong sense of unease aroused by the presence of politically motivated suppliants in a sanctuary in the midst of a town.[47] The scene is set in the town of Corcyra which was plagued by an intense civil war in the 420s BC. While

[44] Thuc. 1. 101–3; Diod. Sic. 11. 84. 8; Paus. 3. 11. 8, 4. 24. 7. For the historical event, see F. E. Adcock, *Thucydides and His History* (1963), 123 f.; H. Bengtson, *Die Staatsverträge des Altertums*, ii (Munich, 1982), 138.

[45] Paus. 4. 6 ff. For the sources used by Pausanias in his treatment of the Messenian Wars, see L. Pearson, 'The Pseudo-history of Messenia and its Authors', *Historia*, 11 (1962), 397 ff.

[46] Paus. 8. 39. 3 f.; also F. Cooper, *The Temple of Apollo at Bassai* (New York and London, 1978), 17 ff.

[47] Thuc. 3. 75. 5–81. 3.

the balance of power was constantly shifting back and forth, the democrats on one occasion got the upper hand and the whole group of oligarchs, more than four hundred fighting men, removed themselves to the sanctuary of Hera in the middle of the town. The democrats saw danger in having their enemy concentrated in a small space in the centre of town. They were afraid that the oligarchs could use the sanctuary as the basis of operations for a military counteroffensive (as had actually occurred at that time in the Delion near Tanagra![48]). So the Corcyrans declared themselves ready to make allowances for the suppliants on condition that they would transfer the site of their *hiketeia* to a place outside the town. The suppliants were then interned on one of the islands lying in front of the town. If a sacred precinct was not available, a suitable substitute was created.

Several Spartan kings driven out of office owed their survival to the fact that they avoided the sanctuaries inside the town and instead chose a distant sanctuary as the place for their *hiketeia*: Leotychides II[49] and Pausanias II[50] in Tegea, Kleombrotos II at Cape Tainaron,[51] and Pleistoanax at Mt Lykaion.[52] King Agis behaved differently.[53] He did not give up his political ambitions and ostentatiously remained in the sanctuary of Athena in the town, thus arousing the mistrust of the new rulers. So he courted his own fate, he was tricked by an extremely sophisticated ruse and met his death.

The Greek towns were repeatedly confronted with the situation in which members of the political opposition came over to their side. On the one hand this was welcomed because it meant that the opponent was weakened. On the other hand the presence of such suppliants attracted the opponents like a magnet, possibly leading them to take revenge on the town sheltering the suppliants. In these circumstances it was understandable that the town-dwellers would be easier in their minds if a suitable place for *hiketeia* could be found far removed from where they lived. This is what the Athenians did in the early fifth century BC when an uprising which they had masterminded on the island of Aegina collapsed. The Athenians of course provided their Aeginetan collaborators with a place of refuge

---

[48] Thuc. 4. 97 f.
[49] Hdt. 6. 72; Paus. 3. 7. 9 f.
[50] Xen., *Hell.* 3. 5. 25; Strabo 8. 5; Diod. Sic. 14. 89. 1; Paus. 3. 7.
[51] Plut. *Agis* 16–18.
[52] Thuc. 2. 21. 1, 5. 16. 3; Plut. *Per.* 22. 3.
[53] Plut. *Agis* 16–21. 2.

—but not in Athens. They sent the fugitives out into the Attic countryside to a place which was as far away from Athens as possible: Sounion.[54]

Herodotus uses the simile that suppliants are naturally to be found in sanctuaries, just as birds are accustomed to make their nests there.[55] Later on Aelian[56] recorded a very popular fable in which the idea of sacred immunity was transferred to the animal world: there were safety zones in the woods which provided absolute security. Once one was inside the boundary the pursuers came to an abrupt halt and the hounds were thrown off the scent. In the middle of these safety zones everything was arranged most satisfactorily for the animals.

The image used by Herodotus and the parable handed down by Aelian both arose from efforts to create more respect for the institution of sacred immunity. But when one plucks these ancient testimonia out of their contexts, they reinforce the notion that is nowadays so popular, to the effect that Greek sanctuaries were retreats where peaceful quiet and greatest harmony reigned—a notion that naturally springs to mind over and over again when one visits the sites of the once heavily frequented places of refuge on capes washed by the waves of the sea, or in quiet bays or in remote mountain landscapes. This point of view so charged with emotion hardly does justice to the true significance of the Greek sanctuaries: the sacred precincts lead us straight into the everyday world of the Greeks. The very existence of these sacred precincts with their specific rights was what made it possible for the Greeks to master the crises of daily life with its private needs and general hazards.

(Translated by Judith Binder)

---

[54] Hdt. 6. 90.   [55] Hdt. 1. 159. 3.   [56] Ael. NA 11. 6.

8

The Archaeology of the Hero

ANTHONY SNODGRASS

My excuse for returning to a well-worn theme is a certain uneasiness about previous work by archaeologists (myself included) on the subject of hero-worship in early Greece. Nearly a century ago, the foundations of our understanding were laid in Erwin Rohde's *Psyche*,[1] a work of many profound insights, some of which have been overlooked or forgotten in more recent scholarship. Rohde saw the ambiguities in the Greek use of the word *hērōs*; he deduced that, in its earliest and profoundest form, hero-worship must have originated as a form of ancestor-worship; he proved that that earliest form was much older than Homer; and he referred it to 'that remote period which is obscured for us by the intervening mass of the Homeric poems'.[2]

Perhaps no one who accuses Homer of 'obscuring' the earlier past can expect his view to prevail for long in Classical studies. Certainly, few archaeologists have taken their cue from Rohde; and the twentieth century has seen the Golden Age of Homeric fundamentalism, thanks mainly to the discoveries of Schliemann. Nowhere was this faith more warmly cherished than among English-speaking scholars. In 1921 appeared L. R. Farnell's *Greek Hero Cults*,[3] a work which placed the Homeric Epic at the centre of its subject. Meanwhile, more by accident than anything else, it was British scholars who were making the discoveries that seemed to support Farnell's case. At the Menelaion near Sparta, they excavated from 1909 the shrine of the heroized Menelaos and Helen; at the Cave of Polis on Ithaka, in 1930, they discovered offerings inscribed as dedications to Odysseus; at a location outside Mycenae, in 1950, they excavated a shrine with

---

[1] *Psyche: Seelencult und Unsterblichkeitsglaube der Griechen* (Freiburg and Leipzig, 1894).

[2] Ibid. 13 (Eng. trans. by W. B. Hillis, London, 1925, 11).

[3] *Greek Hero Cults and Ideas of Immortality* (Oxford, 1921).

dedications naming Agamemnon. Here was a series of major figures from the *Iliad*, proved by archaeology to have been worshipped by the Greeks, and worshipped apparently from an early date. Small wonder that, when the archaeologists (still mainly my fellow-countrymen!) began to produce syntheses of this material evidence, they built their hypotheses round Farnell's work, from John Cook's paper of 1953[4] to Nicolas Coldstream's of 1976.[5]

Of course, since as early as the 1870s, other kinds of archaeological evidence besides the cults of 'Homeric' heroes had begun to be available. These finds were 'archaeological' in a second sense too, in that they showed the ancient Greeks themselves to have practised a kind of archaeology, largely independent of texts. When Schliemann found an Archaic inscription 'I am the Hero's' at one of his Shaft Graves at Mycenae,[6] or when Lolling discovered Geometric and later pottery in the *dromos* of the tholos tomb that he excavated at Menidhi near Athens,[7] the chronology of early Greece was too dimly understood for the exact significance of the finds to be appreciated. Only two generations later, when Carl Blegen found and interpreted a whole series of such cults in the Mycenaean cemetery at Prosymna,[8] was the phenomenon accurately described. By showing that a period of several centuries had elapsed between the last burial in each tomb and the beginning of cult, Blegen proved that there was no question of the immediate descendants having honoured a newly-deceased member of the family. On the contrary, the tombs must have been discovered in antiquity in much the same way as they are sometimes found today, through the collapse of the chamber roof, or as a chance result of agricultural operations. The discoverers can have had no genuine affinity to the prehistoric dead, and can only have guessed at their identity; no wonder that they used anonymous appellations like 'the Hero'. But one consistent feature of the majority of cases was that the beginning of cult belonged to the later eighth century BC— just late enough to be claimed as a manifestation of the influence of the Homeric Epic.

---

[4] 'The Cult of Agamemnon at Mycenae', in *Geras A. Keramopoullou* (Athens, 1953), 112–18.

[5] 'Hero-cults in the Age of Homer', *JHS* 96 (1976), 8–17.

[6] H. Schliemann, *Mycenae* (London, 1978), 115; L. H. Jeffery, *The Local Scripts of Archaic Greece* (Oxford, 1961), 174 no. 6.

[7] H. G. Lolling *et al.*, *Das Kuppelgrab bei Menidi* (Athens, 1880), 5 and 49; P. Wolters, 'Vasen aus Menidi, II', in *JdI* 14 (1899), 103–35.

[8] 'Post-Mycenaean Deposits in Chamber Tombs', in *ArchEph* 1937, i. 377–90.

182 Anthony Snodgrass

But with a subject like this, which involves the behaviour of ordinary people over a long period, it is preferable to look beyond literature to something more fundamental: the language itself. If we turn to the lexicon for enlightenment, we at once remind ourselves that the word *hērōs* had, if not two separate meanings, at any rate two separate contexts of use. The commoner of the two was the use of 'hero' to denote a person who was once alive but has become heroized *only* through death; who is honoured by sacrifice and cult, specifically at his grave where his power is felt to be located; and whose repute and influence are normally confined to the region near the grave, which is a fixed dwelling-place after death. In this sense, 'hero' makes countless appearances in literary (especially prose) and epigraphic documents. But this is *not* the normal sense of the word in Homer and Hesiod, and the lexicon will therefore probably give this not as the primary but as the secondary meaning, 'meaning (b)'. What then is 'meaning (a)'? It is the sense familiar to every reader of Homer, for whom a 'hero' is a hero already in his lifetime; the word is used as a kind of title, awarded not only to warrior and king but (at least in the *Odyssey*) to free men of varied estate. Meaning (a) is further distinguished from meaning (b) in that Homer does not often show the hero being worshipped after death, at his grave or anywhere else. This is no surprise, if his spirit is located not there, but far away in the Underworld, where it cannot easily act as a local force and a local presence. In later centuries, this meaning (a) for *hērōs* becomes less common, occurring mainly in poetic contexts where the setting is the epoch of Homer's 'living heroes'. A subtle example of the avoidance of meaning (a) is Aristophanes' treatment of the warrior Lamachos: in his lifetime, he is called by unflattering names in the *Acharnians* and *Peace*; after his death, he becomes *Lamachos hērōs*, in the sense of meaning (b).[9]

Most of this was set out long ago by Rohde, and his insights have been revived in two important recent discussions by Martin West[10] and Gregory Nagy.[11] Nagy has stressed the possibilities of reconciliation between the two meanings discussed above, or at least between

[9] *Frogs* 1039. The subtlety lies in the fact that a mocking allusion to 'meaning (a)' may be conveyed by the Homeric metre of the line, as A. C. Cassio kindly pointed out to me.
[10] M. L. West (ed.), *Hesiod: the Works and Days* (Oxford, 1978), esp. pp. 186, 190–1, 370–3.
[11] G. Nagy, *The Best of the Achaeans* (Baltimore, 1979), esp. 114–17, 159–61.

the beliefs that lay behind them and the practices to which these beliefs gave rise. Of course the Greeks could have combined the use of both senses in the same living language; but the probable truth is that this awkwardness only briefly arose. Meaning (a) seems to have passed out of normal speech fairly quickly after the time of Homer (or so West has argued from its rather indiscriminate uses in the *Odyssey*). West further suggests that meaning (b) *for the specific word hērōs* could have grown out of the poetic use of meaning (a). But this does not mean that the beliefs and practices associated with meaning (b) were not by far the older: it merely implies that such early beliefs and practices were coupled with other names and terms for the hero-ized dead. Rohde's conclusion has been generally accepted, that the worship of the 'mortal gods', as Hesiod paradoxically called them, was much older than the lifetime of Homer or Hesiod; both poets betray some familiarity with the idea, Hesiod explicitly and Homer by a few almost surreptitious acknowledgments. But they use other words than *hērōes—hēmitheoi* or *daimones*—for the recipients of these honours.

The case may be illuminated by taking up the familiar parallel between the Greek heroes and the saints of early Christendom. Let us imagine that some important body of early Christian literature, such as the Arthurian legends, had habitually used the word 'saint', rather than 'knight', for the main male actors in the narra-tive. It would then be relatively easy for archaeologists and other scholars to discern that 'St Lancelot' or 'St Tristram' had not enjoyed the same status in Christian worship as the conventional body of saints—had not, for example, had churches or shrines dedicated to them. They would soon realize that this literary usage had been a temporary, perhaps a localized one, and recognize it as a distraction from the study of the 'real' saints and their associated monuments. For Greek archaeology, a similar lesson could be applied. Homer's 'living heroes' may have literary pride of place, enabling them to generate that revival which, in many modern languages, allows the colloquial (or in the Soviet Union the official) use of 'hero' in a similar sense. But when it comes to the actual behaviour of ancient Greeks, the 'heroes' of this sense should be seen as a distraction from the older, more enduring, and more geo-graphically widespread use of the word in the religious context of heroization after death.

Now that geography has been mentioned, I should say a little more about it. It is of course true that, in the full Classical period, 'hero' in the sense of meaning (b) was in use wherever Greek was spoken, including Ionia and the colonies. But what was the position in the early stages when, as we have seen, other words may have been preferred to *hērōs*, but where similar beliefs and practices were, beyond doubt, already widespread? How widely, in this same period, was 'hero' accepted in its Homeric sense (meaning (a))? To answer the first question, we shall turn in a moment to archaeology. To answer the second, we may choose to adopt a tentative suggestion of West's, following an even more tentative hint by Rohde. This is, that the 'living hero' was a speciality of Ionian Epic, and as such may have been at first confined, as a usage, to Ionia. Such a state of affairs can have existed only very early on, since by Hesiod's time it had already spread to Boeotia—as is proved by the insertion, in the *Works and Days*, of an 'Age of Heroes' into the traditional sequence of the four 'metallic' ages. The very awkwardness of this insertion has suggested to many scholars that the idea was a new, perhaps extraneous, importation. Another interesting thing about the context in the *Works and Days* is that, in this same passage and a very few lines earlier, Hesiod had indicated his familiarity with the traditional practice of treating the dead of a bygone age as 'spirits of the underworld', in his description of the men of the Golden, and especially of the Silver Age. It is exactly this practice that Rohde held to be the origin of hero-worship.

Is it possible that, before Hesiod, the worship of the transfigured dead was the *only* form of direct contact with the heroic past on the Greek mainland? That it was the advent of the Ionian Epic which brought for the first time the idea of the 'living hero' (together, perhaps, with the word *hērōs* itself) into the consciousness of people there? If so, this would have important consequences for our understanding of the archaeology of this early epoch (and indeed for its art, with which I do not propose to deal here). But in recent years this topic has been studied, at least by the Anglo-Saxon archaeologists, always with an eye on the Epic. We have forgotten Rohde, and instead concentrated on L.R. Farnell's Epic-centred version of Greek hero worship. Let us instead return to the subject with an eye on the older practice of the worship of ancestors and chthonic spirits.

In the past decade or so, the evidence from mainland Greece has become relatively familiar, thanks to the treatment of it by (among others) Nicolas Coldstream,[12] Claude Bérard,[13] and François de Polignac;[14] while a new view of the importance of the colonial evidence has emerged in Irad Malkin's *Religion and Colonization in Ancient Greece*.[15] The best-attested practice is the institution of cults at Bronze Age tombs. From soon after the middle of the eighth century BC, this appears in several (but not all) districts of the Greek mainland; rarely in the islands; not at all in Ionia. That distribution is suggestive, for it at once hints at just such a geographical division as was suggested a moment ago. Since there are no inscribed dedications of this earliest phase, we cannot prove the identity attributed to the prehistoric dead, but the circumstances make it almost certain that their importance was a local, or at most a regional one.

A further argument helps to distance these cults from the heroes of Epic. At the Ischia Colloquium over ten years ago, I drew attention to the fact that the *form* of burial in the prehistoric tombs where cult was installed contradicts, in almost every possible way, the burial-practices of Epic.[16] They are inhumations not cremations; multiple not single; in rock-cut chambers or tholoi, not under tumuli. This seems very hard to reconcile with the suggestion that the cult-practice was inspired by Epic, particularly when combined with the fact that these cults do not apparently occur in Ionia. The suggested dichotomy was followed up by Nagy in his book of 1979,[17] and especially by de Polignac in his of 1984,[18] to show that we are dealing here with a largely independent phenomenon, whose causes are not to be sought purely in the sudden popularity of the Ionian Epic.

There are very strong arguments, I now accept, for the view urged at Ischia by Bérard,[19] and in discussion by Vernant and others, that these causes have much to do with the rise of the *polis*, and that we are looking at the first stage in that glorification of the hero that was to become so central to the *polis* of Classical times. Malkin has indeed

[12] 'Hero-cults'.
[13] 'Récupérer la mort du prince: héroïsation et formation de la cité', in G. Gnoli and J.-P. Vernant (eds.), *La Mort, les morts dans les sociétés anciennes* (Cambridge, 1982), 89–105.
[14] *Naissance*, esp. 127–32.
[15] Malkin, *RC*.
[16] 'Les Origines du culte des héros dans la Grèce antique', in Gnoli and Vernant, *La Mort, les morts*, 107–19.
[17] *The Best of the Achaeans*.
[18] *Naissance*.
[19] See n. 13 above.

gone so far as to trace this practice to the worship of one particular kind of hero, the *oikistēs*, and one particular kind of *polis*, the colony. This takes us on to another and distinct topic which arises first from the archaeological evidence: the worship, not of the prehistoric, but of the recent dead.

Here there is evidence from Athens and Corinth, but the *locus classicus* must remain the case of the burials inside the West Gate at Eretria, so eloquently presented at Ischia by Claude Bérard. The fairly secure relative chronology at Eretria is not fully matched in the more spectacular case since discovered at Lefkandi[20]—more spectacular, because it dates from at least 250 years earlier, and involves a huge building. *If* the Lefkandi find is truly an instance of the institution of cult immediately after the burial of a prominent local figure, then its early date virtually assures us of a further point: this practice, as well as the worship of the prehistoric dead, must have evolved independently of the Ionian Epic. But until the doubts are resolved as to the interpretation of the Lefkandi building as a *hērōön*, it is safer not to rely on this argument.

A third practice attested by archaeology has been brought into the argument, notably by Malkin. It is the occurrence of exceptionally lavish or 'heroic' burial ceremonies for the newly-deceased. This is a phenomenon of wide, indeed partly of non-Greek, distribution in the eighth and seventh centuries BC and, yet again, Homeric influence has been very widely imputed to it. But I prefer to leave it out of the argument, because an extravagant burial is not the same thing as the institution of a lasting cult (and in any case Malkin's account of this particular phenomenon is not free of inaccuracies).[21]

We come now to the fourth and final practice which is thought to be attested in the archaeological record: the early institution of cults to the 'real', Homeric heroes—a fusion, so far as was possible, between the heroes of meaning (*a*) and those of meaning (*b*), by taking the personalities of the one and applying to them the treatment due to the other. But reservations are needed at two points. First, I qualified these cults as being 'thought to be attested', as an acknowledgment of François de Polignac's dissident view that the interpretation of these early instances has been mistaken.[22] He

---

[20] M. R. Popham, E. Touloupa, and L. H. Sackett, 'The Hero of Lefkandi', in *Antiquity*, 56 (1982), 169–74.

[21] *RC*, 261–6.

[22] *Naissance*, 130–1.

argues that the three best-known of these 'hero-cults', the Menelaion near Sparta, the Agamemnoneion near Mycenae, and the 'Cave of Odysseus' at Polis on Ithaka, were quite differently intended at the time of their foundation. At all three sites, a female presence is detectable before or alongside that of the hero. The typical 'Artemis-type' dedications at the Menelaion (to which we may now add the seventh- and sixth-century inscribed dedications to Helen, found in the excavations of the 1970s)[23] show that a 'Helen', who may be the deity long ago identified behind her persona, rather than the figure of the *Iliad*, had at least a share in the sanctuary at this early stage, and may have been in complete possession of it. The female figurines at the 'Agamemnoneion' have a similar message to convey, as have the inscriptions in the cave at Polis which mention the Nymphs, as well as Odysseus. Epigraphical proof of a connection with Menelaos, Agamemnon or Odysseus is not found until Classical or Hellenistic times. Some may say that this argument of de Polignac's is pressed too far; and account needs to be taken of other cases, such as the possible *hērōön* at Sounion of Phrontis, the steersman of Menelaos, where the offerings, such as they are, are both early and typically 'male'.[24] But it is right that the tenuousness of the evidence for these widely-accepted 'Homeric cults' should be brought out.

There is a second area where qualification is needed: the assimilation of the two kinds of hero could only be achieved 'so far as was possible'. For the equation with the grave-cults to be complete, the tomb of the hero should have been the centre of cult. The excavations at the Menelaion have shown that the initiators of the cult, whatever their successors professed, had not succeeded in locating a genuine prehistoric grave. The Agamemnon cult near Mycenae was not, and cannot have been presented as being, located at his tomb; nor of course could the cult in the Polis cave. At Sounion, no definite prehistoric grave has been identified. The whole suggestion of finding a grave, at least for the major heroes, may be irrelevant, since we know that they could be worshipped in two or more places at once (as was Agamemnon, at Amyklai as well as near Mycenae), and that their cults could also be transferred from one place to another. All

---

[23] H. W. Catling, 'Excavations at the Menelaion, Sparta, 1973–76', in *Archaeological Reports*, 23 (1976–7), 24–42, esp. 36–7, figs. 25–9.

[24] Ch. Picard, 'L'Héroön de Phrontis au Sunion', in *RA* 6th ser. (Jul.–Sept. 1940), 5–28; H. Abramson, 'A Hero Shrine for Phrontis at Sunion?', *California Studies in Classical Antiquity*, 12 (1979), 1–19.

this was presumably because these heroes were of more than local importance: they were Panhellenic property. Even if the sites at Sparta, Mycenae, and Sounion were genuine centres of hero-worship from the first, all three of them begin detectably later than the other practices that we have surveyed, and begin at a moment when it is easier to believe that the fame of the Ionian Epic had spread to all parts of the Greek world.

We may finally return for a moment to the cults at prehistoric graves, the prime category of archaeological evidence. Are they all susceptible of a similar explanation, wherever in Greece they occur? Hitherto, we have all tended to assume that they were, whatever our choice of explanation may have been. That view is about to be challenged in a paper by my former pupil James Whitley, forthcoming in the *Journal of Hellenic Studies* for 1988. He argues that the Argolid does indeed present a classic case of the employment of such cults to underline the territorial integrity of the emergent *polis*, and that both Argos and Mycenae used them in this way. But he claims that, for Attica, this interpretation fails. The cults are found only away from the city, and are mostly located in that small group of sites outside Athens where settlement had been established for several centuries before the eighth: Eleusis, Acharnai, Thorikos. He sees their purpose as having been not centripetal, as in the Argolid, but centrifugal: an attempt by the local aristocracies to support separatist claims, against the emergent *polis*, by stressing their association with the rural residences where they had been established for generations past.

But there remains a third area where these grave-cults are especially prominent: Messenia. It is the most difficult case to accommodate to any of the explanations offered for the cults, whether as instruments of *polis* demarcation, or as separatist gestures according to Whitley's view of Attica, or as markers for territorial claims by individual free landowners, according to my own original view. There is another distinctive feature about the Messenian cults: beginning at about the time of the Spartan conquest, they continue and indeed increase in frequency in Archaic and Classical times, more strongly than in the rest of Greece. If they were the work of the Spartan overlords, then it is strange that no such cults have been found on the territory of Lakonia itself. If they are private, or positively separatist, gestures, then it is surprising that the Spartans tolerated or overlooked them. I have no new explanation of the

Messenian cults to offer; but since they continue into the Classical
period, it is possible that one day a helpful inscription will be found
among the offerings in a new Mycenaean tomb.

The message of this paper is in any case a general, not a specific
one. It is that the phenomenon of the installation of cult at prehistoric tombs is to be understood in a way quite independent of the
influence of Homeric Epic, and that the other phenomena considered
here may also be less susceptible to this influence than we have come
to believe. The grave-cults were not directed at the prominent names
made famous by Homer; indeed, they were probably not directed at
named individuals at all, but at the anonymous members of an
alleged ancestral group; a group perhaps not even called by the term
hērōes at first; a group that was of interest only to the local community that claimed descent from them. Only in the other practices
that arose out of, or alongside, the prehistoric grave-cults may we
even tentatively see the incipient influence of Epic—the heroization
of recently deceased leaders like King Teleklos of Sparta,[25] or the
anonymous prince at Eretria, or the oikistai of the early colonies; and
perhaps some of the grandiose burial-rites at actual funerals. Eventually, of course, Homeric heroes did come to benefit from similar
honours, however questionable may be the earliest alleged instances
of this. But the popular understanding of the word hērōs in Classical
times is a sure pointer to the popular beliefs of an earlier age; and
these beliefs were at a level too deep to have been shaped by mere
literary influence.

ADDENDA

It is reassuring for the author to see this particular article, rather
infrequently cited in a subject heavily studied in recent years, reproduced in a more conspicuous place. In the dozen years since the
article went to press, a host of publications on the general themes of
ancestor-worship and tomb-cult have appeared, and I shall have to
be very selective in citing a few of them here.

By far the most comprehensive treatment has been Carla Antonaccio's An Archaeology of Ancestors: Tomb Cult and Hero Cult in Early

---

[25] Paus. 3. 15. 10.

Greece (Lanham, Md., 1995). Antonaccio takes a position fairly close to mine in this article, as is indeed already implied by her title. But other, more particular aspects of the field have also been interestingly taken further. Robin Hägg's paper 'Gifts to the Heroes in Geometric and Archaic Greece', in *Gifts*, 93–9, was not yet known to me when I wrote, and usefully broached the topic of the actual artefacts offered in hero-cult. An important new case-study from the Cyclades is V. K. Lambrinoudakis's paper, 'Veneration of Ancestors in Geometric Naxos', in R. Hägg, N. Marinatos, and G. Nordquist (eds.), *Early Greek Cult Practice* (*AIARS* 38, 1988), 235–46, modifying somewhat the sketchy geographical summary given on my pp. 184–5. Ian Morris, 'Tomb Cult and the "Greek Renaissance": The Past in the Present in the 8th Century BC', *Antiquity*, 62 (1988), 750–61, has emphasized the social versatility and complexity of the attested cults. Finally, the paper by James Whitley mentioned on my p. 188 duly appeared as 'Early States and Hero Cults: A Re-appraisal', in *JHS* 108 (1988), 173–82.

9

Votives and Votaries in Greek Sanctuaries

FOLKERT VAN STRATEN

In this paper I study Greek votive offerings of the Classical period (including some material that may be slightly earlier or later). I have not intentionally restricted myself to the Attic material, but there is probably a certain Attic bias in what follows, as a large proportion of the more interesting material happens to be from that area. The restriction to private votive offerings, however, is intentional.

In the first part we shall look into the placement and arrangement of votive offerings in Greek sanctuaries, basing ourselves on the monuments themselves, as we have them and as they were found. In the second part we shall attempt to view the ex votos through the eyes of the ancient worshippers. Finally, in the third section of the paper, we shall focus on the worshippers as they present themselves through their votive offerings.

I. PLACEMENT AND ARRANGEMENT OF VOTIVE OFFERINGS

The most common words in ancient Greek for 'votive offering' and 'setting up a votive offering in a sanctuary', *anathēma* and *anatithenai*, suggest that they were preferably placed at a certain height from the

The text of this article is substantially the same as that published in 1992, but I have taken the opportunity to add some references to recent publications; for votive offerings with representations of sacrifice I now refer to my *Hierà Kalá. Images of Animal Sacrifice in Archaic and Classical Greece*, Religions in the Graeco-Roman World 127 (Leiden 1995), esp. section 2.2. I am most grateful to Richard Buxton, who was kind enough to correct my English and who also contributed various other improvements. The abbreviations used in the notes are those of the *Archäologische Bibliographie*.

ground. They could be mounted on a pedestal, nailed to a wall, or suspended from the branches of a tree.

Various types of columns and pillars were used as support for votive offerings. Among the Archaic dedications from the Athenian Akropolis, which represent a fair sample, we find small pillars with rectangular or hexagonal cross sections,[1] fluted columns,[2] and smooth unfluted columns such as the one dedicated by Telesinos, which still preserves the bronze base plate of the statuette it once supported (probably a statuette of Athena of roughly the same type as the often illustrated dedication of Meleso).[3]

One particular type of pillar, however, which already occurred in the Archaic period, was to become the most common type of support for votive sculpture in Classical times.[4] It has a rectangular cross section, and tapers slightly from the bottom to the top, where there is a sort of rectangular capital, somewhat wider than the upper part of the shaft, from which it is offset by a concave moulding. A typical example is the votive offering of Lysikleides from the sanctuary of Themis at Rhamnous, dating from around 420 BC (Fig. 11).[5] It consists of a small marble statue of a youth—Lysikleides himself, one assumes—mounted on a pillar of the type just described. The dedication, as is often the case, is inscribed on the capital of the pillar.

Similar pillars were used to support votive reliefs. Some good examples of reliefs and pillars having survived together are the dedication of Xenokrateia found in Phaleron, and the double-relief from the same sanctuary.[6] In a few exceptional instances, relief and pillar were made of one piece. This is the case with an Athenian votive

---

[1] e.g. A. E. Raubitschek, *Dedications from the Athenian Akropolis* (Cambridge, Mass., 1949), no. 191, dedicated by Philea; no. 290, dedicated by Lyson.

[2] e.g. Raubitschek, *Dedications*, no. 10, dedicated by Epiteles.

[3] Raubitschek, *Dedications*, no. 40: Telesinos' dedication. The Athena statuette dedicated by Meleso is Athens NM 6447: A. De Ridder, *Catalogue des bronzes trouvés sur l'Acropole d' Athènes* (Paris, 1896), 312ff. no. 796; W. Lamb, *Greek and Roman Bronzes* (London, 1929), 144; H.G. Niemeyer, 'Attische Bronzestatuetten der spätarchaischen und frühklassischen Zeit', in *Antike Plastik*, iii (Berlin, 1964), 7–31, esp. 21 and pl. 11; C. Rolley, *The Bronzes*, Monumenta Graeca et Romana, v. 1 (Leiden, 1967), 4 no. 42; *IG* I² 426.

[4] Some late Archaic examples: Raubitschek, *Dedications*, no. 233, dedicated by Hierokleides; no. 294, dedicated by Euthydikos.

[5] V. Stais, *AEphem* (1891), 55 pl. 6; S. Karusu, 'Das "Mädchen vom Piräus"', *AM* 82 (1967), 158–69, esp. 160 and Beil. 89; B.Ch. Petrakos, *Prakt* (1976), 51 no. 3; *IG* I² 828.

[6] O. Walter, 'Die Reliefs aus dem Heiligtum der Echeliden in Neu-Phaleron', *AEphem* (1937) i. 97–119.

Fig. 11 Marble votive statue on pillar, from Rhamnous, sanctuary of Themis
(Athens NM 199)

relief dedicated to Zeus Philios by a club of *eranistai*[7] and a votive relief of the banquet type dedicated to the hero Bouthon and the heroine Eudosia.[8] Normally, however, the supporting pillar was made separately, and the votive relief was provided with a tenon which was inserted in a hole in the top of the pillar. This apparently was so much the usual technique that even one of the smallest marble votive reliefs found in the Athenian Agora, which is less than 10 cm. high and little more than 10 cm. wide, has a tenon for mounting it on a separate pedestal.[9] An unfortunate consequence of this practice of making votive sculpture and support of separate pieces is that only a small minority have survived together. In sanctuaries such as the Athenian Asklepieion or the sanctuary of Artemis in Brauron we can still see considerable clusters of pillars which have lost their votive offerings. Since they usually bear the votive inscriptions, they are largely confined to the epigraphical literature. Most of the votive statues and reliefs that we have, on the other hand, are now without their bases or pedestals, and without the inscriptional evidence these might have provided.

Some types of votive offerings naturally lent themselves to being nailed to a wall. An inventory-inscription from Delos mentions a temple key dedicated in the Artemision, and describes it as 'unweighed, because it is nailed to the wall.'[10] Small terracotta votive plaques, which were quite popular in some sanctuaries, were regularly hung on the wall or suspended from the branches of a tree (Fig. 15). They often are provided with suspension holes for that purpose. An early example (*c.* 700 BC) comes from Sounion and is decorated with a painting of a warship.[11] In Athens several painted votive

---

[7] Athens Epigr. Mus. 8783: J. N. Svoronos, *Das Athener Nationalmuseum* (Athens, 1908–1937), 668, pl. 219; O. Walter, 'Kniende Adoranten auf attischen Reliefs', *ÖJh* 13 Beibl. (1910), 229–44, fig. 143; F. T. van Straten, 'Did the Greeks Kneel Before their Gods?', *BABesch* 49 (1974), 164, fig. 7; *IG* II² 2935; dated at 324/3 BC.

[8] Present whereabouts unknown; it was seen at an Athenian art dealer's and a photograph was published in Πολέμων I (1929), 241; the inscription is *IG* II² 4591.

[9] Athens Agora Mus. S1939: E. Mitropoulou, *The Kneeling Worshipper in Votive Reliefs* (Birmingham, 1972), no. 20, fig. 18; van Straten, *BABesch* 49 (1974), 168 no. 10.

[10] *IDélos* 1444 Aa 47–8 (inventory of 141/0 BC): [– – – κλεῖδα] κλειδουχικὴν σιδηρᾶν ἔχουσαν προτόμην λέοντος ἀργυ[ρ]ᾶν [ἐφ᾽ ἧς ἐ]πιγραφή· | [– – – – – Στρατονίκη Ἀντιφῶντος ἐγ Μυρρινούτ]της ὑφιέρεια γενομένη, ἄστατον [διὰ] τὸ καθηλῶσθαι.

[11] Athens NM 14935: *AEphem* (1917), 209; J. Boardman, 'Painted Votive Plaques and an Early Inscription from Aegina', *BSA* 49 (1954), 183–201, 198 no. 1; D. Wachsmuth, ΠΟΜΠΙΜΟΣ Ο ΔΑΙΜΩΝ. *Untersuchungen zu den antiken Sakralhandlungen bei Seereisen* (Diss. Berlin, 1967), 142 n. 246; J. S. Morrison and R. T.

plaques have come to light in the sanctuary of Nymphe on the south slope of the Akropolis.[12] However, the most spectacular collection of such *pinakes* was found at Penteskouphia, near Corinth, more than a century ago.[13] They all date from the Archaic period, and must have come from a sanctuary of Poseidon. As many of these *pinakes* from Penteskouphia have a painted representation on both sides, it would seem probable that they were intended to hang free.

One terracotta plaque, singularly unimpressive in itself, deserves special mention, as it may well be the cheapest votive offering ever to have been hung in an ancient Greek sanctuary. It is a small rectangle (3.6 × 4.1 cm.) with rounded corners and pierced by a single hole at the top. The painting, in Attic red figure technique of the third quarter of the fifth century BC, represents the upper part of a woman carrying a wool basket (Fig. 12).[14] Beazley, after careful study of this piece, concluded that it was not originally manufactured as a plaque, but that it must have been a fragment of a vase, which was trimmed into shape and thus had a secondary use as a votive *pinax*.[15]

Another class of votive offering, which was hung in the same manner as terracotta plaques, consists of painted wooden *pinakes*. There are several indications that these were very popular and occurred in large numbers in many Greek sanctuaries. Owing to the perishability of the material, however, only a few have survived.[16]

Williams, *Greek Oared Ships* (Cambridge, 1968), 73 no. 2, pl. 8b; G. Neumann, *Probleme des griechischen Weihreliefs*, Tübinger Studien zur Archäologie und Kunstgeschichte 3 (Tübingen, 1979), 13, pl. 11b.

[12] J. Travlos, *Bildlexikon zur Topographie des antiken Athen* (Tübingen, 1971), 361–4 with bibliography.

[13] O. Rayet, 'Plaques votives en terre cuite trouvées à Corinthe', *Gazette Archéologique*, 6 (1880), 101–7; M. Collignon, 'Tablettes votives de terre cuite peinte trouvées à Corinthe (Musée du Louvre)', *Monuments grecs publiés par l'Association pour l'Encouragement des Études Grecques en France*, ii, nos. 11–13 (1882–4), 23–32; A. Furtwängler, *Beschreibung der Vasensammlung im Antiquarium* (Berlin, 1885), 47–105; *Antike Denkmäler* I pls. 7–8 and II pls. 23–4, 29–30, 39–40; E. Pernice, 'Die korinthischen Pinakes im Antiquarium der Königlichen Museen', *JdI* 12 (1897), 9–48; H. A. Geagan, 'Mythological Themes on the Plaques from Penteskouphia', *AA* 1970, 31–48; G. Zimmer, *Antike Werkstattbilder*, Bilderheft der Staatlichen Museen Preussischer Kulturbesitz 42 (Berlin, 1982).

[14] Frankfurt Liebieghaus Li. 555; *CVA* Frankfurt 2, pl. 85, 9; F. Eckstein and A. Legner, *Antike Kleinkunst im Liebieghaus* (Frankfurt am Main, 1969), no. 80; P. C. Bol, *Liebieghaus-Museum alter Plastik. Führer durch die Sammlungen. Antike Kunst* (Frankfurt am Main, 1980), 55, fig. 63.

[15] J. D. Beazley *apud CVA* Frankfurt 2, pl. 85, 9.

[16] van Straten, 'Gifts for the Gods', esp. 78–9.

Fig. 12 Attic painted terra cotta votive plaque (Frankfurt Liebighaus Li. 555)

Conversely, for the small gold and silver plates with representations in repoussé relief (*tupoi egmaktoi* or *katamaktoi*), which resembled the *tamata* still found in many Greek churches, it was precisely the intrinsic value of the material that made their chances of survival very slim. So far only one excavated sanctuary, in Thracian Mesembria, has yielded a number of such *tupoi*. Often they were eventually melted down and the gold and silver put to other uses.[17] Fortunately, however, in some cases we still have a record of the *tupoi* that have themselves disappeared, in the form of inventories inscribed on stone. Thus we know that the Athenian Asklepieion in the fourth and third century BC had hundreds of them.[18]

As we saw above, stone reliefs—even small ones—were not normally hung but rather set on a pillar of some sort. There are some exceptions. A limestone plaque from Golgoi (Cyprus), for instance, has two suspension holes in the top centre. This plaque, which dates

---

[17] van Straten, 'Gifts for the Gods', 79–80.
[18] S. B. Aleshire, *The Athenian Asklepieion: The People, their Dedications, and the Inventories* (Amsterdam, 1989), 39: in all the inventories taken together, records of 1347 dedications are fully or partially preserved; van Straten, 'Gifts for the Gods', 108–13.

from the fourth century BC, is of modest dimensions, though not extremely small (31 × 47 cm.), and it is decorated in shallow relief with a representation of people worshipping, dancing, and banqueting in a sanctuary of Apollo.[19] Sometimes hanging may have been regarded as a more convenient method of display even for larger objects, if they were of an irregular shape. Thus, most of the approximately life-size terracotta votive limbs from the Asklepieion of Corinth have suspension holes.[20]

Finally a vast group of small votive offerings remains to be considered, such as the charming bronze figurines from the Arcadian sanctuaries and the Theban Kabirion, or the omnipresent terracotta figurines, which must have overcrowded many a Greek sanctuary.[21] Excavations seldom tell us anything about their original position.[22] When they were first dedicated, the dedicants (subject of course to the permission of the persons in charge of the sanctuary) would tend to put them in a more or less prominent position, close to the altar or the cult image. This is what we read in Herondas' fourth mimiambus: the poor woman who has come to the Asklepieion of Kos to thank the god for having cured her, tells her friend to set her votive offering to the right of Hygieia, that is, close to the image

---

[19] O. Masson, *Les Inscriptions chypriotes syllabiques. Recueil critique et commenté* (Paris, 1961), 287 no. 268; J.-M. Dentzer, *Le Motif du banquet couché dans le Proche-Orient et le monde grec du VIIe au IVe siècle avant J.-C.*, Bibliothèque des Écoles Françaises d'Athènes et de Rome 246 (Rome, 1982), 281–2, 570 R27, fig. 208; F. Ghedini, 'Un rilievo da Golgoi e il culto di Apollo Magirios', *AM* 103 (1988), 193–202.

[20] C. Roebuck, *The Asklepieion and Lerna, Corinth* XIV (Princeton, 1951); M. Lang, *Cure and Cult in Ancient Corinth: A Guide to the Asklepieion, Corinth Notes 1* (Princeton, 1977); van Straten, 'Gifts for the Gods', 123–4.

[21] W. Lamb, 'Arcadian Bronze Statuettes', *BSA* 27 (1925–26), 133–48; M. Jost, 'Statuettes de bronze archaiques provenant de Lykosoura', *BCH* 99 (1975), 339–64; M. Jost, *Sanctuaires et cultes d'Arcadie*, Études Péloponnésiennes 9, École Française d'Athènes (Paris, 1985); B. Schmaltz, *Terrakotten aus dem Kabirenheiligtum bei Theben (Das Kabirenheiligtum bei Theben*, v (Berlin, 1975); B. Schmaltz, *Metallfiguren aus dem Kabirenheiligtum bei Theben. Die Statuetten aus Blei und Bronze. Das Kabirenheiligtum bei Theben*, vi. (Berlin, 1980); B. Alroth, *Greek Gods and Figurines, Boreas* 18 (Uppsala, 1989).

[22] There are some exceptions. In the 'Provisorischer Kultraum' at Kalapodi (Phokis), which was in use between the destruction of the Archaic shrine by the Persians in 480 and the building of the monumental Classical temple *c.* mid-5th cent. BC, the excavators discovered a 'Votivbank', on which various votive offerings were found *in situ*: *inter alia* a small bronze kouros, a terracotta mask, and a terracotta cock. See R. C. S. Felsch *et al.*, 'Apollon und Artemis oder Artemis und Apollon? Bericht über die Grabungen im neu entdeckten Heiligtum bei Kalapodi 1973–1977', *AA* (1980), 38–123. At Kommos in Crete a terracotta bull was found *in situ* on an altar: J. W. Shaw, *Hesperia*, 47 (1978), 142ff., pls. 40–1.

of the deity.[23] One suspects that eventually the temple personnel may have found another place for this humble offering.

In any case, it was not unusual that from time to time, during a clean-up operation or a reorganization of a sanctuary, many of the older and smaller ex votos were buried within the sacred precinct.[24] In this way they had a much better chance of being recovered more or less intact by modern archaeologists, but any information concerning their original position was lost.

II. THE WORSHIPPERS' VIEW OF THE VOTIVE OFFERINGS

Obviously it is not really possible for us to look at the votive offerings through the eyes of the ancient worshippers, but we may try to come close by studying the representational evidence. There is, fortunately, a considerable number of reliefs and vase paintings, mostly from Attika, in which votive offerings are depicted. The most interesting among these are votive reliefs which, in a roughly self-referential manner, include in their scene a small representation of a votive tablet on a pillar.

A good example is the monument of Telemachos of Acharnai, the founder of the Athenian Asklepieion, which has been painstakingly reconstructed from its *disiecta membra* by L. Beschi.[25] Mounted on a pillar of the usual type is a marble plaque decorated with reliefs on both sides, one side showing the interior and the other the exterior of the newly founded sanctuary. On the side with the exterior there is also, on the right, an indication of the Asklepieion in Piraeus, whence Asklepios had come to Athens.[26] The nature of this Piraeus

[23] Herondas 4. 19–20: ἐκ δεξιῆς τὸν πίνακα, Κοκκάλη, στῆσον | τῆς Ὑγιείης μοι.

[24] Schmaltz, *Metallfiguren aus dem Kabirenheiligtum bei Theben*, 4–5.

[25] L. Beschi, 'Il monumento di Telemachos, fondatore dell' Asklepieion ateniese', *ASAtene* 45–6 (1967–8), 381–436; L. Beschi, 'Il rilievo di Telemachos ricompletato', *AAA* 15 (1982), 31–43. The foundation of the Athenian sanctuary is accurately dated at 420/419 BC; Telemachos' monument was probably made about a quarter of a century later.

[26] According to the inscription on the pillar of Telemachos' monument: [ἀ]νελθὼν Ζεόθ[εν], see L. Beschi, *ASAtene* 45–6 (1967–8), 412. On the inscription see also K. Clinton, 'The Epidauria and the Arrival of Asclepius in Athens', in R. Hägg (ed.), *Ancient Greek Cult Practice from the Epigraphical Evidence. Proceedings of the Second International Seminar on Ancient Greek Cult, organized by the Swedish Institute at Athens, 22–24 November 1991* (1994), 17–34. On the coming of Asklepios to Athens: R. Parker, *Athenian Religion: A History* (Oxford, 1996), 175–85 and 345.

sanctuary is suggested, among other things, by a small representation of a votive relief on a pillar, and enough of this miniature votive relief remains for us to recognize the theme. It is an incubation scene: a patient lying on a couch in the *enkoimētērion* (the dormitory which was a regular part of sanctuaries of Asklepios and similar deities) is visited by the healing god.

The iconography of the Telemachos monument as a whole is quite unusual, owing to the unique nature of the event to which it refers. Representations of votive tablets on pillars, however, also occur on a number of regular votive reliefs. An incompletely preserved one from the Athenian Asklepieion shows Hygieia leaning against a tall pillar which supports a votive tablet.[27] The tablet itself is bordered at top and bottom by a raised band, but otherwise it is plain, not carved with a relief of its own. This, in fact, is the case with most of the Classical examples. As it was not unusual for details on votive reliefs to be added in paint, these tablets may originally have been painted with a suggestion of a relief representation.[28] An exceptionally well preserved relief from the same sanctuary, now in the Louvre, depicts a family sacrificing to Asklepios and Hygieia.[29] Again, Hygieia is leaning against a votive offering on a pillar. The shape of the tablet, a thick flat circular disc, is unusual here. One is reminded of the painted marble disc of the doctor Aineas, of late Archaic date, but that almost certainly was a sepulchral monument, and in any case can never have been mounted on a pillar in this fashion.[30]

---

[27] Athens NM 2557: Svoronos, *Ath. NM.* pl. 171; H. K. Süsserott, *Griechische Plastik des 4. Jahrhunderts v. C. Untersuchungen zur Zeitbestimmung* (Frankfurt am Main, 1938), 119, pl. 22, 2; U. Hausmann, *Kunst und Heiltum. Untersuchungen zu den griechischen Asklepiosreliefs* (Potsdam, 1948), 177 no. 143. Second half of the 4th cent. BC.

[28] See S. Karusu, 'Bemalte attische Weihreliefs', in *Studies P. H. von Blanckenhagen* (Locust Valley, NY, 1979), 111–16.

[29] Paris Louvre 755: Süsserott, *Griech. Plastik*, 123, pl. 25, 4; Hausmann, *Kunst und Heiltum*, 178 no. 146, fig. 5; J. Charbonneaux, *La Sculpture grecque et romaine au Musée du Louvre* (Paris, 1963), 119; O. Palagia, 'A Colossal Statue of a Personification from the Agora of Athens', *Hesperia*, 51 (1982), 99–113, pl. 34c; F. T. van Straten, 'The God's Portion in Greek Sacrificial Representations: Is the Tail Doing Nicely?', in R. Hägg, N. Marinatos, and G. C. Nordquist (eds.), *Early Greek Cult Practice. Proceedings of the Fifth International Symposium at the Swedish Institute at Athens, 26–29 June, 1986 (Acta Instituti Atheniensis Regni Sueciae*, Series in 4°, 38) (Stockholm, 1988), 51–67, esp. 53, fig. 6. Late 4th cent. BC.

[30] Athens NM 93, unknown provenance (confiscated in Piraeus), inscription: μνêμα τόδ᾽ Αἰνέο σοφίας ἰατρô ἀρίστο. E. Berger, *Das Basler Arztrelief. Studien zum griechischen Grab- und Votivrelief um 500 v. Chr. und zur vorhippokratischen Medizin* (Basel, 1970), 155ff., figs. 164–5; *IG I²* 1019.

The Amphiareion near Oropos, another healing sanctuary which, like the Asklepieia, enjoyed an increasing popularity during the later fifth and fourth century BC, has produced two votive reliefs that are relevant in this context. The first is the well-known dedication of Archinos.[31] The main scene shows what Archinos experienced when he slept in the *enkoimētērion*: on the left, as he himself saw it in his dream, his shoulder is being treated by Amphiaraos; on the right, as the same event was witnessed by outsiders, a snake is licking Archinos' shoulder while he is asleep on a couch. In the background stands a plain rectangular votive panel on a pillar. The other relief from Oropos has a depiction of an *apobatēs*-race (a race involving four-horse chariots carrying a driver and a foot soldier in full armour, who had to run part of the course alongside the chariot) and, again, a plain tablet on a pillar.[32] Similar plain votive tablets occur on a relief from the Amphiareion at Rhamnous, with a family preparing the sacrifice of a pig (Fig. 13),[33] and another votive relief from the Amphiareion in Athens.[34] In the latter instance, the tablet is framed all round with a raised band.

From the Athenian Akropolis comes a broken votive relief, dedicated by victorious torch racers, which features the by now familiar tablet on a pillar.[35] Possibly of the same provenance is a fragment of a relief dedicated to Athena, which has a tablet bordered by a moulding at top and bottom, but otherwise similarly undecorated.[36]

Next we turn to four representations of votive tablets that are

---

[31] Athens NM 3369: Hausmann, *Kunst und Heiltum*, 169 no. 31, fig. 2; van Straten, 'Gifts for the Gods', 124–5 no. 16. 1, with bibliography. First half 4th cent. BC.

[32] Berlin 725 (K80): C. Blümel, *Die klassisch griechischen Skulpturen der Staatlichen Museen zu Berlin* (Berlin, 1966), 72 no. 85, pl. 121; B. Ch. Petrakos, Ὁ ᾽Ωρωπὸς καὶ τὸ ἱερὸν τοῦ Ἀμφιαράου (Athens, 1968), 121, pl. 38. Early 4th cent. BC.

[33] Athens NM 1384: Svoronos, *Ath. NM.* 329, pl. 39, 2; Hausmann, *Kunst und Heiltum*, 181 no. 181; B.Ch. Petrakos, *Prakt* (1976), 57 no. 34; IG II² 4426. Mid-4th cent. BC.

[34] Athens NM 1383: Svoronos, *Ath. NM.* 328, pl. 38, 4; Süsserott, *Griech. Plastik*, pl. 22, 5; Hausmann, *Kunst und Heiltum*, 171 no. 74. Late 4th cent. BC. This relief was found near the Hephaisteion, during the construction of the Piraeus railway, together with Athens NM 1396, which is an honorary decree with a relief representation of Amphiaraos, Artikleides, and Hygieia, all three with their names inscribed.

[35] Athens Akr. Mus. 3012 and London BM 813: O. Walter, *Beschreibung der Reliefs im kleinen Akropolismuseum in Athen* (Vienna, 1923), no. 213 and 213a; A. H. Smith, *A Catalogue of Sculpture in the Department of Greek and Roman Antiquities, British Museum*, i (London, 1892), no. 813. Late 4th cent. BC.

[36] Athens NM 1389: Svoronos, *Ath. NM.* 349, pl. 58. Inscription: [– –] Ἀθεναίαι ἀνέθ[ηκεν or εσαν].

Fig. 13 Marble votive relief, from Rhamnous, sanctuary of Amphiaraos
(Athens NM 1384)

decorated with relief scenes. They were all part of votive reliefs, but
unfortunately in all four instances only a small fragment is preserved, containing little more than the tablet and part of its pillar, so

that we have no way of knowing what their iconographical context was. On the tablet in the first fragment, from Athens, three female figures are depicted dancing hand in hand.[37] If the traces of an inscription on the capital of the pillar supporting this tablet have been correctly interpreted by Peek as a dedication to Demos and the Charites, they must be the Charites.[38] The date of this relief is difficult to determine; it may still be fourth century, but quite possibly it belongs to the Hellenistic period, as the next three fragments certainly do. One from the Athenian Agora preserves part of a tablet with a Nymph relief (or Charites),[39] a fragment from Chios depicts Hygieia and Asklepios,[40] and finally on one in Corinth we have Apollo, Leto, and Artemis.[41]

Some reliefs have votive tablets that are not mounted on pillars, but attached to the background, which in these cases, one imagines, should be understood as a wall in the sanctuary. A votive relief from Piraeus with a scene of a hero banquet has in its upper left corner a framed relief panel depicting a horseman.[42] Frequently such hero banquet reliefs have a similar panel with only a horse's head. In fact, we have here an interesting example of the flexibility of votive iconography. In a dedication to a hero, some indication of his horsemanship was desirable, though not absolutely indispensable. One

[37] Athens NM 2354: Svoronos, *Ath. NM.* pl. 141.
[38] W. Peek, 'Attische Inschriften', *AM* 67 (1942), 1–217, esp. 58 no. 97.
[39] Athens Agora Mus. S1527: E. B. Harrison, *Archaic and Archaistic Sculpture (The Athenian Agora* XI) (Princeton, 1965), 84 no. 132, pl. 31.
[40] Bonn Akad. Kunstmus. B68: Hausmann, *Kunst und Heiltum*, 168 no. 27; id., *AM* 69/70 (1954–5), 131, 144–5, Beil. 53; H. Kyrieleis, in *Antiken aus dem Akademischen Kunstmuseum, Bonn* (Düsseldorf, 1971), 21 no. 15, fig. 11; P. Kranz, 'Bemerkungen zum Bonner Asklepios-Pinax', in *Beiträge zur Ikonographie und Hermeneutik. Festschrift für N. Himmelmann* (= *BJb* Beih. 47, Mainz, 1989), 289–95. Hausmann suggested a date in the 4th cent. BC, but Kyrieleis and Kranz argue for the 2nd cent. BC. There are traces of an inscription which may be tentatively restored as [- -Ἀσκληπιῶι καὶ Ὑγιε]ίαι | [- - κατ' ἐπιτα]γήν.
[41] Corinth S2567: B. S. Ridgway, 'Sculpture from Corinth', *Hesperia*, 50 (1981). For yet another Hellenistic example of a votive tablet on a pillar, in a relief with a Dionysiac scene: Volos 421, see D. R. Theocharis, *ADelt* 17 (1961–2), 171 pl. 190a. Reliefs with depictions of statues on pillars: Athens NM 3867, see M. Kyparissis and W. Peek, *AM* 66 (1941), 228–32 no. 4, pls. 75–6; Thebes Mus., see *ADelt* 10 (1926), Par. 11 no. 6, fig. 3.
[42] See Svoronos, *Ath. NM.* 536, fig. 243; Dentzer, *Banquet couché*, 594 R226, fig. 481. In a fragment of a similar relief, also from Piraeus, the miniature tablet even has the conventional more elaborate architectural frame of the later classical votive reliefs, see Svoronos ibid., fig. 244. See also the Hellenistic banquet relief from Pergamon: E. Pfuhl and H. Möbius, *Die ostgriechischen Grabreliefs*, ii (1979), no. 1917, pl. 277.

could choose to depict the hero as a horseman, on horseback or dismounted. But if, for some reason, one preferred the other most popular type of heroic votive relief, the banquet, then one could add either a life-size full picture of a horse or rider, or just a horse's head looking in over a wall or through a window, or a horse's head in a frame (window or framed relief panel?), or a relief tablet with a horseman on a reduced scale.[43]

In addition to votive tablets, other types of votive offerings may also be depicted in votive reliefs. For instance the relief of Telemachos of Acharnai depicting the interior of the temple of Asklepios shows a couple of surgical instruments, hanging on the wall between Hygieia and Asklepios.[44] They are a forceps, which may be compared to the *karkinoi iatrikoi* ('medical pincers') mentioned in an inventory of ex votos in the Asklepieion in Piraeus,[45] and a cupping instrument (*sikuē*).[46] Other votive reliefs to healing gods have depictions of anatomical ex votos, seemingly hanging on the background of the relief (which here again may be thought of as a wall in the sanctuary), or suspended from the upper part of its architectural frame.[47] In an often illustrated relief from the Amyneion in Athens, the dedicant, Lysimachides, is seen actually placing his offering, a huge replica of a leg with a varicose vein, in the sanctuary; on the left, in a recessed panel, stand a pair of votive feet (Fig. 14).[48]

It seems most likely that the votive leg that Lysimachides is handling represents his own votive offering. But this raises the broader question, whether an ex voto depicted in a votive relief is always to be understood as specifically the votive offering of the dedicant of this relief, or as a more general indication of the nature of the locality, i.e.

---

[43] F. T. van Straten, 'Unclassical Religion in Classical Greece: The Archaeological Angle', in Πρακτικά του XII Διεθνούς Συνεδρίου Κλασικής Αρχαιολογίας, Αθήνα, 4–10 Σεπτεμβρίου 1983 (Athens, 1988), 288–92. For the hero banquet reliefs (for the votive reliefs of this type I prefer this term to the conventional but misleading 'Totenmahl' or 'funeral banquet'), see R. N. Thönges-Stringaris, 'Das griechische Totenmahl', AM 80 (1965), 1 ff.; Dentzer, *Banquet couché*.

[44] See n. 25.

[45] *IG* II² 47.

[46] See Berger, *Basler Arztrelief*, 63 ff.

[47] van Straten, 'Gifts for the Gods', 105–51, nos. 1.1, 1.2, 9.1, 10.2. On Greek anatomical ex votos see now B. Forsén, *Griechische Gliederweihungen. Eine Untersuchung zu ihrer Typologie und ihrer religions- und sozialgeschichtlichen Bedeutung*, Papers and Monographs of the Finnish Institute at Athens, iv (Helsinki, 1996).

[48] Athens NM 3526: van Straten, 'Gifts for the Gods', 113 no. 2.1, with bibliography. Second half of the 4th cent. BC.

Fig. 14 Marble votive relief, from Athens, sanctuary of Amynos
(Athens NM 3526)

a sanctuary. The answer to this question may have varied from case to case. When someone ordered a votive relief in connection with a cure, and he wanted to make clear the nature of the sanctuary concerned by including a representation of an anatomical votive offering, then it stands to reason that he would choose that part of the body that had ailed him. In the case of the votive relief from the Athenian Asklepieion, however, which presents a fairly complete collection of all the parts of the human body, I think we should take this as an indication of the comprehensive healing power of the god, rather than the manifold complaints of the woman dedicant.[49]

The votive tablets on pillars depicted in votive reliefs, which were discussed above, are probably just general indicators of the nature of the place. There is no good reason to assume that they are self-referential in the strict sense, i.e. that the votive tablet in a relief is a representation of that relief itself. Whenever it is itself decorated with a relief, it is always of a most general, impersonal type: just a picture of the deities and no special reference to any worshippers in particular. In the Telemachos relief, the pillar surmounted by a relief of an incubation clearly serves to indicate that there was a sanctuary, and that it was a healing sanctuary. And certainly in later times, in Neo-Attic reliefs, pillars supporting votive panels were a stock component, used as a general indication of a sanctuary. In one version of the so-called 'Ikarios relief', now in the British Museum, there even are two of those.[50] And in the series of reliefs with Nike and warrior on either side of a Palladion, one replica has the pillar and tablet as an alternative to the Palladion.[51]

The opinion that, in the Classical period too, representations of

---

[49] Athens Akr. M. 7232: Walter, *Beschreibung*, no. 108; van Straten, 'Gifts for the Gods', 106 no. 1.1. 4th cent. BC.

[50] London BM 2190: on the various versions and their genealogy see C. Watzinger, 'Theoxenia des Dionysos', *Jdl* 61/62 (1946–47), 76–87; W. Fuchs, *Die Vorbilder der neuattischen Reliefs* (*Jdl* Ergänzungsheft 20) (Berlin, 1959), 157.

[51] Mantua Pal. Ducale: A. Levi, *Sculture greche e romane del Palazzo Ducale di Mantova* (Rome, 1931), 36 no. 52, pl. 38b; on the type in general see V. H. Poulsen, 'A Late-Greek Relief in Beirut', *Berytus*, 2 (1935), 51–6; Fuchs, *Vorbilder*, 123–6. Another Hellenistic relief type which includes a pillar and votive tablet represents a Muse and a Satyr chorus in a sacred precinct (replicas in Rome and in Naples): M. Bieber, *The History of the Greek and Roman Theater*, 2nd edn. (Princeton, 1961), 85, fig. 308. See also E. Schmidt, *Archaistische Kunst in Griechenland und Rom* (Munich, 1922), 62 n. 19, pl. XIX 3 (relief fragment in Rome MN); G. M. A. Richter, 'A Neo-Attic Crater in the Metropolitan Museum of Art', *JHS* 45 (1925), 201–9.

votive offerings on pillars could be used as a general indication of the sacred surroundings, finds support in the fact that they also occur in vase paintings. For instance, an Attic red-figure krater with a sacrificial scene features a votive tablet on a column next to the altar.[52] There is no good reason to connect this votive offering with any specific person.

There are some other vase paintings with votive panels or statues on pillars.[53] One Boeotian vase painting has a representation of anatomical ex votos.[54] Much more common, however, on vases, are representations of painted votive *pinakes*, to be taken as either terracotta or wood. Fragments of an Attic red-figure krater of the second half of the fifth century BC preserve a picture of Herakles sacrificing in the sanctuary of Chryse (Fig. 15).[55] This is a mythical picture, a scene imagined in the remote past, so the sanctuary is depicted as a simple sacred grove, with a cult statue on a pillar, a rustic altar, and three *pinakes* suspended from the branches of a tree. On a roughly contemporary *chous* (wine jug) a similar open air sanctuary is depicted, with two *pinakes* hanging from a tree, next to an altar.[56] On the left are two women, one holding a *phialē* (flat libation bowl) and a wine jug; facing them on the right is a youth standing beside his horse. Since this iconographical pattern closely resembles a typical class of votive reliefs to heroes, we may perhaps imagine that the vase painter had some Attic hero shrine in mind.

On an Attic red-figured fragment in Bucarest, also of the second half of the fifth century, we see Apollo playing the kithara outside a temple.[57] The temple is rendered in the abbreviated form, usual in

[52] Athens NM 12491: H. Metzger, *Recherches sur l'imagerie athénienne*, Publications de la Bibliothèque Salomon Reinach 2 (Paris, 1965), 116 no. 35; pl. XLVIII 2.

[53] e.g. Cologne Arch. Inst.: A. Rumpf, 'Ein etruskischer Krater', *BJb* 158 (1958), 253–61. New York MMA 08.258.25: *ARV*[2] 776, 3 The Group of Berlin 2415; G. Neumann, *Gesten und Gebärden in der griechischen Kunst* (Berlin, 1965), 82, fig. 41 (statue of Athena on a column, perhaps cult statue rather than votive statue). Paris Louvre L63 (S1662): *ARV*[2] 858, 8 The Trophy Painter; G. van Hoorn, *Choes and Anthesteria* (Leiden, 1951), 169 no. 828, fig. 11; B. Lamprinoudakes, *AAA* 9 (1976), 111, fig. 2 (statue of a boy on a column set in a base; inscription painted on the base: [Tε?]ισίας | [ά]νέθηκεν).

[54] Athens NM 1393: van Straten, 'Gifts for the Gods', 125 no. 17.2 with bibliography.

[55] London BM E494: *ARV*[2] 1079,3 The Painter of London E494; F. T. van Straten, in R. Hägg *et al.* (eds.), *Early Greek Cult Practice* (Stockholm, 1988), 63–4 no. 17 with bibliography.

[56] Paris Louvre L64: *Encyclopédie photographique de l'art. Le Musée du Louvre*, iii (Paris, 1938); van Hoorn, *Choes*, 169 no. 829, fig. 32.

[57] Bucarest NM 03207: *CVA* Bucarest pl. 32, 1.

Fig. 15 Attic red-figure krater (London BM E 494)

vase paintings, consisting of a Doric column and architrave. Suspended from the architrave or from the capital of the column is a *pinax* with a picture of Herakles.

Painted votive plaques occur in several other vase paintings, both Attic[58] and South Italian.[59] Most frequently we find them in combination with a herm and an altar. A red-figure amphora of the first half of the fifth century has a rare picture of *pinakes* being brought to a

[58] Column krater, once Basel: *Münzen und Medaillen*, Sonderliste N (1971) no. 8. Bell krater Brussels A725: *CVA* Brussels 3, IVe/IVc, pl. 2; Metzger, *Recherches sur l'imagerie*, 83 no. 20, pl. 31, 1. Pelike Leningrad 4515: Beazley, *Paralip* 514; A. A. Peredolskaja, *Catalogue of Attic Red Figure Vases in Leningrad* (in Russian) (Leningrad, 1967), no. 133, pl. 95, 3–4. Lekythos London BM E585: *ARV*² 685, 162 Bowdoin Painter. Column krater Naples MN 3369: *ARV*² 523, 9 Orchard Painter; J. Boardman, *Athenian Red Figure Vases: The Classical Period* (London, 1989), fig. 42. Cup Oxford 305: *ARV*² 416, 3 Painter of Louvre G265; *CVA* Oxford 1, pls. 2, 3; 7, 1–2. Skyphos Paris Cab. Méd. 839: *ARV*² 367, 97 Triptolemos Painter. Lekythos private collection: *ARV*² 685, 164 Bowdoin Painter; E. Simon, *Götter der Griechen*, 3rd edn. (Darmstadt, 1985), 308 fig. 294.

[59] A Sicilian red-figure skyphos in Gela, of the second half of the 4th cent. BC, shows Herakles and Silenus sacrificing at an altar. Behind the altar is a pillar, and a considerable number of painted *pinakes* hanging on the wall, nicely overcrowding the picture. See A. Calderone, *ArchCl* 29 (1977), 267–76, pls. 56–7.

sanctuary: a man and a youth each carry a forked branch from which a painted plaque is suspended, and a vessel.[60]

If we look back for a moment, and survey the representations of votive offerings in both votive reliefs and vase paintings, an interesting difference appears. The sculptors of votive reliefs (and their patrons?) had a distinct preference for the inclusion of votive sculpture of a more or less monumental nature, whereas the majority of votive offerings depicted by vase painters are *pinakes* such as, at times, they might paint themselves. Every man to his trade, apparently.

Let us now return to the votive reliefs. Although no one would begrudge the dedicant the pleasure of regarding the ex voto depicted in his votive relief as his own, to the general public visiting the sanctuary it was just another element in the representation that referred to the material surroundings of the sanctuary. It is of the same class, then, as the altars that we see in many (though certainly not all) votive reliefs, and the not too numerous indications of the architecture, to which we shall now turn.

Fourth-century votive reliefs often have an architectural frame consisting of a bottom ledge, two antae or pilasters on the sides, and an architrave topped by something like the lateral edge of a tiled roof (e.g. Figs. 13 and 18; the antae seem to occur from c.420 BC, the complete architectural frame somewhat later). This frame has been variously interpreted as a reflection either of temple architecture, or of the stoa which formed part of so many sanctuaries.[61] The latter opinion seems to find some support in a curious votive monument from the Athenian Asklepieion (Fig. 16).[62] It was carved out of a single block of marble, and consists of a relief depicting the usual procession of worshippers in an architectural frame, and, attached to it at right angles on the left, a higher naiskos or temple-like structure containing the deities. It may be that the sculptor of this monument was exceptionally literal-minded, and that in general we should not take the conventional architectural frame as reflecting any specific type of building, but rather as an indication that the scene depicted

---

[60] *Münzen und Medaillen* Auktion 40 (Basel, 1969), no. 95.
[61] Neumann, *Probleme griech. Weihrel.*, 51.
[62] Athens NM 1377: Svoronos, *Ath. NM.* 294, pl. 48; Hausmann, *Kunst und Heiltum*, 167 no. 11; B. S. Ridgway, 'Painterly and Pictorial in Greek Relief Sculpture', in W. G. Moon (ed.), *Ancient Greek Art and Iconography* (Madison, 1983), 193–208, fig. 13.4 a–b.

Fig. 16 Marble votive relief, from Athens, sanctuary of Asklepios
(Athens NM 1377)

was set within the architecturally defined space of the sanctuary. At least we may agree, I think, that it is not an unmistakable and exact representation of any real building. Still, at least in some cases it was felt by the sculptor as a piece of architecture, so that he could let Hygieia lean against the anta of the architectural frame.[63]

In votive reliefs to the Nymphs the same effect of setting the scene within the space of the sanctuary may be achieved by an irregular frame suggesting the mouth of a cave, which occurs from about the middle of the fourth century. Before that time, in the late fifth and early fourth century, we sometimes see a small stylized cave of Pan in the upper part of the relief field.[64]

That we should beware of taking these frames too literally is emphasized by the fact that sometimes they are, rather illogically, combined. For instance, in a fourth century votive to the Nymphs, found in Piraeus,[65] and in a Thessalian dedication to Artemis of the

[63] Athens NM 1383; see n. 34.
[64] C. M. Edwards, *Greek Votive Reliefs to Pan and the Nymphs* (Diss. New York, 1985); Neumann, *Probleme griech. Weihrel.*, 54.
[65] Berlin 710 (K84): Blümel, *Klass. griech. Skulpt.*, 78 no. 91, fig. 130; Edwards, *Greek Vot. Rel. Pan and the Nymphs*, 540 no. 31.

second century BC,[66] the irregular mouth of the cave is set within the conventional architectural frame.

There are some other indications of architectural elements in votive reliefs. Telemachos' relief, which shows both the interior and the exterior of the sanctuary of Asklepios in Athens, is a rather special case. It is not an ordinary votive relief, but a monument commemorating the founding and construction of the sanctuary.[67]

Two votive reliefs from the same Asklepieion, both incomplete and with a very battered surface, give us a slight hint of the architectural environment. In one, three girls are descending three steps.[68] The other has, in the background behind the worshippers, two isolated columns close together.[69] A fragment from the Athenian Agora shows a herm standing in front of a vertical edge, offset in the background, probably indicating the entrance of a sanctuary.[70] Rather indistinct pillars or pilasters occur in the background of some other fragmentary votive reliefs.[71]

An exceptionally explicit rendering of a special type of sacred building connected with the cult of Herakles, the so-called 'Säulenbau' or columnar shrine, is encountered on some ten votive reliefs and on a series of Attic red-figure vase paintings.[72] It is probably not one specific sanctuary, but rather a specific *type*, for the votive reliefs come from various parts of Greece. The construction (wood or stone?) consists of four columns placed at the corners of a square foundation and supporting an architrave (Fig. 17). On festive occasions this permanent framework was decked with boughs and thus

---

[66] Arndt and Amelung, *Photographische Einzelaufnahmen*, 3401b; *LIMC* s.v. 'Apollon' no. 959.

[67] See n. 25.

[68] Athens NM 1366: Svoronos, *Ath. NM.* 285, pl. 45; Hausmann, *Kunst und Heiltum*, 182 no. 188.

[69] Athens NM 2417: Svoronos, *Ath. NM.* 641, pl. 150; Hausmann, *Kunst und Heiltum*, 176 no. 130.

[70] Athens Agora Mus. S1154: Harrison, *Archaic and Archaistic Sculpture*, 174 no. 233, pl. 61. 4th cent. BC.

[71] Athens NM 1507: Svoronos, *Ath. NM.* 626, pl. 127; Dentzer, *Banquet couché*, 613 R388, fig. 619. Chalkis 913: E. Mitropoulou, *Horses' Heads and Snake in Banquet Reliefs and their Meaning* (Athens, 1976), 15 no. 1.

[72] A. Frickenhaus, 'Das Herakleion von Melite', *AM* 36 (1911), 121–7; S. Woodford, 'Cults of Heracles in Attica', in *Studies Presented to G. M. A. Hanfmann* (1971), 211–25; F. T. van Straten, 'The Lebes of Herakles. Note on a New Decree Stele from Eleusis', *BABesch* 54 (1979), 189–91.

Fig. 17 Marble votive relief, from an Attic sanctuary of Herakles
(Athens NM 2723)

transformed into a pleasant shady pavilion, where Herakles could
enjoy the banquet prepared for him by his worshippers.

To summarize what we have found so far: it would seem that, for the
worshippers in general, votive offerings were a typical component of
a sanctuary. Representations of ex votos could serve to identify the
space in which a scene was set, as a sanctuary, much the same as a
depiction of an altar or a specific architectural element would. Some
further insights into the appreciation of the Greek worshippers for
votive offerings may be gained from literary and epigraphical texts.

Some key words often found in connection with votive offerings
are *agalma*[73] and *kosmos* (*kosmein*): they are something to be enjoyed,
something beautiful, an ornament for the sanctuary. Around the
middle of the fifth century BC a priestess of Demeter and Kore dedicated a votive *agalma* in the Athenian sanctuary of her goddesses,

---

[73] van Straten, 'Gifts for the Gods', 75.

which, in her own eyes, was an adornment of their portal (*prothurou kosmon*).[74] A pillar of a lost votive relief, found in the Athenian Agora, bears the dedication of a cobbler and his sons to the hero Kallistephanos. With this dedication he adorns the hero (*hērō kosmei*).[75] In Cyrene a certain Hermesandros set up a votive offering and two almost identical inscriptions, commemorating his exceptionally rich contribution to the festival of Artemis: 'this stands here as an ornament, a memento of these offerings, and glorious renown.'[76]

In an inscription from a fourth-century choregic monument, found near Vari (Attika), the monument is referred to as a gift to the god in remembrance of the victory, an ornament for the deme.[77]

But not only did the dedicants regard their own dedications as *kosmos* and *agalma*, they were also objects of sightseeing, tourist attractions almost, for the general visitors. This is charmingly illustrated in Euripides' *Ion*, in the conversation between Ion and the handmaidens of Kreousa who have accompanied their mistress to Delphi (184–232). That Ion is well accustomed to sightseers is also clear from his question to Kreousa: 'Has your husband accompanied you to come sightseeing, or for consultation?' (301). In Herondas' 4th mimiambus, the women who have come to the Asklepieion to make a thank offering and set up a votive *pinax* are amazed at what is on display: 'O, dear Kynno, what beautiful statues!' (20–1). And they take the opportunity to have a good look around.

In the normal course of their lives, and even more so when abnormal events occurred, the ancient Greeks had many occasions

---

[74] Athens Agora I 5484: *SEG* 10, 321; M. L. Lazzarini, *Le formule delle dediche votive nella Grecia arcaica* (*MemLinc* VIII, XIX 2, 1976), no. 715.

[75] Athens Agora I 7396: J. M. Camp II, *AJA* 77 (1973), 209. *The Athenian Agora: A Guide to the Excavation and Museum*, 3rd edn. (Athens, 1976), 208 f., fig. 107. M. L. Lang, *Socrates in the Agora* (Excavations of the Athenian Agora, Picture Book, no. 17) (Princeton, 1978), fig. 12. J. M. Camp II, *Gods and Heroes in the Athenian Agora* (Excavations of the Athenian Agora, Picture Book, no. 19) (Princeton, 1980), 28 fig. 56. J. M. Camp II, *The Athenian Agora: Excavations in the Heart of Classical Athens* (London, 1986), 147 fig. 126. Second quarter of the 4th cent. BC.

[76] G. Pugliese Carratelli, 'Supplemento epigrafico cirenaico', *ASAtene* 39–40 (1961–2), 219–339; 312–13 nos. 161–2. 4th/3rd cent. BC.

[77] *IG* II² 3101. According to D. Whitehead, *The Demes of Attica 508/7—ca. 250 BC. A Political and Social Study* (Princeton, 1986), 234–5, δήμωι κόσμον, which he translates 'honor for the deme', refers to the victory. I think that it is much more likely that it refers to the δῶρον, i.e. the concrete monument on which this dedication was inscribed. Some further occurrences of κόσμος, κοσμεῖν in connection with votive offerings: *SEG* 28, 509 = W. Peek, *Griechische Vers-Inschriften aus Thessalien* (SB Heidelberg 1974, 3), 11–12 no. 7 = R. Helly, 'Quarante épigrammes thessaliennes', *RPh* (1978), 121–35; esp. 124. Pind. *Isthm.* 1. 18–23; Plut. *Per.* 12.

on which it was usual to make a dedication to a god. When generation upon generation of worshippers brought their votive gifts, a sanctuary might eventually become so full of them that they would be an impediment as much as an adornment. This is certainly the impression we get from the number of surviving votive offerings, which surely forms only a small percentage of the original number, and those attested in the inventories, of, for instance, the Athenian Asklepieion in the first couple of centuries after its foundation. The situation in many sanctuaries, as described by some later authors such as Diodorus Siculus, Strabo, and Pausanias, was probably not unlike that in some modern Greek churches, where especially the more thaumaturgical icons are largely blocked from view by thick clusters of *tamata*.[78]

This custom of cluttering up the sanctuaries with dedications, set up for every conceivable reason, was a major irritation to Plato: 'To establish gods and temples is not easy; it's a job that needs to be very carefully pondered if it is to be done properly. Yet look at what people usually do—all women in particular, invalids of every sort, men in danger or any kind of distress, or conversely when they have just won a measure of prosperity: they dedicate the first thing that comes to hand, they swear to offer sacrifice, and promise to found shrines for gods and spirits and children of gods. And the terror they feel when they see apparitions, either in dreams or awake—terror which recurs later when they recollect a whole series of visions—drives them to seek a remedy for each individually, with the result that on open spaces or any other spot where such an incident has occurred they found the altars and shrines that fill every home and village.'[79] Even the authorities in charge of the sanctuaries, who would not— one imagines—have shared Plato's prejudices, would for practical reasons sometimes find it necessary to lay down certain rules restricting the placement of ex votos. A Rhodian decree of the third century BC, concerning the Asklepieion, stipulates, 'that no one is permitted to request that an image or some other votive offering be set up in the lower part of the sanctuary (. . .) or in any other spot where votive offerings prevent people walking past'.[80] In an inscription of the same

---

[78] See references in van Straten, 'Gifts for the Gods', 78.

[79] Pl. *Leg.* 909e–910a (trans. Saunders).

[80] LSS 107: (– – –) μὴ ἐξέστω μηθενὶ αἰτήσασ- | [θαι ἀνά]θεσιν ἀνδριάντος μηδὲ ἄλλου | [ἀναθ]ήματος μηδενὸς ἐς τὸ κάτω μέρος | [τοῦ τ]εμένευς (– – –) | ἢ ἐς ἄλλον τινὰ τόπον ἐν | ᾧ στα- | θέντα τὰ ἀναθήματα κωλύσει τοὺς περι- | πάτους (– – –).

period from Miletus we read, 'that it is forbidden to fasten to the woodwork of the new stoa in the sanctuary of Apollo either a votive tablet or anything else, to prevent the woodwork from being damaged, nor to the columns. And if someone wishes to place any votive offering in the new stoa, he must place it against the plastered sections of the walls, underneath the stone course supporting the beams.'[81] In a very damaged inscription from Athens, dating from the second century BC, the priest of a sanctuary is authorized to remove various votive tablets which block the cult image of the god from view, and whatever else is deemed unworthy of the sanctuary, from the temple to the stoa. And in the future, no one is to set up any votive offering in the sanctuary without consulting the priest.[82]

Votive offerings, once they were placed in a sanctuary, were the property of the god, and there could be no doubt about their inalienability. Yet, sometimes it was considered useful explicitly to restate this fact, as in an inscription from Loryma on the Rhodian Peraia (third century BC): 'It is forbidden to remove votive offerings from the sanctuary or to damage any of them.'[83] The remainder of the inscription, which is very fragmentary, probably prohibited the introduction of votive offerings and any alterations in their arrangement without the permission of the priest.

Deisidaimonia (fear of the gods, religiosity), if not common decency, would probably prevent most people from stealing votive offerings.[84] Regrettably, there is always the odd exception. Aelian has a fascinating story about a temple-thief and a dog in the Asklepieion of Athens, which (whatever one may think of its historicity) is too good to be left out. 'A temple-thief who had waited for the midmost hour of night and had watched till men were deep asleep, came to the shrine of Asklepios and stole a number of offerings (*anathēmata*) without, as he supposed, being seen. There was however in the temple an

---

[81] *LSS* 123: (– – –) πρὸς τὴν ξύλωσιν τῆς στοιῆς τῆς καινῆς τῆς ἐν τῶι ἱερῶι τοῦ Ἀπόλλωνος | μὴ ἐξεῖναι πίνακα ἀναθεῖναι μηδὲ ἄλλο μηδέν, ὅπως μὴ βλάπτηται ἡ ξύλωσις, μηδὲ πρὸς τοὺς κίονας· <ἢ>ν δέ τις | βούληται ἀνατιθέναι τι εἰς τὴν στοιὴν τὴν καινήν, ἀνατιθέτω πρὸς τοὺς τοίχους τοὺς ἀλειφομένους ὑποκάτω | τοῦ ἀντιδοκίου τοῦ λιθίνου (– – –). See also *LSS* 43 and 111.

[82] *LSCG* 43.

[83] *LSAM* 74: ἐκ τοῦ ἱεροῦ | μὴ ἐκφέρειν | τῶν ἀν[α]θ[ημά]των | μηδὲ βλ[άπ]τε[ι]ν | μηθέν (– – –).

[84] Cf. Diod. Sic. 5. 63 (concerning the sanctuary of Hemithea in Kastabos): διὸ καὶ πολλῶν ἐκ παλαιῶν χρόνων σεσωσμένων πεπλήρωται τὸ τέμενος ἀναθημάτων, καὶ ταῦτα οὔθ' ὑπὸ φυλάκων οὔθ' ὑπὸ τείχους ὀχυροῦ φυλαττόμενα, ἀλλ' ὑπὸ τῆς συνήθους δεισιδαιμονίας.

excellent watcher, a dog, more awake than the attendants, and it gave chase to the thief and never stopped barking, as with all its might it summoned others to witness what had been done. (. . .) Since however the dog continued to bark when the thief came to the house where he lodged and when he came out again, it was discovered where the dog belonged, while the inscriptions and the places where the offerings were set up lacked the missing objects. The Athenians therefore concluded that the man was this thief, and by putting him on the rack discovered the whole affair. And the man was sentenced in accordance with the law, while the dog was rewarded by being fed and cared for at the public expense for being a faithful watcher and second to none of the attendants in vigilance.'[85]

The question of inalienability might also crop up, though in a less embarrassing fashion, when a decision was taken to melt down old gold and silver ex votos, in order to use the material for one more impressive *anathēma*, or for some useful cult implement. As this could easily be construed as tampering with the god's possessions, an official decision was required of the worldly powers that were in charge of the sanctuary. There are several inscriptions which deal with just such an operation and inform us about the procedure that was to be followed. One of the better-known examples comes from the Athenian sanctuary of the Heros Iatros, north of the Agora (221/0 BC).[86] The *boulē* decrees that the *dēmos* shall appoint a select committee. The members of this committee shall take down the metal reliefs (*tupoi*) and any other silver or gold objects and the coins that are kept as votive offerings in the sanctuary, they shall weigh these and then make them into an *anathēma* for the god as beautiful as they can. The members of the committee must inscribe the names of the dedicants and the weight (of their ex votos) on a marble stele which they must set up in the sanctuary. They must also offer a propitiatory sacrifice to the god worth fifteen drachmae.

This inscription very clearly illustrates that votive offerings constituted a sort of permanent link between the worshipper and his god. Therefore, if votive offerings are interfered with, both parties, dedicant and god, have to be given satisfaction.

---

[85] Ael. *NA* 7.13 (trans. A. F. Scholfield).
[86] *IG* II² 839; *LSCG* 41. For the location of the sanctuary see van Straten, 'Gifts for the Gods', 114 no. 3; also S. Dow, 'The Cult of the Hero Doctor', *BAmSocP* 22 (1985), 33–47. See also *LSCG* 42.

III. THE WORSHIPPERS

Votive offerings may contribute to our understanding of the ancient worshippers: how they saw themselves and how they wanted to be seen. On the one hand there is the iconographical evidence, in particular the votive reliefs with representations of worshippers in the sanctuary. Let us take a closer look at one example (Fig. 13), from the Amphiareion at Rhamnous.[87] In the sanctuary, indicated by the familiar votive tablet on a pillar, a couple with three children have come to offer sacrifice. They are accompanied by one male and one female servant. The names are inscribed above the figures (except, of course, the servants). On the left, at the head of this small gathering, the *pater familias* is taking something from the sacrificial basket (*kanoun*), which is held by the male servant. In the background a glimpse can be seen of the pig which is about to be sacrificed. On the right, behind the man, stand his wife and children, and the maid carrying a cylindrical basket (the *kistē*) on her head.

On the other hand, there is the relevant epigraphical material, such as votive inscriptions, and inventories of votive offerings. Notably the inventories from the Athenian Asklepieion and from the sanctuary of Artemis Brauronia offer a wealth of information, made accessible by the valuable studies of Sara Aleshire and Tullia Linders.[88] With their large number of records they offer the possibility of a quantitative study of, for instance, the sex of the dedicants. It turns out that in the inventories of the Athenian Asklepieion 51.39 per cent of the dedicants are female and 45.82 per cent male (the remaining 2.79 per cent are couples, two men, two women, the Athenian *dēmos*).[89] So there is a hardly significant predominance of women. In the inventories of the *epistatai* (superintendents) of Artemis Brauronia, the dedicants (apart from a couple of possible exceptions) are all female, which is only to be expected, given the particular character of Artemis Brauronia as protectress of pregnant women, women in child bed, etc.[90]

---

[87] Athens NM 1384, see n. 33.

[88] Aleshire, *Ath. Asklepieion*; T. Linders, *Studies in the Treasure Records of Artemis Brauronia found in Athens* (Acta Instituti Atheniensis Regni Sueciae, Series in 4°, 19) (Stockholm, 1972).

[89] Aleshire, *Ath. Asklepieion*, 45.

[90] Linders, *Artemis Brauronia*, 38 and 40f.

In this context, it might seem to be interesting to compare the proportion of male and female worshippers represented on votive reliefs from the same sanctuary, or pertaining to the cult of the same god. On closer inspection, however, things are not as clear cut as one might expect. Let us look at a couple of fourth-century votive reliefs from the sanctuary of Artemis at Brauron.

In the first one, apart from the servants leading the sacrificial animal and carrying the *kistē*, there are twelve worshippers: four couples each with one child.[91] According to the inscription on the architrave, however, this is the dedication of one woman: 'Aristonike, wife of Antiphates of Thorai, set this up as a votive offering to Artemis, in accordance with her prayers.' In all likelihood Aristonike is the woman of the first couple; but she, the dedicant, does not even walk up front. Another votive relief from Brauron was dedicated, according to the inscription on the architrave, by the woman Peisis.[92] Again in the representation the woman dedicant takes second place behind her husband. They are followed by a woman, probably a nanny, accompanying four children.

If we look only at the epigraphical evidence of the inventories, it seems as though the Athenian women by themselves, independently, could make their own dedications. But if we incorporate the iconographical material, we get a substantially different picture: women's dedications there appear as basically a family affair.

Votive reliefs with single female worshippers, or in which a woman is at least depicted in front of the family group, do occur, but they are very rare. There is a small series of reliefs with women kneeling directly in front of the god.[93] And there are a few reliefs in which a woman with both hands raised (normally worshippers in votive reliefs only raise their right hand) is either alone or precedes the rest of the family. One example where the woman is accompanied by her family is a hero banquet from the west slope of the

---

[91] Brauron 1151 (5): *Ergon*, (1958), 35 fig. 37; I. Kontes, 'Artemis Brauronia', *ADelt* 22 A′ (1967), 195, pl. 104a; S. Karusu, 'Bemalte attische Weihreliefs', *Studies P. H. von Blanckenhagen* (Locust Valley, NY, 1979), 111–16, pl. 33, 2; *LIMC* s.v. 'Artemis' no. 974; Travlos, *Bildlexikon Attika*, 72 fig. 77. Second half 4th cent. BC.

[92] Brauron 1152 (83): I. Kontes, *ADelt* 22 A′ (1967), 195, pl. 104b; *LIMC* s.v. 'Apollon' no. 957, s.v. 'Artemis' no. 1127; Travlos, *Bildlexikon Attika*, 72 fig. 78. Second half 4th cent. BC.

[93] van Straten, 'Did the Greeks Kneel before their Gods?', 159–89.

Fig. 18 Marble votive relief, from the sanctuary of Artemis Brauronia
(Brauron Mus. 1153)

Akropolis.[94] In an incomplete relief in Chalkis, the woman dedicant
is the only human figure, but this is an unusual dedication insofar as
the woman is a priestess.[95]

In another votive relief from the sanctuary of Artemis in Brauron,
the woman, by whom or on whose behalf this dedication was set up,
precedes her family, with a small child standing in front of her, closest to the goddess. She is followed by three bearded men, a youth, and
two smaller children (Fig. 18).[96]

This brings us to those few votive reliefs where a child is represented in front of the other worshippers, closest to the god. Some
are probably connected with the introduction of the child into the

[94] Athens NM 3527: O. Walter, 'Ein Totenmahlrelief aus Samos', *Studies D. M. Rob-
inson*, i (1951), 594–605, esp. 600 ff., pl. 58a; R. N. Thönges-Stringaris, *AM* 80 (1965),
78 no. 69, Beil. 10, 1; Dentzer, *Banquet couché*, 590 R192, fig. 450. Late 4th cent. BC.
[95] Chalkis 337: G. Daux, 'Le Relief éleusinien du musée de Chalcis', *BCH* 88 (1964),
433–41. Late 4th cent. BC. See also the relief fragment from Pergamon: O. Deubner,
Das Asklepieion von Pergamon. Kurze vorläufige Beschreibung (Berlin, 1938), 13, fig. 5.
[96] Brauron 1153 (32 + 32a): *Ergon* (1958), 34, fig. 36; A. Kontes, *ADelt* 22 A' (1967),
195, pl. 105a; *LIMC* s.v. 'Artemis' no. 673; Travlos, *Bildlexikon Attika*, 73, fig. 79.
Mid-4th cent. BC.

phratry. Apparently children were introduced twice over, once when they were very small, and again when they reached the ephebic age. The ceremonies could be accompanied by the offering of votive gifts to Zeus Phratrios or Athena Phratria. Connected with the ephebic introduction was the ceremony of the *oinistēria* celebrated in honour of Herakles.[97] The first introduction may be represented on a votive relief from the Athenian Akropolis.[98] Another Athenian relief which shows Herakles next to his columnar shrine, and a boy in front of him, probably refers to the *oinistēria* and the ephebic introduction (Fig. 17).[99]

Apart from these more or less official occasions, children could, of course, be commended to the special care of deities, whenever their parents felt that might be helpful. The large votive relief of Xenokrateia from Phaleron was dedicated, so the inscription on the pillar tells us, to Kephisos and the gods who shared his altar, as a gift for the upbringing of her son Xeniades.[100] Xenokrateia is depicted with her little son before her, stretching out his hand to Kephisos, who is attentively bending over towards his worshippers. They are standing in the midst of a dozen other gods and goddesses, the *xunbōmoi theoi* (i.e. the gods sharing Kephisos' altar) of the inscription.

It is not surprising that among the votive reliefs of Asklepios we should also find some in which small children are placed in a prominent position. In an Athenian one we have a man and woman followed by five daughters, neatly lined up according to size. The sixth and smallest child, also a girl, stands in front of them, close to

[97] O. Walter, 'Die heilige Familie von Eleusis', *ÖJh* 30 (1937), 50–70, esp. 60; O. Walter, 'Die Reliefs aus dem Heiligtum der Echeliden in Neu-Phaleron', *AEphem* (1937), i. 97–119, esp. 103; van Straten, *BABesch* 54 (1979), 189–91; id., 'Gifts for the Gods', 89–90.
[98] Athens AkrM 3030: Walter, *Beschreibung*, no. 46; N. Kontoleon, *AEphem* (1974), 17, pl. 4.
[99] Athens NM 2723: Svoronos, *Ath. NM.* 379, pl. 101, 121; Süsserott, *Griech. Plastik*, 110f., pl. 16, 4; J. Travlos, *Bildlexikon zur Topographie des antiken Athen* (Tübingen, 1971), 276; van Straten, *BABesch* 54 (1979), 189–91.
[100] Athens NM 2756: Svoronos, *Ath. NM.* 493ff., pl. 181; O. Walter, 'Die Reliefs aus dem Heiligtum der Echeliden in Neu-Phaleron', *AEphem* (1937), i. 97–119; Süsserott, *Griech. Plastik*, 97ff.; U. Hausmann, *Griechische Weihreliefs* (Berlin, 1960), 63f., fig. 33; A. Linfert, 'Die Deutung des Xenokrateiareliefs', *AM* 82 (1967), 149–57; M. Guarducci, 'L'offerta di Xenokrateia nel santuario di Cefiso al Falero', *Phóros. Tribute to B. D. Meritt* (Locust Valley, NY, 1974), 57–66; E. Mitropoulou, *Corpus I: Attic Votive Reliefs of the 6th and 5th Centuries B. C.* (Athens, 1977), no. 65; Edwards, *Greek Vot. Rel. Pan and the Nymphs*, 310 no. 3. *c.* 400 BC.

Asklepios and Hygieia.[101] This exceptionally large family, in which all
the children are female, may well be the result of the parents' per-
sistent wish for male offspring. Finally they come to Asklepios for
help.

What about the civil status of the families of worshippers depicted
in the votive reliefs? If they are from Athens, can we determine
whether they are citizens, metics or slaves? If we are to believe the
Old Oligarch, the citizens in Athens were no better dressed than the
slaves and metics, nor did they look any better.[102] And indeed, if there
is no inscription, it is impossible to distinguish between metics and
citizens in votive reliefs on the grounds of visual evidence only.
Whether there are any slaves among the dedicants of votive reliefs is
doubtful. It is perhaps unlikely that they could afford such a rather
expensive gift.

Servants or slaves do occur, however, as accessories in votive reliefs
with families offering sacrifice. Typically they are a relatively small
(not necessarily very young) male figure leading the victim and
carrying the kanoun, and a female figure carrying the kistē on her
head. They are only there as an inevitable extension of the things
that are essential to the sacrifice: the animal and the sacrificial
implements. Consequently, if the composition so demands, they may
be represented disproportionately small or almost invisible in the
background. In a votive relief from the Asklepieion in Piraeus, four
couples are preparing the sacrifice of a bull.[103] In the background,
almost wholly obscured by the other worshippers, is the maid
carrying the quite prominently displayed large kistē. In another
votive relief to Asklepios, found in Thyreatis on the estate of Herodes
Atticus (who probably brought it there from Athens), both the
dedicant and the god brought their family, making the relief very

[101] Athens AkrM: Walter, Beschreibung, 55 no. 96. 4th cent. BC. Other Asklepios
reliefs with children in front: Athens NM 1356: Svoronos, Ath. NM. 276, pl. 50; Hausmann, Kunst und Heiltum, 171 no. 62. Brocklesby Park (from Athens): A. Michaelis,
Ancient Marbles in Great Britain (Cambridge, 1882), 228 no. 10; B. Ashmole, 'An Attic
Relief of the Late Fifth Century', in Antike Plastik. [Festschr.] W. Amelung (Berlin
and Leipzig, 1928), 13–15; Hausmann, Kunst und Heiltum, 166 no. 3. A hero banquet
relief with children in front: Vienna I 1074: Dentzer, Banquet couché, 523 R431, fig. 653.

[102] Ps.-Xen. Ath. Pol. 10: ἐσθῆτά τε γὰρ οὐδὲν βελτίων ὁ δῆμος αὐτόθι ἢ οἱ δοῦλοι
καὶ οἱ μέτοικοι, καὶ τὰ εἴδη οὐδὲν βελτίους εἰσίν.

[103] Athens NM 1429: Svoronos, Ath. NM. 434, pl. 37; Hausmann, Kunst und Heiltum, 181 no. 179; F. T. van Straten, 'Greek Sacrificial Representations: Livestock Prices
and Religious Mentality', in Gifts, 159–70, fig. 4. 4th cent. BC.

crowded.[104] So the sacrificial pig, hardly visible in the background, must make do without the usual servant carrying the *kanoun*. The *kistē* is carried by an all but invisible maid. However, bringing up the rear of the procession of worshippers (two bearded men, a woman, two children), but clearly visible in the foreground, there is a female figure that can almost certainly be identified as a slave girl by her hair style, dress, and the box she holds in her hands. On Classical grave reliefs women are often accompanied by similar handmaidens (e.g. on the well known Hegeso stele). There as here their primary purpose probably is to serve as a status indicator.

Next, I would like to include some observations on the composition of family groups in Classical Greek votive reliefs. There is sufficient material for a cautious statistical analysis. It would probably be best to base such a statistical research on all surviving votive reliefs, but for various practical reasons that is not easily feasible. Limiting the field to one particular sanctuary would seem to be a promising alternative. However, apart from other practical problems, the number of surviving votive reliefs (with worshippers that are identifiable as to their sex and age) from any one sanctuary, is generally too small to produce statistically interesting results. I have tried to steer a middle course, by choosing one specific class of votive reliefs, the hero banquet type, which in the Classical period is as good as restricted to hero cult. Heroes had a broad range of functions. They could be invoked on all sorts of occasions, by people from all walks of life, so there is a reasonable chance that whatever picture emerges may not be too much different from the average.

The total number of Classical banquet reliefs with worshippers that I have found is a little less than 200.[105] Of these *c.* 15 per cent have only one single male worshipper. There is some margin for error, due to the state of preservation of some reliefs, and if we include all the doubtful but possible ones, the single males would amount to *c.* 17 per cent. Single female worshippers there are none. Couples are found in *c.* 74 per cent (maybe 78 per cent) of the reliefs;

[104] Athens NM 1402: Svoronos, *Ath. NM.* 351, pl. 35; Süsserott, *Griech. Plastik*, 114; Hausmann, *Kunst und Heiltum*, 166 no. 7; S. Karusu, 'Die Antiken vom Kloster Luku in der Thyreatis', *RM* 76 (1969), 253–65; P. B. Phaklares, Ἀρχαία Κυνουρία. Ἀνθρωπινή δραστηριότητα καὶ περίβαλλον (Δημοσιεύματα του Ἀρχαιολογικού Δελτίου 43) (Athens, 1990), 96–104 and 192–3. Second quarter 4th cent. BC.
[105] I have used the lists in R. N. Thönges-Stringaris, 'Das griechische Totenmahl', *AM* 80 (1965), 1 ff. and Dentzer, *Banquet couché*, augmented with some stray specimens that for some reason or other were not included in those lists.

this includes all couples, with or without children or other additional figures.[106] Approximately 70 per cent of these couples have children. In other words, in more than half of the reliefs with worshippers (c. 55 per cent), these worshippers are couples with children.[107] There are a few single parents: three or four single men, and three or four single women, with a child or children, which amounts to roughly 2 per cent each. Finally, there are three or four reliefs with rather larger groups of worshippers, consisting of adult male figures only. These, clearly, are not family groups, but probably some sort of clubs or religious associations such as orgeōnes.[108] That there are so few of these among our banquet reliefs reemphasizes the fact that the bulk of this material is really of a private nature.

So what we may conclude (with due caution) from the quantitative breakdown of the iconographical material, is this: (1) Private dedications by men could be regarded as an entirely individual matter. This, however, is only the case in a not too impressive minority of the dedications. (2) Private dedications by women were always regarded as a family affair; they are always portrayed together with their family, or, at the very least, their children. If we look through other types of votive reliefs, we will come across the odd single female worshipper, so instead of 'always' we should rather, more prudently, say 'almost always'.[109]

It is clear from the above that the dedicants of the Classical votive reliefs preferably viewed and represented themselves as members of a family. What, finally, can we learn from these reliefs with regard to their behaviour, their activities in the sanctuary? Even on a cursory perusal of the material it soon emerges that the repertoire of activities depicted is extremely limited.

There is one activity, performed in sanctuaries of healing gods, that is depicted not infrequently: incubation (egkoimēsis, egkatakoimēsis), i.e. the patient is seen lying on a couch, being visited by the god.

---

[106] For the present purpose I have defined 'couple' as an adult male and female figure standing next to each other.

[107] The number of children per couple is as follows: 36 per cent of the couples have one child, 46.5 per cent have two children, 14.9 per cent have three, and 2.6 per cent have four children. On average this works out at a bit more than 1.5 children per family. For another type of votive relief with a larger number of children, see n. 101.

[108] W. S. Ferguson, 'The Attic Orgeones', HarvTheolR 37 (1944), 62–140; W. S. Ferguson, 'Orgeonika', Hesperia, Supp. 8 (1949), 130–63.

[109] See e.g. n. 95.

Here again the patient is regularly accompanied by his family.[110] But otherwise, the only things we see worshippers doing in the scenes on their votive reliefs are worshipping, praying, with one hand raised (sometimes two hands raised or kneeling), and offering sacrifice. The sacrificial scenes usually include an animal. Sometimes only sacrificial cakes (*popana*) are offered, brought to the sanctuary in a *kistē*.

But even of the sacrificial ritual, which encompassed a whole range of consecutive activities, only the initial stage is represented: the presentation of the animal at the altar, and occasionally the deposition of the *olai* (barley corns).[111] Subsequently the animal had to be killed and slaughtered, parts of it were burnt on the altar, most of it was eaten by the worshippers. These interesting and enjoyable activities are (almost) totally absent in votive iconography.[112] Another activity which must have occurred quite frequently in sanctuaries, dancing, is also very rarely depicted on votive offerings.[113]

Why is it that we see so few representations of dancing and banqueting on votive offerings? Some considerations which may have played a part in this iconographical selectivity are the following. Dancing is mainly a collective activity, whereas the votive offerings are predominantly private dedications. And the votive offerings play an essential part in the *do ut des* relationship between men and gods. Therefore perhaps it is understandable that the worshippers, in the representations on their votive offerings, would rather emphasize the fact that they *give*, *offer* a sacrifice, than that they *eat* most of it themselves. These may be relevant points, but I have a feeling that they are, at best, only part of the answer. Perhaps it is wiser, for the moment, to leave the question open.

[110] Hausmann, *Kunst und Heiltum*, Ch. 2; F. T. van Straten, 'Mens en ziekte. De genezingsinscripties van Epidauros', *Hermeneus*, 55 (1983), 181–95 (also in: H. F. J. Horstmanshoff (ed.), *Pijn en Balsem, Troost en Smart. Pijnbeleving en Pijnbestrijding in de Oudheid* (Rotterdam, 1994), 57–70).

[111] van Straten, 'Greek Sacrificial Representations', in *Gifts*, 159–70; id., 'The God's Portion in Greek Sacrificial Representations', 51–68.

[112] Banquets on later votive reliefs: E. Mitropoulou, 'Feasting and Festivals', *Akten des XIII. Internationalen Kongresses für klassische Archäologie, Berlin 1988* (1990), 472–4. See also the relief from Cyprus, n. 19.

[113] e.g. in the pediment of the *pinax* of Niinnion from Eleusis, Athens NM 11036: A. Peschlow-Bindokat, 'Demeter und Persephone in der attischen Kunst des 6. bis 4. Jahrhunderts', *JdI* 87 (1972), 60–157, esp. 105 ff., with bibliography.

PART III
Myths and Rituals

10

Jason, Hypsipyle, and New Fire at Lemnos: A Study in Myth and Ritual

WALTER BURKERT

History of religion, in its beginnings, had to struggle to emancipate itself from classical mythology as well as from theology and philosophy; when ritual was finally found to be the basic fact in religious tradition, the result was a divorce between classicists, treating mythology as a literary device, on the one hand, and specialists in festivals and rituals and their obscure affiliations and origins on the other.[1] The function of myth in society was studied by anthropologists,[2] the interrelation of myth and ritual was stressed by orientalists,[3] but the

---

[1] This chapter was read as a paper at the Joint Triennial Classical Conference in Oxford, September 1968. The notes cannot aim at completeness of bibliography. The preponderance of ritual as against myth was vigorously stated by W. Robertson Smith, *Lectures on the Religion of the Semites* (Edinburgh, 1889;3rd edn., London, 1927), ch. i, pressed further by Jane Harrison: myth 'nothing but ritual misunderstood' (*Mythology and Monuments of Ancient Athens* (London, 1890), p. xxxiii). In Germany, it was the school of Albrecht Dieterich who concentrated on the study of ritual. Thus mythology is conspicuously absent from the indispensable handbooks of M. P. Nilsson (*GF* and *GGR*) and L. Deubner (*AF*), whereas Wilamowitz stated that mythology was the creation of poets: 'Der Mythos . . . entsteht in der Phantasie des Dichters' (*Der Glaube der Hellenen*, i (Berlin, 1931), 42). Mythology tried to re-establish itself in the trend of phenomenology and C. G. Jung's psychology, largely ignoring ritual: cf. the surveys of J. de Vries, *Forschungsgeschichte der Mythologie* (Freiburg, 1961); K. Kerényi, *Die Eröffnung des Zugangs zum Mythos* (Darmstadt, 1967); 'die Religionswissenschaft ist vornehmlich Wissenschaft der Mythen' (K. Kerényi, *Umgang mit Göttlichem* (Göttingen, 1955), 25).
[2] B. Malinowski, *Myth in Primitive Psychology* (London, 1926); C. Kluckhohn, 'Myths and Rituals: a General Theory', *HThR* 35 (1942), 45–79.
[3] S. H. Hooke (ed.), *Myth and Ritual* (Oxford, 1933), defining myth as 'the spoken part of the ritual', 'the story which the ritual enacts' (3); id., *Myth, Ritual, and Kingship* (Oxford, 1958); Th. H. Gaster, *Thespis*, 2nd edn. (New York, 1961). Independently, W. F. Otto, in his *Dionysos* (Frankfurt am M., 1934), spoke of 'Zusammenfall von Kultus und Mythos' (43 and *passim*). In fact connections of myth and ritual had been recognized by F. G. Welcker and, in an intuitive and unsystematic manner, by Wilamowitz ('Der mythische Thiasos aber ist ein Abbild des im festen Kultus gegebenen', *Euripides Herakles*, i (Berlin, 1889), 85, cf. id., 'Hephaistos' (*NGG*, 1895, 217–45 = *Kl. Schr.*

classicists' response has been mainly negative.[4] It cannot be denied
that Greeks often spoke of correspondence of λεγόμενα and
δρώμενα ('what is spoken' and 'what is done'),[5] that rituals are usually said to have been instituted 'on account of' some mythical event;
but it is held that these myths are either 'aetiological' inventions and
therefore of little interest, or that 'well-known types of story' have
been superimposed on 'simple magical rites and spells' as Joseph
Fontenrose concluded from his study of Python: 'The rituals did not
enact the myth; the myth did not receive its plot from the rituals.'[6]

Still, a formula such as 'simple magical rites' should give rise to
further thinking. Life is complex beyond imagination, and so is living
ritual. Our information about ancient ritual is, for the most part,
desperately scanty, but to call it simple may bar understanding from
the start; the simplicity may be just due to our perception and
description. It is true that we do not usually find Greek myths as a
liturgically fixed part of ritual; but this does not preclude the possibility of a ritual origin of myth; and if, in certain cases, there is secondary superimposition of myth on ritual, even the adopted child may
have a real father—some distant rite of somehow similar pattern.
Only detailed interpretation may turn such possibilities into probability or even certainty. But it is advisable to remember that those
combinations and superimpositions and aetiological explanations
were made by people with first-hand experience of ancient religion;
before discarding them, one should try to understand them.

(Berlin, 1937), v. 2, 5–35), 234 f. on the binding of Hera). In interpretation of Greek
tragedy, due attention has been paid to ritual, cf. e.g. E. R. Dodds, *Euripides Bacchae*,
2nd edn. (Oxford, 1960), pp. xxv–xxviii.

 [4] Nilsson, *GGR*, 14 n. with reference to Malinowski: 'für die griechischen Mythen
trifft diese Lehre nicht zu'; cf. id., *Cults*, 10; H. J. Rose, *Mnemosyne*, iv. S. 3 (1950), 281–
7; N. A. Marlow, *BRL* 43 (1960–1), 373–402; J. Fontenrose, *The Ritual Theory of Myth*
(Berkeley, 1966). As a consequence, historians of religion turn away from the Greek,
cf. M. Eliade, *Antaios*, 9 (1968), 329, stating 'daß wir nicht einen einzigen griechischen
Mythos in seinem rituellen Zusammenhang kennen'.

 [5] With regard to mysteries, as Nilsson (cf. n. 4 above) remarks (Gal. *UP* 6, 14 (iii. 576
K.); Paus. I. 43. 2; 2. 37. 2; 2. 38. 2; 9. 30. 12, cf. Hdt. 2. 81; 2. 47; 2. 51; M. N. H. van
den Burg, *ΑΠΟΡΡΗΤΑ ΔΡΩΜΕΝΑ ΟΡΓΙΑ*, Diss. Amsterdam, 1939), not because
there was nothing similar in non-secret cults, but because only the secrecy required
the use of general passive expressions as λεγόμενα, δρώμενα. Ritual as μίμησις of
myth, e.g. Diod. Sic. 4. 3. 3; Steph. Byz. s.v. Ἄγρα. Cf. Ach. Tat. 2. 2 τῆς ἑορτῆς πατέρα
διηγοῦνται μῦθον.

 [6] *Python* (Berkeley, 1959), 461–2, against Hooke (above, n. 3) and J. E. Harrison who
wrote 'the myth is the plot of the δρώμενον' (*Themis*, 3rd edn. (Cambridge, 1927), 331).

One of the best-known Greek myths, from Homer's time (*Od.* 12. 70) throughout antiquity, is the story of the Argonauts; one incident, the 'Lemnian crime' followed by the romance of Jason and Hypsipyle, enjoyed proverbial fame. That it has anything to do with ritual, we learn only through sheer coincidence: the family of the Philostrati were natives of Lemnos, and one of them included details of Lemnian tradition in his dialogue *Heroicus*, written about AD 215.[7] The vine-dresser of Elaius who is conversant with the ghost of Protesilaus describes the semi-divine honours allegedly paid to Achilles by the Thessalians long before the Persian war, and he illustrates them by reference to certain Corinthian rites and to a festival of Lemnos; the common characteristic is the combination of propitiation of the dead, ἐναγίσματα, with mystery-rites, τελεστικόν:

ἐπὶ δὲ τῷ ἔργῳ τῷ περὶ τοὺς ἄνδρας ὑπὸ τῶν ἐν Λήμνῳ γυναικῶν ἐξ Ἀφροδίτης ποτὲ πραχθέντι καθαίρεται μὲν ἡ Λῆμνος † καὶ καθ᾽ ἕνα τοῦ ἔτους† καὶ σβέννυται τὸ ἐν αὐτῇ πῦρ ἐς ἡμέρας ἐννέα· θεωρὶς δὲ ναῦς ἐκ Δήλου πυρφορεῖ, κἂν ἀφίκηται πρὸ τῶν ἐναγισμάτων, οὐδαμοῦ τῆς Λήμνου καθορμίζεται, μετέωρος δὲ ἐπισαλεύει τοῖς ἀκρωτηρίοις, ἔς τε ὅσιον τὸ ἐσπλεῦσαι γένηται. θεοὺς γὰρ χθονίους καὶ ἀπορρήτους καλοῦντες τότε καθαρόν, οἶμαι, τὸ πῦρ τὸ ἐν τῇ θαλάττῃ φυλάττουσιν. ἐπειδὰν δὲ ἡ θεωρὶς ἐσπλεύσῃ καὶ νείμωνται τὸ πῦρ ἔς τε τὴν ἄλλην δίαιταν ἔς τε τὰς ἐμπύρους τῶν τεχνῶν, καινοῦ τὸ ἐντεῦθεν βίου φασὶν ἄρχεσθαι.[8]

On account of the deed that has been wrought about the men by the women at Lemnos, through the instigation of Aphrodite, Lemnos is purified at a certain time in the year; and fire on the island is extinguished for nine days. A ship destined for the sacred embassy brings fire from Delos; and if it arrives before the uncanny offerings, it does not come to anchor at any place in Lemnos but keeps afloat at the promontories, until it becomes religiously sanctioned to move in. For they implore subterranean and secret gods at that time, and hence, I think, they preserve the fire in a pure state at sea. But when the embassy-ship has moved in and they have distributed the fire for the other uses of everyday life and (especially) for the crafts that use fire, they say that from that point on they are starting a new life.

[7] On the problem of the Philostrati and the author of the *Heroicus*, K. Münscher, *Die Philostrate* (Leipzig, 1907), 469ff.; F. Solmsen, *RE* XX (1941), 154–9; on the date of the *Heroicus*, Münscher, 474, 497–8, 505; Solmsen, 154.

[8] Ch. 19 § 20 in the edition of G. Olearius (1709; followed by Kayser) = ch. 20 § 24 in the edn. of A. Westermann (1849; followed by Nilsson, *GF*, 470) = ii. 207 of the Teubner edn. (C. L. Kayser, 1871); critical edns.: J. F. Boissonade (Paris, 1806), 232; Kayser (Zürich, 1844, 2nd edn. 1853), 325. καὶ καθ᾽ ἕνα τοῦ ἔτους is found in three codices (γ, φ, ψ) and apparently in a fourth (p) before correction; the printed editions, from the Aldina (1503), dropped the καί at the beginning; Boissonade and Westermann adopted καθ᾽ ἕκαστον ἔτος found in the other manuscripts. Kayser lists 32 codices altogether.

It is frustrating that one important detail, the time of the festival, is obscured by corruption. The reading of the majority of the manuscripts, καθ᾽ ἕκαστον ἔτος, is too obvious a correction to be plausible. But the ingenious suggestion of Adolf Wilhelm[9] to read καθ᾽ ἐνάτου ἔτους has to be rejected, too: it introduces an erroneous orthography of old inscriptions into a literary text of the Imperial age, it gives an unattested meaning to κατά with genitive,[10] and it fails to account for the καί; it is as difficult to assume two unrelated corruptions in the same passage as to imagine how the misreading of ἐνάτου should have brought forth the superfluous καί. Looking for other remedies, one could surmise that a masculine substantive, required by καθ᾽ ἕνα, is missing, hiding in that very καί: καιρὸν καθ᾽ ἕνα τοῦ ἔτους—an unusual word-order, modelled on Herodotus' frequent χρόνον ἔπι πολλόν and similar expressions and thus combining archaism with peculiarities of later Greek.[11] Of course it is possible that more serious corruption has occurred; still the traditional emendation καθ᾽ ἕκαστον ἔτος may not be far off the mark as to the content: Achilles received his honours which the Lemnian custom is meant to illustrate, ἀνὰ πᾶν ἔτος too (ii. 207, 2, Teubner edn.).

Nilsson, in Griechische Feste (470), has Philostratus' account under the heading 'festivals of unknown divinities'. This is an excess of self-restraint. There is one obvious guess as to which god must have played a prominent role in the fire festival: Lemnos is the island of Hephaistos,[12] the main city is called Hephaistia

---

[9] AAWW, 1939, 41–6, followed by M. Delcourt, Héphaistos ou la légende du magicien (Paris, 1957), 172–3; Nilsson, GGR, 97, n. 6. S. Eitrem, SO 9 (1930), 60 tried καθαίρονται ἡ Λῆμνος καὶ ⟨οἱ Λήμνιοι⟩ καθ᾽ ἕνα κατ᾽ ἔτος.

[10] κατά c. gen. 'down to a certain deadline' in the instances adduced by Wilhelm: a contract κατ᾽ εἴκοσι ἐτῶν, κατὰ βίου, κατὰ τοῦ παντὸς χρόνου. Cf. W. Schmid, Der Attizismus, iv (Stuttgart, 1898), 456.

[11] Moer.: ὥρα ἔτους Ἀττικοί, καιρὸς ἔτους Ἕλληνες, cf. Schmid, loc. cit. in prev. note, 361. For inversion of word-order, cf. Heroicus 12. 2 κρατῆρας τοὺς ἐκεῖθεν.

[12] Il. I. 593, Od. 8. 283–4 with schol. and Eust. 157. 28; A.R. 1. 851–2 with schol.; Nic. Ther. 458 with schol., etc.; cf. Wilamowitz, 'Hephaistos'; C. Fredrich, 'Lemnos', MDAI (A) 31 (1906), 60–86, 241–56; L. Malten, 'Hephaistos', JDAI 27 (1912), 232–64 and RE VIII 315–16. Combination with the fire-festival: F. G. Welcker, Die aeschyleische Trilogie Prometheus und die Kabirenweihe zu Lemnos (Darmstadt, 1824), 155–304, esp. 247ff.; J. J. Bachofen, Das Mutterrecht (Stuttgart, 1861), 90 = Ges. Werke, ii. 276; Fredrich, 'Lemnos', 74–5; Delcourt, Héphaistos, 171–90, whereas L. R. Farnell, Cults of the Greek States, v (Oxford, 1909), 394 concluded from the silence of Philostratus that the festival was not connected with Hephaistos. The importance of the craftsmen was stressed by Welcker, 248, Delcourt, 177. That the festival belongs to Hephaistia, not Myrina is shown by the coins already used by Welcker, cf. n. 35 below.

throughout antiquity, it has the head of Hephaistos on its coins. Incidentally, one Lucius Flavius Philostratus was ἱερεὺς τοῦ ἐπωνύμου τῆς πόλεως Ἡφαίστου ('priest of Hephaistos who bears the name of the city') in the third century AD. (IG XII 8, 27). But Hephaistos is the god of fire, even fire himself (Il. 2. 426): the purification of the island of Hephaistos, brought about by new fire, was a festival of Hephaistos. Philostratus indeed alludes to this: the new fire, he says, is distributed especially 'to the craftsmen who have to do with fire', i.e. to potters and blacksmiths. The island must have been famous for its craftsmen at an early date: the Sinties of Lemnos, Hellanicus said (FGrHist 4 F 71), invented fire and the forging of weapons. The 'invention', the advent of fire, is repeated in the festival. It is true that Philostratus mentions Aphrodite as the agent behind the original crime: she ought to have a place in the atonement, too.[13] But the question: to which god does the festival 'belong', seems to be rather a misunderstanding of polytheism: as the ritual mirrors the complexity of life, various aspects of reality, i.e. different deities, are concerned.[14] The 'beginning of a new life' at Lemnos would affect all the gods who played their part in the life of the community, above all the Great Goddess who was called Lemnos herself.[15]

To get farther, it is tempting to embark on ethnological comparison. Festivals of new fire are among the most common folk customs all over the world; striking parallels have been adduced from the Red Indians as well as from East Indian Burma;[16] and one could refer to the Incas as well as to the Japanese. Nilsson, wisely, confines himself to Greek parallels, not without adding the remark (GF, 173): 'It is a ubiquitous belief that fire loses its purity through daily use.' 'Ubiquitous belief' is meant to explain the ritual. Where, however, one ought to ask, do such ubiquitous beliefs come from? The obvious

---

[13] Cf. A. R. I. 850-2, 858-60; a dedication Ἀ]φροδίτει Θρα[ικίαι from the Kabeirion of Lemnos, ASAA 3/5 (1941-3), 91 no. 12; a temple of Aphrodite at Lemnos, schol. Stat. Theb. 5. 59; the κρατίστη δαίμων in Aristophanes' Lemniai (fr. 365) may be the same 'Thracian Aphrodite'.

[14] The sacrificial calendars regularly combine different deities in the same ceremonies, cf. as the most extensive example the calendar of Erchiai, G. Daux, BCH 87 (1963), 603ff., S. Dow BCH 89 (1965), 180–213.

[15] Phot., Hsch. s.v. μεγάλη θεός = Ar. fr. 368; Steph. Byz. s.v. Λῆμνος. Pre-Greek representations: Fredrich, 'Lemnos', 60ff. with pls. VIII and IX; A. Della Seta, AE (1937), 644, pls. 2 and 3; Greek coins in B. V. Head, Historia Numorum, 2nd edn. (Oxford, 1911), 263.

[16] Fredrich, 'Lemnos', 75; Frazer, GB, viii. 72–5; x. 136; generally on fire-festivals: ii. 195–265; x. 106–xi. 44.

answer is: from the rituals.[17] People, living with their festivals from childhood, are taught their beliefs by these very rituals, which remain constant as against the unlimited possibilities of primitive associations. Thus the comparative method does not, by itself, lead to an explanation, to an understanding of what is going on—if one does not take it for granted that whatever Greeks or Romans told about their religion is wrong, but what any savage told to a merchant or missionary is a revelation. At the same time, by mere accumulation of comparative material, the outlines of the picture become more and more blurred, until nothing is left but vague generalities.

In sharp contrast to the method of accumulation, there is the method of historical criticism; instead of expanding the evidence, it tries to cut it down, to isolate elements and to distribute them neatly to different times and places. The πυρφορία ('fire-bringing') described by Philostratus connects Delos and Lemnos. This, we are told, is an innovation which betrays Attic influence. The suggestion cannot be disproved, though it is remarkable that Philostratus wrote at a time when Lemnos had just become independent from Athens, that the Athenians got their new fire not from Delos, but from Delphi (Plut. Arist. 20), and that the role of Delos as a religious centre of the islands antedates not only Attic, but plainly Greek influence.[18] Still, the critical separation of Lemnian and Delian worship has its consequences: if the Lemnians originally did not sail to Delos, where did their new fire come from? Obviously from an indigenous source: the miraculous fire of Mount Mosychlos.[19] This fire has a curious history. The commentators on Homer and Sophocles and the Roman poets clearly speak of a volcano on Lemnos;[20] this volcano was active in

[17] Usually 'beliefs' are traced back to emotional experience; but cf. C. Lévi-Strauss, *Le Totémisme aujourd'hui* (Paris, 1962), 102f.: 'Ce ne sont pas des émotions actuelles . . . ressenties à l'occasion des réunions et des cérémonies qui engendrent ou perpétuent les rites, mais l'activité rituelle qui suscite les émotions.'

[18] F. Càssola, 'La leggenda di Anio e la preistoria Delia', *PP* 60 (1954), 345–67; there is an old sanctuary of the Kabeiroi on Delos, B. Hemberg, *Die Kabiren* (Uppsala, 1950), 140–53; the Orion myth combines Delos and Lemnos, below, n. 24.

[19] Fredrich, 'Lemnos', 75; with reference to a custom in Burma, Frazer, *GB*, x. 136; Malten, *JDAI* 27 (1912), 248f.; Fredrich, however, thinks that the earth fire came to be extinguished at an early date.

[20] κρατῆρες: Eust. 158. 3; 1598. 44; schol. Soph. *Phil.* 800, 986; Val. Flacc. 2. 332–9; Stat. *Theb.* 5. 50, 87; *Silv.* 3. 1. 131–3. Less explicit: Heraclit. *All.* 26. 15 (echoed by Eust. 157. 37, schol. *Od.* 8. 284) ἀνίενται γηγενοῦς πυρὸς αὐτόματοι φλόγες (F. Buffière, Budé edn., 1962 keeps the manuscript reading ἐγγυγηγενοῦς, 'un feu qu'on croirait presque sorti de terre', but this is hardly Greek); Acc. trag. 532 'nemus exspirante vapore vides . . .' is incompatible with the volcano-, though not with the earth-fire-hypothesis.

literature down to the end of the nineteenth century, with some scattered eruptions even in later commentaries on Sophocles' *Philoctetes*,[21] though geographical survey had revealed that there never was a volcano on Lemnos at any time since this planet has been inhabited by *homo sapiens*.[22] Thus the volcano disappeared, but its fire remained: scholars confidently speak of an 'earth fire', a perpetual flame nourished by earth gas on Mount Mosychlos. As earth gas may be found nearly everywhere and fires of this kind do not leave permanent traces, this hypothesis cannot be disproved. Nothing has been adduced to prove it either. The analogy with the fires of Baku ought not to be pressed; no reservoir of oil has been found at Lemnos.

There is no denying that 'Lemnian fire' was something famous and uncanny. Philoctetes, in his distress, invokes it:

ὦ Λημνία χθὼν καὶ τὸ παγκρατὲς σέλας | ἡφαιστότευκτον (986–7).

O land of Lemnos, all-powerful flame produced by Hephaistos.

Antimachus mentions it in comparison (fr. 46 Wyss):

Ἡφαίστου φλογὶ εἴκελον, ἥν ῥα τιτύσκει
δαίμων ἀκροτάτης ὄρεος κορυφαῖσι Μοσύχλου.

like the flame of Hephaistos which a god produces
at the highest summits of Mount Mosychlos.

This fire on the summit of the mountain is in some way miraculous, δαιμόνιον—but τιτύσκει (after *Il.* 21. 342) is hardly suggestive of a perpetual flame. There is, however, another invocation of Lemnian fire in the *Philoctetes*: τῷ Λημνίῳ τῷδ᾽ ἀνακαλουμένῳ πυρὶ ἔμπρησον ('burn me with this Lemnian fire which is called up (?)') (800f.), the hero cries. ἀνακαλουμένῳ has proved to be a stumbling-block for believers either in the volcano or the earth fire.[23] ἀνακαλεῖν,

[21] L. Preller and C. Robert, *Griechische Mythologie*, 4th edn., i (Berlin, 1894), 175, 178; R. C. Jebb, *Sophocles, Philoctetes* (Cambridge, 1890), 243–5; P. Mazon, *Sophocles, Philoctète* (Budé edn., 1960), note on v. 800.

[22] K. Neumann and J. Partsch, *Physikalische Geographie von Griechenland* (Breslau, 1885), 314–18, who immediately thought of the earth fire, cf. Fredrich, 'Lemnos', 253–4, Malten, *JDAI* 27 (1912), 233, *RE* VIII 316, Nilsson, *GGR*, 528–9; R. Hennig, 'Altgriechische Sagengestalten als Personifikation von Erdfeuern', *JDAI* 54 (1939), 230–46. Earth fires are well attested at Olympos in Lycia (Malten, *RE* VIII 317–19), where the Hephaistos-cult was prominent, and at Trapezus in Arcadia (Arist. *Mir.* 127; Paus. 8. 29. 1) and at Apollonia in Epirus (Theopompus, *FGrHist* 115 F 316) without the Hephaistos-cult.

[23] Meineke and Pearson changed the text to ἀνακαλούμενον, Mazon translates 'que tu évoqueras pour cela', though keeping ἀνακαλουμένῳ; Jebb translates 'famed as', with reference to *El.* 693, where, however, ἀνακαλούμενος is 'being solemnly proclaimed' as victor.

ἀνακαλεῖσθαι is a verb of ritual, used especially for 'imploring' chthonic deities: Deianeira implores her δαίμων (Soph. *Tr.* 910), Oedipus at Colonus his ἀραί (Soph. *OC* 1376). Thus ἀνακαλουμένῳ seems to imply a certain ceremony to produce this demoniac fire; it is not always there. Understood in this way, the verse turns out to be the earliest testimony to the fire-festival of Lemnos; it confirms the guess that the fire was not brought from Delos at that time. How the fire was kindled in the ritual, may have been a secret. Considering the importance of Lemnian craftsmen, the most miraculous method for χαλκεῖς would be to use a χαλκεῖον, a bronze burning-mirror to light a new fire from the sun.[24] Hephaistos fell on Lemnos from heaven, the *Iliad* says (1. 593), on Mount Mosychlos, native tradition held;[25] he was very feeble, but the Sinties at once took care of him. In the tiny flame rising from the tinder in the focus, the god has arrived—alas, this is just a guess. But it seems advisable to send the earth fire of Mosychlos together with the volcano after the volcanic vapours of Delphi, which, too, vanished completely under the spade of the excavators; the miracles of ritual do not need the miracles of nature; the miracles of nature do not necessarily produce mythology.

To get beyond guesses, there is one clue left in the text of Philostratus: the purification is performed 'on account of the deed wrought by the Lemnian women against their husbands'. It is by myth that ancient tradition explains the ritual. Modern scholarship has revolted against this. As early as 1824, Friedrich Gottlob Welcker found a 'glaring contrast' between the 'deeper' meaning of the festival and the 'extrinsic occasion' said to be its cause.[26] Georges Dumézil,[27]

---

[24] Ancient burning-mirrors were always made of bronze; the testimonies in J. Morgan, 'De ignis eliciendi modis', *HSCP* 1 (1890), 50–64; earliest mention: Theophr. *Ign.* 73, Eucl. *Opt.* 30 (burning-glass: Ar. *Nub.* 767); used in rituals of new fire: Plut. *Num.* 9 (Delphi and Athens, 1st cent. BC); Heraclit. *All.* 26. 13 κατ' ἀρχὰς οὐδέπω τῆς τοῦ πυρὸς χρήσεως ἐπιπολαζούσης ἄνθρωποι χρονικῶς χαλκοῖς τισιν ὀργάνοις ἐφειλκύσαντο τοὺς ἀπὸ τῶν μετεώρων φερομένους σπινθῆρας, κατὰ τὰς μεσημβρίας ἐναντία τῷ ἡλίῳ τὰ ὄργανα τιθέντες.
Parallels from the Incas, Siam, China: Frazer, *GB*, ii. 243, 245; x. 132, 137. Fredrich, 'Lemnos', 75. 3 thought of the burning-mirror in connection with the myth of Orion, who recovers his eyesight from the sun with the help of the Lemnian Kedalion (Hes. fr. 148 Merkelbach-West). 'Fire from the sky' lit the altar at Rhodes, the famous centre of metallurgy (Pi. *O.* 7. 48). The practice may have influenced the myth of Helios' cup as well as the theories of Xenophanes and Heraclitus about the sun (21 A 32, 40; 22 A 12, B 6 DK).

[25] Galen xii. 173 K., cf. Acc. trag. 529–31.

[26] *Prometheus*, 249–50.

[27] *Le Crime des Lemniennes* (Paris, 1924).

however, was able to show that the connection of myth and ritual, in this case, is by no means 'extrinsic': there is almost complete correspondence in outline and in detail.

The myth is well known:[28] the wrath of Aphrodite had smitten the women of Lemnos; they developed a 'foul smell' (δυσωδία) so awful that their husbands, understandably, sought refuge in the arms of Thracian slave-girls. This, in turn, enraged the women so much that, in one terrible night, they slew their husbands and, for the sake of completeness, all the male population of the island. Thereafter Lemnos was a community of women without men, ruled by the virgin queen Hypsipyle, until the day when the ship arrived, the Argo with Jason. This was the end of Lemnian celibacy. With a rather licentious festival the island returned to bisexual life. The story, in some form, is already known to the *Iliad*: the son of Jason and Hypsipyle is dwelling on Lemnos, Euneos, the man of the fine ship.

With this myth, the fire ritual is connected not in a casual or arbitrary manner, but by an identity of rhythm, marked by two περιπέτειαι ('reversals'): first, there begins a period of abnormal, barren, uncanny life, until, secondly, the advent of the ship brings about a new, joyous life—which is in fact the return to normal life.

Correspondences go even farther. The mythological *aition* compels us to combine with the text of Philostratus another testimony about Lemnian ritual, which, too, is said to be a remnant of the Argonauts' visit. Myrsilos of Lesbos is quoted for a different explanation of the infamous δυσωδία: not Aphrodite, but Medea caused it; in accordance with the older version ousted by Apollonius,[29] Myrsilos made the Argonauts come to Lemnos on their return from Kolchis, though the presence of Medea brought some complications for Jason and Hypsipyle. The jealous sorceress took her revenge: καὶ δυσοσμίαν γενέσθαι ταῖς γυναιξίν· εἶναί τε μέχρι τοῦ νῦν κατ᾽ ἐνιαυτὸν ἡμέραν τινά, ἐν ᾗ διὰ τὴν δυσωδίαν ἀπέχειν τὰς γυναῖκας ἄνδρα τε καὶ υἱεῖς ('and a foul smell befell the women. And until now, there is a day in the

---

[28] Survey of sources: Roscher, *Myth. Lex.* i. 2853–6 (Klügmann), ii. 73–4 (Seeliger), v. 808–14 (Immisch); L. Preller and C. Robert, *Griech. Mythologie*, 4th edn., ii (Berlin, 1921), 849–59; cf. Wilamowitz, *Hellenistische Dichtung*, ii (Berlin, 1924), 232–48. Jason, Hypsipyle, Thoas, Euneos in Homer: *Il.* 7. 468–9, 14. 230, 15. 40, 21. 41, 23. 747; cf. Hes. fr. 157, 253–6 Merkelbach-West.

[29] Pi. *P.* 4. 252–7.

year (they say) when the women, because of the foul smell, keep away their husbands and sons').[30] Thus one of the most curious features of the myth reappears in ritual, at least down to Hellenistic times: the foul smell of the women, which isolates them from men. Evidently this fits very well into that abnormal period of the purification ceremony. Extinguishing all fires on the island—this in itself means a dissolution of all normal life. There is no cult of the gods, which requires incense and fire on the altars, there is no regular meal in the houses of men during this period, no meat, no bread, no porridge; some special vegetarian diet must have been provided. The ἑστία ('hearth'), the centre of the community, the centre of every house is dead. What is even more, the families themselves are broken apart, as it were by a curse: men cannot meet their wives, sons cannot see their mothers. The active part in this separation of sexes is, according to the text of Myrsilos, played by the women; they are the subject of ἀπέχειν. They act together, by some sort of organization; probably they meet in the streets or the sanctuaries, whereas the male population is scared away. Thus the situation in the city closely reflects the situation described in the myth: disagreeable women rule the town, the men have disappeared.

Dumézil already went one step farther and used the myth to supplement our information about the ritual. There is the famous fate of King Thoas, son of Dionysus, father of Hypsipyle: he is not killed like the other men; Hypsipyle hides him in a coffin, and he is tossed into the sea.[31] Valerius Flaccus (*Arg.* 2. 242ff.) gives curious details: Thoas is led to the temple of Dionysus on the night of the murder; on the next day, he is dressed up as Dionysus, with wig, wreath, garments of the god, and Hypsipyle, acting as Bacchant, escorts the god through the town down to the seashore to see him disappear. It is difficult to

---

[30] FGrHist 477 F 1a = schol. A.R. 1. 609/19e; F 1b = Antig. *hist. mir.* 118 is less detailed and therefore likely to be less accurate: κατὰ δή τινα χρόνον καὶ μάλιστα ἐν ταύταις ταῖς ἡμέραις, ἐν αἷς ἱστοροῦσιν τὴν Μήδειαν παραγενέσθαι, δυσώδεις αὐτὰς οὕτως γίνεσθαι ὥστε μηδένα προσιέναι. Delcourt, *Héphaistos*, 173, n. 2 holds that only the information about Medea goes back to Myrsilos; but the scholiast had no reason to add a reference to 'contemporary' events, whereas Myrsilos was interested in contemporary *mirabilia* (F 2; 4–6). Welcker, *Prometheus*, 250, already combined Myrsilos' with Philostratus' account.

[31] A.R. 1. 620–6; Theolytos, FGrHist 478 F 3, Xenagoras, FGrHist 240 F 31, and Kleon of Kurion in schol. A.R. 1. 623/6a; cf. Eur. *Hyps.* fr. 64. 74ff.; 105ff. Bond; Hypoth. Pi. N. b, iii. 2, 8–13 Drachmann; Kylix Berlin 2300 = ARV² 409, 43 = G. M. A. Richter, *The Furniture of the Greeks, Etruscans and Romans* (London, 1966), 385.

tell how much of this Valerius Flaccus took from older tradition;[32] the general pattern, the ἀποπομπή ('sending off') of the semi-divine king, the way to the sea, the tossing of the λάρναξ ('chest') into the water surely goes back to very old strata.[33] It is fitting that the new life, too, should arrive from the sea—ἀποπομπή and *adventus* correspond.

One step further, beyond Dumézil's observations, is to realize that the bloodshed wrought by the women, the killing of the men, must have had its counterpart in ritual, too: in sacrifices, involving rather cruel spectacles of bloodshed.[34] It would be impossible to 'call secret gods from under the earth' (Philostratus loc. cit.) without the blood of victims, flowing into a pit, possibly at night; the absence of fire would make these acts all the more dreary. Women may have played an active part in these affairs; at Hermione, in a festival called Chthonia, four old women had to cut the throats of the sacrificial cows with sickle swords (Paus. 2. 35). In Lemnos, a ram-sacrifice must have been prominent; a ram is often represented on the coins of Hephaistia.[35] The fleece of a ram, Διὸς κῴδιον, was needed in many purification ceremonies;[36] incidentally, the Argonauts' voyage had the purpose of providing a ram's fleece.

Most clearly the concluding traits of the myth reflect ritual: the arrival of the Argonauts is celebrated with an *agōn*; the prize is a garment.[37] This is as characteristic a prize as the Athenian oil at the

---

[32] Cf. Immisch, Roschers *Myth. Lex.* v. 806. Domitian had made a very similar escape from the troops of Vitellius in AD 69. *Isiaco celatus habitu interque sacrificulos* (Suet. *Dom.* I. 2, cf. Tac. *Hist.* 3. 74; Jos. *Bell. Iud.* 4. 11. 4; another similar case in the civil war, App. *BC* 4. 47; Val. Max. 7. 3. 8).

[33] This is the manner of death of Osiris, Plut. *Is.* 13. 356c. Parallels from folk-custom: W. Mannhardt, *Wald- und Feldkulte*, i (Berlin, 1875), 311ff.; Frazer, *GB*, ii. 75, iv. 206–12; Dumézil, *Le Crime*, 42ff. Hypsipyle is a telling name; 'vermutlich war Hypsipyle einst eine Parallelfigur zu Medea: die "hohe Pforte" in ihrem Namen war die Pforte der Hölle' (Wilamowitz, *Griechische Tragoedien*, 7th edn., iii (Berlin, 1926), 169, n. 1)—or rather, more generally, the 'high gate' of the Great Goddess. The same name may have been given independently to the nurse of the dying child—another aspect of the Great Goddess (*hymn. Cer.* 184ff.)—at Nemea.

[34] Cf. Burkert, 'Greek Tragedy and Sacrificial Ritual', *GRBS* 7 (1966), 102–21.

[35] Cf. *Königliche Museen zu Berlin, Beschreibung der antiken Münzen* (Berlin, 1888), 279–83; Head, *Historia Numorum*, 262–3; A. B. Cook, *Zeus*, iii (Cambridge, 1940), 233–4; Hemberg, *Die Kabiren*, 161. A similar ram-sacrifice has been inferred for Samothrace, Hemberg, 102, 284. Instead of the ram, the coins of Hephaistia sometimes have torches, πῖλοι (of Kabeiroi–Dioskouroi), and *kerykeion*, also vines and grapes; all these symbols have some connection with the context of the festival treated here.

[36] Nilsson, *GGR*, 110–13; Paus. Att. δ 18 Erbse.

[37] Simonides, 547 *PMG*; Pi. *P.* 4. 253 with schol.; cf. A.R. 2. 30–2; 3. 1204–6; 4. 423–34.

Panathenaia, the Olympian olive-wreath in Olympia; the Lemnian festival must have ended with an *agōn*, though it never attained Panhellenic importance. The garment, made by women, ἀγλαὰ ἔργα ἰδυῖαι, is a quite fitting gift to end the war of the sexes; if Jason receives the garment of Thoas (A. R. 4. 423–34), continuity bridges the gap of the catastrophe. There is one more curious detail in Pindar's account of the Lemnian *agōn*: the victor was not Jason, but a certain Erginos, who was conspicuous by his untimely grey hair; the others had laughed at him.[38] Erginos 'the workman', grey-haired and surrounded by laughter, but victorious at Lemnos after the ship had arrived—this seems to be just a transformation, a translation of Hephaistos the grey-haired workman, who constantly arouses Homeric laughter.[39] Thus the myth itself takes us back to the fire-festival: this is the triumph of Hephaistos, the reappearing fire which brings new life, especially to the workmen in the service of their god. It is possible that laughter was required in the ritual as an expression of the new life—as in Easter ceremonies, both the new fire and laughter, even in churches, are attested in the Middle Ages.[40] Another peculiarity seems to have been more decidedly 'pagan': surely neither Aeschylus nor Pindar invented the unabashed sexual colouring of the meeting of Lemniads and Argonauts; in Aeschylus, the Lemniads force the Argonauts by oath to make love to them.[41] Behind

---

[38] Pi. *O.* 4. 23–31; cf. schol. 32 c; Callim. fr. 668. Here Erginos is son of Klymenos of Orchomenos, father of Trophonios and Agamedes (another pair of divine craftsmen, with a fratricide-myth, as the Kabeiroi), whereas A.R. 1. 185, after Herodorus, *FGrHist* 31 F 45/55, makes him son of Poseidon, from Miletus, cf. Wilamowitz, *Hellenistische Dichtung*, ii. 238.

[39] The constellation Erginos–Jason–Hypsipyle is akin to the constellation Hephaistos–Ares–Aphrodite in the famous Demodocus hymn (*Od.* 8. 266–366): another triumph of Hephaistos amidst unextinguishable laughter. A special relation to Lemnos is suggested by a pre-Greek vase fragment, found in a sanctuary in Hephaistia (A. Della Seta, *AE* (1937), 650; Ch. Picard, *RA* 20 (1942–3), 97–124; to be dated about 550 BC, as B. B. Shefton kindly informs me; cf. Delcourt, *Héphaistos*, 80–2): a naked goddess *vis-à-vis* an armed warrior, both apparently fettered. This is strikingly reminiscent of Demodocus' song, as Picard and Delcourt saw, though hardly a direct illustration of Homer's text, rather of 'local legend' (cf. K. Friis Johansen, *The Iliad in Early Greek Art* (Copenhagen, 1967), 38, 59), i.e. a native Lemnian version. The crouching position of the couple reminded Picard of Bronze Age burial customs; anthropology provides examples of human sacrifice in the production of new fire: a couple forced to mate and killed on the spot (cf. E. Pechuel-Loesche, *Die Loango-Expedition*, iii. 2 (Leipzig, 1907), 171 ff.). Surely Homer's song is more enjoyable without thinking of such a gloomy background.

[40] Mannhardt, *Wald- und Feldkulte*, 502–8; Frazer, *GB*, x. 121 ff.; on 'risus Paschalis', P. Sartori, *Sitte und Brauch* (Leipzig, 1914), iii. 167.

[41] Fr. 40 Mette, cf. Pi. *P.* 4. 254; Herodorus, *FGrHist* 31 F 6.

this, there must be ritual αἰσχρολογία or even αἰσχροποιία ('verbal or even physical unruliness') at the festival of licence which forms the concluding act of the abnormal period. Many details are bound to escape us. Hephaistos, at Lemnos, was connected with the Kabeiroi. The Kabeirion, not far from Hephaistia, has been excavated; it offers a neat example of continuity of cult from pre-Greek to Greek population, but it did not yield much information about the mysteries, except that wine-drinking played an important role.[42] Myth connects the Kabeiroi of Lemnos with the Lemnian crime: they left the accursed island.[43] Since their cult continued at Lemnos, they evidently came back, when the curse had come to an end. In Aeschylus' Kabeiroi, they somehow somewhere meet the Argonauts; they invade the houses and mockingly threaten to drink everything down to the last drop of vinegar.[44] Such impudent begging is characteristic of mummery;[45] these Kabeiroi, grandchildren of Hephaistos, reflect some masked club, originally a guild of smiths, probably, who play a leading role at the purification ceremony anyhow. It is tempting to suppose that the ship of the Argonauts arriving at Lemnos really means the ship of the Kabeiroi; being associated with seafaring everywhere, it fits them to arrive by ship. The herald of the Argonauts who rises to prominence only in the negotiations of Argonauts and Lemniads is called Aithalides, 'man of soot';[46] this binds him to the blacksmiths of Lemnos; the island itself was called Aithalia.[47] These Kabeiroi–blacksmiths would, after a night of revel, ascend Mount Mosychlos with their magic cauldron and light the fire, which was then, by a torch-race, brought

---

[42] Preliminary report ASAA i/ii (1939–40), 223–4; inscriptions: ASAA iii/v (1941–3), 75–105; xiv/xvi (1952–4), 317–40; D. Levi, 'Il Cabirio di Lemno', Charisterion A. K. Orlandos, iii (Athens, 1966), 110–32; Hemberg, Die Kabiren, 160–70. Wine-vessels bore the inscription Καβείρων. Kabeiroi and Hephaistos: Akousilaos, FGrHist 2 F 20, Pherekydes, FGrHist 3 F 48 with Jacoby ad loc.; O. Kern, RE X 1423 ff.; this is not the tradition of Samothrace nor of Thebes (where there is one old Κάβιρος, Nilsson, GGR, pl. 48, 1), and thus points towards Lemnos. In the puzzling lyric fragment, adesp. 985 PMG, Kabeiros son of Lemnos is the first man.

[43] Photios s.v. Κάβειροι· δαίμονες ἐκ Λήμνου διὰ τὸ τόλμημα τῶν γυναικῶν μετενεχθέντες· εἰσὶ δὲ ἤτοι Ἥφαιστοι ἢ Τιτᾶνες.

[44] Fr. 97 Radt; that the Kabeiroi are speaking is clear from Plutarch's quotation (Quaest. conv. 633a): αὐτοὶ παίζοντες ἠπείλησαν.

[45] K. Meuli, 'Bettelumzüge im Totenkult, Opferritual und Volksbrauch', Schweizer Archiv für Volkskunde, 28 (1927–8), 1–38.

[46] A.R. 1. 641–51, cf. Pherekydes FGrHist 3 F 109.

[47] Polyb. 34. 11. 4; Steph. Byz. Αἰθάλη.

to the city and distributed to sanctuaries, houses, and workshops—
seductive possibilities.

Equally uncertain is the connection of the purification ceremonies
with the digging of 'Lemnian earth'. Λημνία γῆ, red-coloured clay,
described by Dioscorides and Galen, formed an ingredient of every
oriental drugstore down to this century;[48] superstition can even out-
live religion. Travellers observed how the clay was dug under the
supervision of the priest at the hill which, by this, is identified as
Mount Mosychlos; in the time of Galen, it was the priestess of
Artemis[49] who collected it, throwing wheat and barley on the
ground, formed it into small disks, sealed it with the seal of a goat
and sold it for medical purposes. The priestess of the goddess operat-
ing at the mount of Hephaistos—it is possible to connect this with
the fire festival. Indeed it is all the more tempting because, owing to
the continuity of ritual, this would give a clue as to the date of the
festival: Lemnian earth was collected on 6 August; this corresponds
with the time of Galen's visit.[50] Late summer is a common time for
new-year festivals in the ancient world; incidentally, the μύσται ('initiates') of the Kabeiroi at Lemnos held conventions in Skirophorion,[51]
i.e. roughly in August. Still, these combinations do not amount to
proof.

One question has been left unsolved: what about the recurrent
δυσωδία ('foul smell')? Can this be more than legend or slander?[52] The
simple and drastic answer is given by a parallel from Athens: the
authority of Philochoros[53] (FGrHist 328 F 89) is quoted for the fact
that the women ἐν (δὲ) τοῖς Σκίροις τῇ ἑορτῇ ἤσθιον σκόροδα ἕνεκα

---

[48] Fredrich, 'Lemnos', 72–4; F. W. Hasluck, ABSA 16 (1909–10), 220–30; F. L. W.
Sealey, ABSA 22 (1918–19), 164–5; Cook, Zeus, iii. 228ff.; Diosc. 5. 113; Galen, xii.
169–75 K. (on the date of his visit to Lemnos, Fredrich, 'Lemnos', 73. 1; 76. 1: late
summer AD 166). According to Dioscorides, the blood of a goat was mixed with the
earth, but Galen's informants scornfully denied this. The 'priests of Hephaistos' used
the earth to heal Philoctetes: schol. AB B 722; Philostr. Heroic. 6. 2; Plin. HN 35. 33.
Philoctetes' sanctuary, however, was in Myrina (Galen, xii. 171).

[49] Possibly the 'great Goddess', cf. above, n. 15.

[50] Cf. n. 48 above.

[51] ASAA iii/v (1941–3), 75ff. no. 2; no. 6; but no. 4 Hekatombaion.

[52] General remarks in Dumézil, Le Crime, 35–9. Welcker, Prometheus, 249 thought of
some kind of fumigation. Cf. Frazer, GB, viii. 73 for the use of purgatives in a New Fire
festival. A marginal gloss in Antig. hist. mir. 118 (cf. n. 30 above) mentions πήγανον, cf.
Jacoby, FGrHist III Komm. 437, Noten 223.

[53] E. Gjerstad, ARW 27 (1929–30), 201–3 thinks Philochoros misunderstood the
sense of the ritual, which was rather 'aphrodisiac'; though he recognizes himself that
short abstinence enhances fertility.

τοῦ ἀπέχεσθαι ἀφροδισίων, ὡς ἂν μὴ μύρων ἀποπνέοιεν ('at the festival of Skira ate garlic in order to abstain from sex: they would not give off the scent of perfumes'). Thus we have an unmistakable smell going together with disruption of marital order, separation of the sexes, at the Skira. The women flock together at this festival according to ancient custom,[54] and Aristophanes' fancy has them plan their *coup d'état* on this occasion (*Eccl.* 59). But there is even more similarity: the main event of the Skira is a procession which starts from the old temple of the Akropolis and leads towards Eleusis to the old borderline of Attica, to a place called Skiron. The priest of Poseidon–Erechtheus, the priestess of Athena, and the priest of Helios are led together under a sunshade by the Eteobutadai:[55] Erechtheus is the primordial king of Athens; he left his residence, the myth tells us, to fight the Eleusinians ἐπὶ Σκίρῳ and disappeared mysteriously in the battle; his widow became the first priestess of Athena.[56] Thus we find in Athens, on unimpeachable evidence, the ritual ἀποπομπή ('sending away') of the king which was inferred from myth for the corresponding Lemnian festival. At Athens, the concluding *agōn* has been moved farther away: the 'beginning of new life' is the Panathenaia in the following month Hekatombaion, the first of the year. If the perennial fire in the sanctuary of Athena and Erechtheus, the lamp of Athena, is refilled and rekindled only once a year,[57] this will have happened at the Panathenaia when the new oil was available and used as a prize for the victors. The month Skirophorion coincides approximately with August, the time of the digging of Lemnian earth. The name Σκίρα is enigmatic, but most of the ancient explanations concentrate on some stem σκιρ- (σκυρ-) meaning 'white earth', 'white clay', 'white rock'. The place Skiron is a place where there was some kind of white earth, and Theseus is said to have made an image of Athena out of white earth and to have carried it in procession when he was about to leave Athens.[58] Were the σκίρα some kind of

[54] *IG* II/III² 1177. 8–12 ὅταν ἡ ἑορτὴ τῶν Θεσμοφορίων καὶ Πληροσίαι καὶ Καλαμαίοις καὶ τὰ Σκίρα καὶ εἴ τινα ἄλλην ἡμέραν συνέρχονται αἱ γυναῖκες κατὰ τὰ πάτρια.
[55] Lysimachides, *FGrHist* 366 F 3; schol. Ar. *Eccl.* 18; fullest account: E. Gjerstad, *ARW* 27 (1929–30), 189–240. Deubner's treatment (*AF*, 40–50) is led astray by schol. Luc. p. 275. 23 ff. Rabe, cf. Burkert, *Hermes*, 94 (1966), 23–4, 7–8.
[56] Eur. *Erechtheus* fr. 65 Austin; death and tomb of Skiros: Paus. I. 36. 4.
[57] Paus. I. 26. 6–7.
[58] An. Bekk. 304, 8 Σκειρὰς Ἀθηνᾶ· εἶδος ἀγάλματος Ἀθηνᾶς ὀνομασθέντος οὕτως ἤτοι ἀπὸ τόπου τινὸς οὕτως ὠνομασμένου, ἐν ᾧ γῇ ὑπάρχει λευκὴ ... (shorter *EM* 720, 24); schol. Paus. p. 218 Spiro σκιροφόρια παρὰ τὸ φέρειν σκίρα ἐν αὐτῇ τὸν Θησέα ἢ γύψον· ὁ γὰρ Θησεὺς ἀπερχόμενος κατὰ τοῦ Μινωταύρου τὴν Ἀθηνᾶν ποιήσας ἀπὸ γύψου

amulets 'carried' at the σκιροφόρια, though less successful in superstitious medicine than their Lemnian counterparts? There was another festival at Athens where the women ate garlic in considerable quantities:[59] the Thesmophoria. This festival was among the most widespread all over Greece, and there must have been many local variants; but there are features strikingly reminiscent of the pattern treated so far: there is the disruption of normal life, the separation of sexes; the women gather (cf. n. 59) for three or four days, they live at the Thesmophorion in huts or tents; in Eretria they did not even use fire (Plut. Quaest. Graec. 31). They performed uncanny sacrifices to chthonian deities; subterranean caves, μέγαρα, were opened, pigs thrown down into the depths; probably there was a bigger, secret sacrifice towards the end of the festival. In mythological fantasy, the separation of the sexes was escalated into outright war. The lamentable situation of the κηδεστής ('kinsman') in Aristophanes' Thesmophoriazousai is not the only example. The Laconian women are said to have overpowered the famous Aristomenes of Messene, when he dared to approach them at the time of the Thesmophoria; they fought, by divine instigation, with sacrificial knives and spits and torches—the scenery implies a nocturnal ἀπόρρητος θυσία ('secret sacrifice') (Paus. 4. 17. 1). The women of Kyrene, at their Thesmophoria, smeared their hands and faces with the blood of the victims and emasculated King Battos, who had tried to spy out their secrets.[60] The most famous myth in this connection concerns those women whom Euripides already compared with the Lemniads (Hec. 887): the Danaids. They slew their husbands all together at night, too, with one notable exception, as at Lemnos:

ἐβάστασεν (cf. Wilamowitz, Hermes, 29 (1894), 243; slightly corrupt Et. Gen. p. 267 Miller = EM p. 718, 16, more corrupt Phot., Suda s.v. Σκίρα, who speak of Theseus' return); schol. Ar. Vesp. 926 Ἀθηνᾶ Σκιρράς, ὅτι γῇ (τῇ codd.) λευκῇ χρίεται. R. van der Loeff, Mnemosyne, 44 (1916), 102–3, Gjerstad, 222–6, Deubner, 46–7 (see n. 55 above) tried to distinguish Σκίρα and Ἀθηνᾶ Σκιράς, Deubner, 46, n. 11 even Σκίρα and the place Σκῖρον (Σκίρον? Herodian, Gramm. Gr. iii. 1, 385. 1–4; iii. 2, 581. 22–31 (cf. Steph. Byz. Σκίρος) seems to prescribe Σκῖρον; Σκίρα Ar. Thesm. 834, Eccl. 18); contra, Jacoby, FGrHist IIIb Suppl., Notes 117–18. The changing quantity (cf. σῖρός) is less strange than the connection σκιρ-, σκυρ- (cf. LSJ s.v. σκῖρον, σκῖρος, σκίρρος, σκῦρος) which points to a non-Greek word. On Σκῦρος (cf. Oros EM, 720, 24) Theseus was thrown down the white rock (Plut. Thes. 35).
[59] IG II/III² 1184 διδόναι ... εἰς τὴν ἑορτὴν ... καὶ σκόρδων δύο στατῆρας. On Thesmophoria, Nilsson, GF, 313–25, GGR, 461–6, Deubner, AF, 50–60.
[60] Aelian, fr. 44 = Suda s.v. σφάκτριαι and θεσμοφόρος; Nilsson, GF, 324–5.

Lynkeus was led to a secret escape by Hypermestra the virgin. As the
Argives kept the rule of extinguishing the fire in a house where
somebody had died,[61] the night of murder must have entailed much
extinguishing of fires. Lynkeus, however, when he was in safety, lit a
torch in Lyrkeia, Hypermestra answered by lighting a torch at the
Larisa, ἐπὶ τούτῳ δὲ Ἀργεῖοι κατὰ ἔτος ἕκαστον πυρσῶν ἑορτὴν ἄγουσι
('on account of this the Argives celebrate a festival of torches every
year') (Paus. 2. 25. 4). It is questionable whether this ritual originally
belongs to the Danaid myth;[62] the word-play Lyrkeia–Lynkeus does
not inspire confidence. The myth at any rate has much to tell about
the concluding agōn, in which the Danaids were finally given to husbands.[63] After the outrage against nature, a new life must begin,
which happens to be just ordinary life. But it is Herodotus who tells
us that it was the Danaids who brought to Greece the τελετή ('celebration') of Demeter Thesmophoros, i.e. introduced the festival
Thesmophoria.[64] Thus the similarity of the myths of the Danaids and
Lemniads and the similarity of the rituals of Thesmophoria and the
Lemnian fire-festival is finally confirmed by Herodotus, who connects
myth and ritual.

One glance at the Romans: their μέγιστος τῶν καθαρμῶν ('greatest
of purification rituals') (Plut. Quaest. Rom. 86) concerns the virgines
Vestales and the fire of Vesta, and it covers a whole month. It begins
with a strange ἀποπομπή ('sending away'): twenty-seven puppets
are collected in sanctuaries all over the town, brought to the pons

---

[61] Plut. Quaest. Graec. 24. 296 f.
[62] Cf. Nilsson, GF, 470, n. 5; Apollod. 2. 22, Zenob. 4. 86, etc. point to a connection of
Danaid myth and Lerna (new fire for Lerna: Paus. 8. 15. 9).
[63] Pi. P. 9. 111ff.; Paus. 3. 12. 3; Apollod. 2. 22. Dumézil, Le Crime, 48 ff. discussed
the similarities of the Argive and the Lemnian myth, without taking notice of the
Thesmophoria.
[64] Hdt. 2. 171 τῆς Δήμητρος τελετῆς πέρι, τὴν οἱ Ἕλληνες θεσμοφόρια καλέουσι ... αἱ
Δαναοῦ θυγατέρες ἦσαν αἱ τὴν τελετὴν ταύτην ἐξ Αἰγύπτου ἐξαγαγοῦσαι καὶ διδάξασαι τὰς
Πελασγιώτιδας γυναῖκας. The connection of Danaoi and Egypt is taken seriously by
modern historians (G. Huxley, Crete and the Luwians (Oxford, 1961), 36–7; F. H. Stub-
bings, CAH xviii (1963), 11ff.; P. Walcot, Hesiod and the Near East (Cardiff, 1966), 71);
Epaphos may be a Hyksos name. Now Mycenean representations mainly from the
Argolid show 'Demons' (cf. Nilsson, GGR, 296–7) in ritual functions—procession,
sacrifice—whose type goes back to the Egyptian hippopotamus-Goddess Taurt, 'the
Great One' (cf. Roeder, Roschers Myth. Lex. v. 878–908). S. Marinatos, Proc. of the
Cambridge Colloquium on Mycenean Studies (Cambridge, 1966), 265–74 suggests identifying them with the Δάμιοι of Linear B texts. If these 'Demons' were represented by
masks in ritual (E. Heckenrath, AJA 41 (1937), 420–1) it is tempting to see in this ritual
of the 'Great Goddess', influenced from Egypt, the Thesmophoria of the Danaids. Cf.
also n. 33 above.

sublicius and, under the leadership of the *virgo*, thrown into the Tiber. They are called Argei, which possibly just means 'grey men'.[65] There follows a period of Lent and abstinences: no marriage is performed in this period,[66] the *flaminica*, wife of the *flamen Dialis*, is not allowed to have intercourse with her husband. From 7 to 15 June, the temple of Vesta is opened for nine days; the *matronae* gather, barefoot, to bring offerings and prayers. Especially strange is the rule of the Matralia on 11 June: the *matronae*, worshipping Mater Matuta, are not allowed to mention their sons; so they pray for their nephews. Finally on 15 June the temple of Vesta is cleaned; *quando stercus delatum fas* ('when the refuse has been disposed of') ordinary life may start again. The correspondence with the Lemnian πυρφορία is striking: the ἀποπομπή and tossing into the water, the separation of the sexes, of man and wife, even of mother and son, while the fire is 'purified' on which the *salus publica* is thought to depend.

Enough of comparisons;[67] the danger that the outlines of the picture become blurred as the material accumulates can scarcely be evaded. Whether it will be possible to account for the similarity of pattern which emerged, by some historical hypothesis, is a formidable problem. There seems to be a common Near Eastern background; the pattern of the Near Eastern new-year festival has been summed up in the steps of mortification, purgation, invigoration, and jubilation,[68] closely corresponding, in our case, to ἀποπομπή ('sending away'), ἀπόρρητος θυσία ('secret sacrifice'), abstinences on the one hand, *agōn* and marriage on the other. There appear to be Egyptian influences; more specifically, there are the traditions about the pre-Greek 'Pelasgians' in Argos, Athens, Lemnos (according to

[65] Cf. G. Wissowa, *Religion und Kultus der Römer*, 2nd edn. (Munich, 1912), 420; K. Latte, *Römische Religionsgeschichte* (Munich, 1960), 412–14; on Vestalia: Wissowa, 159–60, Latte, 109–10; on Matralia: Wissowa, 111, Latte, 97–8, G. Radke, *Die Götter Altitaliens* (Münster, 1965), 206–9, J. Gagé, *Matronalia* (Brussels, 1963), 228–35. The flogging of a slave-girl at the Matralia has its analogy in the role of the Thracian concubines at Lemnos and the hair-sacrifice of the Thracian slave-girls in Erythrai (below, n. 67). With the 'tutulum' (= *pilleum lanatum*, Sueton. *apud* Serv. auct. *Aen.* 2. 683) of the Argei, cf. the πῖλοι of Hephaistos and Kabeiroi (above, n. 35).

[66] Plut. *Quaest. Rom.* 86, 284f: no marriage in May; Ov. *Fast.* 6. 219–34: no marriage until 15 June, the *flaminica* abstains from combing, nail-cutting, and intercourse.

[67] There is connection between the Lemnian festival and the Chian myth of Orion (above, n. 24); a cult legend of Erythrai implies another comparable ritual: 'Heracles' arrived on a raft, and Thracian slave-girls sacrificed their hair to pull him ashore (Paus. 7. 8. 5–8).

[68] Gaster, *Thespis*; for necessary qualification of the pattern, C. J. Bleeker, *Egyptian Festivals, Enactment of Religious Renewal* (Leiden, 1967), 37–8.

Athenian tradition), and even in Italy.[69] But there is not much hope of disentangling the complex interrelations of Bronze Age tribes, as tradition has been furthermore complicated by contamination of legends. It may only be stated that similarities of ritual ought to be taken into account in such questions as much as certain names of tribes or of gods or certain species of pottery.

Still there are some definite conclusions, concerning the problem of myth and ritual: there is correspondence which goes beyond casual touches or secondary superimposition. But for the isolated testimonies of Myrsilos and Philostratus, we would have no clue at all to trace the myth back to Lemnian ritual, as we know nothing about the Thesmophoria of Argos. But the more we learn about the ritual, the closer the correspondence with myth turns out to be. The uprising of the women, the disappearance of the men, the unnatural life without love, the blood flowing—all this people will experience in the festival, as well as the advent of the ship which brings the joyous start of a new life. So far Jane Harrison's formula proves to be correct: 'the myth is the plot of the *drōmenon*';[70] its περιπέτειαι ('reversals') reflect ritual actions. The much-vexed question, whether, in this interdependence, myth or ritual is primary, transcends philology,[71] since both myth and ritual were established well before the invention of writing. Myths are more familiar to the classicist; but it is important to realize that ritual, in its function and transmission, is not dependent on words. Even today children will get their decisive impressions of religion not so much from words and surely not from dogmatic teaching, but through the behaviour of their elders: that special facial expression, that special tone of voice, that poise and gesture mark the sphere of the sacred; the seriousness and

---

[69] The evidence is collected by F. Lochner-Hüttenbach, *Die Pelasger* (Vienna, 1960). The Athenians used the legends about the Pelasgians, whom they identified with the Τυρρηνοί (Thuc. 4. 109. 4), to justify their conquest of Lemnos under Miltiades (Hdt. 6. 137 ff.). There was a family of Εὐνεῖδαι at Athens, acting as heralds and worshipping Dionysos Melpomenos. J. Toepffer, *Attische Genealogie* (Berlin, 1889), 181–206; Preller–Robert, *Griech. Mythologie*, ii. 852–3. On Pelasgians in Italy, Hellanikos, *FGrHist* 4 F 4, Myrsilos, *FGrHist* 477 F 8 *apud* D. H. *Ant.* 1. 17 ff., Varro *apud* Macr. *Sat.* 1. 7. 28 f.; on Camillus—Καδμῖλος A. Ernout and A. Meillet, *Dict. étym. de la langue latine*, 4th edn. (Paris, 1959) s.v. *Camillus*.

[70] *Themis*, 331.

[71] Cf. above, n. 3. In Egypt, there were clearly rituals without myths, Bleeker, *Egyptian Festivals*, 19; E. Otto, *Das Verhältnis von Rite und Mythus im Ägyptischen*, SBHeid. 1958, 1. Biologists have recognized rituals in animal behaviour, cf. K. Lorenz, *On Aggression* (London, 1966), 54–80.

confidence displayed invite imitation, while at the same time relent-less sanctions are added against any violation: thus religious ritual has been transmitted in the unbroken sequence of human society. By its prominence in social life, it not only provided stimulation for story-telling, but at the same time some kind of 'mental container'[72] which accounts for the stability, the unchanging patterns of mythical tradition. Thus for understanding myth, ritual is not a negligible factor.

Still one can look at flowers without caring much for roots: myth can become independent from ritual; ritual origin does not imply ritual function—nor does the absence of ritual function exclude ritual origin. Ritual, if we happen to know about it, will be illustrative especially of strange features in a myth; but as these tend to be eliminated, myth can live on by its own charm. Apollonios did not bother about Lemnian festivals, and he dropped the δυσωδία ('foul smell'). The first and decisive step in this direction was, of course, Homer; or to be more exact, Greek myth found its final form in the oral tradition of skilled singers which is behind the *Iliad*, the *Odyssey*, and the other early epics. As a consequence of this successful activity of ἀοιδοί ('singers') and ῥαψῳδοί ('rhapsodes') there took place, of course, all kinds of conflation, exchange, and superimposition of myths, as local traditions were adapted to 'Homeric' tales. Thus myths are often attached to rituals by secondary construction; in this case, the details rarely fit. Poets and antiquarians are free to choose between various traditions, even to develop new and striking combinations. One myth may illustrate or even replace another, the motifs overlap, as the underlying patterns are similar or nearly identical.

Still more clear than the importance of ritual for the understand-ing of myth is the importance of myth for the history of religion, for the reconstruction and interpretation of ritual. Myth, being the 'plot', may indicate connections between rites which are isolated in our tradition; it may provide supplements for the desperate lacunae in our knowledge; it may give decisive hints for chronology. In our case, Philostratus' testimony comes from the third century AD, Myrsilos' from the third century BC, Sophocles' allusion takes us back to the fifth; but as the Hypsipyle story is known to the *Iliad*, both

---

[72] An expression coined by W. F. Jackson Knight, *Cumaean Gates* (Oxford, 1936), 91 for the function of the mythical pattern as to historical facts.

myth and ritual must antedate 700 BC. This means that not even Greeks are concerned, but the pre-Greek inhabitants of Lemnos, whom Homer calls Σίντιες (Sinties), the later Greeks Τυρρηνοί (Tyrrhenians).[73] Excavations have given some picture of this pre-Greek civilization and its continuity into the Greek settlement; in spite of continuous fighting and bloodshed, there seems to have been a surprising permeability in religion, in ritual, and even in myths, between different languages and civilizations, and an equally surprising stability of traditions bound to a certain place.

If myth reflects ritual, it is impossible to draw inferences from the plot of the myth as to historical facts, or even to reduce myth to historical events. From Wilamowitz down to the *Lexikon der Alten Welt*,[74] we read that the Lemnian crime reflects certain adventures of the colonization period, neatly registered in *IG* XII 8, p. 2: 'Graeci ± 800—post 700' inhabiting Lemnos—as if the Lemniads had been slain by the Argonauts or the Argonauts by the Lemniads. To be cautious: it is possible that the crisis of society enacted in a festival breaks out into actual murder or revolution, which is henceforward remembered in the same festival;[75] but actual atrocities by themselves produce neither myth nor ritual—or else our century would be full of both. Another historical interpretation of the myth, given by Bachofen but envisaged already by Welcker, has, through Engels, endeared itself to Marxist historians:[76] the Lemnian crime as memory of prehistoric matriarchal society. The progress of research in

---

[73] Identification of Sinties and Tyrrhenians: Philochoros, *FGrHist* 328 F 100/1 with Jacoby ad loc. Main report on the excavations (interrupted before completion by the war): *ASAA* 15/16 (1932–3); cf. D. Mustilli, *Enc. dell'arte antica*, iii (1960), 230–1, L. Bernabo-Brea, ibid. iv (1961), 542–5. It is remarkable that there are only cremation burials in the pre-Greek necropolis (*ASAA*, loc. cit. 267–72). Wilamowitz, 'Hephaistos', 231 had wrongly assumed that the pre-Greek 'barbarians' would have neither city nor Hephaistos-cult.

[74] Wilamowitz, 'Hephaistos', 231; *LAW* s.v. Lemnos.

[75] In several towns of Switzerland there are traditions about a 'night of murder' allegedly commemorated in carnival-like customs; a few of them are based on historical facts; cf. L. Tobler, 'Die Mordnächte und ihre Gedenktage', *Kleine Schriften* (Frauenfeld, 1897), 79–105.

[76] Welcker, *Prometheus*, 585 ff.; Bachofen, cf. above n. 12; F. Engels, *Der Ursprung der Familie, des Privateigentums und des Staats* (Hottingen–Zürich, 1884), Marx–Engels, *Werke*, xxi. 47 ff.; G. Thomson, *The Prehistoric Aegean: Studies in Ancient Greek Society* (London, 1949), 175 (more circumspect: *Aeschylus and Athens* (London, 1941; 3rd edn., 1966), 287). For a cautious re-evaluation of the theory of matriarchy, cf. K. Meuli in Bachofen, *Ges. Werke*, iii. 1107–15; on the Lycians, S. Pembroke, 'Last of the Matriarchs', *Journ. of the Econ. and Soc. Hist. of the Orient*, 8 (1965), 217–47.

prehistory, however, has left less and less space for matriarchal society in any pre-Greek Mediterranean or Near Eastern civilization.

Indeed Hypsipyle did not reign over men—which *would* be matriarchy—the men have simply disappeared; and this is not a matriarchal organization of society, but a disorganization of patriarchal society, a transitional stage, a sort of carnival—this is the reason why the Lemniads were an appropriate subject for comedy.[77] Social order is turned upside down just to provoke a new reversal, which means the re-establishment of normal life.

If ritual is not dependent on myth, it cannot be explained by 'beliefs' or 'concepts'—which would be to substitute another myth for the original one. Ritual seems rather to be a necessary means of communication and solidarization in human communities, necessary for mutual understanding and cooperation, necessary to deal with the intra-human problems of attraction and, above all, aggression. There are the never-dying tensions between young and old, and also between the sexes; they necessitate periodically some sort of 'cathartic' discharge; it may be possible to play off one conflict to minimize the other. This is what the myth is about: love, hatred, and their conflict, murderous instincts and piety, solidarity of women and family bonds, hateful separation and lustful reunion—this is the story of Hypsipyle, this is the essence of the ritual, too; only the myth carries, in fantasy, to the extreme what, by ritual, is conducted into more innocent channels: animals are slain instead of men, and the date is fixed when the revolution has to come to an end. Thus it is ritual which avoids the catastrophe of society. In fact only the last decades have abolished nearly all comparable rites in our world; so it is left to our generation to experience the truth that men cannot stand the uninterrupted steadiness even of the most prosperous life; it is an open question whether the resulting convulsions will lead to *katharsis* or catastrophe.

ADDENDA

A new edition of Philostratus, *Heroicus*: L. de Launoy, *Flavii Philostrati Heroicus* (Leipzig, 1977). For the *corruptela* καὶ καθ' ἕνα τοῦ ἔτους (above, 229 ff.) de Launoy comes back to the simple text καθ' ἕκαστον ἔτος, with a group of manuscripts: 'Note critique sur Philostrate,

---

[77] Λήμνιαι were written by Aristophanes (frr. 372–91 PCG), Nicochares (frr. 14–17), and Antiphanes (frr. 142–3); cf. Alexis (fr. 139), Diphilus (fr. 53), and Turpilius (90–9).

Heroïkos, 207. 29,' *L'Antiquité Classique*, 42 (1973), 526–31. See, however, καθ' ἕνα καιρὸν ἐν ταῖς κυνάσιν ἡμέραις Plut. *Is*. 73. 380c = Manetho *FGrHist* 609 F 22. See also in general L. de Launoy, 'Le Problème des Philostrate', in *ANRW* II 34, 3 (Berlin, 1997), 2362–449. For archaic Lemnos, see now C. de Simone, *I Tirreni a Lemnos* (Florence, 1996). On Pre-Greeks and Athenians at Lemnos, see R. Parker, 'Athenian Religion Abroad', in R. Osborne and S. Hornblower (eds.), *Ritual, Finance, Politics. Athenian Democratic Accounts pres. to D. Lewis* (Oxford, 1994), 339–46. For 'craters' at Lemnos (n. 20) see also a piece of Hellenistic tragedy, *TrGF* II. *Adespota* 680b: ὦ Λῆμνε καὶ κρα[τῆρες.

The study of Georges Dumézil (n. 27) has been re-edited by B. Leclercq–Neveu (Paris, 1998), with an extensive *Préface* (5–34) on Dumézil and the 'myth and ritual' interpretation. For 'myth and ritual' see also W. Burkert, *SH* 1–58; *HN*, 28–34; 'Mythos—Begriff, Struktur, Funktionen', in F. Graf (ed.), *Mythen in mythenloser Gesellschaft* (Stuttgart, 1993), 9–24.

II

The Locrian Maidens

FRITZ GRAF

Every field of research raises certain problems that are debated vigorously for a while, often because of their relevance to some other matter, and are then left in peace, without anyone in fact having arrived at a satisfactory solution. One example of this is the tribute of the Locrian maidens. Schliemann's discovery of Troy, followed by the exciting discovery of an inscription, gave rise to many discussions of this question, particularly in the first decades of the twentieth century.[1] We shall refer to the opinions put forward in those publications where it is relevant; but first of all we need to reconstruct the ritual on the basis of the copious literary evidence.[2]

I am most grateful to friends and colleagues at Leiden, Utrecht, and Zürich, where I had the opportunity of presenting these ideas, for criticism and advice.

[1] The most important discussions are: A. Brückner in W. Dörpfeld, *Troja und Ilion* (Athens, 1902), ii. 557–63; J. Vürtheim, *De Aiacis origine cultu patria* (Leiden, 1907), 104–24; A. Wilhelm, *JÖAI* 14 (1911), 163–256; W. Leaf, *Troy* (London, 1912), 126–44; P. Corssen, *Socrates*, 1 (1913), 188–202; A. J. Reinach, *Rev. Hist. Rel.* 69 (1914), 12–53; F. Schwenn, *Die Menschenopfer der Griechen und Römer* (Giessen, 1915), 47–54; U. von Wilamowitz-Moellendorff, *Die Ilias und Homer* (Berlin, 1916), 384–94; L. R. Farnell, *Greek Hero Cults* (Oxford, 1921), 293–305; L. Preller and C. Robert, *Griechische Mythologie*, ii.3, 4th edn. (Berlin, 1921), 1268–74; E. Kalinka, *ARW* 21 (1922), 42–6; G. Gianelli, *Culti e miti della Magna Graecia*, 2nd edn. (Florence, 1963), 199–202; E. Bethe, *Homer: Dichtung und Sage*, iii (Leipzig, 1927), 127–46; A. Momigliano, *CQ* 39 (1945), 49–53 = *Secondo contributo alla storia degli studi classici* (Rome, 1960), 446–53; G. De Sanctis, *Ricerche sulla storiografia siceliota* (Palermo, 1958), 59–62; F. Bömer, *Untersuchungen über die Religion der Sklaven*, iii (Abh. Mainz 1961), 4. 310–22; E. Manni in *Miscellanea A. Rostagni* (Turin, 1963), 166–79; G. L. Huxley in E. Badian (ed.), *Ancient Society and Institutions: Studies V. Ehrenberg* (Oxford, 1966), 147–64; H. H. Schmitt in H. Bengtson, *Die Staatsverträge des Altertums*, iii (Munich, 1969), 123–6 (with full bibliography); P. Vidal-Naquet in J. Bingen *et al.* (eds.), *Le Monde grec: Hommages C. Préaux* (Brussels, 1975), 496–507.

[2] The texts are assembled in Leaf, *Troy*, 392–6; Wilhelm (n. 1), 172–87; Wilamowitz, *Die Ilias*, 384–8; P/W ii, 134–5, nos. 331, 332; Schmitt (n. 1), 123; Vidal-Naquet (n. 1), 497 n. 2.

I

One of the most important pieces of evidence comes from Lycophron. In his *Alexandra*, probably composed in the first decade of the third century BC, Alexandra/Cassandra foretells the consequences of the crime of the lesser Ajax, which will affect his descendants, the Locrians.[3] For a thousand years to come, says the unfortunate daughter of Priam, the Locrians will be obliged to send unmarried maidens to the temple of Athena at Ilion; there the maidens will have to stay until they die. They will not even be granted a decent funeral: their bodies will be burnt on a pyre of broken branches, and their ashes will be thrown into the sea (a detail that was already to be found in Timaeus).[4] But for every maiden who dies, another will have to be sent to Ilion, and she will have to enter the temple precinct stealthily, by night, for the Trojans will watch all the entrances and will stone to death any maiden they see—and whoever first catches sight of her will be honoured by the city.

This long account is not always entirely intelligible, but it can be supplemented with the help of numerous other texts. Besides Lycophron, and of course Timaeus (whom Lycophron frequently uses elsewhere as a source), a scholion to the *Alexandra* of Lycophron indicates that Callimachus too gave an account of the tribute.[5] It is not clear how much of the scholion is actually derived from Callimachus,[6] but we may assume that he specifically mentioned the institution of the tribute: we are told that a plague fell upon Locris three years after the Trojan war, which led to the institution of the tribute at the command of the Delphic oracle.

There was a further extremely detailed account in the *Library* attributed to Apollodorus, preserved in the Epitome.[7] Here too it is Ajax' crime that brings the plague upon Locris and leads to the Delphic command to send the tribute of maidens: the first pair to be sent, we

---

[3] Lycoph. *Alex.* 1141–73; cf. the commentary by E. Ciaceri (Catania, 1901), 305–9. On the question of the date, see the survey by A. Lesky, *Geschichte der griechischen Literatur*, 3rd edn. (Bern, 1971), 835, and K. Ziegler in *Kleine Pauly* iii. 815, as well as Momigliano and Manni (n. 1). The discussion by A. Hurst in *Mélanges P. Collart* (Lausanne, 1976), 231–5 argues for a date before 273.
[4] Timaeus *FGrHist* 566 F 146a.
[5] Callim. fr. 35 Pfeiffer.
[6] Cf. R. Pfeiffer, *Callimachus*, i (Oxford, 1949), 41.
[7] Apollod. *Epit.* 6. 20–2.

are told, were called Periboea and Cleopatra. In Ilion their duty was to clean the temple precinct. They were not permitted to step outside the precinct or to approach the image of the goddess. They went barefoot, their hair was shorn, and they each wore only a single garment. A similar account is given in three hexameters of unknown origin quoted by Plutarch,[8] except that it adds that the maidens had no κρήδεμνον: their hair was not fastened.[9] Apollodorus then gives a summary of the history of the tribute: after the death of the first two maidens, others took their place, and finally the Locrians were sending infants, βρέφη. This last statement must be a misunderstanding of the phrase παρθένοι ἐνιαυσιαῖαι (yearly maidens) in the scholion to Lycophron mentioned above: if we could be sure that this too came from Callimachus, we would have established a source for Apollodorus' account.[10] After a thousand years, at the time of the Phocian War, the tribute came to an end. That is remarkable: the Phocian War, mentioned nowhere else, is usually identified with the third Sacred War of 357–46. This fits in well with the fact that Naryca, the city of the Aianteioi, the tribe that was required to supply the maidens,[11] was destroyed during this war.[12] Admittedly, this entails dating the Trojan war to c.1360–50, which is remarkable.[13]

There is also another account in Aelian, though it has to be pieced together from fragments.[14] He begins with the familiar sequence Crime—Plague—Oracle, and he gives what is apparently a paraphrase of the oracle, which (he says) demanded an annual

---

[8] Plut. De sera 12. 557d; despite all conjectures, the origin of the lines is highly uncertain: cf. e.g. Wilamowitz, Die Ilias, 389; Pfeiffer loc. cit.; Vidal-Naquet (n. 1), 499.

[9] Removing the κρήδεμνον (head-covering) allows the hair to flow loose, as we can see from the Homeric Hymn Dem. 41, Eur. Phoen. 1490, Oppian, Cyn. 1. 495–6, and Nonnus, Dion. 2. 95, 5. 375.

[10] Vürtheim, De Aiacis origine, 110–11; cf. Vidal-Naquet (n. 1), 504–5. Apollodorus in his turn is the source for Tzetzes Schol. Lycoph. 1141: see Wilamowitz, Die Ilias, 385; Jacoby FGrHist IIIb (Noten) 346 n. 564.

[11] Servius Danielis (= Servius auctus) on Verg. Aen. 1. 41, and the inscription concerning the Maidens (n. 17 below).

[12] Diod. Sic. 16. 38. 5; cf. Wilhelm (n. 1), 183; Momigliano (n. 1), 446–7; De Sanctis, Ricerche, 60; Huxley (n. 1), 149.

[13] Manni (n. 1), 169 takes this difficulty seriously and therefore identifies the Phocian War with the Gallic invasion of 278/7, which strains the evidence; see also Vidal-Naquet (n. 1), 502.

[14] Ael. fr. 47 Hercher, assembled from the Suda. Reinach (n. 1), 35 is inclined to consider Demetrius of Scepsis as Aelian's source: unfortunately there is no evidence for this.

tribute.[15] Later, he says, the Locrians failed to send the tribute, the maidens grew old in Ilion, and a plague came upon Locris. The god at Delphi at first sent away the Locrians who appealed to him for help, but later he drew their attention to their neglect of the ritual. However, no-one was willing to send their own daughter, until a certain Antigonus intervened and commanded them to.

This puts the date of the reinstitution of the tribute into the early Hellenistic period, and scholars have accordingly associated the break in the tribute with the destruction of Naryca.[16] But there has been no agreement on which Antigonus intervened. It cannot have been Antigonus Doson: the 'Maidens Inscription' discovered at Vitrinitsa in West Locris, which refers to a reinstitution of the tribute, can be dated almost certainly to the first quarter of the third century on the grounds of its letter-forms.[17] It is difficult to decide between Antigonus the One-Eyed (Monophthalmos) and Antigonus Gonatas. Monophthalmos must have intervened before 301, the year of his death. That seems too early for the inscription: we would hardly expect a long interval between the King's intervention and the inscription recording it. That leaves the early years of Gonatas.[18]

II

So the main outlines are established, but there are two problems that still need to be cleared up. On the one hand there is the obvious discrepancy between the sources which say that the maidens had to

[15] The original words of the oracle can still be glimpsed in the phrase ἕως ἂν ἱλεώσητε τὴν θεόν, 'until you have placated the goddess' (P/W no. 332 fail to observe this).

[16] Since Wilhelm (n. 1), 183; 'au prix de quelques imprudences', Vidal-Naquet (n. 1), 503.

[17] Editio princeps Wilhelm (n. 1), 168–9; improved text in A. Nikitsky, Zhurnal Ministerstva narodnago prosvieshcheniia, 43 (Jan.–Feb. 1913), 8–9 (whence E. Schwyzer, Dialectorum Graecarum exempla epigraphica potiora (Leipzig, 1923), 366; C. D. Buck, The Greek Dialects, 3rd edn. (Chicago, 1955), 257 no. 60); IG IX.1² no. 706 (Schmitt (n. 1), 118 no. 472). Wilhelm 249–55 dates it on the basis of Delphic documents to 275–40; Momigliano (n. 1), 453 prefers to extend this time-bracket at both ends; G. Klaffenbach (IG loc. cit.) and, following him, Schmitt 118 n. 125 date it to the early 3rd cent. BC.

[18] Monophthalmos: Corssen (n. 1), 191–2; Reinach (n. 1), 41; Schmitt (n. 1), 125; Vidal-Naquet (n. 1), 503. Gonatas: Wilamowitz, Die Ilias, 384; Manni (n. 1), 174. The question is left open by Wilhelm (n. 1), 186–7; Jacoby FGrHist IIIb (Text) 591; Momigliano (n. 1), 446–7; Huxley (n. 1), 152.

remain in Ilion until they died, and those which speak of an annual tribute. They are irreconcilable. Ilion was a mere village in pre-Roman times, and its sanctuary of Athena could not have accommodated sixty to a hundred 'maidens' of all ages.[19] Moreover, Aelian explicitly states that the Locrians had neglected to send διάδοχοι, successors, and the version of the oracle which he paraphrases in connection with the original institution demands an annual tribute. The Locrian inscription, for its part, also provides for a just exchange for τοῖν πρόσθεν κόραιν (the previous pairs of maidens), in other words it envisages the return of two maidens on each occasion.[20]

This discrepancy is usually explained by saying that the original arrangement was that the maidens were required to remain in Troy, but that this requirement was relaxed by the reorganization, and the length of their stay was reduced to one year.[21] But this is contradicted by Aelian's account of the oracle, which refers to the period before the reorganization, and which states that διάδοχοι (the successive maidens) had been neglected at that time. It is also contradicted by Strabo[22] and Servius,[23] who presuppose an annual tribute from the very beginning. It is also contradicted by a general consideration: the god at Delphi was clearly angry with the Locrians, and the ancient ritual cannot possibly have been made less harsh in order to avert that anger.[24]

---

[19] Stressed by Huxley (n. 1), 150. On the poverty of Ilion at this date see Demetrius of Scepsis in Strabo 13. 1. 27, p. 594; F. W. Goethert and H. Schleif, Der Athenatempel von Ilion (Berlin, 1962), 35.

[20] Line 23 (discussed most recently by Schmitt (n. 1), 125). Line 10, in which it is laid down how long the Maidens had to be given payments for maintenance, is broken off before the end: Nikitsky (followed by Schwyzer) conjectured ἔντε κα [ἐπανέλθωντι . . .] (until they return), Wilhelm ἔντε κα [ἐν ἀνδρὸς ἔλθῃ . . .] (until she marries) or something on those lines; Corssen (n. 1), 197 (ignoring epigraphic considerations) ἔντε κα [ζώῃ] (as long as she lives); Klaffenbach and Schmitt do not offer any supplement.

[21] Thus Vürtheim, De Aiacis origine, 107–9; Wilhelm (n. 1), 219–20; Reinach (n. 1), 37–42; Wilamowitz, Die Ilias, 391; Jacoby FGrHist IIIb (Noten) 346 n. 568. Contra: Corssen (n. 1), 198–9; Schwenn, Die Menschenopfer, 53–4 and Momigliano (n. 1), 448–9 believe that it had always been annual; Farnell, Greek Hero Cults, 295 and Huxley (n. 1), 159 are undecided. For Vidal-Naquet see n. 29 below.

[22] Strabo 13. 1. 40, p. 600.

[23] Servius Danielis on Verg. Aen. 1. 41, derived at least in part from the elusive Annaeus Placidus.

[24] Momigliano (n. 1), 449. His further argument (accepted by Huxley (n. 1), 149), that ἀνὰ ἔτεα πολλά (see n. 30 below for the translation of this phrase) in Aeneas Tacticus 31. 24 indicates a short interval unfortunately has little weight (see also n. 30 below): if the phrase παρθένοι ἐνιαυσιαῖαι (yearly maidens) came from Callimachus (n. 10 above), this might take us back to the period before the reorganization.

There is another possibility. The texts fall into two groups. Those of the first group constitute the evidence for life-long service: Lycophron and possibly his source Timaeus, pseudo-Apollodorus, and the hexameters quoted by Plutarch. It has been suggested that these hexameters come from the Epic Cycle. The account in the *Library* might derive from the same source. Although *Epitome* 6.22 must admittedly be later than the Phocian War, the coherent account in *Epitome* 6.20 f, which covers the story as far as the despatch of the first pair of maidens, could be earlier, and the epic names Periboea and Cleopatra may indicate a source in hexameters, of the kind that was certainly used by the compiler of the *Library*. Moreover, the misunderstanding of the possibly Callimachean phrase παρθένοι ἐνιαυσιαῖαι (yearly maidens) is more likely to have occurred in a source such as the *Library*, which begins by reporting a life-long stay in Ilion, but then found itself confronted with the evidence for annual maidens.

So if the *Library* drew on a source in the Epic Cycle, then Timaeus and Lycophron must also derive from that source: they were both writing at the time during which the tribute had lapsed, so they must have been using an earlier literary source.[25]

The second group of texts, which attest an annual tribute, is more heterogeneous; their main characteristic is the reliability of their authors. If Callimachus[26] is one of them, the quality of his anti-quarian knowledge hardly stands in need of proof; Servius' source is well-informed, and parts of it correspond with the inscription to an astonishing degree;[27] Aelian quotes an oracle, together with many unusual but plausible details; Strabo draws on local tradition;[28] and finally, the inscription itself provides contemporary evidence.

There can be only one conclusion. The actual ritual, reflected in the second group of texts, did not correspond with the mythical account of the institution. The myth presented the ritual with

---

[25] Wilamowitz, *Die Ilias*, 388–9 supposes that Lycophron and Apollodorus used 'a re-working of epic history'; similarly Momigliano (n. 1), 450.

[26] See n. 24.

[27] In stating that the Aianteioi (*ea tribus de qua Aiax fuerat*, 'the tribe from which Ajax came') sent the maidens; that only one maiden, not two, was sent is stated also by the scholiast on Lycoph. 1159, but contradicted by the inscription (cf. also Vidal-Naquet (n. 1), 505).

[28] Demetrius of Scepsis, who indulged in polemic against the inhabitants of Ilium: cf. esp. Strabo 13. 1. 39 p. 600; W. Leaf, *Strabo: On the Troad* (Cambridge, 1923), pp. xxvii–xlvii.

unrelieved harshness, extrapolating so to speak from the actual events to their significance as perceived by those experiencing them. There are many local traditions in Greece that recount how a sacrilegious act caused the god of Delphi to demand a human sacrifice and how, later, this sacrifice was commuted to the harmless form that the local historian or the ancient guide proceeds to describe. In none of these cases should one presume that there really had been human sacrifices at an earlier date.[29]

The other problem concerns the events in Ilion immediately after the arrival of the maidens. Here, too, the literary sources fall into two groups. According to Lycophron the maidens were waylaid, and once they were caught, they might be killed. This detail may have already been in Timaeus, and is included in the *Library*. On the other hand, the inscription envisages the return of each pair, and so does our earliest witness, Aeneas Tacticus, who was probably writing before the lapse. According to him, the maidens were able to enter the *temenos* (sacred precinct) unharmed over a number of years (ἀνὰ ἔτεα πολλά), despite the vigilance of the inhabitants of Ilion.[30]

Once again the gruesome version is found in Timaeus, Lycophron, and Apollodorus; and once again the explanation must be that they reflect, not the cult practice of historical times, but the mythical prototype extrapolated from it. We may compare the Agrionia at Orchomenus, at which the priest of Dionysus, sword in hand, hunted down a group of women and was allowed to kill any that he caught; but when a priest really did kill one of these women (significantly, his name was Zoilus) it was regarded as murder, and brought about the abolition of the ritual.[31] Thus here too the actual ritual does not tally

---

[29] Cf. A. Brelich in J. M. Kitagawa, C. H. Long et al. (eds.), *Myths and Symbols: Studies M. Eliade* (Chicago, 1969), 195–207. Vidal-Naquet (n. 1), 505–7 offers a different explanation of the two branches of the tradition: that there always had to be two maidens at Ilion, and a replacement was sent from time to time. That would be consistent with the texts that recount the more gruesome variant, but it does not explain the evidence for an annual despatch, nor the fact, securely attested by the inscription, that it was always two who returned (the dual form is used).

[30] Aen. Tact. 31. 4. The manuscripts read ανετεα πολλὰ εἰσάγοντες σώματα, but since Orelli it has been customary to read ἀνὰ or ἀν' ἔτεα. That cannot mean 'year after year', as L. W. Hunter, *Aeneas on Siegecraft* (Oxford, 1927) translates it, despite Hdt. 8. 85. 4, where the notion of iteration is conveyed by πάντα. Rather, ἀν(ὰ) ἔτεα πολλά is to be taken together as 'for a period of many years'; Koechly-Rustow's emendation εἰσαγόντες ⟨τὰ⟩ σώματα then becomes practically inevitable.

[31] Plut. *Quaest. Graec.* 38. 299e, already cited by Wilhelm (n. 1), 178 (followed by Reinach (n. 1), 45 and Schwenn, *Die Menschenopfer*, 55; cf. Vürtheim, *De Aiacis origine*, 109); for the ritual at a later date see Burkert, *HN*, 195–6.

with the ideological projection of it, and there is no reason to believe that at some earlier period the priest really did kill the woman.[32] However, it is not possible to gain a clearer picture of the source of these extrapolating, mythical accounts. We have already suggested that it may have been a local epic related to the Epic Cycle;[33] alternatively, it may have originated in local historiography—we know too little about both.[34] But it is important to make two observations in this context. First, that the epic was probably neither the *Ilioupersis* nor the *Nostoi*, but rather it presupposes their existence: there was nothing in these poems about Athena's revenge on the Locrians.[35] Second, details of the ritual, which are essential for its understanding, stem above all from the mythological tradition. But these details—as we shall demonstrate—belong to a definite religious context. They are not random inventions, but evidence of actual cult practice. Accordingly it is legitimate to refer to them in the discussion that follows.

III

It is obvious that the explanation of a ritual which comes closest to the truth is one that, as far as possible, can explain every detail. Yet previous attempts to explain the tribute of the Locrian maidens have collapsed because, for various reasons, they gave arbitrary interpretations of details, or even ignored them completely.[36]

---

[32] Cf. Brelich loc. cit. (n. 29 above), 199, with his reference to Zenobius 4. 29.

[33] The tendency to gruesomeness also recalls poetry in the style of the Epic Cycle: cf. F. Wehrli, *Theoria und Humanitas* (Zürich, 1972), 78.

[34] On Locrian historiography see Jacoby *FGrHist* IIIb (Text) 383; on Philippus of Opus, W. A. Oldfather in *RE* XIII 1284. The recent discovery of the surprising epic from Cos, the *Meropis*, shows that we should take local epic poetry into account even at an early date: L. Koenen and R. Merkelbach, *Collectanea Papyrologica* (Bonn, 1976), 2–13.

[35] Cf. the summary of its contents given by Proclus, printed in T. W. Allen, *Homeri Opera* (OCT) v (1912), 108; J. Davreux, *La Légende de la prophétesse Cassandre* (Liège, 1942), 13 rightly rejects the suggestion that the existence of the tribute was implied by the painting of the Sack of Troy by Polygnotus at Delphi (Preller and Robert, *Griechische Mythologie*, 1268).

[36] The details are completely ignored in the explanation, long current, of the ritual in terms of an ancient human sacrifice ('decided long ago', Wilhelm (n. 1), 179), or of a sacred marriage (Vürtheim, *De Aiacis origine*, 121–3; Reinach (n. 1), 43–53). The euhemeristic explanation given by Farnell, *Greek Hero Cults*, 300–5 is untenable on archaeological grounds: H. L. Lorimer, *Homer and the Monuments* (London, 1950), 451, cf. Huxley (n. 1), 155. On its interpretation as a *pharmakos* (scapegoat) ritual see n. 57 below.

Let us start with the individual accounts of the appearance and dress of the maidens. The Locrian maidens went barefoot, they had only one garment each, their hair was loose, or shorn. That is how mourners must have looked. Greeks expressed grief by cutting off their hair or letting it hang loose;[37] they often went unshod.[38] And their clothing was also significant: they wore a single dark garment, which was possibly not changed throughout the whole period of mourning.[39]

However, hair was also loosened in certain ceremonies, above all in the cults of Demeter and of Dionysus.[40] Witches also wore their hair loose.[41] Conversely, cropping the hair indicates the attainment of maturity, both for youths and for girls.[42] Cropping the hair also plays a part in marriage rituals.[43] Certain mystery cults also prescribed that the feet should be bare,[44] and bare feet were also a sign of

[37] Cropping of hair in general: Eustathius on *Il.* 21. 11 (p. 165. 3); specific examples: e.g. *Anth. Pal.* 7. 146, 489; *P. Michig.* 5. 243. 9; further examples in J. Heckenbach, *De nuditate sacra sacrisque vinculis*, RGVV, ix. 3 (Giessen, 1911), 31–2; L. Sommer, *Das Haar in Religion und Aberglaube der Griechen* (Münster, 1912), 64–79; S. Eitrem, *Opferritus und Voropfer* (Kristiania, 1915), 344–415. Letting the hair hang loose: *Il.* 22. 406–7, 468–9 and in later authors; N. J. Richardson, *The Homeric Hymn to Demeter* (Oxford, 1974), 163; cf. also F. Bömer, *Ovid: Die Fasten*, ii (Heidelberg, 1958), 185; Eitrem, op. cit., 398–401.

[38] Bion 1. 21; Suet. *Aug.* 100; Stat. *Theb.* 572 (*plantis e more solutis*, 'with soles unbound, as was the custom'); cf. P. Sartori, *Zeitschrift für Volkskunde*, 4 (1894), 180; Eitrem, *Opferritus*, 398–9; F. Eckstein, *Handwörterbuch von deutscher Aberglaube*, i. 916; F. Bömer, loc. cit. (n. 37), 366.

[39] Black clothes for mourning: *SIG*³ 730. 24; *Inscriptiones Orae Septentrionalis Ponti Euxini*, i². 59. 6; Livy 45. 7. 4 (Perseus); *Philogelos* 39. At Rome: Tac. *Hist.* 3. 67. 2 with H. Heubner's commentary (Heidelberg, 1972), ad loc.

[40] e.g. the mysteries at Lycosoura: *LSCG* 68. 9–11; Andania: ibid. 65. 22; procession in honour of Demeter at Alexandria: Callim. *Hymn* 6. 124; maenads: Eur. *Phoen.* 1490, *Bacch.* 150, Livy 39. 13. 12, Ath. 5. 28 (198e); Apollo at Thebes: Phot. *Bibl.* 321 b25 (Daphnephoria: cf. Brelich, *Paides e Parthenoi* (Rome, 1969), 413–19); at Actium: *LSS* 45. 43; cult of Isis at Rome: Tib. 1. 3. 31; unidentified cult on Amorgos: *SIG*³ 1123. Cf. also J. Gagé, *Matronalia* (Brussels, 1963), 168.

[41] Hor. *Sat.* 1. 8. 23–4; Ov. *Met.* 7. 182–3; Columella 10. 361; Plin. *HN* 23. 110, 24. 103; cf. Frazer, *GB*, iii. 311 n. 1; Kiessling–Heinze, 8th edn. (Berlin, 1961) on Horace loc. cit.

[42] In general, scholiast A on Hom. *Il.* 23. 142, cf. Eustathius on *Il.* 2. 11 p. 165. 3; on examples later than *Il.* 23. 142 and Hes. *Theog.* 347, see O. Waser, *RE* VI 2778–9; S. Eitrem, op. cit. (n. 37), 366–7; M. L. West, *Hesiod: Theogony* (Oxford, 1966), 263–4. On the cult of Hera Akraia at Corinth see n. 77 below.

[43] Eur. *Hipp.* 1425–7 (see n. 118 below), Paus. 2. 32. 1 (Troizen); Paus. 1. 43. 4 (Megara); Hdt. 4. 34, Callim. *Hymn* 4. 296–8, Paus. 1. 43. 4 (Delos); Stat. *Theb.* 2. 253 (Argos); Pollux 3. 38 (Athens); Plut. *Lyc.* 15. 5 (Sparta).

[44] Lycosoura: *LSCG* 68. 6; Andania: ibid. 65. 15 (obligatory for men), 22–3 (for women); Alexandria: Callim. *Hymn* 6. 124; Eleusis: sculptures discussed in G. E. Mylonas, *Eleusis* (Princeton, 1961), 205, 207, 209–10, cf. 203 (παῖς ἀφ' ἑστίας, a boy initiate); Athena at Lindos: *LSS* 91.

witches,[45] but the Spartan ephebes also went unshod.[46] Finally, a Cretan youth was allowed only one garment,[47] the Attic ephebe wore a black garment,[48] and in certain mystery cults initiates were required to wear white clothing.[49] Ethnologists and folklorists are familiar, then, with such features in the following specific contexts: mourning, magic, the rituals of mystery cults and of puberty and marriage. Their common factor lies in their contrast with normal appearance. Normally hair is bound or plaited and is of medium length; normally garments are of various colours and a person possesses more than just one; normally shoes are worn. Mourning releases people from their routines, and places them, as it were, on the margins of normal society, almost in opposition to it, and so do the various rituals.[50] It is here too, on the fringes of society, that we find the Cynic philosopher, with his long hair and bare feet.[51]

This corresponds with what we are told about the funeral ritual for a maiden who dies in Ilion. The body is either left unburied somewhere on the beach,[52] or it is burnt on a pyre of barren branches, and the ashes are thrown into the sea.[53] The corpses of animals or, in many cases, of criminals, are simply taken outside the city. The most famous order forbidding burial is the case of Polyneices.[54] Polyneices, who attacked his own city, and criminals in general, put themselves outside the bounds of society. But other things that are thrown out

---

[45] Cf. the examples collected in n. 40.

[46] Plut. *Lyc.* 16. 11; distinctive for the *krypteia*: Pl. *Leg.* 1. 633b.

[47] Ephorus *FGrHist* 70 F 149 (= Strabo 10. 4. 2, p. 474); Heraclides Ponticus 3. 3 (*FHG* ii p. 211); Rhianus, *Epigram* 68 Powell = 8 Gow–Page refers to hair-offerings. On μονοχίτωνες (those wearing a single garment) in the service of Dorian Artemis see the scholiast on Eur. *Hec.* 934.

[48] C. Pelekides, *Histoire de l'éphébie attique* (Paris, 1962), 15–16, 115–16; cf. Vidal-Naquet, *Annales ESC* 23 (1968), 947–64; id., *PCPS* 194 NS 14 (1968), 49–64; for Hera Akraia see n. 73.

[49] Cf. n. 40 (Lycosoura, Andania).

[50] Cf. especially V. W. Turner, *The Forest of Symbols* (Ithaca, 1967), 93–111; id., *The Ritual Process* (London, 1969), 88–92 and passim.

[51] Alciphron, *Letter* 2. 38. 2, who calls him μαινόμενος (mad) and παραφρενῶν (crazy). Cf. E. Shmueli, *Cahiers d'histoire mondiale*, 12 (1970), 490–514.

[52] Scholiast on Lycoph. *Alex.* 1155.

[53] Lycoph. *Alex.* 1155–8.

[54] Soph. *Ant.* 26–30. Burial within Attica is forbidden for certain types of criminal: Xen. *Hell.* 1. 7. 22; Lycurg. *Leocr.* 113–14; Hyperides *Lyc.* 20; within the territory of the Second Athenian Confederacy *SIG*³ 147 (= Tod, *Gk. Hist. Inscr.* ii. 123) 61–3. Cf. also *Thule: altnordische Dichtung und Prosa*, v, 2nd. edn. (Düsseldorf, 1963), 104; vi, 2nd edn. (Düsseldorf, 1963), 84–5.

include μιάσματα (objects that pollute) and καθάρματα (scourings, refuse)—they too must be cleared away from the places that are shared by the community.[55] A pyre of barren branches was used in Greece to burn monstrosities: thus Teiresias commanded that the two snakes that had tried to strangle the infant Herakles should be burnt at midnight in such a fire, and their ashes should be carried outside the land.[56] The combination of burning and disposal at sea that is attested for the maidens is also found in the case of the *pharmakos*, the scapegoat, the outcast *par excellence*.[57]

It is clear from Roman practice why the wood of barren trees was used. The Greek ἄκαρπον ξύλον (barren wood) corresponds to the Roman *arbor infelix* (barren tree). Its wood was used to burn *portenta* and *prodigia*, portents and prodigies, and those guilty of high treason were hanged on a tree of this kind.[58] Traitors and monstrosities belong outside normal society, just as the *arbor infelix* stands apart from the useful fruit trees. And even when the *arbor infelix* does bear fruit, it is not like normal fruit, but black, or blood-red.[59]

In the light of all this, it can hardly be doubted that the Locrian maidens are depicted as marginal beings, separated from the normal life of other girls. Such marginalization is a feature of *rites de passage*, the fundamental ritual pattern that is found all over the world, in which Arnold van Gennep[60] identified three stages: separation, marginalization, and reincorporation (*séparation, marginalité, agrégation*). These three stages are played out in the fate of the

[55] Hippocrates *Morb. sacr.* 4. 42–6 Jones (= vi. 362 Littré); cf. also Soph. *OT* 96–8; Arist. [*Ath. Pol.*] 1.

[56] In general, *Lexica Segueriana* s.v. ἀγρίοις κατακαῦσαι ξύλοις (*Anecdota Graeca* i. 10. 26 Bekker); Theoc. 24. 88–100, with further material in A. S. F. Gow's commentary, 2nd edn. (Cambridge, 1952) ad loc; add Eur. *Melanippe, TGF* p. 509 Nauck². Cf. also the pioneering C. Boetticher, *Der Baumkultus der Hellenen* (Berlin, 1856), 301–11.

[57] Tzetz. *Chil.* 5. 736–7; cf. Nilsson, *GF*, 105–15; V. Gebhard, *Die Pharmakoi in Jonien und die Sybakchoi in Athen* (Munich, 1925); id., in *RE* VA 1290–1302; Deubner, *AF*, 179–88. Used ironically as a motif by Lucian, *Alex.* 47.

[58] Portents and prodigies in general: Macrob. *Sat.* 3. 20. 3; *perduellio* Livy 1. 26. 6; cf. C. O. Thulin, *Die etruskische Diziplin*, iii (Göteborg, 1909 = Darmstadt, 1968), 94–6; R. Heinze, *Vom Geist des Römertums*, 3rd edn. (Stuttgart, 1960), 327 n. 26; K. Latte, *RE* IX 1540.

[59] On fruits Macrob. *Sat.* 3. 20. 2 (cf. *Dig.* 48. 9. 9); on the colour red E. Wunderlich, *Die Bedeutung der roten Farbe im Kultus der Griechen und Römer* (Giessen, 1925), 4–72 (magical rites, rites of birth, puberty, and death); for methodology M. Douglas, *Purity and Danger* (London, 1966), 41–57 is exemplary.

[60] A. van Gennep, *Les Rites de passage* (Paris, 1909); developed by e.g. Turner, *Ritual Process*.

maidens, as they leave their native land, spend a year in Ilion (at the edge of the Greek world), and finally return home.

Admittedly, we do not know of any ritual of return in Locris (unless we postulate an immediate marriage). The only thing that might count as a ritual representation of their release would be their pursuit by the men of Ilion[61]—but this occurs, not when they are granted release by their own country, but just before their marginalization. Similar ritual pursuits take place in Crete, when the Cretan lover captures his boy within the framework of Cretan puberty rituals,[62] and—to judge by non-Greek analogies—we may assume that they played a part in the Spartan 'marriage by capture'.[63] Outside Greece such pursuits also occur in death rituals.[64] I do not know of any Greek examples of resistance before marginalization,[65] but it occurs in the marriage and puberty rituals of other societies.[66] Finally, a ritual pursuit, which marks the moment of release, frequently forms part of the *pharmakos* ritual.[67]

However, 'rite of passage' is not a sufficiently specific label: we should, and can, be more precise. At the centre of the whole process there are maidens, παρθένοι. They come from the most distinguished Locrian families. After a year they come home—that seems to indicate a ritual in the realm of puberty rites, of initiations, of the type that underlie rites elsewhere in Greece. For example, there is a clear

---

[61] Aptly characterized as a type of *agōn* by Vidal-Naquet (n. 1), 598.

[62] Ephorus *FGrHist* 70 F 149; the fundamental treatment is H. Jeanmaire, *Couroi et Courètes* (Lille, 1939), 450–60.

[63] Plut. *Lyc.* 15. 4; W. den Boer, *Laconian Studies* (Amsterdam, 1954), 228. On the problem see e.g. E. A. Westermarck, *History of Human Marriage*, 5th edn. (London, 1921), 271–5 and the comments by R. Firth, *Symbols* (London, 1973), n. on p. 110.

[64] G. Widengren, *Religionsphänomenologie* (Berlin, 1969), 399.

[65] The *gephyrismoi* (ritual insults) during the procession of initiates to Eleusis might be regarded as a weakened version of it, if they occurred on the bridge over the Eleusinian Kephissos (Hsch. s.v. γεφυρισταί): cf. Burkert, *HN*, 307; F. Graf, *Eleusis und die orphische Dichtung Athens* (Berlin, 1974), 45–6. J. N. Bremmer discusses this type of resistance in 'Slow Cybele's Arrival', in J. N. Bremmer and N. M. Horsfall (eds.), *Roman Myth and Mythography*, BICS Supplement 52 (London, 1987), 105–11.

[66] South Seas: J. Layard in *Südseestudien, Gedenkschrift F. Speiser* (Basel, 1951), 340–2; Ireland: G. Dumézil, *Horace et les Curiaces*, 4th edn. (Paris, 1942), 32; further examples in Brelich, *Paides*, 65 n. 45. Marriage: van Gennep, *Les Rites*, 179, 181; add E. Thurston, *Ethnographic Notes in Southern India* (Madras, 1906), 16–18; E. Samter, *Geburt, Hochzeit, Tod* (Leipzig, 1911), 162–70. W. Burkert draws my attention to Hdt. 2. 63 (Egypt).

[67] Most clearly in the Βουλίμου ἐξέλασις (expulsion of Bulimia) at Chaironeia, Plut. *Quaest. conv.* 6. 8. 1 (693e–4b), already related to the *pharmakos* ritual by Nilsson, *GF*, 466; cf. also Vernant, *MT*, 157. See n. 79 below. [See now Bremmer, Ch. 12 below.]

parallel with the ritual of the Arrhephoroi at Athens: two maidens, from distinguished families, spent eight months on the Acropolis, separated from their families; like the two Locrian maidens, they were regarded as representatives of their entire age-group.[68] In the Artemision at Brauron, out on the coast of Attica, Athenian girls lived cut off from the world for a certain period of time, during which, as vasepaintings show, they performed ritual dances, barefoot, with their hair loose, and naked or wearing a short garment, the yellow κροκωτός.[69] On Keos the girls spent at least the daytime in the temple; in the evenings they went home and had to work as slaves[70]—this, too, is reminiscent of the Locrian maidens, who were kept ἠύτε δοῦλαι (like slave-girls) at Ilion.[71] Humiliation is often a part of marginalization.[72] At Corinth, children spent a certain period of time in the sanctuary of Hera Akraia, their hair shorn, wearing black garments, as expiation for the murder of Medea's children: this has been interpreted as an initiation ritual.[73] Finally, in some cultures studied by ethnologists, anyone who dies during initiation is denied a normal funeral.[74]

IV

Thus all the details concerning the tribute of the Locrian maidens may be interpreted on the basis of an ancient initiation ritual—although in historical times the ritual no longer involved every girl: as with the Attic Arrhephoroi, it was performed by two representatives.[75]

The Greeks of historical times, admittedly, put a different inter-

---

[68] Interpreted as an initiation ritual by A. Brelich, Le iniziazioni, ii (Rome, 1961), 123–6; cf. Brelich, Paides, 231–8; in detail, W. Burkert, Hermes, 94 (1966), 1–25; id., HN, 169–73; cf. G. S. Kirk, The Nature of Greek Myths (Harmondsworth, 1974), 228–9; Parke, FA, 141–3.

[69] Vase-paintings: L. Kahil, AntKunst 8 (1965), 20–33; ead., Comptes Rendus Acad. Inscr. 1976, 126–30; the κροκωτός: Ar. Lys. 645 (on the text: C. Sourvinou, CQ 21 (1971), 339); cf. Brelich, Paides, 240–79.

[70] Plut. De mul. vir. 12. 249 d–e.

[71] Hexameters cited by Plut. De sera 12. 557d; cf. Timaeus FGrHist 566 F 146a.

[72] Cf. Turner, Ritual Process, 87.

[73] Evidence in Nilsson, GF, 57–61; interpretation: Jeanmaire, Couroi et Courètes, 299–300; A. Brelich, SMSR 30 (1959), 213–54; W. Burkert, GRBS 7 (1966), 117–19; Brelich, Paides, 355–65.

[74] Cf. Brelich, Paides, 60 n. 29; also e.g. J. W. Raum, Wiener Völkerk. Mitt. 16–17 (1969–70), 29; for Männerbünde, S. Wikander, Der arische Männerbund (Lund, 1938), 92.

[75] For a parallel from Cos see Hsch. s.v. ἀγρέται; Greek Inscr. Brit. Mus. iv. 2 no. 968. 6.

pretation on the ritual (indeed, they did not have a word for initiation rites in our sense);[76] they saw it as expiation for the outrage committed by Ajax, just as they interpreted other similar rites as ritual expiation.[77] Following this line, Friedrich Schwenn associated the Locrian practice with the *pharmakos* ritual, in which one or two 'scapegoats' take on all the guilt of the community and are driven out, carrying the guilt with them.[78] We have already associated many features of the practice—those that concern marginalization and expulsion— with *pharmakos* rituals. But some aspects are incompatible with these rituals: the maidens were required to remain for a prescribed length of time in Ilion, humiliated and characterized as marginal, and after that, they were allowed to return home; and this period was the most significant part of the ritual. Even if in certain circumstances a *pharmakos* was able to return home without creating much of a stir,[79] nevertheless this ritual does not include a prescribed period of time for marginalization. The *pharmakos* was chased away, or even killed, and that was the end of the ritual.

The situation in Epizephyrian Locri, a colony probably of the Eastern Locrians,[80] provides some firm support for our arguments, though it also raises further questions. According to Clearchus, the girls here were prostituted as παλαιᾶς τινος ὕβρεως ... ὑπόμνημα καὶ τιμωρία (a reminder and punishment for a certain ancient act of *hybris*).[81] One is tempted to see an allusion here to the myth of

---

[76] The only specific term, μύησις or τελετή, referred to initiation into a mystery cult.
[77] The cult at Brauron is an expiation for the killing of a she-bear, Pausanias the Atticist ε 35; *Anecdota* Bekker 1. 444; scholiast on Ar. *Lys.* 645; Suda s.v. ἄρκτος; cf. the sources cited in W. Sale, *RhMus* 118 (1975), 265–84; that at Corinth as expiation for the murder of the children of Medea: Eur. *Med.* 1378–83; Parmeniscus *FGrHist* 417 F 3; the 'human sacrifice' to Artemis Triklaria at Patrai was interpreted as expiation for the offences of Comaitho and Melanippus, Paus. 7. 19. 4.
[78] Schwenn, *Die Menschenopfer*, 50–2; cf. Reinach (n. 1), 46–8; expressly rejected already by Kalinka (n. 1), 42–3.
[79] As in the case of the Βουλίμου ἐξέλασις (n. 67 above): H. S. Versnel, *Triumphus* (Leiden, 1970), 161.
[80] So F. W. Walbank, *A Historical Commentary on Polybius*, ii (Oxford, 1967), 334.
[81] Clearchus fr. 43a Wehrli. Cf. esp. Gianelli, *Culti*, 197–204; C. Turano, *Arch. Class.* 4 (1952), 248–52; H. Herter in *Éléments orientaux dans la religion grecque* (Paris, 1960), 70; H. Prückner, *Die lokrischen Tonreliefs* (Mainz, 1968), 8–13; C. Sourvinou-Inwood, *CQ* 24 (1974), 186–98; R. van Compernolle, *ASNP* 6 (1976), 367–81. On the ἱερῶν μίσθωμα on no. 23 of the Locrian plaques, interpreted as ritual prostitution since the discussion by S. de Franciscis in *Klearchos*, 9 (1967), 172–6 and in his *Stato e società in Locri Epizefiri* (Naples, 1972), 151, see the refutation, convincing in my opinion, by S. Pembroke, *Annales ESC* 25 (1970), 1270, with C. Sourvinou-Inwood loc. cit. 187; R. van Compernolle, op. cit. 379–81.

Ajax,[82] but there is no evidence for it. Religious prostitution is attested by other authors: according to Pompeius Trogus, the Locrians swore an oath during their war against Rhegion (476/5) that if they won, they would prostitute their daughters every year at the festival of Aphrodite. They won, but allowed the custom to lapse, until Dionysius II reinstituted it, albeit for his own nefarious ends.[83] Even if much that our sources tell us about this re-institution is novelistic ornamentation,[84] there must be some genuinely ancient basis for the conditions under which the girls were prostituted: for the Locrians laid down that these girls might marry earlier than their coevals, and that they should prostitute themselves only to foreigners. This is consistent with widespread pre-marital rites, in which strangers are required to perform the defloration, and the completion of these rites enhances the status of the girls: there are numerous parallels in the ancient world.[85] Ethnologists include these rituals among initiation rites.[86]

In view of these ethnological parallels, the ritual at Locri must have existed in some form at an earlier date, and we must assume a background of pan-Locrian female initiation rites. The fact that Athena is the presiding deity in one instance and Aphrodite in the other is to be explained by the separate development of the rituals during the historic period. In any case, this background would have to be dated earlier than the foundation of Locri Epizephyrii, which Eusebius puts in 679 BC.[87]

---

[82] Gianelli, *Culti*, 200; contra, R. van Compernolle loc. cit. (n. 81 above) 378, whose solution is also unconvincing: Clearchus could hardly speak of an act by the Locrians committed fifty years (at most) earlier as a παλαιὰ ὕβρις, an ancient *hybris*.

[83] Justin 21. 5; a much more gruesome variant in Clearchus fr. 47 Wehrli.

[84] Cf. Periander's trick, Hdt. 5. 92η3.

[85] The material is collected by E. M. Yamauchi in H. Hoffner (ed.), *Orient and Occident: Essays C. H. Gordon* (Kevelaer, 1973), 213–22; cf. also Frazer, *GB*, ii. 282–7, v. 36–59.

[86] van Gennep, *Les Rites*, 100; L. Mair, *Man*, 51 (1951), 63 n. 2; cf. also P. Mayer, *JnlAmerAnthr* 83 (1953), 31; Brelich, *Paides*, 110 n. 159. That splendid scholar L. R. Farnell (*ARW* 7 (1904), 88) had already recognized the Greek examples as 'prenuptial rites'.

[87] Euseb. *Chron.* p. 93. 18 Helm.

V

Nevertheless, the tribute, in the form we know it, must be later. Troy VII was destroyed at the end of the Bronze Age. After that, the hill at Hissarlik remained unpopulated for a lengthy period. A few fragments of pottery may indicate a native settlement in the early Iron Age; there are no traces of Greek influence until the later eighth century. An Aeolian colony settled there around 700 BC.[88] No maidens can have been sent there before the Greek settlement. Moreover, Demetrius of Scepsis knows that the maidens were sent for the first time $\Pi\epsilon\rho\sigma\hat{\omega}\nu$ $\mathring{\eta}\delta\eta$ $\kappa\rho\alpha\tau o\acute{\nu}\nu\tau\omega\nu$, 'when the Persians were already in control', i.e. after 547/6. That sounds precise and credible.[89]

In view of what we have said, it seems unlikely that the rite sprang up at that date ex nihilo. Besides, the myth of Ajax and Cassandra is earlier, even in its cruder form, according to which Ajax raped Cassandra. Even if the tragic poets appear unaware of this version, there are representations from the early sixth century that show a naked Cassandra, and thus seem to refer unambiguously to sexual violence.[90] And this myth of a maiden who is deflowered in the temple[91]

[88] C. W. Blegen, Troy, iv (Princeton, 1958), 249–50; E. Meyer, RE Suppl. 14. 813; J. M. Cook, The Troad (Oxford, 1973), 101.

[89] Demetrius of Scepsis in Strabo 13. 1. 40, p. 600, with Wilamowitz, Die Ilias, 393–4, De Sanctis, Ricerche, 61–2; contra: Vürtheim, De Aiacis origine, 116–17, Schwenn, Die Menschenopfer, 52, Farnell, Greek Hero Cults, 295–6. W. Leaf, Strabo on the Troad (Cambridge, 1923), 192–3, Huxley (n. 1), 153. The tribute is alleged to have begun three years after the destruction of Troy (Apollod. Epit. 6. 20): this derives from the mythological tradition, and is valueless as historical evidence; Polyb. 12. 5. 6 is not evidence that the tribute began before the foundation of Locri Epizephyrii (for the date of which see n. 87 above), but tells us only that the Hundred Houses already existed before the colonization, and that they provided the maidens—at what date, Polybius does not say (Momigliano (n. 1), 447 n. 7, De Sanctis 61, against Vürtheim 105, Wilhelm (n. 1), 175, Farnell 296, Huxley 153).

[90] Thus A. Furtwängler and C. Reichhold, Griechische Vasenmalerei, i (Munich, 1904), 185; Davreux, Légende de Cassandre, 140–1; K. Schefold, Frühgriechische Sagenbilder (Munich, 1964), 88; the earliest example is the Olympic shield-band shown in Schefold 89 fig. 42, dated by him to 590–70.

[91] Early representations prove that the myth in this form did not originate with Callim. (fr. 35 Pfeiffer), as argued by e.g. Preller–Robert, Griech. Mythologie, 1267, with bold conjectures: see the previous note; Davreux, Légende de Cassandre, 12 conjectures that the myth appeared in this form as early as the Iliou Persis. Whether Alcaeus knew it depends on line 22 of fr. 138 in D. L. Page, Lyrica Graeca Selecta (Oxford, 1968) = S 262 (p. 81) in his Supplementum Lyricis Graecis (Oxford, 1974): . . .] $\acute{o}$ $\Lambda o\kappa\rho\grave{o}s$, $o\mathring{v}\delta$' $\H{\epsilon}\delta\epsilon\iota\sigma\epsilon$ ('the Locrian . . . , nor did he fear'). Page himself (Sappho and Alcaeus (Oxford, 1955), 283) had previously restored [$\H{v}\beta\rho\iota\sigma\sigma$'] $\acute{o}$ $\Lambda o\kappa\rho\acute{o}s$ ('the Locrian committed hybris

fits extremely well into the context that we have just outlined. Not only does it function as an explanation of the prostitution at Locri Epizephyrii, but the motifs that appear here are also found in other myths that are related to initiation rites: thus Komaitho, the maiden priestess of Artemis Triklaria at Patrai, had intercourse with her lover in the temple; a plague followed this sacrilegious act, and after a period during which human sacrifice took place, the ritual was instituted that was seen as late as Pausanias.[92]

However, the form that the Locrian ritual took before it was linked with Ilion can only be reconstructed in the roughest outline at most, and even then only very hypothetically. A first clue is the identity of the recipient of the tribute, Athena Ilias. She did not merely receive the maidens in her sanctuary at Ilion. It was in the precinct of Athena Ilias at Physkos in West Locris that the inscription that laid down the new regulations for the tribute was probably displayed.[93] Emancipation decrees are evidence of the regional significance of this sanctuary, which has not otherwise been investigated.[94] The town of Physkos was of some importance in the history of Locris. As inscriptions show, it was the federal capital of the West Locrians in the fourth century, and again after 167 BC.[95] Myth indicates its importance at an earlier date too: the hero Physkos was said to be the father of Locrus and grandfather of Opus,[96] and was regarded as the ancestor of all Locrians.[97]

---

against'); more explicitly H. Lloyd-Jones, *GRBS* 9 (1968), 137 [ἤϊσχυν'] ('the Locrian brought disgrace upon'): in fact, in view of the political stance of the poem (most recently B. Gentili, *Gnomon*, 48 (1976), 743), the poet surely made use of the crudest form of the myth: which was in fact, as the visual depictions show, the version that involved rape. M. L. West in Merkelbach, *ZPE* 1 (1967), 89, proposes yet another restoration (ἔξηλκ', 'the Locrian dragged'); G. Tarditi *QUCC* 8 (1969), 89.

[92] Paus. 7. 19. 1–10. Cf. Nilsson, *GF*, 216–17; J. Herbillon, *Les Cultes de Patras* (Baltimore, 1929), 38–54; M. Massenzio, *SMSR* 39 (1968), 101–32; D. Hegyi, *ActaAntiqHung* 16 (1968), 99–103; Brelich, *Paides*, 366–77.

[93] The inscription was discovered at Vitrinitsa, some 15 km. south of Malandrino (ancient Physkos), and easily accessible by road. The connection of the inscription with the sanctuary at Physkos, cautiously proposed by Wilhelm (n. 1), 163, then more confidently by E. Schwyzer, *Dialectorum Graecarum exempla epigraphica potiora* (Leipzig, 1923), 366, was questioned by L. Lerat, *Les Locriens de l'Ouest* (Paris, 1952), ii. 157. But in view of the significance of the sanctuary, and as the transport of the stone to Vitrinitsa raises no problems, this is hypercritical.

[94] *IG* IX.1 349–52; *SEG* 16. 354–61.

[95] Lerat, *Locriens*, i. 48 and *passim*.

[96] Arist. fr. 561.

[97] Arist. fr. 560. Cf. W. A. Oldfather, *Philol.* 67 (1908), 425–6.

Athena Ilias was also worshipped in South Italy; we are particularly well informed about her cult at Siris.[98] According to Timaeus,
Colophonians founded this city when they fled from Asia Minor in
the face of the Lydian expansion.[99] This foundation date is probably
too early for the oikist to have brought the goddess from Ilion. It is
more likely that she came either directly from Colophon (which in its
turn had foundation myths that refer to central Greece, to Thebes[100])
or directly from central Greece. A Boeotian settlement at Siris, earlier
than the Colophonian colony, has been conjectured on other
grounds.[101] The town was destroyed by its neighbours at an early
date. During the attack, the enemy forces killed fifty youths in the
sanctuary of Athena, among them the boy who served as priest there
in woman's clothing.[102] There is no way of establishing the historicity of this incident: it has indeed been doubted, and the story has
been taken as the legendary *aition* of the cult of Athena at nearby
Polieion.[103] However, initiation themes seem to be perceptible in certain details. Boys were frequently dressed as girls in such contexts;[104]
child-priests may originate in initiation rituals;[105] and the death
of the youths in the sanctuary is reminiscent of the common
mythology of initiation, in which the initiands die.[106]

Thus the cult at Siris may lead us back to central Greece. However,
a recently published inscription attests the cult of the goddess also at
Echinus in Achaia Phthiotis, on the northern side of the Malian Gulf,

---

[98] On its diffusion in South Italy see Strabo 6. 1. 14 p. 264 (Siris, Luceria); Ael. *NA*
11. 5 (Daunia); cf. Arist. *Mir. ausc.* 109. Cf. Gianelli, *Culti*, 93–6; much more critically J.
Perret, *Siris* (Paris, 1941), 225–9, followed by E. Meyer, *Grazer Beitr.* 4 (1975), 162.

[99] *FGrHist* 566 F 51; cf. also Aristotle fr. 584 and Strabo 6. 1. 14 (p. 264). T. J.
Dunbabin, *The Western Greeks* (Oxford, 1948), 34; J. Boardman, *The Greeks Overseas*,
2nd edn. (Harmondsworth, 1972), 180 = 3rd edn. (London, 1980), 184; regarded as a
legend by Perret, *Siris*, 151–73, but the evidence of Timaeus can hardly be rejected.

[100] Details in M. B. Sakellariou, *La Migration grecque en Ionie* (Athens, 1958), 146–72.

[101] Dunbabin, loc. cit. (n. 99).

[102] Lycoph. *Alex.* 984–92 with scholion on 984; Justin 20. 2. 3.

[103] Perret, *Siris*, 199.

[104] Fundamental discussion already in W. R. Halliday, *BSA* 19 (1909), 212–19; cf. C.
Gallini, *SMSR* 34 (1963), 215–16; ethnological material conveniently collected in
Brelich, *Paides*, 31.

[105] The decisive qualification for such a function is generally sexual maturity (Paus.
8. 47. 3; 10. 34. 8), the first growth of facial hair (Paus. 7. 24. 4), or marriage (Paus. 2.
32. 2; 7. 26. 5); or the choice is made on the basis of a beauty contest (Paus. 7. 24. 4).
The subject deserves further investigation. U. Pestalozza, *SMSR* 9 (1933), 173–
202 = *Religione mediterranea* (Milan, 1951), 233–59 is unsatisfactory; meanwhile, cf.
the material assembled by W. Burkert in *Hermes*, 94 (1966), 18 n. 3.

[106] Cf. among others M. Eliade, *Birth and Rebirth* (New York, 1958).

opposite Epiknemidian Locris: it is the dedicatory inscription of her temple, from the late Hellenistic period.[107] Neither at Echinus nor at Physkos have any indications of a special relationship with Ilion been found.

Athena's epithet Ilias, therefore, need not necessarily be derived from Ilion. There is another possible derivation, which was suggested long ago.[108] Aristarchus and Zenodotus discussed whether we should read $A\ddot{\iota}as$ '$O\ddot{\iota}\lambda\epsilon\omega s$ in Homer and not rather $\dot{o}$ '$I\lambda\epsilon\omega s$.[109] In fact the epichoric patronymic is probably $\Phi\iota\lambda\iota\acute{a}\delta\eta s$ and the personal name $\Phi\iota\lambda\epsilon\acute{u}s$.[110] Admittedly there is no direct connection between '$I\lambda\epsilon\acute{u}s$ and '$I\lambda\iota\acute{a}s$; indeed, the feminine adjective implies a masculine adjective '$I\lambda\iota os$ rather than a personal name '$I\lambda os$.[111] Now the epic patronymic of the lesser Ajax, $O\ddot{\iota}\lambda\iota\acute{a}\delta\eta s$, or rather $\Phi\iota\lambda\iota\acute{a}\delta\eta s$, is derived from '$I\lambda\iota os$; the regular patronymic from ('$O)\iota\lambda\epsilon\acute{u}s$ is ('$O)\iota\lambda\epsilon\acute{\iota}\delta\eta s$, which is its metrical equivalent.[112] Thus both '$I\lambda\iota\acute{a}\delta\eta s$ and '$I\lambda\iota\acute{a}s$ are derivatives of a personal name '$I\lambda os$. H. Usener made this suggestion long ago, connecting '$I\lambda os$ with '$I\lambda\epsilon\acute{u}s$ and drawing attention to other examples of similar variations in the suffix.[113]

Thus Athena Ilias becomes the family deity of (O)ileus, the father of Ajax, the hero who is the ancestral hero of all Locrians.[114] That

[107] Arch. Delt. 16 (1960), Chron. 162; on the topography and history of the town see Y. Béquignon, La Vallée du Spercheios (Paris, 1937), 299–303.

[108] H. Usener, Götternamen, 3rd edn. (Frankfurt, 1948), 15–16; id., Kleine Schriften, iv (Leipzig, 1913), 457–8; P. Girard, REG 18 (1905), 70–1; W. A. Oldfather, RE XVII 2175–81; E. Kalinka, ARW 21 (1922), 27–30; Bethe, Homer, iii. 138–42; Lerat, Locriens, ii. 158; E. Meyer, Grazer Beitr. 4 (1975), 161–2.

[109] The passages are collected in e.g. W. A. Oldfather, RE XVII 2175; R. Merkelbach and M. L. West, Fragmenta Hesiodea (Oxford, 1967), 115.

[110] '$I\lambda\epsilon\acute{u}s$ is found in Hes. fr. 235. 1 M–W and in Stesichorus, PMG fr. 226; '$I\lambda\iota\acute{a}\delta\eta s$ in Pind. Ol. 9. 112; cf. the amphora in the British Museum, Beazley ABV (Oxford, 1956), 97 no. 27; F. Brommer, Vasenlisten zur griechischen Heldensage, 3rd edn. (Marburg, 1973), 413; as Vilatas in Corp. Inscr. Etrur. 5264 (from Vulci). Evidence for the coexistence of the two forms is summarized in E. Schwyzer, Griechische Grammatik, 3rd edn. (Munich, 1953), i. 224; cf. also P. Chantraine, Grammaire homérique, i (Paris, 1942), 110–11; for a possible etymology, J.-L. Perpillou, Les Substantifs grecs en -εύς (Paris, 1973), 186.

[111] Cf. P. Chantraine, La Formation des noms en grec ancien (Paris, 1933), 355.

[112] Cf. E. Risch, Wortbildung der homerischen Sprache, 2nd edn. (Berlin, 1974), 148.

[113] H. Usener, locc. citt. (n. 108). Furthermore, Hyg. Fab. 161 in Micyllus' edition (1535) makes Ilios the son of Apollo. H. J. Rose in his edition of Hyginus corrects this to Ileus, perhaps wrongly (as the correction of Argeus to Agreus in the same line is mistaken: A. Henrichs, GRBS 13 (1972), 88). Whether the patronymic is spelt Oilios or Ilios on a cista from Praeneste is disputed: W. A. Oldfather in RE XVII 2178.

[114] Cf. Bethe, Homer, 144; L. Lerat and E. Meyer locc. citt. (n. 108). On Ajax as the chief hero of the Locrians see esp., besides Farnell, Greek Hero Cults, 293, P. von der

this goddess should protect the daughters of distinguished Locrian families during their period of initiation, perhaps in her sanctuary at the central town of Physkos, can no longer seem such a bizarre suggestion.

VI

The myth of Ajax will also have belonged to this context, even if it is impossible to reconstruct it in its early form. In any case, it certainly received its traditional form in the context of the epics about Troy. In the middle of the sixth century, the Locrian cult of Athena Ilias also came under the spell of the epics.[115] The Locrians came to regard the goddess of the Aeolian colony Ilion as the real Athena Ilias, and sent selected maidens to Ilion and no longer to Physkos.[116] We cannot identify the cause of this transformation of the cult. But it is certain that it had come to be understood as an expiation for the crimes of the ancestor of the Locrians: E. R. Dodds has taught us to understand the power of guilt feelings in Archaic Greece.[117] The ambiguity of many of the ritually significant aspects of the cult supported such a reinterpretation in this case as in other cults.[118] Later generations then also forgot the significance of the new interpretation, and tried

---

Mühll, *Der grosse Aias* (Basel, 1930), 14–18 = *Ausgewählte Kleine Schriften* (Basel, 1976), 448–52. Von der Mühll's argument, taken over from C. Robert (*Studien zur Ilias* (Berlin, 1901), cf. Preller–Robert, *Griech. Mythologie*, 1037) that the two Ajaxes were originally one, does not affect the interpretation that I have offered here, since the original Αἴαντε (pair of Ajaxes) would also be Locrian. It is unfortunate that we cannot get any further with the Megarian Athena Aiantis (Paus. 1. 42. 4); nevertheless cf. (in addition to the bizarre thesis of P. Girard, *REG* 78 (1905), 67–8) Farnell, 308–9 and K. Hanell, *Megarische Studien* (Lund, 1934), 49–50.

[115] cf. M. P. Nilsson, *Homer and Mycenae* (London, 1933), 46.

[116] Incidentally the view that the name of the city Ilion has its roots in Greece is defended in particular by Bethe, *Homer*, 144–5; cf. E. Meyer, *RE* Suppl. 14. 814–15.

[117] E. R. Dodds, *The Greeks and the Irrational* (Berkeley, 1951), 28–63.

[118] See n. 77 above. One other example, perhaps, is Eur. *Hipp.* 1425–7: a hair-offering originally made before marriage, which was thus 'initiatory', came to be understood later as a mourning rite: cf. W. S. Barrett, *Euripides: Hippolytos* (Oxford, 1964) ad loc. In the Homeric *Hymn to Demeter* (40–1) Demeter loosens her hairband (see n. 9 above) but does not tear her hair as would be normal in mourning ritual (remarked on by N. J. Richardson in his commentary (Oxford, 1974) ad loc.): this can be explained by the fact that it is the *aition*, not of a mourning ritual but of the loosening of the hair that is customary at the Mysteries.

to put an end to a custom that seemed increasingly alien, and finally
succeeded in doing so.[119]

(Translated by Hazel and David Harvey)

[119] When this was is quite uncertain. Plut. *De sera* 12. 557c is problematic. Were
there no other evidence, the destruction of Ilion by Fimbria would be the most obvious
occasion (sources in F. W. Goethert and H. Schleif, *Die Athenatempel von Ilion* (Berlin,
1962), 36), but this appears to be too early for Plutarch, but later estimates are
unconvincing (Wilhelm (n. 1), 173; Huxley (n. 1), 152); yet the view that Plutarch
copied a late Hellenistic source without acknowledgement (still held by Wilamowitz,
Die Ilias, 384; Walbank op. cit. (n. 80), 335) is a desperate expedient.

12

Scapegoat Rituals in Ancient Greece

JAN N. BREMMER

I

In the Old Testament a curious purification ritual occurs of which the final ceremony is described as follows: 'And Aaron shall lay both his hands upon the head of the live goat and confess over him all the iniquities of the children of Israel, and all their transgressions in all their sins, putting them upon the head of the goat, and shall send him away by the hand of a fit man into the wilderness: And the goat shall bear upon him all their iniquities unto a land not inhabited: and he shall let go the goat in the wilderness' (Leviticus 16: 21–2). It is this ceremony which has given its name to a certain ritual complex: the (e)scapegoat ritual.[1] Similar rituals can be found among the Greeks,[2] Romans,[3] Hittites (§ 111), in

This chapter is a version of a lecture which I had the pleasure of presenting at Princeton and Harvard during the year 1980–81. For helpful comments I am especially indebted to Richard Buxton, Fritz Graf, Albert Henrichs, Theo Korteweg, Robert Parker, and Zeph Stewart.

[1] It seems to me that all previous studies have been superseded by B. Janowski and G. Wilhelm, 'Der Bock, der die Sünden hinausträgt', in B. Janowski *et al.* (eds.), *Religionsgeschichtliche Beziehungen zwischen Kleinasien, Nordsyrien und dem Alten Testament* (Freiburg and Göttingen, 1993), 109–69 (with extensive bibliography).

[2] V. Gebhard, *Die Pharmakoi in Ionien und die Sybakchoi in Athen* (Diss. Munich, 1926), with older bibliography, and *RE* V A (1934), 1290–1304 (with additions and changes which are not always improvements); Nilsson, *GGR*, 107–10; J.-P. Vernant and P. Vidal–Naquet, *Tragedy and Myth in Ancient Greece* (Brighton, 1981), 87–119 (by Vernant); H. S. Versnel, 'Polycrates and His Ring', *Studi Storico-Religiosi*, 1 (1977), 17–46 at 37–43; Burkert, *SH*, 59–77, 168–176, and *GR*, 82–4, 379–80; see also the commentary on Hipponax fr. 118 West by S. R. Slings in J.-M. Bremer *et al.*, *Some Recently Found Greek Poems* (Leiden, 1987), 89–92 and the extensive apparatus to the relevant fragments in H. Degani, *Hipponactis testimonia et fragmenta*, 2nd edn. (Stuttgart, 1991).

[3] Burkert, *SH*, 63–4, 170 (with older bibliography); M. A. Cavallaro, 'Duride, i *Fasti Cap.* e la tradizione storiografica sulle *Devotiones* dei Decii', *ASAA* 54 (1976) [1979], 261–316; H. S. Versnel, 'Self-Sacrifice, Compensation and the Anonymous Gods', in *Entretiens Hardt*, 27 (1981), 135–94; L. F. Janssen, 'Some Unexplored Aspects of the Decian *devotio*', *Mnemosyne* IV, 34 (1981), 357–81.

India,[4] and even in mountainous Tibet (§ VII). In our study we will restrict ourselves to an analysis of the Greek rituals, although we will not leave the others completely out of consideration. The Greek scapegoat rituals have often been discussed. The so-called Cambridge school in particular, with its lively and morbid interest in everything strange and cruel, paid much attention to it.[5] Our own time too has become fascinated once again by these enigmatic rituals: I only need mention here René Girard's well-known *Violence and the Sacred*.[6] Gradually, too, the meaning of these rituals is becoming clearer. Where earlier generations, still influenced by the German Wilhelm Mannhardt, often detected traces of a fertility ritual in the scapegoat complex, Burkert has rightly pointed out that in these rituals the community sacrifices one of its members to save its own skin.[7] Although the general meaning is clear, many details are still in need of clarification. For that reason I shall analyse the ritual complex in a more detailed way, paying special attention to its structure. First, however, I shall present a general survey of the evidence.

II. EVIDENCE

Our fullest evidence comes from the sixth-century poet Hipponax of Kolophon (frr. 5–11 West), who wishes that his enemies be treated as *pharmakoi* or 'scapegoats'. This evidently implies that they will be fed with figs, barley cake, and cheese. Then, in inclement weather, they will be hit on the genitals with the squill and with twigs of the wild fig tree and other wild plants.[8] Tzetzes (*Chil.* 5. 737–9), our source for the fragments of Hipponax, adds that the *pharmakos* was finally burned on 'wild' wood and his ashes strewn into the sea. However,

---

[4] Burkert, *SH*, 60.

[5] J. E. Harrison, *Prolegomena to the Study of Greek Religion* (Cambridge, 1903), 95–119; L. R. Farnell, *The Cults of the Greek States*, iv (Oxford, 1907), 268–84; G. Murray, *The Rise of the Greek Epic* (Oxford, 1907), 13–16, 253–8; J. G. Frazer, *The Scapegoat = GB*, ix. 252–74.

[6] R. Girard, *Violence and the Sacred* (Baltimore, 1977).

[7] Burkert, *SH*, 70 and *GR*, 84.

[8] For the text of fr. 10 West see E. Degani, in *Studi classici in onore di Quintino Cataudella*, i (Catania, 1972), 97–103. L. Koenen, *ZPE* 31 (1978), 86 compares the flogging of Encolpius' penis in Petronius (138). This is highly persuasive, since Petronius evidently was interested in the scapegoat ritual: he is our main source for Massilia (fr. 1) and the only Latin author to use the word *pharmacus* (107).

despite this detailed description Hipponax's information should be used with the utmost care. Invective played an important role in ancient poetry and it is typical of this kind of poetry to disregard the conventions of real life by exaggerating the point the poet wants to make.[9] Thus the mention of inclement weather already shows that Hipponax is not describing the real ritual, since the Thargelia took place in early summer, but conjures up a fate even worse than that experienced at the actual scapegoat ritual.[10] Neither does it seem very probable that the scapegoat was hit on the genitals, since this is not mentioned in our sources for any of the other comparable ceremonies. This too looks much like a product of Hipponax's malicious imagination, even though the scapegoat will have been expelled with the squill and twigs of the wild fig tree, just as the slave in Chaeronea (see below) was chased out with twigs of the agnus castus.

As regards Athens, our sources are divided.[11] One group states that in exceptional times, such as a drought or a famine, certain ugly people were selected and sacrificed.[12] Another group states that at the Thargelia, a festival for Apollo, a man with white figs around his neck was expelled from the city as a purification for the men, and another man with black figs for the women.[13] In Abdera, a poor man was feasted once, led around the walls of the city and finally chased over the borders with stones.[14] In Massilia another poor devil offered himself during a plague. He was feasted for a year and then cast out of the city.[15] In Leukas a criminal was cast off a rock into the sea for the sake of averting evil during a festival of Apollo.[16] Another notice reports that every year a young man was cast into the sea with the words 'Be thou our offscouring'.[17]

From this survey it appears that the ritual was performed during the Thargelia, a festival peculiar to the Ionians, in normal times, but evidently also during extraordinary circumstances such as

---

[9] G. Nagy, The Best of the Achaeans (Baltimore, 1979), 222–42.

[10] For a convincing defence of the transmitted text (fr. 6), see A. Henrichs, 'Riper than a Pear: Parian Invective in Theokritos', ZPE 39 (1980), 7–27 at 26 f.

[11] Unfortunately, POxy 53. 3709 is too lacunose to be informative.

[12] Schol. Ar. Eq. 1136; Suid. s.v. katharma and pharmakos.

[13] Harpoc. s.v. pharmakos; Helladios apud Photius, Bibl. 534a Henry. Hsch. s.v. pharmakos wrongly states that the pair consisted of a man and a woman, see Gebhard, RE V A (1934), 1291.

[14] Callim. fr. 90; Ov. Ibis 467–8 and schol.

[15] Petronius fr. 1; Lactantius on Stat. Theb. 10. 793; schol. Luc. 10. 334.

[16] Strabo 10. 2; Ampelius 8.

[17] Photius and Suidas s.v. peripsēma. The two are connected by Nilsson, GGR, 109 f.

plague, famine, and drought (events which can of course hardly be separated).[18] With these rituals, scholars usually connect a notice of Plutarch that in his home town of Chaeronea every year a ceremony was performed in which *Boulimos*, or 'Famine', represented by a slave, was chased out of the city with rods of the agnus castus, a willow-like plant.[19] Finally, it is related in the romance of Iamboulos (Diod. Sic. 2. 55) that the Aethiopians, in order to purify themselves, put two men into boats and sent them away over the sea, never to return again.

With these rituals in which the elimination of one or two members saves the whole of the community we may compare those stories in which the death of one or two people saves the city from destruction. This is a motif which we frequently find in ancient Greece. During a war of Thebes with Orchomenos two girls sacrificed themselves, as an oracle required, in order that Thebes should win the war (Paus. 9. 17. 1). When a plague had struck Orchomenos the daughters of Orion sacrificed themselves in order to stop the plague.[20] When Eumolpos threatened to conquer Athens, the daughters of Erechtheus sacrificed themselves.[21] Just as noble was the behaviour of the daughters of Leos when Athens was struck by a plague or a famine.[22] Even more interesting is the case of the Athenian king Kodros, which will be discussed below (§ 111).[23] However, not only girls sacrificed themselves. In Euripides' tragedy *Phoenissae* it is the voluntary death of Creon's son Menoeceus which saves the city from catastrophe.

The close connection of these mythical tales with the historical rituals appears also from the fact that on the island of Naxos the girl Polykrite was honoured with sacrifices during the Thargelia, because, as was told, she had died after saving the city from destruction.[24]

---

[18] For the close connection of *limos* and *loimos*, see L. Robert, *Hellenica*, 4 (1948), 128; West on Hes. *Op*. 243; Nisbet and Hubbard on Hor. *C*. 1. 21. 13.

[19] Plut. *Mor*. 693–4, see H. S. Versnel, *Triumphus* (Leiden, 1970), 160f; Vernant, *MT*, 157; V. Rotolo, 'Il rito della *boulimou exelasis*', in *Miscellanea di studi classici in onore di Eugenio Manni*, vi (Rome, 1980), 1947–61. For the chasing of Hunger compare the late epigram of Termessos (*TAM* iii. 103) in which a certain Honoratus is honoured because 'he chased hunger to the sea'.

[20] Ant. Lib. 25; Ov. *Met*. 13. 685.

[21] U. Kron, *Die zehn attischen Phylenheroen* (Berlin, 1976), 196–7 and *LIMC* IV.1 (1988), s.v. Erechtheus, nos. 64–8; C. Collard *et al.*, *Euripides: Selected Fragmentary Plays*, i (Warminster, 1995), 156–94.

[22] Th. Kock, *RE* XII (1925), 2000–1; Kron, *Phylenheroen*, 195–8.

[23] For other possible examples of kings, see Versnel, 'Self-Sacrifice', 144 n. 2.

[24] G. Radke, *RE* XXI (1951), 1753–9; Burkert, *SH*, 72 f.

III. SCAPEGOATS

After this general survey of the evidence I will now proceed to a more detailed discussion, starting with the scapegoats themselves. Who was chosen as a scapegoat, and why these particular people? Some victims were clearly lower class, the poor devils of Abdera and Massilia, for instance, and the *Boulimos* in Chaeronea who was represented by a slave. The Athenian *pharmakoi*, too, are described as 'of low origin and useless' (schol. Ar. *Eq.* 1136) and 'common and maltreated by nature' (schol. Ar. *Ra.* 733). The Leukadians even went so far as to choose a criminal. According to Tzetzes, too, the ugliest person was selected.[25] But in the fictional romance of Iamboulos the scapegoats are strangers, and in the aetiological myth of the Athenian Thargelia they are young men.[26] Finally, we encounter young women and a king.

Now the question naturally arises whether these categories— criminals, slaves, ugly persons, strangers, young men and women, and a king—have something in common (however *bien étonnés de se trouver ensemble!*). Or, to put this question in different terms: do these different *signifiers* perhaps possess the same *signified*? The answer is surely yes. All these categories have in common that they are situated at the margin of Greek society. For the first categories this is obvious enough. Criminals put themselves outside the community, and strangers naturally do not belong to it.[27] Slaves, poor and ugly persons did not count in ancient Greece. As for young women, it has been shown that their place was not inside but at the margin of society.[28] The king distinguished himself from the rest of the population in that he alone could claim contact with the divine. *Diotrephēs*, or 'raised by Zeus', is a stock epithet of kings in Homer.[29] Where

---

[25] Tzetzes, *Chil.* 5. 732; schol. Aesch. *Sept.* 680.

[26] Neanthes *FGrHist* 84 F 16; Diog. Laert. 1. 110.

[27] A. Dorgingfung-Smets, 'Les Étrangers dans la société primitive', *Recueil Jean Bodin*, 9 (1958), 59–73; E. Benveniste, *Le Vocabulaire des institutions indo-européennes* (Paris, 1969), i. 355–61; Ph. Gauthier, 'Notes sur l'étranger et l'hospitalité en Grèce et à Rome', *Ancient Society*, 4 (1973), 1–21; J. Pitt-Rivers, *The Fate of Shechem* (Cambridge, 1977), 94–112, 179–81; O. Hiltbrunner, 'Hostis und *xenos*', in *Festschrift F. K. Dörner* (Leiden, 1978), i. 424–45; G.-J. Pinault, 'Le Nom indo-iranien de l'hôte', in W. Meid (ed.), *Sprache und Kultur der Indogermanen* (Innsbruck, 1998), 451–77.

[28] F. Graf, 'The Locrian Maidens', this volume, 250–70; C. Calame, *Choruses of Young Women in Ancient Greece* (Lanham, Md., 1997).

[29] *Il.* 1. 176, 2. 98, etc.

criminals are marginals at the bottom of society, the king is the lonely marginal at the top.[30] The myth shows, however, that high and low are interchangeable: the Athenian king Kodros who saved the Athenian community by his death was killed dressed up as a woodworker.[31]

When we now survey our material, we are struck by a curious dichotomy. On the one hand we find the poor, the ugly, and criminals, who only occur in the historical rites. This must have been such a recurrent feature of the scapegoat rituals that the words used to denote the scapegoat—*pharmakos*,[32] *katharma*,[33] *perikatharma*,[34] *peripsēma*[35]—soon became terms of abuse.[36] On the other hand there are the attractive, aristocratic, and royal figures, who are found only in the mythical and unhistorical tales.[37]

We can explain this dichotomy as follows. When a catastrophe can be averted from the community by the death of one of its members, such a member must naturally be a very valuable one. This is continually stressed in the mythical tales. For example, the oracle asks

---

[30] Girard, *Violence and the Sacred*, 12; see also G. Widengren, *Religionsphänomenologie* (Berlin, 1969), 360–93; C. Segal, *Tragedy and Civilization* (Cambridge, Mass., 1981), 43 ff.

[31] K. Scherling, *RE* XI (1922), 984–94; Burkert, *SH*, 62–3; C. Sourvinou-Inwood, 'The Cup Bologna PU 273: A Reading', *Métis* 5 (1990), 137–53; E. Simon, *LIMC* VI.1 (1992), s.v. Kodros; add *IG* II² 4258 with the comments by A. Wilhelm, *AAWW* 87 (1950), 366–70, a monument picturing Kodros' death. The name Kodros already occurs in the Linear B tablets: C. A. Mastrelli, 'Il nome di Codro', in *Atti e Memorie VII Congr. Intern. di Scienze Onomast.* (Florence, 1963), iii. 207–17.

[32] Ar. *Eq.* 1405; Lys. 6. 53; Petr. 107; M. Di Marco, 'Pirria *pharmakós*', *ZPE* 117 (1997), 35–41.

[33] J. Wettstein, *Novum Testamentum Graecum*, ii (Amsterdam, 1752), 114–15; Kassel and Austin on Eupolis F 384. 8.

[34] F. Hauck, *Theol. Wörterbuch z. Neuen Test.* 3 (1938), 681 f.

[35] G. Stählin, ibid., 6 (1959), 83–92; C. Spicq, *Notes de lexicographie néotestamentaire* (Göttingen, 1978), ii. 681 f; K. M. Starowieyski, '*Perikatharma* et *peripsema*. Przycznek do historii egzegery patrystycznej', *Eos*, 78 (1990), 281–95.

[36] As was already shown by H. Usener, *Kleine Schriften* (Leipzig and Berlin, 1913) iv. 258; see also Gebhard, *Pharmakoi*, 22–4.

[37] We find a similar dichotomy in Rome, although this has not yet been recognized. According to Macrobius (*Sat.* 3. 9. 9) *dictatores imperatoresque soli possunt devovere*, but he does not give a single historical instance of such a *devotio*. Similarly, all the examples adduced by Versnel, 'Self-Sacrifice'—Curtius, Decius, and the *seniores* at the Celtic invasion of 390 BC—belong to the world of legend, as he himself recognizes (pp. 142–3). Livy (8. 10. 11), however, explicitly says *licere consuli dictatorique et praetori, cum legiones hostium devoveat, non utique se, sed quem velit ex legione Romana scripta civem devovere*. We may safely assume that the members of the Roman élite rather sacrificed a common *legionarius* than themselves. For the Greek inspiration of the Decius legend, see now Cavallaro (above, n. 3).

for the death of the person with the most famous ancestors (Paus. 9. 17. 1), or of the daughters of the king, as in the case of Leos (Ael. *VH* 12. 28) and Erechtheus (Lyc. *Leoc.* 98–9). In other cases the beauty of the scapegoat is stressed. The youth who sacrificed himself in Athens is described by the aetiological myth as a 'handsome lad' (Neanthes *FGrHist* 84 F 16) and Polykrite, the name of the girl who saved Naxos, means 'she who has been chosen by many'.[38]

In real life, during the annual scapegoat ritual, there was of course little chance that the king (if any) would sacrifice himself or his children. Here, society chose one of its marginals. Nevertheless the people realized that they could not save their own skin by sacrificing the scum of the *polis*. For that reason the scapegoat was always treated as a very important person. In Massilia he was kept by the state—a treatment usually reserved for very important people—for one year and then chased from the city, dressed in holy clothes.[39] In Abdera he was treated to an excellent dinner before being chased away.[40] In Athens, too, he was kept by the state, and in the end led out of the city in fine clothes.[41]

In Kolophon the *pharmakos* received in his hand figs, barley cake, and cheese.[42] Hipponax mocks the simplicity of the food, but the ritual is older than his time, and we find a striking parallel in a Hittite scapegoat ritual, which we quote in full:

When evening comes, whoever the army commanders are, each of them prepares a ram—whether it is a white ram or a black ram does not matter at all. Then I twine a cord of white wool, red wool, and green wool, and the officer twists it together, and I bring a necklace, a ring, and a chalcedony stone and I hang them on the ram's neck and horns, and at night they tie them in front of the tents and say: 'Whatever deity is prowling about (?), whatever deity has caused this pestilence, now I have tied up these rams for you, be appeased!' And in the morning I drive them out to the plain, and

[38] Burkert, *SH*, 73. Versnel, 'Self-Sacrifice', 144–5 appropriately compares the Roman examples of Curtius (Liv. 7. 6. 2) and St. Caesarius (*Acta Sanctorum*, Nov. 1, 106–7). Note that J. Toutain, *Annuaire de l'École des Hautes Études*, 1916–17, 1 ff, which is quoted by Versnel 145 n. 2, has been reprinted in Toutain, *Nouvelles études de mythologie et d'histoire des religions antiques* (Paris, 1935), 126–48; also add to Versnel's bibliography on St Caesarius: *Bibliotheca Sanctorum* (Rome, 1963), iii, 1154 f.

[39] Petronius fr. 1; schol. Stat. *Theb.* 10. 793.

[40] Callim. fr. 90; *POxy.* 53. 3709.

[41] Schol. Ar. *Eq.* 1136; Suid. s.v. *katharma*.

[42] Hipp. fr. 8 West, cf. Tzetzes, *Chil.* 5. 734. Barley was considered to be slave's bread: Hipp. frr. 26. 6, 115. 8 West; Aesch. *Ag.* 1041; Wettstein, *Novum Testamentum*, i. 876 f; Bremmer, *ZPE* 39 (1980), 32.

with each ram they take 1 jug of beer, 1 loaf, and 1 cup of milk (?). Then in front of the king's tent he makes a finely dressed woman sit and puts with her a jar of beer and 3 loaves. Then the officers lay their hands on the rams and say: 'Whatever deity has caused this pestilence, now see! These rams are standing here and they are very fat in liver, heart, and loins. Let human flesh be hateful to him, let him be appeased by these rams.' And the officers point at the rams and the king points at the decorated woman, and the rams and the woman carry the loaves and the beer through the army and they chase them out to the plain. And they go running on to the enemy's frontier without coming to any place of ours, and the people say: 'Look! Whatever illness there was among men, oxen, sheep, horses, mules, and donkeys in this camp, these rams and this woman have carried it away from the camp. And the country that finds them shall take over this evil pestilence.'[43]

In this ritual the scapegoats evidently also receive food which we would not term particularly exquisite; nevertheless it is clearly considered as something special. In this prescription of a certain Ashella we are also struck by the adornment of the scapegoats. This must have been a recurrent feature of the Hittite scapegoats, since in the prescription of Uhhamuwa a *crowned* ram has to be sent away, and in the one of Pulisa the god has to be content with a 'lusty, decorated bull with earring'.[44] We find a similar adornment in Israel where a crimson thread was bound around the horns of the goat, the least valuable of the domestic animals.[45] In all these cases a cheap or relatively superfluous animal—for the continuation of the herds only few male animals need be kept from the many that are born—or a woman is sent away after being made more attractive than was originally the case. This structural similarity with our Greek material is a welcome corroboration of our interpretation.

Summing up, we conclude that in historical reality the community sacrificed the least valuable members of the *polis*, who were represented, however, as very valuable persons. In the mythical tales one could omit this stage and in the myths we always find beautiful or important persons, although even then these scapegoats remain marginal figures: young men and women, and a king.

---

[43] O. R. Gurney, *Some Aspects of Hittite Religion* (Oxford, 1977), 49; note also the more recent German translation by H. M. Kümmel in O. Kaiser (ed.), *Texte aus der Umwelt des Alten Testaments*, ii.2 (Gütersloh, 1987), 285–8.

[44] Uhhamuwa: Gurney, 48. Pulisa: Gurney 48 = H. M. Kümmel, *Ersatzrituale für den hethitischen König* (Wiesbaden, 1967), 111 ff.

[45] Thread: Burkert, *SH*, 64. Value: G. Dalman, *Arbeit und Sitte* (Gütersloh, 1939), vi. 99.

IV. VOLUNTARINESS

According to Petronius (fr. 1) the scapegoat offered himself spontaneously in Massilia. Such behaviour is the rule in our mythical examples, where the victims always sacrifice themselves voluntarily.[46] Thus Origen (*C. Cels.* 1. 31) can compare these mythical examples with Jesus:[47]

They [the apostles] not only dared to show to the Jews from the words of the prophets that he was the prophesied one, but also to the other peoples that he, who had been recently crucified, voluntarily died for mankind, like those who died for their fatherland, to avert plague epidemics, famines, and shipwreck.[48]

However, according to another source the scapegoat in Massilia was lured by 'rewards',[49] and in Abdera he had to be bought for money (Callim. fr. 90). These reports must surely be nearer the historical truth; yet the mythical tales, as so often, give a valuable insight into Greek sacrificial ideology. In Greece, as Karl Meuli has brilliantly demonstrated, sacrifice had to be conducted on a basis of voluntariness.[50] People pretended that the victim went up to the altar of its

[46] J. Schmitt, *Freiwilliger Opfertod bei Euripides* (Giessen, 1921); P. Roussel, 'Le Thème du sacrifice volontaire dans la tragédie d'Euripide', *RBPhH* (1922), 225–40; Versnel, 'Self-Sacrifice', 179–85, with an interesting discussion.

[47] Note that Eur. *Bacch.* 963, μόνος σὺ πόλεως τῆσδ' ὑπερκάμνεις, μόνος in which Dodds (ad loc.) rightly sees an allusion to the scapegoat ritual, in *Christus Patiens* (1525) is said of Jesus: μόνος σὺ φύσεως ὑπερκάμνεις βροτῶν (as Charles Segal points out to me), cf. K. Pollmann, 'Jesus Christus und Dionysos. Überlegungen zu den Euripides-Cento *Christus Patiens*', *Jahrb. Österr. Byz.* 47 (1997), 87–106 at 104. For the most recent literature on possible connections between Jesus and the scapegoat ritual/myths see the 'Addenda'.

[48] For human sacrifice at sea, see L. Röhrich, 'Die Volksballade von "Herrn Peters Seefahrt" und die Menschenopfer-Sagen', in *Märchen, Mythos, Dichtung. Festschrift F. von der Leyen* (Munich, 1963), 177–212; H. Henningsen, 'Jonas, profet og ulykkesfugl', *Handelsog Søfartsmuseets Ärbog* (Helsinki, 1966), 105–22.

[49] Schol. Stat. *Theb.* 10. 793 *proliciebatur praemiis.*

[50] K. Meuli, *Gesammelte Schriften*, ii (Basel, 1975), 993–95; for other examples, see, besides Meuli and Burkert, *passim*. For other examples, also outside Greece, see, besides Meuli and Burkert, I. Tolstoi, *Ostrov Belyi i Tavrika na Jevskinskom Ponte* (Leningrad, 1918), 33 n. 2; F. Cumont, 'L'Archevêche de Prédachté et le sacrifice du faon', *Byzantion*, 6 (1931), 521–33; S. Lieberman, *Hellenism in Jewish Palestine*, 2nd edn. (New York, 1962), 158–60; F. J. Oinas, *Studies in Finnic–Slavic Folklore Relations* (Helsinki, 1969), 193–201 ('Legends of the voluntary appearance of sacrificial victims'); A. M. di Nola, *Antropologia religiosa* (Florence, 1974), 201–62; G. J. Tsouknidas, 'Symmeikta', *Athena*, 80 (1985–9), 179–95 at 186–93.

own accord, and even asked for its consent. Whenever the animal did not shake its head in agreement, wine or milk was poured over its head. When, subsequently, the animal tried to shake this off its head, this was interpreted as a sign of its consent! In myth or legend such a trick was not necessary and it was often said that animals went up to the altar voluntarily. Sometimes it was pretended that the animal had committed a crime, but in that case its death was its own fault! We meet this line of reasoning in the *aition* of a scapegoat ritual in an unknown Ionian city. Here it was related that a man, whose very name was Pharmakos, was stoned (§ vi) by the companions of Achilles for stealing holy cups belonging to Apollo.[51] A similar line of reasoning occurs in the legend of Aesop who is pictured as a *pharmakos* and who is thrown over a cliff (cf. the case of Leukas in § ii) after having been accused of stealing a golden cup.[52]

V. PLANTS

According to Tzetzes (*Chil.* 5. 736–7) the *pharmakos* was whipped with squills, twigs of the wild fig tree, and other wild plants, and finally burned on a fire made of 'wild' wood. Why this insistence on wild plants, and what is the connection between these wild plants, on the one hand, and, on the other hand, the squill and the agnus castus, which was used in the Chaeronean ritual? For the discussion of this problem we will take our point of departure in Rome, where the point we want to make is rather more obvious.

In Rome a distinction was made between the fruit-bearing tree, *arbor felix*, and the unproductive one, *arbor infelix*. The latter category comprised not only the unproductive trees—although they constituted its main part—but also those trees which were thorny, had black fruit, or blood-red twigs.[53] It was on an *arbor infelix* that the traitor was hung and scourged to death; monstrosities and prodigies

---

[51] Istros *FGrHist* 334 F 50 and Jacoby ad loc.

[52] A. Wiechers, *Aesop in Delphi* (Meisenheim, 1961), 31–6; F. R. Adrados, 'The "Life of Aesop" ', *QUCC* 30 (1979), 93–112; Nagy, *The Best*, 279–82.

[53] Most important evidence: Macr. *Sat.* 3. 20. 3, cf. J. André, 'Arbor felix, arbor infelix', in *Hommages à Jean Bayet* (Brussels, 1964), 35–46; A. Dihle, *RhM* 108 (1965), 179–83; J. Bayet, *Croyances et rites dans la Rome antique* (Paris, 1971), 9–43; Th. Köves-Zulauf, *ANRW* II. 16. 1 (1978), 262–3; A. Weis, 'The Motif of the Adligatus and Tree', *AJA* 86 (1982), 21–38.

were burned on its wood.[54] The idea seems clear.[55] Trees useful for the community could not be used for persons and animals which had situated themselves outside the community. For the modern city-dweller such a distinction has probably lost most of its significance, but in the Middle Ages it was still of great importance, since the unproductive trees, called *mort-bois*, were free to be taken away from the woods.[56] We meet the same idea in Greece. Monstrosities like the snakes who had tried to strangle Heracles were burnt on 'wild' wood.[57] Theocritus (24. 89–90) mentions that the wood had to be of thorny material which in Rome too was considered as an *arbor infelix*, and even in the Middle Ages was thought to be *mort-bois*.[58] Whenever one of the Locrian Maidens—girls who lived in a state of marginality—died, she had to be burned on 'wild' wood.[59] A connection between death and a wild tree also seems to follow from a fragment of Euripides' *Sciron* (fr. 679 N²) where there is a reference to impaling on the branches of the wild fig tree. Unfortunately, we do not know for whom this unpleasant treatment was meant. It will now hardly be surprising that the *pharmakos* too was reported to have been burnt on 'wild' wood. Ancient Greece evidently made the same connection as ancient Rome between wild trees and persons who had to be removed from the community.[60]

Hipponax tells us that the *pharmakos* was hit on the genitals with the squill.[61] Even though this particular anatomical target seems unlikely (§ 11), the hitting of the body with squills does not seem improbable, since the Arcadians, when returning home from an unsuccessful hunt, used squills to whip the statue of Pan, the god closely associated with the hunt.[62] It seems that the squill was chosen

---

[54] Traitor: Liv. 1. 26. 6 and Ogilvie ad loc.; Cic. *Rab. perd.* 3. Monstrosities: Luc. 1. 590–1; Macr. *Sat.* 3. 20. 3.

[55] Graf, Ch. 11, above, 260.

[56] G. Rabuse, 'Mort Bois und Bois Mort', in *Verba et vocabula. Ernst Gamillschegg zum 80. Geburtstag* (Munich, 1968), 429–47.

[57] Phryn. *PS* p. 15. 12; *Anecd. Bekk.* 10. 26.

[58] Rome: André, 'Arbor felix', 40–1; K. Lembach, *Die Pflanzen bei Theokrit* (Heidelberg, 1970), 75 f. Middle Ages: Rabuse, 'Mort Bois', 442–4.

[59] Lyc. 1157 and schol.; Graf, Ch. 11, above, 259–60.

[60] See also the discussion by R. Parker, *Miasma* (Oxford, 1983), 221.

[61] For the squill see A. Steier *RE* III A (1929), 522–6; Lembach, *Die Pflanzen*, 63–5; Parker, *Miasma*, 231–2; P. Warren, 'Of Squills', in *Aux origines de l'Hellénisme. Hommage à Henri Effenterre* (Paris, 1984), 17–24.

[62] Schol. Theoc. 7. 108, cf. Ph. Borgeaud, *Recherches sur le dieu Pan* (Rome, 1979), 107–17; for a medieval parallel, see Jacob de Voragine, *Legenda Aurea*, 3. 8.

because this plant too was an unproductive one. The status of the squill was very low, as appears from the words of Theognis (537–8) to the effect that a free child will never be born from a slave, just as neither a rose nor a hyacinth will be born from a squill. The plant had the effect of a stinging nettle,[63] and Artemidorus (3. 50) informs us that the plant was inedible, as is also illustrated by an anecdote from the life of the Palestinian monk Kyriakos (Cyr. Alex. Kyr. 227). When Kyriakos had withdrawn into the desert and one day could not find his customary food, the roots of wild plants, he prayed to God to make the squill edible, because, as he argued, God can turn bitterness into sweetness. The Suda (s.v. skilla) even calls the plant 'death-bringing'. Now, when we see that in Rome the parricide was whipped with the red twigs of the cornel tree, an arbor infelix, the conclusion seems evident.[64] Not only for the execution of criminals but also for whipping them wood was chosen which belonged to the category of unproductive trees.

The squill was also used for fighting. We know that in Sicily and Priene the ephebes fought with squills.[65] This probably meant that they pelted each other with the bulbs, although a fight with the leaves cannot be excluded. The connection of the ephebes with the squill will hardly be fortuitous. Just like the pharmakos, the ephebes too are marginal persons.[66]

The distinction between fruit-bearing and unproductive trees also helps to throw light on the chasing away of Famine with rods of agnus castus in Chaeronea. The willow is already called 'fruit-destroying' by Homer (Od. 15. 510), since it was thought to lose its fruit before ripening. During the Thesmophoria the Athenian women slept on twigs of the lygos or agnus castus—a tree usually identified with the lygos—because the plant was thought to promote infertility.[67] Pliny, too, mentions the plant as a means to induce

---

[63] Arist. fr. 223 Rose; Nic. Alex. 254.

[64] Mod. Dig. 48 tit. 9. 1 prooem. virgis sanguineis verberatus, cf. Bayet, Croyances et rites, 36.

[65] Sicily: schol. Theoc. 7. 106/8d, the reading of which is unnecessarily doubted by Wilamowitz apud C. Wendel, Scholia in Theocritum vetera (Leipzig, 1914), 104; Graf, NK, 140. Priene: I. Priene 112. 91, 95.

[66] Bremmer, 'Heroes, Rituals and the Trojan War', Studi Storico-Religiosi, 2 (1978), 5–38; P. Vidal-Naquet, The Black Hunter (Baltimore, 1986), 106–56.

[67] Thesmophoria: Bremmer, Greek Religion (Oxford, 1994), 76. Lygos/agnus castus: Plin. NH 24. 9. 38; Eustath. p. 834. 34; E. Fehrle, Die kultische Keuschheit im Altertum (Giessen, 1910), 152; D. Page, Sappho and Alcaeus (Oxford, 1955), 202; L. Robert, Journal des Savants (1961), 134; G. J. de Vries on Plato, Phaedrus 230b.

infertility.[68] For the early Christian writers the tree has even become the symbol of chastity.[69] This *arbor infelix* aspect of the lygos will help us understand its role in some other Greek myths and rituals. In Sparta Artemis was worshipped under the epithet Lygodesma, or 'willow-bound', because her statue was reputed to have been found in a thicket of willows, and a willow supported her statue (Paus. 3. 16. 9). In Samos Hera was said to have been born near a lygos tree in her Heraion (Paus. 7. 4. 4).[70] The local historian Menedotus (*FGrHist* 541 F 1) even tells a complete *aition* of Hera's connection with the lygos tree. From this tale it appears that her statue was fastened into a mat made of willow. The lygos also occurs in mythical tales. In the story of Dionysos' kidnapping by pirates the god is bound with twigs of the lygos (*h. Bacch.* 7), as was Hermes by Apollo (*h. Merc.* 410).[71]

All these gods—Artemis, Hera, Dionysos, and Hermes—have in common that myths and rituals of reversal play a role in their cults. The late Karl Meuli, to whom we owe a first analysis of this aspect of these gods, even called them 'the fettered gods', because their statues were often fettered and sometimes only untied once a year.[72] A connection of precisely these gods with an *arbor infelix* like the lygos seems therefore completely understandable.

[68] Plin. *NH* 16. 26. 110. This aspect of the plant was taken up by medieval medicine and still in our day by homeopathy which prescribes the plant to promote libido, although scientific tests (as perhaps could have been expected) do not indicate great effectiveness, cf. O. Leeser, *Handbuch der Homöopathie*, B/ii (Heidelberg, 1971), 585–96.

[69] H. Rahner, 'Die Weide als Symbol der Keuschheit', *Zs. f. Kath. Theol.* 56 (1932), 231–53 and *Griechische Mythen in christlicher Deutung* (Zürich, 1945), 361–413. In the Middle Ages the tree became the symbol for infertility and the 'world' as opposed to the Christian way of life, cf. W. Fraenger, *Hieronymus Bosch* (Gütersloh, 1975), index s.v. *Weide*; M. Bambeck, 'Weidenbaum und Welt', *Zs. f. franz. Sprache und Lit.* 88 (1978), 195–212.

[70] For the Samian Hera, see R. Fleischer, *Artemis von Ephesos und verwandte Kultstatuen aus Anatolien und Syrien* (Leiden, 1973), 202–23; Meuli, *Gesammelte Schriften*, ii. 1059–64; H. Walter, *Das Heraion von Samos* (Munich, 1976); Fleischer, *Festschrift Dörner*, i. 343–4; Burkert, *SH*, 129 f.

[71] Dionysos: S. Eitrem, 'Heroen der Seefahrer', *SO* 14 (1935), 53–67; U. Heimberg, *JDAI* 91 (1976), 260–5; L. Kahn, *Hermès passe* (Paris, 1978), 113–17; H. Herter, 'Die Delphine des Dionysos', *Archaiognosia*, 1 (1980), 101–34; Burkert, *HN*, 200 f. Hermes: Kahn, 75–117. L. Radermacher, *Der homerische Hermeshymnus* (Leipzig, 1931), 145–6 already connected this binding with Artemis Lygodesma and Hera of Samos. S. Eitrem, *RhM* 64 (1909), 333–5 also explained the epithet Polygios of Hermes in Trozen as Poly-lygios, or 'with much willow', which is not impossible.

[72] Meuli, *Gesammelte Schriften*, ii. 1035–81; Graf, *NK*, 92–6.

We are, however, not yet finished with the lygos. It was a plant from which wreaths were made. What kind of people wore such wreaths? From our analysis so far we may expect that a lygos wreath was worn by marginal people. This is indeed what we find. In the cult of Hera of Samos it was the Carians, that is to say non-Greeks, who had to wear a lygos wreath (Menedotus, loc. cit.).

According to myth, Prometheus, too, had to wear a lygos wreath, and Prometheus was a kind of culture hero, a being always situated at the margin of society.[73] Our last example is less clear. We have a fragment of Anacreon which says: 'the friendly Megistes has already been wearing a lygos wreath for ten months and is drinking honey-sweet new wine.' Unfortunately, this is all the fragment says, but it seems to us that Gow and Page rightly conclude that Anacreon describes the behaviour of Megistes as being odd.[74] Given this dubious status of the lygos it can hardly be chance that the inhabitants of Magnesia reserved a spot for their cow dung in a place full of willows.[75]

Finally, our classification of the lygos as an *arbor infelix* does not mean that the tree should be considered a useless one. On the contrary, we know that the tree was used for all kinds of basketry. It does mean that the early Greeks in their struggle for survival distinguished primarily between fruit-bearing trees and unproductive ones.

However, we have not yet discussed all the relevant plants. In Athens the *pharmakoi* were led out of the city, one man with black figs around his neck, the other with white ones. Burkert has rightly pointed to the 'marginal' quality of the fig.[76] The fruit has obscene connotations and is in opposition to the fruits of cereal agriculture. We find this symbolic quality again in the rites involving Athenian girls. Aristophanes in his *Lysistrata* (641–5) describes their 'career' as follows:

At the age of seven I immediately became an *arrēphoros*.
Then, at ten, I was an *aletris* for the presiding goddess; then I was a bear at

---

[73] A. Brelich, 'La corona di Prometheus', in *Hommages à Marie Delcourt* (Brussels, 1970), 234–42; M. Detienne and J.-P. Vernant, *Cunning Intelligence in Greek Culture and Society* (Hassocks, 1978), 85.
[74] Anacr. frr. 352, 496 *PMG*; A. F. Gow and D. L. Page, *The Greek Anthology: The Hellenistic Epigrams*, ii (Cambridge, 1965), 421.
[75] I. *Magnesia* 122 fr. e, 12, cf. Robert (above, n. 67), 135–7.
[76] Burkert, *GR*, 83.

the Brauronia with the saffron-robe; and, being a beautiful girl, I carried the basket with a necklace of dried figs.[77]

We do not have many details about this necklace or about the girls who carried the basket (kanēphoroi), but a fragment of the Athenian comedian Hermippos speaks of 'kanēphoroi covered with white flour'.[78] This white flour cannot be separated from the mythical tales of young girls covered with scurvy, as Burkert has demonstrated.[79] Where myth spoke of a real illness, ritual characteristically (§ VII) required only white flour. We infer from this fragment that the carrying of a basket was a duty for girls in a state of marginality and the figs will have signified this state, as the squills did in the case of the ephebes.

The reader may, however, object that the fig tree is a useful and fruit-bearing tree. This is certainly true, and I would therefore add to Burkert's explanation that the black fig came from a wild fig tree (Theophr. HP 2. 2. 8; Plin. NH 17. 256), as did the white one (Athenaeus 3. 76cde). This means that these fruits, too, fit into the pattern we have explored: marginal persons are connected with marginal plants.

VI. LEAVING THE CITY

The elimination of a citizen from the polis was a serious matter. How exactly did it happen? The pharmakos was probably led out of the city in a procession,[80] which in Chaeronea started from the public hearth, as Plutarch (Mor. 693e) informs us. This hearth was situated in the prytaneion, the Greek town hall. Since people who were kept by the state, as happened with the scapegoat in Athens and Massilia, were also entertained in the prytaneion,[81] the conclusion seems reasonable that normally the procession started from the prytaneion.

[77] For the textual problems in this passage see most recently the editions of J. Henderson and A. H. Sommerstein ad loc.
[78] Hermippos F 25 K.–A. For the kanēphoroi, see A. Brelich, Paides e parthenoi (Rome, 1969), 274–90.
[79] Burkert, HN, 170.
[80] A. D. Keramopoullos, Ho apotympanismos (Athens, 1923), 116–19, who compares Aesch. Cho. 98; Plato, Cratylus 396e and schol. Leg. 9. 877; Lys. 6. 53.
[81] F. Gschnitzer, RE Suppl. XIII (1973), 805; S. G. Miller, The Prytaneion (Berkeley, 1978), 13–14; M. J. Osborne, 'Entertainment in the Prytaneion at Athens', ZPE 41 (1981), 153–70.

Elimination from the community started from the heart of that community.

While the procession left the city, flutes played a special melody which was called the 'melody of the wild fig'.[82] We do not know anything more about that melody, but the analogy with folk music does perhaps suggest something about the nature of the music. It has recently been pointed out that music in traditional rites can be divided into harmonious and unharmonious.[83] The latter kind of music was played especially during the removal of persons from the community, as in the case of a charivari. Now Hipponax (fr. 153 West) tells us that his fellow poet Mimnermus (T 5 Gentili/Prato) played this melody. Given the malicious nature of Hipponax, he will hardly have meant this as a compliment. It seems therefore not unreasonable to assume that in this case too the music will not have been particularly harmonious.

Plutarch (Mor. 518b) tells us that cities had special gates for those condemned to death, and for purgations and purificatory offerings. Similarly, the public prison in Athens had a special gate, the gate of Charon, for those condemned to death.[84] The scapegoats, too, will have left the city by a special gate, since at least for Abdera we hear of such a gate, the Prauridian gate (Callim. fr. 90).

After the passage through the special gate the scapegoat was led around the city in a procession. This is certain for Massilia and Abdera, and probable for Athens. The Cynic Diogenes too alluded to this custom. He was supposed to have said during a visit to the Isthmian games: 'One should lead around those potbellies (the athletes!) and purify (the place) all round, and then chase them over the border' (Dio Chr. 8. 14). Deubner denied the circumambulation and thought that the procession only touched upon as many points as possible within the city.[85] However, he had overlooked the text from Dio and, moreover, the two types of procession—going around and staying within the city—are not mutually exclusive, since both rites were performed during medieval and more recent plague

---

[82] Hipp. fr. 153 West; Hsch. s.v. kradiēs nomos.

[83] C. Marcel-Dubois, 'Musiques cérémonielles et sociétés rurales', Proc. 8th Inter. Congr. Anthrop. and Ethn. Sciences, ii (Tokyo, 1968), 340 and 'Fêtes villageoises et vacarmes cérémoniels', in J. Jacquot and E. Konigson (eds.), Les Fêtes de la Renaissance, iii (Paris, 1975), 603–15.

[84] Poll. 8. 102; Zen. 6. 41; H. Lloyd-Jones, ZPE 41 (1981), 28.

[85] Deubner, AF, 181.

epidemics.[86] A circumambulation is a ritual which can be performed in different contexts: apotropaic, cathartic, and as rite of aggregation.[87] In the scapegoat ritual the cathartic aspect was most prominent, since the ritual was called *perikathairein*, 'to purify around', and the scapegoat *perikatharma* (§ 111).

Finally, the *pharmakos* was chased over the border. In Athens and Massilia this happened by means of pelting with stones, and the aetiological myth of the killing of Pharmakos and the story of Polykrite also presuppose a stoning. In a most interesting discussion of this horrific ritual D. Fehling has pointed out that stoning was not always meant to kill; it was often only a kind of *Imponier* behaviour.[88] Whether this was the case with the scapegoat we will discuss in our next section.

It was typical of stoning that everybody present took part in it, and Fehling has suggested that this participation of all people involved was necessary, because those who kept themselves aloof could still think of the expelled person as one of the group; such a thought could become responsible for heavy conflicts within the community.[89] This suggestion is highly persuasive, but there is another aspect too to be considered. The involvement of all persons in the expulsion of one member of the group helps to reconstitute that group, and this fits in well with the general meaning of the Thargelia.

After chasing the scapegoats over the border people probably returned without looking back, as was the rule in the case of purificatory offerings.[90] A prohibition on looking back is typical for the moment of separation: as with the wife of Lot from Sodom, and in modern Greek folklore the bride when leaving the parental home.[91]

---

[86] J. Delumeau, *La Peur en Occident* (Paris, 1978), 139 f.

[87] V. Hillebrandt, 'Circumambulatio', *Mitt. Schles. Gesells. f. Vkd.* 13/4 (1911), 3–8; S. Eitrem, *Opferritus und Voropfer der Griechen und Römer* (Kristiania, 1915), 6–29; E. F. Knuchel, *Die Umwandlung in Kult, Magie und Rechtsbrauch* (Basel, 1919); Weinkopf, *Handw. deutschen Abergl.* 8 (1936–7), 1315–46; W. Pax, 'Circumambulatio', *RAC* 3 (1957), 143–52; H. S. Versnel, 'Sacrificium lustrale: The Death of Mettius Fufetius (Livy I. 28)', *Med. Ned. Instit. Rome* 37 (1975), 1–9 at 5–8.

[88] D. Fehling, *Ethologische Überlegungen auf dem Gebiet der Altertumskunde* (Munich, 1974), 59–82; M. Gras, 'Cité grecque et lapidation', in *Du châtiment dans la cité* (Rome, 1984), 75–89.

[89] Fehling, ibid. 72 f.

[90] Aesch. *Cho.* 98; cf. Keramopoullos, *Apotympanismos*, 116.

[91] For the prohibition on looking back, see E. Samter, *Geburt, Hochzeit, Tod* (Leipzig, 1911), 147–50; Th. Gaster, *Myth, Legend and Custom in the Old Testament* (New York, 1969), 159–60 (Lot's wife); A. S. Pease on Cic. *Div.* 1. 49; A. F. Gow on Theoc. 24. 96; F. Bömer on Ov. *Fa.* 5. 439 and *Met.* 10. 51; J. K. Campbell, *Honour, Family and Patronage* (London, 1964), 136 (modern Greece).

Persons who are looking back still have a tie with what is lying
behind them; the prohibition therefore is a radical cut with all connections with the past. It is, to use the terminology of Van Gennep, a
typical rite of separation. By not looking back the citizens definitively
cut through all connections with the scapegoat.

VII. DEATH?

The final fate of the scapegoats has, understandably, fascinated (and
divided) scholarly opinion. According to some they were killed,
according to others not, and Nilsson even stated that this was a
matter of indifference, since in both cases the goal—the expulsion
from the community—was reached. This is of course true, but does
not solve the problem. We will therefore once again look at the evidence in a systematic way.

We start with Abdera. Till 1934 it was commonly believed that in
this city the scapegoat was stoned to death, since this was reported by
our only source, Ovid (*Ibis* 467–8 and scholion ad loc.). In 1934,
however, a papyrus with a fragment of Callimachus (fr. 90) was published, which stated unequivocally that the scapegoat was chased
over the border with stones but certainly not killed.

We meet a similar discrepancy in Massilia where the scapegoat was
expelled from the city according to Petronius (fr. 1),[92] but according to
later scholia (on Statius, *Theb.* 10. 793) was stoned to death. In Leukas
the criminal was, it is true, thrown from a rock, but birds and feathers
were fastened to him to soften his fall and in the sea boats were waiting
for him to pick him up and transport him over the border. The other
source which reports the hurling from a rock speaks of a sacrifice. In
Athens the scapegoats were expelled over the border in historical
times, but in the aetiological myth the scapegoat was killed. Finally,
the scapegoats in the romance of Iamboulos were put into boats, of
which it is explicitly said that they were seaworthy (Diod. Sic. 2. 55. 3).

---

[92] Petronius, fr. 1 *et sic proiciebatur*. Thus all the manuscripts, but Stephanus (who
has frequently been followed), on the basis of schol. Stat. *Theb.* 10. 793, emended
proiciebatur into *praecipitabatur* 'was hurled from a height'. Frazer, *The Scapegoat*, 253 n.
2, however, already noted that this change was not supported by the textual tradition,
and the recent editions of Servius, our source for Petronius' fragment, and Petronius
have both returned to *proiciebatur*. For *proicio*, 'cast out of a city', see Cic. *Cat.* 2. 2 *quod
(urbs) tantam pestem evomuerit forasque proiecerit*; Ov. *Met.* 15. 504 *immeritumque pater
proiecit ab urbe*.

When we discount the death of the scapegoats in the myths, since it is now generally accepted that the myths are not always an exact reflection of the ritual, we are left with two cases. In Philostratus' *Life of Apollonius of Tyana* (4. 10) it is described how during a plague in Ephesus Apollonius pointed to a squalid beggar and ordered him to be killed, since he was an enemy of the gods. Burkert considers the possibility of a historical background for this tale, and Apollonius is indeed often connected with plague epidemics;[93] yet the passage looks rather novelistic.[94] The eyes of the beggar are full of fire and after his death his body has disappeared. In its place a dog is found as big as the biggest lion. Although this story follows the scapegoat pattern—this is clear and has often been recognized—the event can hardly be considered historical.

The only case left to be discussed is the death of the scapegoat in Hipponax. This death has been much debated, even though our evidence points to a clear solution. Wherever we have a good picture of the historical events, as in Abdera, Athens, Leukas, and Massilia, it appears certain that the scapegoat was not killed but expelled. When we confront this conclusion with Hipponax, our inference can hardly be otherwise than that Hipponax also has derived his description of the end of the scapegoat from an aetiological myth of a legendary version, if it is not his own invention—a possibility which is not at all improbable. An alternative solution, however, is also not completely impossible. The burning of the scapegoat on 'wild' wood, which is not mentioned in any of the Hipponax fragments, may be Tzetzes' own invention.[95] Should this be the case, the burning probably derived from the ritual of the Locrian maidens, since a description of this ritual immediately follows the one of the *pharmakos* (*Chil.* 5. 738 ff.). But whichever solution we choose, in either case our conclusion must be that the *pharmakos* stayed alive.

The Greeks then expelled a living scapegoat as did, e.g., the Hittites. For this expulsion we also have a hitherto neglected parallel from Tibet which shows a striking resemblance to the Greek ritual—the

[93] Burkert, *SH*, 70. For plague epidemics and Apollonius, see E. L. Bowie, 'Apollonius of Tyana: Tradition and Reality', *ANRW* II 16.2 (1978), 1652–99 at 1687.

[94] G. Petzke, *Die Traditionen über Apollonius von Tyana und das Neue Testament* (Leiden, 1970), 126–7; D. Esser, *Formgeschichtliche Studien zur hellenistischen und zur frühchristlichen Literatur unter besonderer Berücksichtigung der Vita Apollonii des Philostrat und der Evangelien* (Diss. Bonn, 1969), 59 suggests an 'aetiologische Lokallegende'.

[95] W. J. W. Koster on Tzetzes Ar. *Ra.* 733a notes Tzetzes' careless handling of the sources in this specific case; Gebhard, *Die Pharmakoi*, 3 ff.; Deubner, *AF*, 184.

occasion of the performance around New Year, the selection of
a lower-class person who is treated as very special,[96] the unharmonious music, the stoning—as appears from the following
description:

At Gyanese, the person selected to act as the scapegoat is fed and clothed at
State expense for a year previous to the ceremony. On the appointed day (just
before New Year) with a bloody sheepskin bound round his head, yak's
entrails hung round his neck, but otherwise naked, he takes his position in
the local Jong, or Fort. In his right hand he carries a fresh sheep's liver, his
left being empty. After blasts from long trumpets, beating of drums, clashing
of cymbals, and incantations by the officiating lamas, the scapegoat
scratches the ground with a stick, to indicate that the season of ploughing
and sowing is at hand, flings the sheep's liver among the crowd, and rushes
down the hill on to the plain below. The people fling after him stones and dirt,
taking, however, great care not to wound him severely, or prevent him from
reaching the open country. Should the scapegoat not succeed in making
good his escape, the devils would remain in the place. Shots from the prong
guns fired into the air increase the pandemonium that accompanies his
flight; in the midst, once he has reached the plain, the lamas perform a
solemn dance of triumph, concluding by burning *torma* offerings.[97]

If, however, the scapegoat was only expelled in historical reality—
why do the mythical tales often speak of a killing? In our analysis we
have repeatedly shown that the myth clarified the meaning of the
ritual. Symbolic acts in the ritual became reality in the myth.[98] This
will also have been the case with the scapegoats. The expulsion of the
scapegoats in practice amounted to a killing, since, like the dead, they
disappeared from the community, never to return. In a way, therefore, Nilsson was right in considering death and expulsion as having
the same effect. However, we may wonder whether the historical
scapegoats will have shared his academic indifference as regards
choosing between these two modes!

---

[96] The person selected is often a beggar: G. Tucci and W. Heissig, *Die Religionen Tibets
und der Mongolei* (Stuttgart, 1970), 197.
[97] D. Macdonald, *The Land of the Lama* (London, 1929), 213f.
[98] Cf. Graf, this volume, pp. 255–6 on a similar discrepancy: 'The myth presented the
ritual with unrelieved harshness, extrapolating so to speak from the actual events to
their significance as perceived by those experiencing them.'

VIII. THARGELIA

We will finally consider the place of the scapegoat ritual in the Greek religious calendar. The scapegoats were expelled on the sixth of the month Thargelion, the first day of the two-day festival of the Thargelia. It is rather surprising to note that on the same day on which the scapegoats were expelled the Greeks also celebrated the fall of Troy,[99] the victories at Marathon and Plataea, and even the victory of Alexander the Great over Darius (Ael. *VH* 2. 25). Evidently the expulsion of evil was felt so intensely that this seemed to be the appropriate day to celebrate these victories.

On the second day of the Thargelia a first-fruit sacrifice was celebrated and a kind of May tree, the *eiresionē*, was carried around.[100] Choirs of men and boys competed in singing hymns and we know of the Thargelia in Miletus that large amounts of undiluted wine and expensive food were consumed. The *eiresionē* and the first-fruit sacrifice are typical signs of seasonal renewal: the first signs of coming prosperity after the scarceness of the winter period.[101] There is a large amount of ethnological material showing that the beginning of a new year—which often coincides with a first-fruit festival—or the arrival of a period of plenty is often celebrated with an *orgia alimentare*: people take an advance on the new harvest.[102] From a psychological point of view the 'orgy' is a kind of collective relaxation by the community, which for a while need not worry any more about the often precarious food situation. In Greece the exceptional character of the meal was stressed by the drinking of undiluted wine, for in normal circumstances wine was always diluted with water.[103]

Since the Thargelia was a festival for Apollo we may expect that the god also shows a connection with seasonal renewal. Such a

---

[99] Damastes *FGrHist* 5 F 7; Hellanikos *FGrHist* 4 F 152a.

[100] For the Thargelia, see Nilsson, *GF*, 105–15; Deubner, *AF*, 179–98; Parke, *FA*, 146–49; W. den Boer, *Private Morality in Greece and Rome* (Leiden, 1979), 129–32.

[101] For the *eiresionē*, see Burkert, *SH*, 134 (sources and bibliography); add W. Klinger, 'L'Irésione grecque et ses transformations postérieures', *Eos*, 29 (1926), 157–74 (with interesting Caucasian material); S. Follet, *RPh* 48 (1974), 30–2 (epigraphical examples).

[102] V. Lanternari, *La grande festa*, 2nd edn. (Bari, 1976), *passim*; add Gregory of Tours, *VP* 6. 2.

[103] For the opposition of mixed and neat wine, see F. Graf, 'Milch, Honig und Wein', in G. Piccaluga (ed.), *Perennitas. Studi in onore di Angelo Brelich* (Rome, 1980), 209–21; add Bremmer, *Arethusa*, 13 (1980), 295 n. 49 and *ZPE* 39 (1980), 32 f.

connection seems indeed to exist. In a hitherto neglected text, Athenaeus (10. 424–5) informs us that the Thargelia in Athens was the festival of Apollo Delius. Although the epithet was most likely added after the Athenians concerned themselves with Delos in 425 BC (Thuc. 3. 104), it seems reasonable to assume that they must have seen a connection between Apollo Delius and the Apollo of the Thargelia. The main festival of Apollo Delius, the Delia, was a festival of seasonal renewal and was connected with the growth of the adolescents.[104] This coincides to a large degree with the festival of the Thargelia where, as we have seen, seasonal renewal and the boys also played an important role. Apollo Delius will thus have been chosen because of the similarity of the Delia and the Thargelia.

This study has thus shown that the expulsion of the scapegoat in the religious calendar preceded a day of seasonal renewal. A similar structure could also be found in Tibet (§ VII) and in Rome where the ancient New Year (the first of March) was preceded by a month full of purificatory rituals. The same alternation could still be found in the carnival rites of western Europe where at the beginning of the year society expelled all kinds of evil.[105] The pattern is fully understandable: no new beginning before a complete *katharsis* of the old situation. This applies of course to the fixed date of the Thargelia as well as to special occasions when a new beginning had to be established after the disturbance of the seasonal and cosmic order through drought or plague. However, it remains enigmatic why the Greeks had to use a human being, whereas the Hittites sometimes and the Israelites always found an animal sufficient. Evidently, to be more civilized does not always mean to be more humane.

ADDENDA

This article had been rejected by *Greek, Roman, and Byzantine Studies* and *Mnemosyne*, before being accepted by *Harvard Studies in Classical Philology*. Its inclusion in the present volume is a good illustration of the radical changes in the study of Greek religion in the last two decades. In the 1960s, Jean-Pierre Vernant and Walter Burkert had pioneered new ways: structuralism, functionalism, and a strict application of the myth–ritual scenario. These new ways became only

---

[104] Calame, *Choruses*, 104–10.
[105] E. Le Roy Ladurie, *Le Carnaval de Romans* (Paris, 1979), 342–4.

generally accepted in the classical world in the 1980s: the initial rejection of my article is just one illustration of this fairly late acceptance. In my own approach, I had been heavily influenced by Walter Burkert, but also by the innovative application of Arnold van Gennep's theories on the rites of passage in the work of the English anthropologist Victor Turner.

As the results of my article have been widely accepted, I have limited myself to correcting some mistakes, replacing foreign publications by English translations and adding a few references to studies with new or overlooked evidence. There have since been four new studies of the scapegoat ritual in general. From these, R. Parker, *Miasma* (Oxford, 1983), 258–80, is an important discussion with many new insights, whereas D. Hughes, *Human Sacrifice in Ancient Greece* (London and New York, 1991), 139–65, 241–8; P. Bonnechere, *Le Sacrifice humain en Grèce ancienne* (Athens and Liège, 1994), 118–21, 293–308, and D. Ogden, *The Crooked Kings of Ancient Greece* (London, 1997), 15–23, do not seem to me to add much. An intriguing problem remains the influence of the Greek scapegoat ritual on the birth of the early Christian idea of the atonement, cf. H. S. Versnel, 'Jezus Soter—Neos Alkestis? Over de niet-joodse achtergrond van een christelijke doctrine', *Lampas*, 22 (1989), 219–42 and 'Quid Athenis et Hierosolymis? Bemerkungen über die Herkunft von Aspekten des "effective death" ', in B. Dehandschutter and J. W. van Henten (eds.), *Die Entstehung der jüdischen Martyrologie* (Leiden, 1989), 162–96, to be read with my discussion, 'The Atonement in the Interaction of Greeks, Jews, and Christians', in J. N. Bremmer and F. García Martínez (eds.), *Sacred History and Sacred Texts in Early Judaism. A Symposium in Honour of A. S. van der Woude* (Kampen, 1992), 75–93.

13
Women and Sacrifice in Classical Greece

ROBIN OSBORNE

There is no doubt that a person's gender could make a difference to their role in Greek sacrifices. But did it normally make a difference in Greece? And why did it make a difference? Two inscriptions from the island of Thasos neatly illustrate the problem. First, one dated to around 440 BC and found in the sanctuary of Herakles:

['Hρα]κλεῖ Θασίωι
[αἶγ]α οὐ θέμις, οὐ-
[δὲ] χοῖρον· οὐδὲ γ-
[υ]ναικὶ θέμις· οὐ-
[δ]' ἐνατεύεται· οὐ-
δὲ γέρα τέμνετα-
ι· οὐδ' ἀθλεῖται.[1]

To Thasian Herakles. Goat is prohibited, so is pig. Women are prohibited. No ninth is given. No perquisite portions are cut. No contests.

Second, one dating to thirty or forty years earlier, and found in the sanctuary of Demeter Thesmophoros:

This chapter was originally written as a paper for Jane Sherwood's Corpus Christi Classical Seminar on Religion and Society. I am grateful to Jane, and to Paul Cartledge, Robert Parker, Richard Seaford, Christiane Sourvinou-Inwood, and participants at the seminar for comments on an earlier draft.

[1] IG XII Suppl. 414, LSS 63. See also B. Bergquist, *Herakles on Thasos: The Archaeological, Literary and Epigraphic Evidence for his Sanctuary, Status and Cult Reconsidered* (Uppsala, 1973), esp. Part II pp. 65–90. The most recent discussion, although not interested in the exclusion of women, is J. Des Courtiles and A. Pariente, 'Problèmes topographiques et religieux à l'Herakleion de Thasos', in R. Étienne and M. T. Le Dinahet (eds.), *L'Espace sacrificiel dans les civilisations méditerranéennes de l'antiquité* (Paris, 1991), 67–73.

'Aθηναίηι Πατρ-
οιηι : ἔρδεται τώ-
τερων ἔτως τέλ-
η : καὶ γυναῖκες : λα-
[γ]χάνωσιν.[2]

To Athena Patroia sacrificial rites are performed every other year and women obtain a cut.

The problem is straightforward: in one of these sacred laws women are prohibited from taking part in the sacrificial cult. In the other women are expressly included in the sacrificial cult as partakers in the sacrificial victim. Are we to take prohibition as normal and the practice at the Thesmophorion as abnormal? Or are we to take inclusion of women as normal and their exclusion from the cult of Herakles as peculiar?

Both these approaches have been taken explicitly by scholars. Farnell writes: 'The general exclusion of women is to be noted in the worship of Herakles; a sufficient proof of it is the proverb preserved by the Paroemiographi, "a woman does not frequent the shrine of Herakles". This was explained in reference to his painful reminiscence of Omphale; but the cause lay deeper than in any fanciful myth; it lay rather in the old religious feeling that the presence of women impairs the warrior's energy, and that it would therefore be detrimental in a hero's shrine which served to consecrate heroic valour; for this reason, as we have noted, they were excluded from the shrine of Agamemnon; and for this reason, as we may believe rather than for any myth, was Herakles called Μισόγυνος, "woman-hater", in Phokis, and his priest was pledged to severe chastity during the tenure of his office.'[3] Sokolowski, pursuing a similar line of trying to explain the exclusion of women from certain cults, suggested that they were excluded from those cults where the ritual dining involved men reclining on sofas.[4]

[2] First published by C. Rolley, BCH 89 (1965), 441–83 n. 6 at p. 447 with trans. on pp. 462–3. For the commonly agreed translation and interpretation see J. Casabona, Recherches sur le vocabulaire des sacrifices en grec (Aix-en-Provence, 1966), 349–50.

[3] L. R. Farnell, Greek Hero Cults and Ideas of Immortality (Oxford, 1921), 162–3. The exclusion of women from sacrifices to Agamemnon relates to Taras: [Aristotle] Mir. ausc. 106. 840ᵃ8–10: 'At Taras ... they hold a separate sacrifice for the Agamemnonidai on their own on another day at which it is not lawful for women even to taste what is sacrificed to them.'

[4] F. Sokolowski, 'Herakles Thasios', HTR 49 (1956), 153–8 at 157.

It is this view that is implicit in most works on Greek religion written before 1979. Scholars show no awareness that there is any problem at all about women and sacrifice, and strongly imply that they think women and men partook equally in sacrifice, even if they played different particular roles in the actual sacrificial ritual. The most egalitarian view of all is perhaps that expressed by Martha, who finds it necessary to employ *a priori* arguments in order to establish that the priestess of Athena Polias did not slaughter with her own hand all the victims consumed at the Panathenaia.[5] But this assumption that there is no problem to be explained is also to be found in such twentieth-century experts as Martin Nilsson and Walter Burkert. Nilsson writes: 'Greek society was an extremely male society, especially in Athens and the Ionian cities. Women were confined to their houses and seldom went outdoors. But religion did not exclude them. There were priestesses in many cults, and women regularly took part in the festivals and sacrifices. Some festivals were reserved for them. Virgins carried the sacred implements and provisions at the sacrifices. These *kanēphoroi*, as they were called, appeared in all processions. Women even had to be allowed to take part in certain nocturnal festivals.'[6] Burkert, in his description of sacrifice in *Greek Religion*, states that 'The sacrifice is a festive occasion for the community' and only specifies the gender of the participants in the case of the *kanēphoros* (a blameless maiden at the front of the procession carries on her head the sacrificial basket), the sacrificer[7] (he cuts some hairs from its forehead) and the sacrificial cry ('As the fatal blow falls, the women must cry out in high, shrill tones'). Elsewhere in his description he talks of 'Everyone hopes as a rule that the animal will go to sacrifice complaisantly, or rather voluntarily'; 'Once the procession has arrived at the sacred spot, a circle is marked out which includes the site of sacrifice, the animal, and the participants'; 'All stand round the altar. As a first communal action water is poured from the jug over the hands of each participant in turn'; 'The participants each take a handful of barley

---

[5] J. Martha, *Les Sacerdoces athéniens* (Paris, 1882), 81.

[6] M. Nilsson, *Greek Popular Religion* (New York, 1940), 96.

[7] Sacrificer may be used in several senses, in the sense of 'slaughterer', in the sense of the person officiating, and in the sense of 'one who causes an animal to be sacrificed', but it is the slaughterer who is in question here. Detienne distinguishes between the sacrifier (French 'sacrifiant'), who offers, and the sacrificer (French 'sacrificateur'), who carries out the sacrifice, including the cutting up of the meat: Detienne and Vernant, *Cuisine*, 11.

groats'; 'To taste the entrails immediately is the privilege and duty of the innermost circle of participants.' Many crucial actions are related in the passive, as if the identity of the agent were of no importance: 'The animal too is sprinkled with water'; 'A bull is given water to drink'; 'The sacrificial knife in the basket is now uncovered'; 'Smaller animals are raised above the altar and the throat is cut. An ox is felled by a blow with an axe and then the artery in the neck is opened. The blood is collected in a basin and sprayed over the altar and against the sides'; 'The animal is skinned and butchered; the inner organs, especially the heart and the liver (*splanchna*), are roasted on the fire on the altar.'[8] Burkert here takes it for granted that men and women play distinct roles in the sacrificial ritual: only women are *kanēphoroi*, only women raise the *ololugē*, only men are sacrificers cutting the hair and, we may add, wielding the axe. But he equally takes it for granted that all alike share in other ritual actions and partake of the meat in the sacrificial feast. When he discusses 'The creation of solidarity in the playing and interplay of roles' he explicitly notes that the exclusion of women from participation in sacrifice is exceptional and that all participants are involved in the sacrifice in one way or another.[9]

It should be clear that this taking for granted will not do: even if the view is basically right we still need to ask why, when gender did play so large a part in determining roles in politics, war, and so on, gender normally played so little role in this area. But in any case the old consensus has been challenged by Detienne who has championed the view that women were normally excluded, not just from the central sacrificial act of slaughtering the animal, but also from sharing in the meat. Detienne considers that what needs explaining are the cases in which women are explicitly included. He writes: 'Just as women are without the political rights reserved for male citizens, they are kept apart from the altars, meat, and blood . . . When women have access to meat, the rules of the cult are careful to specify the precise terms and conditions. For these things are not self-evident.' When he goes on to discuss the Thasos law he seeks to minimise its scope: 'this clause seems only to refer to wives (*gunaikes*) and, undoubtedly, first of all the wives of the citizens who

---

[8] Burkert, *GR*, 56–7.   [9] Burkert, *GR*, 254.

are members of those "countries" that take the place of tribes and phratries.'[10]

It is important to stress how radically Detienne's view of Greek religion differs from that presupposed by Farnell and Sokolowski (and indeed most others). For while Farnell and Sokolowski think that total exclusion of women from cult activity is a peculiar feature of just a few cults, Detienne supposes that women were regularly excluded from taking part in sacrificial ritual or partaking in sacrificial meat. And Detienne's view is the more radical because he also believes that the only meat available for human consumption was meat from sacrifice:[11] if women did not share

---

[10] M. Detienne, 'The Violence of Wellborn Ladies: Women in the Thesmophoria', in Detienne and Vernant, Cuisine, 129–47 at 131. Detienne's article collects and discusses almost all the material which I discuss here, and is far and away the most thorough and most interesting treatment of the subject to have appeared in print.

[11] M. Detienne, 'Culinary Practices and the Spirit of Sacrifice', in Detienne and Vernant, Cuisine, 3, who talks of 'the absolute coincidence of meat-eating and sacrificial practice. All consumable meat comes from ritually slaughtered animals.' Although this view is widely shared it crucially blurs the distinction between two different sorts of ritual killing and neglects the evidence for the availability of meat not slaughtered in any ritual way. G. Berthiaume, Les Rôles du mageiros, Mnemosyne Supplement 70 (Leiden, 1982), 62–70 has shown that, although butcher's meat and sacrificial meat do not form two separate categories, and sacrificial meat was sold in butchers' shops, it was possible to kill animals other than at an altar, even if the slaughter was still ritualised and compassed about with certain offerings to the gods. He acknowledges that in the anecdote told in [Aristotle] Oikonomika 1349ᵇ12–13 'slaughter' (σφάττειν) is used without any religious overtones. Berthiaume also acknowledges (pp. 79–93) that there was meat which came from animals which could be sacrificed but which had not been killed in any ritual way, although he suggests that (p. 89) 'il faut dire que cette consommation de bêtes "non sacrificables", ainsi que celle d'animaux "non sacrificiés" dont nous parlent Athénée [179b–d] et Sémonide [7. 56], pour réelles qu'elles furent, n'en restèrent pas moins essentiellement marginales, et que la manducation de la viande provenant du réseau normal du sacrifice et de l'abattage rituel dans les boutiques des bouchers resta privilégié.' That it was less respectable does not, of course, mean that it was at all times and in all circumstances rare. In addition to the evidence discussed by Berthiaume, I draw attention to the questions arising when sacred laws call for purchase of several animals but only order one to be sacrificed: as with SIG³ 1024. 9–10 (quoted below in n. 21) with Dittenberger's note.

Detienne's view that the killing by butchers in their shops was also 'sacrifice', in the full sense, combines with his view that women were excluded from sacrificial meat to require us to believe that women did not eat meat bought in butchers' shops.

This question also affects the interpretation of visual evidence. A black-figure vase in Boston shows a crowned figure cutting up a joint of meat. This has traditionally been taken as a scene of butchery (cf. J. Boardman, Athenian Black Figure Vases. A Handbook (London, 1974), fig. 287), and Sparkes used the scene to illustrate the chopping block (ἐπίξηνον) and the butcher's knife (κοπίς), remarking of the presence of a tree that this perhaps indicates an 'open-air barbecue' (B. A. Sparkes, 'Illustrating Aristophanes', JHS 95 (1975), 122–35 at 132 and pl. 16b). Durand, however, takes the

in sacrificial meat then they were effectively compelled to be vegetarians.[12]

It is Detienne's view that is coming to be orthodox. Thus Louise Bruit Zaidman begins the second paragraph of 'Pandora's Daughters and Rituals in Grecian Cities' in the first volume of *A History of Women* with the statement: 'Women were excluded from blood sacrifice and the subsequent division of the meat of the sacrificial animal. But blood sacrifice was central to Greek religion; because it made visible the accord between gods and men and renewed the bonds of human community, it was the foundation on which political life was based. The fact that women participated in this ritual only through their husbands was perfectly compatible with their exclusion from active civic and political life.'[13]

In expressing herself in this way, Bruit Zaidman picks up one of the lines, and the most prominent line, laid by Detienne: that there is

---

'chopping block' to be an altar and the scene to be that of cutting up sacrificial meat (so first 'Figurativo e processo rituale', *DdA* NS I (1979), 16–31 at 17–19 with plate on p. 118, a later version of which appears as 'Ritual as Instrumentality' in Detienne and Vernant, *Cuisine*, 119–28 at 122–3, and see further now J. L. Durand, 'Images pour un autel' in Étienne and Le Dinahet, *L'Espace sacrificiel*, 45–55). I find it impossible to see any distinguishing features of an altar about the block on which the meat is being cut, which is unlike any other altar on a vase. On other vases the cutting up of joints after sacrifice seems to be shown being done on the *trapeza*, not on the altar. Durand claims that in this image the meat is not being jointed but merely having the thigh-bone removed to be burnt to the gods, but that seems to me to be far from clear. The table behind the block in this image is itself unlike the *trapeza* shown on other vases. I therefore suspect that this is indeed a butchery scene and that the crown indicates the minimal ritual which attended butchery.

[12] One might compare the early Roman prohibition on women grinding or preparing meat, J. Scheid, 'The Religious Roles of Roman Women', in P. Schmitt Pantel (ed.), *A History of Women, i: From Ancient Goddesses to Christian Saints* (Harvard, 1992), 377–408, at 379. Scheid takes the view that Roman women 'were forbidden to participate in sacrificial rituals' (379), but Valérie Huet has persuaded me that the Roman evidence is actually no more convincing than the Greek for a blanket exclusion.

[13] L. Bruit Zaidman, 'Pandora's Daughters and Rituals in Grecian Cities' in Schmitt Pantel, *History of Women*, i. 338–76 at 338–9. Bruit Zaidman begins the third paragraph: 'This picture is much too simple,' but then immediately goes on: 'It is correct to say that women were generally excluded from blood sacrifice and the handling of meat'; she then again says at the beginning of the fourth paragraph: 'Furthermore, while women were generally excluded from blood sacrifice . . . ' The reader is thus told not once but three times in the space of less than one side that women were excluded from blood sacrifice, though never told exactly what that means. Compare also N. Loraux, *Annales ESC* 36 (1981), 614–22 at 617: 'les femmes n'ont généralement accès à la viande qu'indirectement par le mari.'

an homology between women's place in religion and their place in
the political order.[14] On this line of argument it is to be expected that
if the role of women in sacrifice varies from place to place or cult to
cult there will be associated differences in the political order in that
place or the political unit behind the particular cult, so that the cult
inclusions and exclusions and the political inclusions and exclusions
remain compatible.

Another line of argument emerges most clearly at the end of
Detienne's paper: that there is also an homology between woman
and the sacrificial beast. Detienne draws attention to the way in
which Aristotle in the *Historia Animalium* ($581^{a}31-^{b}2$) compares the
menstrual blood of the newly adolescent girl to 'that of an animal
that has just been stabbed (*neosphakton)'.[15] The reason why women
do not shed blood, it seems to be suggested, is that they themselves
bleed. In myth they shed blood only in response to male transgressions of gender divisions, on occasions when men, by joining the rites
of the Thesmophoria or even by simply refusing 'the male privilege to
shed blood', have somehow ceased to be proper men:[16] hence the
murder of Orpheus, the 'pure man who shuns blood sacrifices and
everything that evokes death and bloodshed'. If we put Detienne's
observations about women bleeding with Helen King's collection of
medical and mythical material on the same subject, with Nicole
Loraux's suggestion, in *Tragic Ways of Killing a Woman*, that women
in tragedy kill themselves by methods that do not involve bloodshed,
and with the fact that the vast majority of those mythical victims
offered in sacrifice (using the term technically) to save a community
are not just women but virgin daughters who have not yet begun
to bleed in their own right,[17] we have a case for thinking that the

---

[14] Detienne, 'Wellborn Ladies', 131: 'As a general rule, by virtue of the homology
between political power and sacrificial practice, the place reserved for women perfectly
corresponds to the one they occupy—or rather, do not occupy—in the space of the
city', and 132: 'At a sacrifice, particularly a blood sacrifice, women cannot function as
full adults. It is precluded by the reciprocity established in the city between a meat-
eating diet and political practice.'

[15] Detienne, 'Wellborn Ladies', 147. For other comparisons between menstrual and
lochial flows and blood shed at sacrifice see H. King, 'Bound to Bleed: Artemis and
Greek Women', in A. Cameron and A. Kuhrt (eds.), *Images of Women in Antiquity*
(London, 1983), 121–2, and compare also R. Girard, *Violence and the Sacred* (Baltimore,
1977), 33–8. On the cultural value of menstruation in Classical Greece see now
L. Dean-Jones, *Women's Bodies in Classical Greek Science* (Oxford, 1994), esp. 225–50.

[16] Detienne, 'Wellborn Ladies', 143.

[17] As well as Iphigeneia, consider Makaria, daughter of Herakles, or the daughter of

shedding of blood was central to Greek conceptions of what it was to be a woman. According to this line of argument, therefore, we would expect women to be systematically excluded from the bloody bits of sacrifice (that is everything after the *ololugē*), at least from menarche to menopause. It is difficult to see what might count as an exception to a rule based on so fundamental a feature of female physiology.

There is no necessary conflict between Detienne's two lines of argument. Although he does not spell this out, it is quite possible to link the fact that women need to shed (their own) blood with women's political status (and various indirect links as well as direct ones might be argued for). If we do so, however, we opt for a basically physiological explanation for women's political standing and for their exclusion from sacrificial ritual. For, if bleeding, not having political rights, and not shedding blood are causally linked, then, whether we take sacrificial exclusion to be a product of having no political rights, or having no political rights to be a product of sacrificial exclusion, the bleeding at least must be the cause and not the product of either sacrificial or political deprivation.

There is something very elegant about the neatness of privileging female physiology, but to do so raises rather than answers questions. The crucial historical question becomes not 'Why should women be treated differently from men in terms of politics and sacrifice?' but, 'Why should such significance be given to menstruation?' To put it another way, we need to ask what grounds there are for putting the emphasis solely on the loss of vital blood in sacrifice, rather than also emphasising the recuperation of vitality through the consumption of meat.[18] But, before speculating on that score, it is as well to ask how well either the physiological or the political explanations, or the explanations of Sokolowski and Farnell based on cult practice, of women's exclusion from sacrifice stand up to the evidence.[19]

In the corpus of sacred laws, cases of specific exclusion of

Embaros. See E. Kearns, *The Heroes of Attica*, BICS Supplement 57 (1989), 56–63 and ead., 'Saving the City', in O. Murray and S. R. F. Price (eds.), *The Greek City from Homer to Alexander* (Oxford, 1990), 323–44, esp. 337–8 with n. 24.

[18] Pertinent remarks on the one-sidedness of many traditional discussions of sacrifice can be found in M. Bloch, *Prey into Hunter. The Politics of Religious Experience* (Cambridge, 1992), Ch. 2.

[19] In what follows I will concentrate on epigraphic evidence, although I believe that the literary evidence of e.g. Eur. *Bacch.* 224 or Paus. 2. 35. 5–8 on the cult of Demeter Chthonia at Hermione is not irrelevant.

women are much more numerous than specific inclusions. Thus three sacred laws from Lindos, two of the fourth century BC and one of the second century BC, exclude women from sacrifices to Athena Apotropaia, Zeus Apotropaios, and Zeus Amalos.[20] In the Mykonos sacred calendar women are expressly excluded from the sacrifice to Poseidon Phukios, though they are not specifically excluded from the sacrifice to Poseidon Temenites on the same day which is listed immediately before, and are not specifically excluded from any other sacrifices listed later.[21] At Elateia in the fifth century women were not allowed to sacrifice at the Anakeion, and on Paros women, and those uninitiated, were excluded from the cult of (Zeus) Hypatos.[22] Exclusions of women from the cult of Herakles are known from inscriptions from other places as well as Thasos,[23] but there are also regulations for cults of Herakles which make no mention of women.[24] Women are excluded from Egyptian cults on Delos in the Hellenistic period (along with men wearing wool).[25]

It is important to note that women are treated differently from men in a number of ways even in the case of cults from which they are not expressly excluded. In certain cases what they wear is regulated and ornate garments are prohibited, as in the cult of Demeter Thesmophoros in fifth-century Arkadia[26] or that of Demeter in third-century Patras (where they are also prohibited from wearing

---

[20] *LSS* 88: (*a*) 'To [Athena] Averter of Evil, a sheep; let the chief sacrificing priest sacrifice; consume what has been sacrificed on the spot; it is not proper for women.' (*b*) 'On the thirteenth of Sminthios: to Zeus Averter of Evil, a ram; to Athena Averter of Evil, a sheep. The chief sacrificing priest sacrifices; consume what has been sacrificed on the spot; it is not proper for women.' *LSS* 89: 'On the eleventh of Hyakinthios, a six-month-old boar to Zeus Amalos; the sacrificing priest Aigelios sacrifices; it is not proper for women.' Sokolowski restores such prohibitions in *LSAM* 42. A. 3 and *LSS* 66 and suggests that they are also involved in *LSS* 68.

[21] *SIG*[3] 1024. 8–9 (*LSCG* 96): 'On the same day an uncastrated white lamb to Poseidon Phukios; it is not proper for women.'

[22] *SIG*[3] 979: 'The sacrificer is to stay in the Anakeion; a woman may not enter.' *IG* XII 5. 183: 'Boundary of Hypatos: it is not right for an uninitiated or a woman.' (Paros, quoted by Dittenberger in commentary on *SIG*[3] 979).

[23] *LSAM* 42 (fragmentary). Sokolowski restores such a prohibition also in *LSS* 66 and suggests in his commentary that such a prohibition also belonged in *LSS* 68.

[24] *LSAM* 83 prohibits burial but makes no mention of women.

[25] *LSS* 56, *ID* 2180.

[26] *LSS* 32. 1–2: 'If a woman wears a garment made of the skin of a wild beast, it is to be consecrated to Demeter Thesmophoros.' For the text and translation see L. Dubois, *Recherches sur le dialecte arcadien*, sect. 2: *Corpus dialectal* (Louvain, 1986), 195–202.

make-up or playing the *aulos*).[27] At Lykosoura in the third century entry to the temple of Despoina was forbidden to those wearing jewelry, black, or shoes or having their hair bound, and if anyone did enter the sanctuary wearing anything forbidden the forbidden object was to be dedicated to Despoina.[28] In other places it was the objects that might be dedicated which were closely regulated by prohibitions which seem similarly aimed at finery: at Sparta a sixth-century regulation, thought to relate to a cult of Demeter, appears to limit the types of woven product that they may dedicate to those approved by the '*polianomos*'.[29] In all these cases the regulations are cult specific and they seem to be a feature of Demeter or Demeter-related cults.

Such regulations are, I think, to be distinguished from regulations relating to the uncleanness resulting from various bodily functions or dysfunctions. In fourth-century Cyrene, in late second-century Delos, and in third-century AD Lindos, a man's sexual contact with a woman, or contact with a woman giving birth, carried impurity; a sacrifice had to be made for newly-wed women at Cyrene.[30] Concern for impurity resulting from contact with other people seems in the Delian case entirely centred on women, with menstruation and miscarriage as the other polluting factors mentioned (along with eating fish and pork), but this is not always the case, for contact with dead relatives of either sex is considered a problem at Lindos and Cyrene.[31] Such regulation may be linked to prohibitions of finery, as at Lykosoura where pregnant and suckling women may not be initiated, but it is notable that most of these regulations are not cult specific—the Cyrene regulation begins:

['*A*]πόλλων ἔχρη[σε·
ἐς ἀ]εὶ καθαρμοῖς κα[ὶ ἁγνήιαις κα[ὶ θε
ραπ]ήιαις χρειμένος τὰν Λεβύαν οἰκ[έν].

Apollo pronounced. You should practice the following purificatory practices and solemnities and cult activities and so inhabit Libya for ever.

[27] *LSS* 33. 1–8: 'At the festival of Demeter the women are not to wear more than an obol's weight of gold jewelry, nor a decorated garment, nor a purple garment, nor to wear make-up, nor to play the *aulos*.'
[28] *LSCG* 68 (*IG* V 2. 514). The Peloponnesian dominance of this evidence is remarkable. A later example occurs in the Mysteries regulations from Andania (*LSCG* 65) which imposes a cash limit on the price of clothing and prohibits jewelry.
[29] *LSS* 28. 1–3.
[30] *LSS* 115 (*SEG* 9. 72) for Cyrene; *LSS* 91 for Lindos. Cf. *LSS* 119 (Ptolemais in Egypt) and the examples quoted by Sokolowski in his commentary on *LSCG* 99.
[31] For sacred laws mentioning death as polluting see R. C. T. Parker, *Miasma: Pollution and Purification in Early Greek Religion* (Oxford, 1983), Ch. 2 and esp. p. 37 n. 17.

Here then we have a strong case for sex-specific regulations that are independent of cult or precise political circumstances and where the physiological argument may have some weight.[32] But such sex-specific rules only make it clearer that exclusions from sacrifice are a different type of regulation altogether.

When we turn to specific inclusion of women, there are certainly cases which make it look as if the political emphasis in Detienne's treatment of the inclusion of women in the Thasos sacrifice to Athena Patroie might have some support. Such is the case of the cult of Artemis Pergaia at Halikarnassos.[33] Here the regulations concerning the priestess of the cult also lay down that the priestess and the wives of the prytaneis in the month Herakleion are to have equal shares of the victim. The invocation of the wives of the prytaneis here makes a clear political link. Detienne compares the situation to that at Athens with the wife of the arkhon basileus and fourteen Gerarai playing a prominent role in activities, including sacrifice, at the sanctuary of Dionysos in the Marshes at the Anthesteria. In that case however we know nothing about the distribution of sacrificial meat.

In other cases it is much harder to see what role politics has. Most important here is the sacred calendar from the deme of Erkhia, modern Spata in the Mesogeia, first published in 1963, which is really five parallel calendars listed in separate columns headed by the first five letters of the alphabet. This specifies, in the first column, that the goat sacrificed to Semele on the 16th of Elaphebolion should be

---

[32] Cf. Parker, *Miasma*, 37 n. 18: 'Documents like the Cyrene law regulate what conditions pollute and for how long; there is no question of being pure enough to visit one shrine but not another.' He also remarks (p. 37): 'it is most implausible that rules of this kind should have been confined to one cult: all our evidence suggests that all the Olympian gods were equally concerned to keep the natural pollutions at a distance.'

[33] *SIG*[3] 1015 (*LSAM* 73), lines 4–25: 'The man who purchases the office of priestess of Artemis Pergaia will provide a priestess who is a citizen woman, descended from citizens on both sides, on the mother's side and the father's side, over three generations. This woman who buys the post will be priestess for her lifetime and will sacrifice the public sacrifices and private sacrifices, and will take the thigh and the joint around the thigh from each victim and a fourth part of the innards and the skins from each of the victims sacrificed publicly, and will take the thigh, the joints around the thigh and a fourth part of the innards of privately sacrificed victims. The Treasurers are to give the Prytaneis a full thirty drachmas for the sacrifice to Artemis. The wives of the Prytaneis in office during the month Herakleion are to take what is given by the city and provide the victim. The priestess is to complete the sacrifice on the twelfth of the month Herakleion. The priestess is to have an equal share with the wives of the Prytaneis who are in charge of the public sacrifice. The priestess is to make, at the beginning of every month, a prayer for aid on behalf of the city, receiving a drachma from the city.' Note also *Suda* s.v. Ἡ Περγαία Ἄρτεμις.

handed over to the women and not taken away, the priestess taking
the skin, and, in the fourth column, that the goat sacrificed to
Dionysos on the 16th of Elaphebolion should be handed over to the
women and not taken away, the priestess taking the skin. The only
parallel specification that an animal be handed over to a particular
group in this document is the handing over to the Pythaistai of the
goat sacrificed to Apollo Pythios in Thargelion in the second column,
of the goat sacrificed to Apollo Apotropaios in Gamelion in the third
column, and of the sheep sacrificed to Apollo Lykeios also in Gamelion (but on a different day) in the fifth column, but notably the prohibition on taking the victim away does not apply to the Pythaistai.[34]
Thus who actually eats the meat is not determined in the case of the
Pythaistai, but the sacrifices to Dionysos and Semele must be consumed by the women. In other cases no specific instructions about
the handing over of the sacrificial victim are made. The calendar
includes sacrifices to Apollo Lykeios and Apollo Apotropaios which
are not handed over to the Pythaistai, but there are no other sacrifices to Dionysos or Semele. The provision that the victim be not
taken away is applied frequently, and not only to the victim handed
over to the women. It is as if the women are like a particular cult
group, but have even more exclusive claim to the cult of Dionysos
and Semele than the Pythaistai have to cults of Apollo other than
Apollo Pythios.

A second equally pertinent piece of Athenian evidence is a decree
of some orgeones found in the Athenian Agora and first published in
1942; it dates to the third century.[35] The orgeones are identified as
πρὸς τοῖς Καλλιφάνους and of the hero Ekhelos. After laying down
some financial regulations the decree specifies the duties of the hesti-
ator to carry out the sacrifice on the seventeenth and eighteenth of
Hekatombaion, sacrificing a pig to the heroines and a full-grown
victim and a table to the hero on the first day and a perfect victim to

---

[34] SEG 21. 541. 144–51 and 433–40, for women; 245–51, 331–7, 531–8 for the
Pythaistai.

[35] LSS 20. 17–23 (Hesperia, 11 (1942), 282–7 n. 55): 'and distribute the meat to the
orgeones who are present and to the [sons] at a half share and to the freeborn wives of
the orgeones the equal share and to the daughters at a half share, and to one maid-
servant at a half share. The woman's portion [to be handed over] to the husband.' This
inscription was subject to full discussion by W. S. Ferguson, 'The Attic Orgeones', HTR
37 (1944), 61–140, and A. D. Nock, 'The Cult of Heroes', HTR 37 (1944), 141–74
reprinted in A. D. Nock, Essays on Religion and the Ancient World, (Oxford, 1972),
575–602.

the hero on the second day. He is to distribute the meat to the orgeones present with half shares for their sons, full shares for free womenfolk and half shares for daughters and for a single slave. The wife's share is to be given to the husband (it is not clear whether the wife is thought to be present at or absent from the sacrifice).

When Detienne discusses these two pieces of Athenian evidence he pleads that the handing over of the victim to the women at Erkhia 'can be justified . . . by Dionysianism alone, by the pre-eminence of its feminine values that serve, here as elsewhere, a subversive intent', and makes much of the fact that the portion meant for the wives is entrusted to the man: 'a woman's equality with respect to meat is subject to two conditions that determine the limits of the hidden citizenship of free women who are lawfully wedded wives. They come third in the hierarchy, after the men, fathers and sons; and their husbands play the role of mediator between them and the shared pieces of the victim. Just as women require a representative in court for any legal proceeding . . . they are admitted into the larger circle of commensals only by the intermediary of someone having the right to obtain for them this favoured treatment.'[36] He concludes discussion of these examples and of two literary testimonia from Pausanias[37] with the statement: 'These are all just so many exceptions that prove the male monopoly in matters of blood sacrifice and everything connected with meat-eating.'

Detienne talks of participation within the sacrificial sphere occurring on (at least) three levels—killing the victim, eating the roasted viscera, and sharing in the meat. Not only does singling out these roles obscure other senses of 'sacrifice' (paying for the victim, praying over the victim) where women's participation is well attested,[38] but to talk of these as 'levels' of participation is to imply that there is some gradation, some ideal progress from 'merely' sharing the meat through eating the viscera to actually killing the victim. That indeed is how Detienne organises his discussion, beginning with the cases in which women share the meat, proceeding to women in sacerdotal functions and ending with women slaughterers. The case for women being excluded from the role of slaughterer is a strong one, and by setting that up as the central activity Detienne is able to imply that

---

[36] Detienne, 'Wellborn Ladies', 133 and 132.
[37] Paus. 5. 16. 2–4, 8. 48. 4–5.
[38] See Herond. 4. 13 for a woman praying; [Dem.] 59. 116 for a case where only the priestess is allowed to pray.

women's exclusion from this activity strengthens the case for their normal exclusion from the other 'levels'. Detienne's talk of levels is no doubt appealing from a Christianising perspective, particularly an Orthodox Christian one, where all can partake of the blessed bread (antidōron), only baptised Orthodox can partake of the body and blood of Christ, and only the (male) priest can make the sacrifice, but it is surely entirely inappropriate in the Greek setting.

That the act of slaughtering is not separable or special is indicated by the way in which the verb θύω, which few would hesitate to translate as 'sacrifice', is used. This verb covers the whole ceremony, not simply the slaughter but including the slaughter.[39] The slaughtering implicit in θύω comes out nicely from the words which Euripides puts in the mouth of Orestes (Orestes 562):

τοῦτον κατέκτειν᾽, ἐπὶ δ᾽ ἔθυσα μητέρα

I killed this man, and I also sacrificed my mother.

This is part of a long passage where, as Casabona points out, θύω, κτείνω, and φονεύω are alternatively employed depending on the viewpoint of the speaker.[40] To sacrifice is 'to put to death . . . for a higher cause';[41] but who wields the knife is not of material interest.

So, for all that Porphyry's famous aetiological myth for the Bouphonia implies a certain anxiety about the act of killing a domestic animal, the role of slaughterer seems not to have been a special or a sacred one,[42] and the cutting up of the meat was the work of butchers not of sacred officials.[43] That butchers were predominantly, even invariably, male is no doubt a fact of interest about the society as a whole, as well as reflecting the physical strength which that job required, but it should not be made into a fact of significance about religion, except in as far as the very unusualness of the female butcher made the image of such an individual a particularly horrific

[39] Casabona, Recherches, 77 and compare 86.
[40] Ibid. 78–9.
[41] Ibid. 79.
[42] Cf. LSCG 151. A. 40–4 (Cos, 4th cent.): 'Let the heralds choose among themselves one to slaughter the ox.' Sokolowski restores the reward of a sausage to the slaughterer in IG I³ 244, but this restoration is quite uncertain.
[43] Berthiaume, Mageiros. It is worth noting, however, the association of priestesses and knives suggested by the finds from the sanctuary of Demeter at Gela published in U. Kron, 'Frauenfeste in Demeterheiligtümern: das Thesmophorion von Bitalemi. Ein archäologische Fallstudie', AA (1992), 611–50, esp. 641–3. I am grateful to Jan Bremmer for drawing my attention to these finds.

one to imagine (as in the stories of the women at the Thesmophoria at Cyrene castrating Battos and of women at the sanctuary of Demeter at Aigila attacking the Messenians with knives, discussed by Detienne) and hence a powerful one to think with, in religious as in other discourses.

Eating the viscera was, undoubtedly, a privilege, but it was one attendant upon having some official role in the ritual, and where there was a priestess, as there will have been in a very large number of cases, the priestess will have shared in the roast viscera.[44] The clearest indication that women might share even the most special parts of the sacrifice comes in a recently published inscription from Chios, dating to around 400 BC, which specifies that the priestess of Eileithuia is to consume her perquisites on the spot 'along with the women who made the sacrifice'.[45]

Detienne writes that 'Powers such as Aglaurus, Artemis, Athena or Demeter require priestesses'.[46] This is hardly an exhaustive list— where has Hera gone?—and the wife of the arkhon basileus was effectively priestess of Dionysos. But it is not the length of the list

---

[44] Priestesses certainly might be given part of the innards to take away, and that would seem to be incompatible with their exclusion from tasting the innards on the spot. Exactly what the priest(ess) got in the way of innards seems to have varied from cult to cult and may be specified when the conditions of a priesthood are laid down: see SIG³ 1013. 3, 8 (Chios, 4th cent.), 1015. 11 (Halikarnassos, priestess, quoted above n. 33), 1016. 3 (Iasos, 4th cent.). Cf. explicit shares of meat for the priestess among other perquisites in IG II² 1356. See now B. Guen-Pollet, 'Espace sacrificiel et corps des bêtes immolées. Remarques sur le vocabulaire désignant la part du prêtre dans la Grèce antique de l'époque classique à l'époque impériale' in Étienne and Le Dinahet, L'Espace sacrificiel, 13–23.

[45] SEG 35 (1985), 923 A. [Πρυτάνεων γν]ώμη· ἱ[ε]ρέ[αι Ἐλει | θίη]ς· ἐ[π]ὴν ἡ πόλις ποιῆ, γί[ν]εσθ | [αι] παρὰ τὸ ἀγωγ[ὸ] ἀλφίτων ἥμυσ | γκτέως [σ]ἱ[τ]ὸ ἡμίεκτον· ἦν δὲ ἰδ | ιώτης ποι[ῆ], δίδοσθαι ἀπὸ τὸ ἱξ | ρ[ὸ], ὥστε ἐς [τὸ] λ[ί]κνον ἐνθεῖ[ν]αι | [μ]οῖραν καὶ γέρας καὶ γλῶσσαν | [καὶ τά]δε ἀναλ[ί]σκεσθαι αὐτὸ μ | [ε]τὰ τῶν γυναικῶν τῶν π[ο]ι[η]σασ | έ[ων] τὰ ἱρά· εἶναι [δὲ] ταυτὰ ταῦτ | α, καὶ ὅταν ἱρὸν καθαιρέωσιν κ | αἱ ϙπ[ον]δ[ὴν] πο[ιέωσιν] ('Decision of the Prytaneis: to the priestess of Eileithuia: when the city sacrifices, there is to be half a hekteus of corn for every one-and-a-half hekteis from the grain consignment; but if a private individual sacrifices, part of the victim is to be given, so as to place in the basket a share and perquisite and tongue and to consume these on the spot with the women who made the sacrifice. The same is to happen whenever they purify the temple and make a treaty.') I am grateful to Christiane Sourvinou-Inwood for drawing my attention to this inscription, and to George Forrest and Robert Parker for help in interpreting it. For the sense of ἀναλίσκεσθαι compare LSS 94. 13–14 κρῆ αὐτῆι ἀναλοῦται (Kamiros, 3rd cent. BC). There seems to be no parallel for a priest(ess) being required to consume her perquisites on the spot. That the sacrifices involved here are to Eileithuia might suggest that the physiological argument is not entirely without force.

[46] Detienne, 'Wellborn Ladies', 135.

which is important but the nature of the cults involved. Many of the cults are cults of *polis* deities (Athena at Athens, Sparta, Tegea, etc., Hera at Argos and Samos and so on) and so it is not merely that any cult involved in the political structure of a city may involve its priest(esse)s in quasi-magisterial duties, but that these priesthoods are in at the foundation of the city, part of the way in which the city identifies itself as a city. Capacity to hold a priesthood is not homologous with political capacity even in cases where the priesthood stands for the *polis*. The privilege of eating, and of being seen publicly to eat, the viscera ignores political limitations. Detienne constructs his account in such a way that the wife of the arkhon basileus at Athens and the wives of the prytaneis at Halikarnassos are made to seem typical, and so he can write that 'in the temple of Artemis the women of Pergea exercise authority in sacrificial matters only when the political rights held by the prytaneis' husbands are temporarily delegated to them';[47] but the priestesses of Athena Polias or other poliad deities cannot be seen as mere 'delegates'. It can hardly be right to argue that priestesses drawn from a particular family stand in for (male members of) that family when newly created priesthoods are equally happy to choose a priestess at random from the whole body of women citizens (as with the priesthood of Athena Nike in fifth-century Athens).[48] There is a strong contrast here to the situation at Rome where 'Public sacerdotal responsibilities were always exercised by men' but there are occasions when sacrifices may be made by the wives of priests.[49]

If it is wrong to see slaughterer, priest, and partaker as on different levels, they clearly do not move entirely independent worlds. Given the presence of priestesses in major 'political' cults (both their acceptance in old cults and their invention in new ones), which seems to establish that there is a perceived divide between serving in a magisterial office and serving in a priestly office (a divide also recognised in (e.g.) the failure at Athens to change inherited life priesthoods into annually elected ones), it seems hard to sustain the view, unless supported by strong positive evidence, that women's exclusion

[47] Detienne, 'Wellborn Ladies', 136.
[48] ML 44. That this priesthood was a highly exceptional doctrinaire democratic innovation does not affect the issue discussed here.
[49] J. Scheid, 'The Religious Roles of Roman Women', in Schmitt Pantel, *History of Women*, 378, 384.

from sharing in the sacrificial meat correlated closely with their political incapacity.[50]

If we look back at the evidence, the political case seems very weak. Far from being highly 'political', the cults from which women are expressly excluded seem more often to be marginal to the city (the cults of Athena Apotropaia and Zeus Apotropaios and Zeus Amalos on Lindos, the cult of Poseidon Phukios on Mykonos, of Zeus Hypatos on Paros, cults of Herakles, of the Anakoin, Egyptian cults). But if in these cases, where the situation is explicit, the exclusion of women can hardly be a product of the cult being limited to those possessing political rights, the extension on political grounds of the prohibition to all cases where women are not expressly included can carry little conviction. Just as it is recognised that prohibitions on finery are cult specific, being particularly linked to Demeter cults, so we should recognise also that prohibitions on women are cult specific. The cult of Herakles on Thasos, with which we began, forbids sacrifice of goats and pigs, forbids ninths and forbids perquisites. In all these respects it is odd and marked out from general Greek practice. It should also be seen as marking itself out when it prohibits women.

In my view we have to conclude that women were not as a rule excluded from sacrificial meat.[51] When Sostratos' mother goes round the deme sacrificing, in Menander's *Dyskolos*, she will have satisfied her appetite as well as her piety.[52] In as far as this restates what was

[50] It is also worth noting that the sons and daughters for whom a share of sacrificial meat is also in some cases explicitly provided would also share women's political incapacity.

[51] It must be admitted that women are, with one famous Dionysiac exception discussed by Detienne, notably rarely important actors in those scenes on painted pots which show episodes close to the moment of slaughter, although they are clearly present in processions leading to sacrifice and are often prominent in votive reliefs. But since it is clear that the scenes of sacrifice which appear on pots are not a random sample of snapshots, but are carefully selected, consciously and unconsciously, discussion of this absence belongs more to considerations of visual ideology than to considerations of actual practice. It needs to be noted that, in addition to the famous Dionysiac scene discussed by Detienne, a fragment showing a woman wielding a knife about to sacrifice a goat has recently been published from German excavations in Athens of what was apparently a brothel. The excavator suggested that the sacrifice shown might be to Aphrodite, on the basis of Lucian, *Dialogues of Courtesans*, 7. 1 (U. Knigge, ''O ἀστὴρ τῆς Ἀφροδίτης', *AM* 97 (1982), 153–70 at 153 and 168 n. 17; pl. 32. 1, Inv. no. 5662). I am grateful to James Davidson for drawing my attention to this piece.

[52] Men. *Dys.* 262–4. There is an excellent discussion of the sacrificial meal in the *Dyskolos* in A. K. Dalby, *Siren Feasts: A History of Food and Gastronomy in Greece* (London, 1996), 2–5. A whole series of pots shows women sitting by tables on which

for a long time believed it is not a very interesting conclusion. But it carries important implications because it negates Detienne's two types of correlation and it distinguishes Greek from Roman practice. To affirm women's sacrificial capacity in Greece is both to deny the homology between women's religious and their political (in)capacity, and also to deny the elegant opposition whereby those who shed the (menstrual and lochial) blood of life are kept from all contact with the blood of death (which is also to deny that the Thesmophoria is quite such a rôle reversal as Detienne claims). Unfashionably, perhaps, I conclude that Greek cult practices must both be seen not to be closely linked to day-to-day politics as carried on in the Assembly,[53] and also not treated as simply a product of the rationalising of natural processes. Religious actions obviously had political effects— the sacrificial ritual itself can be a way of legitimating aggression[54]— but this is by no means incompatible with the independence of religion from political arrangements.

Aristotle, at *Politics* 1280[b]36–8, remarks that '*thusiai*', groups which sacrifice together, are a precondition for the city, along with families, phratries, and other works of friendship. Sacrifices manifest the existence of groups which share a cult, and a city without such groups is unthinkable; but such groups are not subordinated to the city. Just as the Pythaistai are a particular cult group at Erkhia, so women might constitute or be included in other cult groups. As a result, there will have been many sacrificial victims in which women had no share, because they had no part in the group which made the sacrifice, but they will not have been excluded from partaking in the sacrificial victim because it was a sacrificial victim. In some sacrifices, where the occasion was more or less explicitly political, the distribution of meat will have followed political lines: such is the case at the Panathenaia where the prytaneis get five shares, the nine arkhons and the *stratēgoi* and taxiarkhs three, the treasurer of the goddess

---

there are slices of meat: see S. Pingiatoglou, 'Rituelle Frauengelage auf schwarzfiguri-gen attischen Vasen', *AM* 109 (1994), 39–51. These will be further discussed in a forthcoming article by Margot Schmidt, who kindly drew them to my attention.

[53] Detienne himself argues that scholars have traditionally underestimated the political importance of sacrifice, 'Culinary Practices and the Spirit of Sacrifice' in Detienne and Vernant, *Cuisine*, 1–20 at 3–5. I do not dissent from the proposition that religious cult activity is central to the 'life of the *polis*' and is 'political' in that sense.

[54] Compare Bloch, *Prey into Hunter*, Ch. 2, esp. 43–5.

and the *hieropoioi* one, and those Athenians processing and the (female) *kanēphoroi* 'their usual', before the rest is divided between the Athenians.[55] At the Hephaistia the meat reached beyond the political group in that metics were explicitly included among recipients, and at Koressia in the third century not only metics but also freedmen who paid taxes at Koressia were included in the distribution.[56] Women in general certainly enjoyed no meat at all in their own right from the Koressia sacrifices and almost certainly enjoyed nothing from those at the Hephaistia and Panathenaia. But this is not because sacrifice as such is constrained to observe the limits of the political group, but because these are civic festivals in the strong sense of that term. Civic festivals and festivals of other political groups whose membership was entirely male are what we know about most, of course, but there was another side to life, and when Athenaios affords us a glimpse of it, in his account of the Tithenidia at Sparta, we find (unfree?) nurses enjoying sucking pig and probably goat too.[57] Different religious cults in different cities practised different exclusions, and the exclusion of women, implicit in the composition of the cult group or occasionally explicit, must be seen in the context of the other exclusions.[58]

In rejecting Detienne's construction of gender roles in sacrifice, it is important not to return to taking women's presence sharing in the meat for granted. If, where Detienne finds a homology between politics and theology, we find contrast, we should not underestimate the importance of that finding. Political life, in the narrow sense, dominates our ancient sources as it has dominated modern scholarship, but it did not so dominate life as lived and experienced. The world where one might as often find a priestess as a priest, and where men and women ate the sacrificial meat together, may well have been as homologous to everyday life as it was different from life in army, Council, or symposion. The understanding of the world which is reflected in the theology of sacrifice may be a domestic understanding of the world rather than a political one. Relations between cities and between heads of households, which formed the stuff of politics, could, by means of legal devices and army recruitment, be kept to males, but relations with the gods extended to all humans, and

---

[55] *IG* II[2] 334. 8–16.
[56] *IG* I[3] 82 (the same is true in the deme of Skambonidai, I[3] 244); *SIG*[3] 958.
[57] Ath. 138f–9b.
[58] See Sourvinou-Inwood, Ch. 2, above, 47–51.

indeed to the whole of nature. Sacrifice of animals and offerings of natural products gave hope of control of the rest of nature, but it was participation in sacrifice, in a capacity other than that of victim, that secured women's place, as it secured man's place, in the cosmic order of things.

The single woman is condemned to a vegetarian life in Detienne's world. Excluded from sacrifices normally because a woman (and too bloody) she does not enjoy anything from the Thesmophoria either because not married (not bloody enough). Detienne thinks she is excluded from sharing the meat sacrificed to Athene Patroie at Thasos and only allows her a half share of the orgeones' sacrifice at Athens if she qualifies as a daughter. Bleeding or not, we need to restate the claims of the single woman (in fact more likely to be widow than spinster) to share the meat from the sacrifices of any group of which she was a part. And as the Erkhia calendar suggests, the social groups which made up normal life included some that were specifically female. Sacrifice reached parts of society which politics did not reach, and in doing so it reached some parts that were the exclusive domain of women.

PART IV
Boundary Disputes

14
Greek Magic, Greek Religion[1]

ROBERT L. FOWLER

What ordinary parlance terms 'magic'—the use of spells, charms, and other artificial means to enlist the support of supernatural powers in the furtherance of one's aims—was a normal and ubiquitous part of everyday life in the ancient world. This is an undeniable and important fact; it is hardly surprising that it once formed the starting-point for the investigation of Greek religion. Classicists lost sight of it for a while; among anthropologists, by contrast, its role in primitive societies has always been in the centre of discussion. Recently, however, interest among classical scholars has been revived; a spate of publications has forcefully brought to our attention the sheer magnitude of the phenomenon in ancient life.[2] Once

[1] The basis of this chapter is a public lecture delivered on 18 Feb. 1994 at the University of Illinois at Urbana-Champaign, and on 24 March 1994 at McMaster University. I am grateful to audiences on those occasions for their interest and helpful comments, as well as to C. G. Brown, R. Drew Griffith, B. MacLachlan, and W. J. Slater. Particular thanks to Jan Bremmer, Robert Parker, and Christiane Sourvinou-Inwood, who by no means share all the views expressed here and offered vigorous and salutary criticism. The chapter is intended as an orientation and general survey (if a tendentious one) for the non-specialist, though I hope specialists will find points of interest here too; as such it might be considered alongside Jan Bremmer's excellent *Greek Religion*, Greece & Rome New Surveys in the Classics 24 (Oxford, 1994), in which magic receives only brief mention on p. 93. In a discussion as broad as this, a synchronic perspective is unavoidable; I hope the effacing of some of the finer diachronic distinctions will not invalidate the conclusions.

[2] G. Luck, *Arcana Mundi* (Baltimore, 1985), German trans. with revisions, *Magie und andere Geheimlehren in der Antike* (Stuttgart, 1990); D. R. Jordan, 'A Survey of Greek Defixiones Not Included in the Special Corpora', *GRBS* 26 (1985), 151–97; id., 'Inscribed Lead Tablets from the Games in the Sanctuary of Poseidon', *Hesperia*, 63 (1994), 111–26, esp. 116 ff., with bibliography at 116 n. 8; H. D. Betz, *The Greek Magical Papyri in Translation* (Chicago, 1986; 2nd edn. 1992); C. A. Faraone and D. Obbink (eds.), *Magika Hiera: Ancient Greek Magic and Religion* (New York and Oxford, 1991) (= *Magika*); H. S. Versnel, 'Some Reflections on the Relationship Magic–Religion', *Numen*, 38 (1991), 177–97; H. Parry, *Thelxis: Magic and Imagination in Greek Myth and Poetry* (Lanham, Md., and London, 1992); J. G. Gager, *Curse Tablets and Binding Spells from the Ancient World* (New York and Oxford, 1992); C. A. Faraone, *Talismans and*

more the question arises of what relation this material, and the attitudes and beliefs it entails, had with the mainstream of Greek religion.

Although the definition of magic is notoriously difficult,[3] for heuristic purposes its often-noted tendency to be oriented towards the achievement of specific goals (enhancing fertility, securing the attention of one's beloved, etc.) may serve to focus discussion. In what follows I will suggest that this tendency is also found in some important Greek rituals that are not normally thought of as magical, and that, consequently, the distinction between 'magic' and 'religion' does not lie so much in the substance of the ritual acts as in their social context. The second half of the paper will explore the implications of this realization for further study, in the light of the history of the question up to the present day.

It will be useful first to establish the premise, that magical activity was extremely prominent in ancient life. The magical papyri afford a convenient starting-point. Recently Hans Dieter Betz has made available a comprehensive translation, a book of over 300 pages with spells for every conceivable ailment and crisis.[4] Spells and curses from papyri and leaden tablets have also been published by John Gager, selecting from a corpus of over 1,500 items.[5] The spread of dates and findspots of this material shows that, extensive though it is, it represents but a fraction of the ancient reality.

The commonest type of magical spell is known as a 'defixio', or

Trojan Horses: Guardian Statues in Ancient Myth and Ritual (Oxford, 1992); M. García Teijeiro, 'Religion and Magic', *Kernos*, 6 (1993), 123–38; F. Graf, *La Magie dans l'antiquité gréco-romaine* (Paris, 1994); and others. Among earlier contributions, note J. de Romilly, *Magic and Rhetoric in Ancient Greece* (Cambridge, Mass., and London, 1975), 11 ff., and E. R. Dodds, *The Greeks and the Irrational* (Berkeley and Los Angeles, 1951).

[3] Though it might seem a logical priority to define the term 'magic' before discussing its relation to religion, the problem of definition is so intractable that treatment must either become a paper in itself or simply be suspended in favour of a plunge *in medias res*. For a brief survey, see the Excursus below (339–41).

[4] See above (note 2).

[5] Gager, *Curse Tablets*. See also the additional material in R. W. Daniel and F. Maltomini, *Supplementum Magicum* i–ii, Papyrologica Coloniensia 16. 1–2 (Opladen, 1990–2); R. Merkelbach and M. Totti, *Abrasax: Ausgewählte Papyri religiösen und magischen Inhalts* i–iv, Papyrologica Coloniensia 17. 1–4 (Opladen, 1990–6); W. Brashear, *Magica Varia* (Brussels, 1991); R. Kotansky, *Greek Magical Amulets: The Inscribed Gold, Silver, Copper, and Bronze Lamellae. Part I. Published Texts of Known Provenance*, Papyrologica Coloniensia 22. 1 (Opladen, 1994). Two earlier publications worthy of note are C. Bonner, *Studies in Magical Amulets, Chiefly Graeco-Egyptian* (Ann Arbor, 1950) and A. Delatte and P. Derchain, *Les Intailles magiques gréco-égyptiennes* (Paris, 1964).

'binding spell', by which the practitioner seeks to 'bind' or incapacitate an enemy. Such spells were normally written on a metal tablet and buried in a secret place. They were employed for all manner of purposes: to bankrupt a business rival, incapacitate a rival lover,[6] blight someone's crops, cripple an athlete, or silence an orator in a crucial court case. Of this last (very useful) kind of spell, 67 Greek examples and some 46 Latin examples are attested in the archaeological finds, and in literature instances are known from Aischylos and Aristophanes in the fifth century BC, Cicero in the first, and Libanios in the fourth century AD.[7] Demosthenes himself is cursed on one surviving defixio; other famous politicians were not exempt.

To dwell for a moment on the defixiones, a common feature, apart from the keywords 'I bind' (or some other reference to binding or restraining), is their negativity: an individual seeks to harm another or make them do something against their will. The practitioner takes no account of rights or wrongs, and proceeds in secret, perhaps precisely in the awareness that what he or she does is reprehensible.[8] Secrecy is also necessary to obviate the possibility of counter-charms. Other kinds of spells, curses, and imprecations have been found, like the defixiones, on tablets buried in out-of-the-way places, but, lacking the key reference to 'binding', they should not be classified technically as defixiones; however, they share many other features with the defixiones. Some are just as negative in conception, but others appeal to justice, inflicting their curses in the belief that the punishment is deserved.[9] We find imprecations against people who break laws, defile a sanctuary, commit perjury, or pollute a grave, amongst other things. Moreover, the sense of justice allows these curses to emerge into the light of day, so that they may be found carved on gravestones (like Shakespeare's 'curst be he that moves my bones'), set up in public squares, or enshrined into law.[10]

---

[6] For a study of these, see J. J. Winkler, 'The Constraints of Eros', in *Magika*, 214–43; longer version in *The Constraints of Desire* (New York and London, 1990), Ch. 3.

[7] C. A. Faraone, 'Aeschylus' ὕμνος δέσμιος (*Eum.* 306) and Attic Judicial Curse Tablets', *JHS* 105 (1985), 150–4; id., 'An Accusation of Magic in Classical Athens (Ar. *Wasps* 946–48)', *TAPA* 119 (1989), 149–61; id., 'The Agonistic Context of Early Greek Binding Spells', in *Magika*, 3–32, at 15 f.; Cic. *Brut.* 217, *Orat.* 128–9; Liban. *Or.* I. 245–9.

[8] See H. S. Versnel, 'Beyond Cursing: The Appeal to Justice in Judicial Prayers', in *Magika*, 62 f.

[9] Ibid. 60–106.

[10] Curses of this kind are studied by J. H. M. Strubbe in Ch. 2 of *Magika*. See e.g. the Teian curses (*c.* 470 BC), in ML, no. 30 (Strubbe 37 f.). For the similar activity of public

The language of these curses, and indeed of the less savoury defixiones, is often closely similar to the traditional language of good and
pious prayer; for instance, they may remind the god of some service
rendered in the past, with a strong suggestion that he is thereby
obliged to help in the present crisis as well. The procedure is exactly
the same as Chryses' in Book I of the *Iliad*, where the priest reminds
Apollo of his piety on many occasions, so that the god may feel the
readier to punish the Achaeans for their blasphemy.[11] The point will
be important later in our discussion.

Tablets inscribed with magic formulae to guarantee a favourable
reception in the next world were sometimes placed in graves with the
corpse. The celebrated Orphic tablets are merely a special instance of
this practice. From the salvation of the dead we move to the healing
of the quick. Ancient doctors were remarkably learned in the lore of
herbal medicine, and often knew very good recipes for headaches and
other things that ail you; some modern discoveries have proceeded
from such wisdom, for instance the heart drug digitalis, which originated in the purple foxglove. But ancient doctors were careful to
mix in a healthy dose of incantation, like the two sons of Autolykos
in the nineteenth book of the *Odyssey* (19. 457), who healed Odysseus' wound from the boar. Sokrates in Plato's *Charmides* (155e)
reports a headache remedy in the form of the leaf of a certain plant,
which he assures us is useless without the accompanying magic
words.[12] To prevent sickness on a daily basis, or to encourage good
health and luck generally, the use of amulets and charms was
universal.[13]

These instances may suffice to show that magical practices were
very common occurrences in ancient life. I have not even touched
on things like voodoo dolls, love potions, astrology, witchcraft,

---

oath-swearing, and magical activities connected with it, see C. Faraone, 'Molten Wax,
Spilt Wine and Mutilated Animals: Sympathetic Magic in Near Eastern and Early
Greek Oath Ceremonies', *JHS* 103 (1993), 60–80.

[11] Faraone, *Magika*, 6, 17 ff.; Versnel, *Magika*, 92; cf. also F. Graf, 'Prayer in Magic and
Religious Ritual', *Magika*, 188–213.

[12] See R. Kotansky, 'Incantations and Prayers for Salvation on Inscribed Greek
Amulets', in *Magika*, 107–37, at 108 f. The combination of medicines and incantations
is of course well known to anthropologists; see, for instance, E. E. Evans-Pritchard's
classic *Witchcraft, Oracles, and Magic among the Azande* (Oxford, 1937), Part IV.

[13] Further material in G. Lanata, *Medicina magica e religione popolare in Grecia fino
all'età di Ippocrate* (Rome, 1967).

necromancy, instructional books, purifications,[14] and so on. The ever-present fear of these dark forces is sufficiently attested by the ancient foundation of Roman law, the Twelve Tables, which specifically outlawed the use of charms to harm the crops. The admonition is repeated in the codes of Theodosius and Justinian in the fifth and sixth centuries AD. From one end of antiquity to the other, then, and in every walk of life, magic was ubiquitous. Almost everybody used it, in every conceivable situation, and constantly, in such a way as would oppress and suffocate us could we go back in time and live in that environment.

In the past, scholars have denigrated magical activities as the domain of the superstitious, and therefore not worth the attention of serious students of religion.[15] They are the sort of thing you expect to find on strange papyri, or used by the lower classes. It is true that philosophers developed rarefied notions of religion, but they were not at all typical. The universal and commonplace acceptance of magic, among all classes, is easily proved from the evidence. In such a world it is on general grounds not likely that magic was compartmentalized, and its mentality abandoned when the people partook in rituals more readily recognized as 'religious' by the modern scholar. The phenomenon of magic, in fact, cannot be separated from any serious understanding of ancient religion. That it tends to be separated in the minds of students is the result of the historical development of the discipline rather than of any inherent necessity. The second half

---

[14] Rituals for purification of bloodguilt are dramatically illustrated in a new inscription from Selinous: M. H. Jameson, D. R. Jordan, and R. D. Kotansky (eds.), *A Lex Sacra from Selinous*, GRBS Monographs 11 (Durham, NC, 1993; reference from Robert Parker). The date is 460–50 BC. The editors discuss the widespread evidence for such regulations and rituals, and conclude their discussion of the term ἀλάστορες by saying (120): 'Archaic and Classical Greece, one is led to think, was a more violent and spirit-infested world than is usually supposed.'

[15] Cf. Gager, *Curse Tablets*, 3. Wilamowitz spoke of the 'wüste[r] Aberglaube der Zauberpapyri' replacing the 'alte Religion' at *Der Glaube der Hellenen*, 2nd edn. i (Berlin, 1955), 10. Cf. G. Murray, 'Memories of Wilamowitz', *AuA* 4 (1954), 9–14, at 12: 'On Greek religion also he confessed himself "altmodisch"; he did not approve of Jane Harrison's *Themis*, which I had sent him. He has a respect for Jane Harrison but is not disposed to "explain the perfect structure by the embryo nor Plato by the probable superstitions of his grandmother".' Murray here paraphrases letter no. 55 (17 Sept. 1912) in A. Bierl, W. M. Calder III, and R. L. Fowler, *The Prussian and the Poet: The Letters of Ulrich von Wilamowitz-Moellendorff to Gilbert Murray (1894–1930)* (Hildesheim, 1991), 111. See also A. Henrichs, '"Der Glaube der Hellenen": Religionsgeschichte als Glaubensbekenntnis und Kulturkritik', in W. M. Calder III, H. Flashar, and T. Lindken (eds.), *Wilamowitz nach 50 Jahren* (Darmstadt, 1985), 263–305, at 279.

of the paper will trace this development and support this assessment. First, however, let us see whether the general expectation is confirmed in practice—whether magic is merely a self-contained phenomenon, or whether its practices and attitudes are apparent across a broader spectrum of sacred doings. We shall find that public ritual and private magic, though not identical, often overlapped in both style and substance, and that the difference between them should accordingly be interpreted as one of context and social attitudes rather than as a difference in kind.[16]

Some of the examples of magic cited above can certainly be recognized as fringe activity even in the ancient world, and at first blush the contention that magic is not important to an understanding of real religion appears justified. On closer examination this view cannot be maintained. The form of curses, as has already been pointed out, is often indistinguishable from ordinary forms of prayer. In the whole gamut from the most vicious defixiones to the most sanctimonious public denunciations, there is much fluidity of boundaries and much similarity of language and technique. Any attempt to distinguish magic from religion in curses and prayers founders at once.

The writings of the doctors afford pertinent material for thought. The most famous of the Hippocratic writings from the fifth century BC, *On the Sacred Disease*, is justly celebrated for its rationalistic rejection of spells and other magical procedures. It heaps scorn upon charlatans who claim to be able to cause eclipses of the sun or make it rain. Surely, one might say, this is proof that magic was beginning to be regarded merely as the activity of unenlightened, superstitious peasants. Yet this same doctor is quite willing to believe that sleeping in the sanctuary of Asklepios can cure you, and the writers of these treatises elsewhere display a willingness to call upon divination, dreams, and other quite irrational resources to work their wonders. Moreover, in the place of what they reject, they offer the wildest speculations about the human body, which there was not the slightest reason to believe. Rationality in science is sometimes a chimera, and the border between magic and science is easily crossed; it depends on attitude, information available, and

---

[16] It will be clear that the phenomena are being viewed at this stage from the outside; to an insider, differences in context and social attitudes might count as a difference in kind. See the Excursus below.

context.[17] Isaac Newton still devoted much study to alchemy,[18] and science in his day had far to go before its results could always be confidently differentiated from the mysterious and the magical.[19] As for our ancient doctor's contempt of rain-magic, one presumes he refers to individual, unapproved magicians rather than the rain-making rituals carried out on behalf of whole cities in many parts of Greece.[20] The doctor would also be condemning the great Mysteries of Demeter at Eleusis, which included at their centre agrarian magic, as the participants looked to the sky and shouted ὖε, 'rain,' and then poured water into the earth crying κύε, 'conceive.' If the author of On the Sacred Disease meant to include these publicly sanctioned examples of magic in his contempt, he would have been in a distinct minority of determined and anti-social skeptics such as Diogenes the Cynic. But his book does not strike such a pose; indeed, it implicitly allows for the possibility of divine miracles. Moreover, his attitude towards individual, free-lance practitioners can easily be paralleled, whereas the condemnation of the same activities in the public arena cannot. Almost everyone in ancient Greece believed in the efficacy of oracles, provided that one consulted them in the approved manner. But let an unlicensed oracle-monger appear, and watch him be pilloried by the comic poets for a fraud. The Pythia of Delphi is allowed to hear the voice of god; but let a Sokrates claim to hear it, and see what happens to him. Yet these private activities differ not at all in substance from the public ones. Context and social approval make all the difference.

---

[17] G. E. R. Lloyd, Magic, Reason and Experience: Studies in the Origin and Development of Greek Science (Cambridge, 1979), Ch. 1; id., The Revolutions of Wisdom: Studies in the Claims and Practice of Ancient Greek Science (Berkeley, 1987), 11 ff.; id., Demystifying Mentalities (Cambridge, 1990), Ch. 2.

[18] H. D. Betz, 'Magic and Mystery in the Greek Magical Papyri', in Magika, 244–59, at 247.

[19] See K. Thomas, Religion and the Decline of Magic: Studies in Popular Beliefs in Sixteenth and Seventeenth Century England (London, 1971); J. Neusner, E. S. Frerichs, and P. V. M. Flesher (eds.), Religion, Science, and Magic in Concert and in Conflict (New York and Oxford, 1989); S. J. Tambiah, Magic, Science, Religion, and the Scope of Rationality (Cambridge, 1990).

[20] For rain-magic in Greece, see Frazer, GB, 309 f.; J. E. Harrison, Themis, 2nd edn. (Cambridge, 1927), 76 ff.; W. Fiedler, Antiker Wetterzauber (Stuttgart, 1931); L. Radermacher, Mythos und Sage bei den Griechen, 2nd edn. (Baden, 1938), 321 f.; A. B. Cook, Zeus, iii (Cambridge, 1940), 296 ff.; Nilsson, GGR, 110 ff., 116 f., 396 ff. (with further references); R. L. Fowler, 'The Myth of Kephalos as an Aition of Rain-Magic', ZPE 97 (1993), 29–42.

The magical or goal-oriented aspect of some rituals is indeed readily acknowledged by scholars, if not always put front and centre in discussion. The rain-making of the Eleusinian Mysteries was mentioned above; this was not the only agrarian connection of the ritual. Another readily granted example is the Thesmophoria for Demeter, the most widespread religious rites in Greece; these involved throwing a dead pig into the earth, to be excavated later, chopped up, and mixed in with the seed corn of every family participating. The pig is Demeter's fertile animal, and this is simple fertility magic; making the crops grow was a very important purpose of the festival, if not the main one. Although this aspect is usually recognized, modern interpreters normally place more stress on the social function of the festival in providing women an opportunity to express solidarity in the face of oppressive Greek men. This was of course an important part of the festival, but to distribute the stress so may tell us more about our own times and preoccupations than about ancient reality.[21]

Other examples will readily be conceded once pointed out, though they are rarely introduced simply as instances of magic. Scapegoat rituals, by which the evils of a whole city are transferred ceremoniously on to the head of an animal or some unfortunate human, who is then driven beyond the bounds of the country, thus purifying the city, can hardly be described by any other term but magic. Sacred marriages, by which the copulation of humans is ritually performed in the belief that it will enhance the fertility of the crops, are an obviously magical business.[22] The complete destruction of an animal in full view of an enemy army prior to joining battle is another elementary piece of sympathetic magic.

In addition, there are cases in which the magical/instrumental

---

[21] A recent article which strikes an instructive balance is H. S. Versnel, 'The Festival for the Bona Dea and the Thesmophoria,' G&R 39 (1992), 31–55; expanded in *Inconsistencies in Greek and Roman Religion*, ii: *Transition and Reversal in Myth and Ritual* (Leiden, New York, and Cologne, 1993), Ch. 4. See also Bremmer, *Greek Religion*, 76–8.

[22] At ZPE 97 (1993), 35 n. 16 I argued (with many scholars) for a broad application of the term 'sacred marriage', against those who would restrict it to reenactments of the wedding of Zeus and Hera such as were celebrated at the Samian Heraia. The broader definition is a modern construct, but corresponds to something real. I have since been able to see A. Avagianou, *Sacred Marriage in the Rituals of Greek Religion* (Bern etc., 1991), who argues for the restricted definition; but the few festivals to which she will allow the term to apply show, significantly, little homogeneity, and in the case of the Amphitryon myth she has overlooked the revealing Egyptian parallel and probable source of the story (cf. ZPE 97 (1993), 36 n. 23).

aspect has been quite overlooked.[23] First, the Panathenaia. This festival of all Athenians on Athena's midsummer birthday involved a spectacular parade through the city up to the Akropolis, where oxen were sacrificed and a new robe, the peplos, was presented to Athena in the form of her ancient statue in the Erechtheum. Modern discussions of the festival stress its social function in uniting all classes, and make much of its location at the beginning of the civic year.[24] It is, beyond doubt, a New Year's festival of renewal and reintegration. But it is something else too. Scholars who write on the Panathenaia naturally mention the peplos, but seem to regard it merely as a pious gift. Yet it is much more than this. The peplos of ritual is the aegis of myth, Athena's impenetrable armour won in the battle of the Giants, those older, monstrous forces of chaos who threatened the orderly and just government of the Olympian gods. The aegis rendered Athena invulnerable. The ancient statue of Athena on the Akropolis was a talisman upon whose preservation the safety of the city depended, like the Palladion of Troy which had to be stolen by Odysseus and Diomedes before the city could be taken. The goddess who protects the citadel, housed in the king's own palace, is a figure already in Mycenaean religion; this statue is Athena. Putting the peplos on the talisman was an act of simple magic. In its fabric was always woven one theme, and one theme only: the battle of the Giants. The message could hardly be plainer: to give Athena a new robe was to secure the protection of the city.[25] In the fifth century BC, this was surely an important purpose of the proceedings; one can imagine the fears of the citizens were anything to go wrong with the presentation.

Secondly, the Arrhephoria. This curious ritual involved two specially chosen girls, who served Athena for some time on the Akropolis, being given a special chest which contained mysterious and secret items, and into which they must not look under any circumstances; the aetiological myth told of the madness and death of the first two naughty girls who did so. They carried this dread

---

[23] It is prudent to stress again that the magical or the goal-oriented aspect is not the whole of the ritual, merely an important function that deserves to be recognized alongside others.

[24] e.g. J. Neils, in ead. (ed.), *Goddess and Festival: The Panathenaic Festival in Ancient Athens* (Princeton, 1992), 23 ff.

[25] R. L. Fowler, '*AIΓ-* in Early Greek Language and Myth', *Phoenix*, 42 (1988), 95–113, at 106 ff.

burden down from the Akropolis in the dead of night to a sanctuary of Aphrodite; in return they received another, equally mysterious burden, which they returned to the Akropolis. The ritual has been interpreted as a rite of initiation for these pubescent girls. The myth said that the chest originally contained a child, born of an amorous mishap between Hephaistos and Athena; the god's semen fell to the earth, so Athena's virginity was preserved, but the child that Earth conceived and bore was adopted as her own by Athena and entrusted to the daughters of Athens' first king, Kekrops, for safekeeping. The myth speaks of sex, the rite involves girls being separated from their community for months and returning after doing their sacred duty; these slim indications, and a passage in Aristophanes that speaks of the Arrhephoria as a kind of marker of a certain stage of one's growth on the way to adulthood, seem to offer support for the idea that we are dealing with an initiation rite.[26] Of course, any social activity will engender the acclimatization of those involved in it, and if they are young, they will learn something about the ways of their elders; but this is not an initiation or a rite of passage as anthropology understands the term. It is a very curious initiation indeed if only two girls a year out of the whole city are allowed to participate. The real purpose of this ritual may never be known, but the endpoint, the safe delivery of a newborn child who will grow to be king of Athens, suggests that in general the purpose of the annual rite, if properly carried out (and obviously the point of the myth is that everything depends on that), was to secure the prosperity of the city and (in olden days) its king.[27] In other words, the ritual has a specific, concrete goal. Consider also the general character of all these goings on on the Akropolis, involving as they do secret burdens, dark doings in the dead of night, pure young children, and strict rules about the procedure; the ritual has much in common with magical rites, and it would be very hard to maintain any essential difference between them.

Finally, the Arkteia for Artemis at Brauron.[28] Young girls played

---

[26] H. Jeanmaire, *Couroi et Courètes* (Lille, 1939), 264 ff.; W. Burkert, 'Kekropidensage und Arrhephoria. Vom Initiationsritus zum Panathenäenfest', *Hermes*, 94 (1966), 1–25 = *Wilder Ursprung: Opferritual und Mythos bei den Griechen* (Berlin, 1990), 40–59; and many others. The passage in Aristophanes is *Lys.* 641.

[27] Fowler, '*ΑΙΓ*- in Early Greek Language and Myth', 105 ff.

[28] For a good orientation, see H. Lloyd-Jones, 'Artemis and Iphigeneia', *JHS* 103 (1983), 87–102. The most detailed and sensitive discussion is C. Sourvinou-Inwood, *Studies in Girls' Transitions: Aspects of the Arkteia and Age Representation in Attic*

the part of bears and honoured the virgin goddess of the hunt. We can infer from the offerings revealed by the excavation of the site that far more girls participated in these rites than did in the Arrhephoria, but whether they involved a majority of Athenian girls or were compulsory cannot be shown. Let us assume for the sake of argument that as many girls as possible participated, and that their parents thought it a highly desirable part of their upbringing.[29] Several hints, stronger this time, suggest that this was an initiation ritual: separation from the home; extended service to the goddess in a remote setting; alteration of the normal state (or adoption of 'liminality') by acting the role of animals; return to normalcy thereafter; hints of sexuality in the proceedings, including nudity; the passage of Aristophanes already cited. One can readily admit that the cult assumed some initiatory aspects in Classical times, at least as an expected or desirable service of a certain age-class, which was therefore bound to provide opportunities for social acclimatization; and since it must be foolhardy to distinguish between a ritual with initiatory aspects and an initiation ritual pure and simple, the common assessment of the Arkteia may be accepted, however controversial or difficult the interpretation of some details of the initiation may be.

But was this all the ancient girls were doing? To imitate a bear is a most peculiar way to prepare for marriage. To say that it was done for

Iconography (Athens, 1988); see the same author's 'Ancient Rites and Modern Constructs: On the Brauronian Bears Again', BICS 37 (1990), 1–14, criticizing R. Hamilton, 'Alkman and the Athenian Arkteia', Hesperia, 58 (1989), 449–72; 'Lire l'Arkteia—Lire les images, les textes, l'animalité', DHA 16.2 (1990), 45–60. See also P. Vidal-Naquet, 'Le Cru, l'enfant grec et le cuit', Comment faire l'histoire, 3 (1974), 137–68 = 'Recipes for Greek Adolescence', in R. L. Gordon (ed.), Myth, Religion and Society (Cambridge, 1981), 163–85; L. Bodson, 'IEPA ZΩIA: Contribution à l'étude de la place de l'animal dans la religion grecque ancienne (Brussels, 1978), 129–44; J.-P. Vernant, 'Artemis and Rites of Sacrifice, Initiation, and Marriage' [1983], in Mortals and Immortals: Collected Essays, ed. F. I. Zeitlin (Princeton, 1991), 207–19; S. G. Cole, 'The Social Function of Rituals of Maturation: The Koureion and the Arkteia', ZPE 55 (1984), 233–44; R. Osborne, Demos: The Discovery of Classical Attika (Cambridge, 1985), 154–72; P. Brulé, La Fille d'Athènes: La religion des filles à Athènes à l'époque classique. Mythes, cultes, et société (Paris, 1987), 218–61; id., 'Retour à Brauron. Repentirs, avancées, mises au point', DHA 16.2 (1990), 61–90; id., 'De Brauron aux Pyrénées et retour: Dans les pattes de l'ours', ibid. 9–27; K. Dowden, 'Myth: Brauron and Beyond', ibid. 29–43; R. Garland, The Greek Way of Life: From Conception to Old Age (Ithaca, NY, 1990), 187–91; S. H. Lonsdale, Dance and Ritual Play in Greek Religion (Baltimore, 1993), 171–93; R. Seaford, Reciprocity and Ritual (Oxford, 1994), 306–9.
    [29] On the number of participants, see Sourvinou-Inwood, Studies in Girls' Transitions, 111 ff.; E. Simon, Festivals of Attica: An Archaeological Commentary (Madison, 1983), 86.

the vague and abstract reason that it seemed a good way to symbolize liminality, or because the bear symbolized the 'untamed' nature of the virgin, seems to be a common explanation, but it is one that the present writer has always found unsatisfactory, at least as a complete explanation. A religion made only of such ingredients as these is thin spiritual fare, and methodologically (see the second half of this paper) there are grounds for uneasiness when an interpretation stands or falls on a structural relationship alone. Now, the goddess in question is the goddess of the hunt, of childbirth, and the young. The primeval hunting background should be prominent in any discussion; and, by good fortune, we know that a sacred hunt of some kind did in fact form part of the worship of Artemis Brauronia.[30] In the context of hunting, imitating bears makes immediate intuitive sense, whereas in the context of preparation for marriage it does not. In the context of hunting, young girls are the appropriate instrument for the propitiation of the goddess and the securing of her favour. They are pure and virginal like her; the closer they come to puberty, the more sexually attractive they become—like her. The association of the chase of the hunt and the chase of sex is an anthropological commonplace. This is a better place to look for the explanation, in the first instance, of the sexuality in the proceedings, than to Athenian ideas about marriage. One does not preclude the other; indeed, because of the first, the second is easily grafted on to the ritual.

The aetiological myth, which we fortunately possess and which must give us the clue, confirms this analysis of the balance of motifs and impulses.[31] The myth does say that the girls must perform the ritual before they are married, thus supporting the interpretation as a rite of passage (since 'before they are married' is an otiose elaboration of a fact already implicit in the designation παρθένοι);[32] but the main stress of the story lies elsewhere. It speaks of a gentle bear that was wrongly killed, of Artemis' anger and a deadly plague, and of her demand to be appeased. It is that obligation that is most important here, not learning about marriage. If young girls are earnestly

---

[30] Liban. *Hypoth. Dem.* 25; Dein. 2. 12.

[31] W. Sale, 'The Temple-Legends of the Arkteia', *RhM* 118 (1975), 265–84; C. Montepaone, 'Il mito di fondazione del rituale munichio in onore di Artemis', in *Recherches sur les cultes grecs et l'occident* I, Cahiers du centre Jean Bérard 5 (Naples, 1979), 65–76.

[32] In the *Suda* s.v. ἄρκτος ἢ Βραυρωνίοις ('I was a bear at the Brauronia') and the related Ravenna scholion on Ar. *Lys.* 645 some authority has elaborated this hint into the strong statement that no girl could marry unless she had served as a bear—by decree of the assembly. Such elaborations are suspicious.

appeasing an angry Artemis, the natural assumption is that they are appeasing her in her function as the *kourotrophos*, the goddess in whose hands above all the gods rested the health and vigour of girls. The age of the participants—from five to ten years old—has never been easy to explain for those who stress the initiatory aspect to the exclusion of others. A typical summary asserts that the girls 'entered a temporary state of savagery so as to return prepared for the civilized state of marriage';[33] when one thinks that this is meant to apply to five-year-old girls, hardly more than babies, one is inclined to withhold credence. But propitiation of the *kourotrophos* can never start too early; nor can one do it enough. So uncertain was the survival of the young in the ancient world. Artemis the *kourotrophos* was also the goddess of childbirth, the most dangerous of life's experiences, more dangerous than battle, as Medeia knew; more spirits attended this function than anything else in the everyday religion of the Greek world.[34] Should one fail to honor the *kourotrophos*, one's children will not be ἰφιγενεῖς, 'strong-born'. This is what the heroine Iphigeneia, the 'strong-born one', is doing at Brauron.[35] In the same sanctuary the clothes of women who had died in childbirth—not a small number—were dedicated to Artemis. The fact illustrates the nature of the goddess, and her cult, well enough.

Robert Garland points out fairly enough that 'lowering the age-requirement of a rite of passage is widely attested by anthropologists',[36] and what seems appropriate to our notions of human nature can be a deceptive guide. Nonetheless, a putatively original rite of puberty, subsequently modified to include girls of many different ages, must lose some of its focus. Why was the age lowered—not just lowered, but modified to *exclude* pubescent girls? The Brauronia were penteteric, so a range of permissible ages had to be set for practical reasons; but why set the upper limit at an age when the menarche was still some distance away?[37] A simpler explanation sees these rites

[33] R. Seaford, *JHS* 108 (1988), 122.

[34] Garland, *Greek Way of Life*, Ch. 2; T. Hadzisteliou-Price, *Kourotrophos: Cults and Representations of the Greek Nursing Deities* (Leiden, 1978); for a related kind of activity, see J.-J. Aubert, 'Threatened Wombs: Aspects of Ancient Uterine Magic', *GRBS* 30 (1989), 421–49.

[35] C. Calame, *Choruses of Young Women in Ancient Greece* (Lanham, Md., (1997), 166 n. 234.

[36] Garland, *Greek Way of Life*, 190.

[37] P. Brulé, 'Retour à Brauron', 82, acknowledges the difficulty, but suggests that physical readiness for conception was not part of the Greeks' notion of nubility. Such

as originally and *appropriately* performed by children of any age up to puberty, rather than originally performed by pubescent children and subsequently modified for unknown reasons. It is worth recalling that worship on the site, which was inhabited in prehistoric times, is probably far older than the *polis*, which is the necessary context of the prevailing interpretation.[38] As the Athenian *polis* became more cohesive and bourgeois in the late Archaic and early Classical ages, the desire to teach the young about their obligations as citizens and wives of citizens can reasonably be expected to have intruded upon older rites such as the Brauronia, because of the age of the participants. New dimensions were added. But the explicit concerns of the worshippers, as attested by the myth, remained straightforward: the goddess of pristine nature and of the young is angry and unless the children do her dance a plague will strike them dead.[39]

   So much for our more argumentative examples. Whether or not these interpretations recommend themselves in all particulars to the reader, the general assessment may be allowed to have some validity. Magical activity was commonplace, ubiquitous, and instinctive. It is most improbable that the mass of ordinary people, who did not have the benefit of two hundred years of Enlightenment and modern science, and who were steeped from birth in the kinds of magical doings of which I spoke at the outset, somehow put aside this frame of mind

---

an amazing conclusion needs more support than Brulé gives it in his brief remarks. Sourvinou-Inwood (above, n. 28) regards the initiation as one from childhood to the period that leads to and culminates in menarche, but the distinction between 'period leading to menarche' and 'menarche' is one that is often effaced in her own discussion. The difficulty was already acute for Jeanmaire, *Couroi*, 260. Incidentally, though Jeanmaire is normally mentioned as the father of this line of interpretation, Lewis Farnell in 1896 advanced it without ado: *Cults of the Greek States*, ii (Oxford, 1896), 437, with reference to W. Robertson Smith, *Lectures on the Religion of the Semites* (Edinburgh, 1889), 304, 309, for parallels in other societies for initiation ceremonies involving bears. To be sure, Farnell devotes the bulk of his discussion to a totemistic interpretation.

[38] See A. Antoniou, 'Minoische Elemente in Kult der Artemis von Brauron', *Philologus*, 125 (1981), 291–6; B. C. Dietrich, *Tradition in Greek Religion* (Berlin and New York, 1986), 60.

[39] There is the question of how closely related the activities at Brauron were to those of Mounychia; speaking of the latter, W. Burkert, *The Orientalizing Revolution: Near Eastern Influence on Greek Culture in the Early Archaic Age* (Cambridge, MA and London, 1992), 73 ff., thinks that the festival may have originated in a magical rite by which a pestilence was removed; by the Classical period, its nature had changed, so that like other festivals of Artemis it had an 'aura' of girls' initiations. This is a progression very much like the one I have posited for the rites at Brauron.

when they gathered together for the most important festivals of the gods. Instead, they re-directed these same attitudes and impulses and gave expression to them in a different setting. The difference between the 'magical' and the 'religious' acts is thus one of social context and attitude: one is approved, the other almost always is not.

Where to go from here? We have taken one frequently touted characteristic of 'magic'—that its practices are goal-oriented—and found that it crops up repeatedly in 'religion'; the exercise could be repeated with other characteristics. If the distinction between magic and religion must vanish like a soap bubble at the merest touch, it seems fruitless to go past the heuristic stage with any pretence of keeping them separate in point of theory. In purely practical terms, however, there is a well-recognized set of phenomena we all think of in connection with the term 'magic'; it is becoming increasingly clear that this huge body of material must be kept in mind when considering the total phenomenon of Greek religion. And heuresis can take one a long way. The preceding section yielded the understanding that ritual, in broad terms, is twofold: it often entails a straightforward, substantive goal; but as all ritual must inevitably have a place in a social nexus, it will have social purposes, and its forms will be susceptible of reading as a system of signs.[40]

This understanding seems innocuous enough when so expressed, but it is by no means orthodoxy, and brings with it a surprising number of theoretical implications. In the past sixty years, classical scholars have tended to play down magic as a part of Greek religion, and to underestimate the goal-oriented aspect of ritual.[41] Anthropologists do not. Three reasons may be suggested for this state of affairs. Firstly, anthropologists, unlike classicists, have the societies they study before their very eyes and can hardly ignore the patently magical aspects of demonstrative public ritual. A second reason may be snobbery—something of the Frazerian or the Wilamowitzian still lingering; although in a post-Christian age we have found ways to take the Olympian gods seriously, our modernity has subconsciously

---

[40] I find Versnel making the same point in the introduction to *Inconsistencies*, ii, which incorporates several articles I have drawn on frequently in the preparation of this one; see there 12 f.

[41] The influence of W. Burkert's great work, *Greek Religion* (= *GR*), would be hard to overestimate; it devotes but one paragraph to magic, with a clearly polemical intent to deter anyone who might wish to pursue the topic further.

prevented us from extending this courtesy to the manufacturers of voodoo dolls. A third part has to do with the way discussion of the myth/ritual problem has developed in this century.

In the beginning, which is to say in the days of Jane Harrison and her ritualist followers, the relationship of myth and ritual was thought to be straightforward: the myth was the plot of the ritual, the text that backed up the action. For instance, the main ritual action of the Thesmophoria, the burying of a pig underground, was 'explained' by the story of a swineherd who happened to be swallowed up in the chasm created when the lord of the underworld carried off his bride Persephone. Most myth, the ritualists thought, was aetiological in this way. Most ritual, they thought, originated in magical acts, especially those of fertility magic.

The problem of magic and religion also played a vital role in the work of James Frazer. His background lay in nineteenth-century anthropology, which had placed much emphasis on the origins of social customs and the concept of evolution. It was natural for Frazer to see magic as an early and primitive stage of religion, which gradually evolved into a higher stage, characterized not by superstition but by morality, not by attempts to coerce the gods but by a spirit of humble worship and supplication. Christian notions of true religion, and those of the Enlightenment, are easy to detect in this scheme.[42]

Frazer's views on magic and religion have long since been abandoned. In not much time too the views of Harrison on myth and ritual were also seen to be simplistic. A great deal of Greek mythology has no attested connection with ritual, and such myth as does relate to known rituals often has a relationship that is more complex than the ritualists seemed to suggest. To take a simple example, one of the more successful structuralist analyses, that of the Prometheus myth, demonstrates that while the strictly aetiological part is straightforward—Prometheus wrapped the bones in fat, and so do we—the *kind* of story Hesiod invented to account for this central rite of Greek religion is much more significant. Surely many other stories

---

[42] On Jane Harrison and the Cambridge Ritualists, see W. M. Calder III (ed.), *The Cambridge Ritualists Reconsidered*, ICS Suppl. 2 (Atlanta, 1991); R. Ackerman, *The Myth and Ritual School: J. G. Frazer and the Cambridge Ritualists* (New York and London, 1991); on Frazer, see also Ackerman, *J. G. Frazer: His Life and Work* (Cambridge, 1987). Ackerman points out that Frazer's ideas (insofar as they were consistent) changed with time; in particular, he came to disallow the religious element in magic, regarding it merely as religion's precursor, since in his view religion had to have a reflective element. He deliberately distanced himself from the ritualist position in the 1920s.

were possible besides this one with its motifs of deception, the jealousy and hostility of the gods, their departure from earth and the implied end of the Golden Age.[43] Greek views of the gods and life generally are revealed by prying a little bit below the surface of the myth.

In time the pendulum swung fully in the opposite direction. Statements such as 'myth and ritual do not correspond in details of content but in structure and atmosphere' were typical.[44] The summation is remarkable when one thinks about it. Such clearly attested myth/ritual complexes as we do possess from Greece do not bear this claim out; myth and ritual, wherever we can test their relationship, correspond (albeit imperfectly) in *both* content *and* atmosphere.[45]

The problem is that the number of attested myth/ritual complexes is distressingly small, and scholars desperately want a method that will allow them safely to reconstruct rituals from myths alone, thus creating more of these complexes for them to study. With the advent first of structuralism then of semiotics a key seemed to have been provided. These approaches seemed to offer hope because similar structures and signs shared by two myths will allow the scholar, if a ritual connection is known for one of the myths, to infer a ritual connection for the other one, even if its surface content is quite different.[46]

The hazards of this procedure are obvious. To take an example that is pertinent to the myths and rituals discussed earlier: one of the commonest structural motifs used to infer the existence of an initiation ritual behind a given myth is that of separation (for instance leaving one's home and going into the country); this is to produce

---

[43] Vernant, *MT*, 3–32; cf. *Myth and Society in Ancient Greece* (Brighton, 1980), 168–85; G. S. Kirk, *Myth: Its Meaning and Function in Ancient and Other Cultures* (Cambridge, Berkeley, and Los Angeles, 1970), 233.

[44] F. Graf, *ZPE* 55 (1984), 254. In his later work Graf has been less incautious: contrast *Greek Mythology: An Introduction* (Baltimore and London, 1993), 110 ff.; id., 'Römische Aitia und ihre Riten. Das Beispiel von Saturnalia und Parilia', *MH* 49 (1992), 13–25; below, n. 46.

[45] On the correspondence of myth and ritual at the Eleusinian mysteries, the best-known example, see R. Parker's excellent orientation, 'The Hymn to Demeter and the Homeric Hymns', *G&R* 38 (1991), 1–17.

[46] Cf. F. Graf's comments in his learned and valuable *NK*, 5: it is 'impossible, when a myth is attested without a ritual, to infer a ritual by comparing related myths for which rituals are attested—extrapolating, as it were; but where there are at least hints of a ritual, one can make inferences about its mood, structure, and function, though with the greatest of caution and in full awareness of how hypothetical the result is.'

'liminality' or 'marginality', a well-documented aspect of initiation rituals. It is astonishing how often the word 'initiation' occurs in the literature these days, and how many myths are suspected of being vestigially connected with such rituals, on no better grounds than the presence of the separation motif.[47] But almost any myth, given enough subtlety of vision and hard arguing, will conform to the desired pattern. As P. M. C. Forbes Irving has pointedly argued, there is usually no independent evidence for the existence of the rituals.[48] H. S. Versnel astutely observed how often practitioners of this method must assume that the ritual survives only as a fragmentary relic in the myth, so that only the keenest of scholarly bloodhounds, with noses attuned to the initiatory scent, can detect the connection.[49] The assumption of relics is of course exactly how Frazer and the ritualists uncovered fertility rites behind so many myths—a different set of bloodhounds, and differently trained noses.

Yet the problems identified by Frazer and others remain even if their solutions do not. The huge and impressive bulk of data on magical practices also remains and has to be explained. The successors to Frazerism and ritualism have been principally two: structuralism and semiotics. The admirable Ferdinand de Saussure in his famous *Cours de linguistique générale* (published by pupils after his death in 1913) first declared that language is a system of arbitrary signs, none of which has meaning in itself but only insofar as it contrasts or relates to other signs. Structuralism has made many interesting uses of this insight, but semiotics transferred this tenet

[47] See especially K. Dowden's lively and interesting book, *Death and the Maiden: Girls' Initiation Rites in Greek Mythology* (London and New York, 1989); further the same author's *The Uses of Greek Mythology* (London and New York, 1992), 102 ff.

[48] P. M. C. Forbes Irving, *Metamorphosis in Greek Myths* (Oxford, 1990), 50 ff.; cf. F. Graf, *HZ* 253 (1991), 697–9. At *ZPE* 97 (1993), 39 n. 39 I pointed out how easily, and how erroneously, the myth of Kephalos and Prokris could be interpreted as an initiation *aition*. Dowden, to his credit, is genially frank about the lack of evidence, though by the end of his book the joy of discovery has made him look on it as a strength: 'In fact, it is one of the pleasures of our inquiry that rituals and a way of life that cannot otherwise be recovered can be discerned in the mythology' (190). Compare also his remarks in 'Myth: Brauron and Beyond', 36 ff.

[49] H. S. Versnel, 'What's Sauce for the Goose is Sauce for the Gander: Myth and Ritual, Old and New', in L. Edmunds (ed.), *Approaches to Greek Myth*, (Baltimore, 1990), 23–90, at 50 ff. = *Inconsistencies*, ii. 58 ff. See also C. Grottanelli's remarks in *HR* 29 (1989–90), 63. A. Moreau, 'Initiation en Grèce antique', *DHA* 18.1 (1992), 191–244, offers a reply to Versnel, but appears scarcely to have grasped the import of his arguments; his article goes on to claim practically the whole of Greek mythology as initiatory.

about language to other social acts: all social conventions, in fact, form a system of signs like that of language, conveying messages to their users; and in this system, there are no natural signs, only arbitrary ones. The conventional behaviour of society, in turn, expresses its values. The tendency, therefore, is to say that values too must be arbitrary. Now this is suspiciously congenial to our Zeitgeist. Claims to absolute truth advanced in this century of ideological nightmare have become deeply and justifiably suspect; semioticians' argument that all social values are artificially constructed has therefore found ready assent. The idea that a moral value might be either grounded in nature or defensible in metaphysics is instinctively rejected, if not derided by most contemporary scholars. Instead, they argue that the values of any society are merely the product, however complex, of particular historical circumstances. Human nature is not a constant; indeed, there is no such thing as human nature.

Anyone steeped in this manner of thinking ought to be especially alive to the differences in societies, and wary of importing modern ideas into the reconstruction of the past. One school of thought, to be sure, has been especially sensitive to this requirement; the 'new historicism' has been with us for some years now. But there is a seductive danger in semiotics. Its object of investigation is social signs; since such signs can only convey social information, on semiotics' own assumptions, it is inevitable that such meaning as the signs convey will only be *about* social relations (or, in a particularly desperate version, about other signs, so that meaning is endlessly 'deferred'). The danger, therefore, is that one is apt to overemphasize the sociological aspect of ritual and ignore what the participants themselves think they are doing—trying to achieve some substantive goal.[50] Instinctively we recoil from taking *that* seriously; to do so might imply we actually believe, for instance, that the crops will grow

---

[50] The most famous statement of the practical purpose of religion is made by Euthyphro in Plato's dialogue (14b): prayers and sacrifice σῴζει ... τοὺς ἰδίους οἴκους καὶ τὰ κοινὰ τῶν πόλεων· τὰ δ' ἐναντία τῶν κεχαρισμένων ἀσεβῆ, ἃ δὴ καὶ ἀνατρέπει ἅπαντα καὶ ἀπόλλυσιν ('preserve ... private households and public prosperity; and the opposite of what pleases the gods is impiety, which causes universal upheaval and ruin'). This is the original meaning of *sōtēria* ('safe-keeping/salvation'). Many other passages could be quoted; this one is especially important because of the literary context—Euthyphro is meant to be the best possible representative of ordinary, traditional piety. Of course (it should be added at once) passages can also be found that stress the social advantages of religious life in terms of forging and maintaining links between individuals and groups.

better if we chop up a pig. Yet it is the attitude of people who *do* believe that that we must see from the inside. It is the same with modern religion; any believer would regard a purely sociological description of their religion as wholly inadequate.

We are particularly apt to overemphasize that aspect of modern society which most preoccupies us at the moment, one might almost say obsesses us: the nature and roles of the sexes. To the semiotician, gender, like everything else, is a social construct.[51] Gender seems the most important social fact to us; ergo, it must have been to the Greeks. Initiation ritual is the prime means whereby early societies pass on the gender-construct to the next generation; ergo, the Greeks must have had lots of these, and myths that talk about the sexes must be the aetiological myths for initiation rituals. Yet to realize the paucity of independent evidence for these rituals is to suspect at once that the widespread assent these interpretations enjoy is itself culturally determined, a product of late twentieth-century predilections.[52]

---

[51] For some important criticism of this notion, see J. Thorp, 'The Social Construction of Homosexuality', *Phoenix*, 46 (1992), 54–61. It may be of interest to compare the trenchant reaction of a conservative Catholic in 1937 to a similar, if not identical proposition: ' "Works of art are produced by artists," Mr [Anthony] Blunt begins his essay; "artists are men; men live in society and are in a large measure formed by the society in which they live. Therefore works of art cannot be considered historically except in human and ultimately in social terms." By "social" Mr Blunt, as all his colleagues [in *The Mind in Chains*, ed. by C. Day Lewis], means "economic." It would be equally true and fair to say "Men live on the earth, etc. Therefore works of art cannot be considered historically except in geographical and ultimately in meteorological terms." A metaphysician would have little difficulty in demolishing Mr [Edward] Upward's elementary statement of the origin of life in a material universe.' *The Essays, Articles and Reviews of Evelyn Waugh*, ed. D. Gallagher (London, 1984), 199.

[52] A famous and influential article in this category, P. Vidal-Naquet's 'The Black Hunter' of 1968 (reprinted with corrections most recently in *The Black Hunter. Forms of Thought and Forms of Society in the Greek World* (Baltimore, 1986), 106–28; see also 'The Black Hunter Revisited', *PCPS* 32 (1986), 126–44), depends entirely on certain ancient reports that the myth of Melanthos and Xanthios was the *aition* for the service of Athenian ephebes; but it is nearly certain that the connection with the Apatouria is an arbitrary invention of Hellanikos designed to bring the Neleids of Pylos in line with Athens' claims to be the mother of Ionia. The myth of Melanthos and Xanthios therefore has nothing to do with Attic ephebeia. See further my 'Herodotos and his Contemporaries', *JHS* 116 (1996), 62–87 at 73. The point was already implicit in Jacoby's comment on *FGrHist* 323a F 23; it has since been stressed by N. Robertson, *GRBS* 29 (1988), 205 ff.; cf. *AJP* 109 (1988), 284–5. Robertson's vigorous defence of the importance of magic is to be found in numerous articles of recent years, but most provocatively in a review of several influential works on Greek religion in *EMC* 9 (1990), 419–42 and 10 (1991), 57–79; see now also his *Festivals and Legends: The Formation of Greek Cities in the Light of Public Ritual*, Phoenix Suppl. 31 (Toronto, 1992). Robertson's eye-popping interpretations of myths have not won wide assent, but his reminder of the central position of magic is timely.

The tendency of recent years, exactly opposite to the tendency of a century ago, has been to deny the universal aspects of human experience, to deny and even ridicule the concept of human nature, and to develop methods for reconstructing ancient realities that rely as little as possible on our own instincts or common-sense assumptions. The methodological implication seems unobjectionable. Yet the linguistic philosophy underlying all semiological study is anything but invulnerable to criticism and not necessarily more reliable than the imaginative intuition of the learned, patient, sensitive, and intelligent scholar. It is certainly often a good deal less interesting. Although importing modern preconceptions into interpretations of the ancient phenomena is obviously wrong in point of method (as all scholars of all schools since the early nineteenth century have recognized), this is not an argument for abandoning our instincts and common-sense assumptions, since the greatest part of human experience is broadly comparable in all times and places of our history. The basics of life are after all pretty straightforward. Birth and survival; disease, drought, famine, the failure of crops; the pursuit of happiness, the fear of death, the desire for immortality; helplessness in the face of superior, unknown, and hostile powers—these are not social constructs, and they are the very stuff of religion everywhere in human history. To further or hinder them is the goal of goal-oriented ritual. This is why Tylor, Mannhardt, Frazer, Harrison, and the others started where they did; it seemed natural, and *is* natural.

The shortcomings of the Frazerian and ritualist models are plain enough, and progress since then has been spectacular. But there are difficulties in the current models, and the way forward might lie in combining the best of the new with the best of the old. The positive theoretical framework would take a book to work out; but some negatives can be briefly identified. We ought to be suspicious of the one-sided: any interpretation of a myth that relies exclusively on structure, just as any interpretation that arbitrarily decodes the surface content by assigning specific referents to its details (for instance—an old instance—saying that a hero represents the rising sun), without any external evidence in either case, must be regarded as no more than an interesting speculation.[53] If myth and ritual are not attested together, extreme caution is called for when arguing from one to the other. A reading of ancient religious experience that

[53] My interpretation of the myth of Kephalos (above, n. 20) is meant as no more.

is insufficiently aware of the contingencies of ancient life is as weak as one that thinks there are only contingencies in human life.

A fruitful approach might be to investigate magic and other broad categories of ancient religious experience, perhaps from a phenomenological perspective; the time might be ripe for a revival of this branch of philosophy. Other categories can readily be suggested: 'sacrifice', 'prayer', and even 'god' spring to mind.[54] With respect to magic, it seems an urgent need to investigate the deep-level links that must have existed between the part of religious activity normally designated 'magical' and the rest of religion. If the differences between the two are mainly contextual, much careful attention needs to be devoted to the description of these contexts. What exactly about Sokrates' connection with the god of Delphi so provoked people in 399 (and not before)? Why are the oracle-mongers' books acceptable in Rome but not in Athens (at least in some circumstances)? What makes the public scapegoat, repulsive and disgusting though he is, so deeply satisfying, but the private act of spiteful revenge so morally repellent? In what circumstances would a city call in an Epimenides? In what circumstances were individuals allowed to say with impunity that traditional religion is the work of charlatans—to call it, in effect, nothing but 'magic'?

The connections, as I said, are deep-seated; they might find an explanation in psychology and biology as much as in sociology. The interplay of religion, experience, and rationality cannot be adequately studied from any one point of view. Philology, philosophy, and anthropology all have a contribution to make. But the thing is lifeless if we do not at bottom think we are studying ourselves. There is little joy in studying some alien species constructing its own alien reality. The thrill is in the recognition; they are *Menschen wie Du und ich*. The historian of religion, like the historian of politics and any other human endeavour, studies universal human urges as they are manifested in the particular social patterns of the ancient world; and the purpose of that study is to achieve through the imaginative revitalization of our ancestors' mental universe a better understanding of, precisely, human nature.

---

[54] R. Parker's *Miasma* is an outstanding example of this kind of categorical study.

EXCURSUS ON THE DEFINITION OF MAGIC

The problem of definition is clearly central. The bibliography is already ample.[55] I can hardly begin to discuss the problem and its many solutions. Obviously magic can be defined at the very outset as different from true religion. Definition and conclusion are here one. The strict differentiation of the two inevitably involves the view that religion is a higher order of activity than magic, whether it succeeded the other by evolution or not. Modern believers in various religions will share this view. Yet the skeptic is apt to look on the whole apparatus of modern religion as so much mumbo-jumbo, seeing no distinction between, say, the healing rituals of the Azande and the Catholic practice of exorcism. To call this rite 'superstition' must seem offensive to the faithful Catholic. Protestantism, on the other hand, prides itself on having discarded such rituals. Yet there can be few good Protestants who would not feel anxious for an unbaptized child's prospects of salvation, particularly their own, and it is precisely in the realm of Protestantism, with its emphasis on faith, that the miracle-working cults of modern times have thrived. The skeptic will point out these considerations; the more skeptical the point of view, the more 'magic' will be equated with 'religion'.

Many scholars have simply given up. In his contribution to *Magika Hiera*, Roy Kotansky quotes ((above, n. 2) 123 n. 1) J. E. Lowe's *Magic in Greek and Latin Literature*, who already in 1929, on page 1 of his

---

[55] A selection: O. Petterson, 'Magic–Religion: Some Marginal Notes to an Old Problem', *Ethnos*, 22 (1957), 109–19; J. Goody, 'Religion and Ritual: The Definition Problem', *British Journal of Sociology*, 12 (1961), 142–64; M. and R. Wax, 'The Notion of Magic', *Current Anthropology*, 4 (1963), 495–518; D. Hammond, 'Magic: A Problem of Semantics', *American Anthropologist*, 72 (1970), 1349–56; H. Geertz, 'An Anthropology of Religion and Magic', *Journal of Interdisciplinary History*, 6 (1975), 71–89; K. Thomas, 'An Anthropology of Religion and Magic II', ibid. 91–109; M. Smith, *Jesus the Magician* (New York, 1978); D. E. Aune, 'Magic in Early Christianity', *ANRW* II.23.2 (1980), 1507–57; A. B. Kolenkow, 'Relationships between Miracle and Prophecy in the Greco-Roman World and Early Christianity', ibid. 1470–1506; M. Winkelmann, 'Magic: A Theoretical Reassessment', *Current Anthropology*, 23 (1982), 37–66; C. R. Phillips III, 'Magic and Politics in the Fourth Century: Parameters of Groupings', *Studia Patristica*, 18.1 (Kalamazoo, 1985), 65–70; id., 'The Sociology of Religious Knowledge in the Roman Empire to A.D. 284', *ANRW* II.16.3 (1986), 2677–773 (2711–32 on 'Magic and Religion'); J. Middleton, 'Theories of Magic', in *Encyclopedia of Religion*, ix (1987), 82–9; H. D. Betz, 'Magic in Graeco-Roman Antiquity', ibid. 93–7; A. Segal, 'Hellenistic Magic: Some Questions of Definition', in *Other Judaisms of Late Antiquity* (Atlanta, 1987), 79–108; the authorities listed above (n. 2); and several articles in A. D. Nock's *Essays on Religion and the Ancient World* (Oxford, 1972), esp. 'Paul and the Magus' i. 308 ff.

book, declared: 'Many definitions ... have been attempted: none, perhaps, is wholly satisfactory. The word connotes so much, the boundary line between it and religion is so hazy and indefinable, that it is almost impossible to tie it down and restrict it to the narrow limits of some neat turn of phrase that will hit it off and have done with it.' More recently, Gager ((above, n. 2) 24) asserts: ' ... it is our conviction that magic, as a definable and consistent category of human experience, simply does not exist.' Others could be quoted to like effect.

Intrepid souls have not been deterred. At various times scholars have explored the validity of a magic/religion distinction based on attempted compulsion vs. supplication of the divine; secret powers and knowledge vs. throwing oneself on the mercy of the gods; a system aiming at the achievement of immediate goals vs. more general spiritual satisfaction; absence or presence of some kind of theology; or private and individual vs. public and group practice. Exceptions can readily be found to any of these formulations. Magic too has its theology. Religion can be directed towards the attainment of practical goals, and it can appropriate many of the devices of magic.[56] There are groups of magicians who regard their activities as religious. Magic in early societies is ubiquitous in any case; even if magical acts are predominantly done by individuals, since they are done by practically all individuals it is futile to separate this activity out from the general religious consciousness of the public. There are, moreover, many private and individual religious acts. There are many parts of public religion that depend on a private practitioner performing ritual acts with no witnesses. Compulsion is often found in public religion, especially in such rites as public cursing, or the public use of voodoo dolls.[57] Compulsion, or at least the expectation of an obligation on the part of the deity in return for pious service, is still an element in modern religious feeling; it accounts for the instinctive outrage people feel on having Calvin's doctrine of predestination explained to them.

It being impossible to state one characteristic that magic always

---

[56] In *La Magie*, Graf (above, n. 2) devotes a chapter to the manifold interplay between magic and the mystery religions; the same connection allowed Smith to write his book *Jesus the Magician* (previous note), surely one of the few books by a classicist to have earned its author a death threat.

[57] C. Faraone, 'Binding and Burying the Forces of Evil: The Defensive Use of Voodoo Dolls', *CA* 10 (1991), 165–220; id., *Magika*, 9, with other examples of public magic.

has in all places as opposed to religion, several scholars have tried a different approach: magic does not differ in essence from religion; it differs only in the degree of social approval it enjoys, or does not enjoy.[58] This position is congenial to the one espoused in the present paper. Walter Burkert, in an illuminating article on the *goēs* ('sorcerer') in the Greek world,[59] traces the ambivalent status of this figure—often abused, but sometimes integral to the mainstream of religion, particularly in the various mysteries. His explanation for the origin of the *goēs'* bad reputation, however—that it began in the context of the Greek *polis*, which had the effect of clarifying and solidifying what was acceptable to the members of the society in the way of religion—needs a broader perspective, for all societies do this. Deprecation of magic is found already in the Old Testament.[60] 'Bad magic' vs. 'good (religiously sanctioned) magic' is a well-documented anthropological distinction. When Lucius in Apuleius' *Metamorphoses* (11. 15) was initiated into the mysteries of Isis, he became proof against black magic by virtue of the powers of the goddess; but when the world converted to Christianity, the rites of Isis became black magic in their turn.

In a word, one man's magic is another man's religion. In such circumstances the contexts in which denunciations of magic occur, and the criteria by which the denouncer hopes to persuade his peers that the charge is founded, become more interesting and revealing than what is actually called magic. In a similar way, the criteria for detecting quacks laid out in the treatise *On the Sacred Disease*, discussed earlier in this paper, are more important than the alternative theories advanced by the Hippocratic doctor, which are mostly bluff.[61] Or again, when Christianity was sweeping the pagan gods from the field, it is most instructive to see what kinds of sorcery were permitted in the new context, and why. The sign of the cross to this day will keep evil at bay.

[58] e.g. A. A. Goldenweiser, *Early Civilization* (New York, 1922), 348, quoted by the Waxes, 'Notion of Magic', 496; E. R. Goodenough, *Jewish Symbols of the Greco-Roman Period* (New York, 1953), ii. 159, quoted by Phillips, 'Sociology', 2729; Thomas, 'Anthropology', 92; Aune, 'Magic in Early Christianity', 1545; Phillips, 'Magic and Politics', 67; Luck, *Arcana Mundi*, 8; Betz, *Greek Magical Papyri*, xli; cf. Nock, *Essays*, i. 315; Graf, in *Magika*, 196; Versnel (above, n. 2).

[59] W. Burkert, 'ΓΟΗΣ. Zum griechischen "Schamanismus"', *RhM* 105 (1962), 36–55. On the term *magos* ('magus') see also Graf, *La Magie*, 31 ff. The very word, being foreign, designates the outsider.

[60] V. I. J. Flint, *The Rise of Magic in Early Medieval Europe* (Princeton, 1991), 18.

[61] G. E. R. Lloyd, *Magic, Reason and Experience*, 57.

ADDENDA

What was a revival has become a boom. Of recent bibliography I can give only a selection. M. Meyer and P. Mirecki have edited a volume of essays, *Ancient Magic and Ritual Power* (Leiden etc., 1995); another is forthcoming from R. Gordon, *Spells of Wisdom: Magical Power in the Graeco-Roman World*. Fritz Graf's book (n. 2) has been translated as *Magic in the Ancient World* (Cambridge, Mass., 1997). Peter Kingsley, *Ancient Philosophy, Mystery, and Magic: Empedocles and Pythagorean Tradition* (Oxford, 1995) contains much of interest. On magi and *mageia* (and magic/religion) see J. Bremmer, 'The Birth of the Term "Magic"', *ZPE* 126 (1999), 1–12. An issue of *Helios* (21.2, 1994) was devoted to magic. The study of the Greek magical papyri must now start from W. Brashear's exhaustive survey in *ANRW* 18.5 (1995), 3380–684. He supplies a huge list of works on the magic/religion problem at n. 353, and comments: 'Leaving questions of classification and interpretation aside, it should be noted that some practices that seem to us magical were regarded by the ancients as normal procedures of established religion—*haruspicium, augurium, auspicium*, hepatoscopy, ornithomancy, horoscopy and oracle questions— to name but a few.' The same author provides a helpful review article, 'Out of the Closet: Recent Corpora of Magical Texts' at *CP* 91 (1996), 372–83. Most recently, H. Versnel, 'An Essay on Anatomical Curses', in *Ansichten griechischer Rituale. Festschrift W. Burkert* (Stuttgart and Leipzig, 1998), 217–67, provides a typically thorough discussion of one category of curses, with full bibliography on many incidental topics. For the Orphic tablets mentioned on p. 320 see now Christoph Riedweg, 'Initiation—Tod—Unterwelt', ibid. 359–98, who usefully reprints at 389 ff. the texts so far published, with apparatus. The Epigraphic Bulletins in *Kernos* also refer to many works on magic.

Reading similar discussions of problems of definition in J. Hall, *Ethnic Identity in Greek Antiquity* (Cambridge, 1997), 19 ff. and M. S. Silk, *Tragedy and the Tragic: Greek Theatre and Beyond* (Oxford, 1996), 5, it occurs to me that a more fruitful approach would be to think in terms of clusters of characteristics rather than a single characteristic that defines magic; some of these are more apt to be present than others, but none needs always be present. The list of constituent elements in the cluster would be finite and describable. Such a model, like Wittgenstein's idea of family resemblances, enables one to recognize the members of a set without demanding that they all share a single identifier; it accounts for how members can lack key characteristics, and for how key characteristics can be found in non-members without the slightest possibility of misidentification. The clusters will differ from society to society; cross-cultural study would then inquire whether there is a finite list for all societies taken together, and what factors influence the make-up of the cluster in a given society. In all of this, however, the point about social disapproval remains valid. Magic is activity meant to achieve the goals of prevailing religion in ways disapproved by that religion.

My resistance to initiation as the (whole) explanation of many myths struck at least one reader as retrograde, while elsewhere it has been quoted with approval. As it happened, the rituals most suited to making my point that the role of magic is often overlooked were ones currently explained as initiatory; others might have been chosen. Even in the ones I discussed my resistance was not thoroughgoing, as should be clear from my treatment; the real point was that the balance between actor's and observer's categories had become too skewed in favour of the latter.

15
Misconceptualizing Classical Mythology

C. ROBERT PHILLIPS, III

> Whoever turns from work with Greek mythology to Roman mythology cannot long remain unaware that not only does he undertake an entirely different task, but also one which, in more ways than one, is much less profitable.
>
> (Ludwig Preller)

> Roman religion knows no sacred narratives [*hieroi logoi*], no gods' children and marriages, and no world of heroes which builds bridges between divinity and mortal. In a word—Roman religion has no mythology.
>
> (Georg Wissowa)

> Greece is a special case for the comparative mythologist. Being somehow the central reference point for mythology at large, Greek myth tends to carry disproportionate weight in any comparison.
>
> (Jaan Puhvel)

Pity not just the Romans, whose religion and alleged lack of mythology appeared wanting upon application of the Hellenic touchstone.[1] Pity the study of comparative religion, where the Hellenic

[1] I am grateful to the Greco-Roman Religions Group of the Society of Biblical Literature (Larry Alderink and John Helgeland, chairs) for the invitation to present some of the ideas expressed here at the 1989 meeting. The introductory quotes: L. Preller, *Römische Mythologie*, 2nd edn. (Berlin, 1865), 1; G. Wissowa, *Religion und Kultus der Römer*, 2nd edn. (Munich, 1912), 9 (Greek transliterated); Jaan Puhvel, *Comparative Mythology* (Baltimore, 1987), 126. I cite two of my publications as follows: ISO = 'In Search of the Occult: An Annotated Anthology', *Helios*, 15 (1988), 151–70, with editorial corrigenda in *Helios*, 16 (1989), 111; SRK = 'The Sociology of Religious Knowledge in the Roman Empire to A.D. 284', *ANRW* II.16.3, 2677–773. Compiling an

model still influences the conceptualization of mythology. An elderly, if not entirely venerable tradition for which K. O. Müller's enormously influential 1825 production, *Prolegomena zu einer wissenschaftlichen Mythologie*, set the stage; the title implies a general study of mythology but the treatise focuses almost exclusively upon Greek mythology.[2] How have the views of Müller and his epigonoi acquired their long-lasting dominance?

Early nineteenth-century scholars, Germans in particular, fascinated with defining mythology, brought two fundamental assumptions to their enterprise. First, the Enlightenment's favourite straw person, the *homo religiosus* of either primeval past or peasant present, a noble enough 'savage' but one who, through lack of mental ability, had to tell tales to produce theology. Evidence for a golden age, often relying heavily on classical traditions, confirmed her/his presence in times bygone. Further confirmation came from explorers' reports of the New World and studies made of the fraction of European lower orders dwelling in the country.[3] Second, the intelligentsia's conviction of the ineffably noble qualities of Hellenic culture directly influenced those classicists concerned to define mythology, thus ensuring that the evidence of Greek *homines religiosi* would become normative.[4] In consequence mythology received a definition based on fabulistic and Greek parameters; German scholars were largely responsible for the definition, and their country's

---

even tolerably adequate bibliography of this field would take place more fittingly in Tartarus, but the following will prove useful for the current endeavour: M. Detienne, *The Creation of Mythology*, trans. M. Cook (Chicago, 1986), esp. Ch. 1; P. Veyne, *Did the Greeks Believe in Their Myths?*, trans. P. Wissing (Chicago, 1988); W. G. Doty, *Mythography* (Tuscaloosa, 1986). For a superb study of my two themes of interest in folklore and interest in Greece see H. Gockel, *Mythos und Poesie* (Frankfurt, 1981); J. Z. Smith provides a valuable theoretical overview of the relations between anthropology and comparative religion in '*Adde parvum parvo magnus acervus erit*', *History of Religions* 11 (1971–2), 67–90 (= id., *Map Is Not Territory* (Leiden, 1978), 240–64).

[2] (Göttingen, 1825); cf. A. Momigliano, 'K. O. Müller's *Prolegomena zu einer wissenschaftlichen Mythologie* and the Meaning of Myth', in *Settimo contributo* . . . (Rome, 1984), 271–86; Puhvel, *Comparative Mythology*, 126, observed that Greek myth is 'somehow the central reference point for mythology at large'.

[3] Below, at nn. 5–10.

[4] J. Wohlleben, 'Beobachtungen über eine Nicht-Begegnung: Welcker und Goethe', and U. K. Goldsmith, 'Wilhelm von Humboldt: Mentor und Freund von Friedrich Gottlieb Welcker', in W. M. Calder *et al.* (eds.), *Friedrich Gottlieb Welcker, Werk und Wirkung* (Stuttgart, 1986 = *Hermes Einzelschriften* 49), 3–34 and 35–52 respectively with my 'Classical Scholarship Against Its History', *AJP* 110 (1989), 636–57; cf. below, nn. 21–8.

dominance in classical studies ensured a canonical status for a definition which scholars everywhere, from then until now, have contented themselves with expanding. I shall now consider each assumption in detail.

Initially, of course, reports of non-Western religions were simply dismissed as quaint curiosities at best, rude savagery at worst—in either case, the need for Christian missionaries appeared great.[5] The Enlightenment's anti-clerical agenda changed that. Concerned as it was to combat what it conceived to be mendacious clerical obscurantism, the apparently simpler life and religions of the erstwhile savages now seemed a golden age of the simplicity of human thought before Christianity had ruined it. The *philosophes* traced the parallels between the ethnographic material and Greco-Roman religions, combining the two into what they considered a powerful cudgel with which to smite Established Religion.[6] Moreover, one did not need to be a practising *philosophe* to appropriate the idea; William Smith remarked: ' . . . we Christians have as many idle ridiculous Notions and Customs as the Natives of *Guinea* have, if not more.'[7]

Thus the *philosophes* bequeathed to the nineteenth century a way to study non-Christian religions by way of 'mythologies.' Closer to home, the rationalizing Enlightenment had little further use for what it deemed the irrational tales spun by its lower orders. Hegel put it typically: 'How must a folk religion be constituted? (Here folk religion is understood objectively.) (*a*) In regard to objective religion. (*b*) In regard to rituals.'[8] But nationalistic considerations coupled with the rise of the Romantic interest in the irrational (precisely what the *philosophes* had scorned) produced a different view: 'The opposition of Enlightenment and Romantic turns into an ideological test: on the one side the total candor of rationality, on the other side the predilection for the mythic.'[9] Moreover, each nation sought to demonstrate its superior national character through collection and dissemination

---

[5] S. Neill, *A History of Christian Missions* (Baltimore, 1964), Chs. 5–7.

[6] For the period's view of religion, F. E. Manuel, *The Eighteenth Century Confronts the Gods* (New York, 1967). The best general introduction remains P. Gay, *The Enlightenment: An Interpretation. The Rise of Modern Paganism* (New York, 1977), esp. Ch. 4 on classical antiquity and Ch. 6 on Christianity; cf. my SRK, 2700 with n. 64.

[7] *A New Voyage to Guinea* . . . (London, 1744), 267.

[8] H. Nohl, *Hegels theologische Jugendschriften* (Tübingen, 1907), 20. [The quotation comes from the 'Tübingen Essay' of 1793; anglophones may wish to turn to the entire essay in Peter Fuss and John Dobbins (eds. and trans.), *Three Essays, 1793–1795 . . . by G. W. F. Hegel* (Notre Dame, 1984), 30–58.]

[9] Gockel, *Mythos und Poesie*, 16.

of its national folklore-mythologies. Of course there always had been interest in folklore and folksongs, but now they became more than a mere focus of nationalistic pride—they provided the bases for theorizing about religion and also the inspirations for all manner of artistic endeavour.[10] Although Arnim and Brentano's *Des Knaben Wunderhorn*, the collections of the Brothers Grimm, or the Ossian traditions all appear inauthentic from the modern ethnographic perspective, the crucial point here lies in the contemporary acceptance of these bodies of material.[11] The Grimms themselves collected, theorized, and maintained connections with other theorizers, thus ensuring the widespread dissemination of evidence and paradigm.[12]

[10] e.g. the long tradition of such studies in Germany: J. Meier, 'Deutsche und niederländische Volkspoesie', in H. Paul (ed.), *Grundriss der germanischen Philologie* (Strasbourg, 1893) 2.1, 750–860. German folksong: *The New Grove Dictionary of Music and Musicians*, vii. 287–9. The influence of Arnim and Brentano's *Des Knaben Wunderhorn* (next note) on Mahler is famous: D. Mitchell, *Gustav Mahler. The Wunderhorn Years* (Boulder, Colo., 1976) and K. von Fischer, 'Gustav Mahlers Umgang mit Wunderhorntexten', *Melos*, 4 (1978), 103–7—with my thanks to Professor Nadine Sine (Dept. of Music, Lehigh University) for bibliographic orientation. Again, a poet such as Eichendorff could write in a folk/mythological/medieval style (on which see Gockel, *Mythos und Poesie*, 336–7) and see his verse set to music in Robert Schumann's *Liederkreis* Op. 39. For England, R. M. Dorson, *The British Folklorists* (Chicago, 1968); the influence on British fine arts is much less obvious, but cf. E. D. Snyder, *The Celtic Revival in English Literature 1760–1800* (Cambridge, Mass., 1923), H. Trevor-Roper, 'The Invention of Tradition: The Highland Tradition of Scotland', and P. Morgan, 'From a Death to a View: The Hunt for the Welsh Past in the Romantic Period', both in E. Hobsbawm and T. Ranger (eds.), *The Invention of Tradition* (Cambridge, 1983), 15–41 and 43–100 respectively. For the changed attitude to folklore and its contemporary influence, my SRK 2702, n. 73.

[11] For the composition and sources of the *Wunderhorn*, Clemens Brentano, *Sämtliche Werke und Briefe* (Stuttgart, 1975), 17–40. The Grimms: J. M. Ellis, *One Fairy Story Too Many* (Chicago, 1983), with my thanks to the author for additional information; for the relations, R. Steig, *Clemens Brentano und die Brüder Grimm* (Stuttgart, 1914) and next note. Ossian: Snyder, *Celtic Revival*, A. Gillies, *Herder und Ossian* (Berlin, 1933) and cf. Gruppe (next note), 99–103. Another prime example of theorizing relying on a compromised evidence base is Wilhelm Mannhardt: *Germanische Mythen* (Berlin, 1858), *Die Götterwelt der deutschen und nordischen Völker* (Berlin, 1860), *Der Baumkultus der Germanen und ihre Nachbarstämme* (Berlin, 1875), *Antike Wald- und Feldkulte* (Berlin, 1877). Nevertheless, he accomplished much—cf. de Vries (next note), i. 55–6. Fundamental was his (and others') notion that early evidence continued embedded in folk traditions—on this 'doctrine of survivals' see M. T. Hodgen, *The Doctrine of Survivals* (London, 1936).

[12] O. Gruppe, *Geschichte der klassischen Mythologie und Religionsgeschichte* (Leipzig, 1921 = Suppl. 4 to Roscher's *Lexicon*), 154–66; the entire treatise documents the interconnections, with p. 96 onwards of most relevance here; J. de Vries, *Altgermanische Religionsgeschichte* (Berlin, 1956), i. 50–82, with 50–4 on the Grimms. The study has since proceeded rather differently: P. Buchholz, 'Perspectives for Historical Research in Germanic Religion', *History of Religions*, 8 (1968–9), 111–38.

British folklorists were active but accomplished less since Oxbridge
was to remain academically somnolent until the various university
reforms of mid-century—this in contrast to the mighty German university combine.[13]

The rise of anthropology concurrent with Darwin's work on evolution mid-century and the Oxbridge university reform commissions
decisively altered British activity. There had been discussion of evolution in previous centuries, but it remained little more than an intellectual curiosity.[14] Now that Darwin had apparently 'scientifically'
demonstrated its existence, scholars quickly applied the concept of
species evolution to societal phenomena.[15] In consequence the erstwhile 'noble' folk religions seemed to have lost their virtues—at best
they were magical gropings towards either science or real religion
and theology, depending on the investigator's interpretative agenda.[16]
The outcry for 'the endowment of research' then sweeping the British Isles enabled all this work—it was initially a ploy to counter
German technology but soon became an out-and-out competition in
all areas of intellectual endeavour.[17] Nationalism also appeared in
another guise. The British extensively used comparative ethnographic material coming from their far-flung colonial empire while
the Germans, lacking a comparably large empire and consequent
source of data, busied themselves in national traditions while

---

[13] On which see my ISO, 152–6, and 'Classical Scholarship . . . ' (n. 4), 639–40; in
general, for Oxford, A. J. Engel, *From Clergyman to Don* (Oxford, 1983); for Cambridge,
Sheldon Rothblatt, *The Revolution of the Dons* (London, 1968), D. A. Winstanley, *Early
Victorian Cambridge* (Cambridge, 1940) and id., *Later Victorian Cambridge* (Cambridge,
1947).

[14] Notably by Auguste Comte; cf. J. S. Preus, *Explaining Religion* (New Haven, 1987),
107–30, with H. Penner's review, *Journal of the American Academy of Religion*, 57
(1989), 173–80.

[15] On the importance of Darwin for the academic study of religion, E. J. Sharpe,
Comparative Religion (New York, 1975), 47–71, my ISO, 152–4, and SRK, 2686–8 and
2722–4.

[16] Previous note and '*Nullum crimen sine lege*: Socioreligious Sanctions on Magic',
in *Magika*, 260–76. In general, K. Rosengren, 'Malinowski's Magic: The Riddle of the
Empty Cell', *Current Anthropology*, 17 (1976), 667–85, J. Z. Smith, 'Towards Interpreting Demonic Powers in Hellenistic and Roman Antiquity', *ANRW* II.16.1, 425–39; for
modern approaches to the problem of defining 'magic' (which I call 'unsanctioned
religious activity'—cf. my ISO and '*Nullum* . . . ' *passim*); cf. B. R. Wilson (ed.), *Rationality* (Oxford, 1979), esp. I. C. Jarvie and J. Agassi, 'The Problem of the Rationality of
Magic', 172–93, and J. M. Beattie, 'On Understanding Ritual', 240–68; cf. the response
of Jarvie and Agassi: 'Magic and Rationality Again', *Brit. Jour. of Sociology* 24 (1973),
236–45. [Cf. also R. L. Fowler, this volume, 317–43.]

[17] See n. 13; cf. Engel (ibid.), Chs. 3 and 4.

simultaneously criticizing the British enterprise.[18] But all concurred that the study of a religion had to begin with its 'primitive' roots, namely its mythologies. There existed a direct connection with classical studies, since many of the theorizers were either classicists or maintained close connections with classicists.[19] Christianity, incidentally, remained exempt. The Enlightenment had not done much more than advocate deism and orate about the 'treason of the clerics' since it felt that too much was known about the apparent monstrosity, while the nineteenth century, somewhat reversing the position, felt Christianity to be privileged: 'Christianity in its pure form is not a religion alongside other religions, but is The Religion. Yet it is The Religion, because Jesus Christ is not a master alongside other masters, but is The Master.'[20] Thus the legacy of the *homo religiosus.*

The second consideration, the dominance of the Hellenic over the minds of the intelligentsia, also centres on Germany. Goethe, Humboldt, and Schlegel, among others, made strong claims for the resonance between the Hellenic spirit and the Teutonic spirit, constructing

[18] e.g. on India, P. J. Marshall (ed.), *The British Discovery of Hinduism in the Eighteenth Century* (Cambridge, 1970). Those on the scene did not always share the enthusiasm of those at home; Macaulay's famous 'minute' of 2 Feb. 1835 is a classic example of hostility to Indian culture and the Sanskrit language ('fruitful of monstrous superstitions'); cf. C. Hibbert, *The Great Mutiny* (Harmondsworth, 1980), 23–58, and P. Woodruff, *The Men Who Ruled India: The Founders of Modern India* (New York, 1954), 248–65 and 279–305. Cf. Charles Hose and William McDougall, *The Pagan Tribes of Borneo*, 2 vols. (London, 1912)—Hose (preface, 5) spent twenty-four years as a civil officer in the service of the Rajah of Sarawak. Andrew Lang, *Modern Mythology* (London, 1897), 92: 'In all that we say of totemism, as later, of fetishism, we rely on an enormous mass of evidence from geographers, historians, travellers, settlers, missionaries, explorers, traders, Civil Servants, and European officers of the native police in Australia and Burmah [*sic.*]' In general my SRK, 2685–7, and R. Symonds, *Oxford and Empire* (London, 1986). Derision: G. Wissowa commented that *The Golden Bough* did not offer 'anything essential for understanding Roman religion' (*Religion und Kultus*, 248 n. 3, but cf. 104 n. 3, and 121 n. 4), while S. Wide in discussing studies of Greek religion praised the ethnographic material but prefaced it curiously: 'Mannhardt's conceptions gain respect thanks to Frazer, but for the most part Mannhardt collected the folklore material with which Frazer works. . .' ('Griechische und römische Religion' in A. Gercke and E. Norden (eds.), *Einleitung in die Altertumswissenschaft* (Leipzig and Berlin, 1910), ii. 252.

[19] Thus J. Görres (in Gruppe, *Geschichte*, 133–7), O. Gruppe (in de Vries, *Altgerm. Religionsgesch.*, 60–1), and later J. G. Frazer, on whom see my 'Classical Scholarship . . .' (n. 4), 644–50.

[20] A. Harnack, *Die Aufgabe der theologischen Facultäten und die allgemeine Religionsgeschichte*, 2nd edn. (Giessen, 1901), 16; cf. J. G. Gager, *Kingdom and Community* (Englewood Cliffs, NJ, 1975), 4–9, and W. G. Kümmel, *The New Testament: The History of the Investigation of Its Problems*, trans. S. M. Gilmour and H. C. Kee (Nashville, 1972).

in consequence a *Neuhumanismus*.[21] In modern terms: 'For this Greek-Icon contains everything which endangers the contemporary intellect's self-cultivation, or already seems wholly inappropriate. The contemporary mind was itself projected back into a rather arbitrary ideal of an imaginary historical past.'[22] And yet this activity relied on 'Griechen-Dilettantismus'—the image of Greece that was to influence so much of nineteenth-century German classical scholarship, and moreover continue to exert an influence even today, arose from a non-philological, rather emotional base.[23] German classicists either theorized or had close personal ties to the theorizers and thus for all their claims to 'scientific' methodology devoted themselves to explicating a model both scientific (as they used the word) and created by others.[24] The concurrent rise of Sanskrit studies furthered this, as the Vedic material apparently confirmed previous theorizing about the mythologies and at last gave the Germans some non-Western comparative material.[25] Of course, Greek religion and

---

[21] Essential background: C. Diehl, *Americans and German Scholarship 1770–1870* (New Haven, 1978), Chs. 1 and 2; cf. B. Bravo, *Philologie, histoire, philosophie de l'histoire* (Warsaw, 1968), Ch. 2, H. Flashar *et al.* (eds.), *Philologie und Hermeneutik im 19. Jahrhundert* (Göttingen, 1979), A. Grafton, 'Polyhistor into Philolog: Notes on the Transformation of German Classical Scholarship, 1780–1850', *History of Universities*, 3 (1983), 159–92. Useful selection of relevant texts in B. Feldman and R. D. Richardson, *The Rise of Modern Mythology 1680–1860* (Bloomington, 1972) esp. parts two and three. And, of course, scholars could react to those figures in different ways; thus for Welcker, A. Henrichs, 'Welckers Götterlehre', in Calder, *Friedrich Gottlieb Welcker*, 194: 'In opposition to Humboldt's ideal of unity, which was obtained on the basis of individual ethical self-cultivation, indeed Welcker's emphasis lay clearly in the direction of the romantic conception of knowledge, which sought to plumb the Folk-Essence (or Folk-Soul), and this from all the instances when it appeared as a historical reality; thus the object of his inquiry displaced the subject.' Cf. Goldsmith, 'Wilhelm von Humboldt', 48–52, esp. 49 n. 38, and Wohlleben, 'Welcker und Goethe', 4–6, both in Calder ibid.

[22] Wohlleben, (n. 4), 19; cf. Goldsmith (n. 4), 36–41. [I append for this reprinting a brief gloss on the quotation, since it now appears riddling in context. Neohumanism originally accompanied a liberal political agenda. Shortly thereafter, state control of the universities and their tasks intervened—the erstwhile liberal politics were consigned to the Hellenic past, while the aesthetics of neohumanism, apparently politically harmless, became the basis of state-supported university research. Cf. Marchand (Addenda) 34–5, 39–40.]

[23] Wohlleben (n. 4), 12–14; cf. Diehl, *Americans*, 15–18.

[24] Gruppe (n. 12, *passim*, and n. 19) and Diehl, *Americans*, 15–18.

[25] In general, Raymond Schwab, *The Oriental Renaissance*, trans. G. Patterson-Black and V. Reinking (New York, 1984), esp. 21–128 and Gruppe (n. 12), 172–93. In particular, the activities of Max Müller: J. M. Kitagawa and J. C. Strong, 'Friedrich Max Müller and the Comparative Study of Religion', in N. Smart *et al.* (eds.), *Nineteenth Century Religious Thought in the West* (Cambridge, 1985), iii. 179–213, with 187–8 on the controversy with the evolutionist Lang; H. Lloyd-Jones, *Blood for the Ghosts*

mythology were considered to have had 'primitive' sides, but on the evidence of early allegorizers (Xenophanes, Theagenes of Rhegium), Plato, and the reception of Homer into the Neoplatonic tradition the Greeks and their religion had evolved rapidly even by the time of the Homeric poems.[26] Studies proceeded in two related yet divergent directions, starting from the base Wolf and others had established that language constituted the key to understanding a people.[27] Some scholars busied themselves with strictly linguistic and philological concerns although reverencing the principle of *Neuhumanismus*. Others such as F. G. Welcker did not merely reverence it but focused upon it, valuing philology in its own right but seeking by means of that philology to demonstrate further the correctness of *Neuhumanismus*. As for Welcker: 'Thus it is not a scholarly ideal which dominated Welcker, but an ideal of cultivation, to grasp as much as possible the spirit of antiquity and to wed it with his own time's national spirit as well as with the Christian tradition in the West. In this context, the individual bit of knowledge gained by philology contains only secondary value.'[28] Scholars variously evaluated the Greek mythologies in consequence. Creuzer saw Greek popular religion as superficial because of its connection with poetry and the plastic arts; at the same time he believed that religious specialists had also produced a profound, esoteric pantheism.[29] Welcker studied precisely what Creuzer deemed superficial and saw its study as the means to recover

---

(London, 1982), 155–64; G. Stocking, *Victorian Anthropology* (New York, 1987), 56–62. E. Tylor, *Researches into the Early History of Mankind and the Development of Civilisation*, 2nd edn. (London, 1870), 153, felt that Müller had found the 'key' to Indo-European mythology.

[26] R. Pfeiffer, *History of Classical Scholarship* (Oxford, 1968), 8–11; E. Havelock, *Preface to Plato* (Cambridge, Mass., 1963); R. Lamberton, *Homer the Theologian* (Berkeley and Los Angeles, 1986).

[27] Goldsmith (n. 4), 41–2; cf. Diehl, *Americans*, 14–15, and for Wolf, the edition of his *Prolegomena* by A. Grafton *et al.* (Princeton, 1985), 3–35 and 249–54. The rise of Sanskrit studies neatly coincided: Schwab, *Oriental Renaissance*, and Sebastiano Timpanaro, 'Friedrich Schlegel and the Beginnings of Indo-European Linguistics in Germany' in Friedrich Schlegel, *Über die Sprache und die Weisheit der Indier*, ed. E. F. K. Koerner (Amsterdam, 1977), pp. xi–lvii.

[28] G. Pflug, 'Friedrich Gottlieb Welcker und die Entwicklung der klassischen Philologie im 19. Jahrhundert', in Calder, *Friedrich Gottlieb Welcker*, 265.

[29] In general, B. Bravo, 'Dieu et les dieux chez F. Creuzer et F. G. Welcker', *History and Anthropology*, 3 (1987), 263–301.

a Greek 'church'.[30] Nevertheless, many contemporaries could not
forget the alleged 'primitive' background of Greek religion and consequently castigated Welcker's attempts to find order in it: 'Also here
the great scholar has constructed and philosophized too much,
although he often saw the correct solution.'[31]

The German view of philologically interesting mythologies pregnant with sophisticated ideas proved uncommonly congenial to the
British. For example, the Cambridge ritualists took the same comparative evolutionary schemes which had previously worked to the
detriment of the study of early religious mythologies and turned
them to the advantage of Greek religion: the Greek mythologies, as
defined by the Germans, now made sense of the rituals, and vice
versa, while they incidentally provided a way to devalue ·Roman
religion.[32] Durkheim's theorizing allowed further ramifications, particularly since it encouraged the functionalist view that mythologies
by definition had to have some clearly defined role in society.[33] Like
the Germans, the British too felt kindred spirits in the alleged Hellenic
world-view.[34] The long-term results of all this have been insidious for
the study of ancient religion, classical studies generally, and the
study of world religion.

The study of Greek religion has suffered in consequence from a
peculiar dichotomy. Some have studied the mythologies without

[30] Bravo, 'Dieu et les dieux', 287–98. Examples from Welcker's *Griechische
Götterlehre*, 3 vols. (Göttingen, 1857, 1860, 1862): Welcker's Christianity: i. 83, 218,
256–60; Greek religion anticipates Christianity: i. 255–7; idea of a Greek 'church':
i. 106, 123–4; influence of the plastic arts: ii. 101–27.

[31] O. Kern, *Die Religion der Griechen*, 2nd edn. (Berlin, 1963), iii. 295.

[32] On the background W. Burkert, 'Griechische Mythologie und die Geistesgeschichte der Moderne', in *Les Études classiques aux XIXᵉ et XXᵉ siècles: leur place dans
l'histoire des idées* (Vandœuvres-Geneva, 1980 = Fondation Hardt, 26), 172–82, and cf.
a contemporary view of the use of comparative material, Andrew Lang, *Modern
Mythology* (London, 1897), p. xx: 'They have thrown new light on Greek mythology,
ritual, mysteries, and religion.' The group included Cook, Cornford, Harrison and
Murray; cf. S. J. Peacock, *Jane Ellen Harrison* (New Haven, 1988), Chs. 5–7, with bibliography at 248 n. 3, and D. Wilson, *Gilbert Murray OM* (Oxford, 1987), 153–6. Opposition to Frazer: A. B. Cook rev. of J. G. Frazer, *The Golden Bough*, CR 13 (1902), 365–80.
In general, William M. Calder III (ed.), *The Cambridge Ritualists Reconsidered* (Atlanta,
1991 = *Illinois Studies in the History of Classical Scholarship*, 1). For Roman religion,
below at nn. 39–42.

[33] Thus the preface to J. Harrison, *Themis*, 2nd edn. (Cambridge, 1927); cf. P. Q.
Hirst, *Durkheim, Bernard and Epistemology* (New York, 1975), and Sir Edmund Leach,
'Anthropology of Religion: British and French Schools', in Smart, *Nineteenth Century
Religious Thought*, 245–8.

[34] R. Jenkyns, *The Victorians and Ancient Greece* (Cambridge, Mass., 1980), 174–91;
F. M. Turner, *The Greek Heritage in Victorian Britain* (New Haven, 1981), 77–134.

reference to the religion, producing untenable results which border on the ludicrous.[35] Others continue the functionalist and evolutionist paradigm of Durkheim and the Cambridge Ritualists.[36] Others, more sophisticated, such as Burkert, have yoked studies of mythology to religion, but unfortunately have not questioned the conceptual validity of what they utilize as mythologies.[37] Luckily, some scholars then and now have been willing to question the traditions which led both to the dichotomy of Greek religion and Greek mythology and to the heuristically dubious ways those areas have received study: 'Here religion and myth are interwoven with countless threads—it is the task of the Science of Religion to disentangle them and thus to clarify their interrelation.'[38]

The putative primacy of Greek mythology has virtually ruined the study of Roman religion—since the Romans lacked mythology of the Hellenic variety, specialists have assumed either the Romans apparently either had no mythology or else had one notably lacking in comparison to the Greeks. This article's introductory quotes by Preller and Wissowa make the case, while more recently Latte observed 'the absence of . . . mythology and all genealogical connection of the gods'.[39] Again, Michael Grant noted the 'peculiar sort of aridity' of the Roman mythological imagination and most recently Nicholas Horsfall observed, 'But the survival of stories about ghosts and werewolves . . . is one thing, that of myths is quite another.'[40] All of this supported the notion of 'cult acts without belief' for Roman religion, with the unfortunate consequence of doing the nineteenth

[35] Structuralist studies are prime offenders: see the criticism below, n. 46.

[36] Vernant, MT. For the problems with functionalism, Penner (n. 14) and 'The Poverty of Functionalism', History of Religions, 11 (1971–2), 91–7.

[37] Below, n. 46. This is not to denigrate Burkert's immensely valuable contributions, on which see L. Alderink, 'Greek and Ritual Mythology: The Work of Walter Burkert', RSR 6 (1980), 1–13.

[38] Nilsson, GGR, 14, but contrast Veyne, Did the Greeks Believe in their Myths?, 17–26; cf. Detienne, The Creation of Mythology, J. Bremmer, 'What is a Greek Myth?', in id., (ed.), Interpretations of Greek Mythology (London, 1987), 1–9, and J. Gould, 'On Making Sense of Greek Religion', in P. E. Easterling and J. V. Muir (eds.), Greek Religion and Society (Cambridge, 1985), 1–33. For a particular divinity, P. McGinty, 'Dionysos's Revenge and the Validation of the Hellenic World-View', HTR 71 (1978), 77–94, and id., Interpretation and Dionysos (The Hague, 1978).

[39] K. Latte, Römische Religionsgeschichte (Munich, 1960), 62; compare the strong statement of Greek 'belief' in Müller (n. 2), ch. 12—note the emphasis on 'Einheit' and 'Glaube'.

[40] M. Grant, Roman Myths (New York, 1971), 219; N. M. Horsfall, 'Myth and Mythography at Rome', in J. N. Bremmer and N. M. Horsfall, Roman Myth and Mythography (London, 1987 = BICS Suppl. 52), 2.

century one better (or worse).[41] The alleged savages could not think clearly about religion and hence used mythologies. Since the Romans had no mythologies, their thinking was, in consequence, even worse. 'Dumézil has sought to recover Roman mythology through examining the Roman evidence in context of his tripartite scheme, one which, unfortunately, still evokes the normative Hellenic view.'[42] Emphasis on Hellenic-defined mythologies has caused problems in other areas of classical studies. Consider ancient history. If mythology was as important for Greece as many claim, what to make of Thucydides' relatively infrequent mentions? Was it really unimportant or unimportant only in his estimation?[43] If mythologies generally have the very high information content that some would claim (the structuralists come to mind), their absence seems rather odd. But perhaps one should not speak of mythology at all, particularly in historical contexts; the term would better be religious adherence, i.e. rituals devolving upon particular divinities and narratives associated with those divinities as functions of time and place.[44] The relation of Roman religion and politics has fared particularly badly. By comparison with the Hellenic model the Romans allegedly lacked mythology and hence real religion, substituting a series of mindless cult acts which the socioeconomic elite manipulated for its own cynical ends, particularly in the later Republic.[45] This will not do.

---

[41] This is implicit in the Enlightenment position so aptly summarized by Hegel (n. 8); cf. my SRK, III.A with 2697 n. 56.

[42] C. S. Littleton, *The New Comparative Mythology*, 3rd edn. (Berkeley and Los Angeles, 1982), 186–203; A. Momigliano, 'Georges Dumézil and the Trifunctional Approach to Roman Civilization', *History and Theory*, 23 (1984), 312–30. For some specific comments on his view of Roman religion, A. K. Michels, 'Early Roman Religion, 1945–1952', *CW* 48 (1954–5), 30–4. [I am glad to correct here a misstatement of Dumézil, which Mary Beard has kindly pointed out in her 'Looking (Harder) . . .' (see Addenda), 48 n. 9.]

[43] S. Hornblower, *Thucydides* (Baltimore, 1987), 86–7 and 182–3 with bibliography at n. 89. I would generally take Thucydidean evidence as decisive *pace* e.g. R. Meiggs, *The Athenian Empire* (Oxford, 1972). I owe this position, among others, to the distinguished Greek historian George Cawkwell.

[44] For spatial problems, J. Z. Smith, *To Take Place* (Chicago, 1987). Of course there is the immense problem of balancing the synchronic and diachronic: M. Sahlins, *Islands of History* (Chicago, 1985). Cf. my renaming magic as 'unsanctioned religious activity' in my 'Nullum . . .' (n. 16).

[45] Traditional view: L. R. Taylor, *Party Politics in the Age of Caesar* (Berkeley and Los Angeles, 1949), 76–97. But compare the strong criticism in H. D. Jocelyn, 'The Roman Nobility and the Religion of the Republican State', *Journal of Religious History*, 4 (1966–7), 89–104. Bibliographic and source details in my SRK, 2692 n. 43.

Studies of Greco-Roman literature have been infected too. Alleged mythologies have either been isolated as literary topoi, or else considered to be pregnant with literary meaning. The former gives them insufficient credit, while the latter implies too much, absent an integrated view of 'religion' and 'mythology'.[46] As for the arts, the case of Greek vase painting is instructive. The imposing figure of Sir John Beazley still continues to dominate the methodology of the study. That methodology is a kind of aesthetic empiricism, concerned to assign vases to painters and schools by means of both aesthetic minutiae and comparison of treatment of different themes, an 'implicit assurance to his followers that they were playing aesthetic games of style with the best.'[47] Obviously this has meant emphasis on the style and technique of mythic and religious scenes, an emphasis which has seldom gone much beyond noting variant depictions. And what of the significance of the apparent parodies of phlyax vases?[48] In short, throughout the study of classical antiquity the traditional conception of 'Greek mythology' occasions problems.

It requires little effort to see the deleterious effects on the study of world religion, a kind of comparativism run amok. It is bad enough to force the culturally-defined patterns of Greek belief onto often radically different cultures.[49] It is far worse to do so when the whole

---

[46] I regret that for Greek literature I must single out a study by my erstwhile mentor: C. P. Segal, *Tragedy and Civilization. An Interpretation of Sophocles* (Cambridge, Mass., 1981). A deeply learned work, replete with important literary insights—and yet Segal's view of mythology compromises his points. First, he treats it as almost totally divorced from Greek religion. Second, he then interprets it by means of structuralism which not only compromises further its relations with religion, but which does not constitute an adequate interpretative strategy even if one will (mistakenly, in my view) interpret myth by itself. For the problems with structuralism, Burkert, *SH*, 5–14, and M. Heath, *CR* 33 (1983), 68–9. As for Latin literature, consider Ovid's *Metamorphoses* and *Fasti*. In both cases the majority of studies have emphasized the literary reworking of Greek models with scant attention to religious concerns—the overemphasis on Callimachus has only worsened matters. See my 'Rethinking Augustan Poetry', *Latomus*, 62 (1983), 780–818, and 'Roman Religion and Literary Studies of Ovid's *Fasti*', *Arethusa*, 25 (1992), 55–80.

[47] M. Beard, *TLS*, 12 Sept. 1986, 1013.

[48] A. D. Trendall, *Phlyax Vases*, 2nd edn. (London, 1967 = BICS Suppl. 19), 15–17.

[49] Precisely what psychoanalytic interpretation has attempted, the worse when those of its precepts wrongly derived from Greek traditions are then used to interpret those traditions. On this point see B. M. W. Knox, rev. of G. Devereux, *Dreams in Greek Tragedy*, *TLS*, 10 Dec. 1976, 1534–5. For the problems with Freudian theory, my *SRK*, 2695 n. 49, and B. A. Farrell, *The Standing of Psychoanalysis* (Oxford, 1981). I omit Jungian theory as unworthy of serious intellectual attention.

methodology is suspect. Even the methodologically sophisticated Joseph Kitagawa could remark: 'Thus the classical religions retained the language of myth, but speculative inquiry into causal principles and universal laws was no longer inhibited and stultified completely by the mythic mode of thinking.'[50] Put differently and obviously, the world religions do not, unfortunately, know about the Greek model.[51]

Greek mythology, then, was sought, defined, and studied in ways which, while then respectable and valuable, have outlived their utility. That which has been rent asunder should be reunited— narratives of interactions between ordinary mortals and extraordinary beings, and the traditions of the latter, should be taken as an integral part of the way the Greeks made sense of the anomic, related to those things they considered apart from ordinary reality, and legitimated their own secular arrangements.[52] No theory can be taken as forever canonic and the case of Greek mythology is long overdue for a new paradigm.[53]

ADDENDA

History of Scholarship

Suzanne Marchand, *Down From Olympus. Archaeology and Philhellenism in Germany, 1750–1970* (Princeton, 1996) gives detailed discussion of issues I sketched but briefly. Renate Schlesier, *Kulte, Mythen*

---

[50] 'Primitive, Classical, and Modern Religions: A Perspective on Understanding the History of Religions', in id., *The History of Religions* (Atlanta, 1987), 36. Compare R. Needham, *Belief, Language, and Experience* (Oxford, 1972), 179, summarizing the nineteenth-century view: 'As for savages, they were characteristically sunk in ignorance and pathetic incapacities of reason, their imaginations imbued with magical prejudices and their rational faculties stunted for lack of occasion, at best, to elaborate the critical concepts of empirical cosmology.' Further discussion ibid. 176–246.

[51] Puhvel, *Comparative Mythology*, represents a notable exception. Even the idea of a common Indo-European system could cause mischief; thus I am uneasy about the implications of B. Lincoln, *Myth, Cosmos, and Society* (Cambridge, Mass., 1986).

[52] For this definition of religion see my ISO, 159–61, and, in general, P. Berger, *The Sacred Canopy* (New York, 1967), with critiques in my SRK, 2694 n. 47, and M. Spiro, 'Religion: Problems of Definition and Explanation', in M. Banton (ed.), *Anthropological Approaches to the Study of Religion* (New York, 1966), 85–126, and id., *Burmese Supernaturalism*, expanded edn. (Philadelphia, 1978), pp. xii–xxx.

[53] I thus reject the empiricist notion of the immutable truth of a theory promulgated by allegedly 'scientific' methods—see my SRK, 2681–97, and '*Quae per squalidas transiere personas*: Ste. Croix's Historical Revolution', *Helios*, 11.1 (1984), 53–6.

und Gelehrte. Anthropologie der Antike seit 1800 (Frankfurt, 1994) collects ten of her previously published essays, all of which command attention here. Robert Segal (ed.), *The Myth and Ritual Theory* (Oxford, 1998) offers a wide-ranging anthology of texts with valuable introductory material.

Greek Myth

Richard Buxton, *Imaginary Greece: The Contexts of Mythology* (Cambridge, 1994); methodological eclecticism successfully transcends the (inevitable) limitations of any one method—cf. my review in *Method and Theory in the Study of Religion*, 9 (1997), 171–8. Fritz Graf, *Greek Mythology*, trans. T. Marier (Princeton, 1993); the first two chapters discuss the history of the study of Hellenic myth, with p. 22 paralleling my own view of Greek myth's normative tradition. I now feel more optimistic about myth and Greek literature than when I wrote n. 46, and this as the result of Christopher Pelling (ed.), *Greek Tragedy and the Historian* (Oxford, 1997). Note especially in this remarkable volume Robert Parker, 'Gods Cruel and Kind: Tragedy and Civic Theology' (143–60), and Christiane Sourvinou-Inwood, 'Tragedy and Religion: Constructs and Readings' (161–86).

Roman Myth

Fritz Graf (ed.), *Mythos in mythenloser Gesellschaft. Das Paradigma Roms* (Stuttgart and Leipzig, 1993) has a useful collection of individual essays; see especially Mary Beard, 'Looking (Harder) for Roman Myth: Dumézil, Declamation and the Problems of Definition', 44–64. No one should miss Andreas Bendlin's review, *JRS* 85 (1995), 265–6, which sketches a powerful and persuasive view of Roman myth. Denis Feeney, *Literature and Religion at Rome* (Cambridge, 1998) accomplishes a remarkable amount in less than 200 pages; chapters one, two, and four treat, respectively, belief, myth, and ritual.

T. P. Wiseman reviewed Bremmer and Horsfall (above, n. 40) at length in *JRS* 79 (1989), 129–37; expanded to answer Horsfall's reaction to the original review in id., *Historiography and Imagination. Eight Essays on Roman Culture* (Exeter, 1994), 23–36. My 'Walter Burkert in partibus Romanorum', forthcoming in *Religion*, considers several issues surrounding Roman myth. All who would deal with Roman religion must now consider Mary Beard, John North, and Simon Price, *Religions of Rome* (Cambridge, 1998), 2 vols.; cf. my review

article, which includes discussion of Feeney (above), forthcoming in
Religious Studies Review. Finally, I should like to draw attention to
D.H., *Ant. Rom.* 2. 19 and the comment in Emilio Gabba, *Dionysius and
'The History of Archaic Rome'* (Berkeley, 1991), 120: ' . . . the
thoughts of Dionysius in this section represent the first and almost
unique example in antiquity of the realization that Roman religion
was substantially lacking in myth.' I rest my case.

DETAILS OF ORIGINAL PUBLICATION

In the case of all but three contributions (those by W. R. Connor, J.-P. Vernant, and U. Sinn), the authors have revised their original papers for the present volume of *Oxford Readings* so as to incorporate corrections, additions, and/or a section of 'Addenda'. The chapter by F. van Straten appears for the first time with illustrations, and that by F. Graf appears for the first time in English translation.

1 Christiane Sourvinou-Inwood, 'What is *Polis* Religion?', in Oswyn Murray and Simon Price (eds.), *The Greek City From Homer to Alexander* (Oxford: Oxford University Press, 1990), 295–322.

2 Christiane Sourvinou-Inwood, 'Further Aspects of *Polis* Religion', in *Annali dell' Istituto Universitario Orientale di Napoli, Sezione di Archeologia e Storia Antica*, 10 (1988), 259–74.

3 W. R. Connor, 'Tribes, Festivals and Processions; Civic Ceremonial and Political Manipulation in Archaic Greece', in *Journal of Hellenic Studies*, 107 (1987), 40–50.

4 Robert Parker, 'Greek States and Greek Oracles', in P. A. Cartledge and F. D. Harvey (eds.), *Crux: Essays Presented to G. E. M. de Ste. Croix on his 75th Birthday* (Exeter: Imprint Academic, 1985), 298–326.

5 J.-P. Vernant, 'From Oedipus to Periander: Lameness, Tyranny, Incest in Legend and History', in *Arethusa*, 15 (1982), 19–38.

6 Susan Guettel Cole, 'Demeter in the Ancient Greek City and its Countryside', in Susan E. Alcock and Robin Osborne (eds.), *Placing the Gods: Sanctuaries and Sacred Space in Ancient Greece* (Oxford: Oxford University Press, 1994), 199–216.

7 Ulrich Sinn, 'Greek Sanctuaries as Places of Refuge', in Nanno Marinatos and Robin Hägg (eds.), *Greek Sanctuaries: New Approaches* (London: Routledge, 1993), 88–109.

8 Anthony Snodgrass, 'The Archaeology of the Hero', in *Annali dell' Istituto Universitario Orientale di Napoli, Sezione di Archeologia e Storia Antica*, 10 (1988), 19–26.

9   Folkert van Straten, 'Votives and Votaries in Greek Sanctuaries', in A. Schachter (ed.), *Entretiens Fondation Hardt: Le Sanctuaire grec* (Vandoeuvres-Geneva, 1992), 247–84.

10 Walter Burkert, 'Jason, Hypsipyle, and New Fire at Lemnos. A Study in Myth and Ritual', in *Classical Quarterly*, NS 20 (1970), 1–16.

11 Fritz Graf, 'The Locrian Maidens', trans. of German original 'Die lokrischen Mädchen', which appeared in *Studi Storico-Religiosi*, 2.1 (1978), 61–79.

12 Jan N. Bremmer, 'Scapegoat Rituals in Ancient Greece', in *Harvard Studies in Classical Philology*, 87 (1983), 299–320.

13 Robin Osborne, 'Women and Sacrifice in Classical Greece', in *Classical Quarterly*, NS 43 (1993), 392–405.

14 Robert L. Fowler, 'Greek Magic, Greek Religion', in *Illinois Classical Studies*, 20 (1995), 1–22.

15 C. Robert Phillips, III, 'Misconceptualizing Classical Mythology', in *Georgica: Greek Studies in Honour of George Cawkwell*, Bulletin of the Institute of Classical Studies Supplement 58 (1991), 143–51.

SUGGESTIONS FOR FURTHER READING

The books and articles listed below will enable the reader to follow up not only those aspects of Greek religion explored in this volume, but also related topics on which recent scholarship has been focusing. The list is of course highly selective, and does not replace, for example, the richer and more specific bibliographies to be found in the notes to the contributions in this volume.

I. ON WAYS OF APPROACHING GREEK RELIGION AND MYTHOLOGY

BRELICH, A. (1977), 'La metodologia della scuola di Roma', in B. Gentili and G. Paioni (eds.), *Il mito greco. Atti del Convegno Internazionale (Urbino 7–12 maggio 1973)* (Rome), 3–32.

BURKERT, W. (1980), 'Griechische Mythologie und die Geistesgeschichte der Moderne', in *Les Études classiques au XIX⁽ᵉ⁾ et XX⁽ᵉ⁾ siècles: leur place dans l'histoire des idées* (= Entretiens Fondation Hardt 26) (Vandoeuvres-Geneva), 159–207.

BUXTON, R. (1981), 'Introduction', in R. L. Gordon (ed.), *Myth, Religion and Society: Structuralist Essays by M. Detienne, L. Gernet, J.-P. Vernant and P. Vidal-Naquet* (Cambridge), pp. ix–xvii. [On structuralist approaches.]

ELLINGER, P. (1984), 'Vingt ans de recherches sur les mythes dans le domaine de l'antiquité grecque', *REA* 86: 7–29.

GOULD, J. (1985), 'On Making Sense of Greek Religion', in P. E. Easterling and J. V. Muir (eds.), *Greek Religion and Society* (Cambridge), 1–33.

HENRICHS, A. (1985), '*Der Glaube der Hellenen*: Religionsgeschichte als Glaubensbekenntnis und Kulturkritik', in W. M. Calder III, H. Flashar, and Th. Lindken (eds.), *Wilamowitz nach 50 Jahren* (Darmstadt), 263–305.

KEARNS, E. (1995), 'Order, Interaction, Authority: Ways of Looking at Greek Religion', in A. Powell (ed.), *The Greek World* (London), 511–29.

MOST, G. (1999), 'From Logos to Mythos', in R. Buxton (ed.), *From Myth to Reason? Studies in the Development of Greek Thought* (Oxford), 25–47.

SAÏD, S. (1993), *Approches de la mythologie grecque* (Paris).

2. GENERAL STUDIES

BRELICH, A. (1985), *I Greci e gli dei* (Naples).

BREMMER, J. N. (1994), *Greek Religion*. Greece and Rome New Surveys in the Classics No. 24 (Oxford; reprinted with Addenda, 1999).

BRUIT ZAIDMAN, L., and SCHMITT PANTEL, P. (1992), *Religion in the Ancient Greek City* (Cambridge; orig. *La Religion grecque* (Paris, 1989)).

BURKERT, W. (1985), *Greek Religion: Archaic and Classical* (Oxford; orig. *Griechische Religion der archaischen und klassischen Epoche* (Stuttgart, 1977)).

BUXTON, R. (1998), 'Religion and Myth', in P. Cartledge (ed.), *The Cambridge Illustrated History of Ancient Greece* (Cambridge), 320–44.

DODDS, E. R. (1951), *The Greeks and the Irrational* (Berkeley and Los Angeles).

GERNET, L., and BOULANGER, A. (1932), *Le Génie grec dans la religion* (Paris; rev. edn. 1970).

JOST, M. (1992), *Aspects de la vie religieuse en Grèce du début du Ve siècle à la fin du IIIe siècle avant J.-C.* (Paris).

NILSSON, M. P. (1967), *Geschichte der griechischen Religion*, i, 3rd edn. (Munich).

PRICE, S. (1999), *Religions of the Ancient Greeks* (Cambridge).

RUDHARDT, J. (1992), *Notions fondamentales de la pensée religieuse et actes constitutifs du culte dans la Grèce ancienne*, 2nd edn. (Paris).

SCARPI, P. (1994), 'La religione greca', in G. Filoramo (ed.), *Storia delle religioni*, i: *Le religioni antiche* (Rome and Bari), 283–330.

SFAMENI GASPARRO, G. (1994), 'Le religioni del mondo ellenistico', in G. Filoramo (ed.), *Storia delle religioni*, i: *Le religioni antiche* (Rome and Bari), 409–52.

3. BOUNDARY DISPUTES: SOME CONTESTED DEFINITIONS

BREMMER, J. N. (1998), '"Religion", "Ritual" and the Opposition "Sacred vs. Profane". Notes towards a Terminological "Genealogy"', in F. Graf (ed.), *Ansichten griechischer Rituale. Geburtstags-Symposium für Walter Burkert* (Stuttgart and Leipzig), 9–32.

—— (1999), 'The Birth of the Term "Magic"', *ZPE* 126: 1–12.

CALAME, C. (1991), '"Mythe" et "rite" en Grèce: des catégories indigènes?', *Kernos* 4: 179–204.

—— (1996), 'Illusions de la mythologie', in id., *Mythe et histoire dans l'Antiquité grecque* (Lausanne), 9–55.

CONNOR, W. R. (1988), '"Sacred" and "Secular". Ἱερὰ καὶ ὅσια and the Classical Athenian Concept of the State', *Ancient Society*, 19: 161–88.

DETIENNE, M. (1981), *L'Invention de la mythologie* (Paris).

LLOYD, G. E. R. (1979), *Magic, Reason and Experience* (Cambridge), esp. Ch. 1 ('The Criticism of Magic and the Inquiry concerning Nature'), 10–58.

SCHLESIER, R. (1991–2), 'Olympian versus Chthonian Religion', *Scripta Class. Israel.* 11: 38–51.

SCULLION, S. (1994), 'Olympian and Chthonian', *Class. Ant.* 13: 75–119.

VERSNEL, H. S. (1991), 'Some Reflections on the Relationship Magic—Religion', *Numen*, 38: 177–97.

4. MINOANS AND MYCENAEANS

HÄGG, R. (1985), 'Mycenaean Religion: The Helladic and the Minoan Components', in A. Morpurgo Davies and Y. Duhoux (eds.), *Linear B: A 1984 Survey* (Louvain), 203–25.

—— (1998), 'Ritual in Mycenaean Greece', in F. Graf (ed.), *Ansichten griechischer Rituale. Geburtstags-Symposium für Walter Burkert* (Stuttgart and Leipzig), 99–113.

—— and MARINATOS, N. (1981) (eds.), *Sanctuaries and Cults in the Aegean Bronze Age* (Stockholm).

MARINATOS, N. (1993), *Minoan Religion: Ritual, Image, and Symbol* (Columbia, SC).

NILSSON, M. P. (1932), *The Mycenaean Origin of Greek Mythology* (Berkeley; rev. edn. 1972).

RUTKOWSKI, B. (1986), *The Cult Places of the Aegean* (New Haven).

SCARPI, P. (1994), 'Le religioni preelleniche di Creta e Micene', in G. Filoramo (ed.), *Storia delle religioni*. i: *Le religioni antiche* (Rome and Bari), 265–81.

WARREN, P. M. (1988), *Minoan Religion as Ritual Action* (Gothenburg).

5. LOCAL AND REGIONAL STUDIES

BRUNEAU, P. (1970), *Recherches sur les cultes de Délos à l'époque hellénistique et à l'époque impériale* (Paris).

DEUBNER, L. (1966), *Attische Feste*, 2nd edn. (Darmstadt).

FARNELL, L. R. (1896–1909), *Cults of the Greek States*, 5 vols. (Oxford).

GARLAND, R. (1992), *Introducing New Gods: The Politics of Athenian Religion* (London).

GRAF, F. (1985), *Nordionische Kulte: Religionsgeschichtliche und epigraphische Untersuchungen zu den Kulten von Chios, Erythrai, Klazomenai und Phokaia* (Rome).

JOST, M. (1985), *Sanctuaires et cultes d'Arcadie* (Paris).

MIKALSON, J. D. (1977), 'Religion in the Attic Demes', *AJP* 98: 424–35.

—— (1983), *Athenian Popular Religion* (Chapel Hill).

NILSSON, M. P. (1906), *Griechische Feste von religiöser Bedeutung mit Ausschluss der attischen* (Leipzig).

PARKE, H. W. (1977), *Festivals of the Athenians* (London).

PARKER, R. (1989), 'Spartan Religion', in A. Powell (ed.), *Classical Sparta: Techniques behind her Success* (London), 142–72.

—— (1996), *Athenian Religion: A History* (Oxford).

SCHACHTER, A. (1981–), *Cults of Boiotia* (London).

SIMON, E. (1983), *Festivals of Attica* (Madison, Wis.).

6. RELIGION IN SOCIETY

BÖMER, F. (1981–90), *Untersuchungen über die Religion der Sklaven in Griechenland und Rom*, 2nd edn. (Stuttgart).

COLE, S. G. (1984), 'The Social Function of Rituals of Maturation: The Koureion and the Arkteia', *ZPE* 55: 233–44.

CONNOR, W. R. (1991), 'The Other 399: Religion and the Trial of Socrates', in M. A. Flower and M. Toher (eds.), *Georgica. Greek Studies in Honour of George Cawkwell*. BICS Supp. 58 (London), 49–56.

GERNET, L. (1981), *The Anthropology of Ancient Greece* (Baltimore; orig. *Anthropologie de la Grèce antique* (Paris, 1968)).

JAMESON, M. H. (1988), 'Sacrifice and Ritual: Greece', in M. Grant and R. Kitzinger (eds.), *Civilization of the Ancient Mediterranean: Greece and Rome* (New York), ii. 959–79.

MALKIN, I. (1987), *Religion and Colonization in Ancient Greece* (Leiden).

NILSSON, M. P. (1940), *Greek Popular Religion* (New York).

—— (1951), *Cults, Myths, Oracles, and Politics in Ancient Greece* (Lund).

VERNANT, J.-P. (1980), *Myth and Society in Ancient Greece* (Hassocks; orig. *Mythe et société en Grèce ancienne* (Paris, 1974)).

VIDAL-NAQUET, P. (1986a), *The Black Hunter: Forms of Thought and Forms of Society in the Greek World* (Baltimore; orig. *Le Chasseur noir: formes de pensée et formes de société dans le monde grec* (Paris, 1981; rev. edn. 1991)).

—— (1986b), 'The Black Hunter Revisited', *PCPS* 212 (NS 32): 126–44.

7. ARCHAEOLOGY OF THE SACRED

ALCOCK, S., and OSBORNE, R. G. (1994) (eds.), *Placing the Gods: Sanctuaries and Sacred Space in Ancient Greece* (Oxford).

ANTONACCIO, C. (1995), *An Archaeology of Ancestors: Tomb Cult and Hero Cult in Early Greece* (Lanham, Md.).

CORBETT, P. E. (1970), 'Greek Temples and Greek Worshippers: The Literary and Archaeological Evidence', *BICS* 17: 149–58.

DE POLIGNAC, F. (1984), *La Naissance de la cité grecque: cultes, espace et société VIIIe-VIIe siècles avant J.-C.* (Paris).

MARINATOS, N., and HÄGG, R. (1993) (eds.), *Greek Sanctuaries: New Approaches* (London).

MELAS, E. (1973) (ed.), *Temples and Sanctuaries of Ancient Greece* (London; orig. *Tempel und Stätten der Götter Griechenlands* (Cologne, 1970)).

WHITLEY, J. (1988), 'Early States and Hero Cults: A Re-appraisal', *JHS* 108: 173–82.

8. DIVINITY AND DIVINITIES

BORGEAUD, P. (1988), *The Cult of Pan in Ancient Greece* (Chicago and London; orig. *Recherches sur le dieu Pan* (Geneva, 1979)).

CARPENTER, T. H., and FARAONE, C. A. (1993) (eds.), *Masks of Dionysus* (Ithaca).

COOK, A. B. (1914–40), *Zeus: A Study in Greek Religion*, 3 vols. (Cambridge).

DELCOURT, M. (1982), *Héphaistos, ou la légende du magicien*, rev. edn. (Paris).

DETIENNE, M. (1979), *Dionysus Slain* (Baltimore; orig. *Dionysos mis à mort* (Paris, 1977)).

HENRICHS, A. (1982), 'Changing Dionysiac Identities', in B. F. Meyer and E. P. Sanders (eds.), *Jewish and Christian Self-Definition, iii: Self-Definition in the Graeco-Roman World* (London), 137–60, 213–36.

LLOYD, A. B. (1997) (ed.), *What is a God? Studies in the Nature of Greek Divinity* (London).

LORAUX, N. (1992), 'What is a Goddess?', in P. Schmitt Pantel (ed.), *A History of Women in the West: From Ancient Goddesses to Christian Saints* (Cambridge, Mass.), 11–44.

NEILS, J. (1996) (ed.), *Worshipping Athena* (Madison, Wis.).

VERNANT, J.-P. (1991), *Mortals and Immortals: Collected Essays*, ed. F. Zeitlin (Princeton).

9. ORACLES AND DIVINATION

BREMMER, J. N. (1996), 'Modi di comunicazione con il divino: la preghiera, la divinazione e il sacrificio nella civiltà greca', in S. Settis (ed.), *I Greci: storia cultura arte società*, i (Turin), 239–83.

DAKARIS, S. (1998), *The Nekyomanteion of the Acheron*, 3rd edn. (Athens).

FONTENROSE, J. (1959), *Python: A Study of Delphic Myth and its Origins* (Berkeley and Los Angeles).

MORGAN, C. (1990), *Athletes and Oracles: The Transformation of Olympia and Delphi in the Eighth Century B.C.* (Cambridge).

Oracles et mantique en Grèce ancienne = Kernos, 3 (1990), 11–366.

PARKE, H. W., and WORMELL, D. E. W. (1956), *The Delphic Oracle* (Oxford).

PRICE, S. (1985), 'Delphi and Divination', in P. E. Easterling and J. V. Muir (eds.), *Greek Religion and Society* (Cambridge), 128–54.

VAN STRATEN, F. T. (1982), 'Twee orakels in Epirus. Het orakel van Zeus in Dodona en het nekyomanteion aan de Acheron', *Lampas*, 15: 195–230.

VERNANT, J.-P., *et al.* (1974), *Divination et rationalité* (Paris).

10. MYTH

BREMMER, J. N. (1987) (ed.), *Interpretations of Greek Mythology* (London and Sydney).

BRISSON, L. (1982), *Platon, les mots et les mythes* (Paris).

BUXTON, R. (1994), *Imaginary Greece: The Contexts of Mythology* (Cambridge). Revisions incorporated in the translations into French (Paris, 1996), Italian (Florence, 1997), Spanish (Madrid, 2000).

—— (1999), *From Myth to Reason? Studies in the Development of Greek Thought* (Oxford).

DOWDEN, K. (1992), *The Uses of Greek Mythology* (London).

EDMUNDS, L. (1990) (ed.), *Approaches to Greek Myth* (Baltimore).

GANTZ, T. (1993), *Early Greek Myth: A Guide to Literary and Artistic Sources* (Baltimore).

GORDON, R. L. (1981) (ed.), *Myth, Religion and Society: Structuralist Essays by M. Detienne, L. Gernet, J.-P. Vernant and P. Vidal-Naquet* (Cambridge).

GRAF, F. (1993), *Greek Mythology: An Introduction* (Baltimore; orig. *Griechische Mythologie: Eine Einführung* (Munich, 1985)).

KAKRIDIS, I. (1986–7) (ed.), Ἑλληνικὴ Μυθολογία, 5 vols. (Athens).

MARCH, J. (1998), *Dictionary of Classical Mythology* (London).

MOREAU, A. (1999), *Mythes grecs*, i: *Origines* (Montpellier).

VERNANT, J.-P. (1983), *Myth and Thought among the Greeks* (London; orig. *Mythe et pensée chez les Grecs* (Paris, 1965; 2nd edn. 1985)).

11. MYTHS AND RITUALS

BREMMER, J. N. (1984), 'Greek Maenadism Reconsidered', ZPE 55: 267–86.

BURKERT, W. (1979), *Structure and History in Greek Mythology and Ritual* (Berkeley).

—— (1983), *Homo Necans: The Anthropology of Ancient Greek Sacrificial Ritual and Myth* (Berkeley; orig. *Homo Necans: Interpretationen altgriechischer Opferriten und Mythen* (Berlin, 1972; rev. edn. 1997)).

DETIENNE, M. (1977), *The Gardens of Adonis: Spices in Greek Mythology* (Hassocks; orig. *Les Jardins d'Adonis: la mythologie des aromates en Grèce* (1972)).

—— and VERNANT, J.-P. (1989) (eds.), *The Cuisine of Sacrifice among the Greeks* (Chicago; orig. *La Cuisine du sacrifice en pays grec* (Paris, 1979)).

DOTY, W. G. (1986), *Mythography: The Study of Myths and Rituals* (Tuscaloosa).

FARAONE, C. A. (1992), *Talismans and Trojan Horses: Guardian Statues in Ancient Greek Myth and Ritual* (New York).

GOULD, J. (1973), 'Hiketeia', *JHS* 93: 74–103.

GRAF, F. (1980), 'Milch, Honig und Wein', in G. Piccaluga (ed.), *Perennitas. Studi in onore di Angelo Brelich* (Rome), 209–21.

HENRICHS, A. (1978), 'Greek Maenadism from Olympias to Messalina', *HSCP* 82: 121–60.

SCHLESIER, R. (1994), *Kulte, Mythen und Gelehrte: Anthropologie der Antike seit 1800* (Frankfurt).

SEGAL, R. (1998) (ed.), *The Myth and Ritual Theory: An Anthology* (Oxford).

VERSNEL, H. S. (1987), 'Greek Myth and Ritual: The Case of Kronos', in J. N. Bremmer (ed.), *Interpretations of Greek Mythology* (London and Sydney), 121–52.

12. HEROES/HEROINES

BRELICH, A. (1958), *Gli eroi greci* (Rome).

BREMMER, J. N. (1987), 'Oedipus and the Greek Oedipus Complex', in id., *Interpretations of Greek Mythology* (London and Sydney), 41–59.

CLAUSS, J. J., and JOHNSTON, S. I. (1997), *Medea: Essays on Medea in Myth, Literature, Philosophy, and Art* (Princeton).

FRONTISI-DUCROUX, F. (1975), *Dédale: mythologie de l'artisan en Grèce ancienne* (Paris).

GALINSKY, G. K. (1972), *The Herakles Theme: The Adaptations of the Hero in Literature from Homer to the Twentieth Century* (Oxford).

GRAF, F. (1987), 'Orpheus: A Poet among Men', in J. N. Bremmer (ed.), *Interpretations of Greek Mythology* (London and Sydney), 80–106.

KEARNS, E. (1989), *The Heroes of Attica*, BICS Supp. 57 (London).

LARSON, J. (1995), *Greek Heroine Cults* (Madison, Wis.).

LYONS, D. (1997), *Gender and Immortality: Heroines in Ancient Greek Myth and Cult* (Princeton).

MOREAU, A. (1994), *Le Mythe de Jason et Médée* (Paris).
NOCK, A. D. (1944/1972), 'The Cult of Heroes', in id., *Essays on Religion and the Ancient World*, ii (Oxford), 575–602.
PICCALUGA, G. (1968), *Lykaon: un tema mitico* (Rome).

13. GENDER

BLUNDELL, S., and WILLIAMSON, M. (1998) (eds.), *The Sacred and the Feminine in Ancient Greece* (London).
BREMMER, J. N. (1985), 'La donna anziana: libertà e indipendenza', in G. Arrigoni (ed.), *Le donne in Grecia* (Rome and Bari), 275–98.
CALAME, C. (1997), *Choruses of Young Women in Ancient Greece* (Lanham, Md.; orig. *Les Choeurs de jeunes filles en Grèce archaïque* (Rome, 1977)).
COLE, S. G. (1992), '*Gynaiki ou Themis*: Gender Difference in the Greek *Leges Sacrae*', *Helios*, 19: 104–22.
DETIENNE, M. (1989), 'The Violence of Well-born Ladies: Women in the Thesmophoria', in M. Detienne and J.-P. Vernant (eds.), *The Cuisine of Sacrifice among the Greeks* (Chicago; see sect. 11 above), 129–47.
GOULD, J. (1980), 'Law, Custom and Myth: Aspects of the Social Position of Women in Classical Athens', *JHS* 100: 38–59.
KING, H. (1983), 'Bound to Bleed: Artemis and Greek Women', in A. Cameron and A. Kuhrt (eds.), *Images of Women in Antiquity* (London), 109–27.
LEFKOWITZ, M. R. (1986), *Women in Greek Myth* (London).
LORAUX, N. (1993), *The Children of Athena: Athenian Ideas about Citizenship and the Division between the Sexes* (Princeton; orig. *Les Enfants d'Athéna: idées athéniennes sur la citoyenneté et la division des sexes* (Paris, 1981)).
RUDHARDT, J. (1986), 'Pandora: Hésiode et les femmes', *MH* 43: 231–46.

14. RELIGION AND LITERATURE

BOWIE, A. M. (1993), *Aristophanes: Myth, Ritual and Comedy* (Cambridge).
BUFFIÈRE, F. (1956), *Les Mythes d'Homère et la pensée grecque* (Paris).
BUXTON, R. (1988), 'Bafflement in Greek Tragedy', *Métis*, 3: 41–51.
CALAME, C. (2000), *Poétique des mythes dans la Grèce antique* (Paris).
EASTERLING, P. E. (1993), 'Tragedy and Ritual', in R. Scodel (ed.), *Theater and Society in the Classical World* (Ann Arbor), 7–23.
GOULD, J. (1994), 'Herodotus and Religion', in S. Hornblower (ed.), *Greek Historiography* (Oxford), 91–106.

HORNBLOWER, S. (1992), 'The Religious Dimension to the Peloponnesian War, or, What Thucydides Does Not Tell Us', *HSCP* 94: 169–97.

KAHN, L. (1978), *Hermès passe, ou les ambiguïtés de la communication* (Paris). [On the *Homeric Hymn to Hermes*.]

KÖHNKEN, A. (1971), *Die Funktion des Mythos bei Pindar* (Berlin).

KULLMANN, W. (1985), 'Gods and Men in the *Iliad* and the *Odyssey*', *HSCP* 89: 1–23.

MORA, F. (1986), *Religione e religioni nelle storie di Erodoto* (Milan).

PARKER, R. (1997), 'Gods Cruel and Kind: Tragedy and Civic Theology', in C. Pelling (ed.), *Greek Tragedy and the Historian* (Oxford), 143–60.

SFAMENI GASPARRO, G. (1996), 'Plutarco e la religione delfica: il dio "filosofo" e il suo esegeta', in I. Gallo (ed.), *Atti del VI Convegno plutarcheo (Ravello, 29–31 maggio 1995)* (Naples), 157–88.

SOURVINOU-INWOOD, C. (1997), 'Tragedy and Religion: Constructs and Readings', in C. Pelling (ed.), *Greek Tragedy and the Historian* (Oxford), 161–86.

VERNANT, J.-P., AND VIDAL-NAQUET, P. (1988), *Myth and Tragedy in Ancient Greece* (New York; orig. *Mythe et tragédie en Grèce ancienne*, 2 vols. (Paris, 1972–86)).

15. ICONOGRAPHY

ARAFAT, K. W. (1990), *Classical Zeus: A Study in Art and Literature* (Oxford).

CARPENTER, T. H. (1991), *Art and Myth in Ancient Greece: A Handbook* (London).

Lexicon Iconographicum Mythologiae Classicae (= LIMC) (Zürich, 1981–97).

LISSARRAGUE, F. (1990), *The Aesthetics of the Greek Banquet: Images of Wine and Ritual* (Princeton; orig. *Un flot d'images: une esthétique du banquet grec* (Paris, 1987)).

MORET, J.-M. (1984), *Oedipe, la Sphinx et les Thébains. Essai de mythologie iconographique* (Rome).

SOURVINOU-INWOOD, C. (1988), *Studies in Girls' Transitions: Aspects of the Arkteia and Age Representation in Attic Iconography* (Athens).

VERNANT, J.-P. (1990), *Figures, idoles, masques* (Paris).

16. MAGIC

CHRISTIDIS, A.-Ph., and JORDAN, D. R. (1997) (eds.), Γλώσσα και Μαγεία: Κείμενα από την Αρχαιότητα (Athens).

FARAONE, C. A., and OBBINK, D. (1991) (eds.), *Magika Hiera: Ancient Greek Magic and Religion* (New York and Oxford).

FLINT, V., GORDON, R., LUCK, G., and OGDEN, D. (1999), *Witchcraft and Magic in Europe, ii: Ancient Greece and Rome* (London).

GAGER, J. G. (1992), *Curse Tablets and Binding Spells from the Ancient World* (New York).

GORDON, R. L. (1997), 'Quaedam veritatis umbrae: Hellenistic Magic and Astrology', in P. Bilde *et al.* (eds.), *Conventional Values of the Hellenistic Greeks* (Aarhus), 128–58.

GRAF, F. (1997), *Magic in the Ancient World* (Cambridge, Mass.; orig. *Idéologie et pratique de la magie dans l'antiquité gréco-romaine* (Paris, 1994)).

JORDAN, D. R., MONTGOMERY, H., and THOMASSEN, E. (1999) (eds.), *The World of Ancient Magic.* Papers from the First International Samson Eitrem Seminar at the Norwegian Institute at Athens, 4–8 May 1997 (Bergen).

LANATA, G. (1967), *Medicina magica e religione popolare in Grecia fino all' età di Ippocrate* (Rome).

LUCK, G. (1985), *Arcana Mundi: Magic and the Occult in the Greek and Roman Worlds* (Baltimore).

RIBICHINI, S. (1998), 'La magia nel Vicino Oriente antico. Introduzione tematica e bibliografica', in *Magic in the Ancient Near East* (= *Studi epigrafici e linguistici sul Vicino Oriente antico* 15) (Verona), 5–16.

17. OTHER TOPICS IN ANCIENT GREEK RELIGION

BARTON, T. (1994), *Ancient Astrology* (London).

BURKERT, W. (1987), *Ancient Mystery Cults* (Cambridge, Mass.).

DILLON, M. (1997), *Pilgrims and Pilgrimage in Ancient Greece* (London).

LAKS, A., and MOST, G. (1997) (eds.), *Studies on the Derveni Papyrus* (Oxford).

MARTIN, D. B. (1997), 'Hellenistic Superstition: The Problems of Defining a Vice', in P. Bilde *et al.* (eds.), *Conventional Values of the Hellenistic Greeks* (Aarhus), 110–27.

MYLONAS, G. E. (1961), *Eleusis and the Eleusinian Mysteries* (Princeton).

PARKER, R. (1983), *Miasma: Pollution and Purification in Early Greek Religion* (Oxford).

—— (1995), 'Early Orphism', in A. Powell (ed.), *The Greek World* (London), 483–510.

PRITCHETT, W. K. (1979), *The Greek State at War, iii: Religion* (Berkeley).

VERSNEL, H. S. (1981) (ed.), *Faith, Hope and Worship: Aspects of Religious Mentality in the Ancient World* (Leiden).

—— (1990), *Inconsistencies in Greek and Roman Religion, i: Ter Unus* (Leiden).

—— (1993), *Inconsistencies in Greek and Roman Religion, ii: Transition and Reversal in Myth and Ritual* (Leiden).

18. COMPARATIVE STUDIES

BEARD, M. (1993), 'Looking (Harder) for Roman Myth: Dumézil, Declamation and the Problems of Definition', in F. Graf (ed.), *Mythos in mythenloser Gesellschaft: Das Paradigma Roms* (Stuttgart and Leipzig), 44–64.

BERNBAUM, E. (1997), *Sacred Mountains of the World* (Berkeley and Los Angeles). [Contains superlative illustrations.]

BURKERT, W. (1992), *The Orientalizing Revolution: Near Eastern Influence on Greek Culture in the Early Archaic Age* (Cambridge, Mass.; orig. *Die orientalisierende Epoche in der griechischen Religion und Literatur* (Heidelberg, 1984)).

FEENEY, D. (1998), *Literature and Religion at Rome: Cultures, Contexts, and Beliefs* (Cambridge). [On models for understanding Greek and Roman religion.]

JOHNSON, A. W., and PRICE-WILLIAMS, D. (1996), *Oedipus Ubiquitous: The Family Complex in World Folk Literature* (Stanford, Calif.).

LLOYD, G. E. R. (1990), *Demystifying Mentalities* (Cambridge). [On Greece and China.]

PUHVEL, J. (1987), *Comparative Mythology* (Baltimore).

SERGENT, B. (1995), *Les Indo-Européens: histoire, langues, mythes* (Paris).

WEST, M. L. (1997), *The East Face of Helicon: West Asiatic Elements in Greek Poetry and Myth* (Oxford).

19. CONTINUITIES

ALEXIOU, M. (1974), *The Ritual Lament in Greek Tradition* (Cambridge).

DANFORTH, L. M. (1982), *The Death Rituals of Rural Greece* (Princeton).

FELDMAN, B., and RICHARDSON, R. D. (1972), *The Rise of Modern Mythology 1680–1860* (Bloomington, Ind.).

LANE FOX, R. (1986), *Pagans and Christians* (London).

LAWSON, J. C. (1910), *Modern Greek Folklore and Ancient Greek Religion: A Study in Survivals* (Cambridge).

MANUEL, F. E. (1959), *The Eighteenth Century Confronts the Gods* (Cambridge, Mass.).

MILES, G. (1999) (ed.), *Classical Mythology in English Literature: A Critical Anthology* (London). [On Orpheus, Adonis, and Pygmalion.]

REID, J. D. (1993) (ed.), *The Oxford Guide to Classical Mythology in the Arts, 1300–1990s*, 2 vols. (Oxford).

SEZNEC, J. (1953), *The Survival of the Pagan Gods* (Princeton; orig. *La Survivance des dieux antiques* (London, 1940)).

WARNER, M. (1994), *From the Beast to the Blonde: On Fairytales and their Tellers* (London).

—— (1998), *No Go the Bogeyman: Scaring, Lulling and Making Mock* (London). [On images of monstrosity in various cultures, including ancient Greece.]